THE PAPERS OF
THOMAS JEFFERSON

THE PAPERS OF
Thomas Jefferson

Volume 6
21 May 1781 to 1 March 1784

JULIAN P. BOYD, EDITOR

MINA R. BRYAN AND ELIZABETH L. HUTTER,

ASSOCIATE EDITORS

PRINCETON, NEW JERSEY
PRINCETON UNIVERSITY PRESS

1952

Printed in the United States of America by
Princeton University Press, Princeton, New Jersey

DEDICATED TO THE MEMORY OF

ADOLPH S. OCHS

PUBLISHER OF THE NEW YORK TIMES

1896-1935

WHO BY THE EXAMPLE OF A RESPONSIBLE

PRESS ENLARGED AND FORTIFIED

THE JEFFERSONIAN CONCEPT

OF A FREE PRESS

FOREWORD

THIS volume requires a particular explanation of some matters touched upon in the general outline of editorial policies and methods set forth in Volume 1 and further developed in the Foreword to Volume 2.

Record Entries. In addition to the comments about record entries in the Foreword to Volume 2, it should be pointed out that, beginning with the present volume, all such entries are to be enclosed in a special form of bracket—⟦thus⟧. This was made advisable by the occasional need for enclosing brackets within brackets in record entries. It was also thought advantageous to provide a device that would enable the reader to distinguish at a glance the difference between a summary of a document and a record entry. It may also be noted that the present volume contains the first record entry for a document previously attributed to Jefferson but now known to have been written by someone else. For example, the resolutions concerning peace with England, printed under date of 25 May 1782, were thought by Edmund Pendleton to have been written by Jefferson, an attribution followed by Ford, II, 160, but, for reasons indicated in the record entry under that date, these resolutions were drafted by another hand. In similar instances in future volumes where it is deemed advisable to note and present evidence against Jefferson's supposed authorship of a document, the record entry form will be employed for this purpose.

Summary Journal of Letters. Since none of the preceding five volumes contains any entry drawn from Jefferson's list of correspondence registered in a document of 656 pages (including its alphabetical index), the decision to refer to it as the "Epistolary Record," as was done in Volume 1, page xii, has been reconsidered. Beginning with the present volume and with the first entry to be drawn from this source (TJ to John Key, 11 Nov. 1783), the term which Jefferson applied to the first page of the record beginning on that date will be employed—that is, "Summary Journal of letters." For convenience, this will be abbreviated as SJL.

Though this is Jefferson's own term, it is inadequate as a descriptive title to the remarkable record of correspondence kept in his own hand and extending from 11 Nov. 1783 to 25 June 1826. For what began as an effort to summarize in journal or calendar form the contents of letters written by Jefferson soon developed into a simple register. The document referred to in these volumes as SJL is in DLC: TJ Papers and is accompanied by an earlier and somewhat halting attempt at a journal of correspondence covering Jefferson's terms as governor. It contains entries dating from 19 June 1779 to 28 May 1781, but is very incomplete and covers only two pages. Its entries are usually, however, summaries of contents of letters written by Jefferson. From 11 Nov. 1783 through 19 Sep. 1785 the entries in SJL for both outgoing and incoming letters appear in a single sequence, the latter of course being entered under the date of receipt. Incoming letters during this period were rarely summarized but outgoing letters were usually given a cryptically brief or a very full summarization. In utilizing SJL in the years 1783-1785, the editors have quoted in full the summaries of outgoing letters, whether the documents are available and printed or are missing and represented only by a record entry. The date of an entry taken from SJL is always to be understood as being the same as that given in the letter itself unless noted to the contrary. Discrepancies in dates occasionally are to be found and where they appear will always be indicated in notes.

In June 1785 the summaries of contents begin rapidly to drop out of SJL, and the notation "see copy" (later shortened to "s.c." and still later dropped altogether) begins to appear. The explanation for this lies in the fact that at this time Jefferson began to use regularly a Watt copying press and to file press copies of all of his outgoing letters. With the entries for 20 Sep. 1785 Jefferson began a new arrangement of his register which was to be maintained to the end. In the left-hand column of each page appear the entries for "letters written by me," and in the right-hand column are those for "letters received" (with the place where written and the date sent added as regular parts of the entry). A few refinements followed at a later period, such as the uniform use of "directory style" for all personal names, &c. But the pattern was now fixed.

The chronological portion of SJL is complete for the 43-year span covered except for a gap of one year, 1788, for which entries once existed but cannot now be found. To this daily record Jefferson added a key or index alphabetically arranged by the names of his correspondents, enabling him to determine readily what letters had passed between him and any given correspondent. There are actually four of these indexes, covering (1) the period from Jefferson's arrival in France "to the establishmt. of my Copying press," Aug. 1784 to June 1785; (2) the period of his service as minister to France, June 1785 to Sep. 1789 (including the year missing in the chronological section); (3) the period from his appointment as secretary of state through and a little beyond his first term as President, Sep. 1789 to the end of 1805; and (4) the remainder of his second term as President, 1 Jan. 1806 to 3 Mch. 1809. The first two of the indexes are in his hand; the others in one or more amanuenses' hands. No alphabetical index for the daily register as kept during the remainder of Jefferson's life appears to have been compiled.

The reliability of SJL, with respect to both its completeness and its accuracy, is very high. From the appearance of the MS itself and from other evidence, it seems likely that Jefferson did not record each letter as it was written or received but, rather, that he kept his copies of outgoing letters and the original incoming letters (each carefully docketed with date of receipt as soon as read) until a considerable number had accumulated, then entered the lot in the register and filed the letters themselves. Unimportant notes, dinner invitations, and occasionally a highly personal letter of which he did not make a copy (e.g., his letter to Mrs. Cosway of 5 Oct. 1786) are therefore not entered. On the whole the omissions are negligible.

The value to the editors of Jefferson's papers of such a careful and unique record cannot be adequately stated. It has proved indispensable in identifying and dating mutilated, incomplete, undated, and misdated letters, of which there were bound to be many in an archive as large as Jefferson's and one handled by so many persons since 1826. It also tells us, from the day it begins to within ten days of his death, precisely what letters are missing from that archive. Since the present edition is planned to include, in full or in summary, all of Jefferson's correspondence, the editors have decided not to print SJL as a separate document but to extract all pertinent information from it and to distribute that information throughout this first or chronological series of volumes where it will be most useful. For this purpose SJL has been checked against the TJ Editorial Files. When it reveals the date of receipt of a letter or other data not found in the letter itself, these data are incorporated in the notes. When it records a letter unknown except from the entry in SJL, the missing letter is given a record entry, as noted above. But when a missing letter is known through an acknowledgment in a reply as well as through an entry in SJL, the missing letter will be accounted for in the note to the letter acknowledging it. After 11 Nov. 1783 it is to be assumed that all outgoing letters are recorded in SJL unless there is a note to the contrary.

Codes. The present volume also contains the first appearance in this edition of a letter involving the use of a code (TJ to Madison, 31 Jan. 1783). A statement concerning editorial method in the treatment of letters partially or wholly in code is therefore necessary.

In general it may be said that the method decided upon is intended to achieve the maximum of flexibility, readability, and simplicity of presentation consistent with accurate and precise designation of all coded words and passages. Where a fixed method is employed, such as the use of italics or brackets, the text of a document is made needlessly complex and difficult for the reader and the chances of erroneous readings multiplied (e.g., Madison to TJ, 20 Aug. 1784, Madison, *Writings*, ed. Hunt, II, 68-75; Virginia delegates in Congress to Gov. Harrison, 23 Apr. 1782, Burnett, *Letters of Members*, VI, No. 487). Even in the use of these and other fixed methods, footnotes keyed to the text by superscript numerals are almost invariably necessary. Since this is so, the editors have decided to depend in all cases upon textual notes and superscript numerals *for the complete and precise designation of all coded words and passages.* Such notes will always be employed but, where advisable, will be supplemented by the use of italics. For example, italics will be utilized in a letter having one or two words or a number of widely-scattered words in code. This, of course, results in an undesirable appearance of the text from the standpoint of readability, but it is less objectionable than a use of brackets or than the obviously cumbersome method of attaching a superscript numeral to every isolated word in code. In cases where the coded passage can be precisely and conveniently described in a textual note (such as a consecutive passage involving a whole sentence or paragraph), italics will usually be dispensed with for the sake of readability. The test determining the method to be employed will be simplicity and effectiveness of presentation of the text. But, to repeat, whatever the method utilized, every word and passage in code will be indicated.

All codes known to have been employed by Jefferson will be grouped together and published with appropriate commentary in the second or topical series of volumes in this edition (see Vol. 1: xiv-xvi). There they will be arranged in a sequence arbitrarily numbered in accordance with the time of their appearance in the present or chronological series of volumes. Thus the code which first comes to light in the letter from Jefferson to Madison of 31 Jan. 1783, having been concerted by the two men in Philadelphia a few days earlier and being based on Thomas Nugent's *New Pocket Dictionary of the French and English Languages* (London, 1774), is arbitrarily designated in TJ Editorial Files as Code No. 1. It will be so referred to throughout this edition. Occasionally, as in this particular instance, there will be a brief description of the code when this is made necessary in order to explain how the editors have decoded a particular passage, but in general the notes in the chronological series will merely indicate the code by number and the full description will be deferred until all are grouped in the topical volumes. Some of the codes employed by Jefferson are cited or described in Edmund C. Burnett, "Ciphers of the Revolutionary Period," *Amer. Hist. Rev.*, xxii [1916-1917], p. 329-34.

In many instances involving code, as in the letter from Jefferson to Madison of 31 Jan. 1783, the recipient of the letter either inserted interlineally or wrote on a separate page a transliteration of part or all of the coded words. In such cases the fact will be indicated in the note accompanying the letter itself. Occasionally the recipient made a partial or erroneous transliteration: a notable example of the latter which seriously misled all previous editors is that of Madison's decoding of Jefferson's letter of 14 Feb. 1783. Because of this, the editors plan to check the recipient's decoding in all cases where a key to the code is available and, as in the instance just cited, to provide a reading for passages not decoded (or erroneously decoded by the recipient) in all cases where the editors have been able to make a usable reconstruction of a missing key. In every case the appended textual note will indicate whether the decoding was done by the recipient, by someone else, or by the editors and will show which text for the decoding was employed.

Letters from Virginia Delegates in Congress to the Governor of Virginia. In the present and succeeding volume a number of letters from James Monroe, Samuel Hardy, and John Francis Mercer to Benjamin Harrison are to be found. These letters report occurrences in Congress and transmit intelligence in accord with a plan conceived by Jefferson whereby one member each month had the duty of communicating for the whole delegation (TJ to Harrison, 17 Dec. 1783). These letters passed under the eye of all members of the delegation and may, therefore, be considered in effect as being as much letters by all as if the entire delegation had signed them, as had been the custom theretofore and as, indeed, was the case in extraordinary instances while the plan was in

operation, such as the letter of 22 Mch. 1784 in which the delegation transmitted the exemplification of the Virginia Deed of Cession. The scheme of rotation, typical of Jefferson's liking for system, unfortunately did not work well because of Hardy's illness
and Mercer's volatile personality. Jefferson, though ill himself
much of the time during the early weeks of 1784, not only carried
the lion's share of drafting reports in Congress during that time
but was also Harrison's most reliable and most frequent informant,
a fact of which Harrison was duly appreciative. Jefferson appears
also to have been the only member of the delegation who considered
it important to communicate timely intelligence to the Speaker of
the House of Delegates and to the Speaker of the Senate. This he
did in an obvious effort to influence Virginia legislation and bring
state policies into alignment with the exceedingly important
legislation he was engaged in drafting in the national body.

As a logical result of this plan of rotation of correspondence,
letters from Gov. Harrison to the correspondent of the month are
included here because they are to be regarded as being addressed
to all members of the Virginia delegation. This interchange is
therefore in effect a part of the Jefferson corpus and is certainly
essential to an understanding of the progress of legislation and of
the relations between local and national interests and attitudes.

Papers of the Continental Congress. The abbreviation PCC is
explained in previous volumes as having reference to "Papers of
the Continental Congress, in the Library of Congress." This designated location is no longer accurate, since on 6 June 1952 the
enormously rich collection of historical documents comprising the
Papers of the Continental Congress was transferred from the custody of the Library of Congress to that of the National Archives.

It is also important at this time to note another fact of such consequence to the editorial process in this and future volumes that it
cannot be accommodated by such explanations of editorial method
as the foregoing or, regrettably, by any other device or stratagem.
This is the first volume of the series whose title page does not carry
the name of Dr. Lyman H. Butterfield as Associate Editor. No one
can know better than those who were his colleagues in the editorial
office from March 1946 to July 1951 what this omission means to
them and to this edition. Dr. Butterfield contributed to the work a
contagious enthusiasm, a friendly and engaging spirit, an unflag-
ging industry, a devotion to high standards of scholarship, and a
knowledge of American history and literature as remarkable for

FOREWORD

exactness and copiousness as for the generosity with which he made it available to all at whatever cost to himself. These qualities caused him to be an almost inevitable choice for the Directorship of the Institute of Early American History and Culture, an important center of historical scholarship for the whole colonial period of American history. The responsibilities of his new office will deprive this edition of Dr. Butterfield's talents in the daily routine of editing, but the editors take comfort in the fact that Thomas Jefferson and his papers create no incompatibility between the field of Dr. Butterfield's new responsibilities and his continuing interest in this edition. As evidence of this fact and as assurance that his advice and experience will be available in an official, though different, capacity, the editors take much satisfaction in announcing that he has accepted an invitation to become a member of the Editorial Advisory Committee of *The Papers of Thomas Jefferson.*

GUIDE TO EDITORIAL
APPARATUS

1. TEXTUAL DEVICES

The following devices are employed throughout the work to clarify the presentation of the text.

[. . .], [. . . .]   One or two words missing and not conjecturable.

[. . .]¹, [. . . .]¹   More than two words missing and not conjecturable; subjoined footnote estimates number of words missing.

[   ]   Number or part of a number missing or illegible.

[roman]   Conjectural reading for missing or illegible matter. A question mark follows when the reading is doubtful.

[*italic*]   Editorial comment inserted in the text.

⟨*italic*⟩   Matter deleted in the MS but restored in our text.

〖   〗   Record entry for letters not found.

2. DESCRIPTIVE SYMBOLS

The following symbols are employed throughout the work to describe the various kinds of manuscript originals. When a series of versions is recorded, *the first to be recorded is the version used for the printed text.*

Dft   draft (usually a composition or rough draft; later drafts, when identifiable as such, are designated "2d Dft," &c.)

Dupl   duplicate

MS   manuscript (arbitrarily applied to most documents other than letters)

N   note, notes (memoranda, fragments, &c.)

PoC   polygraph copy

PrC   press copy

RC   recipient's copy

SC   stylograph copy

Tripl   triplicate

All manuscripts of the above types are assumed to be in the hand of the author of the document to which the descriptive symbol pertains. If not, that fact is stated. On the other hand, the follow-

ing types of manuscripts are assumed *not* to be in the hand of the
author, and exceptions will be noted:

FC   file copy (applied to all forms of retained copies,
such as letter-book copies, clerks' copies, &c.)

Tr   transcript (applied to both contemporary and later
copies; period of transcription, unless clear by
implication, will be given when known)

3. LOCATION SYMBOLS

   The locations of documents printed in this edition from originals
in private hands, from originals held by institutions outside the
United States, and from printed sources are recorded in self-ex-
planatory form in the descriptive note following each document.
The locations of documents printed from originals held by public
institutions in the United States are recorded by means of the symbols used in the National Union Catalog in the Library of Congress;
an explanation of how these symbols are formed is given above,
Vol. 1: xl. The list of symbols appearing in each volume is limited
to the institutions represented by documents printed or referred to
in that volume.

CSmH	Henry E. Huntington Library, San Marino, California
Ct	Connecticut State Library, Hartford, Connecticut
CtY	Yale University Library
DLC	Library of Congress
DNA	The National Archives
ICHi	Chicago Historical Society, Chicago
IHi	Illinois State Historical Library, Springfield
MHi	Massachusetts Historical Society, Boston
MdAA	Maryland Hall of Records, Annapolis
MeHi	Maine Historical Society, Portland
MiU-C	William L. Clements Library, University of Michigan
MoSHi	Missouri Historical Society, St. Louis
MWA	American Antiquarian Society, Worcester
NHi	New-York Historical Society, New York City
NN	New York Public Library, New York City
NNP	Pierpont Morgan Library, New York City
NcD	Duke University Library

NjP Princeton University Library
PHC Haverford College Library
PHi Historical Society of Pennsylvania, Philadelphia
PPAP American Philosophical Society, Philadelphia
PPL-R Library Company of Philadelphia, Ridgway Branch
PU University of Pennsylvania Library
RPA Rhode Island Department of State, Providence
Vi   Virginia State Library, Richmond
ViHi Virginia Historical Society, Richmond
ViU University of Virginia Library
ViWC Colonial Williamsburg, Inc.
WHi State Historical Society of Wisconsin, Madison

4. OTHER ABBREVIATIONS

The following abbreviations are commonly employed in the annotation throughout the work.

TJ Thomas Jefferson

TJ Editorial Files Photoduplicates and other editorial materials in the office of *The Papers of Thomas Jefferson*, Princeton University Library

TJ Papers Jefferson Papers (Applied to a collection of manuscripts when the precise location of a given document must be furnished, and always preceded by the symbol for the institutional repository; thus "DLC: TJ Papers, 4:628-9" represents a document in the Library of Congress, Jefferson Papers, volume 4, pages 628 and 629.)

PCC Papers of the Continental Congress, in the National Archives

RG Record Group (Used in designating the location of documents in the National Archives.)

SJL Jefferson's "Summary Journal of letters" written and received (in DLC: TJ Papers)

5. SHORT TITLES

The following list includes only those short titles of works cited with great frequency, and therefore in very abbreviated form, throughout this edition. Their expanded forms are given here only in the degree of fullness needed for unmistakable identification.

Since it is impossible to anticipate all the works to be cited in such very abbreviated form, the list is appropriately revised from volume to volume.

Atlas of Amer. Hist., Scribner, 1943.   James Truslow Adams and R. V. Coleman, *Atlas of American History*, N.Y., 1943

Biog. Dir. Cong.   Biographical Directory of Congress, 1774-1927

Bland Papers   The Bland Papers: Being a Selection from the Manuscripts of Colonel Theodorick Bland, Jr.

B.M. Cat.   British Museum, *General Catalogue of Printed Books*, London, 1931—. Also, *The British Museum Catalogue of Printed Books, 1881-1900*, Ann Arbor, 1946

B.N. Cat.   Catalogue général des livres imprimés de la Bibliothèque Nationale. Auteurs.

Burk-Girardin, *Hist. of Va.*   John Burk, *The History of Virginia . . . Continued by Skelton Jones and Louis Hue Girardin*

Burnett, *Letters of Members*   Edmund C. Burnett, ed., *Letters of Members of the Continental Congress*

C & D   See *Va. Gaz.*

Cal. Franklin Papers   Calendar of the Papers of Benjamin Franklin in the Library of the American Philosophical Society, ed. I. Minis Hays

Cal. Wash. Corr. with Officers   Library of Congress, *Calendar of the Correspondence of George Washington . . . with the Officers*

Clark Papers   See *George Rogers Clark Papers*

CVSP   *Calendar of Virginia State Papers . . . Preserved in the Capitol at Richmond*

D & H   See *Va. Gaz.*

D & N   See *Va. Gaz.*

DAB   *Dictionary of American Biography*

DAE   *Dictionary of American English*

DAH   *Dictionary of American History*

DNB   *Dictionary of National Biography*

Evans   Charles Evans, *American Bibliography*

Ford   Paul Leicester Ford, ed., *The Writings of Thomas Jefferson*, "Letterpress Edition," N.Y., 1892-1899

Fry-Jefferson Map   *The Fry & Jefferson Map of Virginia and Maryland: A Facsimile of the First Edition*, Princeton, 1950

George Rogers Clark Papers, 1771-1781; also *1781-1784*
    George Rogers Clark Papers, ed. James A. James, Illinois State Historical Library, *Collections*, VIII, XIX

HAW   Henry A. Washington, ed., *The Writings of Thomas Jefferson*, Washington, 1853-1854

Heitman   Francis B. Heitman, *Historical Register of Officers of the Continental Army*, new edn., Washington, 1914; also the same compiler's *Historical Register and Dictionary of the United States Army* [1789-1903], Washington, 1903

Hening   William W. Hening, *The Statutes at Large; Being a Collection of All the Laws of Virginia*

JCC   *Journals of the Continental Congress, 1774-1789*, ed. W. C. Ford and others, Washington, 1904-1937

JHD   *Journal of the House of Delegates of the Commonwealth of Virginia* (cited by session and date of publication)

Johnston, "Jefferson Bibliography"   Richard H. Johnston, "A Contribution to a Bibliography of Thomas Jefferson," *Writings of Thomas Jefferson*, ed. Lipscomb and Bergh, xx, separately paged following the Index

L & B   Andrew A. Lipscomb and Albert E. Bergh, eds., *The Writings of Thomas Jefferson*, "Memorial Edition," Washington, 1903-1904

L.C. Cat.   *A Catalogue of Books Represented by Library of Congress Printed Cards*, Ann Arbor, 1942-1946; also *Supplement*, 1948

Library Catalogue, 1783   Jefferson's MS list of books owned and wanted in 1783 (original in Massachusetts Historical Society)

Library Catalogue, 1815   *Catalogue of the Library of the United States*, Washington, 1815

Library Catalogue, 1829   *Catalogue. President Jefferson's Library*, Washington, 1829

Marraro, *Mazzei*   Howard R. Marraro, *Philip Mazzei: Virginia's Agent in Europe*, New York, 1935

MVHR   *Mississippi Valley Historical Review*

OED   *A New English Dictionary on Historical Principles*, Oxford, 1888-1933

Official Letters   Official Letters of the Governors of the State of Virginia, ed. H. R. McIlwaine

P & D   See *Va. Gaz.*

PMHB   *The Pennsylvania Magazine of History and Biography*

Randall, *Life*   Henry S. Randall, *The Life of Thomas Jefferson*

Randolph, *Domestic Life*   Sarah N. Randolph, *The Domestic Life of Thomas Jefferson*

Randolph, "Essay"   Edmund Randolph, "Essay on the Revolutionary History of Virginia," VMHB, XLIII-XLV (1935-1937)

Sabin   Joseph Sabin and others, *Bibliotheca Americana. A Dictionary of Books Relating to America*

Simcoe, *Military Journal*   John Graves Simcoe, *Military Journal*, New York, 1844

Swem, *Index*   E. G. Swem, *Virginia Historical Index*

Swem, "Va. Bibliog."   Earl G. Swem, "A Bibliography of Virginia," Virginia State Library, *Bulletin*, VIII, X, XII (1915-1919)

Swem and Williams, "Register of the General Assembly of Va." Appended to: Virginia State Library, *Fourteenth Annual Report*, 1917

TJR   Thomas Jefferson Randolph, ed., *Memoir, Correspondence, and Miscellanies, from the Papers of Thomas Jefferson*, Charlottesville, 1829

Tucker, *Life*   George Tucker, *The Life of Thomas Jefferson*, Philadelphia, 1837

Tyler, *Va. Biog.*   Lyon G. Tyler, *Encyclopedia of Virginia Biography*

Tyler's Quart.   Tyler's Quarterly Historical and Genealogical Magazine

Va. Council Jour.   Journals of the Council of the State of Virginia, ed. H. R. McIlwaine

Va. Gaz.   Virginia Gazette (Williamsburg, 1751-1780, and Richmond, 1780-1781). Abbreviations for publishers of the several newspapers of this name, frequently published concurrently, include the following: C & D (Clarkson & Davis), D & H (Dixon & Hunter), D & N (Dixon & Nicolson), P & D (Purdie & Dixon). In all other cases the publisher's name is not abbreviated

VMHB   *Virginia Magazine of History and Biography*

Wharton, *Dipl. Corr. Am. Rev.   The Revolutionary Diplomatic Correspondence of the United States*, ed. Francis Wharton

WMQ   *William and Mary Quarterly*

CONTENTS

·◄┣ 1781 ┫►·
continued

[xxi]

CONTENTS

CONTENTS

CONTENTS

CONTENTS

1782

CONTENTS

1783

CONTENTS

CONTENTS

CONTENTS

CONTENTS

CONTENTS

1784

CONTENTS

CONTENTS

CONTENTS

ILLUSTRATIONS

ILLUSTRATIONS

VOLUME 6

21 May 1781 to 1 March 1784

1781 3 June. Retired from governorship.

  4 June. Tarleton's troops raided Monticello. TJ took refuge with friends and, later, retired with his family to Poplar Forest.

  12 June. House of Delegates voted an enquiry into the conduct of the Executive for the past twelve months.

  14 June. Congress appointed TJ a commissioner to negotiate peace.

  26 July. Returned to Monticello from Poplar Forest.

  4 Aug. Declined appointment to serve as a peace commissioner.

  26 Nov. House of Delegates ordered appointment of a committee to state charges and receive information concerning the Executive.

  10-22 Dec. Attended General Assembly as member of House of Delegates.

  12-15 Dec. General Assembly agreed unanimously to a resolution of thanks to TJ for his services as governor.

  20 Dec. Sent replies to Marbois' queries concerning Virginia.

1782 Apr. Chastellux visited TJ at Monticello.

  6 May. Declined serving as member of House of Delegates.

  8 May. TJ's daughter, Lucy Elizabeth, was born.

  30 May. Appointed by House of Delegates to a committee to investigate and publish findings concerning Virginia's western claim.

  6 Sep. Martha Wayles Jefferson died.

  12 Nov. Appointed by Congress as a peace commissioner.

  26 Nov. Accepted appointment as a commissioner.

  27 Dec. Arrived in Philadelphia.

1783 20 Jan. Awarded honorary degree by College of William and Mary.

  26 Jan. Left Philadelphia.

  30 Jan. Arrived in Baltimore to await passage to Europe.

  14 Feb. Appointment as peace commissioner suspended by Congress.

  26 Feb. Returned to Philadelphia.

  1 Apr. Released from his mission to Europe.

  12 Apr. Left Philadelphia to return to Virginia.

  May-June. Drafted proposed constitution for Virginia.

  6 June. Elected delegate to Congress.

  4 Nov. Took seat in Congress at Princeton.

  5 Nov. Returned to Philadelphia.

  22 Nov. Departed for Annapolis.

  13 Dec. Congress reconvened at Annapolis.

  13 Dec. Appointed to a committee to report on the definitive treaty with Great Britain.

  23 Dec. George Washington resigned his commission as commander-in-chief of the army.

1784 14 Jan. Definitive treaty of peace ratified by Congress.

  1 Mch. Congress accepted Virginia's cession of the territory northwest of the Ohio River.

  1 Mch. TJ presented the report of a plan for the government of the western territory.

THE PAPERS OF
THOMAS JEFFERSON

◖════════◗

From James Callaway

SIR   Bedford May the 21st. 1781

I am Extreemly Sorry to inform you that in place of the three Hundred and eighty four Militia, Requested by your Excellency to be sent from this County to the Assistance of General Green, I have only been able to send out One Hundred and thirty some Odd men, Exclusive Officers, Notwithstanding the Utmost exertion has been Used. The Extreem Busy Season of the Year, among the Common People, Exceeds their Conception of the Necessity of Turning out, Especially as the enemy is not immediately Pressing upon them. I shall Endeavour to Punish the Delinquents Instantly, and send them down Agr[ee]able to the Instructions already given me. I am not at this time able to inform your Excellency, what Number of Militia can be sent from this County to Join Majr. General Marquis Fayette, as Tomorrow is the day on which they meet, tho' I am Doubtfull of Marching any Considerable Number for the Reasons I have Mentioned. At the same time you may Rest Satisfied, that Nothing shall be Wanted on my Part, toward forwarding this, or any Other Publick Business Commited to my Charge, as I conceive Our Publick affairs Requires the Strictest attention. I am your Excellencys Very Hble Servant,

JAMES CALLAWAY

P.S. The Militia Ordered to General Green from this County have been Marched some time, 130 odd Privates.   J.C.

RC (Vi); addressed in part: "℗ favr. of Mr. Talbot"; endorsed.

To the County Lieutenants of Powhatan, Chesterfield, Prince George, and Dinwiddie

SIR   Charlottesville May 21st 1781

You will be pleased to order all Cattle and Horses which may at any Time be within twenty Miles of the Enemys Camp to be

[3]

removed beyond that Distance excepting only such Horses as are unfit either for Cavalry or Artillery. Should the Owners not perform this Order within such short and reasonable Time as you shall prescribe, you will be pleased to order out proper Officers and men of your Militia to carry such Horses and Cattle to the Marquis Fayette's Head Quarters for the use of our Army having them duly appraised. I am &c., THOMAS JEFFERSON

FC (Vi).

To the County Lieutenants of Goochland and Henrico

SIR   Charlottesville May 21st 1781

Should the Marquis Fayette give you Notice at any Time that there is Reason to apprehend the Enemy will cross James River, you will be pleased to order all Cattle and Horses which may be within twenty Miles wherever they shall at any Time be to be removed [&c. as in the Letter to Powhatan.]¹ I am &c.,
THOMAS JEFFERSON

FC (Vi).   ¹ Brackets supplied; for remainder of text see preceding letter.

To the County Lieutenants of Hanover and New Kent

SIR   Charlottesville May 21st 1781

Whenever the Honble. Major Genl. Marquis La Fayette shall think it necessary and shall so inform you, you will be pleased to have collected all the Boats and other smaller vessels, whether Public or Private, on Pamunkey either on or opposite to the Shore of your County and to have them carried to such Places as he shall direct. I am &c.,   THO JEFFERSON

FC (Vi).

To Benjamin Harrison, Jr.

SIR   Charlottesville May 21st. 1781

The Council some Time ago came to a Resolution that they would advance Money for the Pay of the Virginia Continental

Troops but for no others. It is therefore not in my power to say that any Money shall be advanced you out of the Treasury for the Payment of any other Troops.

I suppose them in this Instance not liable to Imputation till a precedent can be produced where the Troops of one State have been paid off by another State. The other Burthens which lie on us are greater than we can go through with and if our Northern Brethren will advance Money for any Southern Purpose surely they will for the Payment of their own Troops.

You shall have a Warrant for one hundred thousand pounds whenever you please which you will be at Liberty to lay out in the Purchase of hard Money according to the Desires of the Marquis. I am &c., THO JEFFERSON

FC (Vi).   Benjamin Harrison, Jr. was Deputy Continental Paymaster General. The minutes of Council do not show that he received the warrant for £100,000 until 18 July 1781 (*Va. Council Jour.*, II, 358).

To Robert Lawson

SIR   Charlottesville May 21st 1781

I received yesterday your favor by Mr. Archer and will lay the recommendations before Council as soon as they shall assemble. When that will be I cannot precisely say, there being at present five members only and they much dispersed. In the mean time from what passed on the former occasion (as I mentioned to you in my Letter from Colo. Skipwith's) I think you may safely call the gentlemen into command *as far as there shall be men for them to command* of those formerly ordered to reinforce Genl. Greene, and of whom Genl. Greene furnished you with a copy of the list I had sent him. As soon as a council shall assemble, the business shall be done and dispatched to you by Express. I am with much respect Sir Your most obedt. servt.,   TH: JEFFERSON

RC (NcD); addressed and endorsed. FC (Vi).
YOUR FAVOR BY MR. ARCHER: See Lawson to TJ, 16 May 1781. MY LETTER FROM COLO. SKIPWITH'S: See TJ to Lawson, 11 May.

To Matthew Pope

SIR   Charlottesville May 21st 1781

I got the favor of Colo. Senf to be the Bearer of a note to Colo. Davies or in his absence to any person having the Packages in his hand to have them opened and the Articles you desire taken out and sent to you in a Cart or Waggon.

Necessity is Law, in times of war most especially. You will therefore take possession of any church, barn or other vacant house or houses convenient and necessary for the establishment of a Hospital for which this shall be your warrant. I am &c.,

THO JEFFERSON

FC (Vi); at head of text: "Doctor Pope."

To David Ross

SIR   Charlottesville May 21st 1781

As there will be wanting a very considerable number of Saddles, Bridles, Boots and other Accoutrements immediately, I shall be obliged to you if you will be so good as to employ as many Shops as you can in preparing them. There will be no Danger of having too many made before I shall receive such Returns as will enable me to fix the numbers. I am &c.,   THOMAS JEFFERSON

FC (Vi).

William Lewis to James Maxwell

SIR   Renown of turky Island M, 22, 81

Yours of 20th I got yesterday after the boat past, and shoud have Answered it by the boat. The vessels are all in want of Powder Match Rope and Carterage paper and Grape shot (Except[1] my own Vessel). There is a Waggon here with those Articles but I have not a line concerning them nither do I know what is to be done with them after to day we shall have no provisions. I wish the Governor would apoint a Comissary for to supply the Men in the fleet for I find it dificult to keep my own people that have allways had aplenty. And you must think with what difficulty it tis on board the other Vessels to keep there people that have never had a drop of spirits since they have been in service. I have mentioned those circumstances to his Excellency frequently. I wish you would come down or direct in what manner and when we are to git supplys. Mrs. Reaves I am told has rum to sell. I am sorry to trouble you about these matters but realy If we are not better suply'd We shall lose all our people.

I am Sir your Most Obedt   WILLIAM LEWIS

P.S. We had a sloop of Mr. Pleasants in service and when we were ordred up by the Baron and sent of those small Vessels first Mr Pleasants before we got up took her away and now we want her for to put those Military Stores in. I wish you would represent the Matter to his Excellency. I have wrote Mr. Pleasant on t[he] subject.

RC (Vi); addressed: "Capt. James Maxwell Richmond"; endorsed.

¹ Lewis wrote "Expect."

To the Rev. James Madison and Robert Andrews

GENTL   Charlottesville May 22d 1781

I have just received a Letter from President Reid acknowledging the Receipt of mine on the subject of running our joint Boundary, deferring answering the particulars respecting the mode of running the line till he can confer with their Commissioners on the subject and in the mean time proposing as the season is fast advancing that your meeting shall be on the 12th. of June. I have informed him that I received his Letter but yesterday which left three weeks only to the day proposed for meeting, that, being now removed to a considerable distance from you, a part of the time will efflux before I can receive your answer; that the movements of the enemy may perhaps render it necessary for you to take measures for the safety of your families and therefore begging leave to consider it as his desire that as early a day as possible after the 12th. of June may be fixed on and to take the liberty of communicating to him by a future letter the earliest at which you will be able to attend at your two stations according to the answer I shall receive from you. I must now beg the favor of you to let me know what will be the earliest Day by a letter which the Quarter Master at Williamsburg must hand on through the line of expresses to this place.

I write now to Capt. Young the Quarter Master to have two good Horses for each of you and a covered Waggon of the best kind to carry the Instruments to Pittsburg in readiness at such time and place as you shall direct. I am &c.,

THOMAS JEFFERSON

FC (Vi); at head of text: "The Revd. Messrs. Madison & Andrews."

I WRITE NOW TO CAPTAIN YOUNG: This letter from TJ has not been found, but at this moment the colorful and explosive quartermaster was having horse troubles of his own. On the 23d he wrote Davies from Richmond: "My difficulties and misfortunes are without number; I have lost my Horses, I fear they will fall into the hands of the Enemy, and what is still worse, I fear John, my faithfull Servant will share the same fate. . . ." (CVSP, II, 114). Three days later Young had better news for Davies: "I found my horse in King-William and the fellow who had him refused to give him up. I wish I was Dictator for 1. Day, I would proscribe every person in the State of suspicious caracter—I am not a rash man, but should my horse fall into the hands of the Enemy by means of his being detained by that villian, if God spares me, I will assassinate him, if I can't [get] satisfaction by law, which I don't expect" (same, 120-1).

To Joseph Reed

SIR   Charlottesville May 22. 1781

Your Excellency's Favor of the 6th Inst. came to Hand Yesterday. The Movements of the Enemy since I did myself the Honor of writing to your Excellency on the Subject of our joint Boundary having rendered it necessary in the Opinion of the General Assembly for them to adjourn to this Place, the Executive have of Course come hither for a Time. This has placed us at a great Distance from Mr. Madison and Mr. Andrews two of the Commissioners appointed for the Purpose of running the Boundary. These Gentlemen also unfortunately reside in Williamsburg, a Place supposed to be an Object with the Enemy, and I am not without Fears that this new Circumstance will create Difficulties in the Time of their Attendance. I shall immediately dispatch an Express to them with a Communication of your Excellency's Letter, and will on Receipt of their Answer do myself again the Honor of writing to you. In the mean Time as there remain but three Weeks between this and the 12th. of June, the Day proposed by your Excellency for the meeting of the Commissioners, as a Part of this will be effluxed before I can receive a Letter from our Commissioners and it is probable they have to provide for the Safety of their Families before their Departure, I will beg Leave to consider it as your Excellency's Desire that as early a Day as possible after that may be fixed on, and take the Liberty of communicating the earliest at which they will be able to attend according to the Answer I shall receive from them.

I have the Honor to be with great Respect your Excellency's most obedient and most humble Servant,   TH: JEFFERSON

RC (PHi); in a clerk's hand; endorsed. FC (Vi).

From the Virginia Delegates in Congress

Sir   Phila: 22d. May 1781

Mr. Nicholson we presume will communicate to your Excellency or his principal the State of the business committed to his care. He has we believe been greatly embarrass'd for want of money, and it has not been in our power to afford him assistance, although our endeavours have been exerted for the purpose.

The Chevr. Luzerne has received within a few days past Dispatches from his Court. The Contents of them have not yet transpired, but we expect they will in a day or two be communicated to Congress. No doubt but from the present State of Affairs in Europe, they must be important and interesting to America. Mr. Carmichael writes the Committee of Correspondence, that Mr. Cumberland had left Spain, and returnd to England through France, but notwithstanding his negociations are at an end in consequence of his departure, Mr. Carmichael conjectures conferences will be soon opend for the accommodation of the disputes between the belligerent powers, under the mediation of the Emperor. He gives this as his conjecture and not from Official authority.

Ct. Rochambeau, in consequence of advices receivd by his Son who arrived in the Ship that brought over the Admiral to take command of the French Fleet at Rhode Island, requested a Conference with General Washington. They are now together and the Operations of the ensuing Campaign will we expect be digested, and we hope the forces of our Ally be put in motion. We are really reduced to extremities for want of money. The State paper passes under great depreciation and not willingly received by the people. Specie appears to be the money chiefly in circulation. How the State will furnish us with that article we know not, unless the Assembly will authorize Mr. Ross their Agent to purchase flour for the Southern Department and exchange it for the Specific supply of Maryland, so far as to answer our exigencies. The Maryland flour may be deliverd at the Head of Elk, and we apprehend disposd of for gold and Silver. Unless something is done to furnish us with money to bear our reasonable expences in this place we must sell what little property we possess here or return to Virginia. Your Excellency will pardon our giving you the trouble of representing to the Assembly any matter that particularly respects ourselves, but our present Situation will we hope apologize for Your Obt. Servts.,

JOS: JONES

JAMES MADISON JUNR.

THEODK. BLAND

M. SMITH

Tr (MiU-C: Clinton Papers); endorsed: "Copy of an intercepted Letter from the Delegates to Congress from Virginia to the Governor." Another Tr (Public Record Office, London); endorsed: "Copy of a Letter from The Delegates to Congress from Virginia to The Governor 22d. May 1781. (3) In Sr. Henry Clinton's Letter of the 13th. July."

For the matters touched on in Carmichael's letter, see Burnett, *Letters of Members*, VI, No. 122, note 4 and S. F. Bemis, *The Hussey-Cumberland Mission and American Independence* (Princeton, 1931).

To Richard Claiborne

SIR   Charlottesville May 23d. 1781

Your letters of the 18th and 19th inst. came to hand yesterday. Experience has for some time past convinced the Council that as the mode of acquiring[1] waggons, horses &c. by Impress is the most irritating, so it is the most expensive which can be adopted. They therefore have generally meant to discontinue Impresses and to have purchases made wherever a delay can be admitted. And indeed it is questionable where necessity obliges the public to have an article on the spot whether any price which the owner would ask to part with it voluntarily would not be less than appraisers would rate it at.

In answer therefore to your Letter I can only advise your procuring the necessaries required by purchase. In a conversation which I had with Mr. Lyne, I mentioned the necessity of paying your Warrants as quickly as possible. He was sensible of it and I can say will pay it as soon as he has as much money. I am[2] with much respect Sir your obt. servant,   TH: JEFFERSON

FC (Vi). Two Tr (NHi: Steuben Papers): one in the hand of Richard Claiborne.

On 30 May Claiborne wrote to Capt. Charles Russell, asking him to wait on Steuben and inform him that "in answer to my proposalls to the Council respecting the requisition he made upon the Department, I receiv'd the Inclosd copy of a letter from the Governor. By this Government propose to do nothing more in the matter, than to advance the money for the purchases. Had I the cash, I do not suppose the Business could be done in less than five or six days, but I have been with Colo. Brook this morning and he tells me there is no possibility of getting any shortly, as the press is not prepared to print the money. . . . But should we fail, the Baron's only recourse must be to Impress. Indeed, I am Apprehensive it must be the case, as [I] do not think Any person will hire his waggon and team to go out of the state" (Claiborne to Russell, 30 May 1781. NHi). Steuben seems to have placed part of the blame for failure upon Claiborne, for on 3 June the latter wrote acknowledging Steuben's letter of 31 May: "The step which you have been induced to take by making a regular complaint against my Conduct as Deputy Quarter Master for the State of Virginia I make no doubt was done from a motive of zeal for the public interest"; Claiborne protested that he too had acted "with unwearied diligence for the public good," stated that he was prepared to receive an arrest whenever Steuben should order it, and enclosed copies of his letter to TJ of 18 May with enclosures and of TJ's reply, "by which," he concluded, "you may judge of my prospects. . . . I should have made this report to you some time since; but waiting for the Governor's answer, which I did not receive until about the time of my leaving Richmond, and being almost constantly on the move since in finding a place for my office rendered it impossible" (Claiborne to Steuben, 3 June 1781, NHi). Apparently Steuben did not reply, for on 7 July Claiborne wrote that he had not heard from him since the charges were made and added: "I consider, Sir, that your reputation is likewise at stake in this affair as you did me the honor to be present at my appointment, and gave your approbation that I should conduct the business, so that as it appears to you I have not transacted it properly an enquiry should be made both in public and private points of view" (Claiborne to Steuben, 7 July 1781, NHi). Claiborne continued in office, though in June he appealed directly to the House of Delegates for assistance in solving the difficult problems confronting him (CVSP, III, 164, 171).

[1] Tr reads "equiping."
[2] FC ends at this point; complimentary close supplied from Tr.

From George Rogers Clark

SIR   Yohogania, C. House May 23d 1781

A few days past I Receivd despatches from the Illinois-Kantuck &c. of a late date. I am sorry to Inform your Excellency that near 100.000 ℔ of Beef at the Kantucky is Spoilt by the persons who Engag'd to procure it. About the same Quantity on hand Excellent good and 250 Head of Cattle promis'd by the inhabitants. The Indians have done considerable damage there. The Enclosd copies are all that is worth your notice from the Illinois but what you already know of by former letters from that country.

You will see the measures that have been taken Respecting Shannon and Moore and the Issue. Colo. Broadhead would not agree to suffer Colo. Gibsons Regiment to go on the Expedition as he said he could not answer for it. I have wrote to Genl. Washington in consequince as ℔r Enclosd copies. The Continental officers and soldiers of this Department, to a man, is anxious for the Expedition supposd against the Indians. The country in general wishing it to take place but too few think of going and so great a Contrast between the people of the two states in this Quarter that no method I doubt Can be taken to force them to war. Wee are taking Every step in our power to Raise Volentiers. What number we Shall get I cant as yet Guess, I doubt too few. The disapointment of Seven Hundred men from Frederick Berkly and Hampshire I am afraid is too great a Stroke to recover as in fact the greatest part of this country is in Subordination to neither Pensylvainia or Virga. Genl. Washington informs me that he had Recievd information that Colo. Connoly had left new york with a design to make a diversion in these Countries to be Reinforced by Sr. John Johnson in Kanady. I doubt Sir we shall as utial be obligd to play a desperate gaim this campaign. If we had the 2,000 men first proposd such Intelligence would give me pleasure. The greatest part of our Stores have come to hand. The Remainder I Shortly Expect. By the greatest Exertion and your timely supplies of money we have the Coats and provisions Expected in this Quarter nearly compleat. I propose to leave this about the 15th June if we can Imbody a Sufficient number of men by that time. I do not yet Despair of seeing the proposd object on tolerable terms although our Circumstances is Rather gloomy. Colo. Crockett and Regiment arivd a few days past who Informed me that a Company or two of Volentiers might be Expected from Frederick and Barkly. I am Sorry we are so circumstancd as to be glad to Receive them. I have the Honr. to be with Great Esteem Your Devoted Servt,

G R CLARK

RC (Vi); addressed; endorsed in part: "inclosg a Court of enquiry on Wm. Shannon & alia." Enclosures: (1) Proceedings of the court of inquiry on William Shannon and others (missing), see George Slaughter to TJ, 13 and 14 Apr. 1781, and enclosures. (2) Copy, in Clark's hand, of his letter to Washington of 20 May 1781 (Vi). The text indicates that Clark also enclosed a copy of his letter to Washington of 21 May (missing); both letters to Washington are printed in *George Rogers Clark Papers, 1771-1781*, p. 551-4.

From David Ross

SIR   Point of Fork 23d May 1781

I am just now favoured with your Letter of the 21st. I expected the waggons would have come to this place in consequence of what your Excellency mentioned to me, and the instructions which I had lodged at Fredericksburg for the Waggoners. Orders had been given by the Baron to deliver the Arms at the barracks, other orders to deliver them at the Town, and lastly to deliver them at the old Courthouse. This latter station he fixes upon, and has given orders accordingly for the arms to be carried there to-morrow. The cloathing and other stores I think had better be stored here, and I have directed the bearer to do so, unless you order it otherwise. I have engaged a Mr. Richard Mathies to inspect, pack and prize the hemp in the several Counties and to employ waggons [that it] may be forwarded to Philadelphia immediately. The inspecting and prizing the hemp is very necessary and can only be done by people of some experience in the business, wherefore I think it will [be] best to load those waggons with the rope yarns and hemp, which I saved from the works at Warwick before the Enemy got there. I dont know but there is a sufficient quantity to load the whole of them with the hemp in this county. If so it will be best not to interfere with the operations of Mr. Mathies.

I expect to engage all those waggons to return here again with the other arms which are now ready.

Inclosed I send you a short state of the case relative to the stores lost at Petersburg. This is a most provoking transaction, and I hope the several persons concerned in it will be punished for their conduct.

I have this moment received your letter by Col. Sinf, I shall send to the most likely places for procuring Saddles immediately but am apprehensive it will take some time to procure any considerable number of them.

I do not know where Mr. Armistead has carried his Stores. I wish some place was appointed where things should be collected. I fear [there are] many things lost, and others [much] wanted and not known that they are on hand.

The Baron wants Blankets and many other articles for the equipment of the new recruits. I have advised him to obtain your order and they shall be furnished. He also wants some Stores for himself, which he begs me to procure for him. I hinted that your order should be obtained for them. He said he would give a warrant for the money, and seemed much hurt at my requiring any other security. His demands are moderate and I believe it will be best to comply with them. I am Sir With great respect Your very humble Servant,

DAVID ROSS

RC (Vi); addressed to TJ in "Albemarle"; endorsed. Enclosure (missing): See below.

YOUR LETTER OF THE 21ST: Evidently a letter from TJ concerning the arms received from Philadelphia, and not the letter to Ross printed above under 21 May which Ross acknowledges as YOUR LETTER BY COL. SINF. The following letters in Vi are concerned with the confusion in the INSTRUCTIONS for the delivery of arms from Philadelphia: On 18 May Samuel Patteson wrote to William Davies that the arms had arrived in Charlottesville "last night" and that the "Wagoners say they will not move any further because they are greatly injured by the depreciation of continental money to the Northward on which was their agreement." On the same day Reuben Lindsay wrote to Davies that Col. Febiger's orders were to carry the arms to Richmond, but that Gen. Weedon, at Fredericksburg, had given verbal orders to carry them to Charlottesville; not knowing where to store them in the latter place, Lindsay requested further orders. On 21 May Ross wrote to Lindsay from Point of Fork, instructing him to have the wagons proceed to that place and receive loads of hemp to carry to Philadelphia, and also to send the wagons loaded with clothing. On 22 May Steuben's aide-de-camp instructed the "Conductor of the waggons which brought the arms on from Philadelphia" to return at once to the place where the arms had been unloaded and "immediately . . . have the arms . . . reloaded and carried on to Albemarle old Court house with the greatest haste." Such orders and counter-orders enabled the irrepressible Henry Young to coin a phrase: writing to Davies from Richmond on 23 May, Young said that "One day I receive orders from ten persons, the next day they are countermanded by twenty. I fear this regular confusion (if I may be allow'd the expression) will end in our total ruin" (Vi). Two days earlier Young had called to Davies' attention a new factor in the confused situation: "The people in this country dont like people that they cant understand so well as they uster to do. I fear the Marquis may loos his Credit; Deserters, British —Cringing Duchmen and busy *little* French men swarm about Head Quarters. The people do not love French men, every person they cant understand they take for a French man" (Young to Davies, 21 May 1781, Vi). THE INCLOSED STATE OF THE CASE RELATIVE TO THE STORES: Ross wrote to Davies on the same day, addressing him at Albemarle old Courthos," enclosing a similar statement (Vi, enclosure missing) and adding: "I think Benjamin Baker of Nansemond is [also very] reprehensible, he engaged to Mr. Crew (who I sent to examine and pack up the goods) that agreeable to my desire, he would send an Officer and 12 men as a guard, and never sent a man. Col. Walker in Dinwiddie also refused to furnish Baird with the assistance of a guard." See also David Ross to TJ, 16 May and enclosure.

From Samuel Huntington

Philadelphia, *24 May 1781*. Encloses the following resolves of Congress of 22 May, and expects "the Necessity as well as the Importance of those Measures will have a suitable Impression upon the States universally, and excite them to a vigorous and punctual Compliance": (1) "That the whole Debts already due by the united States be liquidated as soon as may be to their Specie Value, and funded, if agreeable to the Creditors as a Loan upon Interest"; (2) that the calculation of expenses of the present campaign be made in solid coin and "Experience having evinced the Inefficacy of all Attempts to support the Credit of Paper Money by compulsory Acts, it is recommended to such States, where Laws making paper Bills a Tender yet exist, to repeal the same"; (3) that the treasurer of the United States is directed to draw orders on the treasurers of the states, payable at 30 days' sight, for the quotas called for on 26 Aug. 1780 which were due before 31 Dec. 1780, and that the treasurer will continue to draw such orders for subsequent requisitions, the states being expected to direct their treasurers to accept the orders and "take effectual Measures to enable their respective Treasurers to pay them punctually."

FC (DLC: PCC, No. 15); at head of text: "Circular." Enclosure (Vi): Resolutions of Congress on the "Report of the Committee appointed to devise farther Ways and Means to carry on the present Campaign," printed in JCC, XX, 524-5.

This letter was not received until after the Assembly had adjourned on 4 June to meet at Staunton. William Fleming transmitted the letter and its enclosure to Benjamin Harrison on 7 June (*Official Letters*, III, 1).

From the Continental Board of War

[*Philadelphia, 25 May 1781.* Extract of a letter from Col. William Fleming to Benjamin Harrison, Staunton, 7 June 1781 (*Official Letters*, III, 1): "I . . . take the liberty through you Sir of communicating a letter from the board of war of the 25th of May with a resolve of Congress of the 23d directing the removal of the Convention prisoners out of this State and requesting the necessary guards and provisions might be furnished by the States through which they may pass, and the requisition of the board of War for the prisoners taken in the Southern department to be sent to Fort Frederick in Maryland." The letter from the Continental Board of War, doubtless addressed to TJ, has not been found. The enclosed resolutions of Congress of 23 May (vi) authorized the Board of War "to remove the Convention Troops, in such manner and to such place, as they think most conducive to the [good of the] Union in general," and requested the states "to furnish the necessary Guards, and to supply the said prisoners and Guards with provisions, through their respective States, to the place or places to which they are removed" (printed in JCC, xx, 530). The Board also wrote to George Washington on 25 May concerning the removal of the Convention troops (DLC: Washington Papers).]

To William Davies

Sir   Charlottesville May 25. 1781.

I have just received a letter from Baron Steuben informing me that at the date of it (the 23d) he was on his way to the old Court house to fit the new recruits for the feild, and supposing it might be in your power to aid them with some articles necessary for them. If any thing can be done by the state in this way I think it will be of essential good, as, wherever these recruits are to be employed, the sooner they are carried into the feild the better: and will therefore venture to assure you of the concurrence of the executive in every aid which can be afforded for this purpose from your department. I am with much respect Sir Your most obedt. sert.,

Th: Jefferson

RC (CSmH).   Steuben's letter of 23 May has not been found.

From John Nelson

Sir   Hanover Town 25th. May 81

The reduced Situation of my Corps has inducd the Marquis to order me to this Place, for the Purpose of recruiting the Horses, and geting equiped as fast as possible; to expedite which, Capt. Read will wait upon your Excellency with a State of our Wants to obtain Orders for what is necessary. When I had the Honor to see your Excellency at Wilton, you told me I should be furnished with what we wanted; to prevent Loss of Time, upon this Occasion, I made Application to Mr. Ross in Richmond, who furnished me with two Hundred pr. of Overalls and one Hundred Stable Waistcoats, of Light Canvis, upon a Promise, from me, to obtain an Order from you for them; he has also sent out Agents to procure Boston Spurs and Curry-Combs for us. As to our Saddles and Bridles, they were never good for any thing, tho' I shall have as many fitted up as possible, but it will be better to have a new Set made complete, as what we have, with all the Repairs we can give them, will not last long; and to let you know the true Situation of the Horses, they were never fit for Dragoons, and are so much worn down with hard Service, that I should despare of geting many of them into Order in Six Months, and when in the best Plight, they are only fit for Express and Waggon-Horses. The Marquis has ordered some to be purchased on Continental Account and desired me to apply to your Excellency for Forty more, upon Receipt of which we can deliver nearly the same Number. Capt. Read informs me he has not been able to purchase a single Horse for the Price he was limited to; Horses have become so scarce, from the great Demand for them, that they are not to be had under a great Price; indeed it is not a Time to think of what a Horse costs, when the Enemy are out-numbering us so much in Cavalry. If your Excellency thinks proper to have the Horses purchased, and will send me either Money or Instructions to get them, I will soon do it, as no one is so much interested in geting good ones as myself, and there is a saving to the Country in every Horse purchased by an Officer; as Individuals expect to be paid for their Trouble.

The Behaviour of Capt. Fearer, in absenting himself so long from Service, without Leave, has determined all the Officers never to serve with him. I must request, therefore, that you will be pleased to send Lieut. Armistead a Captain's Commission, and at the same Time a Blank Cornet's Commission for a very deserving Young Man. Capt. Read has an Estimate of the Money due to the Corps, tho' it is impossible to make out Pay-Rolls, as we are unacquainted with the Mode in which it is to be drawn; it is necessary, also, that a Sum of Money should be drawn on Account to procure many Things which we suffer for, that can not be had without Cash. I have writ to the Assembly for Permission to recruit one Hundred Infantry to be joined to my Corps, and hope to have the Assistance of your Excellency, as I have it much at Heart to ta[ke] the Field with a Corps that may render some Service; if the Assembly vote the Men to be raised the sooner I can get the Bounty Money, the better. With great Respect & esteem, I have the Honor to be Sir yr mo: obedt. hble: Servt.,   J. NELSON Majr VLD

P.S. Since writing I have been informed by the Officers that they will not draw their Pay at forty for one, as the Quarter Masters and many others have been paid at Eighty for one and some even higher.   JN

RC (Vi); addressed; endorsed: "Major Nelson's Lr 25th May 1781 not yet answer'd."

CAPT. FEARER: On 20 July 1781 representation was made to the Council that Fearer had "long absented himself from the Corps of Cavalry to which he belongs, notwithstanding repeated orders for his return; and that he has now with him three or more horses the property of the state and a trooper as his servant," whereupon the board directed that a court of enquiry be set up to examine evidence and to report their opinion of the propriety or impropriety of his being superseded (*Va. Council Jour.*, II, 361). Apparently the Council felt that the report of the court would go against Fearer, for on 10 Aug. it promoted Lieut. William Armistead to a captaincy "to take rank from the day on which it shall be determined by a board of officers that Captain Fearer ought to have been superceded" (same, 373; Armistead is recorded as a captain in Nelson's corps in 1782: Gwathmey, *Hist. Reg. of Virginians in the Revolution*).

To David Ross

SIR   Charlottesville May 25th 1781.

The Clothing which came here from Philadelphia is ordered to the Point of Fork in the Waggons which brought it. The other Waggons also proceed there.

The Baron Steuben has written to me on the Subject of having the New Levies immediately equipped which I think with him to be very important. You will please to provide for them such articles as he shall inform you are wanting. According to the late Regulations every Thing of the clothing kind should pass through the hands of the Cloathier (Mr. Armistead or Peyton) one of whom, if not attending, should be sent for.

Though it is not incumbent on the State to provide Stores for the Officers yet the General Officers are so much taken up with the Business of Command that they can scarcely do it themselves. I think indeed their Applications would be more proper to the Continental Quarter Masters. However Harmony with them is so essential for the public Good, and the present Requisition of Baron

Steuben being as you say very moderate I think it will be better to comply with it taking from him a proper Voucher to debit the United States. I am &c., THOMAS JEFFERSON

FC (Vi); at head of text: "David Ross Esq Commercial Agent."
BARON STEUBEN HAS WRITTEN ME: This was probably Steuben's (missing) letter to TJ of 23 May (see TJ to Davies, 25 May).

From Lafayette

DR. SIR   Richmond 26 May 1781

The returns of the Men serving from the different Counties I have not yett been able to obtain, as soon as they are made out, I shall have the honor of inclosing them. By Genl. Lawson's letter herewith sent your Excellency will learn the small progress He has made; request to have the letter returned. Baron de Steuben informs me that only two men had been imployed in repairing the damaged Arms. No doubt this matter on being represented by the Baron has been enquir'd into, and every man sett to work who cou'd possibly be procured. The times of the Militia expire daily and they are discharged, but very few come in to supply their place. One Company of rifflemen only have arrived tho' they might be very usefully employed.

Very few Horses have been impressed. I hope your Excellency and the Councill will give some Orders on this head. Capt. Davenport who just now returns from Amelia and Brunswick assures me that by impressing every fourth Horse, We shou'd be able to raise 200 in those Counties. We are in the outmost want of Cavalry; the Enemy's great superiority in Horse giving them such an advantage over us that they have it almost in their power to over run the Country, in spight of all our efforts. You will observe by Colo. White's memo inclosed, that there are 50 of the 1 Regiment at Staunton, cou'd We mount those and Nelsons Corps who are at Hanover, getting Cloathing made up, it wou'd be a great acquisition, as our whole force in Cavalry at present is about 60 and the Enemy have 500 Horse. The mounted Militia are all gone home except Capt. Royall whose time is out next Thursday. Notwithstanding positive Orders to the contrary they carried of their Accoutrements which has incapacitated us from remounting others.

I herewith send some letters for your Excellency's opinion as to the propriety of sending them in, I have daily applications for Flags but do not grant any but such as are allowed of by the Order of Councill. Lord Cornwallis arrived at Petersbo. the 20th. The 23d. Colo. Tarleton, with 300 Horse of his Legion, profitting by the very heavy rain which rendered the Continells Arms unfitt to fire, and having intercepted the Videtts, surprised a party of Militia in Chesterfield about 2 Miles S. W. of Colo. Cary's Mill. They killed 6, and took about 40 Prisoners. 24th. the British evacuated Petersbo. and destroyed the Bridge they had constructed on Appamatox. They marched to Maycox and crossed about 1000 Men that Evening to Westover. The next day they were employed in crossing the rest of their Army. Same Night We sent off our Stores and Baggage. Had Genl. Wayne joined me (who writes 20th. from Yorktown that He woud March 23d) I shoud certainly have disputed the heights of Richmond with them, but in our present situation I dare hardly risk the smallest matter. Our opposition must be only such as will Check Ld. Cornwallis, without giving him an opportunity of ingaging us further than We wish, or than prudence will justify. Mr. Day, A Quarter Master at Wmsbg. writes informing of a Fleet having passed Jastown. the 22[d.] but of this your Excellency will have the fullest intelligence from Mr. Travers who viewd them himself.

The Marquis sett off at Noon to reconnoitre Brook's Bridge as He has sent in Orders to move on the Troops to that place. I take the liberty of sending your Excellency this rough Copy as it may afford some little intelligence. The Inclosures mentioned are not to be come at. We learn from Phila. and from Genl. Wayne's letter, that 10 Sail of the line and 3000 Troops sailed from Sandy Hook about the 13th. Genl. Sumner writes that report says Ld. Rawdon evacuated Camden. I have the Honor to be with the Highest respect Your Exc'ys most Hble Servt.,

Wm Constable Aid deCamp

RC (Vi); addressed; endorsed in part: "℔ Express." Enclosures not identified and not sent. Although signed by Constable, this letter was really from Lafayette as proved by the context and by the explanation in the final paragraph. What Constable meant by "this rough Copy" was that Lafayette had left it in that state; the present text is a fair RC with no distinction between the part by Lafayette and the part added by Constable.

From David Ross, Enclosing a Letter from James Maury

Sir   Point of Fork 26th. May 1781

I have just now received the inclosed letter from Mr. James

Maury which I send for your perusal. Any thing that you think in my power to do for him I will Chearfully perform it.

Agreable to your desire I furnished him with every thing I thought necessary for his embarking and instructed him to take a passage from the E. Shore if he found any inconvenience in going from Hampton.

The Money he mentions in his letter is an order for £10,000 which I gave him on the Treasurer to pay his expenses and lay in provisions for the voyage. I have just now received a letter from the Marquis recquesting me to meet him at Richmond. I shall sett off tomorrow morning but expect to return in 2 days.

The Greatest Part of the Powder belonging to the State is now at this Place under a Guard of 7 men.

Mr. Anderson is now in such a way as to repair 100 muskets ⅌ week and from the additional number of hands which he'll be able to sett to work next week I suppose he will then repair at the rate of 150 ⅌ week. I am with great respect Sir Your very huml Serv,

DAVID ROSS

I Have got a piece of Ravens Duck at this place for you to make the addition to your Marque[e]

ENCLOSURE

James Maury to David Ross

DEAR SIR   Richmond 24 May 1781

Not having been able to procure the Money, Horse or Servant for my Journey to Hampton, I am still here. General Cornwallis too, in the Interim, having reached Petersburg, I am desirous of making another application for my Vessell. It occuring to me also that every obstacle to negociating for the permission of sending Tobaccoe to our prisoners being now removed, the Governor would willingly endeavor to have it effected here, by which much Time, much Trouble and much Expence would be saved. No Misunderstanding as yet between the opposite Commanders. The Marquis sent in a Flag the day before yesterday with a passport from Congress for the Vessell loaded with necessaries for the Convention Troops, which Flag Lord Cornwallis admitted notwithstanding it so soon followed after the Affronts recieved by his predecessor. We have now some Tobaccoe and some vessells which we can call our own. If you think as I do I pray you urge these Considerations to his Excellency and send the Bearer my Brother with your Dispatches to him. If his Excellency approves our proposal blank Commissions of Flag of Truce should be sent for as many vessells as will answer the purpose that in Case of Success they might be protected. I refer you to my Brother for the News. I am with much regard Dr Sir yr very humble Servant,   J. MAURY

RC (Vi); addressed to TJ at Charlottesville, "favored by Mr. Maury"; endorsed. Enclosure (Vi); addressed to Ross at "Point-fork By Favor of Mr. F. Maury."

It is probable that TJ had requested a MARQUEE because of a shortage of housing in Charlottesville, for the sudden influx of a large number of state officials and members of the legislature no doubt taxed the capacity of homes and taverns in that village. William Davies, for example, had sent to John Peyton for a marquee for his own use and on 25 May Peyton wrote him: "Agreeable to your request I have sent up my waggon with your Marquee. . . . I presented your order to Captain Russell for the thin duck to mend your Marquee, which he refused delivering without the barrons orders" (Peyton to Davies, 25 May, Vi). But, as he expected to leave office almost at once, TJ must have requested the marquee for the use of his successor; TJ, of course, not only stayed at Monticello himself but reported that the "Speakers of the two houses and some other Members were lodging with us" (Vol. 4: 265). THE AFFRONTS RECEIVED BY HIS PREDECESSOR: TJ, of course, was the one who felt that he had been first affronted and the present letter, containing what must have been the first news he received that Lafayette had tendered the passports for the *Riedesel*, would not seem to have been the most diplomatic method that Maury could have chosen to present his cause (see TJ to the Virginia delegates, 10 May; Lafayette to TJ, 28 May; and Ross to TJ, 28 May). EVERY OBSTACLE . . . BEING NOW REMOVED: That is, removed by the death of General Phillips. See Ross to Davies, 4 Aug. 1781, CVSP, II, 291.

To David Ross

SIR   Monticello May 26th. 1781

I am exceedingly at a Loss to judge whether it be better to try the Method of Application to the new Commanding Officer for a Passport and run the Risk of losing another Month or two, or to pursue the former plan of applying immediately to Charlestown. With Respect to myself however I can more easily determine that the sending to Charlestown having had the Approbation of Council and having a Prospect within two Days of divesting myself of my Office it would not be proper for me to enter on a new Plan. Nevertheless I think it would be adviseable for Mr. Maury to wait a few Days, that my Successor who will have to go through with any Plan that may be adopted may also chuse such one as he shall think best. I am &c.,   THOMAS JEFFERSON

FC (Vi). TJ apparently changed his mind; see his second letter to Lafayette of 30 May 1781.

From Francis Taylor

SIR   Winchester May 26. 1781.

I wrote you the 16 Instant, that a Board of Officers, who were ordered by Colo. Wood to enquire into the titles of the Soldiers to discharges, had sat, and were of opinion that nearly all of the men were entitled to discharges from their removal from Albemarle Barracks. They have since been discharged, and a small Militia Guard is now on duty at the Barracks near this place.

The small number of men we have left being too inconsiderable to be serviceable, I doubt not but your Excellency will think proper to order them to be discharged as also the Officers, which I did not think myself authorised to do without your order.

The Arms of those men of the Regiment who were discharged at Albe. Barracks, were sent away by orders received by Capt. Porter who was at that place. About One hundred and Sixty are here, and on application from the County Lieutenant of Frederick, I have let him take One hundred and forty, to arm some of the Militia who are to march against a body of Tories in Hampshire, which arms are to be returned after the expedition. The rest of the Arms here are delivered to the Quarter master and want repairing. I shall as soon as I can, make a return of the Cloathing drawn by each Soldier and transmit to you. Please inform me what to do as soon as possible, as the expence of keeping Officers without men I imagine will not be approved.

Colo. Wood went to Maryland last week, and I expect will not be here, before the return of an Express sent by him to Congress. I am Sir, Your most obedt Servant,   FRA TAYLOR

RC (Vi); addressed and endorsed. This letter had an enclosure (missing) of a return of the regiment (see Taylor to TJ, 1 June 1781).

Samuel Patteson to William Davies

SIR   Hendersons 27. May 81.

Agreeable to your Instructions I have sent on four hundred stand of arms. The Waggon that brought your Marque to Colo. Lewis's went off before I received your Letter which was this morning. Carver lost two of his horses last night, however, Mr. Southall procured Waggons for the purpose. Your Marque I have paid particular attention to. I have reserved six shirts, one I believe Colo. St[arke] directed West to put on, the ballance 36 I have sent which makes a deficiency of two agreeable to Capt. Pendleton's number. The worthy officer you mention I have treated with the utmost respect. There are no boxes to be had to put the arms in, and I hope but little injury will result from their being sent loose, as we have been as careful as possible in storing them. Fryday I sent an express to point of fork requesting (as you directed me) that all the superfluous stores should be sent here. He arrived there that night and returned to Mr. Lewis yesterday afternoon. I every moment expect a fleet of canoes. Yesterday I met his Excellency in the road. He gave me a letter which with two more I have enclosed. I informed him the stores were coming to Hendersons, and I think his words were these following. "The Council have passed a resolution that all the stores should be sent up the great river and I would wish you should not have more than one load brought to Hendersons before I can confer with Colo. Davies on the subject. Canoes and Batteaus will be much less expence to the public than Waggons, and it is my opinion at all events that there should not be a sufficiency of stores at Hendersons to draw the Enemy's attention for it will be impossible to procure Waggons to move them off." Would his Excellency's magnificent building be illuminated if the Enemy should come? Mr. Andrew Moore from Rockbridge says those mutinyous rascals in Augusta and Rockbridge amount to a majority, a great majority in Augusta! There are but few Waggons in this county and the demand for Waggons I expect will be very great. I know of my own knowledge there is the greatest plenty the other side of the mountains. Except you have an impress Warrant procured and give positive orders on the subject I fear we shall be in a bad situation with respect to our stores; without you follow the Council plan. If you have not wrote to point of fork when the Canoe men arrive I shall direct them after unloaded to go down, load, and wait for your orders which river to take.

I am good Colo. with sentiments of the highest respect your most obed. and most humble servant.   SAMUEL PATTESON

I have found my horse half dead, tenderfooted and sore backed.

RC (Vi); addressed to Davies at "Albemarle old Cthouse"; endorsed: "From Mr. Saml Patterson, in answer to his instructions respecting the removal of Arms &c. from Henderson's." HE GAVE ME A LETTER: This may possibly have been TJ's letter of 25 May to Davies, q.v. THE COUNCIL HAVE PASSED A RESOLUTION: There are no recorded actions of the Council between 15 May and 12 June (Va. Council Jour., II, 345-7). On the question of removing the stores from Point of Fork, David Ross wrote William Davies from that place on 27 May: "I am of opinion a considerable part of the powder ought to be removed immediately as 'tis at any rate too great a risque to have such a quantity in one place, in an indifferent house, and only a guard of seven men. . . . If you think the middle country cannot be defended, tis highly proper to have the stores removed beyond the mountains. I have recommended to your people here to make their movements with as little noise and all the discretion in their power. The people at present are really panic struck and have lost much of their military ardor. I need not tell you the force of imagination. If an idea goes abroad that we are not able to oppose the British, it will have an unhappy effect. Indeed this seems too much the case already. My brother writes to me from Bedford that a pretty general consternation has seized the people there" (Ross to Davies, 27 May 1781, Vi). On 28 May Steuben wrote to John Walker: "I have about 500 men for whom I yesterday received the Arms. I march today with them to the fork where I shall cover the removal of the stores and keep open the communication" (Steuben to Walker, 28 May 1781, NHi).

To the County Lieutenants of Washington and Certain Other Counties

SIR   Charlottesville May 28th 1781

Lord Cornwallis from Carolina and a Reinforcement of 2000 Men from New York having joined the hostile Army which was before here and crossed James River renders it necessary for us to bring a very great Force into the Field. As I have reason to believe you have not sent the whole Number ordered to the Southward by my Letter of   [1] You will now be pleased to send under proper Officers whatever number you were deficient to join immediately our Army under Major General Marquis Fayette. As it is uncertain whether he will retire Northwardly or Westwardly, I would advise that your men come by the Way of Charlottesville should no movement of the Enemy render it unsafe. You will be pleased to understand that the number you are now required to send, with those actually marched to the Southward are to make up   [2] as formerly required. Let every man who possibly can, come armed with a good rifle and those who cannot must bring a good smooth Bore if they have it.

They must expect to continue in the Field two months from the Time of their joining the Army.

Cavalry in a due proportion being as necessary [&c. as in the Letter of May 5th to the County Lieut of Culpeper.][3]

I need not urge you to the most instantaneous execution of these Orders. Till the Reinforcements now called for get into the Field the whole Country lies open to a most powerful Army headed by the most active, enterprising and vindictive Officer who has ever appeared in Arms against us. I am[4] with great respect Sir your most obedt Servt.,   TH: JEFFERSON

FC (Vi); at head of text: "County Lieutenants of Washington, Montgomery & Botetourt." Following this letter in the Executive Letter Book (Vi) there is this entry: "County Lieutenants of Rockbridge, Augusta, Rockingham, Amherst," and after the same salutation, place, and date, "Lord Cornwallis from Carolina &c. as in the Letter to Washington." Since there is no variation in text noted, it is probable that TJ decided to call on these four additional counties after letters to the first three had been dispatched. RC (Vi) to the county lieutenant of Montgomery; in a clerk's hand, with signature and several insertions in TJ's hand.

¹ Blank in FC; "Mar. 29" inserted in TJ's hand in RC.

² Blank in FC; "187" inserted in TJ's hand in RC.

³ Brackets supplied; the paragraph beginning with these words in TJ's let-ter to the county lieutenants of Lunenburg &c. of 8 May, q.v., follows at this point in RC. The letter of 5 May to the county lieutenants of Culpeper was made from the same master copy.

⁴ FC ends at this point; the complimentary close and signature have been supplied from RC.

To James Hunter

SIR   Charlottesville May 28th 1781

I formerly desired Mr. Ross to write to you for five hundred horsemen's Swords made on the Model of the one lodged with you (I believe) by order of Colo. Washington. I must now desire you will add five hundred more to that Number and urge you in the strongest Terms to employ every hand you possibly can in making them; also to let me know what number are ready and how many we may expect by the Week.

Should Colo. Fitzgerald have sent the Incyclopedie to you I shall be obliged to you to contrive it to Winchester if possible as that place will be safer even than this: should he not have sent it be so good as to forward to him the inclosed Letter.

Lord Cornwallis from Carolina and a Reinforcement of 2000 Men from New York have joined Arnold and crossed James River. I am &c.,   THOMAS JEFFERSON

FC (Vi). TJ's letter to John Fitzgerald, enclosed with the present letter to Hunter, has not been found; but see TJ to Fitzgerald, 27 Feb. 1781 and Fitzgerald's reply, 1 Apr. 1781.

To Samuel Huntington

Charlottesville, 28 May 1781. This letter is virtually identical with the first part of TJ's letter to George Washington, same date, q.v. for variations in the two texts.

RC (DLC: PCC, No. 71, II); 2 p.; in a clerk's hand, signed and addressed by TJ; endorsed in part: "Read June 4. Referred to the board of War." FC (Vi). Tr (DLC: TJ Papers).

From Lafayette

SIR   Gold Mine Creek May 28th. 1781

The Enemy's intention has been to distroy this army and I conjecture would have been afterwards to distroy the Stores which it covers. They have now undertaken another movement and it appears they are going through the country to Fredericksburg. Their Dragoons were this morning near Hannover Court House and (unless this is a feint) I expect the Army will be there this evening.

Our small corps moves this evening towards Andersons Bridge. We shall be upon a parallel line with the Enemy keeping the upper part of the Country. I have sent orders to General Weedon to collect the Militia but by a letter recieved from him find that He cannot properly do it as He has no powers from Your Excellency. General Wayne was to leave York Town on the 23d.

Your Excellency will be sorry to hear that all the fine Horses in the Country are falling into the Enemy's hands. This will in the end prove a ruin to this State. But the owners will not remove them. Your orders to impress do not extend farther than twenty miles, and unless the executive give a warrant for 50 miles we cannot get a single Horse. The British have so many Dragoons that it becomes impossible either to stop or reconnoitre their movements, and much more so to send impressing parties around their Camp.

There Has been a Cartel setled between General Greene and Lord Cornwallis. This last I have requested to keep the Virginia Militia in the State untill we can exchange them for Carolina Militia in British service. I request your Excellency will please to give me some informations Respecting the British Prisoners in this State as we must soon send a body of them to Lord Cornwallis, but I presume General Greene will have wrote on the subject. As soon as Your Excellency will please to write me a letter respecting our Prisoners at Charles Town I shall get from Lord Cornwallis a pasport for every kind of supplies you will think proper to send to them. Their Friends ought also to get notice of it that they may collect private supplies for our unfortunate Brother Soldiers.

No Riflemen, no Cavalry, no arms, and few Militia coming. The Culpeper Militia were desirous to take their rifles but were prevented from doing it as the Executive had not called for arms so at least the Officer says. I wish Your Excellency will order Riflemen to join us. Without them and without Horse we can do nothing.

With the highest respect I have the honor to be Your Obt. Humble Ser, LAFAYETTE

N.B. Camden is evacuated. General Greene has ordered General Lawson to join him. Having received a late letter from him it becomes my duty to recommend the execution of these orders. The Barron will probably know Genl. Greenes intentions. To him I refer Genl. Lawson, and beg only leave to observe General Greenes successes may greatly releave us.   l.F.

RC (CSmH); in a clerk's hand, signed by Lafayette; endorsed by TJ: "LaFayette."

From David Ross

Sir   Point of Fork 28 May 1781

I Have just now time to advise you that my agent in Philadelphia on the 9th. instant forwarded 275 Stand of arms and 1 ton of Gunpowder, to Fredericksburg, on the 11th. he forwarded a ton of Gunpowder on the 18th. he forwarded 600 Stand of arms and by this date he expected to forward the remainder of the 2000 Stand. This Supply of Arms, the Arms over and above what the Baron has taken for his Men together with the number that Mr. Anderson can repair may I think be reckon'd at 4,000 Stand more than are at present in the hands of our people, so that I think there will not be a want of arms.

Neither our Delegates in Congress, nor the Generosity of our Northern friends have as yet given any assistance to my agent. The repairs of the Arms, the purchase of Bayonets and the advance of Specie to the Waggoners has been done by loans from private people.

The bearer Mr. Maury will give you the News. He thinks there is a fair prospect now of negotiating matters with Lord Cornwallis for sending Tobacco to Charlestown. He wishes to be sent in with a Flag on this business. I am Sir with great respect Yr huml Serv.,

DAVID ROSS

RC (Vi); addressed and endorsed.

ASSISTANCE TO MY AGENT: Either Ross was in error in saying that the Virginia delegates had given no assistance or the delegates themselves were, for in their letter to TJ of 1 May they pointed out that, before Nicolson's arrival as Ross' agent, they had already undertaken to have the 2,000 rampart muskets sawn off and made acceptable for infantry. The Board of War, in acknowledging Steuben's letters of 16 and 21 Apr. 1781, wrote that they had previously "directed two thousand rampart musketts to be delivered to the Delegates of Virginia for the use of that state and which they conceived might be very serviceable to the militia: The Delegates have contracted with a workman to cut them to a proper length and to put them in perfect repair. From the essay which has been made on two of them, the Board have no doubt that they will fully answer the purpose for which they are intended" (Board of War to Steuben, 30 Apr. 1781, NHi). Ross must have meant that the Virginia delegates had not been able to assist Nicolson in financing the purchase of arms and supplies, a fact which they acknowledged in their letter to TJ of 23 May 1781, q.v. William Grayson of the Board of War added the following in a letter to Weedon: "There never was more manoeuvring than to get the rampart arms, and have them repaired. I really now cant tell how it has been effected. I shall consult the Delegates of the state and fall upon all the ways and means upon the face of the earth to get you swords and pistols. As to Musketts I think you are in a pretty good way. Wayne has at last marched. . . . 600 new levies will shortly join you from Maryland and Delaware. Moylans horse will go in fourteen days amounting to 60 dragoons: Pray with Steubans 1200 and this force canot you look Cornwallis in the face? . . . Since writing the above, we have screwed out fifty pair of pistols, and a thousand cartridge boxes. Pray inform me what you want. Everything shall be done that can be done" (Grayson to Weedon, 29 May 1781, PPAP). A few days later Grayson wrote: "I am now *authorized* to tell you you will be supplyed to a much greater extent than I expected. By the first day of July, there shall be a sufficient quantity of arms in Virginia *for all your purposes*" (same to same, 5 June 1781, PPAP). Daniel of St. Thomas Jenifer informed Weedon that Grayson himself was responsible for much of this activity: "The Board of War has promised to have ready in 7 days 1500 stand of arms for our state [Maryland]. Grayson is indefatigable" (Jenifer to Weedon, 5 June, 1781, PPAP). See also TJ to the Virginia delegates, 6 Apr. 1781.

To the Speaker of the House of Delegates

SIR   Charlottesville May 28th. 1781

Since I had the honour of addressing the General Assembly by Letter of the 14th instant I have received a second Letter from the Honble. Major General Greene on the subject of cavalry and another in answer to one I had written communicating to him information I had recived as to the conduct of a particular officer employed by him in impressing, which I transmit herewith.

I also inclose a Letter which I have received since the same date from the Honble. Dudley Digges resigning the office of Member of the Council of State.

Further experience, together with recent information from the Commanding Officer within this State, convince me that something is necessary to be done to enforce the calls of the Executive for militia to attend in the field. Whether the deficiencies of which we have had reason to complain proceeded from any backwardness in the militia themselves or from a want of activity in their principal officers, I do not undertake to decide. The Laws also to which they are Subject while in the field seem scarcely coercive enough for a state of war.

The Commanding Officer also represents that great evils and dangers are to be apprehended from the total want of authority of the military power over citizens within the vicinities of his and of the enemy's encampments. Many of them tho' well disposed are led by an attachment to their property to remain within the power of the enemy, and are then compelled to furnish horses, procure provisions, serve as guides and to perform other offices in aid of their operations: while others of unfriendly disposition become spies and intelligencers and if taken in the very fact are not subject to that speedy justice which alone can effectually deter. He supposes that the lives of our soldiers and citizens entrusted to his care might be rendered much more secure by some legal provision against the unrestrained right of passing to and fro in the neighborhood of the encampments and by subjecting the inhabitants within some certain distance to such immediate trial and punishment for leading attempts against the safety of our army or in aid of that of our enemies, as the rights of the citizens on the one hand and necessities of war on the other may safely admit. I have the honor to be with very great respect Sir your mo: obt & mo: hble. servt.,

Th: Jefferson

RC (Vi); in a clerk's hand, signed by TJ; endorsed: "Governor's Letter May 28th: 1781. Stating sundry Matters May 28th. 1781. Referred to Committee of whole on State of Commw." FC (Vi); at head of text: "The Speaker of the House of Delegates." Enclosures (now separated from RC): Copies of Nathanael Greene's letters to TJ of 28 and 30 Apr. 1781 and Dudley Digges to TJ, 14 May 1781.

SINCE . . . ADDRESSING THE GENERAL ASSEMBLY BY LETTER OF THE 14TH INSTANT: This must have been an error on TJ's part, and may have been caused by the fact that he had before him Digges' letter of the 14th which he enclosed with this (and the date of which TJ himself inserted, perhaps at this time); he must have been referring to his letter to the speaker of the House of 10 May. Endorsements of both letters (10 and 28 May) show that they were referred to the committee of the whole, but there is a reference to only one letter from TJ in the proceedings of the House of 28 May (JHD, May 1781, 1828 edn., p. 5), perhaps because the present letter was considered as a supplement to that of 10 May. It is possible that at this time TJ transmitted other letters to the speaker of the House, either as enclosures with the present letter or without covering letters. For example, on 28 May the speaker presented a letter from George Washington; this may have been Washington's letter of 16 May to TJ (same, p. 4). Also, on the same day, the speaker "communicated to the House a letter from John Walker, Esq. addressed to his excellency the Governor, containing information respecting the enemy, and stating the desire of the honorable Major General Marquis de La Fayette on the subject of impressing horses" (same, p. 4-5). This letter from Walker to TJ has not been found, but it was written on 25 May (see TJ to Lafayette, 29 May). It is possible, too, that TJ's reference to FURTHER EXPERIENCE, TOGETHER WITH INFORMATION FROM THE COMMANDING OFFICER, meant that he enclosed Lafayette's letter of 26 May. See Hening, x, 411, for an Act establishing martial law within 20 miles of the American army, no doubt adopted in pursuance of TJ's advice.

From Steuben

I have the honor to inclose to your Excellency a representation to the House of Delegates of the State of the Virginia Line.

As this is a matter which requires the consideration of that House I beg your Excellency to lay this representation before them as early as possible. with the highest respect I have the honor to be Your Excellencys Most Obed Sevt.

ENCLOSURE

Representation of the State of the Virginia Line

[28 May 1781]

Major General Baron Steuben thinks it his duty to lay before the honorable house of Delegates the present situation of the Virginia Line.

At the General's arrival in this State in November last, the line consisted of about 1400 men, chiefly drafts for 18 months raised the preceeding summer. Of these, 500 were [sent] to the southward under Col. Buford, but were so naked as to be unfit for service; the remaining 900 were at Chesterfield destitute as well of arms as cloaths. With great difficulty 800 of these by the unexpected arrival of some cloathing from Philadelphia were at length equipped and sent in two detachments to General Greene, and joined him before the action at Guilford; since which time he has received no reinforcement of regular troops from Virginia. By the last arrangements of Congress, 8 regiments of infantry 2 of cavalry and one of artillery are required as the quota from this state, amounting in the whole to 5898 effective men exclusive of officers, staff &c. By the act of assembly passed in the fall session, the legislature determined that 3,000 men should be raised which were to be embodied in the month of February last. This law, however has not been enforced: the invasion of the state and a variety of unfortunate circumstances have so far defeated the execution of it, that in very many counties there has been no draft at all, and the whole number of recruits which has yet arrived does not exceed 450 men, and should the enemy continue in the state during the campaign, that number will probably be all that will be collected.[1]

After the action of Guilford the Virginia infantry then

with the army from extraordinary desertions did not exceed	700
Col. Washington's Cavalry consisted of about	120
Col. White's	80
The Artillery	54

Amounting in the whole to no more than	954[2]

which is not the sixth part of the quota required from the State. Since that period the line has been considerably diminished from the continuance of the same causes, without the addition of a dozen recruits.[3] Under these circumstances how the several regiments of this line are to have existence is a matter worthy the most serious attention of the honorable house.

The opposition made to the law in some counties, the entire neglect of it in others, and an unhappy disposition to evade the fair execution of it in all afford a very melancholy prospect: A prospect the more truly distressing, when it is remembered that the Virginia quota alone, would of itself be far more than sufficient not only to exterminate the whole force of the enemy from this state, but to endanger all the conquests they have made to the southward. The recital of the distresses which will follow from a perseverance in these measures is too painful to be attempted. Certain it is, however, that unless some mode is adopted to punish desertion and enforce the execution of the laws, unless some check is devised to prevent the shameful evasions and impositions, which to the disgrace of individuals are too successfully attempted, this country will sink under the power of her enemies, or be dependent for support solely upon foreign assistance.[4]

The equipment of the cavalry is of the highest moment. Three hundred horses are wanting to complete them, but the sum limitted by a law of the state being no more than £5000, is utterly inadequate, nor can one horse fit for service be procured at that price. Without the interposition of the legislature, the cavalry cannot be mounted; and in the present situation of affairs, without a formidable cavalry there can be but little security for anything below the mountains.[5]

FC (NHi); endorsed: "Copy to Govr Jefferson with a memorial to house of delegates 28 May 1781." Of the enclosure there are two drafts in NHi: (1) A draft in the hand of William North, which was perhaps the first to be composed and represented Steuben's initial views; and (2) a draft entirely in the hand of William Davies, which was obviously made subsequent to that in North's hand and was a revision of it, containing one or two slight omissions and some additions as indicated below. The revision by Davies is the text followed above. Under date of 23 May there are in NHi copies of letters from Steuben to Washington and to the Board of War containing a summary account of his effort to raise troops in Virginia for Greene's army, in which some of the phraseology of Davies' version of the memorial is used, indicating that both texts of that document were composed at least five days before Steuben transmitted the final version to TJ. The revision by Davies bears at its head the following dateline: "Albemarle O C House 28 May 1781," but this is not in Davies' hand and was obviously added at the time and place from which Steuben dispatched the covering letter to TJ.

TJ submitted Steuben's letter and the memorial in his letter to the speaker on 31 May (JHD, May 1781, 1828 edn., p. 7). Steuben was somewhat franker in his comment to Greene about the state of the Virginia line: "The Desertion that prevails among the Recruits is astonishing, and equals that of the Virginia troops with you. . . . You mention the great want of Officers to the Virginia troops with you. Inclosed you have a list of those who have returned from your Army on various pretences; and when once they get in this state it is impossible to assemble them again. In a word, my dear General, I despair of ever seeing a Virga Line exist. Everything seems to oppose it. . . . The few recruits we have are formed into a Regt under Colo Gaskins. About 150 are armed. I shall order them in a couple of days to the forks of James River where, at the same time that they in some measure satisfy the people of the state by protecting their magazines which are all collected there, they may be disciplining and equipping the men" (Steuben to Greene, 14 May 1781, NHi).

[1] The draft in North's hand differs somewhat from this sentence, though the substance is the same.

[2] The draft in North's hand adds the number of "440" recruits (450 in pres-

ent text) and the words "which makes the whole Virga. Line 1394 Men."

3 This sentence is not in the draft in North's hand.

4 This entire paragraph is lacking in the draft in North's hand.

5 The corresponding sentence in the draft in North's hand merely reads: "The Service of the Cavalry is so Essential to the Operations of the Army as to make this an Object of the most important consideration."

To George Washington

Sir   Charlottsville May 28th. 1781.

I make no doubt you will have heard, before this shall have the honour of being presented to Your Excellency, of the junction of Lord Cornwallis with the force at Petersburg under Arnold who had succeeded to the command on the death of Major General Philips. I am now advised that they have evacuated Petersburg, joined at Westover a Reinforcement of 2000 Men just arrived from New York, crossed James River, and on the 26th. Instant were three Miles advanced on their way towards Richmond; at which place Majr. General the Marquiss Fayette lay with 3000 men, regulars and militia, that being the whole number we could Arm till the arrival of the 1100 Arms from Rhode Island which are about this time getting to the place where our public Stores are deposited. The whole force of the Enemy within this State from the best intelligence I have been able to get, I think, is about 7000 Men, Infantry and Cavalry, including also the small Garrison left at Portsmouth. A number of Privateers and small Vessels which are constantly ravaging the Shores of our Rivers prevent us from receiving any aid from the Counties lying on Navigable Waters; [and powerful Operations meditated against our Western Frontier by a joint force of British and Indian savages have, as your Excellency before knew, obliged us to embody between two and three thousand Men in that quarter. Your Excellency will judge from this state of things and from what you know of your own Country what it may probably suffer during the present Campaign. Should the Enemy be able to produce no opportunity of annihilating the Marquis's Army a small proportion of their force may yet restrain his movements effectually while the greater part is employed in detachment to waste an unarmed Country and to lead the minds of the people to acquiescence under those events which they see no human power prepared to ward off. We are too far removed from the other scenes of war, to say whether the main force of the Enemy be within this State, but I suppose they cannot any where spare so great an Army for the operations of the field: Were it possible for this Circumstance to justify in Your Excellency a determination to lend us Your personal aid, it is evident from the universal voice that the presence of their beloved Countryman, whose talents have been so long successfully employed in establishing the freedom of kindred States, to whose person they have still flattered themselves they retained some right, and have ever looked up as their dernier resort in distress, that your appearance among them I say would restore full confidence of salvation, and would render them equal to whatever is not impossible. I cannot undertake to foresee and obviate the difficulties which stand in the way of such a resolution: the whole Subject is before you of which I see only detached parts; and your judgment will be formed on view of the whole. Should the danger of this State and its consequence to the Union be such as to render it best for the whole that you should repair to it's assistance, the difficulty would then be how to keep men out of the field. I have undertaken to hint this matter to your Excellency not only on my own sense of its importance to us, but at the sollicitations of many members of weight in our legislature which is not yet assembled to speak their own desires. A few days will bring to me that period of relief which the Constitution has prepared for those oppressed with the labours of my office, and a long declared resolution of relinquishing it to abler hands has prepared my way for retirement to a private station: still however as an individual citizen I should feel the comfortable effects of your presence, and have (what I thought could not have been), an additional motive for that gratitude, esteem & respect with which][1] I have the honour to be Your Excellency's Most obedient & Most humble servant,

TH: JEFFERSON

RC (DLC: Washington Papers); in a clerk's hand, signed by TJ; endorsed in part: "Ansd. 8: June." FC (Vi); Tr (DLC: TJ Papers). Tr (PPAP).

On 28 May TJ sent a virtually identical letter to Samuel Huntington, but with the difference noted below.

[1] The text in brackets (supplied) was sent only to Washington. The letter to Huntington reads, instead: "and the very powerful operations preparing by a joint force of British and Indian Savages on our frontier oblige us to embody an army there of between two and three thousand men. These facts with those which I have heretofore been constrained to trouble your Excellency with will enable Congress to form a proper judgement of the situation of this State and to adopt such measures for its aid as it's circumstances may require and their powers effect."

From the Commissioners of the Specific Tax in Fairfax County

SIR   Fairfax County May 29th. 1781

Inclosed we transmit your Excellency the Amount of each Commissary's Return of the Produce received this last Spring, in payment of the Tax payable in enumerated Commodities, in this County. The Wheat, Rye, and Oats, and three thousand four hundred and ninety seven 5/8th Bushels of Corn We have delivered to Mr. James Lawrason of Alexandria, Mr. John Brown's Deputy in this County, in pursuance of your Excellency's Order of the 23d February last. The remainder of the Corn vizt. one hundred and seventy one Bushels was delivered out for the use of the Troops under the Command of the Marquis De la Fayette, when They passed through Colchester, as by the inclosed Copies of the receipts and Orders. We shall take care to have the Tobacco prized up and keep it at your Excellency's Disposal. We have the Honour to be Your Excellency's most Obedt. Servts.,

MARTIN COCKBURN
RICHARD CHICHESTER
Commissioners of the Specific Tax

RC (Vi); addressed to TJ at Richmond; endorsed. Enclosures not found. TJ's ORDER OF THE 23D FEBRUARY LAST has not been found.

To the County Lieutenants of York and Certain Other Counties

SIR   Charlottesville May 29th 1781

Information having been given me that a considerable number of Men have deserted from the French Army and Navy in America which the Commanding Officers are very urgent to have apprehended, I must desire you to give orders at the several Ferries in your County, that all Foreigners offering to cross at them and having the Appearance of Soldiers or Seamen be examined with great Strictness and if there be good Reason to believe them to be Deserters that they then be delivered to such Persons as you shall appoint to guard them till you can have an Opportunity by Militia or otherwise to send them with a State of the Circumstances of Suspicion to the Headquarters of Major General the Marquis La Fayette. I am[1] with much respect Sir Your most Obd. Servt.,

TH: JEFFERSON

FC (Vi); at head of text: "County Lieutenants of York, New Kent, Hanover, Gloucester, King & Queen, King William, Middlesex, Essex, Caroline, Spotsylvania, Lancaster, Richmond, King George, Northumberland, Westmoreland, Stafford, Prince William, Fairfax, Loudoun & Berkeley." RC (ViU); in a clerk's hand, signed by TJ; at foot of text: "Westmoreland."

1 FC ends at this point; complimentary close supplied from RC.

From Andrew Donnally

SIR   Green Brier County 29th. May 1781

Agreeable to your Excellency's Instructions I have held a Court Martial to enquire into the Delinquencies which have happened by Persons of the Militia neglecting to perform their Tour of Duty, the Number of Delinquents here are few; and am at a loss how to have them Marched to the place directed to, in your Instructions, as no person here will undertake to perform the Duty upon the Terms mentioned in your Excellency's Letter; this makes me request your farther Instructions how I am to proceed in this affair. I am Sir Your Excellency's Obt. Hble Servant,

ANDW. DONNALLY

RC (Vi); addressed and endorsed. YOUR . . . INSTRUCTIONS: See TJ to the county lieutenants, 12 Apr. 1781, in which YOUR EXCELLENCY'S LETTER of 30 Mch. 1781 is referred to.

To Lafayette

SIR   Charlottesville May 29th. 1781

I am honored with your Favor of the 26th as I had been by one of the Day before from Colo. John Walker who informed me that he wrote at your Request on the Subject of horses. I have now the Pleasure to inclose to you eight Impress Warrants accompanied with Resolutions of the House of Delegates, which I obtained yesterday and to inform you that as soon as the other Branch of the Legislature is convened I believe they are disposed to strengthen you with Cavalry to any Amount you think proper and with as good Horses as you shall think Oeconomy should induce us to take. Stud Horses and Brood Mares will be always excepted because to take them would be to rip up the Hen which laid the Golden Eggs.

I am sorry it has not been in your Power to send me the County Returns of Militia. I assure you that such Returns weekly are indispensably necessary to enable the Executive to keep Militia in the Field. I did however, on receiving Information from Colo.

Walker that the Enemy were reinforced, call for one Fourth of the Militia of Washington, Montgomery, Botetourt, Rockbridge, Augusta, Rockingham and Amherst which (the last excepted) are our best rifle Counties. They will rendezvous at Charlottesville and there expect your Orders.

Baron Steuben informed me also that only two men were employed in repairing the damaged Arms. I am at a Loss what to think on this Subject as I have received Assurance that one hundred a Week are repaired there and that very shortly they will be enabled to repair 150 a Week. I will take immediate Measures for procuring a State of the Repairs.

I sincerely and anxiously wish you may be enabled to prevent Lord Cornwallis from engaging you till you shall be sufficiently reinforced and be able to engage him on your own terms. This may be the Case when your Superiority in Cavalry shall become decided which I have the most sanguine hopes the Assembly will immediately provide for. In the mean Time the upper Country will afford you a secure Retreat presenting Hills inacessible to Horse and approaching them to their most dangerous Enemies the Riflemen.

I will take the Liberty of recommending to you that the two Field Officers to be appointed for valuing the Impressed horses be skilled in that Business, and that the same two may go through the whole Business that all may be valued on the same Scale. Also that Officers of mild and condescending Tempers and manners be employed and particularly instructed while they prosecute their Object steadily to use every soothing Art possible.

A high Tone of Conduct will as it did in a former Instance revolt the People against the Measure altogether and produce a Suppression of it. I have the honor to be &c.,

THOMAS JEFFERSON

FC (Vi); John Walker was probably the bearer of the (missing) RC of this letter (see Walker to TJ, 30 May). Enclosures (missing): (1) eight impress warrants, one of which was transmitted by Thomas Nelson to Colonel Josiah Parker on 8 June 1781; it was signed by TJ, dated at Charlottesville on 28 May 1781, executed in blank, and authorized the holder to "impress in the counties contiguous to the march of the enemy such and so many horses as the Honble Major General Marquis Fayette shall direct, following . . . the sense and intention of the House of Delegates ex-pressed in their resolutions of this date as amended and hereto annexed" (VMHB, XXII [1914], 261). (2) Resolutions of the House as noted below (same, p. 261-2; MS in Vi).

YOUR FAVOR OF THE 26TH: This is undoubtedly the letter that Constable wrote TJ on 26 May, part of which was Constable's fair copy of Lafayette's rough draft. ONE OF THE DAY BEFORE FROM COLO. JOHN WALKER: Walker's letter to TJ of 25 May has not been found, but its subject is apparent from the present letter and from the action taken on it by the House of Delegates.

On May 28 the "Speaker communicated to the House a letter from John Walker, Esq. addressed to his excellency the Governor, containing information respecting the enemy, and stating the desire of the honorable Major General Marquis de La Fayette on the subject of impressing horses." This letter was referred to a committee which reported at once and the following resolutions were agreed to by the House on the same day: that the Governor be advised to issue his warrant to Lafayette empowering him to impress in the counties contiguous to the march of the enemy all such horses as he should think necessary; that all such horses should be appraised in specie by two field officers and that this valuation should be paid in specie or "in paper money at the real exchange"; that impress warrants ought to be issued only to commissioned officers; that stud horses and others actually employed in moving the families or effects of the owners ought not to be impressed; and that Lafayette ought to be asked to have an exact return made giving names of owners, amount of valuation, and purposes for which impresses were made" (JHD, May 1781, 1828 edn., p. 4-5). In view of the often-expressed view that TJ's legalistic views and philosophical temperament unfitted him for the severely practical tasks of a war governor, two actions taken on 28 May are pertinent: (1) he issued warrants in accordance with the terms of the House's resolution despite the fact that the Senate did not concur in that resolution until almost two weeks later (same, 12 June, p. 14); (2) he amended this resolution as follows: a MS copy of the resolution (Vi), attested by John Beckley, has the following notation in TJ's hand: "By an amendment brood mares are not to be impressed unless the owner fails on reasonable notice to remove them out of the way of the enemy, in which case Stud horses are also to be subject to impresses. Th:J." There is no record of such an amendment in the journals of the House and TJ's notation is written at the bottom of Beckley's attested copy; hence it is safe to assume that the amendment was by executive decision rather than by legislative action (VMHB, XXII [1914], p. 261-2). Indeed, the present letter shows that "the other Branch of the Legislature," the Senate, was not then in session and the form of TJ's impress warrant (see above) shows that the resolution was "amended" on 28 May when he annexed a copy to each warrant. Here, as elsewhere throughout the governorship, TJ never forgot either that a war was being fought or that it was being fought by and for free men. But he recognized that "Necessity is Law, in times of war most especially," as he wrote Matthew Pope on 21 May 1781, though even so he kept in view "the rights of the citizen on the one hand and necessities of war on the other" (see TJ to the speaker of the House, 28 May). A HIGH TONE OF CONDUCT . . . IN A FORMER INSTANCE: This was a delicate warning to Lafayette not to yield to the temptations that had ensnared Greene and Steuben and had helped to defeat their efforts to obtain cavalry horses. Lafayette's need was desperate, as theirs had been, but the fact that such a warning was necessary could not have been more dramatically underscored than by the remarkable coincidence that, on this same day, Lafayette was being used by the same individual who, more than any other, had caused most of the difficulty in the "former Instance" and whose "high Tone of Conduct" toward TJ had earned him a reprimand by Congress—Col. Anthony Walton White (see Vol. 3: 587; TJ to White, 24 Mch. 1781; and White's haughty reply, 5 Apr. 1781). For the letter that Lafayette wrote TJ on this day was not only not couched in his usual friendly style, but was a rather imperious demand. It was signed by Lafayette, but the handwriting—and probably the choice of words—was that of Col. White himself, a fact whose full implications could not have been known to Lafayette but which were in all probability not lost on TJ, for he had dealt with that blustery cavalryman under Gates, under Greene, and under Steuben. Nevertheless, TJ complied with Lafayette's request concerning arms and accoutrements (TJ to the county lieutenants of Powhatan, &c. 31 May). THE DAMAGED ARMS: TJ obtained his figures of the number that could be repaired from David Ross (see Ross to TJ, 26 May). Steuben, who by the middle of May had lost all interest in remaining in Virginia and was, as he wrote Greene, "heartily disgusted at the Conduct and proceedings in this Quarter" (Steuben to Greene, 14 May 1781, NHi), was engaged in making more than habitually harsh criticism of Virginia. What he had actually said to Lafayette was this: "I cannot flatter you with hopes of another supply [of arms]. However astonishing it may be, it is true that only two men have been employed by the State for the reparation of arms since January. At present there are six added to them from the Battalion of Continental troops which are here [at Point of Fork]. This shamefull neglect I have acquainted Government with, but scarcely hope for an amendment" (Dft, Steuben to Lafayette, 22 May 1781, NHi). This was manifestly untrue and was not altogether fair to Lafayette, besides being quite unfair to Steuben's loyal supporter, Col. Davies. For, since Steuben already had Greene's permission to join him in South Carolina and was waiting only for arms to be given to the drafted men then assembling at Albemarle barracks, he was reluctant to send even the 327 arms that went with his letter of 22 May and therefore said nothing about the 1,100 stand of arms that arrived at Albemarle Old Courthouse on the very

day that he wrote Lafayette. While Steuben was making this criticism of the government, his friend Davies was writing him as follows on the same day from Charlottesville: "I am also taking measures for sending down the 1100 stand of arms which have just arrived from Philadelphia. From a conviction that the interests of the state and continent are inseparably connected, I had directed all the state gunsmiths to work upon the continental arms, and I flatter myself you must have seen with satisfaction the hands that are employed in that business at the point of fork. As I arrived here last evening, I have not yet seen the Governor, but shall immediately forward the arms down to the fork to be given to the men. . . . My horses being much fatigued and reduced with constant riding will unavoidably make it the afternoon of tomorrow before I can reach you, in case I should still be required to attend you" (Davies to Steuben, 22 May 1781, NHi).

From Lafayette

SIR   Head Quarters May 29h: 1781

The Enemy's Movements into the Country, and our great deficiency in Cavalry, makes it absolutely necessary that two hundred dismounted Dragoons, under the Command of Col: White are immediately furnished with Horses. For this purpose I have directed Col: White to fix upon some Place of safety to equip his Men, and send them to the Feild; to accomplish which I must request the favor of your Excellency to Order all the accutrements, and arms in the possession of the Militia, and in the different parts of this State to be sent to Col: White and he impowered to employ Persons to impress two hundred Horses fit for the Dragoon Service, on the South side of James River and in any other part of the State your Excellency may please to direct. I flatter myself the adopting this mode, without loss of time, will meet with your Excellencys approbation, as I can assure you nothing else will put it in my power to prevent the Enemy from raveging the Country in small Parties. I have the honor to be your Excellencys Most obedt: & very H: Sevt.,   LAFAYETTE

RC (Vi); it is a significant fact that this letter is in the handwriting of Col.

Anthony Walton White, who must in fact have composed it (see note to preceding letter from TJ to Lafayette); signed by Lafayette; endorsed. Gottschalk, *Lafayette and the Close of the American Revolution*, Chicago, 1942, p. 241, misinterprets this letter as evidence that Lafayette had "on his own responsibility . . . issued orders to Colonel White to impress two hundred horses."

For TJ's action on this letter, see his orders to the county lieutenants of Powhatan and certain other counties, 31 May, and his letter to Lafayette of 31 May. It is to be noted that TJ did not empower Col. White "to employ Persons" to impress horses or agree to issue a warrant to him, but that he referred the latter decision back to Lafayette and avoided the former altogether by suggesting that White be given one of the impress warrants that TJ had sent to Lafayette; by this action he was assured that impresses made by White would be in accord with the resolution of the House, a copy of which was attached to each warrant.

From the Virginia Delegates in Congress

〚*Philadelphia, 29 May 1781*. In Col. William Fleming's letter to TJ of 14 June 1781, q.v., he enclosed a "paper" which "came under cover from Our members in Congress of the 29th of May," in which letter "mention is made of a letter from the King of France of a late date to Congress the contents of which will be sent to the respective legislatures, without hinting the purport." The letter from the delegates, doubtless addressed to TJ, has not been found. See Samuel Huntington to TJ, 1 June 1781, and references there.〛

From the Continental Board of War

SIR   War office May 30. 1781.

The board do themselves the honor to transmit to you, a resolution of congress of the 23d. instant also a resolution of the 11th. of april last, by which you will discover that they depend upon the arrears of specific supplies for the last campaign which have not yet been furnished by the different States to make good their engagements with the Court of France.

As the honor and faith of the united [States] is so materially concerned, there is every reason to expect, the most decided exertions in the States to enable Congress to comply with their contracts. The board request you will be pleased to acquaint them with your expectations on this head and what they may probably depend on. I have the honor to be with the highest respect, Sir, Yr. Most Obedt. & very hble Servt.,   WILLM. GRAYSON.

By order of the Board

Tr (Vi). Enclosures (missing): Resolutions of Congress of 11 Apr. and 23 May 1781 ordering the Board of War to form magazines of the specific supplies required by the resolution of 25 Feb. 1780 (JCC, XIX, 373; XX, 528; see also Samuel Huntington to TJ, 26 Feb. 1780).

From John Gibson

Fort Pitt May 30th. 1781.

This will be delivered to your Excellency by Ens. Tannehill paymaster to the 7th. Virg Regiment whom I have sent Express to Richmond in order to procure the 4 months pay allowed by the Honorable the Assembly of Virga. towards the Depreciation of their former pay, for the noncommissioned Officers and soldiers of the same regiment. I hope when your Excellency is Assured that they have not recieved a single shilling for these twenty months past, you will interest yourself in their Behalf, and dispatch Ens. Tannehill Back. Inclosed is also my Account of Expences in forwarding the Powder from Carlisle to this place for Genl. Clarke which Considering the depreciation, I think is low, and I am certain much less than what I Expended. You will please to order it to be paid. Ensn. Tannehill will also deliver an account for the making up of the Cloathing and shirts for the regiment, which I hope your Excellency will order to be paid.

General Clarke will write your Excellency by this Opportunity, and I make no doubt give you every information relative to the intended Expedition. I am much afraid he will not be able to get many of the militia from this quarter, as I have just heard that three hundred men from the Counties of Monongehala and Ohio have crossed the Ohio at Weeling and are gone to Cut of the Moravian Indian towns, if so they will hardly turn out on their return. Indeed it appears to me they have done this in order to evade going with Genl. Clarke. The Moravians have always given the most convincing proofs of their attachment to the cause [of] America, by always giving us Intelligence of every party that Came against the frontiers, and on the late Expedition they furnished Colo. Brodhead and his party with a large Quantity of provision when they were Starving.

For the news of this post permit me to refer your Excellency to the Bearer Ens. Tannehill. I have the honour to be your Excellencys most obedient Humble Servt., JNO. GIBSON
Colo Comdr. F pitt

RC (Vi); endorsed: "Colo: John Gibson & Mr. William Harrison their Letters. June 11th: 1781. to lie on table."

As indicated in the endorsement, Gibson's letter, together with the letter of William Harrison to TJ of 2 June 1781, q.v., was presented to the House on 11 June (JHD, May 1781, 1828 edn., p. 13). GENERAL CLARKE . . . BY THIS OPPORTUNITY: Gibson wrote to Clark on the same day, sending the letter by ENS. TANNEHILL, requesting him to write the Governor on the same subject; no letter from Clark, complying with this request, has been located (*George Rogers Clark Papers, 1771-1781*, p. 559-60).

From James Hunter

Stafford 30h May 1781

I have but just time to acknowledge receipt of your Excellencys Favor of 28h. inst. as Tarlton with 500 Horse is reported to have been at Hanover Court yesterday, and last night within five miles of Bowling Green on his way to distroy my works. If that be true, (Fredericksburg is thereby nearly deserted) he may do the mischeif to night.

A Troop of Colo. Nelsons Horse just now crossed the Ferry, its said, on their way back, to recruit their Horses.

I have long ago informed the Officers in every department that there was no Sword Cutler, or other Artificer at my works that could make the Swords, and unless they are returned on furlough from the Army, shoud the Works remain, it will be impossible to furnish them, or many other Military Stores on hand for the Southern and this Army, much retarded by the Hands being taken from me. At present, I am removing my Tools, and a total stopage to every thing. I am wth the utmost Respect Yr Excellencys most obedt. & obliged Sert., JAMES HUNTER

RC (Vi); addressed to TJ at Charlottesville; endorsed.

To Miles King

Sir Charlottesville May 30th 1781

The passports for the British flag vessel was by me put under cover to Genl. Phillips and delivered to an Officer appointed by Major Genl. Baron Steuben to carry it in with a flag and to attend the vessel to and from her port of destination.

The movements of the enemy and uncertainty with what part of them Genl. Phillips was, prevented the Officer from going on before the arrival of the Major Genl. Marquis Fayette who then undertook to have it forwarded. Since this I have heard nothing of it and did not doubt it was gone on. I advise your messenger to go by the Marquis head quarters to whom I will write by him that you may be certainly informed where it is and when to expect it. Your messenger said you have lately written to me but I have not received the Letter. We are still doubtful of the Arrival of a Fleet talked of. I am &c., THOMAS JEFFERSON

FC (Vi).
King's letter, to which this is an answer, was enclosed in TJ's letter to Lafayette of the same day, following,

and has not been found. YOUR MESSEN-GER SAID YOU HAVE LATELY WRITTEN TO ME: This probably refers to King's letter of 11 May which, though endorsed as "recd May 81," may have arrived in Richmond after TJ had departed on 15 May and may not have come to his attention before the present letter was written. SINCE THIS I HAVE HEARD NOTHING OF IT: This is a surprising statement, for, if TJ read the letter of James Maury enclosed in that of David Ross of 26 May (which TJ received and answered on the same date), he knew that Lafayette had sent to Cornwallis the passport for the flag *Riedesel* on 22 May. It is apparent that on 30 May he *had* read Maury's letter of 24 May (see second letter to Lafayette of this date).

To Lafayette

SIR   Charlottesville May 30th. 1781

I inclosed to Genl. Phillips a passport for the British flag vessel the Genl. Riedesel and delivered it to Captn. Jones who called on me for that purpose by order of Major General Baron Steuben and was to have accompanied the vessel to and from her port of Destination.

The movements of the enemy and uncertainty where Genl. Phillips was then to be found delayed his going till you had arrived. I think Baron Steuben afterwards informed me you would be so kind as to send in the Letter by a flag and an Officer to go with the vessel.

The inclosed Letter from Mr. Miles King written at the request of Captain Gerlach the flagmaster I take the Liberty of transmitting to you by the person who brought it who is returning to Mr. King and will carry any line of information with which you will be so kind as to favor him. I am &c.,   THOMAS JEFFERSON

FC (Vi). Enclosure not found; see note to preceding letter.

James Monroe conducted the *Riedesel* in place of CAPTN. JONES: on 17 June Weedon wrote to Lafayette: "The Flag Ship going to Alexandria is Con-ducted by Colo. James Monroe who had full direct[ions] how to Act" (Weedon to Lafayette, 17 June 1781, PPAP); see also Monroe to TJ, 18 June 1781.

To Lafayette

SIR   Charlottesville May 30th. 1781.

Mr. Maury informs me there is Reason to expect from Lord Cornwallis a permission to export to Charlestown tobacco for our Officers and Soldiers in captivity there. As you have been fully apprised of what has been done heretofore and a negotiation for the relief of Officers and soldiers of the Continental Line which you have honored by accepting the command seems equally reconcileable to your Office and humanity, I will beg leave to inform you that the State will provide as far as nine hundred hogsheads of tobacco to be sent to Charlestown for the above purpose and to ask the favor of you to negotiate with Lord Cornwallis for the License. The Distance of the Executive from his Lordship is an additional reason for asking this favor of you. Mr. Maury will lend any aid in his power to promote this business, and is still recommended as a proper person to attend the tobacco to Charlestown. I have the honor to be &c., THOMAS JEFFERSON

FC (Vi). This letter was written before TJ received Lafayette's letter of 28 May in which he said that as soon as he heard from TJ he would get a passport for Charleston. See note to TJ to Miles King, this date; see also TJ to Ross, 26 May 1781, for TJ's earlier and different decision.

To Robert Scot

SIR   Charlottesville May 30 1781

There is an Indian Chief from Kaskaskia with some companions arrived here, whose rank, services, disposition and proposals are such as require attention from us and great respect. He has particularly desired to be distinguished by a medal, and we think it of so much Importance as to send the bearer express to wait till you can make a medal of the kind formerly made and send it up by him. As he is impatient to return I must endeavour to retain him by such devices as I can and in the mean time press you to lay aside all other work and make one which I shall hope to receive by the return of the bearer as speedily as possible.

That we may not be at the like loss hereafter I must desire you to make half a dozen more and send them to the Executive. I am &c,   THOMAS JEFFERSON

FC (Vi). At head of text: "Mr Robert Scott."

AN INDIAN CHIEF FROM KASKASKIA: Jean Baptiste Ducoigne (variously spelled); see TJ's speech to Ducoigne, printed under 1 June 1781. A MEDAL OF THE KIND FORMERLY MADE: See Robert Scot's invoice for executing an Indian medal, with TJ's memoranda, 13 Oct. 1780.

From John Walker

DEAR SIR   Belvoir 30th. May 1781

When I had the pleasure of seeing you yesterday, I forgot to inquire in what manner the horses to be impressed for public service, were to be equiped with Saddles, Bridles, Harness &c. Unless some mode is pointed out by which this may be effected, the horses will be useless.

Have you heard any material News from below? If you have and are not too much engaged pray communicate it. I propose to set out for Camp as soon as my horses are fit to take the road which will I hope be in about two days. I am My Dear Sir Your most obedt. Servt.,   JN. WALKER

RC (Vi); addressed and endorsed. Walker apparently had left Steuben's staff as liaison officer sometime in April, but he may have joined Lafayette's staff in a similar capacity (Walker to Steuben, 17 Apr. 1781, NHi). At any rate he wrote Steuben from Belvoir: "I hoped to have had the pleasure of seeing you on James River, but am desired by the Governor to return to the Marquis's camp for certain purposes, and tomorrow I am to set off" (same to same, 31 May 1781, NHi).

From Vivian Brooking

SIR   Amelia May 31st. 1781

Fearing least my Letter of the 26th. Inst. may have miscarried, This is to inform you I was unfortunately taken by a Party of British Light Horse the 14th. Inst. and restricted to the Town of Blandford for Ten Days then was to return Home on Parole which I thought more eligible than to be committed to close Confinement. As I was acting under your Orders of the 8th. Inst. to imbody and arm the Militia I think myself justifiable in signing a Parole, and expect not to be considered as an acting Officer of Militia untill exchanged or my Parole shall be altered. I am Sr. Your mst. obedt Servt.,   V. BROOKING Co. Lt.

RC (Vi); addressed and endorsed.   Brooking's LETTER OF THE 26TH. INST. has not been found. YOUR ORDERS OF THE 8TH. INST.: See TJ to the county lieutenants of Lunenburg, and certain other counties, 8 May.

From George Corbin

SIR   Accomack 31st. of May 1781

The danger and difficulty of sending a cross the Bay, have prevented me from informing before this, the particular situation of Affairs in this County.

Our draft was appointed the 23d. ulto., but the disaffected (encouraged by the example of Northampton) about two hundred in number appeared in order to prevent it by force. Being informed of their design, I was prepared to meet them on their own ground, having previously ordered out a party of chosen men with a field peice to attend near the place appointed for the draft. But upon consideration I was of opinion that it would be impolitic to make use of force, as I found by enquiry many men who had always been accounted honest good citizens mislead by false representations from the disaffected, might by cool reasoning be set right again. I therefore postponed the draft for two days, and promised myself with the assistance of others that the people might be reasoned to their duty: however [goo]d that reason altho' it quieted the minds of the greater part of the rioters [who] appeared the first day, yet a considerable number were still determined the second day to oppose it at the risque of their lives; therefore thought it prudent to inform the people that I would a second time put of the draft, but was under a necessity of returning those soldiers for the War, who had opposed it, and requested them to give in their names to a person appointed to list them, which a number of them to the amount of twenty or upwards accordingly did; these with a few others equally guilty were adjudged the day following by a court martial to be soldiers during the war. Several others have since been discovered who were concerned but concealed their arms in the woods to prevent suspition. Those who appeared to head the mob the first day were John Custis (sea side) and William Garrison, but upon reasoning with them, they left the mob and seemed sorry for what they had done; however penitent they might be, I yet view them as the most dangerous persons concerned being the only persons of property amoungst them. I was induced to adopt mildness rather than force for the following reasons: From the detached situation of this County aid or Supplies of any kind could not be expected from the State; nor could we expect it from our neighbours the Marylanders, who would generally rejoice at our distress, and many of them rather plunder than assist us; The enemy's barges continually hovering around our sea and bay coasts, threatening to burn and plunder all who should oppose their wicked designs; The disaffected daily increasing by their clandestine trade with the british at Portsmouth, their threats thrown out against all who shall fail to apply for protection, and accept the profered mercy in the british Proclamations, which have been very industerously and artfully circulated and enforced; and I may add the exhausted state of our magazine. For these reasons I forced moderation on the friends to the State, tho' much against the inclination of many of them, least the contrary should be productive of the general ruin of both parties, without gaining the least advantage to our Independence.

Several inhabitants of this county living near the water have been lately plundered even to the cloths on their backs, and their houses burnt to ashes. This has occasioned an address from the principle inhabitants of this shore to the commanding officer of the continental forces desiring his influence to prevent a mode of war so cruel and inhuman, as we are taught to believe that those barge gentry who are the authors of this mischief have no such commission being confined to high water mark. We think by a representation of facts (established by affidavits) through a proper chanel to the british commanding officer to whom they are amenable, might prevent in future such acts of cruelty. The field officers of this Shore have also requested if it can be consistent with the good of the State to order the men raided by their counties under a proper officer to be stationed for their defence. This guard, tho' small, aided by volunteers, and a barge of fifty feet long mounting one six and two four pound cannon with swivels and muskets and fifty men, which I hope will be compleat in fifteen days, will be sufficient to protect us against the insults we are daily experiencing, should we get assistance from no other quarter. Since the enemy came last to this bay, have been obliged to station guards on the inlets on the bay coast, and am under the necessity of asking for the public money and Stores in the county for their support, as public credit with us is entirely dead, and our paper currency almost in the same condition. The military Stores of the Accomack and Diligence Gallies are not sold, it being the opinion of the Gentlemen Commissioners and myself that they would be more useful to the State, than their produce in money if sold. Some of these I must beg the liberty of equiping the barge with.

I have also taken the liberty of lending to the State of Maryland one of the large guns belonging to the Accomack, and the two nine pounders from the fort on Wollop's Island to arm a barge building at Snow-Hill, which is 65 feet straight, this and ours are to cruize in consort for the protection of the eastern Shore of Maryland and Virga.—Tho' I hope the liberty I have, and must take with the public money and Stores, will be fully authorised by necessity.

The Gentlemen who have generously undertaken the Barge desire, if it is not inconsistend, that the necessary Commissions and Bonds blank for the Captain and two Lieutenants may be inclosed to me, or the commanding Officer of the County with directions for the due execution thereof, with what fees, if any should be taken, as soon as possible.

You will please observe from the Clerk's certificate inclosed that several vancancies have happened in the Militia, and that Commissions are desired for those recommended; the appointment of Col. Cropper as County Lieutenant meets not only mine but the entire approbation of every field officer of the county, as he is warmly attached to his country, an[d ha]d the experience of two years service and upwards in the Con[tinen]tal army. Perhaps your excellency will wonder why I have not incl[osed] my Commission as county Lieutenant, having resigned; you will please be informed that on the death of Col. S. Simpson, which happened in the begining of the year 1777, the Court was pleased to recommend me, but as I was of a weak constitution, and by no means capable of filling so important a commission, I would not suffer my recommendation to be sent over, but was determined to serve the County to the best of my ability, untill some person more equal to the task should be proposed by the Court, this I flattered myself would happen soon, but to my great disappointment did not take place untill Mar. last, so have not, nor never had, any Commission as County Lieutenant but acted under the Court's recommendation, and the Commission I then had as Colonel to the first Battalion. We have had several late arrivals on our shore from the west Indies, but no news, by them. Pardon me for having Called your attention so long from matters of greater importance. I am Your most obedt. humbl. Servt.,   GEO. CORBIN

RC (Vi); addressed to TJ at Richmond, "Favd Capt Levin Walker"; endorsed in part: "Answered."

TJ probably never saw this letter because it was not sent until 17 June, with the following letter (Vi), which was also addressed to TJ, but doubtless delivered to Nelson: "The Bearer of this will deliver you mine of the 31st. Ulto. to which I refer you for a particular State of affairs in this County, and have only to observe that since that period matters wear a much better aspect, and for further particulars I refer you to the bearer Captn. Abraham Outen who now waits on you for the Commission I mentioned in my last." Corbin also requests other commissions for persons who cannot attend in person. The notation, "Answered," in the endorsement may refer to a letter from William Davies to Corbin of 23 July, acknowledged in Corbin's letter to Davies of 18 Aug., stating with some exaggeration that Davies' letter is the "only instance of friendly attention in two years past, paid by the Executive to this Shore" (CVSP, II, 339).

To the County Lieutenants of Powhatan and Certain Other Counties

SIR   Charlottesville May 31st. 1781

It having become essentially necessary to raise immediately a large body of Cavalry and having no means of providing Accoutrements we are obliged to attempt the recovery of All the public Arms and Accoutrements for Cavalry dispersed in private hands through the state, which if they can be secured will arm and equip a very respectable force. I am therefore to press you instantly and diligently to search for any such in your County, not in the hands of men in actual Service and send them to such place as Colo. White shall appoint, and if collected before such appointment is known to you, then to send them to the Head quarters of the Marquis Fayette. I am &c.,   THOMAS JEFFERSON

FC (Vi); at head of text: "Circular. County Lieutenants of Powhatan, Chesterfield, Amelia, Prince Edward, Cumberland, Dinwiddie, Prince George, Henrico, Goochland, Hanover, Louisa, James City, York, Warwick & Elizabeth City."

This order was issued in compliance with Lafayette's request of 29 May, q.v. See also note to TJ's letter of that date to Lafayette.

To William Davies

SIR   Monticello May 31. 1781.

Mr. Patterson and Mr. Southall communicated to me your orders for removing the stores to Henderson's on the North river, and thence upwards. The superior expediency of removing them to the main river appeared to the council so evident that they had fixed on that river as the proper line of deposit: I have consulted with many gentlemen of judgment now at Charlottesville, and the same measure seems to meet their universel approbation: I must confess it is what I think best. I have therefore taken the liberty of directing Mr. Southall to remove them immediately to the old court house, where they will either be kept or removed to such higher parts of the river as you shall think proper to direct. You will be pleased to determine whether it will be best to have all at one place or to disperse them, on the river. There are some good houses at Irving's at the mouth of Rockfish. There are houses I beleive at Lynch's ferry which is near the head navigation of the river and has a very good road leading through the Blue ridge, tho' should you send a person up the river on purpose it is probable they may find other houses and perhaps better. I have excepted out of my order to Mr. Southall the arms (about 200 stand) which will be immediately wanting, and the 256 barrels of powder of which article I understand a very great quantity is already gone up James river. These he will carry to the house at Rockfish gap provided by your order.

After delivering to the Baron as many of the new muskets as he has men, I wish the residue could by any safe route be thrown into the Marquis's way, as he has militia unarmed. On the 29th. he was at Goldmine creek in Hanover, and the enemy at Hanovertown. Unless they press forward to Fredericksburg, I imagine his retreat will be by Charlottesville towards the Blue ridge. As you are where you can consult with the Baron, be so good as to settle with him the best way of keeping or getting these arms so situated as that the militia coming in to the Marquis may be armed with them. I am with much respect Sir Your most obedt. sert.

TH: JEFFERSON

RC (PHi); addressed: "Colo William Davies at the Fork."; endorsed.

I HAVE . . . TAKEN THE LIBERTY OF DIRECTING MR. SOUTHALL: Stephen Southall also wrote Davies on 31 May (RC, Vi), stating in part: "I have . . . procured Six Canoes and three hands from Colo. Joseph Cabell, and am to have Several Waggons to morrow which shall be dispatched immediately down to the Fork. The Governour yesterday told him [me?] he had consulted the members of the Assembly and it was their universal Opinion that the stores shoud be sent to Albemarle old Court house even the stores that are now at Hendersons. I am in Consequence at a loss what to be at. I shewed the Governour your letter respecting the Stores being carried to the Mountains, and he observed when the Stores where on navigation we not only had the same Oppertunity to remove by land, but the water also. I then urged the Security of the mountain, but he still presisted. Pray write me by this Express respecting that matter." In this letter Southall also explained about the 256 BARRELS OF POWDER: "There were two hundred and fifty six barrels of powder that came to Mr. Hendersons Yesterday. I went down last night to see what number of stores were there and the situation they were in. I found them stored, but to my great surprize in bad Order the Canoes not being Clamped together the barrels were put in the bottoms of the Canoes and by some means . . . the Canoes were near half full of Water some of them, tho' the tops of the barrels were kept dry and One barrel fell short of the invoice brought up. Now from the Governours direction to me I shou'd suppose no more of the stores will come here, but in the case more powder comes pray Order the Canoes to be Clamp'd as we must inevitable be ruin'd with such management." See Patteson to Davies, 27 May 1781 and note there.

To the Speaker of the House of Delegates

⟦*Charlottesville, 31? May 1781.* JHD, May 1781, 1828 edn., p. 7 (31 May): "The Speaker laid before the House a letter from the Governor, enclosing one from Baron Steuben, with a representation of the present state of the Virginia line; which was read and ordered to be referred to the committee of the whole House on the state of the Commonwealth." TJ's letter has not been found; the "one from Baron Steuben" is his to TJ of 28 May, which enclosed the state of the Virginia line, printed above.]

To Lafayette

SIR   Charlottesville May 31st. 1781

I had the honor last night of receiving your favor of the 28th. from Goldmine Creek and this morning that of the 29th. I shall be very happy indeed if against such a Superiority of Cavalry you shall be able to keep out of the way of the enemy till you are fully reinforced. I imagine Genl. Weedons observation as to his want of power to call forth the militia respects the Counties round about Fredericksburg, but all those on the South Side of Rappahannock have been called on by the Executive, and as to those on the North side they may be called out under our Invasion Law which directs that the Commanding Officer of the militia of any County hearing of the approach of an enemy shall call on so many circumjacent Counties as he shall think necessary, which Counties by their Officers are obliged to obey his call. I have the pleasure to inform you that Mr. Ross's Agent in Philadelphia on the 9th. instant forwarded 275 Stand of Arms and a ton of Powder to Fredericksburg; on the 11th he forwarded another stand of Arms; on the 18th. he forwarded 600 stand of Arms, and by this time expected the remainder of the 2000 engaged from Congress, by the board of War. I must pray you to take such measures through Genl. Weedon or otherwise as may secure these Stores from falling in with the enemy and moving them to where they may be useful to you. Your knowledge of the movements of the enemy will enable you to do this with safety whereas at the distance I am from them my orders however proper when given might by a change of their route lead the Arms into their way. Besides the preceeding Arms Genl. Washington has sent on 1000 Stand and the board of war were sending on 2000 more from Springfield. As to the eleven Hundred and odd stand which lately came on from Rhode Island the property of this State, I desired Colo. Davies after delivering to Baron Steuben as many as he has new Recruits, to return the rest for the militia of your Camp. Will you be so good as to advise him by what route you will have them sent to your Camp or to what other place? Two hundred of them being yet in your neighbourhood I have ordered them for present Safety to Rockfish Gap from which place they shall be moved according to any order you shall give.

With respect both to those Arms and the new Levies, I am desired to communicate to you the inclosed Resolution of General Assembly. The representation there directed of the present State, quantity and condition of the public Arms would be unnecessary to you who know already more of them than I do, nor can any body be more sensible than yourself of the reasons which would urge the detention of the New Levies till other effectual force can be assembled. I shall therefore in Compliance with the resolution only add my desire that you will be pleased to retain all those Arms within the State for its particular defence.

Two Days before the receipt of your letter of the 28th I had dispatched one to you inclosing eight Impress Warrants to provide horses from the Counties contiguous to the line of the enemys March. The Assembly used this undefined Expression in order to give you a latitude of impress, knowing that a precise circumscription might defeat their Intention altogether. This therefore anticipated your desire expressed in that Letter of extending your powers to 50 miles round. It also takes in your second request in the letter of the 29th to authorize Colo. White to impress on the South side of James River. The Counties through which the Enemy marched or bordered on them are within the extent of the impress warrants sent you, one of which therefore being given to Colo. White will authorize him to impress in Amelia, Powhatan, Chesterfield, Dinwiddie, Prince Edward, Brunswic and the other Counties there abounding with good horses. I will immediately direct the County Lieutenants to collect all Accoutrements for horse belonging to the Public in their Counties and to send them to such place as Colo. White shall appoint and in the mean time to your Camp.

The prisoners of war in this State are most of them in the hands of Colo. Holmes continental Commissary of prisoners at Winchester. There are a few at Staunton. Your orders to either place will be effectual. I have the honor to be &c.,

THOMAS JEFFERSON

FC (Vi). Enclosure: Resolutions of the House of Delegates of 29 May that "a representation be made to the Hon. Major General Marquis La Fayette, by his excellency the Governor, stating the present state, quantity and condition of the public arms; the urgent reasons that appear for detaining the new levies now collected at Albemarle old courthouse, to oppose the invading enemy, until effectual exertions can be made for providing other means of defense" and instructing the Governor to advise Lafayette "that this state, under its present circumstances, can in no wise consent that the public arms in the hands of the said new levies, be sent out of the State" and that TJ give orders countermanding such as may have been delivered for that purpose and detaining them for immediate defense (JHD, May 1781, 1828 edn., p. 6).

From Lafayette

I have receiv'd your Excellencys letter enclosing some Resolves respecting the imports[1] of Horses, and thought it was my best way to intrust General Nelson with the care of carrying them into execution. Inclosed your Excellency will find the Returns of General Mullenbergs Brigade.

I have the pleasure to inform you that Camden is evacuated, that the posts of fort Motte, Orangeburg, Fort Watson, Fort Granby have surrendered to General Greens Army. The General writes me the 16th. and was then on his way to Ninety Six and Augusta, in these several places 50 Officers, 380 private 375 tories have been captured. The vast superiority the Enemy have acquired in Virginia is not without some loss in other Quarters. Over running a Country is not to conquer it, and if it was construed into a right of possession, the french could claim the whole German Empire.

To my great satisfaction the Virginia Recruits and the Virginia Militia will remain in this State. I was guarding against Motives of self Interest, but am happy to see that the new levies, General Lawsons Men, and the Pensylvanians will cooperate with us against the same Army.

In case the Baron was gone, I request the enclosed may be immediately sent after him. It contains an Order to remain in the State, and cannot be forwarded too soon. I wish the Stores may be carried very high up, as they will the less require our attention.

Lord Cornwallis was this day at little pages Bridge, and it is said busy in repairing of it. We are marching on a parallel with him, and keeping the upper part of the Country. Tomorrow I form a junction with General Weedon at Mattapony Church, and shoud General Waine arrive our inferiority will not be quite so alarming. My Lord is going from his Friends, and we are going to meet ours, with the highest respect I have the honor to be Dear Sir, Your Excellencys Most Obedient Humble Servt,   LAFAYATE

General Greenes Requests are to impart you the Southern Intelligence. He was engaged in very important business and requests you will excuse his not writing himself.

TR (MiU-C: Clinton Papers); endorsed: "Major General the Marquis Lafayate to Governor Jefferson 31 May 81." Another Tr (Public Record Office, London), enclosed in a letter from Sir Henry Clinton to Lord George Germain, 13 July 1781.

Since this letter was intercepted by

the British, it is very improbable that TJ ever saw it. It is possible that it arrived at Charlottesville (and was taken) at about the same time that Tarleton's men were there (4 June). If so, the British deprived TJ of what would have been a satisfying communication. In choosing Nelson to supervise the impressment of horses, in expressing the wish that the militia and recruits would remain within the state and operate in conjunction with the forces of Lawson and Wayne, and in ordering Steuben to remain in Virginia, Lafayette acted in marked contrast with the behavior of Steuben at this time, who desired most of all to leave Virginia at the first opportunity and who was endeavoring to carry with him not only Lawson's men but such arms as he could obtain from Virginia and such men as he could raise in North Carolina.

[1] Thus in MS, obviously a transcriber's error for "impress."

From Matthew Pope

HONBLE. SIR   Henrico County May 31st. 1781

Doctor Wilson, who has the superintendance of the Continental Medical department in this State, informs me that the Medecines which were coming on from Rhode Island (and belonging to this State) have been taken for the use of the Continental Army; owing he tells me to their being no directions on them. This Sir is a double misfortune at this juncture, for the State is almost without every useful Medecine, and what is to be done I know not, if some method is not fallen upon to recover them, or others in lieu of them. Such treatment as this surely deserves the highest censure and I should think corporal punishment on the offenders. I shall leave your Excellency to take such steps in the affair as you shall think proper.

Having been lately much with the Army I have seen how they suffer and what difficulties they labour under for almost everything they want and what great discontent prevails amongst all ranks of People, and I must say I think with great cause: and unless some mode is fallen upon to satisfie the people, and supply the Army better; I see little prospect of our supporting it long. The remedy is easy and very expeditiously to be accomplished, and in a manner whereby impressing necessarys &c. which so exasperates the people at large may be avoided, and I hope Sir you have influence enough to effect so desireable an end. If the assembly will allow such a price as one Neighbour gives to another, or the market price for every necessary the Army stands in need of, or if they will allow the person authorised to provide the necessarys for the army to give certificates to be paid in kind, or as much money as will replace the commodity when paid, I am fully convinced the Army would be well supplied and a number of Waggons might be dispenced with;

the People would bring in the different articles the Army stand in need of; and both Army and people contented and happy. I would have the same mode adopted with respect to Waggons, Carts, or Horses, you will pardon the liberty I have taken leaving you Sir to improve on the hint and earnestly to recommend it to the assembly to be instantly adopted; I do not think there is any time to lose.

I am sorry to inform your Excellency I have never yet received the necessarys, I wrote for, by Colo. Senf; Colo. Davis nor a quarter Master was to be found. I have since inclosed the memorandum by Major Claiborne to Colo. Davis. I must beg the favour of you Sir to write to Colo. Davis desireing the articles may be sent on to the General Hospital which at this moment is at Allen's Creek Church in Hanover. Where it may be to morrow I know not as we keep moving with the Army, transporting all our Medecines and Stores with the Hospital. Fearing that list may miscarry I have inclosed another and must beg your Excellency will order Colo. Davis to procure such articles as he has not, especially Oznabrigs for Bedding, for should we have an Action we have no Beds to lay our wounded Men [on. I] have repeatedly applied in vain to Mr. William [. . .] and sent to Mr. Ross for that purpose, I beg [my] most respectful compliments to your Lady and [am] With the highest Esteem and Regard Your Excellencys most Obt and Respectful Servt.,
MATTW. POPE

ENCLOSURE

May 31st. 1781

List of Necessarys wanted for the immediate use of the General Hospital
Twelve Pounds of Tea
Twelve quire Writing Paper
Twenty five Yards new Linnen
all the old that was sent from Richmond
Twenty five Pounds of Coffee
Forty or Fifty Gallons of Molasses
Two pieces of Oznabrigs
Three Pounds of brown thread

MATTW POPE D:G:

This Sir, is the list I wish to have if the other has not been complied with.

RC (Vi); addressed to TJ at Charlottesville; endorsed. Enclosure (Vi).
WE HAVE NO BEDS TO LAY OUR WOUNDED MEN ON: There is in Vi another letter, written at "Albemarle O Ct House" on 31 May from Capt. Arthur Lind to William Davies that gives a graphic account of distresses suffered by ill and wounded soldiers: "Dr. Monro when he marched with the Troops, under Colo. Gaskins, left with me—(By what rule of propriety I leave you to judge) twenty five sick two thirds of them very bad cases, without the least means in my power to Alleviate their distresses—some of them with-

out Blankets. They are stowed in two very bad Negro Quarters. I have wrote to Doctor Gillmore on the subject, desiring him to take into his care the aforesaid miserable beings, which I shall send to him in three or four days. I understand that he has no right to receive Continental troops. I hope you'l point out to him the Humanity and necessity that there is for his receiving them."

From George Slaughter

Sir   Louisville 31st. May 1781

Haveing never recieved any kind of Clothing, or pay shall be much oblig'd to you to let the bearer Mr. Chapman Austin have what money due me, Capt. Benjamin Roberts and Eight months pay for Ensign William Roberts, if not already drawn by Lieutenant Saunders. As to the news of this place I refer you to Mr. Austin who appears to be an intelligle young Gentleman & I am Yr Excellencies Mo. Ob. Hum Servant,

GEORGE SLAUGHTER Commd at Falls Ohio

RC (Vi); addressed and endorsed.

Recommendation of the Justices of the Peace for Bedford County

Bedford May Court 1781.

Thomas Watts one of the Justices of the Peace for this County having been charged as guilty of High Treason and by this Court Ordered for further Trial—It is the Opinion of this Court, that it be recommended to his Excellency the Governor to Issue a New Commission of the peace for this County and that the said Thomas Watts be left out of the same.   A Copy Teste

JA. STEPTOE Cl:

MS (Vi); in hand of Steptoe. This opinion of the Bedford co. court was probably transmitted to TJ by letter during May, but no such letter has been found. Bedford court met on the fourth Monday of each month (Hening, VIII, 519) and presumably, therefore, this opinion was transmitted on or soon after Monday, 28 May 1781.

Petition of Robert Poage and Others

TO THE HONOURABLE THE GENERAL ASSEMBLY OF THE COMMONWEALTH OF VIRGINIA.

The Memorial of a Number of faithful Citizens humbly represents, That your Memorialists have from Sentiment, as well as a regard to the Authority of our Country, cordially espoused the common Cause of America. We have invariably endeavoured to cultivate unanimity, Fortitude and Perseverance amongst our fellow Subjects, and joined our most fervent prayers with our Endeavours that the Measures adopted by Legislation may render the War in which we are engaged successful. But after seriously contemplating the manner in which this War has been lately prosecuted by our Enemies in contrast with the Manner in which they are resisted by us, we begin to be greatly alarmed at what may be the Event. By the repeated and extensive Incursions which the Enemy have lately made into our Country, it appears that they are rather attempting to conquer by Famine than by the Sword. We have reason gratefully to acknowledge that Divine Providence has repeatedly interfered on our behalf, and may boast of many singular Instances of the Conduct and Bravery of our Troops, both regular and Militia; but Experience now fully evinces, that our Regulars have not been enlisted in sufficient Numbers and in general not for a sufficient length of Time, to afford a rational Prospect of final Victory. By this Means tho'tful Men are deterred from entering into the Service. Knowing that a large Army only promises a speedy and honourable Peace, the Enemy are encouraged to persevere and almost assured of Success, and our General Officers, who must know that such Measures are like to prove abortive, are under the strongest Temptations to make their Peace with the Enemy by Treachery, and thus by a sudden Revolution bring us into a State of unconditional Subjection.

To supply this Defect, the Militia has been considered as the natural Strength of a Nation, the cheapest and surest Defence, on whose protection we are ultimately to depend; and accordingly great pains hath been taken to arrange and Discipline the Militia. But after frequent Experiments it evidently appears, that in a Country of such vast extent, where the Enemy have the Dominion of the Seas, these cannot answer our Expectations and ought not to be our main Dependance; but should only be considered as an useful Supplement to our Armies in Cases of Emergency. Not to mention the want of Arms and the other Furniture of War, which is an accidental Defect, it is impossible that an Army chiefly composed of troops without Experience should meet an Army of Veterans upon equal Terms. Or if the Militia really did answer all the Ends of an Army, other Objections of great Weight cannot be removed. The long and rapid Marches, the Duties and Manner of living in a Camp, to which the Militia are little practized, is exceedingly injurious to their Health; so that not a few after performing a Tour perhaps without effecting any thing of Consequence, either die of sickness, or return home with irreparable loss of Constitution. And if the Militia are repeatedly draughted in large numbers especially in Seed Time and Harvest, Multitudes of their Families will be deprived of the Means of Subsistance, the Price of Commodities will rise in rapid Progression, and our Currency depreciate in Proportion; so that in a short time we shall be destitute of the Sinews of War, and the Provisions of a Camp, as well as a regular Army; and if we may judge by what we frequently hear in common Conversation, nothing is so likely to break the Spirit of the Body of the People, and dispose them tamely to submit to the British Yoke. We beg leave to subjoin to the Deficiencies which we think it our Duty thus freely to represent, that we believe in God as the Disposer of all human Events; and we are as firmly persuaded that the prevalence of Vice in our Camps, and too generally amongst all Ranks of People, has justly provoked the heavenly Majesty to correct us by continuing the War; and we have reason to fear that without Reformation the Scourge will be continued untill we are absolutely subjected to our Enemies. We are well informed of the excellent Rules of War, and the Laws which have been established for the suppression of Prophanity and other prevailing Iniquities; but there is great reason to lament that these are not generally observed, nor their penalties inflicted. And this is a principal Reason why so many Parents of good Principles, do not encourage their Sons to take up Arms in Defense of Liberty, being in Doubt which is the greatest Evil, Slavery or the loss of Morals.

Therefore, that the Evils which we fear may be prevented, to remove in some Measure those which we feel, and to obtain the object of our most zealous Wishes, we would with the greatest Deference submit the following Plan to the Consideration of our Legislature, Viz.

That our United States be divided into Districts, having a joint regard to the Equality of Property and the Number of Militia in each District. Suppose the Number of Districts to be Fifty Thousand, and supposing the Number of Militia in each District to be six, who with the Addition of Invalids, Superanuated and other exempted Persons will make about Ten. That each District furnish one Soldier *in Perpetua*, and supply him with Sufficient Arms and Clothes, when, and as often, as the Executive of the State to which he belongs, or the General Congress shall direct, and that every six Districts furnish one Tent. That when there is not a Call for so large a Number in the Field, they shall serve in Rotation during one Year or one Campaign, and the Surplus be left to follow their proper Callings at Home, during which time their pay as Soldiers shall be suspended, except that they shall be obliged to attend their Officers three days in every quarter of a Year, to be properly disciplined; for which Time they shall have Wages and Provisions; and they shall constantly hold themselves in readiness to take the Field when required. If the Soldier has a Family, they shall be taken Care of and provided for by the District, agreeable to some general Regulation; for all which Expences they shall have Credit in the payment of their Taxes. And one of the District shall be chosen Annually, who shall have Authority to execute this plan, as far as it relates to his District. That the Soldier be exempted from personal Taxation and £_____ of his Estate, agreeable to the Valuation of the Assessors. If he be an unmarried person, and it appears that he hath a Parent or Parents which are supported by him, they and their Family with their Estate shall be provided for and have the same Privileges as if they belonged to him, and the Expences defrayed the same way. That a Soldier thus enlisted shall not be compelled to serve more than seven Years; and if he shall die, or be otherwise disqualified for Duty, before his Term expires the District shall procure another to serve out the Term. These Soldiers shall be formed into Battalions and Brigades as usual, allotting a proper Proportion for light Infantry and Dragoons, and all Care taken to allot these Brigades to the Northern, Southern, Eastern and Western Service, as may be most contiguous to their places of Residence; and if this should be regarded, we presume it will be judged expedient, that the two Brigades most contiguous to our Western Frontiers, be chiefly armed with Rifles. That the Troops now in Continental or State Service be continued on the present Establishment, as if this plan had not taken place, Except that they be allowed more adequate Wages; And that the Soldiers to be enlisted in Consequence thereof have the same or equal Advantages with them. That the Militia also stand enroled and be subject to the same Regulations as if this plan had not taken Place, except that they shall not be obliged to attend more than one General and Two Petet Musters in the Year: nor shall they in common Cases be called into actual Service, unless to resist an Invasion or quell an Insurrection in their own County or Counties adjacent. And in no Cases shall they be detained any longer than regular Forces can be marched to their relief. That one Chaplain of Exemplary Piety and good moral Deportment be appointed to each

Brigade, who shall rank with a Lieutenant Colonel, be obliged constantly to attend his Brigade when they are in the Camp or in the Field, and also he shall be bound by the most sacred Obligations to discharge the Duties of his Function, and be fully impowered and bound by Law to have the Acts for restraining Vice in the Army punctually executed. The Chaplain to be chosen by the Major Voice of the Brigade, Officers and Soldiers. That all in Office, civil and military, be also bound by Law and by their Oath of Office to suppress Vice, by their own Example and by legal Process, and that they be also bound to maintain and support the Rights of Conscience, and the several religious Denominations, that are Friends to the Freedom of America. That Days of publick Fasting and Thanksgiving be appointed from Time to Time, as the Case may require; and that on these Occasions all our fellow Subjects be exhorted and Charged to cultivate good Morals and a friendly and Christian Intercourse, without regarding religious Distinctions.

We would now only farther trouble our Honourable Legislature to Assure them that these Sentiments might easily have been recommended to your Consideration by the Names of Multitudes, had we not apprehended that popular Petitions in the Case would be inexpedient, and been fully persuaded that you will be more attentive to the Sentiments than the Names or Rank of the Subscribers. We wish to suggest a plan that when corrected and amended, shall obtain your approbation, that of the General Congress, and all the United States of America, be generally adopted by them, and bring a War that has been too long protracted to a speedy and happy Conclusion, which is the Prayer of

ROBERT POAGE

CALEB WALLACE

DAVID RICE

WILLIAM READ

JOHN W. HOLTE

JOSHUA EARLY

MS (Vi).

This petition, reflecting a belief widespread in Virginia in the late spring of 1781 that "the measures adopted for the prosecution of the war and the defence of the State have been founded on ill policy and conducted improperly," does not appear to have been aimed directly at TJ's administration. But it was undoubtedly representative of the general dissatisfaction with the functioning of both civil and military authority, of which Nicholas' resolution calling for an investigation of the conduct of the Executive, Davies' request for an extension of powers and reorganization of the War Office, Claiborne's appeal for similar aid in the quartermaster's department, and the General Assembly's resolution calling for an inquiry into the responsibility for loss of stores at Point of Fork were further expressions. In these respects the petition was fairly typical. But in one particular it seems to have been unique: it is perhaps the earliest suggestion that, at least in respect to military organization, the government of the United States should operate directly on individuals rather than through state authority. It may have been this unorthodox proposal that influenced the House of Delegates on 30 May 1781 to lay the memorial on the table (JHD, May 1781, 1828 edn., p. 7). The legislature itself did not, of course, escape the feeling that measures for prosecuting the war were "founded on ill policy": on 29 May a petition was presented from Amherst county calling for legislation to correct the irregular manner of calling militia into service, "tours of duty not being fixed by law" (same, p. 5).

Speech to Jean Baptiste Ducoigne

Charlottesville, [ca. 1] June, 1781.

BROTHER JOHN BAPTIST DE COIGNE

I am very much pleased with the visit you have made us, and particularly that it has happened when the wise men from all parts of our country were assembled together in council, and had an opportunity of hearing the friendly discourse you held to me. We are all sensible of your friendship, and of the services you have rendered, and I now, for my countrymen, return you thanks, and, most particularly, for your assistance to the garrison which was besieged by the hostile Indians. I hope it will please the Great Being above to continue you long in life, in health and in friendship to us; and that your son will afterwards succeed you in wisdom, in good disposition, and in power over your people. I consider the name you have given as particularly honorable to me,[1] but I value it the more as it proves your attachment to my country. We, like you, are Americans, born in the same land, and having the same interests. I have carefully attended to the figures represented on the skins, and to their explanation, and shall always keep them hanging on the walls in remembrance of you and your nation. I have joined with you sincerely in smoking the pipe of peace; it is a good old custom handed down by your ancestors, and as such I respect and join in it with reverence. I hope we shall long continue to smoke in friendship together. You find us, brother, engaged in war with a powerful nation. Our forefathers were Englishmen, inhabitants of a little island beyond the great water, and, being distressed for land, they came and settled here. As long as we were young and weak, the English whom we had left behind, made us carry all our wealth to their country, to enrich them; and, not satisfied with this, they at length began to say we were their slaves, and should do whatever they ordered us. We were now grown up and felt ourselves strong; we knew we were free as they were, that

[60]

we came here of our own accord and not at their biddance, and were determined to be free as long as we should exist. For this reason they made war on us. They have now waged that war six years, and have not yet won more land from us than will serve to bury the warriors they have lost. Your old father, the King of France, has joined us in the war, and done many good things for us. We are bound forever to love him, and wish you to love him, brother, because he is a good and true friend to us. The Spaniards have also joined us, and other powerful nations are now entering into the war to punish the robberies and violences the English have committed on them. The English stand alone, without a friend to support them, hated by all mankind because they are proud and unjust. This quarrel, when it first began, was a family quarrel between us and the English, who were then our brothers. We, therefore, did not wish you to engage in it at all. We are strong enough of ourselves without wasting your blood in fighting our battles. The English, knowing this, have been always suing to the Indians to help them fight. We do not wish you to take up the hatchet. We love and esteem you. We wish you to multiply and be strong. The English, on the other hand, wish to set you and us to cutting one another's throats, that when we are dead they may take all our land. It is better for you not to join in this quarrel, unless the English have killed any of your warriors or done you any other injury. If they have, you have a right to go to war with them, and revenge the injury, and we have none to restrain you. Any free nation has a right to punish those who have done them an injury. I say the same, brother, as to the Indians who treat you ill. While I advise you, like an affectionate friend, to avoid unnecessary war, I do not assume the right of restraining you from punishing your enemies. If the English have injured you, as they have injured the French and Spaniards, do like them and join us in the war. General Clarke will receive you and show you the way to their towns. But if they have not injured you, it is better for you to lie still and be quiet. This is the advice which has been always given by the great council of the Americans. We must give the same, because we are but one of thirteen nations, who have agreed to act and speak together. These nations keep a council of wise men always sitting together, and each of us separately follow their advice. They have the care of all the people and the lands between the Ohio and Mississippi, and will see that no wrong be committed on them. The French settled at Kaskaskias, St. Vincennes, and the Cohos,[2] are subject to that council, and they will punish them if they do you any injury.

If you will make known to me any just cause of complaint against them, I will represent it to the great council at Philadelphia, and have justice done you.

Our good friend, your father, the King of France, does not lay any claim to them. Their misconduct should not be imputed to him. He gave them up to the English the last war, and we have taken them from the English. The Americans alone have a right to maintain justice in all the lands on this side the Mississippi,—on the other side the Spaniards rule. You complain, brother, of the want of goods for the use of your people. We know that your wants are great, notwithstanding we have done everything in our power to supply them, and have often grieved for you. The path from hence to Kaskaskias is long and dangerous; goods cannot be carried to you in that way. New Orleans has been the only place from which we could get goods for you. We have bought a great deal there; but I am afraid not so much of them have come to you as we intended. Some of them have been sold of necessity to buy provisions for our posts. Some have been embezzled by our own drunken and roguish people. Some have been taken by the Indians and many by the English.

The Spaniards, having now taken all the English posts on the Mississippi, have opened that channel free for our commerce, and are in hopes of getting goods for you from them. I will not boast to you, brother, as the English do, nor promise more than we shall be able to fulfil. I will tell you honestly, what indeed your own good sense will tell you, that a nation at war cannot buy so many goods as when in peace. We do not make so many things to send over the great waters to buy goods, as we made and shall make again in time of peace. When we buy those goods, the English take many of them, as they are coming to us over the great water. What we get in safe, are to be divided among many, because we have a great many soldiers, whom we must clothe. The remainder we send to our brothers the Indians, and in going, a great deal of it is stolen or lost. These are the plain reasons why you cannot get so much from us in war as in peace. But peace is not far off. The English cannot hold out long, because all the world is against them. When that takes place, brother, there will not be an Englishman left on this side the great water. What will those foolish nations then do, who have made us their enemies, sided with the English, and laughed at you for not being as wicked as themselves? They are clothed for a day, and will be naked forever after; while you, who have submitted to short inconvenience, will be well supplied through the rest of your lives. Their friends will be gone and their enemies left behind; but your friends will be here, and will make you strong against all your enemies. For the present you shall have a share of what little goods we can get. We will order some immediately up the Mississippi for you and for us. If they be little, you will submit to suffer a little as your brothers do for a short time. And when we shall have beaten our enemies and forced them to make peace, we will share more plentifully. General Clarke will furnish you with ammunition to serve till we can get some from New Orleans. I must recommend to you particular attention to him. He is our great, good, and trusty warrior; and we have put everything under his care beyond the Alleghanies. He will advise you in all difficulties, and redress your wrongs. Do what he tells you, and you will be sure to do right. You ask us to send schoolmasters to educate your son and the sons of your people. We desire above all things, brother, to instruct you in whatever we know ourselves. We wish to learn you[3] all our arts and to make you wise and wealthy. As soon as there is peace we shall be able to send you the best of school-masters; but while the war is raging, I am afraid it will not be practicable. It shall be done, however, before your son is of an age to receive instruction.

This, brother, is what I had to say to you. Repeat it from me to all your people, and to our friends, the Kickapous, Piorias, Piankeshaws and Wyattanons. I will give you a commission to show them how much we esteem you. Hold fast the chain of friendship which binds us together, keep it bright as the sun, and let them, you and us, live together in perpetual love.

MS not located; text from *The Writings of Thomas Jefferson*, ed. Lipscomb and Bergh, XVI, 371-7. This appears to be the sole printing from the MS, which is recorded among the TJ Papers before their transfer in 1903 from the State Department to the Library of Congress as a draft written on 2 quarto pages; in the Papers as then bound it was located in Series 1, vol. 1, No. 13 (*Calendar of Jefferson Correspondence*, in *Bulletin of the Bureau of Rolls and Library of the Department of State*, No. 6, Washington, 1894, p. 91). Diligent search among the TJ Papers as rebound in the Library of Congress has failed to disclose it. If the original actually was a draft in TJ's hand, the editors of the L & B edition certainly repunctuated it in printing it, and they probably made several errors in transcribing it (some are noted below).

TJ's first recorded Indian address shows him already well skilled in a species of peculiarly American diplomacy he was very often called upon to use in later years. It shows his deep interest in Indian ethnology, expressed earlier in his excavation of an Indian burial site, in his recording of Logan's speech to Governor Dunmore in 1774, and in his plan to collect data on the Indians' "laws, customs, religions, traditions, and more particularly their languages" through the agency of the College of William and Mary (see the Revisal of the Laws, Bill No. 80, Vol. 2: 540, above). And it sets forth most of the sympathetic and far-sighted views on the status and future of the Indian that were to be embodied in TJ's Indian policy as President. He was here addressing Jean Baptiste Ducoigne (De Coigne, Decaigne, De Coin, Duquoin,

&c.), a half-breed chief of the dwindling Kaskaskia nation, from whose name was taken that of the town of Duquoin, Perry co., Ill. There is a sketch of Ducoigne in Hodge's *Handbook of American Indians*, I, 405. From *The St. Clair Papers* (ed. William Henry Smith, Cincinnati, 1882, II, 139) it appears that Ducoigne served with Lafayette in Virginia, and it is clear that TJ in his letter to Robert Scot, 30 May 1781, was writing for a medal to bestow on Ducoigne. There is no mention in the Assembly or Council Journals of Ducoigne's appearance in Charlottesville, though from TJ's speech it is clear that the assembled legislators heard the Indian's "friendly discourse." That TJ at this critical moment and in the very last hours of his governorship took the trouble to show the Kaskaskia chief every honor and to give him sound and sincere advice is a measure of his feelings for the Indians as a race. Nor was the advice wasted. Ducoigne, who had already named his little son Jefferson (perhaps the earliest among a great many namesakes), was to become a kind of model of the "good Indian" who had thrown in his lot with government authority, and he was for that reason to suffer persecution at the hands of his fellows, including some of the tribes inhabiting the Illinois country mentioned toward the close of TJ's address. Ducoigne visited Philadelphia early in 1793, and TJ reported a remarkable speech by him to President Washington (see TJ to Washington, 4 Feb. 1793). When TJ's French friend Volney traveled to the Mississippi in 1796, he carried a letter of introduction from TJ to Ducoigne that was couched in the most affectionate terms and offered to undertake the care of "my name sake Jefferson," who "was at his mother's breast" when Ducoigne visited Charlottesville in 1781 (TJ to Ducoigne, 21 June 1796). In the correspondence of William Henry Harrison, territorial governor of Indiana from 1800, with TJ as President and Henry Dearborn as secretary of war, may be traced the decline of Ducoigne and of his tribe, who were the victims of circumstances from which TJ's personal sympathy and his protective policy toward friendly Indians could not rescue them; see Harrison's *Messages and Letters*, ed. Logan Esarey, *Ind. Hist. Colls.*, VII, Indianapolis, 1922, *passim*.

TJ's remark that he has CAREFULLY ATTENDED TO THE FIGURES REPRESENTED ON THE SKINS refers to the interesting gifts which the Kaskaskia Indians had presented to him. These were paintings on buffalo skin and were presumably among the "Indian curiosities" mentioned as later visitors at Monticello as hanging on the walls of the main hall and library in TJ's home. See Sir Augustus Foster's "Notes on the United States, 1804-1812," ed. Margaret Bailey Tinkcom, WMQ, 3d ser., VIII (1951), 100-1; Baron de Montlezun's *Voyages en 1815 et 1816 . . .* , quoted by J. M. Carrière and L. G. Moffatt, Albemarle Hist. Soc., *Papers*, IV (1943-1944), 46; George Ticknor to Elisha Ticknor, 7 Feb. 1815, in Ticknor's *Life, Letters, and Journals*, Boston, 1876, I, 34. Which of the several Indian paintings described by these travelers had been presented by Ducoigne and which may have been sent or brought back by Captains Lewis and Clark from beyond the Mississippi is not ascertainable. This speech, coming at the close of TJ's governorship and at a time when public morale was exceedingly low, is also a remarkable evidence of TJ's unshaken faith in an early and victorious peace. Much of his comment on the military situation, despite an obvious effort not to delude the Indians by promises that could not be fulfilled, was hyperbole: "They . . . have not yet won more land from us than will serve to bury the warriors they have lost" was a statement that avoided the ludicrous only by being the kind of expression that was expected at Indian treaties and conferences. But in defining the causes of the war and in outlining the world picture, TJ was clearly expressing a confident belief. He was doing this and perhaps laying a foundation for something more when he added: "The Americans alone have a right to maintain justice in all the lands on this side the Mississippi." The COMMISSION that TJ gave to Ducoigne at this time has not been found.

[1] There is probably an omission here in the printed text, which ought to read: "I consider the name you have given your son as particularly honorable to me."

[2] Probably an error in transcription for "Cahôs," one of the names of the French settlement at Cahokia (now in Illinois) on the east bank of the Mississippi, opposite and a little below St. Louis.

[3] Probably an error in transcription for "We wish you to learn."

Bond of John Ellyson and Richard Harvie

[*Without place*] *1 June 1781*. John Ellyson and Richard Harvie give bond to TJ, or his successor as Governor, in the amount of 20,000 weight of merchantable tobacco, under the condition that they will appear before the Governor and Council when called for and that John Ellyson will not go "within Ten Miles of any post, encampment or party of the enemy."

MS (Vi); 2 p.; signed by Ellyson and Harvie, witnessed by Foster Webb, Jr., and John Bryan; the words "encampment or party" in the text are inserted in TJ's hand.

From Samuel Huntington

Sir   In Congress June 1st. 1781.

I am directed to inform you that Congress have received undoubted intelligence both from their Minister at the Court of Versailles, and the Minister of France in America by order of his Court, that the Courts of Vienna and Petersburgh have offered their mediation to the belligerent powers for the re-establishment of Peace; That these overtures had been eagerly embraced on the part of Great Britain; That France had declined her full acceptation thereof, until the concurrence of her Allies could be obtained for that purpose, at the same time observing that should she again be pressed on this head, she would be obliged to enter into a previous plan of negotiation conditionally, for herself and Allies; That Spain had answered in such manner to the proposals of the mediating powers as to shew her eventual acceptance. The intervention of such formidable powers will undoubtedly prove an event the most favorable to these United States, if by a great and timely exertion we sufficiently reduce the force of the Enemy now operating in our Country. But should languor and inaction subject us to the contempt of the negotiators all the consequences will be chargeable upon ourselves.

This is a conjuncture that calls for the most serious consideration of these States. Congress have not a doubt in their minds, but that each State in the union is determined to support the confederacy, that has been so solemnly entered into through every difficulty, and hand it down unimpaired to their posterity. Under these impressions Congress can with confidence call on their constituents for such exertions as are proportionate to the truly critical situation of our Affairs. The plan of operations for the present campaign having been preconcerted on the principle of obliging the enemy to abandon their possessions in every part of these States, therefore an unequivocal compliance with the demands heretofore made by Congress for provisions, men and money are what we have at present to ask for, should these means be expeditiously and punctually put into our hands, we have the most pleasing prospect of putting a speedy and happy issue to the war; by driving the Enemy from their present possessions in every part of these States: but at all events to confine them to the sea coasts; in order to give as little room as possible to the enemy's claim of Uti possidetis which will undoubtedly be most strenuously insisted on by them in the course of the negotiation—a claim totally inadmissible on our part, of course. Then nothing should be left unessayed by these States, to prevent the embarrassments that such a claim must inevitably produce. Of consequence it is become indispensably necessary by our immediate and, under providence, successful efforts, to place ourselves in such a situation as to enable our negotiators to speak a firm and decided language becoming the Characters of Ministers of free sovereign and Independent States. We conclude with observing that from the foregoing communications we are so thoroughly convinced of the most strenuous exertions of every State in the union to accomplish the great objects herein pointed out, that Congress will immediately proceed to carry into full execution their plans adopted for defeating the ambitious views of our enemies; and be prepared to accept of peace, upon no other terms than the Independence of the thirteen United States of America in all their parts.

By order of Congress. SAM. HUNTINGTON President

RC (PHC); entirely in Huntington's hand; endorsed: "Pt. of Congress of 3d June 81. Virginia." This letter was transmitted under cover of Huntington's letter to TJ of 2 June 1781, q.v.

The INTELLIGENCE outlined in this letter was received by Congress on 22 May 1781 through La Luzerne. A letter from the King of France of 10 Mch. 1781, another from La Luzerne of 25 May 1781, and a report of a conference between La Luzerne and a committee of Congress on these important occurrences are printed in JCC, XX, 556-69. See also Board of War to TJ, 30 May 1781, and Virginia delegates to TJ, 29 May 1781.

From Francis Taylor

SIR   Winchester June 1st. 1781.

I wrote you the Sixteenth and Twenty sixth of May, and mentioned in both letters, that a board of Officers had sat and were of opinion that most of the soldiers of the Regiment of Guards were entitled to discharges. There are only one Corporal and four privates left, a Fifer having received his discharge on the opinion of a Court martial since, and a soldier for being in an ill state of health.

In each of those letters were inclosed a Return of the Regiment, and I hoped to have been favoured with an answer by this time and orders to discharge the Officers and Soldiers left; who can be of but little service, as they are so few, and I did not think myself authorised to discharge them without your orders. The Officers are very desirous to go home, having no expectation to be continued in service. I beg that a messenger may be sent to inform me what to do. I am Sir, with great respect Your most obedt. humble servant,

FRA TAYLOR

RC (Vi); addressed in part: "Favoured by ⟨Colo Holmes⟩ Mr. Ritter."

In a letter to Davies of this date, Taylor reported that he had allowed the county lieutenant of Frederick to have 140 arms of the discharged men "to put into the hands of Militia, who are gone against the Tories in Hampshire," and added: "I have wrote twice . . . to the Governor and expected his order to discharge the Officers and remaining soldiers, who are of little service in proportion to their expence to the publick. I imagine my letters have but lately been received, and hope soon to hear from him" (Vi). The "Militia . . . gone against the Tories in Hampshire" were authorized by TJ's letter to Garret Van Meter of 27 Apr. 1781. On June 16 Van Meter reported that "In consequence of a letter I received sometime ago, from his Excellency Governor Jefferson, relative to a late Insurrection in this County, I ordered out a Company of my militia as Mounted Infantry, together with Three Companies of Foot, as the Rioters had embodied themselves, and the numbers very considerably increased"; but on approach of the militia the rioters dispersed, some were apprehended, and Van Meter applied for a special commission of oyer and terminer for their trial, which was granted by the Council on 22 June 1781 (CVSP, II, 163; see also note to Van Meter to TJ, 20 Apr. 1781).

From Robert Wooding

SIR   Halifax Coty. the 1st. June 1781.

Agreeable to Your Order You have Inclosed the State of the Militia of this County (as ℔ Returns made to me by the Captains in April last) consisting of 20 Captains, 40 Lieutenants, 20 Ensigns and 1004 Rank and file, Eighty Eight of which are under 18 years of age. Of the Remaining part we have about 350 at this time in Actual Service in this State and Carolinia. I am Sorry to assure your Excellency that those of the Militia who are now at home are in a Defensless situation, they having been, in a manner, Dis[pers]ed to Supply those who Marched out on Duty upon former I[nvasions]. I wish it were Possible for the Public to furnish about 250 Stand of Arms and a proper Proportion of Amunition. I know we have good Men among us who would be Glad to use those Arms upon Every Proper Occation, against the Common Enemy; who at this time are much Dispirited the having neither Arms Amunition nor Even a flint to Put to any kind of Gun Could they get one. I have Caus'd Court Martials to be held for the Examination of those who Refused to March when Ordered; the Court have Sentanced about 40 to Six Months Service in this State, they will be sent down as soon as Possible. I have the Honour to be Sir yr. most Obt. Servt.,

Ro. Wooding C. Lt.

RC (Vi); addressed and endorsed. Enclosure not found.

From John Cabeen

PLEASE YOUR EXCELLENCY   Charlott's Ville, June 2d. 1781

I make bold to Inform you, of the melancholly and Deplorable Situation I am in at present. I inform your Excellency that I have been taken prisioner, by the Americans, at the Southren Department about Three years ago, and after being Taken, got a Parole from Governor Caswell to go to any part, of the Country, to work for the Country. I accordingly Proceeded and advanced, Settled in Richmond, and married, my Inclination was never to Interfere at either Side. I Resided and Lived in Richmond when the British were there, my Inclination did not Lead me to go with them, as being married in this Country. I afterwards rented a place in Newcastle, and Coming to Richmd. to get Money, which was Due to me, for work I had Made for Some of the Inhabitants, as I am a Shoemaker by Trade (misfortunately) altho' not having ill Intention, going to Richmond, at the time the British Lately Came up the River, was apprehended, and Carry'd before Colo. Davis, on Suspicion of being not a friend to America. I am a Prisioner of War, but do not want to be Exchanged. I have not had any hearing, am now Confined in Irons among Criminals of the Greatest Crimes. There are Some here, which are Guilty of Murder, that is without any Irons, and walks in and out as they please. I humbly Request your Excellency will order me to be Released from Irons, as it is Beyond all humanity to treat prisioners of War after Such a manner, without being Guilty of Some misbehaviour. Now if it be agreeable to the Benignity of your Excellency I should be glad if I Could have the Priviledge of Going home, to my family, which I Suppose is Now Suffering, as they have Nothing to Subsist on, as I am Confined. I always Intend to be an Inhabitant of America, as long as I live. The above is the Circumstances and Nature of what is alledged against me, and your Excellency Duly Considering my Situation, will Cause you the prayers of the Distressed and I Remain your Excellency's Most Obedient and Very Humble Servant,

JOHN CABEEN

RC (Vi); addressed to TJ at Charlottesville; endorsed in part: "not yet consider'd."

From William Harrison

SIR   Yohogane Coty. 2nd Jun 1781

I have the pleasure to Inform your excellencie that the Provision required for the Western expedition is nearly Compleat and will be at Fort Pitt with Boats sufficient to Transport it by the fifteenth Inst. I find the expence Considerabley augmented from My first expectation. Owing to the Depreciation of the Currency, the Money Sent Me from the Treasurey with 100000 pounds furnished me by Genl. Clark is intirely expended and my Self Considerabley in debt. I find that I Cannot possibley Close My Accounts with less than 400000 pounds as the General urges the Needecessity of that furnished by him being replaced. You will therefore please to Order that Sum Sent Me by Lieut. Tannehill who will hand you this. My Honour Word and fortune is at Stake for the Debts I have Contracted, in behalf of the Commonwealth, which I hope your excellencie will Consider and Order the Money Sent me without delay. I have the Honour to be your Excellencies Very Hubl Servt.,   WILL. HARRISON

RC (Vi); addressed: "His Excellency the Governour of Virgia. ⅌ Lieut Tannahill"; endorsed.

This letter, together with that of John Gibson to TJ of 30 May, q.v., was presented to the House on 11 June and ordered to lie on the table (JHD, May 1781, 1828 edn., p. 13). Whether these letters were transmitted in a covering letter from TJ is not known.

From Samuel Huntington

SIR   Philadelphia June 2. 1781

My Letter of yesterday addressed to your Excellency and which accompanies this, contains such important Intelligence, that Congress have thought it indispensible to communicate the same to the Legislatures of the several States through their respective Supreme Magistrates as soon as possible; at the same Time the Intelligence is of a Nature that ought to be kept secret as may be at present. I am therefore directed to request that effectual Measures be observed to prevent Copies or Extracts of the Letter of the 1st Instant from being taken or published.

I have the Honor to be, with very great Respect Your Excellency's Most obedient & most humble Servant,

SAM. HUNTINGTON President

RC (Vi); in a clerk's hand, signed by Huntington; at head of text: "Circular"; endorsed. FC (DLC: PCC, No. 16). Enclosure: Huntington to TJ, 1 June 1781, q.v.

To Lafayette

SIR   Charlottesville June 2d. 1781

The House of Delegates and so many of the Senate as were here having reason to believe that Genl. Morgan might probably have it in his power to raise a number of volunteers to join in our present defence, have come to a Resolution of which I do myself the honor of inclosing you a Copy. I have transmitted it to him also.

Should you find it not inconsistent with any orders under which he may be acting I make no doubt you will give it the aid of your additional Recommendations to that brave and useful Officer.

I am &c.,   THOMAS JEFFERSON

FC (Vi). Enclosure: Resolution of House of Delegates of 2 June concerning Gen. Morgan (see TJ to Morgan, following).

To Daniel Morgan

SIR   Charlottesville June 2d. 1781

I have the pleasure to inclose to you a resolution of the House of Delegates assented to by so many of the Senate as were here, by which you will perceive the confidence they repose in your exertions, and the desire they entertain of your lending us your aid under our present circumstances. I sincerely wish your health may be so far reestablished as to permit you to take the field, as no one would count more than myself on the effect of your interposition. I inclose you Commissions for the officers of three battalions. They are of necessity dated at the time of my signing them, and it will be well if you endorse on each the date from which it is to give rank. [The more immediate this aid the more valuable it will be.]¹ I am with great respect Sir Your mo. obd. & most [hble. Servt.,

TH: JEFFERSON]

RC (NN); MS mutilated, the signature and possibly some of the text being cut out (see note 1, below); in a clerk's hand, addressed by TJ: "Brigadr. Genl. Morgan Berkeley; endorsed. Enclosures: (1) Resolution of the House of Delegates of 2 June 1781, requesting the Governor to "call for the immediate assistance of Brigadier General Morgan to take the command of such Volunteers, Militia or others as he may be able speedily to embody and march to join the army under command of the Honble Major General Marquis la Fayette; that this Assembly have the utmost confidence in the active exertions of General Morgan in the present emergency; and that the Governor do transmit to the said General so many proper Commissions as may be necessary for the field officers, Captains, Subalterns and others to be by him appointed" (Tr in the hand of John Beckley, signed and attested by him, in Vi; JHD, May 1781, 1828 edn., p. 9-10). (2) Commissions as specified in the resolution (missing). FC (Vi).

This resolution was not agreed to by the Senate until 11 June, but TJ had dispatched the above letter and Morgan had accepted the call by that date (CVSP, II, 154-5; Morgan's letter of acceptance is missing, but he refers to it in another to the Speaker of 15 June; same, 162). Morgan, in consequence of this resolution, appealed to Horatio Gates, Col. William Darke, Maj. John Smith, Col. John Nelson, county lieutenant of Frederick, John Morrow, county lieutenant of Berkeley, Col. David Kennedy of Frederick co., Major George Scott, Captain Francis Willis, Jr., and Col. Charles Mynn Thruston. These gentlemen, with Morgan met at Winchester on 14 June 1781 "to consider of the most speedy and proper methods of carrying a late Act of Assembly [sic] for General Morgan to raise a number of Volunteers for the defense of this Country and for other purposes into Execution." They met as "a Convention" and adopted various resolutions making recommendations to the legislature: (1) that magazines for provisions, carriages, entrenching tools, axes, and all kinds of military stores be laid up at Winchester and other places; (2) that proper persons be impowered to "make, repair, and collect all kinds and sorts of Millitary implements, from every person with whom such necessaries may be found, for the general defence"; (3) that "it appears absolutely necessary that a number of horses to mount the light dragoons be had . . . and that some method be immediately fallen upon for the supply thereof; (4) that Gen. Morgan be impowered to employ "all kinds of Artificers and make use of all proper material necessary . . . which materials we are of opinion are abundant, if proper authority be given to take them"; (5) that Gen. Morgan's "commissaries have power by Legislative authority to furnish necessary provisions, and that his Quartermasters have sufficient powers to execute their office according to such directions as they shall receive from him"; (6) that, because the "approach of Harvest and the criticalness of the spring crops, have prevented the inhabitants from becoming Volunteers in such numbers as was hoped and expected," the legislature "provide some decisive measure for procuring the number necessary"; and (6) that George Rootes bear the foregoing resolutions to the General Assembly and "answer such questions as they may please to ask him . . . and that he do take a letter from Genl. Morgan and demean himself therefrom" (Vi; the minutes of this "Convention" were signed by all of those named above, including Morgan, whose letter of 15 June is in CVSP, II, 162-3). Morgan's letter and "other papers on the subject" were presented to the House by the Speaker on 18 June and were laid on the table (JHD, May 1781, 1828 edn., p. 21). Many of the extensive powers recommended were embraced in the Act "for giving certain powers to the governour and council," for example the power "to procure by impress or otherwise . . . provisions of every kind, all sorts of cloathing, accoutrements and furniture, proper for the use of the army, negroes as pioneers, horses both for the draft and cavalry, waggons, boats or other vessels . . . and also all other necessaries as may be wanted for supplying the militia or other troops employed in the public service"; this Bill was already engrossed and passed its third reading at the time Morgan's communication was laid before the House (Hening, x, 412-13). Morgan was in the field by July and continued in service for several months, though in the latter part of 1781 he was in command at Winchester. On 20 Sep. 1781, ill and still suffering from his old wounds, he wrote to Gov. Nelson: "I am in hopes we have that old Fox Cornwallis pretty safe. Nothing this sid of heaven would make me so happy as to be at the takeing him, if my health would permit, but I am afraid it will not. [I] must therefore pray for your success, which I shall most fervently do" (CVSP, II, 473). Unhappily, the patriotic old warrior was denied the gratification of being present at Yorktown.

[1] The sentence in brackets (supplied) appears only in the FC. It is probable that this was added as a postscript to the RC, in TJ's hand, and was cut away with the signature at some later date.

To the Speaker of the House

SIR   Charlottesville June. 2. 1781.

I beg leave to refer to the consideration of the General assembly the inclosed letters from the County Lieutenants of Augusta, Rockbridge and Rockingham, and have the honour to be with great respect Sir your most obedt. humble servt.,   TH: JEFFERSON

RC (Vi); addressed by TJ: "The honble Benjamin Harrison esq. Speaker of the House of Delegates." Enclosures (missing): These were probably George Moffett to TJ, 5 May 1781; Samuel McDowell to TJ, 9 May 1781; and Garret Van Meter to TJ, 14 and 20 Apr. 1781. TJ's letter with its enclosures was laid before the House on 2 June. The letters from Augusta and Rockbridge were referred to the committee of privileges and elections and the letter from Rockingham was ordered to lie on the table

(JHD, May 1781, 1828 edn., p. 10). Apparently no further action was taken by the House. But on 23 June the Council, "conceiving the late insurrections . . . to have been occasioned by the artifice of a few disaffected and designing men," advised the Governor to offer pardon on condition that they would deliver up their ringleaders or, in case they should refuse, to call on "the whole strength of the aforesaid counties for apprehending and bringing them to justice" (Va. Council Jour., II, 351).

To Robert Andrews and Rev. James Madison

GENTLEMEN   Charlottesville June 3d. 1781

The advance of the season has induced his Excellency President Reid to propose deferring the final Settlement of our boundary till the first Day of May 1782 which we have agreed to. You will be pleased therefore to consider that as the time at which your Services will be hoped for by the public. I am &c.,

THOMAS JEFFERSON

FC (Vi); at head of text: "The Revd. Robert Andrews and James Madison."

From Theodorick Bland

SIR   Philadelphia June 3d 1781

The letter from the delegation to your Excellency will apprize you of the Situation of Public affairs at this time, and of our endeavors to promote every thing that can give energy to the operations of the Army in defense of our distressed Country. I should not therefore have troubled your Excellency with the perusal of this which relates to myself did not my own peculiar Situation render it necessary and had I not reason to conjecture from the several late ineffectual applications I have been *driven through dire necessity to make*, that my letters may have miscarried. I can hardly suppose them to have passed unnoticed. The long expected and long wishd for remittance which was to have come through the hands of Mr. Braxton has afforded us no relief and has evaporated into smoke. My Finances are as well as my Credit entirely exhausted, my Private resources in Virginia Cut off by the Enemy, and I am at this moment without the means of buying a dinner or of procuring money even to purchase a bait of oats for my horses. I have even offerd my Horses for sale, (but can not meet with a Purchaser) in order to procure a present Subsistance for my family. The money I have Borrowd with the most solemn assurances to repay, and which I am disappointed in doing, is this day exhausted to the last Shilling. The anxiety I feel in this Situation (new, to me) is insupportable especially as it in some degree incapacitates me from turning my thoughts with that application I would wish to do to those important concerns which I would wish to engross my whole attention. The Subject is such an one as I cannot but with the utmost Sense of pain commit to Paper, and with feelings which I cannot so well describe as your Excellency may concieve. I must therefore cease to prosecute it further by assuring you I am Yr. Excelly's obedt. Svt,   THEOK: BLAND

RC (Vi); addressed to TJ; franked by Bland and endorsed.

On 19 June the House passed a resolution, agreed by the Senate, instructing the Governor and Council "to use every means to make remittances to our delegates in Congress in discharge of their allowance, either by giving orders for the purchasing and transmitting to them tobacco or hemp, or by pursuing such other mode as to them shall appear most effectual" (JHD, May 1781, 1828 edn., p. 23, 28). This action may have been taken as a result of TJ's forwarding the letter to the legislature in Staunton.

From Samuel Huntington

SIR   Philadelphia June 3. 1781

I have been honored with your Excellency's Letter of the 28th Ulto., previous to which Congress had adopted the Measures contained in their Act of the 31st Ulto., Copy of which is enclosed, for sending Assistance to repel the Enemy in Virginia. No Means in the Power of Congress will be left unessayed to give you all necessary Aid. I am informed some Arms are now on the Way for Virginia, and the Board of War are still using their Endeavors, not without Prospect of Success, to procure more Arms to supply such Troops from Maryland and this State as may be raised and march to join the Marquis de la Fayette.

Enclosed are Extracts of Intelligence from the West Indies which you may not have received.

I have the Honor to be, with very great Respect Your Excellency's Most obedient Servant, SAM. HUNTINGTON

RC (Vi); in a clerk's hand, signed by Huntington; endorsed. FC (DLC: PCC, No. 16). Enclosures: (1) Resolve of Congress of 31 May 1781 recommending to the states of Pennsylvania, Delaware, and Maryland to raise troops to be sent to Virginia at once, since the "Deficiency of the Continental regular Lines makes it absolutely necessary to call forth a respectable Body of Militia till those Lines be completed"; it was recommended that Pennsylvania raise four battalions of infantry, one company of artillery, and one corps of horse; Delaware one battalion of infantry and one corps of horse; and Maryland two battalions of infantry and one corps of horse. Each of the infantry battalions was to consist of nine companies of 64 men rank and file (Vi; printed in JCC, XX, 583-4). (2) Tr of extracts of letters of 3 and 8 May 1781 announcing the arrival of De Grasse's fleet in the West Indies and stating that "Rodney is now at Statia dividing the Spoil of the poor Dutch and Americans" (Vi; printed in CVSP, II, 84-5).

To Joseph Reed

SIR   Charlottesville June 3. 1781.

The proposition made in your Excellency's letter of May 14. for deferring the ultimate settlement of our boundary till the 1st. of May 1782. is perfectly agreeable. The observations necessary to fix it with accuracy could not be made in the present season. I also concur in the further proposal to extend Mason and Dixon's line twenty three miles by an ordinary surveyor and to have it marked in the slightest manner to answer present purposes. For this end I have written to the Surveyor of the county of Monongalia, who will concur in the work with any person whom your Excellency shall be pleased to appoint on your part. These gentlemen may settle together the time of proceeding on the business. I have the honor to be with very great respect,   TH: JEFFERSON

RC (NN); endorsed. FC (Vi). Tr by Thomas Meriwether, Assistant Clerk of Council (Vi).

Steuben to the Speaker of the Senate

[3 June 1781]

Quelques jours passé J'ai eu L'honneur de vous informer de L'Etat de La Ligne de Virginie en General. J'espere que Vous avez fait connaitre a L'honorable Assemble le contenue de cette Lettre. Croyant necessaire que Les Legislative soient au fait du nombre des trouppes que cet Etat tiens en Campagne.

A present je prens la Liberté de vous depeindre La situation des trouppes presentement assemblée a cette place. Par le retour cy joint vous verrez le nombre qui est entres. La pluspart de ces gens arriverent depourvue de toute article d'habillement.

Par mon ordre les souliers, chemisses et autres articles qui se trouverent dans les magazins de l'Etat furent distribues. Le Retour cy joint vous marquerat le nombre, et en le comparent avec le nombre d'hommes present, vous trouverai combien il en qui sont depourvue des necessaire pour etre en etat de faire service.

C'est avec douleur que je vois augmenter tout les jours le nombre des malades, consequence naturelle quand les gens sont expose a L'humidite sans avoir L'habillements necessaires. La desertions on ete un autres suite. Le soldat qui sacrifierai volontier sa vie dans un combat a sa patrie devant L'Ennemie revolte de se voir prise de misere faute d'habillemen.

Pour tout habillement je n'esperai, que des chemisses, des soulier des overals, des petits jackets de toile des hunting shirts et des blanquettes, Articles que je croyais obtenir facilement puisqu'ils peuvent etre fait dans le pais. Et je n'esperai pas que dans le mois de juin toute L'Etat de Virginie n'aurait pas fournis ces articles pour 500 hommes, qui ne sont que la sixieme partie du draft que L'assemblee a vouer dans le mois de Nov.

Le Battaillion du Collonel jaskins [Gaskins] est armé des Arms qui sont arrivée de Philadelphie, mais il n'y avait pas une Giberne. Gen. Greene et moi meme ont mentionné cet objet dans nos requisitions dans le mois de novembre. Plusieurs fois J'ai reitire ma demande sur cet Article au Gouvernement, representant que parmi les Articles necessaires, les selles pour la Cavallerie et les Gibernes pour L'Infanterie devrait etre les premiers objets puisqu'il demandait plus de temps a les faire. Cependent Monsieur pas une seule Giberne peut maintenant etre fournié de L'Etat et J'ignore meme si jamais une seule a été commandé.

Je vous suplie Monsieur de mettre ceci devant L'honorable Assemblé. C'est avec douleur que je doit representer des Choses de cette nature Mais je m'interest de me vois justifier devant L' Assemble et devant le bon peuple de cet Etat que le retard de mettre ces trouppes en Campagne n'est point une suite de ma negligence.

Voila cet pauvre Battaillion campé dans le bois perissant sans pouvoir L'Employer pour la Service, sans meme pouvoir les Exercer faute de soulier et des chemises. Je vous suplie M: de m'indiquer a qui je doit m'addresser pour pouvoir remedier a cette triste situation.

Dft (NHi), entirely in Steuben's hand; endorsed in the hand of William North: "To Mr. Cary Speaker of the Senate 3 June 1781." This is in effect a supplement to Steuben's communication on the state of the Virginia Line, transmitted to the Speaker of the House by TJ on 31 May (see Steuben to TJ, 28 May 1781); for obvious reasons Steuben did not send the present letter through TJ; why he chose to address it to the Speaker of the Senate rather than of the House is not known. Translated in part in Palmer, *Steuben*, p. 275. Enclosures missing.

LE NOMBRE DES MALADES: See Matthew Pope to TJ, 31 May 1781. PAS UNE SEULE GIBERNE: On 3 Mch. 1781 TJ authorized George Muter to contract for 3,000 cartridge boxes to be completed by the end of May, but apparently the terms offered by the Council were unacceptable to the contractor (see Muter to TJ, 3 and 5 Mch. 1781, and TJ to Steuben, 5 Mch. 1781).

To the Surveyor of Monongalia County

SIR   Charlottesville June 3d. 1781.

It having become impracticable to settle the boundary between this State and Pensylvania by Astronomical Observations during the present Season, it is referred by mutual Consent till the next year. In the mean time it is agreed that Masons and Dixons line shall be extended twenty three miles with a Surveyors Compass only in the usual manner marking the Trees very slightly. I am therefore to desire you to undertake to do this in Conjunction with such person as shall be appointed by his Excellency President Reid, and report your work to the Executive. We shall rely on your engaging Chain Carriers markers &c. the expense of which shall be paid by the public. I am &c.,   THOMAS JEFFERSON

FC (Vi).

From the Virginia Delegates in Congress

D'R S'R   [3? June 1781]

The delegates have done all they could to hasten Wayne as well as to forward other assistance to our State foreseeing what occasion you would have for aid but could only get the Pen[nsy]lvanians under March very lately and a Resolution a few days past to send forward some Militia from this State and our Neighbour Maryland. Your situation no doubt you have occasionally communicated to the Commander in Chief and must refer you to him for such consolation as he has in prospect. The Delegates endeavours to second your efforts in that quarter have not been wanting and we have no doubt the General will do all in his Power.

[P.S.] 7 Battalions of Militia-Infantry in the whole and 1 Do Horse.

MS not found. Text from Burnett, *Letters of Members*, VI, No. 144, where it is printed from a copy then in the possession of Stan. V. Henkels, Phila. See Huntington to TJ, this date.

From James Callaway

Bedford, 4 June 1781. Has not been able to send two companies of militia from the county in response to the instructions of 8 May. Those who have marched are a part of those who have just finished serving three months at Portsmouth; has assured them they will be relieved in six weeks and hopes the executive will approve; "these men are generally poor . . . their Subsistance depending Totally upon their own Labour." It has been impossible to get into the field any of the militia subjected to six-month service by court-martial; part of those brought in "Broke Jail, and Others Escaped from their Guards." These "Disaffected and Disobedient Wretches" stay much together and are very troublesome; "Near forty of the Enlistments that were made in this County last Summer for Eighteen Months, have long since Deserted and are Secreted by them." Encloses a militia return and asks for new blank commissions.

RC (Vi); 3 p.; addressed to TJ "favr. of Mr. Innis."; endorsed. Enclosure not found.

See Callaway to TJ, 21 May 1781. The last letters written by TJ in his official capacity as Governor were dated 3 June. Letters known to have been addressed to him after that date which were of an official nature, and which were obviously handled by Col. William Fleming or Thomas Nelson, have been summarized or listed in this edition because they do not properly belong to TJ's correspondence and in most cases were never in his hands. Exceptions will be made, however, in such cases as those in which the context indicates that the writer, unaware that TJ had left the governorship, conveyed information to or requested advice from TJ himself.

For a recent and dependable account of TJ's retirement from the governorship, see Malone, *Jefferson*, I, ch. xxv, in which, however, the traditional overemphasis upon the extent of the collapse of state government is moderately repeated; TJ's speech to Ducoigne and his letter to Washington of 28 May, to say nothing of the continued functioning of such important agencies as the war office, indicate that the state of moribundity of government was far from being as total as sometimes indicated. Indeed, the sudden raids on Charlottesville and Point of Fork appear to have obscured the concurrent massing of aids whose foundation had been laid in weeks of previous effort, not only on the part of TJ's administration but also on the part of the Continental Board of War, the

Virginia delegates in Congress, and others. Gottschalk notes this, but indicates that the "Credit for this burst of energy was due to the new governor of Virginia [Nelson], but not entirely, for the initial steps had been taken even while Jefferson was still governor" (Gottschalk, *Lafayette and the Close of the American Revolution*, p. 250). The fact is, however, that the last days of TJ's administration and the first weeks of Nelson's have been generally juxtaposed in the minds of historians and public alike as evidence of weakness of the former and strength of the latter (see *Virginia Cavalcade*, I [1951], No. 2, p. 40-2, for a typical representation of the popular view). But even after Cornwallis had turned and begun his "retreat," William Davies wrote from Richmond such a comment about the Executive as he had not had occasion previously to express: "The enemy's light troops are at Petersburg, the Marquis at Holts forge, and the executive at this place without a guard, an express or a single vidette. I think we shall be swept off one of these days. I see nothing in the world to prevent it. There is nobody here knows where the Governor is, nor have we heard the least tittle from him or about him since he left Charlottesville. I hardly know how to account for it" (Davies to Steuben, 12 July 1781, NHi). Even with Tarleton's men in Charlottesville and Simcoe's at Point of Fork, Davies had not felt as unprotected or as isolated from other parts of government as he did a month after Nelson's election. TJ's last few months and Nelson's first few weeks stand in need of reappraisal.

Malone correctly points out that TJ would have guarded himself better against later controversy if he had produced a formal statement of his unwillingness to serve longer (*Jefferson*, I, 354). There is no evidence that he did so and the exact date of his exit from office can be established only inferentially. For some time he had been giving notice of his intention of retiring, as in his letters to Page of 22 Sep. and 20 Oct. 1780, and to Marbois, 4 Mch. 1781. But these were private communications. Perhaps he regarded no formal statement as necessary, for, as he wrote Washington on 28 May 1781, "A few days will bring to me that period of relief which the constitution has prepared for those oppressed with the labours of my office, and a long declared resolution of relinquishing it to abler

hands has prepared my way for retirement to a private station." Some significance attaches to the fact that Girardin, in printing this letter, adds a footnote to the effect that "Mr. Jefferson's term of office expired on the last day of May," since TJ advised Girardin and corrected parts of his MS (Burk-Girardin, *Hist. of Va.*, IV, 493). But it is apparent that, at the time, TJ regarded the "period of relief which the Constitution has prepared" as beginning for him on 2 June, for he had taken office on that date in 1779 and had been re-elected the same date in 1780 (see Vols. 2: 277 and 3: 410). The House of Delegates resolved on 30 May 1781 to proceed "on Saturday next" (2 June) to ballot for governor and the Senate was informed of this; when the day came, however, action was postponed to Monday, 4 June. TJ continued to function as Governor on Sunday, 3 June, as indicated in the letters written that day. These actions apparently constitute his final acts as Executive and he himself certainly regarded Sunday, 3 June 1781, as his last day in office; on 9 June 1781 he referred to "the alarm on the day succeeding my exit from office" (Tarleton's dragoons appeared early on the morning of 4 June). See also TJ to Marbois, 24 Mch. 1782: "I retired from office in the month of June last and was obliged by the movements of the enemy to retire from my house at the same time." Benjamin Harrison, as Speaker of the House and as guest at Monticello until Tarleton's raid, was entitled on public and private grounds to know TJ's mind on the subject better than anyone else except the Governor himself. On 8 June 1781 Harrison wrote to Joseph Jones: "We have now no Executive in the State. For want of a Senate the governor will act no more, and the remainder of the council will not get together. I hope we shall set these matters right next week" (*Letters of Joseph Jones*, ed. W. C. Ford, 1889, p. 83; this letter was sent by Harrison from Staunton express to Jones at Philadelphia, who copied it in his of 20 June to Washington). This significant letter may indicate that TJ had been approached by Harrison, at least informally, *after* Tarleton's raid and asked to serve in the interim, for the Senate had been in session on 2 June. It apparently did not meet again until sometime between 8 June, when Harrison wrote, and 12 June, when Nelson was elected Governor (JHD, May 1781, 1828 edn., p. 10, 11, 15). No Senate journal for this session is known to be extant either in MS or printed form, but it has been stated that TJ was nominated in the Senate and received some votes there (Eckenrode, *Revolution in Virginia*, p. 227 and Henry, *Henry*, II, 143, both cited by Malone, *Jefferson*, I, 360; while the Constitution of 1776 required both Houses to elect the Governor by joint ballot, it also stipulated that this ballot was to be made in each House separately). Whether this is fact or not, the explanation for Harrison's statement may be that TJ, who certainly regarded his term of office at an end and he himself reduced by constitutional requirement to private status, felt that he could not continue to act even in the interim without formal validation by both houses, even though he had been willing to act on Sunday and for one extra day beyond his legal term. This was a natural as well as a legal position to take, for while TJ was barred from exercising the Executive powers, those powers could be exercised by one or more continuing members of the Council—which, of course, is precisely what happened when William Fleming acted as Executive in the interim between 7 and 12 June 1781.

Richard Henry Lee, in his letter to Washington, 12 June 1781, stated that TJ had "resigned" (Malone, *Jefferson*, I, 358), but there is no evidence to support this. The statement of Madison in a letter to Mazzei, 7 July 1781, is both succinct and accurate: "Mr. Jefferson's year having expired, he declined a re-election, and General Nelson has taken his place" (Madison, *Writings*, ed. Hunt, I, 143). Had Tarleton delayed his raid only twenty-four hours, TJ would in all likelihood have been spared the charge that he had abandoned the government whereas, as Malone has well said, it "would be nearer the truth to say that the government abandoned him" (*Jefferson*, I, 358).

From Arthur Campbell

S**IR**   Washington June 4th. 1781

Okana-Stotes Baggage was first possessed by a detachment mostly Carolinians. The Medals, Belts of Wampum said to be of curious construction were secreted. Colo. Martin has lately purchased one of the Belts; curious enough, he says the wampum in it will answer the purposes at the Treaty (if any). A number of Papers, some curious and perhaps interesting were delivered to me, others I hear is since delivered into the Hands of the Commanding Officers of the Regiment from Carolinia. I will endeavour to collect the whole, and as soon as I can take copies of some that may be interesting to me, I will with pleasure send you the originals.

I am with great Respect your Obedient Servant,

A**RTHUR** C**AMPBELL**

RC (DLC).

This letter was transmitted to TJ by Col. William Fleming in his letter of 14 June 1781. For other letters bearing on the matter of the archives of the Cherokee nation, see Campbell to TJ, 15 Jan. 1781; TJ to Huntington, 17 Feb. 1781; Huntington to TJ, 27 Apr. 1781; Campbell to TJ, 20 June 1781; TJ to McKean, 20 Dec. 1781; and Madison to TJ, 26 Mch. 1782.

From Arthur Campbell

Sir   Washington June 4th. 1781

This day your Orders of the 28th. of May came to hand, and I am sorry our situation at present is such that I have but a small prospect of forwarding the aid required. The murmuring and distresses occasioned by the misconduct of Commissaries and the want of pay for Militia services performed last year, together with the dread a Man commonly has to leave his Family exposed to the danger of being destroyed by the Indians before his return, are objections not easily answered. If they Militia were paid off, I believe I should succeed well in complying with your Excellencys orders of the 12th. of April last, and to this I have hopes to add one Troop of Horse.

Our frontier is now threatned with an Invasion from the Creek Indians, Cherokees, Tories &c. By a Letter from Colo. Sevier to Colo. Isaac Shelby which he favored me with the perusal, a certain Crawford just made his escape from the Cherokees; says that the British Agent, some Tories, and a large body of Indians, were preparing to come in, in order to give a blow to confound the project of a Treaty. The account is so far believed in Carolinia that part of their Militia are embodied. To me it is doubtful, on account of the want of provisions; and information I have from Georgia, that Governour Galvis has succeeded against Pensacola, treated with the Creek Indians in behalf of America as well as the Spaniards, And that General Pickens at Ninety-Six, and Colo. Clarke at Agusta were in a fair way to reduce those Posts. General Greenes Head Quarters at Orangeburg, Sumpter at Monks Corner, and Marian carrying off a Picquet from the Quarter-House.

I am Sir Your most Obedient Humble Servant

ARTHUR CAMPBELL

P.S. We are in want of Ammunition. None of that ordered last Fall are come to hand, neither has Colo. Preston received it.

RC (Vi); endorsed in part: "A Campbell to Govr. Jefferson."
YOUR ORDERS OF THE 28TH. OF MAY: See TJ to the county lieutenants of Washington and certain other counties, 28 May 1781.

From La Luzerne

Sir   Philadelphia, June 4, 1781.

Unavoidable obstacles have prevented the dispatching of our

second division at the time when it had been purposed to send it. I can not enter just here into a detailed account of the reasons for this change in our plans; but I have done so in part to Congress, and that body, notwithstanding the hurtful effect this may have upon the campaign, could not refrain from appreciating the wisdom and prudence of the King in the part which he has pursued. We await however some reinforcements; but they are in no sense equal to what the King's friendship towards the United States has induced him to do to make up for this delay in the plans previously arranged; he has granted them a gratuitous subsidy the disposition of which has been left to Congress. Mr. Robert Morris, Superintendent of the finances, has been charged to consider the gradual application which he shall make of it to the needs of the army of the South. For the rest, Sir, although I can not enter into the detail of the plans which are to be adopted for the assistance of the United States, I can assure you that they will be efficacious, that the King is firmly resolved to aid them to the full extent of his power, and that if they will on their side make efforts to resist the enemy some time longer, they may count confidently upon a happy issue of the glorious cause for which they are striving. I can assure you, moreover, that the calamities and peril of the Southern States furnish an additional motive for His Majesty to redouble his interest in their behalf, that his affection derives therefrom additional stimulus, and that the event will prove that they are perfectly justified in not allowing themselves to be discouraged by the difficulties of the present juncture.

I have the honor to be, Sir, with the most sincere and the most respectful attachment, Your Excellency's Very Humble and Very Obedient Servant, DE LA LUZERNE

MS not found; text from *Magazine of American History*, XXIX [1893], 382-3, where it is printed from a copy furnished by Walter R. Benjamin, N.Y. MS sold American Art Association, Catalogue of Gable Collection, Lot 459, 24 Nov. 1924.

From Edwin Conway

Lancaster County, 6 June 1781. Encloses a return of militia for Lancaster co. and asks for supplies.

RC (Vi); 2 p.; addressed: "Thomas Jefferson Esqr. Governor of Virginia favoured by Capt Currell"; endorsed. Summarized in CVSP, II, 145.

Although this letter is addressed to TJ, there is no evidence that it was ever in his hands.

From Samuel Huntington

Philadelphia, 6 June 1781. Circular letter to the Governors enclosing a resolution of Congress of 2 June.

FC (DLC: PCC, No. 16); 1 p.; at head of text: "Circular." Summarized in CVSP, II, 144, from the recipient's copy which was addressed to TJ.

From George Washington

DEAR SIR   HeadQrs. New Windsor 8th. June 1781

I have had the honor of receiving your Excellency's favors of the 9th. and 28th. of May. The progress which the enemy are making in Virginia is very alarming not only to the State immediately invaded but to all the rest; as I strongly suspect, from the most recent European intelligence, that they are endeavouring to make as large seeming conquests as possible that they may urge the plea of uti possidetis in the proposed mediation. Your Excellency will be able to judge of the probability of this conjecture from the Circular letter of the President of Congress of the 1st Inst.

Were it prudent to commit a detail of our plans and expectations to paper I could convince Your Excellency by a variety of reasons that my presence is essential to the operations which have lately been concerted between the French Commanders and myself and which are to open in this quarter provided the British keep possession of New York.

There have lately been rumours of an evacuation of that place, but I do not place confidence in them.

Should I be supported by the Neighbouring States in the manner which I expect, the enemy will, I hope, be reduced to the necessity of recalling part of their force from the Southward to support New York or they will run the most eminent risque of being expelled with a great loss of Stores from that Post which is to them invaluable, while they think of prosecuting the War in America, and should we, by a lucky coincidence of Circumstances, gain a Naval Superiority their ruin would be inevitable. The prospect of giving relief to the Southern States by an operation in this quarter, was the principal inducement for undertaking it. Indeed we found upon a full consideration of our affairs in every point of view, that, without the command of the Water it would be next to impossible for us to transport the Artillery, Baggage, and Stores of the Army to so great a distance and besides, that we should loose at least one third of our force by desertion, sickness, and the heats of the approaching Season even if it could be done.

Your Excellency may probably ask whether we are to remain here for the above reasons should the enemy evacuate New York and transfer the whole War to the Southward? To that I answer[1] that we must, in such case, follow them at every expence, and under every difficulty and loss; but that while we remain inferior at Sea, and there is a probability of giving relief by diversion (and that perhaps sooner than by sending reinforcements immediately to the point in distress) good policy dictates the trial of the former.

Give me leave before I take leave of your Excellency in your public capacity to Express the obligations I am under for the readiness and Zeal with which you have always forwarded and supported every measure which I have had occasion to recommend thro' you, and to assure you that I shall esteem myself honored by a continuation of your friendship and corrispondence shou'd your country permit you to remain in the private walk of life.

I have the honor to be with every Sentiment of respect & regard Dr Sir Yr. Most Obt. & Hbl Ser,   GO: WASHINGTON

RC (PHi); endorsed. FC (DLC: Washington Papers); with several insertions and complimentary close in Washington's hand; endorsed.

For the proceedings of the Wethersfield conference at which the decision was reached to move the combined American and French armies against New York so as to threaten that post or to be prepared to move "against the enemy in some other quarter, as circumstances shall dictate," see Washington, *Writings*, ed. Fitzpatrick, XXII, 105-107.

[1] Inserted in FC at this point, in Washington's hand: "without hesitation"; all other insertions in FC are in RC.

From Josiah Parker

[*Place unknown, before 9 June 1781*. Extract of a letter from Josiah Parker to the Speaker of the House of Delegates, "Carters Meades Mills," 9 June 1781 (Vi): "A few days since I wrote Mr. Jefferson respecting my peculiar situation being in the field with a few men from Isle of Wight and Nancemond and from a request of the Marquiss de la Fayette to embody as many of the Militia as I could down James River below the Enemy, in consequence of which in addition to the men before mentioned [I] have ordered from Southampton 200 and from Surry 100 Men. The last County has nearly sent their number but the former contrary to their common custom has only furnished a small proportion. . . . I have employed Smiths to repair the Arms, to make horsemans Swords and Mechanicks of different sorts in the different branches without sufficient authority, which may probably ruin me without even the approbation of my Country, and for what? To expose my person, my property, my family and all, 'tis a horrid Situation and altho I have wrote the Governor on the Subject, he treats it with contempt, and does not deign to answer me. I fear my Dear Sir the root of Springs of Government is rotten, and I dread the Consequence. Nothing but my zeal coud induce me to write thus freely. I am foolishly proud of my Country, and cannot bear to see her neglected." Parker's letter to TJ has not been found; it is possible that it was not received.]

To Col. William Fleming

SIR   Monticello June 9. 1781.

The alarm which took place on the day succeeding my exit from office prevented my depositing with you the public papers in my hands. I now transmit them by express. The labels on them were true formerly; but in preparing for flight I shoved in papers where I could.

You will be pleased to recollect that the militia of several counties now with the Marquis are to leave him at the close of this month. It was the intention of the Executive to relieve them from the same counties. The counties I speak of are Frederic, Hampshire, Berkeley, Orange, Fauquier, Loudon and Spotsylvania.

I am with great respect Sir Your most obedt. servt.,

TH: JEFFERSON

RC (The Rosenbach Company, Phila., 1946); endorsed. The enclosed public papers, consisting of two packages, have not been identified; see Fleming to TJ, 14 June 1781.

Henry Young to William Davies

DR SIR   Staunton 9th. June 1781.

The Iron Chest that was put in your Waggon contains a number of Papers of consequence, you will be pleas'd to take it with you to this place. We have reason to apprehend that the Enemy are within twelve miles of Charlottesville. I apprehended two days ago a Desserter on suspicion of his being a spie. Circumstances are strong against him but no positive proof. He says that the Enemy will be hear in a day or two. Some confidence is repos'd in his opinion by many, for my part I give no credit to any thing that he says. Two days ago Mr. Nicholas gave notice that he shou'd this day move to have a Dictator appointed. Genl. Washington and Genl. Greene are talk'd of. I dare to say your knowledge of those worthy Gentlemen, will be sufficient to convince you that neither of them will or ought to except of such an appointment. Genl. Wayn join'd the Marquis yesterday with a very respectable Corps—perhaps it might be the day before, accounts differ. We have but a thin House of Delligates, but they are Zealous I think in the cause of Virtue.

I want to see you much. I think, this session of Assembly will be very strict.

I am Yr. unshaken frd.,

H YOUNG

RC (Vi); addressed to Davies without indication of place; endorsed.

A DICTATOR: If George Nicholas announced his intention to introduce a motion to this effect on 7 June (as reported by Young), he did so on the first day the House met at Staunton, whither they had adjourned on the approach of Tarleton's troops to Charlottesville on 4 June, having already resolved "That during the present dangerous invasion, forty members be a sufficient number to compose a House to proceed upon business" (JHD, May 1781, 1828 edn., p. 10). Though the journal of this session contains no record of such a motion on the 9th or any other day, there is no doubt that the motion was made and that it touched off a bitter controversy. The fullest account is in a letter from Archibald Stuart to TJ, dated at Staunton, 8 Sep. 1818 (MH: Sparks Transcripts). Stuart was not a member of the House of Delegates, but he was a spectator of its proceedings at Staunton in June and stated that Nicholas spoke in favor of establishing "a Dictator . . . in this Commonwealth who should have the power of disposing of the lives and fortunes of the Citizens thereof without being subject to account." Nicholas proposed George Washington for this post and "refered to the practice of the Romans on similar occasions. After Mr. Nicholas sat down Mr. Henry addressed the Chair; he observed it was immaterial to him whether the Officer proposed was called a Dictator or a Governor with enlarged powers or by any other name yet surely an Officer armed with such powers was necessary to restrain the unbridled fury of a licentious enemy and concluded by seconding the Motion." The motion, Stuart continued, was opposed by Mann Page of Spotsylvania and others. "After a lengthy discussion the proposition was negatived," and it was obvious that the proposal "was not relished by the people. . . . I communicated these facts to you,"

Stuart concluded, "shortly after they took place."

The information from Stuart (perhaps communicated orally in the summer of 1781) was no doubt the cause of TJ's long and vigorous denunciation of attempts to establish dictatorships in Virginia in his *Notes on Virginia* at the conclusion of his answer to Query XIII (Ford, III, 231-5); he here replies directly to the arguments used by Nicholas and Henry and states that the dictatorship proposal "wanted a few votes only of being passed." In a MS addition in his own copy (ViU) of the Stockdale edn. of *Notes on Virginia*, London, 1787, p. 207, TJ stated that the motion "was rejected by a majority of 6. only." (This more precise statement, evidently based on later information, was included in a footnote in the Randolph edn. of the *Notes*, Charlottesville, 1853.) TJ's bitterness on this subject was unquestionably owing to his conviction that Patrick Henry himself aspired to this post of unlimited power and that Henry's initiative in the move to censure TJ's administration (see under 12 June, below) was part of a concerted plan to gain that end. This is clear from the narrative of these proceedings by Girardin, who wrote under TJ's eye and with his approval.

"At length," wrote Girardin about 1814, "a powerful army under Cornwallis was poured into Virginia, which was only aided by an inconsiderable regular force under La Fayette; and the Assembly was driven by the enemy over the mountains to Staunton. At this juncture, some of its members turned their eyes towards a dictator; and measures for effecting the project were suddenly taken, with the zeal inspired by a belief that its execution was necessary to save the country. An individual, highly conspicuous for his talents and usefulness through the anterior scenes of the great revolutionary drama, was spoken of as the proper person to fill the contemplated office, to introduce which, it was necessary to place Mr. Jefferson *hors de combat*. For this purpose, the misfortunes of the period were ascribed to him; he was impeached in some loose way, and a day for some species of hearing, at the succeeding session of Assembly, was appointed. However this was, no evidence was ever offered to sustain the impeachment; no question was ever taken upon it, disclosing, on the part of the Assembly, any approbation of the measure; and the hearing was appointed by general consent for the purpose, as many members expressed themselves, to give Mr. Jefferson an opportunity of demonstrating the absurdity of the censure. But the impeachment, sour as was the temper of the Legislature, failed to produce the two ends it had in view, namely, to put down Mr. Jefferson, and to put up the project for a Dictator. The pulse of the Assembly was incidently felt in debates on the state of the Commonwealth, and, out of doors, by personal conversations. Out of these a ferment gradually arose, which foretold a violent opposition to any species of Dictatorship, and, as in a previous instance of a similar attempt, the apprehension of personal danger produced a relinquishment of the scheme" (Burk-Girardin, *Hist. of Va.*, IV, Appendix, p. xi-xii).

Edmund Randolph, writing in 1809 or earlier, comments on TJ's "great bitterness [in the *Notes on Virginia*] against those members of the assembly in the years 1776 and 1781, who espoused the creation of a dictator." Randolph does not mention the name of any person proposed for this office; he attributes both moves to panic and declares that neither had the remotest chance of succeeding: "Let it be understood, that the power, which may have saved Rome, would have made Virginia revolt" ("Essay," VMHB, XLIV [1936], 314-15). William Wirt in his biography of Henry, first published in 1817, thought it "highly probable, that Mr. Henry was the character who was in view for that office," but that "The project came from other quarters" than Henry himself (*Sketches of the Life and Character of Patrick Henry*, Philadelphia, 1817, p. 231; see also Henry, *Henry*, II, 145-8). What Henry's own inner thoughts were on this subject—as on many others—will probably never be known. For what another prominent Virginian, not present at Staunton, was thinking on the question of a dictatorship, see R. H. Lee to the Virginia Delegates in Congress, 12 June 1781, below.

From George Rogers Clark

Yohogania Court House, 10 June 1781. Capt. Bentley of Illinois has presented a number of bills which Clark has countersigned; Bentley has presented other bills drawn by Col. Montgomery which cannot be properly credited without further investigation. Mr. Charles Gratiot has also sent bills to the executive, some of which are known to be just, as that "Gentleman as well as Capt. Bently have taken great Pains to subsist our troops." Capt. Bentley wishes to undertake supplying Fort Jefferson for a garrison of 100 men; "I don't know any person more likely to accomplish such a task."

RC (Vi); 2 p.; endorsed.

This letter was acknowledged by Gov. Nelson in a (missing) letter of 26 June 1781 in which he directed Clark to "consider Detroit not as the principal object of his expedition, but to employ his forces in the first instance in chastising the hostile Indians"; on the same day the Council authorized a warrant to be issued "to Thomas Bently in part paiment of certain bills" (*Va. Council Jour.*, II, 353).

From Robert Morris

Sir   Philadepa. June 11th 1781

No doubt you have seen in the Publick Papers, the plan of Establishing a National Bank, the necessity of which every body sees that allow themselves the least time for reflection on the present State of Public Credit. All the Publick Bodies in America, have more or less lost the Confidence of the World as to Money Matters, by trying Projects and applying Expedients to stop a Course of depreciation which Original errors had fixed too deep to Admit of any radical Cure. It is in vain to think of carrying on War any longer, by means of such Depreciating Medium and at same time an Efficient circulation of Paper that Cannot depreciate is Absolutely Necessary to Anticipate the Revenues of America. A National Bank is not only the most Certain but will prove the Most Usefull and Oeconomical Mode of doing so. It is therefore of the Utmost Importance that this first Essay, confined as it is in point of Capital, should be brought into Action with the greatest Expedition. I am sensible that Plans of Publick Utility however Promising and pleasing they may be on their first Appearance soon grow languid unless it be the Particular Business of some Man or set of Men to Urge them forward. This may be said to be my Duty in the present instance but I cannot be every where. I must apply for Support to Gentlemen of your Character and Zeal for the service of their Country requesting in the most Earnest Manner you will urge your Friends and Fellow Citizens to become Proprietors of this Bank Stock. Every Subscriber will find his Own Interest benefitted, in proportion to the Capital he deposits. And I dare say few will find the Other parts of their Fortunes to yield them so large or so certain an income as the Stock they have in the Bank. And at the same time they will have the Satisfaction to be Consider'd for Ever as promoters of an Institution, which has been found beneficial to other Countries, and inevitably must be so in the highest degree to this. An institution that most probably will Continue as long as the United States, and that will probably become as usefull to Commerce and Agriculture in the days of Peace as it must to Government during the War.

The Capital proposed is but small when the Extent and Riches of the United States are Considered, but when put in Motion, the Benefits flowing from it will be so perceptible that all difficulty about Encreasing the Capital will vanish, And we shall only have to Appeal to the interest of Mankind, which in most Cases will do more than Patriotism, but there have been and will Continue to be instances where Interest have been Sacrificed to Patriotism And in that belief, I ask you to devote some of your time to Promote this infant Plan which as it gathers Strength may in the end prove the means of saving the Liberties, Lives and property of the Virtuous part of America. My good Opinion of you is an excuse for Giving you this interuption. I am Sir Your Most Obedt. Servt.,

ROBT MORRIS

RC (Vi); in a clerk's hand, signed, and addressed by Morris: "His Excelly Thos Jefferson Esqr Govr of Commr in Chief Virginia"; endorsed in part by a clerk: "Robt Morris's Lre to Gov Jefferson."

There is no indication that this letter ever reached TJ, but it was obviously intended for his personal attention. On 26 May 1781 Congress agreed to certain resolutions approving "of the Plan for establishing a national Bank in these United States, submitted to their Consideration by Mr. R. Morris the 17th day of May 1781" (MS, Vi; printed in JCC, XX, 546-8; Morris' plan is printed in same, p. 545-6). On 6 May 1782, Benjamin Harrison, then Governor, transmitted to the speaker of the House "two letters from the Financier, one inclosing the resolution of Congress establishing a public bank" (*Official Letters*, III, 214).

From John Beckley, enclosing a Resolution of the House of Delegates

SIR   Staunton 12th. June 1781.

I am directed by the House of Delegates to convey to you information respecting a Resolution of their House, of this Date, for an Enquirey into the Conduct of the Executive for the last twelve Months; I therefore, Sir, do myself the honour to inclose a Copy of that Resolution: And remain with great regard, Sir, Your obedient humble Servant,   JOHN BECKLEY

ENCLOSURE

In the House of Delegates, the 12th. of June 1781.

Resolved that at the next Session of Assembly An enquirey be made into the Conduct of the Executive for the last twelve Months.
Teste,   JOHN BECKLEY C.h.d.
                                                 a Copy
                                                 JOHN BECKLEY C.h.d.

RC (DLC); addressed: "The Honourable Thomas Jefferson Esquire Albemarle"; endorsed by TJ: "recd Aug. 7. 1781." Enclosure (DLC); also in Beckley's hand. From the address and endorsement it seems probable that the letter went from Staunton to Charlottesville to Poplar Forest (near Lynchburg) and back to Monticello, where TJ had returned from Poplar Forest on 26 July. From TJ's exchange with George Nicholas, 28 and 31 July, it is clear that he had received unofficial word of the proposed legislative inquiry long before receiving Beckley's official communication; see Archibald Cary to TJ, 19 June 1781.

Among other items of business performed by the diminished General Assembly this day were the following, in this order: a committee of the House met with a committee from the Senate, examined the ballots cast for "a Governor or Chief Magistrate of the Commonwealth for the ensuing year . . . and found a majority of votes in favor of Thomas Nelson, jun. Esq."; the House adopted the resolution printed above; the House and Senate jointly elected William Cabell, Samuel Hardy, and Samuel McDowell members of the Council "in the room of those who have resigned"; and the House resolved "That the Executive be desired to present to Captain John Jouett, an elegant sword and pair of pistols, as a memorial of the high sense which the General Assembly entertain of his activity and enterprize, in watching the motions of the enemy's cavalry on their late incursion to Charlottesville, and conveying to the Assembly timely information of their approach, whereby the designs of the enemy were frustrated, and many valuable stores preserved" (JHD, May 1781, 1828 edn., p. 15). As Malone remarks, the proceedings of this day "marked the nadir of the entire public career of Thomas Jefferson" (Jefferson, I, 361). For a confidential account by a participant who strongly supported TJ, see Archibald Cary's letter of 19 June, below. See also Randolph's "Essay," written in 1809 or earlier, which flatly states that "Colo. George Nicholas and Mr. Patrick Henry were those who censured Mr. Jefferson" (VMHB, XLIV [1936], 321).

Though this point was later lost sight of, the term THE EXECUTIVE used in the resolution was clearly intended to embrace the members of the Council as well as the Governor; moreover, Nicholas himself (in his letter to TJ of 31 July) used the expression "persons entrusted with the administration." So far as attending to duty is concerned, the inquiry would have been much more appropriately directed toward the conduct of the members of Council alone. During the first half of 1781 TJ could not obtain a full board (four members besides the Governor) between 4 and 19 Jan., 13 and 20 Feb., 25 Apr. and 10 May; the last full meeting of the Council during TJ's governorship occurred on the last-mentioned date (Va. Council Jour., II, 271-3, 292-6, 341-6). Two members of Council resigned during these hectic months (see Joseph Prentis to TJ, 8 Apr., and Dudley Digges to TJ, 14

May); and one person declined to serve (see John Tyler to TJ, 1 Apr.). After the junction of the British armies at Petersburg, the situation may be summed up in a phrase used by Betsy Ambler, daughter of Councilor Jacquelin Ambler: "everybody scampering." Miss Ambler in this same letter found the Governor's precipitate flight to Carter's Mountain "laughable," but her very next letter describes how her father slept in a coach guarded by a slave these nights and how the family were carried hither and yon at every rumor of the enemy's approach ("An Old Virginia Correspondence," Atlantic Monthly, LXXXIV [1899], 537-9). During these alarms and excursions the late president of the Council, Dudley Digges, was captured (R. H. Lee to Virginia Delegates in Congress, 12 June 1781, below); and the sole member present and active from 1 to 12 June was William Fleming, whom TJ on 13 May had urgently summoned to Charlottesville in order to "make a Board."

By some remarkable oversight (perhaps indicating that the anti-Jefferson group were not really interested in attaching blame to anyone but the former Governor), the members of TJ's executive board who had remained in office did not receive notice of the resolution of inquiry until the middle of July. (There had been a full board meeting on 20 June at Staunton, and on 23 June the Assembly had adjourned until October. The Council sat at Charlottesville from 2 July.) Under date of 16 July the following entry appears in Va. Council Jour., II, 356:

"This day the following resolution of the House of Delegates, passed at Staunton, the 12th of June last was received under cover directed to David Jameson, William Fleming, Andrew Lewis, George Webb and Jaquelin Ambler esquires.

" 'Resolved that at the next session of Assembly an inquiry be made into the conduct of the executive for the last twelve months.'

"The underwritten members, who till now were strangers to such a resolution having passed, think it their bounden duty to declare, that conscious of the rectitude of their intentions through the course of the most arduous and expensive attendance on public business, however unsuccessful their endeavours may have been, they are very ready and willing to have their public conduct enquired into with the most scrupulous exactness:— That as they cannot but feel most sensibly this implied censure on them, so they should not, from motives of delicasy alone, if there were no other, continue their attendance at the Board, at least till the result of the intended enquiry shall have convinced their fellow Citizens that their honest and best endeavors have not been wanting to serve their country, but that a secession of the members, to whom the fore-mentioned resolution was addressed would leave the State without a legal Executive at a time when the want of one may be productive of the most fatal consequences.

"Signed in the minutes by David Jameson Andrew Lewis and Jaquelin Ambler." (George Webb and William Fleming did not sign because they were not present at this meeting of Council.)

With respect to TJ's partners in the executive office during his governorship the matter of the inquiry seems to have ended here. They were never called upon to defend themselves, and TJ, who correctly judged himself to be the target of the critics in the legislature, did not feel it necessary to defend them.

Richard Henry Lee to the Virginia Delegates in Congress

DEAR GENTLEMEN   Chantilly June the 12th. 1781

I am not informed who of our Delegates remain at Congress and therefore this letter is addressed to you whom I have good reason to suppose are yet there. The unhappy crisis of our countrys fate demands the closest attention of all her sons, and calls for the united wisdom and the strongest exertions of all others who may be affected by our ruin. I suppose you have been informed of the junction of the enemies forces on James river and of many of their subsequent movements—that they have quickly mounted a very formidable Cavalry by seising on all the fine horses in that part of our country where most they abound to the number of 5 or 600. Being thus provided, and greatly superior in numbers and quality of troops to the Marquis, they moved as if intending to cross the Country to Fredericksburg. Our army keeping at a prudent distance advanced upon their left or western flank. The Marquis proceeding forward in daily expectation of being joined by Gen. Waynes long, very long delayed force, approached Rappahanock above Falmouth, when the enemy halted their main body in the forks of Pomunkey, and detatched 500 Cavalry with an Infantryman behind each to Charlottsville where our unformed Assembly was collecting by adjournment from Richmond. The two houses were not compleated, and Mr. Jefferson had resigned his office and retired, as some of our dispersed Delegates report, when the enemy entered Charlottsville this day sennight and dispersed the whole taking Mr. Digges the Lieutenant Governor prisoner and some Delegates, Mr. Lyons the Judge and many others. I find that several of the Delegates have returned home dispersing the news of our misfortune and their disgrace without expressing a thought about any future collection of the Legislature. It seems that our Stores were collected in the North fork of James river, below Charlottsville and not above 40 miles from where the main body of the enemies army had placed themselves, that these Stores were under protection of Baron Steuben with 7 or 800 new Levies. These then being nearly between the enemies horse above and their army below which had moved towards the North fork, it remains extremely probable that the Barons force and the Stores are one or both e'er now destroyed. You will then judge of the situation of this country, without either executive or Legislative authority, every thing in the greatest possible confusion, the enemy far superior in force to that with the Marquis, and practising every thing that force and fraud can contrive. I do give it to you gentlemen as my serious opinion, uninfluenced by vain apprehensions, that if immediate and powerful interposition does not take place, commensurate to the certain danger, that all the country below the Mountains will be in the power of the enemy in a few months. It is true that we have in Virginia a number of Men much greater than the enemies force, but it is also true that their dispersed, unarmed, and unadvised condition; without government and without system of any kind, renders them an easy prey to the combined force and concerted system of our enemies. Upon the principle therefore of duty to my country, and deep affection for the liberties of America I have ventured to give you this intelligence of our true state, and mean to close it with my opinion of the remedy best fitted, and most likely to baffle the designs of our enemies and to secure the liberty of this country. In the popularity, the judgement, and the experience of Gen. Washington we can alone find the remedy. Let Congress send him immediately to Virginia, and as the head of the Fœderal Union let them possess the General with Dictatorial power until the general Assembly can be convened, and have determined upon his powers, and let it be recommended to the Assembly when met to continue this power for 6, 8, or 10 months as the case may require. The General should be desired, on his arrival here, to call a full meeting of the Legislature where he shall appoint to consider of the above plan. Both antient and modern times furnish precedents to justify this procedure, but if they did not, the present necessity not only justifies but absolutely demands the measure. In the winter of 1776 Congress placed such powers in the General, and repeated the same thing (if I mistake not) with regard to Pennsylvania in 1777 after its new government was formed and organised. There is no time to be lost gentlemen in this business, for the enemy are pushing their present advantages with infinite diligence and art. The efforts of this country have certainly not been equal to its powers, but however feeble they may have been under republican government, you may be assured that when it shall come under the sword of a Conqueror, such resources and such power will appear from Virginia as to put the liberties of the rest of N. America in eminent peril. The inferiority of our Army here to that of the enemy renders it very necessary that 2 or 3000 regulars be sent with the General, or at least to follow him quickly, and if they are to be got, accoutrements for 1000 horse, with a good supply of Arms and Ammunition for Infantry. The better to distract us, and keep our force divided, the Armed vessels of the enemy are pushing vigorously into the rivers, and committing depredations on the shores both of Bay and rivers. Is it not possible, by any solicitation to procure a superior Marine force for these southern waters. It is reported here than Gen. Wayne has objections to Act under the Marquis's command. If there should be any disagreement, or any objection of this kind, the consequences are too obvious to escape your notice, And will furnish an auxiliary reason for the Commander in chief coming here, if any additional reason can be requisite, when the very being of the state certainly demands it.

I am dear gentlemen sincerely and affectionately yours,

RICHARD HENRY LEE

P.S. By the Delegates who have returned from Charlottesville it is supposed that the last remaining press in this Country has been taken by the Enemy as it was sent out of Town but a few hours before the light Horse entered. I reckon the want of a press here a most essential injury to our Cause and Country. Should the commander in chief come here upon the plan above mention'd he will find himself much distressed for want of a press thro' which to communicate his desires to the People; I submit it to you therefore whether every nerve ought Not be strain'd to get a press immediately removed to Winchester or Stanton in this State, even tho' it should be furnish'd with but a moderate collection of Tipes it may answer the above purposes and furnish the public with a small Gazette to convey intelligence, the People being now destitute of information and left a prey to Tory lies and bad influences. What is become of Dunlap and his Press which ought to have been here long since? Be pleased to fill up the direction of the letters for Gen. Washington and forward them securely.   R. H. LEE

RC (DLC: Rives Papers); endorsed in an unidentified hand: "June 12. 1781 R. H. Lee." One enclosure must have been R. H. Lee's letter to Washington of this date, printed in Lee's *Letters*, II, 233-5; and another was Lee to James Lovell, same date, forwarded via Washington, printed in same, p. 235-8.

The enclosed letters set forth Lee's plan for a dictatorship in terms similar to those found in his letter to the Virginia Delegates. To Washington he observed: "It would be a thing for angels to weep over, if the goodly fabric of human freedom which you have so well labored to rear, should in one unlucky moment be levelled with the dust." Lee's INTELLIGENCE OF OUR TRUE STATE was, of course, exaggerated: both the executive and legislative powers were in being and were active; TJ had already appealed to Washington to lend the vast support of his presence, though he was not frightened into the expedient of recommending establishment of a dictatorship; Congress had already taken action to send forward troops; the Board of War was laboring, successfully, to dispatch arms and equipment for troops —in brief, succor was fast approaching and in large part this was due to groundwork laid by the retiring Governor who, like General Morgan, did not share in the fruitful climax of these efforts. Nevertheless, Lee's letter is an illuminating reflection of the near panic that gripped the minds even of some of Virginia's leaders at this time; its frantic appeal needs to be set beside TJ's confident speech to Ducoigne of 1 June 1781. In this connection it is worth noting that Lee had warmly supported Steuben's proposal of late March to send two thousand troops (with badly needed arms, of course) southward to support Greene; "I find," he wrote Steuben, "that the excellent plan you had projected has not been carried into execution. . . . Thus, instead of effecting our business by great Master strokes we must expect the consequences of much delay and tedious defensive operations" (Lee to Steuben, 18 Apr. 1781, NHi). Had TJ and the Council approved this proposal, the situation in June in respect to both arms and men would in all likelihood have been much worse than it was. It is surprising, however, that Lee did not know that Dunlap's PRESS had arrived and had been set up by Hayes in Richmond early in April. MR. LYONS THE JUDGE was Peter Lyons of Hanover co. (*Tyler's Quart.*, VIII [1927], p. 184-5).

From Col. William Fleming

SIR   Stanton June 14th. 1781.

I was honored with your favour of June 9th. and two packages of publick papers. From the pressing instances of the Marquis for rifle men, by a resolve of the Legislative, the Militia of Pittsilvania, Henry, Amherst and Albemarle below the Mountain and of Botetourt, Rockbridge, Augusta, Rockingham, Frederick, Hampshire, Berkly and Shenando above the Mountain, are caled into the field. Many of them will join the Marquis this day, and I expect the whole of them in Six or Seven days more. I will mention the counties of Orange Faquier Loudon and Spotsylvania to the board, when there is one. The present vacancies are filled up with Colo. Wm. Cabel, Saml. McDowal and Mr. Hardy. The inclosed paper came under cover from Our members in Congress of the 29th. of May. In theirs, mention is made of a letter from the King of France of a late date to Congress the contents of which will be sent to the respective legislatures, without hinting the purport. No Steps have yet been taken relative to the Flags. Mr. Braxtons remittance only reached them the 28th of May, and on Account of the great depriciation they have declined receiving it, unless Mr. Braxtons Agent will make the payment on equitable principles. A letter from Colo. Arthr. Campbell of a private nature accompanies this. I have the honor to be with great esteem. Your most obt. Humble Servt.,

WILLM. FLEMING

RC (DLC). Enclosure: (1) Arthur Campbell to TJ, 4 June 1781, printed under that date. (2) "The inclosed paper . . . from Our members in Congress" has not been identified.

Major John Pryor wrote William Davies concerning the considerable reinforcements of RIFLE MEN for Lafayette, asking that "one thousand weight of the best powder and fifteen hundred weight of lead" be provided for the making of loose ammunition for their use (Pryor to Davies, Charlottesville, 13 June 1781, Vi). The next day Pryor discovered a sufficient quantity of powder in Charlottesville (same to same, 14 June 1781, Vi).

From Arthur Campbell

Washington [co.] *15 June 1781.* Encloses a letter from Joseph Martin which explains the reference in Campbell's letter of 4 June "respecting an attack from the Indians and Tories from the South"; in that letter Martin informs Campbell that about 300 Indians are on their way to attend the proposed treaty; recommends that Campbell come immediately; has sent an express to Col. Sevier to come as soon as possible; is informed that the alarm spread by Crawford is not to be credited but it has drawn all the forces that can be raised to the frontier.

RC (Vi); 2 p.; addressed to TJ; endorsed. Enclosure (Vi): Joseph Martin to Arthur Campbell, Long Island, 4 June 1781.

From Samuel Huntington, enclosing a Resolution of Congress Appointing Peace Commissioners

SIR   Philadelphia 15. June 1781

Before this comes to Hand your Excellency will have received my Letter of the 2d Instant with it's Enclosures, by which you will be informed that a Negotiation for Peace between the Belligerent Powers may probably take Place through the Mediation of the Empress of Russia and Emperor of Germany.

In Consequence of which Congress have thought proper to add four other Plenipotentiaries to the Honorable John Adams Esquire to assist in the expected Negotiation, of which you are elected one, as you will be informed by the enclosed Resolve. You will doubtless come this Way to embark, if Circumstances will admit of your Undertaking this important Service. The Commissions will be prepared immediately, as no Time should be lost.

Your Appointment is ordered to be kept secret that the Enemy may not get Intelligence of your Embarkation.

With very great Respect I have the Honor to be Your Excellency's Most obedient & most humble Servant,

SAM. HUNTINGTON President

ENCLOSURE

By the United States in Congress assembled   June 14. 1781

Resolved That four persons be joined to Mr. Adams in negotiating a peace between these United States and Great Britain.

The following were elected
The honble. Benjamin Franklin
The honble John Jay
The honble. Henry Laurens
The honble. Thomas Jefferson
Extract from the minutes.   CHAS THOMSON secy.

RC (MHi); endorsed by TJ: "Huntington Saml. Presidt. of Congress. Philadelphia. June 15. 1781. appmt. Plenipoty. to Peace with Adams Franklin Jay Lawrens." FC (DLC: PCC, No. 16). Enclosures (MHi): (1) Resolution of Congress appointing TJ and others to serve as peace commissioners, printed herewith, and (2) extract of the minutes of Congress recording the election. Both MSS are in the hand of Charles Thomson.

Huntington's letter was transmitted to TJ through Lafayette, by whom TJ returned his reply (Lafayette to TJ, 26 June; TJ to Lafayette, 4 Aug.; TJ to Thomas McKean, 4 Aug. 1781).

From James Monroe

DEAR SIR   Fredricksbg. June. 18. 1781.

I sometime since address'd a letter to you from a small estate of mine in King George whither I had retir'd to avoid the enemy from the one I lately dispos'd of on the Potowmack river. I had then the pleasure to congratulate you on your safe retreat from Richmd. to Charlotsville and anticipated the joy yourself and family must have felt on your arrival at Montichello from which the misfortune of the times has long seperated you. I lament your felicity on that head was of but short duration. I hope how'eer that neither yourself nor Mrs. Jefferson have sustaind injury from these obtrusions of the enemy. In former I advis'd you I would not stay at home in the present state of the country and should be happy to bear some post in her defence. For that purpose I sate out to join the Marquis's army to act in any line either himself or Council would em-

ploy me in. Being confin'd here some few days with small indisposition Genl. Weedon has requested of me to sit out this Evening
to manage the Brittish flag on its way to Alexandria. So soon as I
disingage myself from this affair I shall join the army and serve
till the enemy leave this State. I earnestly wish to leave the Continent and shall not alter my plan unless our publick affairs change
materially. Whither you continue in or retire from office I hope
[to see] both yourself and family in the [course] of the year. [If
we . . . and in the former instance I should find you at Stanton on
my] way to the Springs. Otherwise God knows where we shall be.
Be so kind as make my best respects to Mrs. Jefferson & believe
me with the greatest esteem & regard yr. friend & servant,

JAS. MONROE

RC (DLC); MS mutilated, the text in
brackets being supplied from Monroe,
Writings, I, 11-12.

Monroe's LETTER from King George
co., which must have been written some
time late in May—certainly not earlier
than 15 May and not later than 4 June
—has not been found. THE BRITTISH
FLAG: That is, the *Riedesel*; see TJ to
Lafayette, 30 May 1781.

From Archibald Cary

DEAR SIR   Staunton 19th June, 1781

Mr. Innes will deliver you this. The News of the Town he will
give you. You must have heard Nelson is your successor. He got
here last Night, left the Marquis nigh Nat Dandridge's, the Enemy
from West Ham as low as Richmond. He can give no Particular
Accounts of the losses individuals have sustain'd, but they must be
very great. We hear yours has been so, but hope not so bad as
reported. We have letters of a late date from Congress, they give
us reason to expect a Peace this Winter. Petersburg and Viena have
offerd their Mediation between the Beligerent Powers. Great Britain has Signified her assent, Spain seems Inclined, France waits
our answer, which I judge will be to agree. The Push made on
this State gives us reason as well as other Matters, that Each Power
are to remain possessed of what they hold at the Close of the War;
this must rouse us and I hope it will. At length the Assembly are
giving Ample Powers to the Executive. The Bill for that purpose
stands for a Committee of the Senate this day and will Pass. It is
what that body have long Wished. A Bill has Passed both Houses
for establishing Martial Law 20 Miles round both Armys. I hope
it will have a good effect. The Militia Law will Come to the Senate
this day. Several other Bills are on the Carpit but Are Short, and

tend to defence. One has passed both Houses, for Stoping Currancy of Continental bills Next Month, New Bills for exchanging them not to Issue but by order of executive, old ones to be received in Taxes. Also a Bill Impowering Congress to Lay a duty of 5 pr. C: on Imports and Prises. So Much for Assembly but I must give you one more peice of News respecting your Self. An Address was ready to be offered the Senate to you. What Can you think Stopt it? George Nicholas made a Motion in the Delegates House for an Inquire into your Conduct, a Catalogue of omissions, and other Misconduct. I have not Seen the Particulars. Your Friends Confident an Inquire would do you Honor Seconed the Motion. I presume you will be Serv'd with the order. As this Step was Taken I persuaided Winston not to make his Motion; I had heard something of this Kind was to be brought on the Carpit, and If I know you, it will Give you no pain.

We hear Moylands Horse will be with the Marquis this Week also that General Washington will March if any more Troops are Sent here. I think we can cope with those now in the Papers[1] and private letters Mention as if New York was to be Evacuated, if so we may Expect their whole Force, nor shall I be disappointed if it happens, as this state and Maryland are worth all the rest to Britaign. We have a report but not to be depended on that 45 Sail of vessels were the begining of last Week in our bay, no credit given to it. Our Army about 6000 strong, Lord Cornwallis under 5000. Lessley has Moved from Portsmouth, has been above Suffolk, we Know not what Force. Some Say the Enemy have been at Edenton. The French Fleet of 24 line of battle with 153 Transports Arrived in 37 days all Safe in their Islands. They met with Hood Gaurding St: Lucia, beat him and have drove the british Fleet to the North. St. Lucia was attack'd and offerd to Surrender but the French General refused the Terms, and Insisted on a Surrender at discretion. This must be Comply'd with, and indeed as the French fleet now Amounts to 30 Sail of the Line and before this are joind by 17 or 18 Spanish the whole British Islands will be at their Mercy. It is Said 7 Sail of the Line and a body of Land Troops bound to America Parted from their Grand Fleet off the Western Islands. I wish it may be so. Jn. Walker, Hardy and Mr. Web of our Council observe that Baron Stuben deserves to be hanged for his Conduct. He has Positive orde[rs] which it is Say'd At length he obays to join the Marquis, this with Morgan and Wayn will Increase our Army to about 8 or 9 M: We Know not the Cause of his Lordships Giving up his design on Fredericksburg, unless Wayns Junction was the Cause. Tarelton would have made an attempt here, but for the Motion [of] the Marquis, as that also obliged Cornwallis to move South, as if to Cover Tarlton and Simpco's retreat, but we are at a loss to Account for his moveing down the River, perhaps to Fight with More Advantage to his Cavelry. I have now Given you all the News and shall Conclude with Complments to Yr. Lady and an assurance that I am with Great regard Your Affte Friend and Hble Servt.,

ARCHD. CARY

RC (DLC); addressed: "To Thos. Jefferson Esqr Bedford Pr Favr Mr Inness." MS faded and in places almost illegible.

On TJ's LOSSES to British troops at his Elkhill plantation on the James, see his statement printed under date of 27 Jan. 1783. The bill for GIVING AMPLE POWERS TO THE EXECUTIVE was passed by the House on the 18th and agreed to by the Senate on the present date as Cary predicted (JHD, May 1781, 1828 edn., p. 21, 23; Hening, x, 413-16). Cary's NEWS RESPECTING YOUR SELF was with little doubt the first information that TJ had concerning the proceedings in the Assembly calling for an investigation of the Executive; see John Beckley to TJ, 12 June 1781. The ADDRESS of thanks to TJ was to have been presented by Edmund WINSTON, who represented the Bedford-Henry-Pittsylvania district in the Senate; it is worth noting that TJ stopped at Winston's home late in July while on his way back from Poplar Forest to Monticello (Account Book under date of 25 July 1781). George WEB (Webb) had been a member and regular attendant at Council meetings during TJ's administration; Samuel HARDY was elected a member 12 June 1781; and John WALKER was elected on 19 June to take the place

of William Cabell, who had been elected on 12 June but declined to serve (JHD, May 1781, 1828 edn., p. 15, 21, 23). Hardy qualified as a member of the Council on the present date but Walker declined to serve (Va. Council Jour., II, 348; Official Letters, III, 100). The opinion of these three that BARON STUBEN DESERVES TO BE HANGED FOR HIS CONDUCT reflected a fairly widespread opinion and was supported officially three days later by the resolution of the House calling for an investigation concerning the loss of stores at Point of Fork. HE HAS POSITIVE ORDERS WHICH . . . AT LENGTH HE OBAYS: Lafayette had forwarded these orders to TJ in his letter of 31 May 1781, q.v. It is to be noted that Cary says nothing about Steuben's letter to him as Speaker of the Senate of 3 June 1781, in which the Baron made an effort to exculpate himself and to place some of the blame for the condition of affairs on the Executive.

1 Thus in MS. Cary not only omitted essential punctuation, but probably a word as well. What he intended, perhaps, was the following: "I think we can cope with those now in the State. The Papers and private letters Mention as if New York was to be Evacuated."

From Arthur Campbell

SIR   Washington June 20th. 1781

I send by this conveyance part of the Papers you desired in your Letter of the 23d. of May last. I have not yet received those that are in the hands of the Carolinia Officers, but this being so good an oppertunity I am desirous of forwarding what I have, at the same time you will please to consider them as sent to you as a private Gentleman or a member of the Philosophical Society, and not as a public Officer in Virginia. The treatment I met with at the March Session is such, that I don't mean to produce farther proofs for vindicating my conduct in attacking the Cherokees. To good men and to posterity I wish to be free from blame in all my public transactions. When I took the field and undertook to lead a Body of men into the Wilderness to oppose the enemy, I neither had honorary or pecuniary emoluments in view. The recent inhuman butcheries in Georgia roused our indignation, and to give safety to my own Neighbourhood, and confer a blessing on posterity were my main motives, and encouraged me to attempt what numerous and well appointed armies had hitherto failed to effect. The event much exceeded most peoples expectations, and those immediately in danger will long remember the effort with gratitude, and it will no doubt answer beneficial purposes to all if properly improved by Government.

I intend with the next collection to send you a copy of my order book, and some remarks on the proper extent of the Cherokee Country their origins, manners and government, with a scheme to abolish their present form, and to introduce agriculture and civilization.

I am Sir very Respectfully Your most Obedient Servant,

ARTHUR CAMPBELL

RC (DLC: PCC, No. 71, II); addressed: "For Thomas Jefferson Esquire Fvd by [. . .] Eppes"; endorsed.

TJ enclosed this letter in his to Thomas McKean, 20 Dec. 1781. See

Arthur Campbell to TJ, 4 June 1781 (first letter) and references there. TJ's letter of 23D OF MAY LAST to Campbell has not been found.

From Meriwether Smith

DEAR SIR   Philadelphia, June 21st. 1781.

Congress having received some important Communications from the Minister plenipotentiary of France respecting the Intentions of the Courts of Petersburgh and Vienna, have come to some Determinations thereupon which are not only interesting to the united States in general, but to the State of Virginia in particular; I took the Liberty therefore to insist that you should be added to the Ministers of these States already in Europe, that the State of Virginia particularly and the united States in general might have the Benefit of your abilities in a Negociation that may probably take place. I am not at Liberty to communicate to you explicitly by *a Letter* their *Objects* that will require your attention, or the *Nature* of the

Restrictions by which you will be bound: You will therefore not be able to determine whether the Embassy will be *agreeable* and *honourable*; but, I am confident that you cannot fail of rendering very essential Services to the State by your intimate Knowledge of its Interests; and I am persuaded that it can only be requisite to suggest to you that the Business will be very important and your Usefulness in negociating it very great, to induce you to accept the Appointment.

Exertion and Unanimity are now more than ever requisite in the State of Virginia. Assistance will come but slowly; but I beseech you to avoid Despair. It can only produce Divisions which will encrease your Distresses without procuring for you one valuable End. This State and some others in the union enjoy most of the Blessings of Peace; and, attentive to other objects more pleasing, they are not willing to behold the Distresses of Virginia. Congress is so destitute of Money and consequently of Power, that if there was the most cordial Disposition to give immediate and effectual assistance to the State, it is not practicable. I have no Doubts however, but that the Campaign will end favourably for us, and it is not improbable that it may be the last. This latter Circumstance will depend greatly upon the firmness and Exertions of Virginia; as the Influence of the mediating Powers in Europe will probably be exerted in our favour [in pr]oportion to our Success. At all Events, it [will be] very important for us to deprive Britain of an Alliance which her Successes in America may encourage.

My Situation here is really distressful. I have not had any authentic Intelligence concerning my family and Estate since the month of April, having designed to leave this City on the first of May, which prevented any Letters from being written to me, if the Communication had not otherwise been cut off. I am the more distressed because my funds will not enable me either to stay or to go from hence. However the Virginia Delegates are not the only suffering Delegates here, and they must submit to the Hardship of the Times. I hope it will not be of long continuance; and [be] assured that while I do remain here, I shall not neglect to try every Expedient which may promise any Relief to the State.

I am Dr. Sir, yr. most obedt. & hble Servt.,   M. Smith

RC (DLC); at foot of text: "His Excelly. Thos. Jefferson Esq Govr. of Virga."; addressed, in another hand: "Thomas Jefferson Esquire Albemarle"; endorsed by TJ: "Smith Meriwether."

I took the liberty to insist that you should be added: John Witherspoon strongly objected to sending several ministers and gave it as his opinion that "it would be much better to assign to one the commission already given [to Franklin]" (Burnett, *Letters of Members*, VI, No. 154).

From Lafayette

Dr. Sir   Rawsons ordinary 26 June 1781.

I have the honor to forward a dispatch recommended by the president of Congress, to be sent to you by a particular conveyance. Lieut. Stokely is charged with it, and directed to deliver it into your own hands.

Lord Cornwallis was at Birds yesterday, from which place he retired with his main body, into Williamsburg. We have been pressing his rear, with our light parties, supported by the army, but his Lordship has proceeded so cautiously, and so covered his marches with his cavalry, that it has been, under our circumstances, next to impossible to do him any injury.

From present appearances, it would seem, that the antient capital is to be a garrisoned place, and, perhaps, a small post will be established at york.

With the greatest regard, I have the honor to be Dr Sir, your most obt. Sv.,   LAFAYETTE

RC (DLC); in a clerk's hand, signed by Lafayette. Enclosure (MHi): Samuel Huntington to TJ, 15 June 1781.

From Nathanael Greene

                 Camp near the Cross Roads between
Sir   Broad river and the Catawba June 27. 1781.

The tardiness, and finally the countermanding the Militia ordered to join this army has been attended with the most mortifying and disagreeable consequences. Had they taken the field in time and in force we should have compleated the reduction of all the enemy's out posts in this Country; and for want of which we have been obliged to raise the seige of 96 after having closely beseiged it for upwards of twenty days and when four days would have compleated it's reduction. For want of the Militia the approaches went on slow and the seige was rendered bloody and tedious. My force has been unequal to the operations we had before us, but necessity obliged me to persevere, tho' under every disadvantage; and we should have been finally successfull had not the enemy recieved a large reinforcement at Charlestown generally agreed to amount to 2000 Men, which enabled them to march out and raise the seige. The place might have been taken ten days sooner if our force had been equal to the labor necessary to facilitate it's reduction. Every post the enemy held either in S. Carolina or Georgia have been taken or evacuated except Charlestown, Savannah, and Ninety six, and our success would have been compleat had our force been equal to the plan. However I hope the operations this way will be accompanied with many advantages. Certain it is, the enemy were about to detach from this quarter to Lord Cornwallis a greater force than we have had operating here. The reduction of their posts, destruction of the stores, their loss in killed, wounded and prisoners together with the increase of our friends and the decline of theirs are matters highly injurious to the enemy's interest and favourable for ours. And the operations would have been rendered still more so had the militia come forward agreeable to my application and your first order.

The high respect which I ever wish to pay to the prerogatives of every State induces me to question with all due deference the propriety of your Excellency's order for countermanding the militia which were directed to join this Army. No general plan can ever be undertaken with safety where partial orders may interrupt it's progress; nor is it consistant with the common interest that local motives should influence measures for the benefit of a part to the prejudice of the whole. I conceive it to be the prerogative of a Governor to order the force belonging to a State as he may think necessary for the protection of it's inhabitants. But those that are ordered out upon the Continental establishment are only subject to the orders of their Officers. Without this just and necessary distinction there would be endless confusion and ruinous disappointments. I only mention these things to avoid a misunderstanding in future. I have no wish for command further than the interest and happiness of the people are concerned, and I hope every body is convinced of this from my zeal to promote the common safety of the good people of these Southern States. I feel for the circumstances of Virginia, and if I had been supported here in time, I should have been there before this with a great part of our Cavalry. But though I have not had it in my power to join the army, I hope your Legislature are convinced that I have left nothing unattempted to afford you all possible protection. You may remember in some of my former letters that I had solicited the Commander in Chief for the return of the Marquis with his detachment to the Southward from a persuasion you would be oppressed, and I have great reason to believe it had the desired effect. The moment I got intelligence that Lord Cornwallis was moving Northwardly I gave orders for the Marquis to halt and take the Command in Virginia and to detain the Pensylvania Line and all the Virginia drafts. With this force aided by the militia I was in hopes the Marquis would have been able to have kept the enemy from over running the State.

The importance of Cavalry and the consequences that might follow the want of it, your Excellency will do me the justice to say, I early and earnestly endeavoured to impress upon your Legislature, and they must blame themselves if they experience any extraordinary calamities for the want of it. You would have been in a tolerable situation had your Cavalry been sufficiently augmented, and the last reinforcement from N. York had not arrived. This gave the enemy such a decided superiority that there appears nothing left but to avoid a misfortune untill reinforcements can be got from the Northward. I have the highest opinion of the abilities of the Marquis and his zeal, and flatter myself that nothing will be left unattempted to give all the protection to the States that his force will admit. Your militia are numerous and formidable and I hope if Genl. Morgan is out with them, they will be usefull. Tho' Virginia is oppressed she is not a frontier State to the Southward, which would have been the case had I not moved this way, and all the force in North and South Carolina and Georgia would have been lost. Besides the disagreeable impression it would have made upon the northern States to see those to the Southward over run. To divide the enemy's force as much as possible I have ever considered as favourable to our purposes, as it enables us to employ a greater body of Militia and to more advantage.

My heart is with you, and I only lament that the cross-incidents in this quarter have prevented hitherto my pursuing my inclinations that way.

I have the honor to be with great respect Your Excellency's Most Obedient Humble Servant,   NATH GREENE

RC (Vi); at foot of text: "His Excellency Governor Jefferson"; endorsed.

From Nathanael Greene

SIR
Camp near the cross roads between broad River and the Catabaw June 27th [29?] 1781

The importance of partizan Corps as well as the necessity for augmenting our Cavalry is more and more felt every day. Capt. Rudolph belonging to Lt. Col. Lee Legion comes to Virginia with a view of augmenting that useful and necessary Corps. Whether the circumstances of other Corps of Cavalry and the peculiar situation of Virginia will admit of enlarging this Corps your Excellency will judge and direct accordingly. I have only to observe that what ever aid is given to this business will essentially promote the service, and the force so formed shall be employed in Virginia while the State continues to be oppressed.

I have the honor to be with great respect Your Excellencys Most Obedt hum Sv, N GREENE

Dft (MiU-C); dated 27 June, but endorsed: "Govr. Jefferson June 29h. 1781. Exd. Rudolph sent to get Reinforcements for Lees Corps." Tr (CSmH) is also dated 29 June.

From Lafayette

[SIR] [Tyree's P]lantation[1] July the 1st 1781

I Have Been Honoured with your favor of the 14th and while I am to thank you for the pains You took of Acquainting me with particulars Relative to Col. Ross, I feel a sincere pleasure in this opportunity to Continue our Correspondance. The Honor of Hearing from you Shall Ever Be wellcome, and I Beg leave from time to time to present You with the Camp Gazette, and with the assurance of My affectionate Regard.

I Had Some days ago the Honor of transmitting a letter which the president of Congress Called a very important one. Should my Suspicions prove true I Congratulate the Cause in General upon this Choice, and Beg leave to Assure you that on Every [. . .][2] Be Happy to Make Any Commun [. . .][2] to Your present purposes.

With the Highest Regard and a Sincere Attachem[ent] I Have the Honor to Be Dear Sir Your Most obedient Humble Servant,

LAFAYETTE

Since My last His Lordship Has Remained into Williamsburg.

RC (DLC); MS mutilated. TJ's FAVOR OF THE 14TH has not been found.

1 Place supplied from Gottschalk, *Lafayette and the Close of the Amer. Rev.*, p. 261. 2 Three or four words missing.

To George Nicholas

SIR Monticello July 28, 1781.

I am informed that a resolution on your motion passed the House of Delegates requiring me to render account of some part of my administration without specifying the act to be accounted for. As I suppose that this was done under the impression of some particular instance or instances of ill conduct, and that it could not be intended just to stab a reputation by a general suggestion under a bare expectation that facts might be afterwards hunted up to boulster it, I hope you will not think me improper in asking the favor of you to specify to me the unfortunate passages in my conduct which you mean to adduce against me, that I may be enabled to prepare to yield obedience to the house while facts are fresh in my memory and witnesses and documents are in existence. I am Sir Your most obedt. Servt.

Dft (DLC); at foot of text: "Colo. George Nicholas."

I AM INFORMED: TJ had not yet received the official notification of the proposed inquiry sent him by John Beckley on 12 June, but he had heard about it from Cary (see Cary to TJ, 19 June), probably from Archibald Stuart (see note on Henry Young to William Davies, 9 June), and probably also from Edmund Winston, a member of the Senate, at whose house TJ had stopped three days before he wrote the present letter (TJ's Account Book under 25 July 1781).

From George Nicholas

SIR   July 31st. 1781.

By the resolution of the House of Delegates an enquiry is to be made into the conduct of the executive for the last twelve months. No particular instance of misconduct was specified. They seemed to think and I am still of opinion that the persons entrusted with the administration ought to be ready to give an account of the whole and of every part of it.

You consider me in a wrong point of view when you speak of me as an accuser. As a freeman and the representative of free Men I considered it as both my right and duty to call upon the executive to account for our numberless miscarriages and losses so far as they were concerned in or might have prevented them. In doing this I had no private pique to gratify, and if (as I hope it may) it shall appear that they have done everything in their power to prevent our misfortunes I will most readily retract any opinion that I may have formed to their prejudice.

I shall exhibit no charges but only join in an enquiry.

At your request I will mention such things as strike me at present as want[ing] explanation and if any thing shall hereafter occur I will inform you by letter.

The total want of opposition to Arnold on his first expedition to Richmond.

The dissolution of a considerable body of militia on our Southern frontier at the time of Green's retreat for want of orders from the executive.

The want of timely orders to the counties of Amherst Augusta &c. after the adjournment of the Assembly from Richmond.

The great loss that the country has sustained in arms &c. exclusive of those destroyed by the enemy.

The rejection of an offer made by Cols. Campbell Christian and McDowell to raise regiments for the Southern Service.

I am Sir Yr. most obdt. Servt,   G NICHOLAS

RC (DLC); addressed: "Thomas Jefferson Esqr. Monticello."
I SHALL EXHIBIT NO CHARGES: This is a puzzling statement, since Nicholas immediately proceeded to mention several charges informally and later furnished a formal list of allegations that were more extensive and largely different from those mentioned in this letter (see the following document). Though the present list is manifestly a personal selection by Nicholas, there is every reason to believe that TJ's critics in the Assembly had discussed or were later to discuss in some detail the errors of the late Executive; thus Archibald Cary (letter to TJ, 19 June 1781) mentions "a Catalogue of omissions, and other Misconduct," implying that, though he had "not Seen the Particulars," some had been drawn up.

Charges Advanced by George Nicholas, with Jefferson's Answers

[After 31 July 1781]

OBJ. That Genl. Washington's information was that an embarkation was taking place destined for *this state*.

ANS. His information was, that it was destined for the Southward as was *given out* in N. York. Had similar informations from Genl. Washington and Congress been considered as sufficient ground at all times for calling the militia into the feild there would have been a standing army of militia kept up; because there has never been a time since the invasion expected in Dec. 1779, but what we have had those intimations hanging over our heads. The truth is that Genl. Washington always considered it as his duty to convey every rumor of an embarkation: but we (for some time past at least) never thought any thing but actual invasion should induce us to the expence[1] of calling the militia into the feild; except in the case of Dec. 1779 when it was thought proper to do this in order to convince the French of our disposition to protect their ships. Inattention to this necessary œconomy in the beginning went far towards that ruin of our finances which followed.

Where were the post riders established last summer?

ANS. They were established at Continental expence to convey speedy information to Congress of the arrival of the French fleet then expected here. When that arrived at Rhode island these expresses were discontinued. They were again established on the invasion of October, and discontinued when that ceased, and again on the first intimation of the invasion of Dec. But it will be asked, why were they not established on Genl. Washington's letters? Because those letters were no more than we had received upon many former occasions, and would have led to a perpetual establishment of post riders.

OBJ. If a proper number of men had been put into motion on Monday for the relief of the lower country and ordered to march to Wmsburg. that they would at least have been in the neighborhood of Richmond on Thursday.

ANS. The order could not be till Tuesday because we then received our first certain inform[ation].[2] Half the militia of the counties round about Richmond were then ordered out, and the whole of them on the 4th,[3] and ordered not to wait to come in a body but in detachments as they could assemble. Yet were there not on Friday[4] more than 200 collected, and they were principally of the town of Richmond.

OBJ. That we had not signals.

ANS. This tho' a favorite plan of some gentlemen and perhaps a practicable one, has hitherto been thought too difficult.

OBJ. That we had not look-outs.

ANS. There had been no cause to order lookouts more than has been ever existing. This is only in fact asking why we do not always keep lookouts.

OBJ. That we had not heavy artillery on travelling carriages.

ANS. The gentlemen who acted as members of the B. of W. [Board of War] a twelvemonth can answer this question by giving the character of the artificers whom during that time they could never get to mount the heavy artillery. The same reason prevented their being mounted from May 1780 to December. We have even been unable to get those heavy cannon moved from Cumberland by the whole energy of government. A like difficulty which occurred in the removal of those at S. Quay in their day, will convince them of the possibility of this.

OBJ. That there was not a body of militia thrown into Portsmouth, the Great bridge, Suffolk.

ANS. In the Summer of 1780, we asked the favor of Genl. Nelson to call together the County Lieutenants of the lower counties and concert the general measures which should be taken for instant opposition on any invasion until aid could be ordered by the Executive, and these county Lieutenants were ordered to obey his call. He did so. The first moment to wit on Sat. Dec. 31. 8. o'clock A.M.[5] of our receiving information of the appearance of a fleet in the bay, we asked the favor of Genl. Nelson to go down, which he did, with full powers to call together the militia of any counties he thought proper, to call on the keepers of any public arms or stores, and to adopt for the instant such measures as exigencies required till we could be better informed.

Qu. Why were not Genl. Nelson and the brave officers with him particularly mentioned?

Ans. What should have been said of them? The enemy did not land nor give them an opportunity of doing what nobody doubts they would have done, that is, somewhat worthy of being minutely recited.

Qu. Why publish Arnold's letter without Genl. Nelson's answer?

Ans. Ask the printer. He got neither from the Executive.

'As to the calling out a few militia and that not till late.'

Ans. It is denied that they were few or late. 4700 men (the number required by Baron Steuben) were called out the moment an invasion was known to have taken place; that is on Tuesday[6] Jan. 2.

Obj. The abandonment of York and Portsmouth[7] fortifications.

Ans. How can they be kept without regulars on the large scale on which they were formed? Would it be approved of to harrass the militia with garrisoning them?

MS (DLC: TJ Papers, 6: 1014-15); without caption. From the handwriting and the presence of some interlined corrections it seems probable that this is the original statement drawn up by TJ in the summer or fall of 1781. Filed with it (DLC: TJ Papers, 6: 1011 and 1016) are two fair copies of the same paper in TJ's hand, one of which is a polygraph copy of the other; these are identical in phrasing with the MS described above, but they differ from it in some spellings and are more carefully punctuated. Both fair copies originally had the same caption, but the caption of that at 6: 1016 contains a later insertion by TJ, enclosed in square brackets in the following transcription: "Heads of charges proposed by Mr. George Nicholas to be urged against Mr. Jefferson before the

H. of Representatives of Virginia [obtained from Mr. Nicholas in writing (by a friend) and communicated by a friend] with the heads of answers proposed to be given by Mr. Jefferson." The date when the fair copies were made has not been ascertained; it could not have been before June 1804, when TJ began regular use of the polygraph, and a plausible conjectural date would be 1805, when TJ prepared a statement on his conduct in 1781 (see notes and documents relating to the British invasions in 1781, Document I, printed above under date of 31 Dec. 1780). Still another text of the charges and answers is embedded in the enclosure in TJ's letter to Joseph Delaplaine, 26 July 1816; this text is identical in substance with the others except for a single inserted phrase which is noted below.

TJ himself provided the best introductory comments on this paper, and they may be read in the several versions of his vindicatory statement printed above among the notes and documents relating to the British invasions in 1781, 31 Dec. 1780; see Vol. 4: 261-2, 264, 268, notes 15-16. But these by no means answer all the questions posed by this paper. The principal unanswered question is of course: What relation does the present paper have to the informal series of charges set forth in George Nicholas' letter of 31 July, preceding? Nicholas there offered five matters for investigation, only the first and third of which relate to Arnold's invasion in January; but the formal series of charges is eleven in number, and all bear directly on the January invasion. TJ himself says that the formal charges were "obtained from Mr. Nicholas in writing and communicated by a friend," but no such paper by Nicholas has been found, the "friend" who communicated it has not been identified, and the time and circumstances of its being communicated are unknown. It is possible that the formal list of charges here given is the "Catalogue of omissions, and other Misconduct" mentioned by Cary (letter of 19 June, above); more probably this list was drawn up by the anti-Jeffersonian group after 1 Oct. when the Assembly met again, since the legislature had already adjourned when Nicholas received TJ's letter of 28 July. It is unlikely that these charges were prepared by the committee of investigation appointed on 26 Nov. (see John Harvie to TJ, 27 Nov. 1781 and enclosure), since TJ obtained his list *privately* and since that committee had been instructed to convey "in writing, to the members which composed the Executive" any accusations brought before them. Besides, that committee never brought any charges on the floor of the House. (TJ himself voluntarily read these charges, with his answers, to the House on 12 Dec. 1781.)

Some of the questions asked and answered in this paper are puzzling in themselves. There had evidently been discussion during TJ's term of office about SIGNALS (perhaps the use of flaming tar barrels), but that discussion is not on record. The question WHY WERE NOT GENL. NELSON AND THE BRAVE OFFICERS WITH HIM PARTICULARLY MENTIONED raises the further questions: mentioned when and where? In his "communiqué" on the January invasion published in the *Virginia Gazette* for 13 Jan. (printed above, Vol. 4: 269-70), TJ *does* mention Nelson's action. The question WHY PUBLISH ARNOLD'S LETTER WITHOUT GENL. NELSON'S ANSWER is partly explicable, though the gaps in the file of the *Virginia Gazette* at this period make it impossible to state in what issue of that paper Arnold's letter was published. The letter in question (now in NHi: Steuben Papers) is from Arnold "On Board his Majestys Ship Hope," 2 Jan. 1781, to "The Officer commanding the forces on shore," professing surprise at "the Hostil appearances of the Inhabitants under Arms on shore" and inquiring if they intend "to Offer a vain opposition to [. . .] Troops under my command in their landing." According to a letter to Steuben (same location) from James Fairlie, aide-de-camp, Williamsburg, same date, "Genl. Nelson sent his compliments back to Mr. Arnold, *Viva Voce*, appologising that he had not pen and Ink, that he would oppose him, as long as he has a Man to fight."

See resolution of thanks to Jefferson by the Virginia General Assembly, 12-19 Dec. 1781.

1 In the 1816 version of the charges and answers sent to Delaplaine, the phrase "and harrassment" was added here.

2 This sentence is interlined in MS for the following, deleted: "The fact however was otherwise."

3 This passage is much corrected in MS, which reads, with interlineations and deletions, as follows: "Half the militia of the counties round about Richmond were then [*preceding word interlined*] ordered out ⟨on⟩ ⟨Monday⟩ ⟨Tuesday⟩, and the whole of them on ⟨Tuesday⟩ ⟨the next day⟩ ⟨Wednesday⟩ the 4th." This series of alterations shows that TJ's memory of these events tended to be over-favorable to himself but that he corrected it by reference to records. See the Council's proceedings for 1-4 Jan. 1781 (*Va. Council Jour.*, II, 268-72) and TJ's letters to various county lieutenants, 2 and 4 Jan. 1781.

4 Interlined in MS for "Thursday," deleted.

5 From the words "to wit" this passage is interlined in MS. The 31st was, however, a Sunday, not a Saturday.

6 Interlined in MS for "Monday," deleted.

7 Interlined in MS for "Hampton," deleted.

From Horatio Gates

Dear Sir   Berkely 2d: August 1781.

Your Favour of the 17th: Febry: and the many Marks of Respect and Attention with which you at Times have Honoured me, claim my most Thankfull Acknowledgements. I went to Philadelphia in April. Inclosed are Copies of what passed, in respect to my particular Affair between Congress, General Washington, and Myself. I earnestly Hoped, that (without being covered with Disgrace) I could have been indulged to have served this Campaign. A Motion for rescinding the Resolve of the 5th: of October has been several Times made in Congress, but once to my Astonishment was prevented being Carried by a Mr: Maddison of This State, a Gentleman I do not know, and who I am satisfied does not know me. But the Spirit of party, and Cabal, will constantly infest all popular Government. Without their balefull influence, The World had long ago been all Republican; Heaven Grant They may not in the End Poison all we have been doing and at length leave us a prey to Avarice, Ambition and Tyranny.

I am exceedingly Anxious to know how things are circumstanced from James River to Charles Town. Cornwallis has Spun his Thread too Fine. I think it must break somewhere, but His Escapes renders him confident.

Report says the French Fleet are Triumphant in the West Indies; Tobago and Barbadoes taken by the Marquis de Bouille. Our Main Army, Join'd by the French Troops from R: Island, are at Kingsbridge; Reinforced by Mr: La Touche Treville. With a Fleet Superior to the British, and 10,000 more French Troops, New York and Long Island must Fall; but are these two last mention'd Succours to be depended upon. In the mean Time, the Year Wears. By the last Account all things looked well in Europe. England notwithstanding every Ministerial Boast, without an Ally upon that Continent.

You will Oblige me by shewing the inclosed papers to The Governour, Mr. Henry, Rich. H. Lee, and General Lewis; and any unprejudiced Gentleman of your acquaintance.[1] The Bearer has something to say in regard to his late Office, but as I am resolved for the Future to be carefull not to be thought Officious, I shall leave him to tell his own Tale.

Should the Warm Springs, or any other inducement, bring you and Mrs. Jefferson into Berkeley, I beg you to take up your Quarters at my House, in this, as well as in most respectfull Compliments to Your Lady, I am joined by Mrs. Gates.

With Great regard I am Dear Sir, Your Obliged Humble Servant,   HORATIO GATES

RC (DLC); at foot of text: "Honourable Thomas Jefferson Esq." Dft (NHi); with numerous deletions and corrections, only one of which has been noted here (note 1). Enclosures (DLC): Copies of (1) Gates to Samuel Huntington, 24 Apr. 1781, requesting that immediate consideration be given his case. (2) Gates to Washington, 29 Apr. 1781, stating that Gates can testify concerning his conduct to the satisfaction of his superiors, but that he hopes it will not be his lot to continue in stagnation until he has proved himself. (3) Washington to Gates, 12 May 1781, replying that he was in no way responsible for the delay in the investigation and adding, "No particular Charges having been Lodged with me, I neither had nor have I any to make" (printed in *Writings*, ed. Fitzpatrick, XXII, 76-8). (4) resolution of Congress of 21 May, "That the Resolutions of the 5th: of October last, directing a Court of Inquiry to be Held on the Conduct of Majr: Gen: Gates, as Commander in Cheif of the Southern Army; and Directing The Commander in Chief to appoint an Officer to Command the Southern Army, in the room of Maj: Gates, until such Inquiry be made, did not operate as a Suspension of General Gates from His Command in the Line of The Army at Large, as a Major General; And as from the Situation of Affairs in Said Department, such Court of Inquiry cannot be Speedily Held, that Major Gen: Gates be inform'd he is at Liberty to repair to Head Quarters, and take such Command, as the Commander in Chief shall direct" (printed in JCC, XX, 521-2). (5) Huntington to Gates, 22 May, transmitting the resolution of Congress of 21 May (printed in Burnett, *Letters of Mem-*

bers, VI, No. 118). (6) Gates to Huntington, 22 May, stating that he regrets the inquiry must be postponed because "the uninformed public still believe that the Resolve which recalled me from the Command of the Southern Army was Grounded upon positive Charges against me" and that he cannot resume his position in the army before he is "Publickly restored to Esteem of the Soldiers." (7) Gates to Washington, 22 May 1781, informing Washington that he can "neither with Advantage to The Public nor Honour" to himself accept under the present circumstances "the proferred indulgence of Congress" (printed in Sparks, *Correspondence of the American Revolution*, III, 319-20).

THE BEARER has not been identified but it is obvious from the remark in Gates' letter to TJ of 15 Nov. 1781 that the present letter, together with its packet of enclosures, was carried to Richmond and back again to Gates. The MOTION FOR RESCINDING the resolution of 5 Oct. 1780 is printed in JCC, XX, 533, note 2, and was introduced by James Mitchell Varnum. This letter, therefore, arrived when TJ was in the midst of his own tribulations at the hand of political opposition; see his reply to Gates, 14 Dec. 1781. GENERAL LEWIS was probably Gen. Andrew Lewis.

[1] At this point the following is deleted in the draft: "Columbus was rewarded with Chains for adding a World to His Masters Dominions. The Great Raleigh was Sacrificed to Gondomar [Spanish minister], and Sydney for His patriotism. You see Congress have Great Examples before their Eyes of the Corruption of all Good Government."

To Lafayette

SIR   Monticello Aug. 4. 1781.

I am much obliged by the trouble you took in forwarding to me the letter of his Excellency the President of Congress. It found me in Bedford 100 miles Southward of this where I was confined till

within these few days by an unfortunate fall from my horse. This
has occasioned the delay of the answer which I now take the liberty
of inclosing to you as the confidential channel of Conveyance
pointed out by the President. I thank you also for your kind sentiments and friendly offers on the occasion, which th[at] I cannot
avail myself of has given me more mortification than al[most] any
occurrence of my life. I lose an opportunity, the only one I ever
had and perhaps ever shall have of combining public service with
private gratification, of seeing count[ries] whose improvements in
science, in arts, and in civilization it has been my fortune to [ad]-
mire at a distance but never to see and at the same time of lending
further aid to a cause which has been handed on from it's first
origination to [its] present stage by every effort of which my poor
faculties were capable. These however have not been such as to
give satisfaction to some of my countrymen and [it] has become
necessary for me to remain in the state till a later period in the
present [year] than is consistent with an acceptance of what has
been offered me. Declining high[er] objects therefore my only one[1]
must be to shew that suggestion and fact are different things and
that public misfortunes may be produced as well by public poverty
a[nd] private disobedience to the laws as by the misconduct of the
public servant[s]. The independance of private life under the protection of republican laws will I hope yeild me that happiness from
whi[ch] no slave is so remote as the minister of a Commonwealth.
From motives of private esteem as well as of public gratitude I
shall pra[y it to] be your lot in every line of life as no one can with
more tru[th] subscribe himself with the highest regard and respect
Sir Your mo. ob. & mo. hble servt.

Dft (DLC); with deletions and corrections which are chiefly changes in
phraseology; MS mutilated; endorsed by
TJ: "Fayette the Marquis." Enclosure:
TJ to Thomas McKean, same date, following.

On 14 Aug. 1781 Lafayette wrote La
Luzerne concerning TJ's refusal of the
appointment as commissioner: "Mr. Jefferson refuse, mais si on lui permet de
passer plus tard je crois qu'il acceptera;
c'est un Homme d'esprit, un habitant du
sud, et un Eminent lawyer, trois quali-
tés qui sont en sa faveur" (*Am. Hist.
Rev.*, xx [1914-1915], 605). TJ was
wrong, of course, in thinking that this
was the only opportunity of the sort he
had ever had; he had been asked in 1776
to go to France as minister (see Vol. 1,
521-2).

[1] TJ first wrote, "sole ambition";
then substituted, "future ambition";
then inserted the present reading.

To Thomas McKean

Sir   Albemarle Aug. 4. 1781.[1]

The letter of June the 15th. with which your Excellency was pleased to honor me came unfortunately when I was absent on a journey to the county of Bedford an hundred miles Southward of this. I there received it on the 9th. of July, and a return to this place was necessary to furnish me certain informations on which depended materially my powers to obey the wishes of Congress. This return was retarded till within these few days by an unlucky fall from a horse which rendered me unable to travel and produced so much of the delay of this answer as has occurred with me.[2]

I fully feel how honourable is the confidence which Congress has been pleased to repose in me by their appointment to the high and arduous duty of assisting in the negotiations for peace, and do sincerely[3] lament the existence of circumstances which take from me the right of accepting so desireable an office. But when I consider the abilities which will be opposed to those who undertake this great work, the knowledge and talents requisite to weigh and discuss the great interests of the contending powers and of all their members, and to investigate and foil the various combinations which artifice and intrigue will form against them, I am conscious of nothing within myself which fits me for such an encounter. To this disqualification which is perpetual in it's nature, is added a temporary and indispensable[4] obligation of being within this state till a later season of the present year than the duties of this appointment would admit. After begging your Excellency therefore to make my most grateful acknowledgements to Congress for the honor they destined me, I must ask their leave to decline the undertaking; in doing which I should not render justice to myself were I not to declare my zealous wishes to serve our common country on the most general principles, and at the same time the particular pleasure with which I should have undertaken this appointment had it depended on circumstances within my power to controul.

I have the honor to be with infinite respect Your Excellency's Most obedient & most humble servt.,   TH: JEFFERSON

RC (DLC: PCC, No. 78, XIII); endorsed in part: "Read 27 to be considered only." Dft (DLC: TJ Papers); at foot of text: "Pr. of Congress." TJ began his draft of this letter the day after he received Huntington's letter of 15 June (see note 1, below). The ink is faded and portions of the text are illegible; the sheet was folded and is worn at the folds, indicating that TJ probably carried it about with him until he revised it. When the letter was revised, presumably on or about 4 Aug., TJ used a different ink, which is unfaded. Thus the later revisions may be clearly distinguished from his first composition.

The LETTER OF JUNE THE 15TH was, of course, Huntington's to TJ; McKean succeeded Huntington as president of Congress on 10 July 1781 (JCC, XX, 733). The present letter was transmitted to Congress through Lafayette (see TJ to Lafayette, this date); it was read in Congress on 27 Aug. and ordered to "be considered on Wednesday next," but nothing further appears in the journals until 8 Oct. 1781 when a motion to assign a date "for electing a minister plenipotentiary to negotiate &c. in the room of Mr. Jefferson, who has declined the appointment" was lost on a roll-call vote (JCC, XXI, 910, 1043; the motion and vote were recorded "only in the More Secret Journal"). When TJ failed to respond promptly to Huntington's letter of 15 June, McKean wrote again 20 Aug., to which TJ replied 7 Sep. 1781. On 23 Nov. 1781 the secretary for foreign affairs laid before Congress heads of a verbal communication from La Luzerne informing him, among other matters, that Vergennes, in a letter of 7 Sep. 1781, had assured La Luzerne that the "King of France had received with great pleasure an account of Mr. Adams, Mr. Franklin, and Mr. Jay's appointment" and also expressed "favourable sentiments of them, and Mr. Jefferson, from his general reputation" (same, XXI, 1138).

[1] The first date line read: "Poplar Forest Bedford July 10. 1781"; in the revision, TJ first wrote, "Monticello," then substituted "Albemarle."

[2] The text to this point is entirely in the ink of the revision; and was substituted for two sentences, only the first of which is legible: "I had yesterday the honor of receiving your Excellency's letter of June 15."

[3] The words "do sincerely" were substituted in the later revision for "thoroughly."

[4] The words "and indispensable" were inserted in the revision.

From Philip Mazzei

SIR   Florence, 8. August 1781.

I have at last been honored with your Excellency's commands. The following papers (the first I have received from Virginia, except a short letter from Mr. Bellini last year) came to my hands yesterday; viz,

Copy of a letter from the Board of Trade, dated Williamsburg Novr. 13. 1779.

Your private letter dated Williamsburg April 4. 1780.

Three official ones, dated Richmond, one May 12; and two May 31st. 1780.

Copy of my Commission dated April 22d. 1779, and certifyed by Your Excellency at Richmond the 16th. of May 1780.

Copy of my Instructions relative to it, dated and certifyed as above.

Copy of my Commission, dated April 24th., certifyed as above.

Copy of my Instructions of the same date, certifyed as above, and deficient of the Invoice therein mentioned.

Two bundles of my private papers, as mentioned in the said private letter.

[114]

I have received no instructions relative to the business intended at first to be transacted by Mr. Smith, although the letter of 12 May says, "It was found most expedient after your departure to relinquish the purpose of sending Mr. Smith to Europe, and to put on you the execution of his duties, as you will perceive by the Instructions."

The above papers arrived in France in July last year. Such a delay is really scandalous, but it don't surprise me. In letter 8, dated Paris March 4th, 1780, I mentioned my apprehensions on the subject very plainly; I extended my diffidence in several of my following; and in letter 24, after having desired that my letters might be inclosed always to Mr. Lynch, I concluded "I have reasons to apprehend, that they may be mislead [mislaid], or at least retarded, if they are not inclosed to him." I shal take proper steps to find out where the fault lyes, and will give your Excellency a full information of it.

I don't expect that Messrs: Penet & Co: will pay the money you order me to draw on them in one of the above mentioned letters. The sum cannot certainly be adequate to my wants, especially as it is now better than a year since I ought to have received it, but it would be infinitely better than nothing.

You will be sensible, Sir, from the contents of letter 22, that the duplicates of my first Commissions and Instructions must have eased my mind in one respect; but you know likewise from letters 13 and 21, that nothing can be done in regard to the Loan without new powers, which I requested in the first of the two, dated Paris April 21st. 1780, 3 copies of which must have arrived in the Alliance, the Dove, and the Luzerne, only one of the 4 having been lost in the Committé.

I have already mentioned that I have received no Instructions relative to the business intended at first to be transacted by Mr. Smith; and the letter from the Board of Trade forbids me to contract for goods on the terms prescribed in my first Instructions. Such as I had been ordered to contract for, I could have sent you, as you will have observed in said letter 22, dated Florence October 20th, 1780; but now I must remain quite inactive for want of new orders on every point. Till then I shall continue to go on endeavouring to be of some use to our Cause, through all those means I can think of as far as my poor abilities and influence can assist my zeal. In the mean time I have the honour to be most respectfully, Sir, Your Excellency's most Humble & most Obedient Servant,

PHILIP MAZZEI

RC (CtY); at head of text: "1st. Copy"; endorsed in part, in an unidentified hand: "recd. Febry 21. 1782." The "3d. copy" is in NN and is dated, erroneously, "8. April 1781."

Before this letter was received, Gov. Harrison had written Mazzei, in consequence of a resolution of the Assembly, discharging him from further service (Harrison to Mazzei, 31 Jan. 1782, *Official Letters*, III, 142). So far as known, TJ wrote Mazzei only one letter on 31 May 1780; Mazzei states, in his *Memoirs*, p. 275, that of all of the letters written by TJ to him while Governor, only one had reached him. The copies of Mazzei's commission and instructions as certified by TJ on 16 May 1780 have not been found, though copies of the originals as issued by Gov. Henry in Apr. 1779 are in War Office Letter Book (MiU-C; photostats in TJ Editorial Files).

From Thomas McKean

Sir   Philadelphia August 20th. 1781.

My Predecessor sent you the Copy of a vote of Congress of the 14th. of June last, appointing you a Minister for negociating a peace: As no answer has been yet received, a doubt has taken place, whether the information had reached you, and therefore I now inclose you a Duplicate.

Permit me, Sir, to congratulate you on this evidence of the full confidence and esteem of your Country, and to hope that so very honorable an appointment may meet with your acceptance.

I am, Sir, with the most respectful attachment Your most obedient humble Servant,   Tho M:Kean President

RC (MHi); endorsed by TJ: "McKean Tho. Presid of Congress Phila. Aug. 20. 1781. Duplicate of appmt to negotiate peace." Tr (PHi); endorsed. FC (DLC: PCC, No. 16). Enclosure (missing): Copy of the resolution of Congress of 14 June 1781, printed as enclosure to Huntington to TJ, 15 June 1781.

To Thomas McKean

Sir   Albemarle Sep. 7. 1781.

Your Excellency's favor of the 20'th Ult. inclosing a duplicate of the resolution of Congress which honoured me with an appointment is just come to hand. I received the Original on the 9th. of July, and was prevented answering it till the 4th. of Aug. by accidents which I therein endeavored to explain. This answer I took the liberty of putting under cover to the honble. Majr. Genl. Marquis la Fayette, being the channel thro which the one addressed to me had come. I am in hopes it will have come to your Excellency's hands very soon after the date of the one I have now the honor to receive. Lest however any accident should have intercepted it I now take the liberty of inclosing a duplicate and have the honour to be with the highest respect Your Excellency's most obedient & most humble servt,   TH: JEFFERSON

RC (DLC: PCC, No. 78, XIII); addressed and endorsed in part: "Read 25." Dft (DLC: TJ Papers). Enclosure (missing): Copy of TJ to McKean, 4 Aug. 1781, q.v.

From Edmund Randolph

DEAR SIR   Philadelphia Sepr. 7. 1781.

By the last post I suggested to you that our European affairs would probably bear greater delay than you apprehended. What you call your temporary disability will be removed early enough, to allow you to reach France by January. From Colo. Laurens's account I am induced to believe, that Great Britain will never admit an American plenipotentiary into the congress, before which a general pacification is to be agitated, until some humiliating stroke of war and that until such admission, France will not negotiate on the subject. These considerations fully answer your objection, and give me an opportunity of wishing for authority to say, that you will embark upon the embassy.

I am Dr. Sir yrs. sincerely,   EDMUND RANDOLPH

RC (NNP).   Randolph's letter BY THE LAST POST has not been found, nor was it received by TJ; see letter following.

To Edmund Randolph

DEAR SIR   Monticello Sep. 16. 1781.

I have received your letter of the 7th. inst. That mentioned to have been sent by the preceding post has not come to hand nor two others which Mrs. Randolph informs me you wrote before you left Virginia, nor indeed any other should you have been so kind as to have written any other.

When I received the first letter fr[om the President of C]ongress inclosing their resolution, and mentioning [the necessity of an] expeditious departure, my determination to attend at the [next session of] assembly offered a ready and insuperable obstacle to my acceptance of that appointment and left me under no necessity of deliberating with myself whether that objection being removed, any other considerations might prevent my undertaking it. I find these are many and must therefore decline it altogether. Were it possible for me to determine again to enter into public business there is no appointment whatever which would have been so agreeable to me. But I have taken my final leave of every thing of that nature, have retired to my farm, my family and books from which I think nothing will ever more separate me. A desire to leave public office with a[1] reputation not more blotted than it has deserved will oblige me to emerge at the next session of our assembly and perhaps to accept of a seat in it, but as I go with a single object, I shall withdraw when that shall be accomplished.

I should have thought that N. Carolina rescued from the hands of Britain, Georgia and almost the whole of S. Carolina recovered, would have been sufficiently humiliating to induce them to treat with us. If this will not do, I hope the stroke is now hanging over them which will satisfy them that their views of Southern conquest are likely to be as visionary as those of Northern. I think it impossible Ld. Cornwallis should escape. Mrs. Randolph will be able to give you all the news on this subject as soon as you shall be able to release her from others. I am with much esteem Dr. Sir Your friend & servt.

P.S. Pray let me know whether you will want Collé another year. Mrs. Randolph supposes not, but could not positively determine me.

Dft (DLC); MS stained, some words supplied from Ford, III, 49-50.

[1] TJ first wrote: "A necessary attention to my own."

From Hugh Rose, enclosing Affidavits respecting Jefferson's Orders for Militia

DEAR SIR   Geddes, Septr. 26th. 1781

Herewith you will receive my Affidavit with my Certificate agreeable to your Request in your Favour by Jupiter. If either of them from my Aversion to Prolixity shou'd not contain a due Portion of the Facts which came within my Knowledge, I hope you will not scruple to require my Attendance upon the Assembly, for be assured, that no Person will more readily step forth in Exculpation of injured Virtue, as far as Integrety and Honour will permit, than your affectionate Friend & Servt.,   HUGH ROSE

P.S. Mrs. Rose and the greatest part my Family being upon a Visit at Coll. Jordans I am for the first time in my Life reduced to the disagreeable Necessity of commencing Housekeeper as such present my Compliments to Mrs. Jefferson &c. in Lieu of ———

ENCLOSURES

Amherst, September 25th. 1781

On Tuesday Evening the second of last January (being in Richmond) I received a Letter from the Governor, earnestly requesting me to take Charge of and to convey by some safe Hand the Despatches therein enclosed; they were for the commanding Officers of Albemarle, Amherst, Fluvanna and Goochland, requiring them immediately to send forth certain Proportions of their Militia in order to oppose Arnold, whose Movements indicated an Intention of penetrating into the Country. After having received the said Despatches, and having dismist the Messenger, reflecting upon my Situation (my Horses not having arrived and that Period being uncertain) I was very uneasy, and resolved to deliver them to his Excellency early the next Morning; but fortunately as I conceivd shortly after Day Light on Wenesday Morning, I met with Coll. Nall of Rockingham on his Passage Home, to whom (as his Rout was through the Counties of Goochland and Albemarle) I deliverd the Despatches of those Counties with the Governors pressing Injunctions for the speedy and safe Delivery of them. I waited upon the County Lieutenant of Goochland the next Day with other Despatches, and he inform'd me that he had received those sent by Coll. Nall on the preceeding Evening.

Amherst Sct.   HUGH ROSE
      Sworn to before me
      Gabl. Penn

Amherst, Septr. 25th. 1781

I do hereby certify that on the twenty second of March last, the Executive granted a Suspension from the Draft of the Militia of the said County untill further Orders, which Suspension was taken off by an Order of Council dated April the twelvth which Order I receiv'd about the eighteenth of the same Month and drafted the Militia on the eighteenth Day of May.

HUGH ROSE C.Lt.

RC (DLC); addressed: "Thomas Jefferson Esqre. Monticello." Enclosures are also in DLC and are in Rose's hand, with attestation by Penn on the first of them; they are on separate pages and have a separate cover addressed as above.

This letter and enclosures were prepared and sent in response to a written REQUEST by TJ (missing) for attested information respecting orders given by TJ as governor. The accuracy of Rose's statement concerning orders for militia in January is verified by a letter he wrote to George Muter from Amherst, 8 Jan. 1781 (Vi, partly quoted above in note

to TJ's letter to the county lieutenants of Charlotte, &c., 2 Jan. 1781). The actual LETTER FROM THE GOVERNOR of 2 Jan. 1781 covering the dispatches Rose was to deliver, however, has not been found. TJ wanted the information here furnished for his defense in the forthcoming legislative investigation, and he may well have written to others besides Rose for similar testimony, though no other correspondence on the subject has been found. Rose's first statement seems to be a reply to the third charge in George Nicholas' letter of 31 July 1781, though it may also pertain to the third charge in the formal

paper also printed under that date. *Hist. Reg. of Virginians in the Revolu-*
COLL. NALL was lieutenant-colonel of *tion.*
the Rockingham militia; see Gwathmey,

From George Mason

DEAR SIR   Gunston Hall Septemr. 27th. 1781.

It gives me great pleasure to hear that you have determined
again to accept a Seat in the House of Delegates; where I am sure
Your Assistance, on many Occasions, will be greatly wanted.

You have, no Doubt, been informed of the factious, illegal, and
dangerous Schemes now in Contemplation in Congress for dismembering the Commonwealth of Virginia, and erecting a new State
or States, to the westward of the Alleghany Mountains. This power,
directly contrary to the Articles of Confederation, is assumed upon
the Doctrine now industriously propagated "that the late Revolution has transferred the Sovereignty formerly possessed by Great
Britain to the United States, that is to the American Congress,"
A Doctrine which, if not immediately arrested in it's progress will
be productive of every Evil; and the Revolution instead of securing,
as was intended, our Rights and Libertys, will only change the
name and place of Residence of our Tyrants. This, that Congress
who drew the Articles of Union were sensible of and have provided
against it, by expressly declaring in Article the 2d. that "Each
State retains it's Sovereignty, freedom and Independence, and
every power, Jurisdiction, and right which is not by this Confederation expressly delegated to the United States in Congress assembled." And in Article the 13th. that "the Articles of this Confederation shall be inviolably observed by every State and the union shall
be perpetual; nor shall any alteration at any time hereafter be made
in any of them; unless such alteration be agreed to in a Congress of
the United States, and be afterwards confirmed by the Legislatures
of Every State." In the 9th Article defining the Powers of Congress,
least the power of deciding Disputes concerning Territory between
any of the States shoud be attended with dangerous Consequences,
it is provided "that no State shall be deprived of Territory for the
Benefit of the United States," and the 11th. Article declares that
"Canada, acceding to this Confederation, and joining in the Measures of the United States, shall be admitted into, and entitled to all
the advantages of this Union: but *no other Colony* shall be admitted
into the same, unless such Admission be agreed to by nine States."
This Article holds out an immediate Offer to Canada; and the words

no other Colony plainly relate to the other British Colonys of Nova Scotia, and East and West Floridas, and clearly exclude the Idea of any absolute Power in Congress to erect new States. I had almost forgot to mention the Beginning of the 13th. Article, declaring that "Every State shall abide by the Determinations of the United States in Congress assembled, on all Questions which by this Confederation are submitted to them." From whence arises, by the strongest Implication, a negation and Disclaimer of any other powers, and a Declaration that no State is bound by them if they shou'd at any time be assumed. I shou'd not have troubled You with these Quotations, but that I apprehended in the late Confusions and sudden removals of public, as well as private Papers, the Articles of Confederation may have been sent to some distant place. I think they will prove that Congress are now arrogating to themselves an unwarrantable and dangerous power, which is in it's nature subversive of American Liberty; for if they can stride over the Line of the Confederation, and assume Rights not delegated to them by the Legislatures of the different States, in one Instance, they can in every other that the Lust of Power may suggest. I hope our Assembly will take this Subject up with the Coolness and Attention which it's Importance merits, and with proper Firmness endeavour immediately to put a Stop to such Proceedings, by positive Instructions to the Virginia Delegates in Congress. And as much will depend upon the Disposition of the Inhabitants in the western parts, it will be prudent to secure their Affections by giving them all the advantages of Government; which will require that the executive and judiciary Powers shall be exercised among them; this may be a difficult plan, but it is an absolutely necessary one; permit me Sir to recommend it to your particular attention. I do it, because I really know no Man whom I think so capable of digesting a proper plan, and I know, from some former Conversation, that You have heretofore turn'd your Thoughts to this Subject. I am at this time very unwell, and hardly able to sit up; which I hope will excuse the loose Manner in which I have written.

I beg my Compliments to Your Lady; and am, with the truest Esteem & Respect, dear Sir Your affecte. & obdt. Servt.,

G. MASON

RC (DLC); addressed; endorsed by TJ: "Mason George"; the following note appears on the address leaf: "forwarded by your most obed Svt J. H. Norton The Assembly have adjourned to the 5Th of next month."

TJ had indeed theretofore turned his thoughts to this subject; in 1776 he provided specifically for the establishment of new states in the West in his draft Constitution for Virginia (see Vol. 1: 363). Though agreeing with Mason that the Confederation was a government of limited and expressly delegated powers,

TJ nevertheless did not permit his strict constructionism to interfere with his consistently held view of the western lands as a national rather than a state resource. Mason, of course, was interested in the subject as a personal as well as a public question, since he was involved in land-jobbing schemes (see Vol. 2: 133-8); Abernethy, *Western Lands and the Revolution*, p. 224-9).

Jefferson's Certification of William Short as an Attorney

Sep. 30. 1781.

At the desire of the Executive I have examined Mr. William Short and report it as my opinion that he is duly qualified to practise the law as an Attorney. Given under my hand on the day above-mentioned.

TH: JEFFERSON

MS (Vi); entirely in TJ's hand; endorsed in part: "Feby 18. [1782?]."

Below TJ's statement is the following in the hand of George Wythe: "Nov. 2. 1781. From an intimate acquaintance, of some standing, with Mr. W. Short, and from several exercises I have heard him perform, I am fully persuaded, and accordingly report it as my opinion, that he is duly qualified to practice the law, as an attorney. Given under my hand. G. Wythe." This MS is filed in Vi with Short's undated petition to the Governor and Council, stating that, "having been for a considerable time engaged in the Study of the Law, and being now desirous of entering into the practice thereof, he begs to be referred to some proper Gentlemen to be examined therein, in order . . . to his obtaining a legal Licence." On the verso of this MS is David Jameson's statement referring the petitioner to "Thomas Jefferson, George Wythe, John Blair, Jerman Baker and Henry Tazewell esquires, or any two of them . . . to examine into his abilities to practice . . . and to make report thereof to the Executive" (dated 19 Sep. 1781; the names of Wythe and Blair are interlined in the hand of Tazewell). Short, "having been examined and reported as fit to practice as an attorney in the County and other inferior courts," was granted a license on 18 Feb. 1782 (MS Va. Council Jour., Vi).

To James Madison

DEAR SIR   Monticello Sep. 30. 1781.

I beg leave to introduce to your acquaintance the bearer Mr. Short who comes to Philadelphia in hopes of being able to prosecute in greater quiet there than he can here the studies in which he is engaged: and I chearfully add to what you may already have heard of him my testimony of his genius, learning and merit. I do this the rather as it gives me an opportunity of saving the right of correspondence with you which otherwise might be lost by desuetude, acknoledging not to have written to you these five months before and lamenting that the same space has occurred since I heard from you. Tho ours is at present the busy and interesting scene yet I have nothing to communicate to you of the military kind, as I am so far from the scene of action and so recluse that I am persuaded you know every event before I do and more especially as Mr. Short does not set out immediately. I pray you to consider me as being with very sincere respect & esteem Dr. Sir your friend & servt., TH: JEFFERSON

Intended as RC, but not sent (DLC); written on a sheet which TJ subsequently used for a summary of the case of Blair v. Blair; addressed: "The honourable James Madison Philadelphia. favoured by Mr. Short."

The presence of this letter in TJ's papers would ordinarily indicate that it was a draft. However the care with which this letter and the three following letters to McKean, Morris, and Peters were written—all being signed and addressed—indicates that they were intended as recipients' copies of letters which were never sent. This supposition is strengthened by the fact that TJ used the paper on which all of the letters were written for notes or summaries of legal cases, writing across or over the letters, these summaries probably being written during his retirement in 1781 to 1783 while putting his private papers in order. Since Short did not propose to "set out immediately" and since Cornwallis surrendered a few days after this letter was written, perhaps the young lawyer decided that quiet for study, after all, could be had in Virginia. Short was certainly in Virginia early in 1782 (see Ambler to TJ, 16 Mch. 1782, and Monroe to TJ, 6 May 1782). TJ's admission that he had not written THESE FIVE MONTHS refers, inferentially, to a missing letter that Madison referred to in a letter of 1 May 1781 (Madison, *Writings*, ed. Hunt, I, 132).

To Thomas McKean

SIR   Monticello in Virginia Sep. 30. 1781.

The bearer Mr. William Short purposing to Philadelphia for the prosecution of his studies, I do myself the honor under authority of the acquaintance I had the pleasure of forming with you in Philadelphia, of introducing him to your notice, persuaded that should you give him an opportunity of being known to you, you will think it a circumstance not merely indifferent to add to the number of your well wishers a gentleman of very uncommon genius, erudition and merit.

I have the honour to be with very great respect Your Excellency's most obedt. & most humble servt.,   TH: JEFFERSON

Intended as RC, but not sent (DLC); written on a sheet which TJ subsequently used for a summary of the case of Blair v. Blair; addressed: "His Excellency Thomas McKain President of Congress. favored by Mr. Short."

To Robert Morris

Monticello, 30 Sep. 1781. This letter is identical in substance with TJ's letter to Thomas McKean, this date.

Intended as RC, but not sent (DLC); written on a sheet which TJ subsequently used for a summary of the case of Hunt v. Tucker's executors; addressed: "The honourable Robert Morris Philadelphia favored by Mr Short."

To Richard Peters

Monticello, 30 Sep. 1781. This letter is identical in substance with TJ's letter to Thomas McKean, this date.

Intended as RC, but not sent (DLC); written on a sheet which TJ subsequently used for a summary of the case of King *v.* Dugard; addressed: "The honourable Richard Peters Philadelphia favored by Mr Short."

From James Monroe

DEAR SIR   Caroline Octor. 1. 1781.

I propos'd to myself the pleasure of visiting yourself and family before this at Montichello but the prospects below and the arrival of Genl. Washington in the State induc'd me to postpone the trip of pleasure to the less agreeable one to camp upon the Idea of bearing some small part in bringing about the event we all so anxiously wish for. With this view I waited on Gov. Nelson and solicited some command in the militia but was inform'd the militia in the field was officer'd and of course that I could procure none whatever. This would have mortified me much had I not discover'd during my continuance with the army that Genl. W. had under his command 16000 regular troops, a force certainly very sufficient to reduce the post at York. On the contrary upon being well inform'd of our force and the propriety of the appointments thro' the whole, I was the rather surpris'd the militia were detained at all, more especially when we take into consideration the difficulty of supply, for surely in the present state of things the militia will not render sufficient service to counterbalance the quantity of provisions they consume. I had however the good fortune to effect a point which since interruption of our civil affairs in this State I have been very desirous to accomplish and in the expedience whereof was so happy as to have your concurrence when with you last at Richmd. Colo. Josiah Parker has a ship just ready to sail for France and has been so kind as offer me a passage in her, which I have accepted. I should be happy to wait on you before I sail and shall be sincerely sorry to leave the Continent without wishing yourself and family health and happiness in person, but as we sail the 10th or 12. of next month from some port south of Portsmouth and I have much business to transact in these few days I shall be at home am unfortunately depriv'd of that pleasure. I have to desire of you a letter to each of our Ministers and also your advice upon the plan I had better pursue as also where I had better visit. Since my return from Richmd. I have liv'd a very sedentary life upon a small estate I have in King George in course of which time have read all the books you mention on the subject of law. I have made such a disposition of the property I sold in Westmoreld. as to give me an interest nearly competent to my purpose without injuring the principal. I mean to convey to you that altho' I shall most probably be glad sometime hence to acquire more by the practice of the law (if I have it in my power) I would still wish to prosecute my studies on the most liberal plan to qualify myself for any business I might chance to ingage in. This if not profitable will be agreable, for surely these acquirments qualify a man not only for publick office, but enable him to bear prosperity or adversity in the capricious turns of fortune with greater magnanimity and fortitude by giving him resources within himself, of pleasure and content, which otherwise he would look for in vain from others. I wish you to say whither if I am so fortunate as to sail and arrive safe you would advise me to reside altogether in the South of France or (if possible) spend a year at the Temple in London before my return. I write you on my return home from below from Mr. Taliaferro's and as I have not a moment to lose have only time to add that whatever commands you will favor me with I shall be happy to execute and that I am with my best respects for Mrs. Jefferson, Yr. sincere friend & very humble servant,   JAS. MONROE

RC (DLC).

From Philip Mazzei

[*Florence*, 2 *Oct. 1781*. Mazzei's "Representation" of his conduct as agent for Virginia in Europe states that in a letter of this date, his dispatch "No. 26" to TJ, he wrote: "My Bill drawn by your Excellency's order, on Messr. Penet, D'Acosta, Freres & Co., has been protested. I am at a loss what to do. It was my intention to tell my circumstances to this Sovereign, and was I to do it, I think I might obtain what I want; but am afraid of prejudicing the Affair of the Loan, lest the difficulty I must confess of receiving remittances for my maintenance, should raise doubts on the possibility of paying the Annual Interest in time of war, which I am instructed to engage for" (Marraro, *Mazzei*, p. 96). No copy of this dispatch has been found.]

To Benjamin Franklin, to John Adams,
and to John Jay

DEAR SIR   Virginia Oct. 5. 1781.

The bearer hereof Colo. James Monroe who served some time as an officer in the American army and as such distinguished himself in the affair of Princetown as well as on other occasions, having resumed his studies, comes to Europe to complete them. Being a citizen of this state, of abilities, merit and fortune, and my particular friend, I take the liberty of making him known to you, that should any circumstances render your patronage and protection as necessary as they would be always agreeable to him, you may be assured they are bestowed on one fully worthy of them.

He will be able to give you a particular detail of American affairs and especially of the prospect we have thro' the aid of our father of France, of making captives of Ld. Cornwallis and his army, of the recovery of Georgia and South Carolina, and the possibility that Charlestown itself will be opened to us.

I have the honour to be with the most profound respect & esteem, Your Excellency's Most obedient & most humble servt,

TH: JEFFERSON

RC (DLC: Madison Papers); addressed: "His Excellency Benjamin Franklin American Minister at the Court of Versailles. favored by Colo Monroe." 2d RC (DLC: Madison Papers). 3d RC (Stuart W. Jackson, Gloucester, Va., 1946).

TJ enclosed the three letters in his to Monroe of this date, explaining that the second and third were intended for John Adams and John Jay but that they were not addressed. These copies differ from that addressed to Franklin only in the complimentary close in which "Dr. Sir" is substituted for "Your Excellency." None of the letters was ever presented by Monroe because he was disappointed in obtaining passage for Europe (Monroe to TJ, 6 May 1782).

To James Monroe

DEAR SIR   Monticello Oct. 5. 1781.

I should have been and shall always be happy to see you at Monticello, but could not expect so much of the little time you have to prepare for your journey. I inclose you three letters, the one directed to Dr. Franklin, the other two for Mr. Jay and Mr. Adams but not directed because I really do not know the address of those two gentlemen. This you will be able to learn before you shall have an opportunity of delivering them and you will be so good as to superscribe it. With respect to the part of France or even of Europe in which it will be best for you to reside you will certainly be the best judge yourself, when you get there. Paris itself would no doubt be agreeable, and like all other great cities would admit of so much perfect retirement as you should chuse. But the South of France might be preferable in climate and other circumstances. In fact these and your own good judgment must and ought to govern your determination. The books noted in the paper I once took the liberty of putting into your hands, are amply sufficient in the line of the law. Adding to them any new publications of the same kind in England I should not think further reading necessary. The other branches of science noted in the same paper will afford you agreeable and useful employment, and in some of them you will find better books in Paris than those I named. An entrance in the Temple, or gown from thence, would hardly add to your character here, but could you attend Westminster hall a term or two, no doubt you would catch something in the manner of doing business which, formed as our habits are on that model, might be of advantage to you. An attendance on parliament would be useful in the same way. When I left Richmond in May I put into the hands of Mr. Buchanan for you a small box containing the Parliamentary debates and Historical register, between 30 and 40 vols., and left with Mrs. Sherrar a letter to you, begging your acceptance of them as a small memorial of the esteem I entertain for you. The books are still with Mr. Buchanan. They may be of use when you shall become a parliamentary man, which for my country and not for your sake, I shall wish to see you.

I think with you that the present force of regulars before York might admit a discharge of the militia with safety. Yet, did it depend on me, perhaps I might not discharge them. As an American, as a Virginian, I should covet as large a share of the honor in accomplishing so great an event as a superior proportion of numbers could give.

I shall be very happy to hear from you whenever you can spare time to write, tho' can not promise a full return of American news, secluded as I am and mean to be from the news-talking world. Yet you shall certainly have the best I can give you if you will let me know how and where to address you. The Annual register, Monthly reviews and Parliamentary debates, no doubt, will obtain your perusal wherever you settle. In our present dearth of science nothing would be more acceptable after you are done with them and they should be preserved for you till your return. Mrs. Jefferson joins me in wishes for a safe and pleasant voiage and return, and beleive me to be with great sincerity, Dr Sir Your affectionate friend & servt.,   Th: Jefferson

RC (DLC: Madison Papers); without name of addressee which has been supplied from internal evidence; endorsed by Monroe: "1781. Octr 5." Enclosures: Letters of introduction to Franklin, Adams, and Jay, same date, preceding.

The list of books noted in the paper i once took the liberty of putting into your hands has not been found, but this must have been in 1780 when, on the advice of Monroe's uncle, Joseph Jones, Monroe began studying law under TJ's direction (DAB; see also Monroe to TJ, 9 Sep. 1780). This list of books must have been similar to that drawn up for Robert Skipwith in 1771 and revised at various times (see Vol. 1: 76). I . . . left with mrs. sherrar a letter to you: See TJ to Monroe, 15 May 1781.

From Edmund Randolph

Dear Sir   Philadelphia Octr. 9. 1781.

I was much distressed on the receipt of your late favor by Mrs. Randolph, to find your irrevocable purpose of sequestering yourself from public life. If you can justify this resolution to yourself, I am confident, that you cannot to the world. There remains now no alternative, but either to consign southern interests wholly to the management of our present ministers, or to interdict them from the exercise of all discretionary power.

My distance from Colle prevents me from attending to George Hay so minutely, as my knowledge of his genius and application inclines me to do. I must request you, as a friend to rising abilities, to give him a hint of such books, as my little stock will afford, and are suited to his progress. I am certain that an apology for consigning this trouble to you is unnecessary.

Mr. Adams has been harrassing the pensionary of Holland with overtures of a treaty of commerce. He seems to have committed the dignity of America by his importunities, and being so often repudiated. This he has done against the opinion and advice of Count de Vergennes. Our country does not rest, I hope, upon the prospect of a loan from Holland, or of any new pecuni[ary] aid from France. France has embarrassed herself by her advances for America, and forewarned us to rely on ourselves alone for fresh supplies of Money. I must intreat you to add one other object to your journey to the assembly—enforce the necessity of a state of our accounts against the continent being forwarded to us, and of establishing sufficient funds to enable congress to carry on the war with effect.

Capt. Gillon, who took on board of his ship in France about

10,000 £ Ster: worth of clothing and was supposed to be lost, is arrived at Falmouth in Casco bay.

Mrs. Randolph would tire me with a narrative of Mrs. Jefferson's and your attention to her since my absence, did I not take pleasure in professing myself to be at all times Yr. friend & Servt.,

EDM: RANDOLPH

RC (DLC).

From David Watson

[*Monticello, before 28 Oct. 1781.*] Watson would be "much obleadged" if TJ would consider his state, for he is "full of want" and has not "Any Spair Clothing to Change my Self." He [had been given?] "sume Stockings . . . publicklly" which caused him "very much Concern: as I have a Spirit above thos things although Never So poor: has Come of Good people and good principle is Sorey to be Accomodated by Neagros."

RC (DLC); MS badly faded and partly illegible; the draft of TJ's letter to Washington of 28 Oct. 1781 is written on verso. The date of this letter may be presumed to be between early Apr. and 28 Oct. and to have been written when TJ was not at Monticello. For under date of 3 Apr. 1781, TJ's Account Book shows that he "sent David Watson a British deserter, house joiner by trade, to work at Monticello @ 3000 ℔. tobo. a year or it's worth in paper."

TJ's Account Book for 1781 shows that he had paid Watson a total of £1395 between 9 June and 25 Sep. Possibly one reason for Watson's being "full of want" was that he was also, much of the time, full of whiskey. The Account Book for Jan. 1782 gives an impressive record of Watson's consumption: 12 Jan.: "Watson has had 3 galls. whiskey. 3 galls. do. ½ galln do." (this probably represents a cumulative record, since it is the first in the Account Book dealing with Watson's whiskey consumption); 14 Jan.: "Watson 1 qt. do."; 16 Jan.: "1 qt. do"; 30 Jan.: "Charge Watson & Orr 3 galls. whiskey"; and 1 Feb.: "charge do. 4. gall. do." See also TJ to John Key, 2 Mch. 1784.

To George Washington

SIR   Monticello Oct. 28. 1781.

I hope it will not be unacceptable to your Excellency to receive the congratulations of a private individual on[1] your return to your native country, and above all things on the important success which has attended it. Great as this has been however, it can scarcely add to the affection with which we had looked up to you, and if in the minds of any the motives of gratitude to our good allies were not sufficiently apparent the part they have borne in this action, must amply evince them. Notwithstanding the state of perpetual decrepitude to which I am unfortunately reduced, I should certainly have done myself the honour of paying my respects to you personally, but that I apprehend those visits which are meant by us as marks of our attachment to you must interfere with the regulations of a camp, and be particularly inconvenient to one whose time is too precious to be wasted in ceremony.

I beg you to beleive me among the sincerest of those who subscribe themselves Your Excellency's Most obedt. & most humble servts., TH: JEFFERSON

RC (PHi); addressed to Washington at "Head-Quarters"; endorsed in part: "ansd 30th." Dft (DLC).

[1] TJ first wrote in Dft: "I beg leave to tender to your excellency my congratulations on," then changed the sentence to read as printed.

From Horatio Gates

DEAR SIR   Berkeley 15th: November 1781

The Packet which Gen: Stephen does me the Favour to deliver you with this Letter, has Travelled to Richmond, and back again to my Hands. Had the person to whom I intrusted it, been half as keen for your receiving it, as he is in the pursuit of his Own Interest, I am confident you would have got my First Letter in due Time. On the 7th: of October I wrote Gen: Washington the Letter, of which the inclosed is a Copy, but have not as yet received an Answer. Are you not ready to fall down, and Worship Louis the Sixteenth, for Saving our Country? Tobacco is all he asks for in Return, surely you will Supply France, in preference to every other Market. Just as we were in the Jaws of Ruin, and Dependence, to have The Compte de Grasse come, and Secure the Capture of The Conqueror of the South, with his whole Army, is so important, and Decisive a Service, as our Utmost Gratitude only can repay.

As I can now only hope to see you in your way to Warm Springs next Summer, I beg You, and Your Lady, will consider the Invitation in my other Letter, as transferred to that period. With a Gratefull remembrance of your many Civillities, and Attentions, I am Sir Your much Obliged Humble Servant,   HORATIO GATES

RC (DLC). Dft (NHi); endorsed. Enclosure (Tr in Gates' hand, DLC; another Tr in an unidentified hand, with corrections by TJ, DLC): Gates to Washington, 7 Oct. 1781, stating that he regrets that he did not have an opportunity to pay his respects to Washington on his return to Virginia; inquiring whether his letter of 22 May had been received; and reaffirming his desire to serve his country but that he thinks Washington would not want him to serve "under the Stigma that has so ungenerously been laid upon" him.

THE PACKET . . . MY FIRST LETTER: Gates here refers to his letter to TJ of 2 Aug. 1781 and its enclosures, as proved by internal evidence and TJ's reply of 14 Dec. 1781.

From James Madison

Dear Sir   Philada. Novr. 18. 1781.

By the conveyance through which you will receive this the Delegates have communicated to the State the proceedings in Congress to which the territorial cessions have given birth. The complexion of them will I suppose be somewhat unexpected, and produce no small irritation. They clearly speak the hostile machinations of some of the States against our territorial claims, and afford suspicions that the predominant temper of Congress may coincide with them. It is proper to recollect however that the report of the Committee having not yet been taken into consideration no certain inference can be drawn as to its issue, and that the report itself is not founded on the obnoxious doctrine of an inherent right in the U. States to the territory in question, but on the expediency of cloaking them with the title of New York which is supposed to be maintainable against all others. It is proper also to be considered that the proceedings of the Committee, which we laboured in vain to arrest, were vindicated not by the pretext of a jurisdiction belonging to Congress in such cases, but alledged to have been made necessary by the conditions annexed to the Cession of Virginia. Although the Cession of Virginia will probably be rejected on the whole, I do not think it probable that all the principles and positions contained in the report of the Committee will be ratified. The Committee was composed of a Member from Maryland, Pennsylvania, N. Jersey, Rhode Island and N. Hampshire all of which States except the last are systematically and notoriously adverse to the claims of the Western territory and particularly those of Virginia. The opinion of the Committee is therefore no just index of the opinion of Congress, and as it is a rule observed since the Confederation was completed, that seven votes are requisite in every question, and there are seldom more than 7. 8. 9. or 10. States present, and even the opinion of a Majority of Congress is a very different thing from a Constitutional vote. I mention these particulars that you may be the better able to counteract any intemperate measures that may be urged in the legislature. I do not hesitate to declare my opinion that the State will not only find in the communications we have made to them ample justification for revoking or at least suspending that Act of Cession, and remonstrating against any interference with respect to cases within their jurisdiction, but that they ought in all their provisions for their future security, importance and interest to presume that the present Union will but little survive the present war. I am equally sensible nevertheless of the necessity of great temper and moderation with respect to the first point, and in the last that they ought to be as fully impressed with the necessity of the Union during the war as of its probable dissolution after it. If the State wishes any particular Steps to be pursued by the Delegates, it would be well for particular instructions to that effect to be given. These will not only be a guide to us, but will give greater weight to whatever is urged by us.

I inclose you a paper containing two of the many letters lately published in New York with the subscription of Mr. Deane's name. The genuineness of some of them and particularly that to Mr. Morris is generally doubted. There are some who think the whole of them spurious. However this may be there is, through another channel, indubitable proof that no injustice is done in ascribing to him the sentiments advanced in these letters. Either from pique, interested projects of trade, or a traitorous correspondence with the Enemy, he has certainly apostatized from his first principles.

Colo. Willet has lately defeated and dispersed a party from Canada amounting 6 or 700 few of whom will escape captivity, the sword, or famine in the Wilderness. The action commenced near Johnstown.

The Minister of France has dispatches from [France] by a late arrival which confirms the expedition from Cadiz against Minorca, and the actual landing of the troops on the Island.

With great respect & sincere regard I am Dr Sir Yr Obt & hbl Servt.,   J MADISON JUNR.

RC (DLC); addressed to TJ at Richmond, with the following note: "Capt Irish is requested to deliver this to the Govr of Virga. with the letter addressed to him."; endorsed by TJ: "Madison Nov. 18. 1781 recd Jan. 9. 1782." Enclosure (missing): The 14 Nov. 1781 issue of *Freeman's Journal* (Philadelphia), containing a reprint from a New York paper of two letters written by Silas Deane to William Duer and Robert Morris (McRee, *Life of James Iredell*, I, 560, cited by Burnett, *Letters of Members*, VI, No. 384, note 4).

The letter addressed to the Governor, containing the PROCEEDINGS IN CONGRESS on the cessions of western territory, was that of 17 Nov. 1781, to which Harrison replied on 11 Jan. 1782 (Bur-

nett, *Letters of Members*, VI, No. 387; *Official Letters*, III, 126). The suggestion that INSTRUCTIONS be given the delegates was one that had already occurred to others (see George Mason to TJ, 27 Sep. 1781), but it was 9 Jan. 1782 when Captain Irish arrived with the letter and proceedings and the General Assembly had already risen (Harrison to delegates, 11 Jan. 1782, *Official Letters*, III, 126). See Madison to TJ, 15 Jan. 1782. The letter to Harrison and the proceedings have not been found, but see the delegates' letters to Nelson of 9, 16, and 23 Oct. 1781 (Burnett, *Letters of Members*, VI, Nos. 340, 353, and 360). THE OBNOXIOUS DOCTRINE OF AN INHERENT RIGHT: See George Mason to TJ, 27 Sep. 1781.

From William Fleming

DR. SR.   Castle Hill, 23d. Novr. 1781.

As I lately passed thro' Orange in my way to Culpeper, I heard of a British deserter at one Proctor's, about five miles beyond Orange court house, who is an excellent stone cutter. If you have occasion for such an artist, you may probably engage him by sending to Proctors.

I intended myself the pleasure of spending a [d]ay at Monteciello before my return home, but on my arrival at Colo. Champe's, found he was gone to my house, by way of Fredericksburg.

Be pleased to present my respects to Mrs. Jefferson, & believe me with great esteem yr. friend & obed servt.,   WM. FLEMING

RC (DLC).   William CHAMPE was colonel of Culpeper militia (Gwathmey, *Hist. Reg. of Virginians in the Revolution*).

From John Harvie, enclosing a Resolution to Inquire into the Conduct of the Executive

DEAR SIR   Richmond Novr. 27th. 1781

Being Anxious that the Inclosed Resolution of the House of Delegates should reach you as early as possible, I have prevail'd on Capt. Dalton to be the Bearer of it to your House. I should be unhappy to think that any Accident should prevent the State from Deriveing the Advantage of Council from her ablest Citizens, by the Cavil of party on the Illiberality of the Inviduous, wherefore, shall esteem it as much my Duty as it is Assuredly my Inclination to Attend the ensueing Election in our County, to give my Sanction to a choice that will Confer Honour on the Electors in particular, as well as Benifits on the Community at large. Doctor Arthur Lee is Chosen a Member, and I have heard that Mr. Mason will again Consent to Serve. The Assistance of men of Real Abilities I should hope will be a Stimulous to others of like Character to lend their aid to the tottering Condition of the Commonwealth. I have the Satisfaction to find that in the Opinions of all men I here Converse with, that the Administration before the last, is now View'd as haveing been Honorable to the Cheif Magistrate, and preservative of the Rights of the people, and the Constitution of the Land. In short I think Sir in no period of your life, has your Character shown with a Superior Lustre, to what it will do on your appearance in the Assembly, to which place may your own Inclination and the Voice of the people Speedily send you.   JNO HARVIE

ENCLOSURE

IN THE HOUSE OF DELEGATES

Monday the 26th. of November 1781.

RESOLVED, that this House will on Wednesday the 12th of December next proceed agreeable to Resolution of the 12th: of June last to enquire into the conduct of the Executive of this State for the last twelve Months next preceeding the said Resolution; and that as well the Information against the said Executive, as their defence be received and heard on that day.

ORDERED, that a Committee be appointed to state any Charges and receive such Information as may be offered respecting the administration of the Executive, of which, the said Committee shall give notice if any accusation should be made in writing, to the members which composed the Executive within the time referred to.

AND a Committee was appointed of Mr. Banister, Mr. Tyler, Mr. Nicholas, Mr. Southall, and Mr. Morgan.

Teste JOHN BECKLEY C.h.d.
A Copy JOHN BECKLEY C.h.d.

RC (DLC); addressed: "The Honble. Thomas Jefferson Esqe. of Albemarle." Enclosure (DLC); in Beckley's hand and attested by him.

Harvie was not a member of the Assembly at this time, but wrote as a private individual; this suggests the possibility that he was the "friend" who communicated to TJ the formal charges printed above under date of 31 July. THE ENSUEING ELECTION IN OUR COUN-

TY: In April James Marks and Isaac Davis had been elected delegates for Albemarle (James Gilmer to TJ, 13 Apr.), but on 21 Nov., by a ruling of the House of Delegates, Davis was obliged to vacate his seat on accepting the post of deputy commissary of provisions (JHD, Oct. 1781, 1828 edn., p. 9). A special election was therefore held, and TJ was enabled to come into the House.

From George Washington

SIR   Philadelphia 30th Novemr 1781

Your very agreeable Favor of the 28th ulto. which I have had the pleasure to receive, and which is filled with such sincere Marks of Cordiality and Affection, could not fail to be very acceptable to me.

I thank you Sir for your Congratulations on the late Success in Virginia—a Success which must be productive of happy Relief to that State in particular; and I trust if properly improved, will be conducive of very extensive good Consequences to the united States. The very important Share which our great Allies have taken in this Event, ought to endear them to every American, and their Assistance should be remembred with perpetual Gratitude.

I am most sincerely sorry for the Misfortune which prevented me the pleasure of seeing you in Virginia. Among the Number of my Friends, who made me happy in their Company while I was in that State, it would have afforded me a peculiar Satisfaction to have added you in the List.

With very great Regard & Esteem I am Sir Your most Obedient & most humble Servt.,   GO: WASHINGTON

RC (DLC); in the hand of Jonathan Trumbull, Jr., signed by Washington. FC (DLC: Washington Papers).

Jefferson's Account and Attendance Record in the General Assembly for October 1781

[10-22 December 1781]

1781 [The Commonwealth of Virginia to] Thomas Jefferson [Dr.]
Dec. Travelling to & from the Assembly 150 miles @ 2d

300 [℔. Tobo.]

To 13. days attendance from Dec. 10th. to 22d inclusive   650

Entries in TJ's hand in record of accounts and attendance of the members of the General Assembly, 1781-1782 (Vi).

TJ was more precise in giving the dates of his attendance than the other members from Albemarle (Isaac Davis, James Marks, and Thomas Walker) who entered their accounts on this page, but he appears to have erred in writing "@ 2d." The record of his colleagues makes clear that the mode of reckoning is in pounds of tobacco: 2 lbs. per mile

for coming and going, and 50 lbs. for each day of attendance. On 10 Dec. TJ also signed the oath prescribed for state officers; the original as subscribed by members of this Assembly is in Vi; the text is the same as that in the Revisal of the Laws, Bill No. 98, printed above, Vol. 2: 589, which was drafted by TJ in 1779. TJ, of course, had already taken the oath of fidelity and the oath of office as governor as prescribed by the Act of 1779 (Hening, x, 22-3).

Resolution of Thanks to Jefferson by the Virginia General Assembly

Wednesday the 12th. of December 1781.

A Motion was made that the House do come to the following Resolution

RESOLVED, that the sincere Thanks of the General Assembly be given to our former Governor Thomas Jefferson Esquire for his impartial, upright, and attentive administration *of the powers of the Executive*, whilst in office; *popular rumours, gaining some degree of credence, by more pointed Accusations, rendered it neces-*

sary to make an enquirey into his conduct, and delayed that retribution of public gratitude, so eminently merited; but that conduct having become the object of open scrutiny, tenfold value is added to an approbation founded on a cool and deliberate discussion. The Assembly wish *therefore* in the strongest manner to declare the high opinion which they entertain of Mr. Jefferson's Ability, Rectitude, and Integrity as cheif Magistrate of this Commonwealth, and mean by thus publicly avowing their Opinion, to obviate *all future*, and to remove all *former* unmerited Censure.

And the said Resolution being read a second time was on the question thereupon agreed to by the House Nemine Contradicente.

Teste

JOHN BECKLEY C.H.d.

1781. Decr. 15th.
Agreed to by the Senate with
amendments unanimously.

W. DREW. *C.S.*

MS (Vi). The body of the Resolution is in Beckley's hand and bears his signature and a note below signed by William Drew, clerk of the Senate. The amendments, five in number, were all made by the Senate and are indicated in MS by being underscored and here by being italicized; they are listed in Drew's hand on a separate leaf and are signed by him and by Beckley: "1781 December 19th. Agreed to. J. Beckley, C.H.D." Endorsement on verso of resolutions reads: "Reso. of thanks to Thomas Jefferson Esqr. former Governor of this State. 12 Decr. 1781." Two copies of the Resolution as amended by the Senate's deletions and agreed to by the House (i.e., the text above *without* the italicized words and without the final paragraph, which was not part of the Resolution) are in DLC; one of these (TJ Papers, 7: 1185) is in John Beckley's hand and was originally enclosed in Nathaniel Harrison's letter to TJ, 22 Dec. 1781, q.v.; the other (TJ Papers, 7: 1186) is a copy in the hand of William Drew and is endorsed in the hand of Henry Tazewell.

In accordance with the resolution of 26 Nov. (see enclosure in John Harvie's letter to TJ, 27 Nov.), the committee appointed to state charges and receive information respecting the conduct of the executive, reported on 12 Dec. John Banister read the report, which was as follows:

"that the committee did, according to order, convene for that purpose, and no information being offered on the subject matter of the said inquiry, except that some rumors prevailed, which appeared to the committee to have been the cause of the original order of the 12th of June, directing the said inquiry; that the committee had come to a resolution thereupon, which he read in his place, and afterwards delivered in at the clerk's table, where the same was again twice read, and agreed to by the House, as followeth: *Resolved, that it is the opinion of this committee*, That the said rumors were groundless" (JHD, Oct. 1781, 1828 edn., p. 37).

Presumably it was at this point (though the Journal does not record it) that, since Nicholas had absented himself "and no other undertaking to bring them forward," TJ himself rose in his place and read Nicholas' charges, "from his paper, answering them seriatim to the house" (above, Vol. 4: 262; see Nicholas' charges and Jefferson's answers, printed under 31 July 1781). The motion herewith printed was then made (the mover not being named), and, having been read a second time, was agreed to unanimously. John Talbot, a member from Bedford, was ordered to carry it to the Senate. The MS here printed was, of course, the one that Talbot carried. The Senate's amendments were made on 15 Dec. and on the 19th "The House proceeded to consider the amendments of the Senate . . . and the same being read, were agreed to" (JHD, Oct. 1781, 1828 edn., p. 42, 48). On the same day TJ resigned his appointment as delegate to Congress in place of John Blair, to which he had been elected on 30 Nov. before coming into the House (same, p. 49, 23; copy of resolution of appointment in DLC). Having obtained what he desired from the legislature, he immediately turned to pursuits he loved better than politics (see his letters of 19 and 20 Dec. 1781 to Clark, Marbois, and Thomson). On the 22d, the day he received from Speaker Harrison of the Senate a copy of the resolution of thanks, he stopped attending the Assembly; and on the 24th he expressed his innermost feelings on the whole affair of the investigation with a bitterness probably unmatched anywhere else in his surviving writings (see letter to Isaac Zane under that date).

The comment of an interested spectator of these events is found in a letter from Edmund Pendleton to James Madison of 31 Dec. 1781: "Since my last Mr. Jefferson's honorable acquittal of the loose censure thrown out at random on his character, hath come to my hand, which I doubt not you'll have published in one of the Philadelphia papers, that this stain may be wiped out wherever it may have reached. I am assured by a member of the assembly that it was entered unanimously in the House of Delegates, and he believes in the Senate, tho' the clerk has omitted it in my copy." Pendleton goes on, significantly, to report that Gov. Thomas Nelson, who had resigned earlier in the month, will also probably "receive a vote of thanks and approbation of his conduct, from a conviction that what he did wrong was imputable to a mistake in his judgment, and not from a corrupt heart. I am satisfied of the integrity of his mind, but whether that should intitle to more than indemnity, I doubt" ("Unpublished Letters of Edmund Pendleton," Mass. Hist. Soc., *Procs.*, 2d ser., XIX [1905], 144-5). The resolution of thanks to TJ was printed in Hayes' *Va. Gaz.*, 22 Dec. 1781.

To Duncan Rose

DEAR SIR   Richmond Dec. 13. 1781

I have the pleasure of your favors of the 10th. and 13th now before me. Should the report of the Committee of Trade on your claim come on while I am here I will propose the order that the Commercial agent pay your balance on a supposition that the account does in it's nature belong to that department. This being done it will be easy for you and he so to accomodate your matters as that any purchases you may make may be placed against his debt to you.

The warrants for £10,000 and 11680£ which you mention to be expressed for tobacco due on public account I suppose to be in part of your salary. I am informed since I came to town that the assembly either have passed or will certainly pass an act for paying all the public debts now outstanding, with their depreciation. When this will be done is not so easy to foresee, but it gives a hope of justice some day or other. With respect to the warrant for £11250 it would be just that the public should pay on this the depreciation which incurred between the 18th. of Apr. and 23d. of July, that is between it's date and paiment had it never been paid I suppose it would come in on the footing of the two warrants first abovementioned: but being paid, it stands in an immense croud of private losses by depreciation incurred while the treasury was without money, into which I apprehend the assembly will never enter on account of the multiplicity and intricacy of the accounts of that kind which in that case would be brought in to be overhauled. This loss therefore, however unjustly, will I fear fall on you. The depreciation from July 23. to Oct. 15., that is from your receipt of the money at the Treasury till paid to Mr. Cox for Genl. Morgan, cannot with justice be made the loss of any person but yourself unless there was any default in Mr. Smith. The paiment made on the 15th. of October to Mr. Cox (whom I understand to have been duly authorised to receive the money either for Genl. Morgan or Mr. Beall) should in honour, as it does in law, discount so much of the 15M tobacco as it was worth at that time, and of course that you are liable either in law or honour for the balance only.

Make no apologies to me for giving me opportunities of serving you. The obligation is on my part and so will ever be deemed, as I am with very great sincerity Dr Sir Your friend & servt.,

TH: JEFFERSON

RC (ViHi); addressed to Rose at Richmond; endorsed.

Rose's FAVORS OF THE 10TH. AND 13TH have not been found. On 29 Nov. 1781 Rose presented a petition to the House of Delegates requesting settlement of his claim against the commonwealth for money and tobacco advanced "during the exhausted state of the treasury," and for pay due him as a member of the board of trade. His petition was referred to the committee of trade, which made its report on 15 Dec. and presented a resolution allowing Rose's claim in the amount of 145,749 pounds of tobacco, together with another resolution, "That so much of the aforesaid tobacco as respects the trading department, ought to be paid to the petitioner by the agent of that department, as soon as the circumstances thereof will admit, with interest

until paid." The House agreed to the committee's resolutions on 15 Dec. and the Senate did so on 18 Dec. (JHD, Oct. 1781, 1828 edn., p. 20, 41, 45). AN ACT FOR PAYING ALL THE PUBLIC DEBTS NOW OUTSTANDING, WITH THEIR DEPRECIATION: A bill "to exchange and fund outstanding auditors' warrants" was defeated on 28 Dec. and a bill "for the more effectual settlement of the accounts of public agents, and for other purposes" was considered, but postponed to the next session (same, p. 61, 68-9). The Act that TJ was led to anticipate was, no doubt, the Act establishing a scale of depreciation as "a just standard whereby to settle and adjust debts and contracts" entered into between 1 Jan. 1777 and 1 Jan. 1782 (Hening, x, 471-4).

To Horatio Gates

DEAR SIR
Richmond Dec. 14. 1781.

I have received your friendly letters of Aug. 2. and Nov. 15. and some of the gentlemen to whom you wished them to be communicated, not being here, I have taken the liberty of handing them to some others so as to answer the spirit of your wish. It seems likely to end as I ever expected it would, in a final acknowlegement that good disposition, and arrangements will not do without a certain degree of bravery and discipline in those who are to carry them into execution. This, the men whom you commanded, or the greater part of them at least, unfortunately wanted on that particular occasion. I have not a doubt but that on a fair enquiry the returning justice of your countrymen will remind them of Saratoga and induce them to recognize your merit. My future plan of life scarcely admits a hope of my having the pleasure of seeing you at your seat: yet I assuredly shall do it should it ever lie within my power, and am assured that Mrs. Jefferson will join me in sincere thanks for your kind sentiments and invitation, in expressions of equal esteem for Mrs. Gates and yourself, and in a certain hope that should any circumstance lead you within our reach you will make us happy by your company at Monticello. We have no news to communicate. That the assembly does little, does not come under that description. I am with very sincere esteem Dr. Sir Your friend & Servt.,

TH: JEFFERSON

RC? (DLC); addressed: "The honble Majr. Genl. Gates Berkeley."

To George Rogers Clark

DEAR SIR   Richmond Dec. 19. 1781.

Having an opportunity by Colo. Boon I take the liberty of calling to your mind your kindness in undertaking to procure for me some teeth of the great animal whose remains are found on the Ohio. Were it possible to get a tooth of each kind, that is to say a foretooth, grinder &c. it would particularly oblige me. Perhaps you know some careful person at Fort Pitt with whom they might be safely lodged till our Mathematicians go out in the spring to settle the Pennsylvania boundary, who could readily bring them in for me in their baggage waggon. I beleive we spoke of the expediency of securing them in a box. I hope you will pardon the freedom I take in being so minute. The retirement into which I am withdrawing has increased my eagerness in pursuit of objects of this kind. Hoping the acquaintance I had the pleasure of making with you was not merely official I take the liberty of subscribing myself Dr. Sir Your friend & servt.,   TH: JEFFERSON

RC (American Museum of Natural History); addressed: "General Clarke Louisville"; endorsed: "Govr. Jefferson. Decmr: 19 1781 Mamoth Bones."

A Bill for the Relief of Military Pensioners

[19 Dec. 1781]

Whereas by the act of General assembly for establishing a board of Auditors the said board was authorized to allow pensions and sums in gross to a certain extent to officers and souldiers of the army or navy raised by act of general assembly and disabled in the service and to the widows of those slain or dying therein, which allowances having been made in paper currency have by the depreciation of that become inadequate to the benevolent purposes of the said act: Be it therefore enacted by the General assembly that all such allowances made or to be made shall be paiable in specie, the Auditors taking care that they be properly reduced where in consideration of such depreciation they shall have been made larger than they be when to be paid in specie.

MS (Vi); entirely in TJ's hand; endorsed by TJ: "a Bill for the relief of Military pensioners"; docketed by a clerk: "December 19th: 1781. read the first time. December 20th: 1781. read the second time & Committed to Mr: Jefferson Mr: Henry & Mr: Richard Lee Engrossed."

On 18 Dec. Richard Lee, for the committee of trade, reported on a number of petitions concerning claims for pensions; whereupon the House ordered Lee, TJ, and Patrick Henry to bring in a bill or bills pursuant to the resolutions of the committee. On 19 Dec. TJ presented the above bill, which was read the second time on 20 Dec. and recommitted to the same committee (the Journal lists Arthur Lee, but see docketing above). On 22 Dec. TJ reported that the committee had considered the bill but had made no amendments. On 21 Dec. the House granted TJ leave of absence for the remainder of the session and he left Richmond before the bill was read the third time and passed, on 24 Dec. Richard Lee carried the bill to the Senate which approved it on 27 Dec. (JHD, Oct. 1781, 1828 edn., p. 47, 50, 52, 53, 54, 58; Hening, x, 461). During his attendance at the legislature TJ was added to the committee on finance, to the committee on county petitions, to a committee to prepare a bill for better government of the western counties, and to the committee to draft a naval bill (same, p. 34, 39, 46, and 51), but the present bill is the only evidence that he took any really active part in the legislation proposed at this session, his one object being to defend his administration against the charges that had been made. The "Bill to impower the Executive to fitt out a certain naval force" was read the first time on 21 Dec. and was in accord with recommendations for defense that TJ had made in his letter to the Speaker of the House of Delegates on 10 May 1781 (Hening, x, 458); however, there is no evidence on the MS bill (Vi) to show that TJ had a hand in its authorship. It is also possible that TJ may have been the author of a bill introduced by Southall on 10 Dec. 1781, the day he entered the legislature, whose purpose was the relief of those persons who had been or might be injured by the enemy's destruction of county records in June 1781 (MS, Vi; JHD, Oct. 1781, 1828 edn., p. 33-4). He was certainly the first and perhaps the only one to take advantage of the provision in the Act which authorized the governor to commission magistrates in any county whose records had been destroyed empowering them to hear witnesses and take depositions of any persons whose "Estates, Titles, and interests" had been affected by such destruction (Hening, x, 453-4). On 10 Jan. 1782 the Council, "on application from Thomas Jefferson esqr. of Albemarle County," advised the governor to issue such a commission to the nine senior magistrates of Albemarle and at the same time urged "that the Printer be directed to publish in his paper so much of the . . . Act as empowers the Governor to issue such Commissions" (MS Va. Council Jour., 10 Jan. 1782, Vi).

To Thomas McKean

Richmond Dec. 20. 1781.

I had the honour of receiving a letter from your excellency desiring that application might be made to Colo. Arthur Campbell of Washington for certain papers taken on his expedition against the Cherokees, and described, in his relation of that, as the Archives of the nation. The application was immediately made, and he has transmitted to me the packet which accompanies this, with a promise of some other papers of a like nature within a short time. So soon as received they shall be forwarded to your Excellency. I have the honour to be with the highest respect Your Excellency's Most obedt. & most humble servt., TH: JEFFERSON

RC (DLC: PCC, No. 71, ii); addressed: "His Excellency The President of Congress"; endorsed: "Governor Jefferson respecting Letters taken by Col. Campbell on his expedition against the Cherokes. Decr. 20th. 1781." A LETTER FROM YOUR EXCELLENCY: Samuel Huntington to TJ, 27 Apr. 1781, q.v., and references there. THE PACKET WHICH ACCOMPANIES THIS: The papers which Arthur Campbell sent to TJ and which he, in turn, forwarded to McKean with this letter are in DLC: PCC, No. 71, ii, p. 143-221, and include the following: (1) Alex. Cameron to Chiefs of Cherokees, 16 Jan. 1775; (2) Lord Dunmore's talk to Little Carpenter and other Cherokee Chiefs, 23 Mch. 1775; (3) instructions of the King to governors concerning Indian territory, signed by John Stuart, 4 July 1763; (4) Alex. Cameron, speech to Cherokees, 7 July 1774; (5) speech by an unidentified person to Cherokees, 3 June 1773; (6) abstract of treaty of cession to the King by Creeks and Cherokees, Augusta, 1 June 1773; (7) Alex. Cameron, speech to Cherokees, 30 Mch. 1773; (8) Alex. Cameron, warrant of protection for "the Great Warrior of Chote," 1 Mch. 1771; (9) Alex. Cameron, speech [to Cherokees] 5 Feb. 1772; (10) John Stuart to the Cherokees, 14 Jan. 1764; (11) Edw. Wilkinson to "the Great Warrior Onconnistota," 5 July 1778; (12) Wm. Preston to the Cherokee chiefs, 12 Apr. 1775; (13) David Taitt to Oconastota, 24 Jan. 1777; (14) John Stuart to "OuKonnestotah," n.d.; (15) map of "the New Province" at the junction of Scioto and Ohio Rivers, n.d.; (16) John Stuart, speech of "Oucconnastoté," 6 Feb. 1777; (17) St. Andrews Club, Charles Town, S.C., membership card for "Oucconnastotah," signed by John Stuart, President, 30 Nov. 1773; (18) Patrick Henry to "Ouconostotah," 3 Mch. and Nov. 1777; (19) Patrick Henry to "Ouconostotah," n.d.; (20) John Stuart to the Cherokees, 30 June 1763; (22) treaty between state of Virginia and the Cherokee nation, Fort Henry, 20 July 1777.

To Marbois

Sir Richmond Dec. 20. 1781.

I now do myself the honour of inclosing you answers to the quaeries which Mr. Jones put into my hands. I fear your patience has been exhausted in attending them, but I beg you to be assured there has been no avoidable delay on my part. I retired from the public service in June only, and after that the general confusion of our state put it out of my power to procure the informations necessary till lately. Even now you will find them very imperfect and not worth offering but as a proof of my respect for your wishes. I have taken the liberty of referring to you my friend Mr. Charles Thompson for a perusal of them when convenient to you. Particular reasons subsisting between him and myself induced me to give you this trouble.

If his Excellency the Chevalier de la Luzerne will accept the respects of a stranger I beg you to present mine to him, and to consider me as being with the greatest regard & esteem Sir Your most obedient and most humble servt., Th: Jefferson

RC (Bibliothèque Nationale); addressed: "Monsr. de Marbois Secretary to the embassy of his most Christian majesty Philadelphia." Enclosure (missing): Answers to Marbois' queries concerning Virginia, q.v. under date of 30 Nov. 1780, and references there; see also Marbois to TJ, 29 Jan. 1782, Ambler to TJ, 16 Mch. 1782, and TJ to Marbois, 24 Mch. 1782.

To Charles Thomson

Dear Sir   Richmond Dec. 20. 1781.

I received notice from the secretary of the American Philosophical society some time ago that they had done me the honour of appointing me a counsellor of that body. The particular duties of that office I am quite a stranger to, and indeed know too little of the nature of their institution to judge what objects it comprehends. In framing answers to some queries which Monsr. de Marbois sent me, it occurred to me that some of the subjects which I had then occasion to take up, might, if more fully handled, be a proper tribute to the Philosophical society, and the aversion I have to being counted as a drone in any society induced me to determine to recur to you as my antient friend, to ask the favor of you to peruse those answers, and to take the trouble of communicating to me your opinion whether any and which of the subjects there treated would come within the scope of that learned institution, and to what degree of minuteness one should descend in treating it; perhaps also you would be so friendly as to give me some idea of the subjects which would at any time be admissible into their transactions. Had I known nothing but the load of business under which you labour I should not have ventured on this application, but knowing your friendly disposition also I thought you would take some spare half hour to satisfy a friend who can assure you that he is with great sincerity & esteem Your most obedt. humble servt.,

Th: Jefferson

P.S. I have mentioned to Monsr. de Marbois my request to you to ask of him the perusal of the papers I sent him without however communicating the purpose of that request.

RC (DLC: Thomson Papers); addressed: "Charles Thompson esq. Philadelphia"; endorsed: "Letter Decr. 1781 from Thos Jefferson Esq & Answer March 9 1782."

From Nathaniel Harrison

SIR [Sena]te Room Decr. 22. 1781

I have the Pleasure to inclose you the Resolution of the General Assembly for your impartial upright and attentive administration whilst Governor. This is the more pleasing to me as it intirely coincides with my own Sentiments. I have the Honor to be with the greatest [es]teem Sir Yr. mo. obt. Hble Servt,

NATHAL HARRISON. S.S.

RC (DLC); addressed: "The Honble Thomas Jefferson." MS mutilated. Enclosure (also DLC): Resolution of thanks to TJ by the General Assembly, 12-15 Dec. 1781, q.v. (the copy actually enclosed in Harrison's letter is the fair copy of the amended text in TJ Papers, 7: 1185).

To Isaac Zane

Richmond Dec. 24. [1781]

I am sorry to be told here that you are sick in Philadelphia. I had hoped to have had the pleasure of seeing you. You have heard probably of the vote of the H. of Delegates at the last session of assembly. I came here in consequence of it, and found neither accuser nor accusation. They have acknowledged by an express vote that the former one was founded on *rumours* only, for which no foundation can be discovered: they have thanked &c. The trifling body who moved this matter was below contempt; he was more an object of pity. His natural ill-temper was the tool worked with by another hand. He was like the minners which go in and out of the fundament of the whale. But the whale himself was discoverable enough by the turbulence of the water under which he moved. But enough of this—I had abundance of reasons for wishing to see you. Among others I have been answering to a gentleman of science a number of quæries mathematical, meteorological, geographical, physiological &c. &c. and I wished to have drawn much information from you. Should you come within reach of Albemarle pray let me see you: otherwise I shall certainly visit you in Frederic as soon as the mild season sets in. I wish you much better health. Adieu!

RC (PHi); at head of text: "Th:J to Isaac Zane"; endorsed by Zane: "from Tho Jefferson Richd. Decr. 24—81. Ansd. by C. Logan feby. 25th. 1782."

THE TRIFLING BODY WHO MOVED THIS MATTER: George Nicholas; see Archibald Cary to TJ, 19 June; the exchange between TJ and Nicholas, 28-31 July 1781; and notes and documents relating to the British invasions in 1781, above, Vol. 4: 261-2. ANOTHER HAND: It was TJ's conviction that this was Patrick Henry; see note on Henry Young's letter to William Davies, 9 June 1781. A GENTLEMAN OF SCIENCE: See TJ to Marbois, 20 Dec. 1781. See further, Zane's answer to the present letter, 25 Feb. 1782. BY AN EXPRESS VOTE: This, of course, refers to the vote of the House of Delegates of 12 Dec.; the acknowledgement in the resolution of thanks of the same date that "popular rumours" made it necessary to have an inquiry was struck out by the Senate and acceded to by the House.

From George Wythe

GW TO TJ   Williamsburg. 31 Dec. 1781.

A few days after the reduction of York I returned to Williamsburg, and accompanying Mr. Madison, waited on general Washington, with an address of the university among other things, desiring him to give orders, that the college, which we found employed as an hospital, might be evacuated so soon as it could be done conveniently. He was very civil, and gave a kind answer; but for that business referred us to count de Rochambeau and general Nelson: from the latter of whom as we saw no prospect of redress, we made no application to the other. But some conversation, which I had with general Chastellux, and a letter, which he wrote to me, since, give me some hopes that the college will be restored, in two or three months. During that interval, I know not a place, at which my time would pass so happily as at Monticello, if my presence at Chesterville were not indispensibly necessary to adjust my affairs left there in some confusion by the manager who hath lately eloped. I can therefore only thank you for your friendly invitation and offer. You must allow me to insist that you send me but one horse, in exchange for him you had of me, without compensation for difference of value if any there be and even that one I desire not unless you can spare him conveniently. In our dealings, you, and not I, if either, ought to have the advantage, for more reasons than I can enumerate. I desired Martin to take the roan horse then in good plight to assist him in carrying home the servant he recovered in my neighbourhood. Send me a description of the other servants belonging to you, whom you suspect to be in the lower part of the country. I have heard of several lurking there, supposed to be slaves.

Present my best respects to Mrs. Jefferson, and Patsy, and Poll, & accept my wishes of many happy years to you all, not forgetting my friend Peter. Adieu.

RC (DLC); addressed: "Hon. Thomas Jefferson Monticello Albemarle"; endorsed by TJ: "Wythe George 81. Dec. 31."

From John Lyne, with Jefferson's Memoranda for a Legal Opinion

SIR   Richmond 13 Janry. 1782.

The inclosed copy of Mr. Todds Will and money I receiv'd a few days ago from the Gentleman who has married the Widow. He requisted that I would inclose it to you for your Advice for all matters relative to the Widow and perticular to the question below. If the money inclosed is short of your demand for Advice I will pay you or Order the balance on demand. I shall be glad to be favoured with your Answer by the first Opertunity. I am Sir Yr Most H Servt,   JOHN LYNE

QUESTIONS

What increse does the Testator Mean of the Mare Lucretia, is it all the Colts and their increse in the possession of the Testator at his death? Or is it Only the futer increse?

What part of the Personal Estate and Slaves has the Testator given his Widow, and what Title has She in such Estate?

What Estate has the Widow in the Testators Houses and Lands After Marriage?

JEFFERSON'S MEMORANDA FOR A LEGAL OPINION

Better for the widow to reject the will because on the most favourable construction she gets no more by it than the law gives her: for the law gives her a third of the lands and slaves for life, and   of the personal estate after debts are paid in absolute property; which is perhaps equal or more than equal to the mare, clock, looking glass.

An estate for life jointly to the widow and two daughters determinable by moieties on the attainment of age or marriage by the daughters respectively.

Proportionable part means inheritable part, i.e. moiety.

1. Because the testator, after supposing both to have received *'their proportionable parts'* and to be dead without issue and that too in the life of the wife, makes a disposition which goes to the whole of his

estate, viz. in that event he gives all the negroes who came by his wife and all the horses with ¾ of the rest of his personal estate to his wife, *all* his lands to his two godsons in fee, and the residue not comprehended in this description to his sister Eliz. for life, remainder to his brothers and sisters children. This shews that he meant his first devise as a gift of his whole estate to his daughters on their age and marriage and considered that devise as separate. On their death without issue: that he contemplated this event as it might happen in the life of his wife is proved by his making her one of the reversionary legatees.

2. If it be supposed he meant by their proportionable part, one third part only, then he has given the widow her life in one third and leaves that third undisposed of after her death. It would of course descend equally on his daughters in fee, not subject to the cross remainders on the death of one daughter, nor to the remainder over on both their deaths. Now it does not seem improbable he meant to separate this third from the rest of his estate and put it into a different channel of transmission. This improbability therefore will weigh in determining the meaning of a doubtful expression, and induce us to beleive that by the words 'proportionable part' he meant the inheritable proportion, that is a moiety and not a third only.

'Increase' does not pass the offspring living at the time of making the will. Bullock v. Bullock G.C.

LAW	WILL
1. In the lands one third for life	1. In the lands one third for life if the above opinion be wrong.
2. In the slaves one third for life	2. In the slaves one third for life.
3. In the other personal estate one third in absolute property after debts are paid.	3. In the other personal estate, the mare Lucretia a clock and looking glass in absolute property and one third for life of the rest of the personal estate after debts paid and specific legacies taken out.
	4. On the death of both daughters without issue in the life of the wife, all the negroes which came by her, the horses and ¾ of the rest of his personal estate in absolute property.

RC (DLC); addressed to TJ, "Albemarle"; endorsed by TJ: "Todd's case a limn. of lands." TJ's notes on the queries in Lyne's letter, doubtless an outline of a (missing) reply, are written on the verso of the sheet. Enclosure (missing): Copy of Todd's will.

Under date of 16 Jan. 1782 in TJ's Account Book there is the following: "recd from John Lyne for opinion on Todd's will 28/."

From James Madison

Your favor of the   [1] day of   [1] written on the eve of your departure from Richmond came safe to hand by the last week's post. The result of the attack on your administration was so fully anticipated that it made little impression on me. If it had been consistent with your sentiments and views to engage in the new service to which you were called, it would have afforded me both unexpected and singular satisfaction, not only from the personal interest I felt in it but from the important aid which the interests of the state would probably have derived from it. What I particularly refer to is her claim to Western territory. The machinations which have long been practised by interested individuals against this claim are well known to you. The late proceedings within the walls of Congress in consequence of the territorial cessions produced by their recommendations to the States claiming the Western Country were many weeks ago transmitted for the Legislature by a Capt. Irish. By the same conveyance I wrote to you on the subject. We have the mortification to find by our latest letters from Richmond that this Gentleman had not at the date of them appeared there. As it is uncertain whether that information may not have totally miscarried it will be proper to repeat to you that the States besides Virga. from which the cessions came were Connecticut and N. York. The cession of the former consisted of all her claim west of N. York as far as the Missisipi. That of the latter of all her claims beyond a certain western limit drawn on the occasion. The cession of Cont. [Connecticut] extended to the soil only expressly reserving the jurisdiction. That of N.Y. made no reservation. These cessions with that of Virga. and Sundry memorials from the Inda. [Indiana] and other land Companies were referred to a Committee composed of a Member from N.H. R.I. N.J. Pa. and Maryld. The ingredients of this composition prepared us for the complexion of their proceedings. Their first Step was to investigate and discuss the respective titles of the States to the territory ceded. As this was directly in the face of the recommendation of Congress which professed to bury all such discussions and might prejudge future controversies between individual members of the Union, we refused to exhibit any evidence in favor of the title of Va. and endeavoured though in vain to prevail on Congress to interdict the Committee from proceeding in the enquiry. The next step of the Committee was still more obnoxious. They went fully into a hearing of the

Memorialists through their Agents, and received all the evidence adduced in support of their pretensions. On this occasion we renewed our remonstrances to the Committee and our complaints to Congress, but with as little effect as on the first occasion. The upshot of the whole was a report to Congress rejecting the Cessions of Virga. and Connt. and accepting that of N.Y.; disallowing also the claims of the Companies N.W. of the Ohio, but justifying that of the Inda. Compy. The report seems to distrust the doctrine hitherto maintained, of territorial rights being incident to the U.S. Collectively which are not comprehended within any individual State; substituting the expedient of recognizing the title of N.Y. stretching it over the whole country claimed by the other ceding States, and then accepting a transfer of it to the U.S. In this state the business now rests. The report having never been taken into consideration, nor do we wish it should, till it shall have undergone the consideration of Virga.

In whatever light the policy of this proceeding may be viewed it affords an additional proof of the industry and perseverance with which the territorial rights of Virga. are persecuted and of the necessity of fortifying them with every precaution which their importance demands. As a very obvious and necessary one we long since recommended to the State an accurate and full collection of the documents which relate to the subject. If the arrival of Capt. Irish had taken place before the adjournment of the Assembly and during your stay with it we flattered ourselves that this recommendation would have been attended to and that the task would have fallen on you. As this was not the case we have no hope at present of being enabled from any other sources than the voluntary aids of individuals to contradict even verbally the misrepresentations and calumnies which are daily levelled against the claims of Va. and which cannot fail to prepossess the public with errors injurious at present to her reputation and which may affect a future decision on her rights. Col. Masons industry and kindness has supplied us with some valuable papers and remarks. Mr. Jones has also received from Mr. Pendleton some judicious remarks on the subject. We are still notwithstanding far from possessing a complete view of it. Will you permit me to ask of you such information as your researches have yielded, with the observations which you have made in the course of them. I would not obtrude such a request on you if the subject were not of public importance and if it could have been addressed with equal prospect of advantage elsewhere. Indeed if you would prevail on yourself to spare as much time as would survey the whole subject, beginning with the original charter, pursuing it thro' the subsequent charters and other public acts of the crown thro' the Governors of Virga. and referring to all the transactions with the Indians which have been drawn into the question, the public utility I am persuaded would sufficiently reward you for the labor.

Pray did you ever receive a letter from me enclosing a proposition declaratory of the coercive power of Congress over the States? It went by an Express while you were at the head of the Executive.

We have not a word of news from Europe. The French are assembling a force in the W. Indies which presages further calamities to the English. The Spaniards are also in motion but their object will probably be both a small and a selfish one. I shall cheerfully send you a line as often as I have a subject for it, tho' I shall be so selfish as to hope for some return for it. I am Dr. Sir Yrs sincerely,   J. MADISON JR.

RC (DLC: Madison Papers); endorsed by TJ.

YOUR FAVOR . . . RICHMOND: TJ's letter, written just before he left Richmond on 22 Dec., has not been found. THE NEW SERVICE TO WHICH YOU WERE CALLED: TJ was elected to serve as a delegate to Congress on 30 Nov. 1781 and resigned the appointment on 19 Dec. (JHD, Oct. 1781, 1828 edn., p. 23,

49). The letter to TJ, together with one to the Governor of Virginia TRANSMITTED . . . BY A CAPT. IRISH, was that of 18 Nov. 1781; a LETTER FROM ME ENCLOSING A PROPOSITION DECLARATORY OF THE COERCIVE POWER OF CONGRESS was that from Madison to TJ, 16 Apr. 1781.

1 Blank in MS.

From Marbois

MONSIEUR   A Philadelphie le 29. Janvier 1782.

Il y a quelques jours que M. Charles Thompson me parla d'un ecrït contenant des reponses à des questions que j'ay pris la liberté de vous adresser l'année derniere, et me dit que vous desiriés que je lui en donnasse communication: Je l'aurois fait avec beaucoup d'empressement, Monsieur; mais elles ne me sont point parvenues quoiqu'il y ait deja quelque tems que M. Thompson m'en a parlé et que M. le Chevalier d'Annemours m'en a ecrit. Je ne puis vous exprimer combien je suis sensible à cette perte. Je desire que vous ayiés gardé une copie de ces reponses, et je l'espere: dans ce cas, je vous supplie d'avoir la bonté de me l'adresser par une voye sûre et d'être bien persuadé de toute ma reconnoissance: Elle est d'autant plus grande que je sais combien vos momens ont été et sont precieux et nous avons vu avec la plus grande satisfaction que vos compatriotes se sont empressés à le reconnoitre et à vous marquer la gratitude qu'ils ont des services que vous leur avés rendus pendant la durée de votre gouvernement.

Je suis avec respect, Monsieur, Votre très humble et très obéissant serviteur, DE MARBOIS

RC (ViWC).

Marbois' QUESTIONS . . . L'ANNEE DERNIERE may possibly have been repeated in his missing letter to TJ of 5 Feb. 1781 (see TJ to Marbois, 4 Mch. 1781), but they were first carried to TJ by Joseph Jones sometime before 30 Nov. 1780 (see TJ to D'Anmours 30 Nov. 1780 and preceding document). For an explanation of the delay of TJ's letter to Marbois of 20 Dec. 1781, see Ambler to TJ, 16 Mch. 1782, and TJ to Marbois, 24 Mch. 1782.

From Charles Bellini

SIGE. TOMMASO AMATISSMO. Dallo Spedale Febbio. 13. 1782

Il Sige. Gen'le Conte di Rochambeaux va a spasso per il Paese, ed è probabile ch'egli venga a Monticello, almeno Egli ne à l'intenzione; il Sige. Coleau, un uffiziale di rango nell' Armata lo accompagna, ed io non voglio perder l'occasione di rinnuovarle i miei più rispettosi Sentimenti, e ringraziarla dell' affettuosa Lettera ch' Ella si compiacque di scrivermi da Richmond in Data de' 23 Xbre. 1781. Io non ò espressioni bastanti per esprimere la consolazione che quella Lettera somministrò al mio spirito oppresso, e totalmente destituto d'ogni filosofico aiuto: S'io potessi avere una lettera simile ogni giorno, Non dubito ch'io potrei senza pena restare allo Spedale, e vedere con filosofica indifferenza le miserie della vita, da alcuni tanto desiderata.

Ella certamente avrà occasione di render un Servizio considerabile a questa, una volta Università in generale, ed al restante dei Professori in particolare, Se parlando col Sige. Generale Ella vorrà fargli sentire con quanta ingiustizia, per non dir barbarie, Noi Siamo Stati trattati, ed io più degli altri in particolare, Non per altro delitto che d'esser Straniero, Nobilmente povero, e privo di assistenza ed aiuto.

Se la nobil mia povertà, e l'aria pestifera ch'io son forzato di respirare non me l'impedi[scono] io Spero di venir io stesso a Monticello, per mai più partir[ne] e per contestarle ch'io Sono, di Lei, della Sua Sigra. Consorte e Famiglia universa, presente e futura. Divotissmo. ed Obbligatissmo. Servitra., C. BELLINI

RC (DLC). The editors are indebted to Prof. A. T. MacAllister, Jr., Princeton University, for a transcription of this letter, as well as for a translation on which the summary below is based.

Rochambeau is traveling about the country and intends to visit Monticello, accompanied by "Mr. Coleau," an officer in the army; Bellini takes this occasion to renew his friendship and to thank TJ for his letter from Richmond of 23 Dec. 1781. "I cannot adequately express the consolation which that letter administered to my spirit, oppressed and totally destitute of every philosophical aid. If I could have a letter like that every day, I don't doubt that I could remain in the Hospital without difficulty and view with philosophical indifference the miseries of life. . . ." Informs TJ that he can render the "once" university and the professors a great service if, in speaking to "the General," he can make him realize "with what injustice, not to say barbarity" they have been treated; Bellini especially, "for no other crime than for being a foreigner, nobly poor,

and deprived of aid and assistance." If his poverty and the "pestilential air" he is compelled to breathe do not prevent it, he hopes to visit Monticello.

The reference to MR. COLEAU is doubtless to Chastellux. THE HOSPITAL: That is, the College of William and Mary, where Bellini was professor of languages (WMQ, 1st ser., XV [1906-1907], p. 175, 265-6). The college had been in use as a hospital in 1781 (see George Wythe to TJ, 31 Dec. 1781). The "affectionate letter" that TJ wrote Bellini from Richmond on 23 Dec. 1781 has not been found. See also Bellini to TJ, 8 Apr. 1782.

The Case of Mace Freeland

I. JEFFERSON'S STATE OF THE CASE AND OPINION THEREON

II. PETITION OF MACE FREELAND TO THE GOVERNOR AND COUNCIL

III. PETITION OF MACE FREELAND TO THE HOUSE OF DELEGATES

15 February 1782

EDITORIAL NOTE

This case, along with others that came to him during 1782, reveals Jefferson as turning seriously to the practice of the law. Perhaps the fact that the case of Mace Freeland seemed to offer an opportunity to reinforce those "principles of moderation and justice which principally endear a republican government to it's citizens" may have induced him to accept it. At any rate on 12 Feb. 1782, when Freeland presented the facts, Jefferson made the following entry in his Account Book: "Mace Freeland's case. recd. 22/5¼ viz. a pistole for advice. (Buckingham)." Three days later the rough draft of the state of the case and opinion was completed. Freeland accepted the advice and commissioned Jefferson to draft the petitions that had been recommended. Apparently Jefferson made both the rough drafts and the fair copies on or about 23 Feb. 1782, for on that date another entry was made in the Account Book: "Mace Freeland, recd. of him for drawing 2 petitions 21/." Freeland signed the fair copies, one addressed to the Governor and Council and the other to the House of Delegates.

No manuscript or printed journal of the House of Delegates exists for the May 1782 session and the legislative history of this highly interesting case must therefore be pieced together from other sources. But these are sufficient to indicate that Mace Freeland was not the only claimant. From the clerk's docketing on the petition it is clear that Freeland's appeal was presented on 7 June and was referred to the committee on propositions and grievances. That committee reported back and found that it was "reasonable," which was equivalent to a recommendation that the petition be granted. Thereupon a snag appeared, and the petition was ordered to be recommitted. The committee reported again, its recommendation was approved, a bill was drawn, and it presumably passed both houses without further ado. From the docketing on the petition and from the Act as adopted it is easy enough to discover what the snag was. It appears that Mace Freeland, uncle of the unfortunate Robert Williams, had a sister named Spice Pendleton. She obviously desired a share in Williams' residuary claim to the estate and presumably filed her petition. It further appears that Robert Williams had cohabited with one Elizabeth Jones and "by her left issue." The evidence for the statement that "the said Robert Williams was engaged to be married" to Elizabeth Jones is lacking, but it must have been sufficient to convince the General Assembly, for its unqualified assertion as a fact became law (Hening, xi, 65). Presumably Elizabeth Jones also had filed a petition. In any event, the bill as finally drawn and as passed vested title in the entire real and personal estate of James Freeland, "whether in possession or remainder," equally in Mace Freeland, Spice Pendleton, and Elizabeth Jones. The life interest of Mary Williams, mother of the suicide Robert Williams, was not drawn in question and presumably she continued to enjoy her use of the estate during her widowhood. There is no evidence in the journals of the Council that Freeland presented the petition to that body.

I. Jefferson's State of the Case and Opinion thereon

Monticello Feb. 15. 1782.

James Freeland having cohabited with Mary Williams and by her had issue a son Robert Williams, and having afterwards intermarried with the said Mary, made his last will and testament bearing date the 14th of Mar. 1770. duly proved and recorded and therein lent[1] to his wife Mary for her life or widowhood all his estate real and personal, consisting of lands, slaves and mere personalties and after her death or marriage gave it to the said Robert Williams in fee. The testator died. Robert Williams became felo de se during the life of the widow leaving neither wife nor child. And the question is What goes with the estate?

The remainder to Robert Williams was a vested remainder[2] and therefore capable of transmission to his heirs had he had any (1. Salk. 237, ib. 224). But a doubt is expressed whether, as having been a bastard, he could have any heirs? And if he could, whether the transmission to them be not cut off by the felony committed on himself? With respect to the latter question, a felo de se does not forfeit his lands of inheritance, and this by the rules of the common law, and by our act of assembly of 1727 slaves are not forfeitable except in cases where lands are subject to forfeiture. Therefore they are not forfeitable for a felony de se. But all his other chattels real and personal are forfeited for this cause. In answer to the former part of the question Whether Robt. Williams could have any heirs I observe that a bastard being deemed in law the child of nobody can have no heir who is obliged to derive his descent through the blood of the father[3] or mother. That is, he can have no collateral heir: but heirs of his body he may have. However the bastard in the present case having none such, his lands of inheritance whether in possession[4] or remainder are escheated to the commonwealth for defect of blood.[5] As the bastard can have no heirs but of his body to claim the inheritance of his lands, so is he denied relations, except they be of his body, to claim his personal estate. (Jones v. Goodchild 3. P.W. 33). Under our former government therefore the king became entitled to his personal estate and by letters patent granted it to such person as he thought proper and administration was thereupon granted to the patentee, Manning v. Napp, 1. Salk. 37. Under our present government the commonwealth becomes entitled instead of the king to the personal estate[6] in such a case. As to the slaves a doubt may be raised on the proviso of the act of assembly of 1705, declaring that slaves shall not escheat on the death of a person without lawful heirs but that in that case they shall be accounted and go as chattels and other personal estate. But to me this proviso appears to carry a contradiction [. . .] in itself and therefore to be nugatory for I know no instance wherein lands of inheritance are liable to escheat but [not?] the personal [estate which?] goes to the public also. When therefore the first member of the proviso says that slaves shall not escheat, and the second that they shall in that case go as personal estate, it is saying first that they shall not go to the commonwealth, and then that they shall. If however we must give some meaning to this proviso I should suppose it would be extended only to the cases of persons convicted of capital crimes where it might be allowed to revive the rights of relations in these instances wherein the law acknowleges such relations to exist but I do not think it should be further extended to the double of effect first of creating a relations heir between a bastard and his collaterals contrary to one fundamental principle and then in opposition to another to give to those collaterals his personal estate.[7]

Upon the whole then my opinion is that the lands, slaves and personalties of Robert Williams whether in possession or remainder are become the property of the commonwealth for defect of heirs and next of kin to him.

As to the lands, the act of May 1779 concerning Escheators has made it a duty in the escheator of the county to proceed to have the escheat found by inquest, to return that inquest to the General court where after it shall have laid one year without traverse he is to proceed to sell them to the highest bidder. But I think there has been[8] one instance where on escheat from an alien and application to the General assembly they have granted the lands to a relation of the decedent, and would therefore advise Mr. Mace Freeland uncle to Robert Williams on the side of the father[9] to apply to the assembly for a grant of them, and to rest his application on the ground of natural relationship, but more especially on that of the lands having been[10] originally the inheritance of his house.

As to the slaves and personal estate, no cases have arisen under the present government to determine whether the Executive may by letters patent grant either the property or care of them to any one, or whether the application must be to the assembly. I would therefore advise a petition to the Executive for such letters patent, and that the petition to the assembly before recommended be extended to the slaves and personalties also.   TH: J.

Dft (DLC); much revised and inter-lined, some of the more important alterations being indicated below.

THE ACT OF MAY 1779 CONCERNING ESCHEATORS was drawn by TJ, as was its predecessor of 1777 (see Vol. 2: 168-71, 279-85).

[1] TJ wrote "gave" and then deleted it, interlining the word "lent."

[2] TJ wrote "sufficient . . . had he died a natural death to transmit" and then deleted the words.

[3] TJ first wrote "which is obliged to derive his line of descent through a father or mother" and then altered the words to read as above.

[4] TJ first wrote "reversion" after the word "possession" and then deleted it.

[5] TJ first wrote and then deleted: "but it is not so as to his slaves."

[6] At this point TJ added the words: "of such a person, but no cases have arisen to settle the question whether the Executive may issue letters patent disposing of the personal property or whether [. . .]" and then altered the passage to conclude the sentence as above.

[7] This passage interpreting the effect of the Act of 1705 appears to have given TJ more difficulty than any other part of the case, if one is to judge by the number of alterations, interlineations, and marginal revisions. It would needlessly complicate the presentation of the text to attempt to follow these many revisions, none of which seems to vary in important particulars from the final version.

[8] TJ first wrote: "I have known one instance" and then altered the clause to read as above.

[9] TJ first wrote and then deleted: "[. . .] by whom the lands came."

[10] TJ first wrote and then deleted "[. . .] transmitted from his father."

II. Petition of Mace Freeland to the Governor and Council

To his Excellency Benjamin Harrison esq. Governor of the Commonwealth of Virginia and the honourable the Council of state the Petition of Mace Freeland of the county of Buckingham humbly sheweth

That James Freeland your petitioner's father being seised and possessed of a considerable estate in lands slaves and personalties, and having issue James Freeland your petitioner's elder brother by one venter, and your petitioner by another devised to the said James Freeland your petitioner's brother a considerable part of his estate, and died; that the said James Freeland had cohabitation with a certain Mary Williams, and by her had issue Robert Williams, after which he intermarried with the said Mary; that the said James by his last will and testament bearing date the 14th. of Mar. 1770. devised to his said wife his whole estate real and personal for her life or widowhood, and the remainder after her death to the said Robert Williams his natural son, in fee; that the said Robert Williams hath lately become Felo de se, leaving neither wife, nor issue of his body; that for want of such issue (as your petitioner is advised that no others[1] are acknowledged by the law as heirs or next of kin to a bastard) the slaves and personalties of the said Robert Williams in possession and remainder are escheated to, and vested in the Commonwealth; that your petitioner hath been advised that under the British government it was usual for the crown, in mitigation of the rigours of the law, to regrant by letters patent such property as had lapsed by the misfortunes of individuals to the families from which the property had been derived; that your petitioner, under such usage, would have obtained a grant, as standing in the place of uncle, heir, and next of kin on that side from which the estate came, that is to say, on the part of the father of the decedent; that your petitioner hath been further advised that under the present form of government the disposal of confiscated chattels is in your Excellency and your honors,[2] and hopes it will appear to you that the rigourous laws of escheat and forfeiture, invented by a spirit of rapine and hostility of princes towards their subjects in the most bar[barous][3] times, and relinquished in practice by them in later and more humanized ages will be thought inconsistent with the principles of moderation and justice which principally endear a republican government to it's citizens; and that

[155]

these ruling principles will proscribe the idea of supplying by the misfortunes of individuals those fiscal necessities, which being incurred for the good of all, it is most just and most politic should be raised by equal contributions on all.

Your petitioner therefore humbly prays that your Excellency and your honours will be pleased to regrant to him by letters patents[4] the slaves and personalties of his said nephew Robert Williams in possession and remainder and your petitioner as in duty bound shall ever pray &c.   MACE FREELAND

MS (Vi); entirely in the hand of TJ; signed by Mace Freeland; endorsed by TJ: "Petition to the Governour"; and in another hand: "From Mace Freeman [*sic*]." Dft (DLC); endorsed by TJ: "Freeland's case. Bastard. his heirs. Escheat. lands. slaves. Distribution. Felo de se. Forfeiture. Lands. slaves. personalties."

[1] TJ, evidently copying from the fair copy of the petition to the House of Delegates, wrote at this point: "can be heirs to a bastard (the estate of the said Robert Williams" and then deleted the line.

[2] In Dft TJ first wrote: "your petitioner doth not know whether under the present form of government the exercise of this power resides in the hands of the Executive, but that if it does," and then altered the passage to read as above.

[3] With this word TJ came to the end of page one, wrote "bar-," and then forgot to close the word at the top of page two.

[4] The words "the remainder in" were interlined at this point and then erased, the subsequent words "in possession and remainder" then being interlined in turn.

III. Petition of Mace Freeland to the House of Delegates

To the honourable the Speaker and the House of Delegates the petition of Mace Freeland of the county of Buckingham humbly sheweth

That James Freeland, your petitioner's father being seised and possessed of a considerable estate in lands slaves and personalties, and having issue James Freeland your petitioner's elder brother by one venter, and your petitioner by another, devised to the said James Freeland your petitioner's brother a considerable part of his estate and died; that the said James Freeland had cohabitation with a certain Mary Williams, and by her had issue Robert Williams after which he intermarried with the said Mary; that the said James by his last will and testament bearing date the 14th. of Mar. 1770 devised to his said wife his whole estate real and personal for her life or widowhood, and the remainder after her death to the said Robert Williams, his natural son, in fee; that the said Robert Williams hath lately become Felo de se, leaving neither wife nor issue of his body; that for want of such issue (as your petitioner is advised that no other can be heir or next of kin to a bastard) the estate of the said Robert Williams in lands, slaves, and personalties, whether in possession or remainder, is escheated and transferred to the Commonwealth; that your petitioner is further advised that under the British government, it was usual for the Crown, in mitigation of the rigour of the law, to make restitution of estates which had lapsed by the misfortunes of individuals, to the families from which they were derived; that accordingly King Charles the second, by his charter to the colony of Virginia, bearing date the 10th. day of Octob. in the 28th. year of his reign had converted into a right what had been before a matter of grace, by granting "that all lands possessed by any subject inhabiting in Virginia which should escheat to him his heirs or successors, should and might be enjoyed by such inhabitant or possessor his heirs and assigns for ever, paying the usual composition." That in execution of this charter it had been a rule of government to issue[1] a new grant to such of the relations of the deceased as would have stood in the place of heir had there been no corruption of blood, or want of inheritable blood, and to consider such person in possession under the charter as ought in justice to be in possession; under which charter and rule of construction your petitioner would have been entitled to a grant of the said estate of Robert Williams, as standing in the place of uncle and heir of the part of the father from whom, and from your petitioner's father the said estate moved; that your petitioner understands that the Escheator of the county, under the act of assembly concerning Escheators is proceeding to find an office as to the said estate in possession and remainder in order to institute a sale of the same to the highest bidder; that your petitioner humbly hopes that the rigourous laws of escheat and forfeiture invented by the spirit of rapine and hostility of princes towards their subjects in the most barbarous times will be thought inconsistent with the principles of moderation, justice and perfect equality which principally endear a republican government to it's citizens; that these ruling principles will proscribe the idea of supplying by the misfortunes of individuals those fiscal expences which being incurred for the good of all, it is most just and most politic should be raised by the equal contributions of all; and especially that our new and happy form of government will not be ushered in by the destruction of rights restored to us and rendered sacred even by an arbitrary government, and which reason, generosity and humanity concur to establish.[2]

Your petitioner therefore humbly prays that you will be pleased to pass an act for vesting in your petitioner the said estates of his said nephew Robert Williams whether in possession or remainder and your petitioner as in duty bound shall ever pray &c.

MACE FREELAND

MS (Vi); entirely in the hand of TJ; signed by Freeland; endorsed in TJ's hand: "Petition to the House of Delegates"; docketed in hand of John Beckley: "Mace Freelands petition June 7th 1782. Referred to [committee on] propositions [and grievances]. (reasonable) recommitted. report drawn to vest Estate in Mace Freeland Spice Pendleton and Eliza. Jones—bill drawn." Dft (DLC); with numerous deletions and interlineations.

¹ TJ first wrote in Dft: "it had been a rule with the privy council to advise" and then altered the passage to read as above.

² This latter part of this paragraph, beginning with the words "that your petitioner humbly hopes," was originally phrased as follows in Dft, and then altered by TJ to read as above: "that your petitioner considers it as inconsistent with the spirit of our new and happy change of government to take from it's citizens any rights which were made sacred under a more arbitrary form of government and which reason generosity and humanity concur in establishing; and that the magnanimity of a Commonwealth will be far from striving to [. . .] supply by the total ruin of individuals those expenses which being incurred for all, it is most politic and most just should be produced by the equal contributions of all."

From Harry Innes

Dr Sir

Bedford Feby. 18th. 1782

Your favor of the 3d. Instant came safe to hand yesterday and I can not forbear returning you my most grateful thanks for the particular manner in which you answered my Letter of Novr. I am again going to mention something farther in behalf of those people who wish to contest the Titles of Patton's and Buchannan's Representatives, and in this I am encouraged by your polite and freindly Letter from Richmond of Decr. 15th.

On serious reflection on the case before the receipt of your last favor I was inclined to think that as the Grantees had complied apparently with all the requisitions of Government for obtaining Titles to Lands, that the several Claimants would be defeated in a prosecution before the Court of Chancery upon this principle, of having suffered the Grantees and their Representatives to obtain Decrees quietly before the Court of Appeals. But quæ. whether it might not be adviseable to address the Assembly on this head and get an Amendatory Act to direct the Court of Appeals to reconsider their Decrees in this instance, for certain it is, they were surprised into their determination, for the Claimants tho' settled on the Land were never summoned to contest the matter before the Court by the Representatives of the Grantees, nor did they even know that such a Law existed till the matter was determined; Or whether the Legislature on having the matter fairly investigated before them and the many frauds and abuses which were commited by Patton and Buchannan, proved, quash the whole of their Pattents and Grants by an express Law for that purpose.

I am induced to be thus far troublesome to you Sir, for two reasons, 1st. as an Attorney who wishes for the best information on so important a point, and 2dly as a freind to the oppressed and injured, reasons which I hope will be a sufficient Appology for my petulance on this subject.

An answer delivered to the bearer Mr. Allison on his return from Doctor Walker's would meet with a ready convayance.

I am Dr. Sir with respect & esteem Your mo. ob.

HARRY INNES

RC (DLC); addressed to TJ, "Albemarle"; endorsed by TJ.

Innes' LETTER OF NOVR. 1781 has not been found, nor have TJ's two letters to Innes of 15 Dec. 1781 and 3 Feb. 1782. On 29 Sep. 1779 Innes was appointed a commissioner by TJ to determine claims to unpatented lands and in the same year was appointed escheator for Bedford co. (DAB; see Vol. 2: 158-61; TJ's commission to Innes was sold 21 Mch. 1911, Item 171, by the Merwin-Clayton Sales Co., Cleveland, Ohio, but has not been found).

From George Rogers Clark

DEAR SIR   Louisville Feby 20th 1782

I Received your favor by Colo. Boon. I am unhappy that it hath been out of my power to procure you those Curiosities you want except a large thigh Bone that dont please me being broke. I expect to get the whole this spring as a strong post is to be fixed at the mouth of Licking Creek within a small distance of the place. Parties Marching by, I shall have the largest and fairest got—a Thigh and Jaw Bone Grinders and Tusk. The Animal had no foreteeth that I could ever discover and by no means Carnivorious as many suppose. You may be assur'd that I shall embrace the first opportunity to get them and have them Convey'd to some part of the Frontier Convenient to you. Their is very Curious Shells found in many parts of this Cuntry. I shall send you a few of them. Nothing of this nature escape me am anxious of being possessd of your Sentiments Respecting the big bones, what those Animals ware and how they Came into this part of the Globe. I am nearly Satisfied myself but expect to be more So. You scarcely ride a day through many parts of the Western Cuntry but you meet with Some Curious work of Antiquity, the Cituation of the Cuntries whare they are found Respecting Each other fully Evince the uses they ware for, and the powerfull nations that Inhabited those Regions and make no doubt but those Beasts ware in being at that time as the great number of bones found only at that particular Spot and their preservation to the present time I think very easily accounted for by any penetrating Eye that view the place. I hope that you think me worthy of a Correspondence and favour me as such during my Stay in the back Cuntry which I am determind shall be as short as possible. I cant with propriety leave it at present nor can I be easy untill I see some of those my cuntrymen that speak so loudly of what they are pleasd to call Quixotic Scheams. I shall recommend it to them to learn a little more of the Geografy of their own Cuntry and its true Interests before they presume to Speak so frely for the future. I am Sr. with Esteem your Hbl Servt.,   G R Clark

RC (MHi).

From Isaac Zane

Dear sir   Marlbro' Iron Works Feby. 25th. 1782.

I was favor'd with yours of the 24th of decemr. last while in Phila. and should have acknowledg'd it, had opportunity Offered. I was heartily pleased to see that justice done you, at the last session which I would feign have done in June last. But probably all is for the best, and Slander reproved. I should have been happy to have accompanied the bearer Mr. Charles Logan to Albemarle, but my long indisposition, and absence, has so disconcerted affairs that it will take much assiduity to have them reclaimed to their former order. No visit would be more gratefully received at Marlbro', than one from Th. J. If probable to be, I pray let me know when it may be expected, and no attention shall be wanting. Mr. Logan is a grandson to the noted James Logan of Pensila. [Pennsylvania] and son to the late honble. W. Logan. He married the heires of the Pleasants family, is now on his way to his possessions by his Wife, any civillity shewn him will be esteemed as done your most respectful & Affectionate friend,   Isaac Zane

RC (DLC).

From D'Anmours

Dr Sir   Baltimore feby. 27. 1782.

The Bearer hereof is Col. Ternan of armand's Legion. As an intimate friend of mine, I beg leave to introduce him to the honour of your acquaintance. His hobby-horse is like mine, natural history; But speaks also very well upon Every other subjects, so as to mistake them for so many hobby-horses. I Recommend him to the fate every man of merit meets with at *monte-cielo*.

I have been obliged to leave Richmond without pursuing the Plan I had formed to visit you and Mrs. Jefferson in albermarle. I very often do those things I wish not to do, and leave undone those I have most at heart; therefore the lord have mercy upon me; But Like Stern I am merely led By Circumstances. I hope next Spring I will be able to make that agreable trip.

I Send you a Couple of news-papers that Contain all the news we have. By Calculation, there is about two hundred ships of the line, and two hundred thousand men at Sea Ready to Knock down one another. The Party that will have the Blessing of Destroying a Larger part of the human Race, will, to be sure, thank very devoutly the Supreme Being for that Great Good luck. And yet all this happens between the politest, and more civilized nations of the Globe, the Chiefs of which are at Versailles, L'Escurial and St. James Dancing and frolicking as Deliberately as if they were not the principal Causes of all that havock.

On my way here I Call'd at Col. mercer, who now is Become a Compleat farmer. This piece of news is for Mrs. Jefferson, who will Scarce believe it. Yet Madam, nothing is truer. By his present appearance you Could never guess that he was once one of the first-Rate-Beaux. Red coats, Gold frogs, Gold and Silver embroider'd Jackets, Powder, Puffs, Smelling Bottles, &c. all is vanished. And if you, now and then, see some Remains of them, they appear Like the Ruins of those ancient magnificent cities, which serve to show what they once were: indeed the Reformation is as Compleat as Can be imagined.

Col. ternan who is just mounting his horse Leaves me only time to assure you of the sincere sentiments of everlasting attachement with which I am Dear Sir & Madam Yr mst obdt & hble servt,

LE CHEVR D'ANMOURS

RC (DLC); endorsed by TJ: "D'Anmour Chevelr."

COL. TERNAN: Jean, Chevalier de Ternant, who had been associated with the American army in various capacities, was taken prisoner at Charleston in May

1780, and exchanged in Jan. 1782. Ternant was appointed French minister to the United States in 1791 (Lasseray, *Les français sous les treize étoiles*).

From David Jameson

DR. SIR   Richmond Mch 7. 1782

I inclose you the Revenue Act and the act for Specific's passed last Session. By the former the old Specific law is repealed and the exemption done away and not revived in the last.

You say nothing of the Mule. I hope you received it safe. with the highest esteem I am Dr Sir Yr obt hb Servt,

DAVID JAMESON

RC (DLC); TJ's draft of his letter to Overton Carr, 16 Mch. 1782, q.v., is written on the blank pages of Jameson's letter. Enclosures (missing): Copies of "An act for ascertaining certain taxes and duties, and for establishing a permanent revenue" and "An act for laying taxes in certain enumerated commodities" (Hening, x, 501-17; 490-2).

The two Acts sent by Jameson must have been requested by TJ in a letter in which he failed to say anything of the MULE; no such letter, if written, has been found. Mules were rare in America at this time, but there is apparently no evidence to show that TJ shared Washington's great enthusiasm for that hybrid.

From Philip Mazzei

Florence, 8 Mch. 1782. Five months have elapsed since the capitulation of Cornwallis and several vessels have arrived in France which sailed from America after that event; does not complain of being neglected before that time but is "greatly disappointed and mortified" by the present silence. Recapitulates the substance of his earlier dispatches; has received no financial aid; has lived too long on his own credit; his "honour is at stake." "I only ask for an ostensible letter (conceivd in a manner as to rise no doubts in regard to the possibility of paying the annual interest of the Loan) with which I think that I could be supplied as I have often said, by this sovereign, whose friendship for us is great, and whose partial curiosity I had the mortification never to be able to satisfy with direct american news, which is the first thing he asks every time he sees me. But in case it should be resolved otherwise, I must beg the favor of an immediate remittance, to enable me to discharge with honour my engagements in Europe, and to return to my home." Encloses "3 of the pieces I have written in Europe concerning our American affairs. They are those which have made the deeper and more general impression in our favour."

RC (DLC: Mazzei Papers); 4 p.; at head of text: "31 [i.e., dispatch No. 31] 2d. Copy"; in a clerk's hand, with complimentary close, signature, and "His Eccelly. Ths. Jefferson Govr. of Virginia" in Mazzei's hand; printed in Marraro, *Mazzei*, p. 96-100; Garlick,

Mazzei, p. 73-7. The enclosed "pieces" have not been precisely identified but they are probably the same as those mentioned in Mazzei's letter to Madison, 15 Mch. 1782 (Garlick, *Mazzei*, p. 79).

On 31 Jan. 1782 Gov. Benjamin Harrison wrote Mazzei: "The Assembly have passed a Resolution directing the Executive to discharge from Office such of their Servants as are not absolutely necessary and to adopt the most rigid Economy in the disposal of public Monies . . . in obedience to which order many valuable Officers have been reduced. . . . You will not therefore I presume take it amiss that you should share in this general regulation, particularly when you reflect that no advantage has hitherto arisen to the State from your appointment nor none likely to arise in future. You will therefore consider yourself as henceforth discharged from the service of the State. I cannot however be the instrument of that recall without returning you the thanks of the Executive for your good intentions towards us." On 26 Apr. 1782 Mazzei wrote Harrison that he was greatly humiliated by not being informed that a change in the governorship had taken place, and on 6 Sep. 1782 acknowledged Harrison's letter of 31 Jan. 1782 (*Official Letters*, III, 142; Marraro, *Mazzei*, p. 100, 101).

From Charles Thomson

DEAR SIR   Philadelphia March 9. 1782

I received the letter which you did me the honor to write on the 20 of December last, and immediately waited on Mr. Marbois who informs me that he has not received the Answers you refer to.

I am ashamed to acknowledge that I am as ignorant as you declare yourself to be of the particular duties of a counsellor of the American philosophical society, although I have been honored with that appointment.

With regard to the institution of the society I can inform you that it has for its object the improvement of useful knowledge more particularly what relates to this new world. It comprehends the whole circle of arts, science and discoveries especially in the natural world and therefore I am presuaded your answers to Mr. Marbois queries will be an acceptable present.

This Country opens to the philosophic view an extensive, rich and unexplored field. It abounds in roots, plants, trees and minerals, to the virtues and uses of which we are yet strangers. What the soil is capable of producing can only be guessed at and known by experiment. Reasoning from Analogy we may suppose that all the rich productions of Asia may in time be transplanted hither. Agriculture is in its infancy. The human mind seems just awakening from a long stupor of many ages to the discovery of useful Arts and inventions. Our governments are yet unformed and capable of great improvements in police, finance and commerce. The history, manners and customs of the Aborigines are but little known. These and a thousand other subjects which will readily suggest themselves open an inexhaustible mine to men of a contemplative and philosophical turn. And therefore though I regret your retiring from the busy anxious scenes of politics, yet I congratulate posterity on the Advantages they may derive from your philosophical researches. I am with sincere esteem and Affection Your Most obedient and Most humble Servt.,   CHAS. THOMSON

RC (DLC). Dft (DLC: Thomson Papers). Dft is identical in substance with RC, but interlineations, substitution of words, and the rearrangement of a sentence, which are not noted here, indicate that Thomson revised his original draft with great care before preparing the fair copy.

From Arthur Lee

DEAR SIR   Philadelphia March 13th. 1782

In your retird situation it will not I hope be disagreable to you to hear what is going on at this place.

You will see in what state our western Country rests in Congress, by the Extract that I shall subjoin. The report has not been taken up because the Enemy think they shall acquire an accession of strength, by their usual arts, and by the admission of Vermont, as a state. On our part, not being strong enough to give it a final dismission, we can only watch their motions, and act on the defensive. I doubt whether Vermont will be admitted. The publication of the names of all the Adventurers in these land Companies, woud I conceive greatly lessen their influence by showing that they are interested, Jo[hns]on, Chase and Carroll, who have committed Maryland into a quarrel with Virginia on this subject, are among them. But I shall bring authenticated Copies of them to the next Session of Assembly, when I suppose this question will be fully discussd. I hope you will be in the House. My Brother R. H. will be in the House of Delegates, and, I believe, Col. G. Mason. Should you see the Attorney, with whom this goes, he will give you a full and satisfactory account of this business, as he has with great diligence and discernment collected and digested all the arguments relating to it. My Colleagues seem to me to be as faithful to, and watchful over, the interests of our Country as you can possibly wish.

The latest news from France says that the fleet and Convoy destind for the W. Indies, after the british fleet had taken some of the transports, were obliged by a storm to return to port much injurd. The beginning of Feby. they were ready to sail again. Rodney with 12 Ships, saild for the W. I. the 10th of Jany. It is said St. Kitts is taken, but we have no authentic account of that or of the engagement between de Grasse and Hood. I beg my respects to your Lady, & have the honor to be with the greatest esteem, dear Sir Yr. Most Obedt. Servt.,   A. LEE

RC (DLC). Enclosure (DLC): "Extract from a report of a Committee (Mrs. Boudinott, Jenifer, Livermore, Smith & Varnum) on the Western Lands, read Nov. 3d. 1781." Although the report was presented on 3 Nov. 1781 it was postponed, and is printed in the *Journals* under date of 1 May 1782, when it was considered. The extract enclosed in Lee's letter includes that portion of the report which states the reasons of the committee for not accepting "the cession proposed to be made by the State of Virginia" or guaranteeing "the tract of country claimed by them in their act of cession" (JCC, XXII, 227-8).

THE ATTORNEY was Attorney General Edmund Randolph, who left Philadelphia after 18 Mch. (see Madison to TJ of that date).

From Jacquelin Ambler

DEAR SIR   Richmond March 16. 1782.

When you left the letters with me you seemed desirous that more attention should be paid to safety than dispatch in the conveyance of the two larger ones: I was not so particular therefore in forwarding the smaller letters, but reserved those for the President of Congress and Monsr. Marbois to be sent by some hand that would not fail to deliver them safely. Several Weeks elapsing and none such casting up, I was exceedingly uneasy, and asked the favor of Mr. Jameson, who is personally known to Count Rochambeau, to inclose and recommend them to him to be forwarded: not doubting but they would go with much greater certainty by one of the Counts Couriers than by any of the express riders from hence. The Count politely wrote in answer that he had sent them by a trusty Messenger. I assure you I was very unhappy for their long detention, and lament that I did not think of the Count sooner. Mr. Short left Richmond a few hours before your favor reached me, or I should certainly have written by him. Being obliged to attend the Board, I had not the pleasure of seeing him when he called at our House, but had desired Mrs. Ambler to inform him how I had sent the letters. She forgot to do so it seems. Be pleased to present our respectful Compliments to your Lady and believe me Dear Sir with very great esteem Your Friend & Servt.,   J: AMBLER

RC (DLC). Ambler's letter was enclosed in TJ to Marbois, 24 Mch. 1782, q.v.

The present letter was doubtless in response to a letter of inquiry from TJ to Ambler (YOUR FAVOR) written after he had received Marbois' letter to him of 29 Jan. 1782, but no such letter from TJ to Ambler has been found. THE TWO LARGER ONES: These were the letters of 20 Dec. 1781 to McKean and Marbois, with their fairly bulky enclosures. THE SMALLER LETTERS have not been identified, though one of them was certainly TJ's letter of 20 Dec. 1781 to Charles Thomson (see TJ to Marbois, 24 Mch. 1781).

To Overton Carr

I take the liberty of addressing you on the subject of the common trust confided to us by our deceased friend Mr. D. Carr, the others who were joined with us in that sacred charge having either declined it or been withdrawn by death. My avocations from every thing of a private nature left of course the management of the interests of the estate on my sister, in which she was greatly aided by Mr. Sam Carr while he lived. These have been conducted I beleive as well as they might be. Order and œconomy have been observed, and indeed they were necessary to support so numerous a family on so moderate an income. The girls, three in number, are now become marriageable and of course require to be clothed more expensively than at any earlier period. This being done, the taxes to government paid and mere necessaries provided for the rest of the family you may readily conceive that little or nothing remains for the education of the boys. The estate may be pronounced incompetent to this purpose, and the boys, of very hopeful genius, must be abandoned to nature, and lost to themselves their families and their country unless their friends will take them by the hand.[1] I knew intimately the value which their father justly set on the blessings of science, the schemes for their education which he had fondly anticipated, and how vitally he would have been distressed could he have imagined that his own untimely fate and incompetence of fortune would leave them to that barbarism which of all things he most abhorred. I know too what he would have done for us had our lots been changed. These considerations have induced me to write to you, for whom I think he had more affection and in whom he placed more confidence than in any other person living, to apprize you of the situation of his estate and family and the advancing age of the boys, circumstances which distance of place would probably keep from your notice. I have taken the eldest son upwards of a twelvemonth past, bestowed on him while in public life the few moments I had to spare, and latterly have been able to pay more attention to him. He is reading Virgil, will shortly begin French and gives me great expectations that my attentions will not be lost on him. I have not been without hopes that you might be able to reconcile to yourself the same cares of the second, whom, that no time might be lost while I should consult you on his behalf, I have also taken, have carried him thro' his grammar and about half through Cordery. By the time the third shall be ready for beginning the Latin I think Peter will be so far advanced as that under my eye, and with some additional trouble to me I shall be able to take care of him also. They are all going to be inoculated within about a fortnight, after which should such be your pleasure Sam may with safety wait on you. I am sure you will be so kind as to send me a line on this subject and to advise me what you can do or think best to be done; as it will not be in my power to take care of the three. Mr. Maury at Fredericksbg. will be the most likely channel of conveyance for a letter; tho' even thro' him it will not be so certain as I could wish. The inclosed letter to Mr. Stone being of considerable consequence to me give me leave to ask your particular care of it. I am Sir with very great esteem & respect your mo. ob. & mo hble servt.

Dft (DLC); with numerous deletions and corrections, only one of which is noted below; written on the verso of David Jameson to TJ, 7 Mch. 1782; endorsed by TJ on the recto of Jameson's letter: "Carr, Overton." Enclosure: TJ to Thomas Stone, same date, following.

CORDERY: *The Colloquies of Corderius*, familiarly known as the Cordery in English (and presumably colonial) schools. Overton Carr was Dabney Carr's brother who had moved to Maryland; apparently two of Dabney's sons married two of Overton's daughters (VMHB, V [1897-1898], 441).

[1] TJ first wrote and then deleted at this point: "from a ⟨sense⟩ remembrance of the precious worth of their father, a sense of the distress which he would have felt could he have foreseen ⟨that neither his industry nor frugality⟩ ⟨could⟩ ⟨had secured a sufficiency to give his sons that education of which he so⟩ ⟨much⟩ ⟨well knew the worth nor his merit provided friends⟩ the fatal loss to them which his untimely fate would produce, and that neither his fortune nor friends would rescue those."

To Thomas Stone

DEAR SIR   Monticello Mar. 16. 1782.

You will probably be surprised at the receipt of a letter from one who has been so long withdrawn from your notice, but who still retains a proper sense of that worth with which his service with you in Congress brought him acquainted. There resides within the limits of your state a Mr. Overton Carr, formerly of this country, whose opinions, or conduct, or some other circumstances have unfortunately exposed him to the censures of your government. I knew this gentleman at a very early period of his life and then formed a good opinion of his abilities and worth. What his political tenets may have become in the present contest I am unapprized though report strengthened by some knolege of the connections he formed in your state makes them not favourable to us. He is of a family here very numerous and as remarkeable for their integrity as their zealous whiggism. But, which more particularly calls my attention to him, he had a brother, the dearest friend I possessed on earth, who had every excellence which good sense, learning, or virtue could give, who entertained a most particular affection for this gentleman, whose affections, were every other motive withdrawn, I feel myself religiously bound to respect, and whose memory is still revered in this country as having been one of the earliest and most distinguished leaders in the opposition to British tyranny. Give me leave therefore, influenced by these motives, so far to avail myself of the acquaintance I had the pleasure to contract with you, as to bring the case of this gentleman under your notice, and sollicit you to procure for him all those indulgencies which shall not be inconsistent with the safety of your state or that of our common cause. Our independance is now too far matured to be endangered by the feeble whisperings of an obscure individual, and I am sure if this gentleman has not sinned very seriously, your state would rather find in him an object for it's magnanimity than it's vengeance. If however his disposition be not only malignant but marked with any peculiar spirit of enterprize, if indulgences to him be really inconsistent with the public safety (for I am totally uninformed as to all the particulars of his conduct) I shall be forced however reluctantly to estimate these circumstances as superseding all motives of private duty in me, and as obliging me to withdraw my intercession for him.[1] Otherwise I cannot but commit him to your patronage and beg you to interest yourself for him as far as in conscience you think you can, which will add a new motive for the great esteem & regard with which I have the honour to be Dr. Sir your most obedt. & most hble servt.

P.S. Tho' for want of another opportunity I send this letter through the hands of Mr. Carr, yet I have not apprized him of it's object that no new disappointment may add to his sufferings.

Dft (DLC); endorsed by TJ: "Stone Mr of Maryland." The first name of the recipient has been assigned from internal evidence; Thomas Stone served with TJ in Congress in 1776 (Burnett, *Letters of Members*, II, p. 1).

On 2 Mch. 1781 the Maryland Council ordered Overton Carr and Garland Callis arrested and brought before Council, with their papers, to "be dealt with according to Law," since there was good reason to believe that their "general Conduct and Conversation" tended to encourage and spread "Dissatisfaction and Disaffection amongst the Subjects [*sic*] of this State" and their example and influence were therefore prejudicial to the interest of the state (*Maryland Archives*, XLV, 336). On 4 Jan. 1782 the following action was taken by the Council: "Whereas Overton Carr of Prince Georges County, did on the 16 Day of March 1781 enter into Bond with this Board in the penal Sum of two thousand pounds gold or Silver, that he would not depart the County . . . without leave being first obtained of the Governor and Council. Be it known . . . that from a change of Circumstances it is no longer deemed necessary to confine Mr. Carr . . . and he is therefore to go at large and to remove from place to place as Business or Inclination may prompt him . . ." (same, XLVIII, 39).

1 The following passage was first written and then deleted at this point: "and to be considered by you as no longer his intercessor . . . in this case I wish him to remain uninformed of my having."

From James Madison

DEAR SIR   Philada. March 18th. 1782

In my last to you on the subject of the map in the hands of Dr. Smith I informed you of the little chance of getting a copy of it for you. Nothing has since occurred which affords the least expectation from that quarter. But I have met with a bundle of old pamphlets belonging to the public Library here in which is a map published in 1650 which from this and other circumstances I am pretty confident is of the same impression with that of Doctr. Smith's. It represents the South sea at about 10 days travel from the heads or falls I forget which of James River. From the tenor however of the pamphlet to which it is immediately annexed and indeed of the whole collection there is just ground to suspect that this representation was an artifice to favor the object of the publications which evidently was to entice emigrants from England by a flattering picture of the advantages of this Country, one of which dwelt on in all the pamphlets is the vicinity of the S. Sea, and the facility it afforded of a trade with the Eastern World. Another circumstance which lessens much the value of this map to the Antiquary is that it is more modern by 25 years than those extant in Purchase's pilgrim, which are referred to in the Negociations between the British and French Commissaries touching the bounds of N. Scotia as the first of Authenticity relating to this part of the world. If notwithstanding these considerations you still desire that a copy be taken from the map above described I shall with pleasure execute your orders, or if you wish that a copy of Virga. or of the whole country may be taken from those in Purchase, your orders shall be equally attended to. I much doubt however whether that book be so extremely scarce as to require a transcript from it for the purpose you seem to have in view.

You will find in the inclosed gazette all our latest intelligence both from Europe and the W. Indies. The Ministerial speeches in Parliament as well as other considerations render it pretty certain that the system for recovering America will be changed. A peace with Holland and a suspension of the expensive operations in

America are to give their resources full play against France and Spain, whilst all the arts of division and seduction will probably be practised on the U. States.

Congress have taken no step in the business of the Western territory since the report of the Committee of which I have already given you an account, and which we hear arrived at Richmond on the day of the Ajournment of the Assembly. We wish it to undergo their consideration, and to receive their instructions before we again move in it. Mr. Randolph by whom this goes will probably be present at the May Session and will be possessed of every information that may be necessary. I refer you to the interview with him which I hope that occasion will afford you for other congressional intelligence.

I am this moment told that pretty certain information is come to hand of the final reduction of St. Kitts.

With great regard I am Dr. Sr. Yr. obt. friend & Servt.,

J. MADISON JR.

RC (DLC: Madison Papers); endorsed by TJ: "Madison Jas. Mar. 18. 1782." Enclosure not found.

Madison's LAST . . . ON THE SUBJECT OF THE MAP was apparently his letter to TJ of 3 Apr. 1781. The MAP PUBLISHED in 1650 was Nicholas, John, and Virginia Farrer's "Faithfull Map of Virginia in America" (1651), which identified the "peacefull Indian Sea" as "10 dayes march with 50 foote and 30. horsemen from the head of the Jeames River" (copy in PPL-R, where Madison saw it).

To James Madison

Dr Sir   Monticello Mar. 24. 1782

I have received from you two several favours on the subject of the designs against the territorial rights of Virginia. I never before could comprehend on what principle our right to the Western country could be denied which would not at the same time subvert the rights of all the states to the whole of their territory. What objections may be founded on the Charter of N. York I cannot say, having never seen that charter nor been able to get a copy of it in this country. I had thought to have seized the first leisure on my return from the last assembly to have considered and stated our right and to have communicated to our Delegates or perhaps to the public so much as I could trace, and expected to have derived some assistance from antient M.S.S. which I have been able to collect. These with my other papers and books however had been removed to Augusta to be out of danger from the enemy and have not yet been brought back. The ground on which I now find the question to be bottomed is so unknown to me that it is out of my power to say any thing on the subject. Should it be practicable for me to procure a copy of the charter of N.Y. I shall probably think on it, and would cheerfully communicate to you whatever could occur to me worth your notice. But this will probably be much too late to be of any service before Congress who doubtless will decide ere long on the subject. I sincerely wish their decision may tend to the preservation of peace. If I am not totally deceived in the determination of this country the decision of Congres, if unfavourable, will not close the question. I suppose some people on the Western waters who are ambitious to be Governors &c. will urge a separation by authority of Congress; but the bulk of the people Westward are already thrown into great ferment by the report of what is proposed, to which I think they will not submit. This separation is unacceptable to us in form only and not in substance. On the contrary I may safely say it is desired by the Eastern part of our country whenever their Western brethren shall think themselves able to stand alone. In the mean time on the petition of the Western counties a plan is digesting for rendering their access to government more easy.

I trouble you with the inclosed to Monsr. Marbois. I had the pleasure of hearing that your father and family were well yesterday, by your brother who is about to study the law in my neighborhood. I shall always be glad to hear from you; and if it be possible for me, retired from public business to find any thing worth your notice, I shall communicate it with great pleasure. I am with sincere esteem Dr Sir Your friend & servt.

Dft (DLC). Enclosure: TJ to Marbois, same date, following.
Madison's TWO SEVERAL FAVOURS ON . . . THE TERRITORIAL RIGHTS OF VIRGINIA were those of 18 Nov. 1781 and 15 Jan. 1782.

To Marbois

SIR   Monticello Mar. 24. 1782.

I am very sorry that the papers I had taken the liberty to trouble you with have been so unfortunately delayed. I retired from office in the month of June last, and was obliged by the movements of the enemy to retire from my house at the same time, to which I did not return till the month of Aug. I immediately engaged in the work of digesting the materials I had collected in answer to your quæries, and supplying their defects. This I completed in a short time[1] except as to some few articles which requiring information from very distant parts of the country, I referred forwarding the whole to you till our assembly should meet in October when I hoped to get the information I wanted. That meeting was unexpectedly protracted so that I did not go to Richmond till December. On leaving that place without having had a good opportunity of sending my letter to you, I put that and some others into the hands of the honbl. Mr. Ambler a member of the council desiring he would forward them by some of those safe conveyances which I supposed government would have. On receipt of your favor of January—[29] I became uneasy lest they should have miscarried, and wrote to Mr. Ambler to be informed of the channel of conveyance. I take the liberty of subjoining his answer as it will explain to you the cause of the one letter being delayed while it's companion went on safely. The trifle which has exposed you to this detail was not worth a thought on your part and I trouble you with it merely to satisfy you of the attention I payd to your wishes. I hope before this you will have received it safely and that it will have effected the sole purpose I could expect which was that of shewing you with how much respect I have the honour of considering whatever comes from you and of the very profound regard with which I am Sir Your mo. ob. & mo hble servt.

Dft (DLC); endorsed by TJ: "Marbois Monsr. de." Enclosure: Jacquelin Ambler to TJ, 16 Mch. 1782. The present letter was enclosed in TJ's to Madison, preceding.

THAT MEETING WAS UNEXPECTEDLY PROTRACTED: The Assembly met according to adjournment on 1 Oct. 1781 but there were not enough members present to conduct business until 19 Nov. when the House was organized. I . . . WROTE TO MR. AMBLER: TJ's letter to Ambler has not been found, but HIS ANSWER is that of 16 Mch. 1782, q.v.

[1] TJ first wrote and then deleted the following: "a few days."

From James Madison

DEAR SIR   Philadelphia, March 26, 1782.

A letter has been lately received from you by the President of Congress, accompanied by a bundle of papers procured from the Cherokees by Colonel Campbell. As it appears that these papers were transmitted at the request of the late President, it is proper to apprize you that it was made without any written or verbal sanction, and even without the knowledge of Congress; and not improbably with a view of fishing for discoveries which may be subservient to the aggressions meditated on the territorial rights of

Virginia. It would have been unnecessary to trouble you with this, had it not appeared that Colonel Campbell has given a promise of other papers; which if he should fulfil, and the papers contain any thing which the adversaries of Virginia may make an ill use of, you will not suffer any respect for the acts of Congress to induce you to forward hither.

MS not found. Text printed from *Papers of James Madison*, Henry D. Gilpin, ed., Washington, 1840, I, 116.

The LETTER ... RECEIVED FROM YOU BY THE PRESIDENT OF CONGRESS was TJ's letter to McKean, 20 Dec. 1781. Technically Madison was no doubt correct in stating that Huntington's request of TJ of 27 Apr. 1781 was made WITHOUT ANY WRITTEN OR VERBAL SANCTION of Congress, for there is no evidence in the Journals that Hazard's letter, forwarded by Huntington to TJ on the date mentioned, was read or referred to in Congress; yet Huntington was certainly acting in line with if not under authority of a former action of Congress (see Vol. 1: 144-8).

From Charles Bellini

CARISSMO. SIGNE. TOMMASO   Williamsburg 8. Aprile 1782.

Rispondendo all'umanissma. Sua de 25. Marzo scorso, nella quale Ella mi domanda una lista classata di Traduzioni degli autori più Celebri Greci e Latini, Le dirò che io, particolarmente in questo genere, sono il più ignorante tra gl'ignoranti, forse perchè in Italia simili autori si leggono ne' loro originali solamente, se Latini; e si comparano gli originali con le Traduzioni Latine, se Greci. Io conosco bensí una stupenda, ottima traduzione uguale, se non superiore all'originale, di Lucrezio, fatta dal Famoso Marchetti, e due di Virgilio, una da Annibal Caro, l'altra da Antonio Ambrogi già Gesuita: Se io meritassi la permissione d'opinare sopra di ciò io preferirei quella dell' Ambrogi, perchè, non solamente egli è fedele nella sua traduzione, ed à conservato tutto il nobile ed il Poetico dell' autore, [ma] di più, ed in preferenza del Caro, egli à tradotto in Toscano, e l'altro in Lingua Lombarda che gli era più conveniente, perchè Nativa. Relativamente al restante degli Autori Latini e greci dei quali Ella desidera le traduzioni; io ne ò data La Lista al Sige. Genle. Chastleux che viene Costà: Egli certamente e ad ogni riguardo è il Soggetto più capace di darle le migliori notizie per le traduzioni Francesi ugualmente che per l'Italiane. Per quel che concerne poi quelle Traduzioni i di cui Autori Ella à trovati nei Cataloghi, io non saprei che dirne; solamente ardirei di porle in veduta che, alla riserva di Strozzi di cui La Repubblica Letteraria Italiana non fa gran' caso, tutti gli altri sono Lombardi; ed in conseguenza il Loro linguaggio non è certamente nè il più dolce nè il più armonico, nè il più stimato nel mondo, e quand' anche le Loro traduzioni siano ottime, esse avranno sempre il difetto della Lingua. Io non pretendo di pronunziare dogmaticamente, ma solo darle la mia opinione, alla quale Ella darà quel valore ch'ella merita.

S'io non avessi la gotta, avrei certamente accompagnato il Sige. Generale, ma io non ò creduto prudente di espormi a rimanere per una Strada, e poi non ò creduto decente di lasciar la mia moglie allo Spedale in cura ad una tregenda infinita di malattie. Se il tempo si cambierà mai in meglio, io verrò certamente a rivedere, e Lei e l'amabilissma. Sua Sigra. Sposa e Famiglia. La mia moglie ed io siamo moltissmo. obbligati alla buona memoria che Mrs. Jefferson e Lei anno avuto la bontà d'avere per noi; E pregandola a continuarmi l'onore della Sua benevolenza, mi protesto Con tutto il rispetto Suo Divotmo. Obblmo. Servre. ed Amico

C: BELLINI

RC (DLC). The editors are indebted to Prof. A. T. MacAllister, Jr., Princeton University, for a transcription of this letter, as well as for a translation on which the summary below is based.

Replies to TJ's letter of 25 Mch. (missing), in which he requested a classified list of translations of the most famous Greek and Latin authors; is ignorant in this matter, perhaps because in Italy such authors are read in the original only if Latin and the original is compared with the Latin translation if Greek; however he knows of an excellent translation of Lucretius by Marchetti which is equal, if not superior, to the original, also of two translations of Virgil—one by Caro and the other by Ambrogi, formerly a Jesuit, of which he prefers Ambrogi "because he is faithful in his translation and has kept all the noble and poetic qualities of the author," and also because he translated into Tuscan and Caro translated into Lombard. Bellini has given the rest of the list to Gen. Chastellux who comes to Monticello because he is capable of giving the best information on French translations as well as Italian; can say nothing concerning the translations TJ found in the catalogues except to point out that with the exception of Strozzi, who is not highly regarded by Italian men of letters, all the others are Lombards and "consequently their language is certainly not the sweetest nor the most harmonious nor the most esteemed in the world." If Bellini did not have the gout he would certainly have accompanied the General but he did not think it prudent to risk having to be left behind on the road; also he did not think it proper to leave his wife "at the Hospital grappling with an infinite horde of diseases." If the weather improves he will come to see TJ and his wife and family; he and his wife are deeply obliged for the thoughtfulness which TJ and Mrs. Jefferson have shown them and begs the continuance of that benevolence.

Election Return for Delegates from Albemarle County

At an Election held for Albemarle County the xith day of April Anno Domini MDCCLXXXII, By the Freeholders of the said County I have Caused to be Chosen Two Burgesses To Wit

Thomas Jefferson, and Thomas Walker, Esqrs. to Act as Burgesses for the said County as by Law is Required, given under my hand and seal the day and Year above Written.

JAMES QUARLES S. Al.

MS (Vi); endorsed: "Albemarle Return May 1782."

James Quarles evidently came to Albemarle co. around 1776 from King William, and no doubt he had served as sheriff prior to the Revolution, as indicated in his use of the word "Burgesses" (Woods, *Albemarle County*, p. 299-300).

To Benjamin Harrison

SIR   Charlottesville April 13. 1782.

The legion of Colo. Armand which was stationed here to be refitted for service has for some time been on sufferance for provisions. Flour they have had and still have, but of animal food the supplies have almost totally failed, and failed from a cause which is without remedy, that is, the want of it in the neighborhood. The former calls for beef by fifteenths and tenths had reduced the stocks of cattle here in common with those in other parts of the country; and that of the sixth which was punctually complied with here has left the people without beef for their own use. It never was a country abounding with pork, few raising more than served their own families. In this situation I fear their supplies of animal food will become worse instead of better. Forage has been brought in pretty plentifully till within these few days; but now that also fails, the season being come on in which most of the farmers begin to be out of that article. These things have induced Colo. Armand to think of changing his quarters, and as Genl. Washington's orders seem to restrain him from going any distance from hence, he has cast his eyes on Staunton. By information from the inhabitants of that place it seems probable his legion might be subsisted there, could he have the aid of the Specific tax of the county in which it is. As your Excellency had favoured him with the aid of that resource in this county we are in hopes the same may be extended to him there. It really seems necessary, to render the horses fit for the feild, that they should be removed to some place where better supplies of forage may be had. Their situation will no doubt be represented to you by Colo. Armand, who wished me to trouble you on this subject also, as being able to give you some information as to the circumstances of this neighborhood and the little probability there is of his situation being bettered here. It must give your Excellency satisfaction I am sure to be informed that Colo. Armand has been very successful in recruiting, taking for granted that his recruits in this state will be applied to it's credit as part of it's quota.

I have the honour to be with the highest respect & esteem Your Excellency's Most obedt. & most humble servt.,

TH: JEFFERSON

RC (PHi); addressed: "His Excellency Governour Harrison Richmond"; endorsed. THEIR SITUATION WILL NO DOUBT BE REPRESENTED TO YOU: Armand's letter to Gov. Harrison, dated 13 Apr. 1782, is printed in part in CVSP, III, 129-30.

From James Madison

DEAR SIR   Phila. April 16th 1782

Your favor of the 24 of March with a letter inclosed for Mr. Marbois came to hand yesterday.

I intreat that you will not suffer the chance of a speedy and final determination of the territorial question by Congress to affect your purpose of tracing the title of Virga. to her claims. It is in the first place very uncertain when a determination will take place, even if it takes place at all; and in the next it will assuredly not be a final one, unless Virga. means to be passive and silent under aggression on her rights. In every event therefore it is proper to be armed with every argument and document that can vindicate her title. Her adversaries will be either the U. States or N.Y. or both. The former will either claim on the principle that the vacant country is not included in any particular State and consequently falls to the whole, or will cloath themselves with the title of the latter by accepting its cession. In both cases it will be alledged that the Charter of 1609 was annulled by the resumption of it into the hands of the Crown, and that the subsequent grants to Maryland &c. denote this to have been the construction of it; that the Proclamation of 1763 has constituted the Allegheny Ridge the Western limit of Virga. and that the letter of Presidt. Nelson on the subject of a New Colony on the Ohio relinquishes on the part of Virga. all interference with the Authority of the Crown beyond that limit. In case the title of N.Y. should alone be opposed to that of Virginia, it will be further alledged against the latter that the treaties of 1684. 1701. 1726. 1744 and 1754 between the Government of the former and the 6 nations have annexed to it all the Country claimed by those nations and their tributaries, and that the expence of N. York in defending and protecting them ought in equity to be reimbursed by this exclusive advantage. The original title of N.Y. is indeed drawn from the charter to the Duke of York in 1663-4, renewed after the treaty of Westminister in 1674. But this Charter will not I believe reach any territory claimed by Virga.

Much stress will also be laid on the Treaty of Fort Stanwix particularly as a bar to any corroboration of the Claim of Virga. from the Treatys of Lancaster and Loggstown. It is under this Treaty that the companies of Ind[ian]a. and Vandalia shelter their pretensions against the claims of Virga. &c. &c. see the pamphlets entitled "Public good" and "plain facts." As these pretensions can be of no avail unless the Jurisdiction of Congress or N. York at least can be established, they no otherwise deserve notice than as sources of calumny and influence in public councils. In both which respects it is the interest of Virga. that an antidote should be applied.

Mr. Randolph during his stay here was very industrious and successful in his researches into the territorial claims of all the States, and will be able to furnish you with many valuable hints. Your visit to Richmond in May will give him an opportunity.

Our information from Europe has been peculiarly defective of late. It seems little probable that any decisive steps have been or will speedily be taken towards either a partial or general peace. The weight of the war will probably fall on the West Indies at least in the early part of the Campaign. Whither it will then be shifted is altogether uncertain.

With very sincere regard I am Dr Sir Yr Obt Servt,

J Madison Jr.

RC (DLC: Madison Papers); endorsed by TJ.

From Marbois

Monsieur   A Philadelphie le 22. avril 1782.

J'ai reçu les lettres que vous m'avés fait l'honneur de m'ecrire le 20. decembre et le 24. mars dernier. J'ai mis sur le navire marchand *le Philadelphie* les paquets pour l'Europe joints à la premiere et je crois que ce vaisseau a heureusement decapé malgré la vigilance des corsaires anglois.

Je ne puis vous exprimer à quel point je suis reconnoissant de la peine que vous avés prise pour rediger des reponses detaillées aux questions que j'avois pris la liberté de vous adresser. La Philosophie qui les a Dictées, les lumieres que cet écrit me donne sur un des plus importans etats de l'union et les circonstances dans lesquelles vous avés pris la peine de les ecrire en font l'ouvrage le plus precieux que je pusse emporter de ce pays-ci.

J'ai vu surtout, Monsieur, avec un plaisir inexprimable la candeur et la Franchise avec laquelle vous vous expliqués sur les objets que des Politiques à vue courte apelleroient secrets d'Etat. Vous avés jugé en veritable homme d'Etat que s'il y a des secrets dans les societés qui sont en decadence et tendent à leur ruine ou leur dissolution, il ne doit point y en avoir dans une republique qui se fortiffie et s'aggrandit tous les jours, et qui ne pourroit decroître quand même l'administration seroit momentanement vitieuse. Je vous prie d'etre bien persuadé, Monsieur, qu'on ne peut être plus touché que je le suis de vos bontés en cette occasion, et que j'en sens toute l'etendue, quelque peu de prix que vous vouliés y mettre vous même.

Je viens de communiquer cet ouvrage interessant à M. Thompson qui est trop bon juge pour n'en pas connoitre tout le merite.

M. le Chev. de la Luzerne est bien sensible à votre souvenir, Monsieur, et me charge de vous presenter ses sinceres complimens. Il regrette beaucoup de n'avoir pas eu l'honneur de vous voir pendant son dernier sejour en Virginie; mais, le peu de tems qu'il pouvoit y passer ne lui a pas permis de s'eloigner jusqu'à l'endroit que vous habités; mais ne pouvant vous entretenir vous même, il a eu le plaisir d'entendre les temoignages du respect et de l'estime que les personnes qu'il a eu occasion de voir ont conservés de votre administration et il a joint bien volontiers sa voix à celle du public.

Je suis avec un profond respect, Monsieur, Votre très humble et très obéissant serviteur,   MARBOIS

RC (ViWC).

From James Monroe

DEAR SIR   Richmond May 6. 1782

Mr. Short being just sitting out for Monticello I am happy to take the opportunity to assure you how sincerely I thank you for the late instance of your kindness and attention to me, which I particularly value as a testimony of your regard for me, and at the same time to assure you that nothing but a series of disappointments in the vessels I had appointed to sail in deprivd me of the opportunity of availing myself in that instance of the advantage it would have given me. Mr. Short will inform you of my appointment in the House, upon declining the other plan, and how very anxiously I wish your arrival and how very sincerely I join the better part of this community in my desire that a few days more will give us your aid in the House and society to your friends. I have only time to desire my best respects to Mrs. Jefferson and assure I am with great respect esteem yr. sincere friend & servant,

JAS. MONROE

RC (DLC).   MY APPOINTMENT IN THE HOUSE: Monroe had been elected a member of the House of Delegates from King George co.

To the Speaker of the House of Delegates

SIR   Albemarle May 6. 1782.

Purposing to decline the office of delegate for this county to which I have been lately elected, I take the liberty of declaring to you that I do not accept of the appointment, and of begging that this my act of renunciation may through your favor be communicated to the honourable the House of Delegates with every assurance to them and yourself[1] of the very great respect with which I have the honour to be their & your most obedient & most humble servt.,

TH: JEFFERSON

Dft (DLC); endorsed by TJ: "Speaker of the H. of Delegates."

The General Assembly convened on 6 May 1782 and John Tyler was probably elected Speaker of the House that day or the following, though this fact, of course, could not have been known to TJ at the time the present letter was written. No journal of the House for this session is known to be extant, either in manuscript or printed form. See Tyler to TJ, 16 May, and TJ to Monroe, 20 May 1782. There is in Vi, however, "a very sketchy minute book for the House for this session" which, under date of 16 May 1782, contains the following: "Mr. Jeffersons Letter—read & to lie" (William J. Van Schreeven to editors, 29 Feb. 1952). Edmund Randolph, the same day, wrote Madison: "Mr. Jefferson has . . . tendered a resignation. This they refuse to accept, grounding the refusal upon his own principles, delivered on a similar occasion" (Randolph to Madison, 16 May 1782, DLC: Madison Papers).

[1] TJ first wrote and then deleted the following: "that I am with the most profound respect their and your."

From Thomas Watkins, with Jefferson's Opinion concerning a Will

SIR   May the 9th 1782.

As the Trustees mentioned in my Fathers Will, are at a loss to know, whether they have a right to divide his real Estate among his Children as they think fit, or not; I do, at their request, beg you that you would give us your Opinion on that head; and if you should think that they cannot, we would willingly know whether a division could be procured by a Suit in Chancery agreeable to the two depositions which I have sent inclosed. I am Sir Yr Hbl Svt, T WATKINS

OPINION

Considerations on the will of Mr. B. Watkins and the declarations of Mrs. Watkins and the Revd. Mr. Leigh.

I. Taking the will alone, separately from extrinsic testimony, the first question which presents itself is whether the estate of Mr. Watkins real and personal must be divided equally among his widow and children or whether the Trustees therein named may divide the same among them in any proportion they shall in their discretion think proper. After devising the estate to the Trustees in fee the testator expresses the trust to be 'for the maintenance and education of his wife and children.' These words hold up no idea of inequality; on the contrary they do by universal acceptation give an equal interest to all the devisees described, which interest is the nature of a jointenancy subject to severance, or to survivorship if not severed, according to the well known rules of jointenancy. This being the legal effect of these words if they stood single and unconnected with any others, are there others in the will which will alter their legal import? Giving them (i.e. the trustees) says the will by these presents full power to sell if they 'judge it necessary all or any part thereof and to make conveyances to the purchasers in fee-simple, with power also to make purchases with the money arising from such sale for the use of my wife and family.' These words are so far from changing the effect of the former and giving rise to an inequality of partition that they confirm the equal bequest by naming again it's objects, that is his wife and family, in terms of equality.

He proceeds 'and to make division of my estate among my said wife and children *at any time* when they shall think it convenient to do so.' These only give to the trustees a power of dividing *at such time* as they shall think proper, saying nothing of the proportions.

'And finally to do every thing with regard to the said estate in as full and ample manner as I could myself while living.' These words may be considered either 1. as meaning to invest the trustees with those full powers necessary for an advantageous execution of the trust, as for instance to submit to them the arrangements, the objects of pursuit, the management in general, the mode of partition &c. under which construction they neither lessen nor enlarge the equal rights of the cestuy que trusts given before; or 2. as meaning to authorize them to alter the trust itself at their will, and literally to give them a power 'of doing every thing with the estate which the testator himself might have done.' But this construction would be so large as eventually to defeat any possible purpose imputable to the testator, for under it they might not only divide the estate unequally, but might give all to some, and more to others, or might give the estate totally out of the testator's family to strangers for this he himself could have done, a power which the judges governing themselves by technical and fixed rules of construction would probably never admit the testator to have intended and therefore that they will adopt the meaning first mentioned which is rational and sufficient to satisfy those words.

Cases have frequently occurred before the courts wherein these discretionary powers have been confided to trustees, executors &c. on which these general observations may be made; that the judges are so far from favouring them and straining the force of words to produce them that they only tolerate them when given in the most unequivocal terms; that they have sometimes rejected them when given explicitly and at others have defeated them by controuling even attempt at unequal partition. It is observable too that these are the later authorities which discourage them the most.

2. Vern. 383. Warburton v. Warburton.	(Com. ple. 420)
2 Vern. 149.	(287.)
1. Ca. Ch. 309.	(1284.)
2. Ca. Ch. 198.	(1372.)
2. Ca. Ch. 228.	(1389)
198.	(1537)
Pr. Ch. 256.	(1901.)

Supposing that the widow and children are by the will become jointenants of the trust, the next question is What is the duration of their estates? As to the personal estate it is perpetual, and so also as to the slaves who by the act of ass. pass by deed or will as personal chattels do: but as to the lands it is as certain that the widow and children take by the will estates for life only, there being no words of limitation annexed to the devise of the trust. The reversion of the trust therefore after the death of the jointenants for life descends to the heir at law as being undisposed of by the will. This being the case of a trust is not therefore different from that of an estate in possession, the determinations being that limitations of a trust either of real or personal estate are to be construed as those of a legal estate. Any of the jointenants may by a bill in chancery compel a severance of the trust and conveyance of their equal share, which as to the slaves and personal estate is necessary to prevent their share surviving to the other legatees on their death to the exclusion of their own children where they have any and as to the real estate it will on the death of the particular tenant give the heir a right of entry into the severed part. — Garth v. Baldwin 2. Vezey. 655

II. In forming the preceding opinions, the parol declarations of the testator's intention have been purposely kept out of view. If they can be admitted as proof they decide in favor of the power of the trustees. The question whether they may or may not is of no importance indeed as to the slaves and personalty because the will conveys in those what the parol evidence says the testator intended. But it becomes of consequence when applied to the real estate because by the depositions he meant that his trustees should divide his lands among his three sons by certain bounds which is very different from the effect of the will. I think however that the parol evidence will not be admitted in this case. Because it tends to what the courts have so much endeavored to prevent, that — 2. Vez. 216. 5. Co. 68. 1. Freem. 292.

is the putting it in the power of witnesses to make wills for testators and because parol evidence has been expressly rejected where it was to alter the estate devised. The alteration here would not be in the duration of the estate but in the quantum, which is full as material.

On the whole then it seems to me that rejecting parol proof the will will be found to have given equal estates to the widow and children in jointenancy, that these estates are absolute as to the slaves and personalties but for life only in the lands, which on the death of the jointenants successively will survive to those overliving them, and on the death of the last will revert to the heir at law in fee. That as to the slaves and personal estate those who have children should sever immediately to enable themselves to transmit their own parts to their own children.

As it will probably be disagreeable to the trustees to divide the lands so differently from what they know to have been the testator's intention, so long as there may be a chance of being permitted to fulfill that intention, and as it would be perillous for them on the other hand to pursue his intention while there is so much room for ⟨them to⟩ doubt whether the law will justify it, I would advise them to file a bill of Interpleader in the *High* court of chancery, stating the will of their testator the conviction they are under of the division he wished to have made, and for which alone he entrusted them with discretionary powers, their desire to exercise those powers for the fulfilling his real will if the laws will authorize them, and the doubts which have been suggested to them whether they are so authorized, praying the Chancellors to call before them the several parties interested. to cause them to interplead and assert their respective claims and if it shall appear to them that the power of apportioning the land rests in the discretion of the trustees that then they may be permitted to apportion them among the three sons according to the bounds described by the testator and that this apportionment may be confirmed by decree of the court; but that if they possess no such power that then the court will decree such partition as the law requires. Under such a decree the trustees will act safely, what they do will be firm, it may be done on motion any day of the ensuing session of the Chancery, and need cost the estate the fee of one lawyer only as the proceeding being amicable, he may state it for all parties and leave it to the judgment of the court.

RC (DLC); addressed; endorsed by TJ: "Watkins T's case. Discretionary power of divisn to trustees Parol evidence to explain will." The "two depositions" have not been found, but may be identified from TJ's caption to his opinion on the will. Dft of opinion (DLC) is undated, but presumably was written soon after the receipt of Thomas Watkins' letter.

Benjamin Watkins, first clerk of Chesterfield co., was the father of Thomas Watkins and the father-in-law of THE REVD. MR. LEIGH (Meade, *Old Churches and Families of Va.*, I, 451). He appears to have died about 1779, for he was clerk of Chesterfield until his death and Thomas succeeded him in that office in that year (Frederick Johnston, *Memorials of Old Va. Clerks*, Lynchburg, 1888, p. 164).

From James Monroe

As I so lately wrote you by Mr. Short and have since daily expected to see you here I did not propose writing you till after I should have that pleasure; but as I begin to fear you will not abate that firmness and decision which you have frequently shewn in the service of your country even upon this occasion, and as I have had an opportunity since I wrote last of being better informed of the sentiments of those whom I know you put the greatest value on, I think it my duty to make you acquainted therewith. It is publickly said here that the people of your county inform'd you they had frequently elected you in times of less difficulty and danger than the present to please you, but that now they had call'd you forth into publick office to serve themselves. This is a language which has been often us'd in my presence and you will readily conceive that as it furnishes those who agree on the fundimental maxims of a republican government with ample field for declamation, the conclusion has always been, you should not decline the service of your country. The present is generally conceiv'd to be an important era which of course makes your attendance particularly necessary, and as I have taken the liberty to give you the publick opinion and desire upon this occasion, and as I am warmly interested in whatever concerns the publick interest or has relation to you it will be unnecessary to add it is earnestly the desire of Dear Sir yr. sincere friend & servant,   Jas. Monroe

RC (DLC).

From John Tyler

I receiv'd your Letter by Doctor Walker, and have agreeable to your desire laid it before the House of Delegates, but the Constitution in the Opinion of the Members will not warrant the acceptance of your resignation.

I am sorry most sincerely for my Country that she is depriv'd of your services, and I am sorry for myself in particular, that I cou'd not have the pleasure of yielding to you the Office which I hold, and which you cou'd fill with so much more propriety. However, I suppose your reasons are weighty, yet I wou'd suggest that good and able Men had better govern than be govern'd, since 'tis possible, indeed highly probable, that if the able and good withdraw themselves from Society, the venal and ignorant will succeed. I am sure you can readily discover how miserable a Situation the country wou'd be reduced to, and how wretched the reflection to a person of sense and merit. In times of Peace Men of moderate abilities perhaps might conduct the affairs of the State, but at this time when the Republic wants to be organized and requires but your influence to promote this desirable End, I cannot but think the House may insist upon you to give attendance without incuring the Censure of being siezed.

I am Sir, with very sincere respect your most obt. humble [Servant], JNO: TYLER

RC (DLC); addressed to TJ "in Albemarle"; endorsed by TJ: "Assembly Genl." For Tyler's own resignation as a member of the Council at an even more critical time, see his letter to TJ, 1 Apr. 1781.

To James Monroe

DEAR SIR Monticello May 20. 1782.

I have been gratified with the receipt of your two favours of the 6th. and 11th. inst.[1] It gives me pleasure that your county has been wise enough to enlist your talents into their service. I am much obliged by the kind wishes you express of seeing me also in Richmond, and am always mortified when any thing is expected from me which I cannot fulfill, and more especially if it relate to the public service. Before I ventured to declare to my countrymen my determination to retire from public employment I examined well my heart to know whether it were thoroughly cured of every principle of political ambition, whether no lurking particle remained which might leave me uneasy when reduced within the limits of mere private life. I became satisfied that every fibre of that passion was thoroughly eradicated. I examined also in other views my right to withdraw. I considered that I had been thirteen years engaged in public service, that during that time I had so totally abandoned all attention to my private affairs as to permit them to run into great disorder and ruin,[2] that I had now a family advanced to years which require my attention and instruction, that to this was added the hopeful offspring of a deceased friend whose memory must be for ever dear to me who have no other reliance for being rendered useful to themselves and their country, that by a constant sacrifice of time, labour, loss, parental and friendly duties, I had been so far from gaining the affection[3] of my countrymen[4] which was the only reward I ever asked or could have felt, that I had even lost the small estimation I before possessed: that however I might have comforted myself under the disapprobation of the well-meaning but uninformed people yet that of their representatives was a shock on which I had not calculated: that this indeed had been followed by an exculpatory declaration, but in the mean time I had been suspected and suspended in the eyes of[5] the world without the least hint then or afterwards made public which might restrain them from supposing I stood arraigned for treasons of the heart and not mere weaknesses of the head. And I felt that these injuries, for such they have been since acknowleged, had inflicted a wound on my spirit which[6] will only be cured by the all-healing grave. If reason and inclination unite in justifying my retirement, the laws of my country are equally in favor of it. Whether the state may command the political services of all it's members to an indefinite extent, or if these be among the rights never wholly ceded to the public power, is a question which I do not find expressly decided in England. Obiter dictums on the subject I have indeed met with, but the complection of the times in which these have dropped would generally answer them, and besides that, this species of authority is not acknowleged in our profession. In this country however since the present government has been established the point has been settled by uniform, pointed, and multiplied precedents. Offices of every kind, and given by every power, have been daily and hourly declined and resigned from the declaration of independance to this moment. The General assembly has accepted these without discrimination of office, and without ever questioning them in point of right. If a difference between the office of a delegate and any other could ever have been supposed, yet in the case of Mr. Thompson Mason who declined the office of delegate and was permitted by the house so to do that supposition has been proved to be groundless. But indeed no such distinction of offices can be admitted;[7] reason and the opinions of the lawyers putting all on a footing as to this question and giving to the delegate the aid of all the precedents of the refusal of other offices,[8] the law then does not warrant the assumption of such a power by the state over it's members. For if it does where is that law? Nor yet does reason, for tho' I will admit that this does subject every individual if called on to an equal tour of[9] political duty yet it can never go so far as to submit to it his whole existence.[10] If we are made in some degree for others, yet in a greater are we made for ourselves. It were contrary to feeling and indeed ridiculous to suppose a man had less right in himself than one of his neighbors or all of them put together. This would be slavery and not that liberty which the bill of rights has made inviolable and for the preservation of which our government has been changed. Nothing could so completely divest us of that liberty as the establishment of the opinion that the state has a *perpetual* right to the services of all it's members. This to men of certain ways of thinking would be to annihilate the blessing of existence; to contradict the giver of life who gave it for happiness and not for wretchedness, and certainly to such it were better that they had never been born. However with these I may think public service and private misery inseparably linked together, I have not the vanity to count myself among those whom the state would[11] think worth oppressing with perpetual service. I have received a sufficient memento to the contrary. I am persuaded that[12] having hitherto dedicated to them the whole of the active and useful part of my life I shall[13] be permitted to pass the rest in mental quiet. I hope too that I did not mistake the mode any more than the matter of right when I preferred a simple act of renunciation to the taking sanctuary under those many disqualifications (provided by the law for other purposes indeed but) which afford[14] asylum also for rest to the wearied. I dare say you did not expect by the few words you dropped on the right of renunciation to expose yourself to the fatigue of so long a letter, but I wished you to see that if I had done wrong I had been betrayed by a semblance of right at least.

I take the liberty of inclosing to you a letter for Genl. Chattlux for which you will readily find means of conveyance. But I meant to give you more trouble with the one to Pelham who lives in the neighborhood of Manchester and to ask the favor of you to send it by your servant express which I am in hopes may be done without absenting him from your person but during those hours in which you will be engaged in the house. I am anxious that it should be received immediately. Mrs. Jefferson has added another daughter to our family. She has been ever since and still continues very dangerously ill. It will give me great pleasure to see you here whenever you can favor us with your company. You will find me still busy but in lighter occupations. But in these and all others you will find me to retain a due sense of your friendship & to be with sincere esteem Dr Sir Your mo. ob. & mo. hble servt.

P.S. Did you ever receive a copy of the Parl. debates and Histor. Register with a letter left for you with Mr. Jas. Buchanan?

Dft (DLC); with numerous deletions and corrections, the more important of which are noted below. The enclosed letters to Chastellux and to "Pelham who lives in the neighborhood of Manchester" have not been found, nor has Pelham been identified. He may have been William Pelham, a surgeon's mate in Virginia, with whom TJ later corresponded (see WMQ, 2d ser., VIII [1928], 42-5).

There is no doubt, as Malone suggests, that this embittered letter was written at a moment of anxiety about Mrs. Jefferson's health so intense as to result in almost a lack of normal capacity to judge issues reasonably and in proper proportion. But it is perhaps wrong to conclude, as he does, that there was no occasion for TJ "to go into legalities . . . in the effort to determine whether or not the state might *require* public services of its citizens through an indefinite period" (Malone, *Jefferson*, I, 395) and that presumably TJ would not have done so had he been functioning more normally. On the contrary, there was a very specific occasion for him to raise and set forth the legal argument—that is, the blunt threat of an arrest contained in the letter from TJ's old schoolmate, John Tyler, who, as Speaker of the House, warned that "the House may insist upon you to give attendance without incurring the Censure of being siezed" (Tyler to TJ, 16 May 1782). The threat of an arrest by a sergeant-at-arms undoubtedly reopened the deep wounds of the preceding year and, of course, made it necessary that TJ should consider what legal grounds he could stand upon if the House made good Tyler's warning. The present letter, therefore, may be considered as less an explanation to Monroe than a reply to Tyler. It was certainly shown to others in Richmond, as TJ may have intended. "I saw a letter from Mr. Jefferson to Col. Monro," Randolph informed Madison, "in which he assigns reasons for refusing his seat in the house of delegates. The pathos of the composition is really great; and the wound, which he received by the late impeachment, is, as he says, to be cured only by the all-healing grave. His triumph might certainly be an illustrious one over his former enemies were he to resume the legislative character: for in the constant division between the two leaders, Henry and Lee, he might incline the scale to whichsoever side he would" (Randolph to Madison, 1 June 1782, DLC: Madison Papers).

[1] At this point TJ first wrote, then deleted: "which gave me the first information."

[2] At this point TJ first wrote, then deleted: "that so far from receiving or wishing compensation from the public I had been from time to time impairing for my support that capital which a growing family had a right to expect entire as I received it at least if not improved, that."

[3] TJ first wrote: "esteem."

[4] TJ deleted at this point: "which would indeed have been a full reward for all, a solace for everything."

[5] TJ first wrote, then deleted: "my countrymen without so much as an intimation hung out which might prevent their suspicions going to my heart as well as my head."

[6] TJ first wrote: "nothing in this world could ever heal."

[7] TJ deleted at this point: "for besides that the English."

[8] TJ deleted at this point: "such distinction could not be founded in law or reason."

[9] TJ deleted at this point: "to a certain rotine of duty if called on for that duty."

[10] The final part of this sentence read, before being altered: "to submit his whole existence to his fellow creatures."

[11] TJ first wrote: "might think proper to oppress."

[12] TJ first wrote: "now serving my 40th year and."

[13] TJ first wrote: "may."

[14] TJ first wrote "afford" and then, presumably intending to strike out "which," altered it to "affording"; the recipient's copy probably reads: ". . . for other purposes indeed but) affording asylum" &c.

From John K. Read

SIR   Solitude 22 May 82

The inclosed note of Hand, was taken a few days ago, by my
young Man, for a debt of considerable amount. The manner of its
being drawn is new to me and I have taken the freedom to inclose
it to you for your opinion, for which I shall be extremely obliged
to you, the bearer being directed to wait for that Purpose. The
matter is thus—a certain Mr. Moseley sold to Capt. Geo. Hancock
of Powhatan, his estate in that county, for 800,000 wt. Tobo. who
gave his Bonds, payable at different periods to Moseley, for that
amount, Pollock wins, of Moseley, one of Hancocks bonds for 200.
hhds. Hancock purchases *his* bond of Pollock, and gives him three
negroes, and a note for 58.000 wt. tobo. payable in 85. for the
ballance. Hancock sells his estate to Jno. and Lachlan McIntosh,
who agree to receive and pay his debts. In consequence the note
due from Hancock to Pollock is taken in by the McIntoshes, and
theirs given in exchange. This is the note I have taken the liberty
to inclose for your opinion. Pollock (tho curious en[ough)] en-
dorses the note to me, but it is not binding on me, unless I please,
as my young man was uncertain if it was sufficiently valid. You
will be so oblidging allso to inform me, if the endorsement of Hancock, on the back, is sufficiently obligatory on him or the McIntoshes, for the Payment in May next. I am very respectfully Sir,
Your mo ob[lidg]   J. K. READ

RC (DLC). Enclosure (missing): Note of John and Lachlan McIntosh.
The following entry appears in TJ's account book under May 1782: "22. charged
Doctr. John K. Reed an opinion on Mc.intoshes bond."

Resolutions concerning Peace with England

[25 May 1782]

[Ford, II, 160, prints a series of resolutions under the date "[June?
1778]" to the effect that "a Proposition from the Enemy to all or any
of these United States for Peace or truce separate from their Allies
is insidious and inadmissable." A copy of these resolutions in the hand
of John Beckley is in DLC: TJ Papers, 3:448, bearing an endorsement
in the hand of Edmund Pendleton which reads in part: "Caveat against
treaty. I believe, but am not certain, these were the work of Mr. Jefferson in Spring 1778." It was this endorsement which misled Ford
and caused him to publish the resolutions on the supposition that TJ
was the author. But these resolutions, important as they were in rejecting the idea of separate peace negotiations on the part of the individual

states; in declaring the intent of Virginia to prosecute "the war with vigour and effect, until peace shall be obtained in a manner consistent with our national faith and fœderal union"; and in binding the Virginia delegates by instructions to this effect, with probable influence over the resolution of Congress of 4 Oct. 1782 [JCC, XXIII, 637-9], were adopted by the House of Delegates on 24 May 1782 and by the Senate on the following day (Hening, XI, 545). TJ, not being a member of that session of the General Assembly and being withdrawn from all public affairs, was certainly not the author of the resolutions.]

Appointment by the General Assembly of a Committee to Investigate and Publish Findings concerning Virginia's Western Claim

In the House of Delegates

Thursday the 30th: of May 1782

Resolved that a Committee of five to wit George Mason, Thomas Jefferson, Arthur Lee, Edmund Randolph and Thomas Walker Esquires be appointed and vested with full Powers to collect all Documents and Proofs necessary for establishing the Right of this State to it's Western Territory as stated by the Act of Government in 1776. To state such Right and apply the Proofs in Support thereof. That the said Committee or a Major Part of those who undertake the Business aforesaid be authorized to publish from time to time in Part, or in the whole such of their Proceedings as they shall think proper. That the public Printer be directed to publish such of the Proceedings of said Committee as he shall be desired by them to publish. That the said Committee shall have power to apply so much of the public Money as shall be necessary for the Purpose of publishing the whole or any Part of their Proceedings in Philadelphia. And that one Copy of their Work when compleated shall be sent to the Legislature of each State in the Federal Union and one Copy thereof presented to Congress.

Teste

JOHN BECKLEY C.H.D.

1782 June 1st
　Agreed to by the Senate
　　Will: Drew C. S.

A Copy

JOHN BECKLEY C.H.D.

Tr (DLC); endorsed by TJ: "Assembly Genl." See Appendix III.

From Chastellux

J'apprend dans le moment, monsieur, que Mr. Jamisson est prêt a partir pour Richmond ou il espere que vous vous rendrés de votre côté, et qu'il s'est même chargé d'une lettre de Mr. d'Oyré pour vous. Je me hate donc de profiter de cette occasion pour vous remercier, non du soin que vous avés bien voulu prendre de mon cheval dont je vous ai pourtant mille obligations, mais des momens heureux que vous m'avés fait passer a Monticello et de l'indulgence extrême que vous m'avés montrée. Elle est telle, monsieur, que j'oserois presque me flatter d'avoir acquis un ami dans celui qui etoit deja l'ami des lettres, des sciences et des arts. Je n'avois pas de droit au partage de votre esprit, qui est si bien occupé; mais je voudrois en avoir obtenu enfin votre coeur et je m'estimerois tres heureux d'y conserver, du moins prétendre quelque place. J'ai eté ettonné du *pont naturel* malgre ce que vous m'en aviés dit. Quand il auroit eté placé plus loin, je n'aurois pas regretté mes pas. J'ai trouvé deux choses en virginie qui valent la peine de les aller chercher bien loin, l'une est le *Pont naturel*, l'autre . . . votre modestie vous empecheroit-elle de la deviner? J'espere, monsieur, que la première sera mieux connue désormais. J'ai envoyé un ingenieur très bon dessinateur en lever les plans et en prendre les perspectives. La seconde sera gravée dans ma memoire; et ce que j'en ai pensé se retrouvera quelque jour dans un journal que j'ai fait de mon voyage, et dont je voudrois soumettre a votre critique tous les articles, excepté un seul. Je me laisse entrainer, monsieur, au plaisir de converser avec vous et je ne pense pas qu'on attend ma lettre dans ce moment-cy. Seroit-il possible que vous vinssiés a Richmond sans descendre jusqu'a Williamsburg et ne puis-je me flatter de vous assurer de vive voix des sentimens sinceres et inalterables avec lesquels j'ai l'honneur d'etre, monsieur, votre tres humble et tres obeissant serviteur,   LE CHR DE CHASTELLUX

Plus j'ai examiné votre lapin d'amerique plus je le trouve semblable a celui d'Europe. Tout ce qu'on peut dire c'est qu'il y a une espece de lapin qui ne terre pas et c'est la votre. M. *d'ulloa* dans ses *noticias americanas* dit que les lapins de l'amerique meridionale ne terrent pas non plus, mais il ne met pas en doute qu'ils ne soient de vrais lapins.

Voules vous bien presenter mes respects a Mde. Jefferson?

RC (DLC).
This letter marks the beginning of a distinguished correspondence between TJ and the Chevalier de Chastellux

(François-Jean, later Marquis de Chastellux), who held the rank of maréchal de camp in Rochambeau's army and who made a tour in the spring of 1782 from Williamsburg to the Natural Bridge, spending four days at Monticello in April. Chastellux kept a journal of his tour and published it as part of his *Voyages . . . dans l'Amérique septentrionale*, Paris, 1786; English translation, London, 1787. His account of TJ's domestic life is the best available for the period before Mrs. Jefferson's death, and his description of Monticello ("Mr. Jefferson is the first American who has consulted the fine arts to know how he should shelter himself from the weather") is of the highest interest. It was undoubtedly at TJ's suggestion that Chastellux went on to view the Natural Bridge in Rockbridge co., on property which TJ had himself acquired in 1774 (see list of his lands in MS of Farm Book, p. 32; quoted in Randall, *Life*, II, 238) and which TJ himself designated "the most sublime of Nature's works" (*Notes on Virginia*, Ford, III, 109). Chastellux furnished a very full description of the Natural Bridge in his *Voyages*, together with plans made by a French military engineer (Baron de Turpin) which were published as engravings in his book; see Chastellux to TJ, 30 June 1782. This was one of the DEUX CHOSES EN VIRGINIE which he had found worth the great trouble to seek out. Chastellux's companion on his tour was MR. D'OYRE (see following letter). M. DE ULLOA: Antonio de Ulloa, whose *Noticias Americanas* (Madrid, 1772) was an important contribution to American natural history (see Sabin 97687; TJ's Library Catalogue, 1815, p. 125).

From D'Oyré

MONSIEUR   a Williamsburg le 10. juin 1782.

Je n'ay point oublié la promesse que je vous ai faite de vous Envoyer Le journal du Siege d'York; Le mémoire de M. Necker sur les finances de France; et le Sermon du docteur Cooper.

M. Le Cher. de Chastelus, qui vous ecrit, vous rappellera probablement, Monsieur, votre Engagement de lui communiquer vos notes si intéressantes sur la Virginie: j'y suis intéressé, par la permission que vous m'avez donnée d'en prendre copie.

M. Jamisson vous dira combien je lui ai parlé de vous, Monsieur; et de Mde. Jefferson. C'est par lui que j'ay appris que vous aviez eté choisi représentant à L'assemblée générale; cette destination contrarie sûrement vos occupations et vos gouts; mais vous trouverez Le dédomagement de vos sacrifices dans l'utilité de vos concitoyens.

Je ne vous dis rien de notre affreux désastre, dont je suis nâvré jusqu'au fonds de L'âme, et comme français, et comme désirant vivement La paix et le bonheur de L'amérique, qu'un tel Evênement ne peut que retarder.

Je suis avec Les sentimens d'Estime et de considération Monsieur Votre très humble et très obéissant Serviteur,

D'OYRÉ

Mrs. Lynch et Dillon me chargent de vous faire Leurs compliments.

[191]

RC (DLC).

François-Ignace, Chevalier d'Oyré, major in Rochambeau's army (Contenson, *La Société de Cincinnati de France*), had accompanied Chastellux on his tour to Monticello and the Natural Bridge in Apr. 1782. NOTRE AFFREUX DESASTRE: Rodney's great naval victory over De Grasse off Dominica, Apr. 1782. M[ES-SIEU]RS. LYNCH ET DILLON: Chastellux's aides-de-camp, who had also accompanied him on his tour in Virginia; Dillon's first name is given as Frank in Chastellux's narrative (*Travels*, London, 1787, II, 2), but neither officer has been further identified.

From James Monroe

DEAR SIR   Richmond June 28. 1782

I am sorry I have had no opportunity or should have answer'd your favor by your servant sooner. Indeed should have wrote by him but was so unlucky as not to see him while in town. I have been much distress'd upon the subject of Mrs. Jefferson and have fear'd, as well from what you suggested yourself as what I have heard from others, that the report of each succeeding day would inform me she was no more. Indeed this was awhile reported and believ'd but I flatter myself that in this instance I shall experience that common fate, who when she has propagated reports unfavorable to myself and my friends I have rarely found to be groundless, has fail'd and that it may please heaven to restore our amiable friend to health and thereby to you a friend whose loss you would always lament, and to your children a parent which no change of circumstance would ever compensate for. You will forgive this obtrusion on an affair which tho' greatly you are not singly interested in, and as I necessarily suppose you are entirely engaged in an attention to and discharge of those tender duties which her situation unhappily requires from you and so anxious and deeply interested in the prospect of an event which so materially concerns the peace and tranquility of your family, I shall forbear to trouble you with an answer to that part of your letter which respects your retreat from publick service. This I shall postpone either till I see you or till I hear the situation of your family will leave your mind more at ease and leasure to attend to a disquisition of the kind, and in the meantime beg leave to assure you that nothing will give me so much pleasure to hear of Mrs. Jefferson's recovery, and to be informed of it from yourself. I forgot in my last to inform you I had receiv'd the parliamentary debates and annual register from Mr. Buchanan and to assure you I will keep them forever as a testimony of your friendship and esteem. Believe me to be Dear Sir very sincerely your friend & servant,   JAS. MONROE

P.S. Your letter to Pelham I sent off instantly and receiv'd a verbal message by my servant that no answer was necessary. You have perhaps heard of my appointment in Council. Engag'd as you are in domestic duties permit me to assure you I wish regularly, as soon as circumstances will permit you, to correspond with you and to have your advice upon every subject of consequence.

RC (DLC).

From Chastellux

a Williamsburg le 30 juin 1782

Quoique les circonstances ne vous ayent pas permis, Monsieur, de vous rendre au desir que j'avois de vous posseder quelques jours a Williamsburg, je ne puis quitter la virginie sans me figurer que je me sépare de vous une seconde fois. Recevés donc avec mes adieux l'hommage de ma reconnoissance pour toutes les prévenances que j'ai recues de vous, et pour le bonheur dont vous m'avés fait jouir a Monticello. Mais en meme tems que je m'avoue votre débiteur a cet égard, permettés moi de vous faire souvenir, que vous etes aussi le mien. Vous avés contracté avec moi un engagement dont je ne pourrai jamais vous dispenser; vous m'avéz promis differentes observations que vous ne m'avés pas envoyées, et que je vous demande avec instance. Si vous voulés, Monsieur, les adresser a Philadelphie, je les recevrai a mon passage dans cette ville.

J'aurois bien desiré vous montrer de très beaux plans du *Pont naturel* faits par l'ingénieur que j'y ai envoyé. Je compte les porter en Europe où ils seront gravés, et feront connoitre dans un autre hemisphere des merveilles de la nature presqu'ignorés dans celui cy. Mais le tems approche ou les américains auront le loisir de regarder autour d'eux, et de compter les tresors qu'ils possedent. Ce ne sera pas la nature brute qui leur ofrira ceux qu'ils doivent le plus estimer. Ils en trouveront un qui se cache dans les montagnes, mais qui doit, tôt ou tard, en sortir pour enrichir et illustrer la virginie.

J'ai l'honneur d'etre, Monsieur, avec le plus sincere attachement, votre très humble et tres obeissant serviteur,

LE CHR. DE CHASTELLUX

J'ai appris avec beaucoup de douleur que Madame Jefferson avait eté malade. J'espere qu'elle est maintenant retablie et je vous suplie, Monsieur, de lui presenter mes plus respectueux hommages.

M. le ch. d'Oyré, M. Lynch et M. Dillon me chargent de les rappeler a votre souvenir.

RC (DLC). TJ did not receive the present letter until 17 Oct., more than a month after Mrs. Jefferson's death (see TJ's answer, 26 Nov. 1782).

From Benjamin Franklin

DEAR SIR   Passy, July 15. 1782.

I was in great Hopes when I saw your Name in the Commission for treating of Peace, that I should have had the Happiness of seeing you here, and of enjoying again in this World, your pleasing Society and Conversation. But I begin now to fear that I shall be disappointed, as I was in my Expectation of your Company when I first undertook the Voyage hither.

Mr. Jones, who possibly may have the honour of delivering this into your hands, is a particular Friend of Mine, and a zealous one of our Cause and Country. I am sure you will be pleas'd with his Conversation, and therefore I make no Apology for recommending him to your Civilities. His Fellow Traveller too, Mr. Paradise an amiable and worthy Character, will merit, your Regards. He has affairs in Virginia, in which possibly your Counsels and Countenance may be of use to him, and which I therefore beg you would afford him. If in anything I can render you or your Friends any Service here, you will do me a Pleasure in commanding freely, Dear Sir, Your most obedient and most humble Servant,

B FRANKLIN

RC (CtY).

On John Paradise and his AFFAIRS IN VIRGINIA, see Franklin to TJ, 6 May 1781, and note there. On 15 July, in Paris, William Jones and Paradise wrote Franklin in part as follows: "Mr. Paradise and Mr. Jones present their grateful respects to their inestimable friend Dr. Franklin . . . requesting him . . . if he has not had leisure to write the letters, with which he kindly intended to favour them, to send them by the post directed to Mr. [Jonathan] Williams at Nantes, as they propose to set out towards Orleans as soon as the heat of the day is a little abated. They wish him perfect health and all possible happiness, hoping again to pay their respects to him on their return from America" (Jones and Paradise to Franklin, 15 July 1782, PU).

From Thomas Turpin

DEAR SIR   [Before 7 August 1782]

Not having had the Pleasure of Seeing or even of hearing from you for a long time I am at length oblig'd to apply to you for Payment of the rent of my Tenemen[t] at Richmd. I have forborn to apply to the Assembly for Pay as I think I had no right having had your Promise for the Payment of the rent tho' you have Promised to Pay me 8000 wt. of Tobo. I think 10000 is no extravagant demand as tenements of less value then rented at near three times that Sum. I hope Sir you will Send or order the Tobo. as soon as you can for as I told you above, I am &c Your Affectn. Friend,

THOS. TURPIN

RC (Vi); addressed: "To Mr. Thos. Jefferson." This letter was enclosed in TJ to Benjamin Harrison, 7 Aug. 1782, following.

YOUR PROMISE FOR THE PAYMENT OF THE RENT: See TJ to Turpin, 23 Dec. 1780 (Vol. 4: 225).

To Benjamin Harrison

SIR   Monticello Aug. 7. 1782.

The inclosed letters from Colo. Turpin will in some measure explain to you the reason of my troubling you with the present application. On the removal of the seat of government I engaged his house on the hill. A house having been always found for the Governor I took for granted that the rent of that would be considered as a public charge. Tho' from the nature of my application to Colo. Turpin I became personally liable to him, I flatter myself it will still be the opinion that it should be paid by the public. I therefore take the liberty of asking your interposition so far as to have a determination of the point by the Executive if you think it properly within their determination, or a reference to the Auditors if you judge that more proper. But what I most particularly sollicit your favor in is that it might be paid immediately if possible, as I shall otherwise think myself bound to pay it which I really cannot do without much inconvenience. My tobaccoes of the last year having been destroyed by the enemy, I with great difficulty contrive the paiment of my taxes and can provide the additional sum of this rent, if I am to pay it, by no other means than a sale of some part of my estate. You will observe what Colo. Turpin sais in his last letter as to the quantum of the rent, as also in the former letters every thing which has passed on that subject. I thought his first letter left it in my power to fix it at 8000 ℔. of tobo., and after advising with Mr. Buchanan I closed it at that. It is one year's rent for which I stand answerable. I have written to Colo. Turpin that I would apply to you on this subject and taken the liberty of desiring him to ask from you the result.

I have the honour to be with very real esteem & respect Your Excellency's Most obedt. & most humble servt.,

Th: Jefferson

RC (Vi); addressed and endorsed. Enclosures (Vi): Turpin's letters to TJ of 22 and 30 Dec. 1780 and that printed under 7 Aug. 1782, preceding.

On 24 Sep. 1782 the Council authorized payment to Turpin (see Harrison to TJ, 3 Oct. 1782). TJ's letter TO COLO. TURPIN has not been found.

Lines Copied from Tristram Shandy by Martha and Thomas Jefferson

Time wastes too fast:[1] every letter
I trace tells me with what rapidity
life follows my pen. The days and hours
of it are flying over our heads like
clouds of windy day never to return——
more every thing presses on[2]——and every
time I kiss thy hand to bid adieu, every absence which
follows it, are preludes to that eternal separation
which we are shortly to make!

MS (James Monroe Law Office, courtesy of L. G. Hoes, Fredericksburg, Va.); in the hand of Martha Wayles Jefferson with additional lines by TJ as indicated below; endorsed on verso by Martha Jefferson Randolph: "A Lock of my Dear Mama's Hair inclosed in a verse which she wrote." The original is wrapped around a lock of Mrs. Jefferson's hair and is accompanied by an authentication in the hand of a granddaughter.

There is no date on this affecting exchange of sentiment between two gifted people whose marriage was one of consummate happiness, but the lines must have been written in the weeks—perhaps days—immediately preceding Martha's death on 6 Sep. 1782. Martha Jefferson Randolph later recalled that her father had been in constant attendance on her mother during this last illness: "For four months that she lingered he was never out of Calling. When not at her bed side he was writing in a small room which opened immediately at the head of her bed" ("Reminiscences of Th J. by MR," from MS copy made by Mary and Anne Cary Randolph, ViU). We may imagine that sometime during these months, facing an eventuality too painful to be spoken about, Martha turned to the lines of *Tristram Shandy* that both recalled, and he continued the passage. The full text from Sterne is as follows: "I will not argue the matter: Times wastes too fast: every letter I trace tells me with what rapidity Life follows my pen; the days and hours of it, more precious, my dear *Jenny!* than the rubies about thy neck, are flying over our heads like light clouds of a windy day, never to return more——every thing presses on ——whilst thou art twisting that lock, ——see! it grows grey; and every time I kiss thy hand to bid adieu, and every absence which follows it, are preludes to that eternal separation which we are shortly to make.——Heaven have mercy upon us both!" (*The Life and Opinions of Tristram Shandy, Gentleman. By Laurence Sterne*, Shakespeare Head Edition, Oxford, 1926, III, 166-7). The editors wish to express their grateful appreciation to Professor Edward L. Hubler of the Department of English, Princeton University, for identifying these lines. Though this identification proves that the lines were copied from another rather than composed by Martha and TJ, they are included here because they represent the only known writing of any sort exchanged between the two that has been preserved. Martha Jefferson Randolph evidently thought that her mother had composed the lines and that they were intended as verse.

¹ The colon is in dark ink and is written over some mark or letter (perhaps "e"). TJ evidently corrected Martha's transcription of the lines.

² Everything preceding this point is in a faded ink in the handwriting of Martha Wayles Jefferson; all that follows is in a darker ink and in TJ's hand. MS is here given line for line and verbatim save for the fact that the first word in first line and fifth word in third line are begun with initial capitals.

To Benjamin Harrison

SIR   Monticello Sep. 22. 1782.

I do myself the honour of inclosing you a letter received from Mr. Thomas Smith as agent for Mr. Nathan. I have no idea that the laws, as they stand at present, can give him an action against me for assumpsits of public debts, made in council and so expressed with their unanimous advice, and this in the presence of Mr. Nathan, who knew the debts to be public, who applied to me as a public officer for paiment, and who has never before pretended to consider it but as a public affair. And even were it possible that the present laws should leave me exposed to shipwreck where there never was anything in the nature of a private assumpsit, I suppose it not possible they should be permitted to remain so. The purpose of the present trouble I give your Excellency is to ask whether, should any suit be brought against me, I may take the liberty of remitting the defence wholly to the public whose concern alone it is? I had had some thoughts of abstracting myself awhile from this state by a journey to Philadelphia or somewhere else Northwardly; but I suppose it would not be safe for me to leave a state by whose laws I must certainly be protected and trust myself in another where that protection would be doubtful.

MS not found. Text printed from Ford, III, 60-1, where the letter is printed from a copy then in Vi. The enclosed letter from Thomas Smith to TJ has not been found.

On the Nathan matter, see TJ to Board of Trade, 18 Mch. 1780, and TJ to Randolph, 18 July 1783, and references there.

To Henry Tazewell

SIR   Monticello Sep. 30. 1782.

The unhappy circumstances which have abstracted me from all business during the preceding summer will I hope apologize for my being so late in acknowleging the receipt of your letter of June 8. on the subject of the papers in the case of Kennon's trustees. I have copies [of the] Bill, Mr. Kennon's answer, Mr. Wayles and Hardyman's joint answer, the separate answer of Acrill, the joint one of Baker & Thompson, list of the suits wherein Mr. Wayles and Hardyman were bail and the decree. But these are all of them copies, and so attested by Mr. Davenport. If I ever saw the original papers, be assured that they did not remain in my possession, as I never trusted myself with the custody of such papers. I kn[ow tha]t I have seen the original instrument of exoneration sig[ned by] the creditors, but I have no copy of that. I am Sir Your very humble servt,   TH: JEFFERSON

P.S. On recurring to another bundle of papers I find an attested copy of the instrument of exonerat[ion.]

RC (Lloyd W. Smith, Madison, N.J., 1951); slightly mutilated; addressed to Tazewell at Williamsburg; endorsed: "Thos. Jefferson Oct: 1782." Tazewell's letter of 8 June 1782 has not been found.

To Elizabeth Wayles Eppes

MY DEAR MADAM   [3? October 1782]

The girls being unable to assure you themselves of their welfare the duty devolves on me and I undertake it the more willingly as it will lay you under the necessity of sometimes letting us hear from you. They are in perfect health and as happy as if they had no part in the unmeasurable loss we have sustained. Patsy rides with me 5 or 6. miles a day and presses for permission to accompany me on horseback to Elkhill whenever I shall go there. When that may be however I cannot tell; finding myself absolutely unable to attend to any thing like business. This miserable kind of existence is really too burthensome to be borne, and were it not for the infidelity of deserting the sacred charge left me, I could not wish it's continuance a moment. For what could it be wished? All my plans of comfort and happiness reversed by a single event[1] and nothing answering in prospect before me but a gloom unbrightened with one chearful expectation. The care and instruction of our children indeed affords some temporary abstractions from wretchedness and nourishes a soothing reflection that if there be beyond the grave any concern for the things of this world there is one angel at least who views these attentions with pleasure and wishes continuance of them while she must pity the miseries to which they confine me.

But I forget that I began this correspondence on behalf of the children and am afflicting you at the distance of 70 or 80 miles with sorrows[2] which you had a right to think yourself out of the reach of. I will endeavor to correct myself and keep what I feel to myself that I may not dispirit you from a communication with us. News from hence you will not expect. Mrs. Gilmer's getting better and better is the only event I recollect which can be interesting to you. I say nothing of coming to Eppington because I promised you this should not be till I could support such a countenance as might not cast a damp on the chearfulness of others. I shall begin to expect Jack in a week or ten days. When he shall have been with me some time he will I hope furnish me with a pleasing subject for a letter to Mr. Eppes. At present having neither business, politics nor news to communicate, I do not trouble him with an epistle of small stuff as your injunctions have obliged me to do you. Be so good as to tender my sincere esteem to him and to the family and sometimes to recollect yourself the fr[iend]ships & affection with which I am Dr. Madam your most obedt hble servt.,

Dft (MHi); written on the address-leaf of a letter addressed, in the hand of Edmund Randolph, to "Thomas Jefferson esquire Monticello Albemarle." This draft contains many alterations, deletions, and interlineations, of which two are noted below.

This appears to be the first intimate, personal letter written by TJ after his wife's death and the great care which he took in its composition, to say nothing of the expressions that he allowed to remain, testify to the overwhelming grief that he experienced. Randolph may have visited Monticello about this time and he certainly gave one of the most graphic accounts of Jefferson's grief: "Mrs. Jefferson has at last shaken off her tormenting pains, by yielding to them, and has left our friend inconsolable. I ever thought him to rank domestic happiness in the first class of the chief good; but scarcely supposed that his grief would be so violent as to justify the circulating report of his swooning away whenever he sees his children" (Randolph to Madison, 20 Sep. 1782, quoted in Henkels Catalogue 694 [1892], lot 86). James Madison thought TJ's "philosophical temper renders the circulating rumor which you mention altogether incredible" (Madi-

son to Randolph, 30 Sep. 1782, DLC: Madison Papers), but TJ's daughter Martha left an account which validates the basis for the rumor that Randolph reported: ". . . after her death, during the first month of desolation that followed I was his constant companion, while we remained at Monticello.... As a nurse no female ever had more tenderness or anxiety; he nursed my poor Mother in turn with aunt Carr [Mrs. Dabney Carr] and her own sisters [Randall, *Jefferson*, I, 382, gives the reading as "sister," who, of course, would have been the recipient of the present letter] setting up with her and administring her medecines and drink to the last. For four months that she lingered he was never out of Calling. When not at her bed side he was writing in a small room which opened immediately at the head of her bed. A moment before the closing scene he was led from the room almost in a state of insensibility by his sister Mrs. Carr who with great difficulty got him into his library where he fainted and remained so long insensible that they feared he never would revive. The scene that followed I did not witness but the violence of his emotion, of his grief when almost by stealth I entered his room at night to this day I dare not trust myself to describe. He kept his room for three weeks and I was never a moment from his side. He walked almost incessantly night and day only lying down occasionally when nature was completely exhausted on a pallet that had been brought in during his long fainting fit. My Aunts remained constantly with him for some weeks, I do not remember how many. When at last he left his room he rode out and from that time he was incessantly on horseback rambling about the mountain in the least frequented roads and just as often through the woods; in those melancholy rambles I was his constant companion, a solitary witness to many a violent burst of grief, the remembrance of which has consecrated particular scenes of that lost home beyond the power of time to obliterate" ("Reminiscences of Th.J. by MR," from a MS copy made by Mary and Anne Cary Randolph, ViU; one word supplied from text in Randall, *Jefferson*, I, 382, who states that these recollections were drawn up in answer to some queries from Tucker for use in his biography of TJ). Though written nearly half a century afterwards, this comment by Martha (who was ten at the time of her mother's death) is so clear in its details as to leave little doubt of its general accuracy. It may be safely assumed, therefore, that the statement "He kept his room for three weeks" and the assertion "My Aunts remained constantly with him for some weeks" are dependable and that TJ began to emerge from his deep withdrawal sometime in late September. Presumably Mrs. Eppes had returned to Eppington by the end of that month; the date of 3 Oct. 1782 has been assigned to the present letter as the probable date of its composition on the ground that, on that date, TJ entered in his Account Book: "gave . . . [Jupiter] to pay ferrges by Eppington to Richmd 5/." I SHALL BEGIN TO EXPECT JACK: This was probably John Wayles Eppes, who later married TJ's daughter Mary.

[1] TJ deleted the following at this point: "and myself thrown on the world at a time of life when I should be withdrawn."
[2] TJ deleted at this point: "of another you participated in recently while here."

From Benjamin Harrison

DEAR SIR   In Council October 3d. 1782.

Payment has been some time order'd for the rent of the House you lived in whilst Governor of the State and Colo. Turpen may receive the Money whenever he pleases to apply to the Agent.

Should Mr. Nathan, Mr. Smith or any other person bring a Suit against you for any Contracts or Acceptances made by you on behalf of the State, whilst chief Magistrate, the Executive will take your defence on them in behalf of the State and in every respect protect you from Damage, which will fully appear to you by the enclosed Order. I am Dear sir, &c.,   B.H.

FC (Vi). Enclosures: Order in Council of 2 Oct. 1782 and possibly of 24 Sep. 1782 (see below).

THE RENT OF THE HOUSE: See TJ to Harrison, 7 Aug. 1782; on 24 Sep. the Council ordered that "A demand being made by Colo. Turpin of eight thousand weight of Tobacco for the rent of his house for the use of the Governor: The Commercial Agent is desired to discharge the same according to Mr. Jef-fersons contract out of the first public tobacco he may receive" (MS Va. Council Jour., Vi; this order was revoked 23 Nov. 1782 and the treasurer ordered to deliver to Henry Young "Nine hhds. of Upper Rappahanock Tobacco amounting as near as may be to 9600 lb. . . . to be paid to Doctor Turpin for one years rent of the Governors house"; same). THE ENCLOSED ORDER: On 2 Oct. 1782 the following is recorded in the proceedings of the Council: "The Governor having laid before the Board a Letter from Mr. Jefferson touching the acceptance of sundry Bills in the possession of Mr. Simon Nathan, of Philadelphia, drawn by General Clarke and others on the State of Virga. and enclosing a Letter from Thomas Smith Agent for the said Nathan: The Board on considering the Subject Matter of the Several Letters, advise that a Letter be written to Mr. Jefferson assuring him that should Mr. Nathan institute a suit against him on account of his acceptance of the said Bills as Governor of this State, the whole expence that may be incurred either in defending the said Suit or that may be recovered in consequence of it shall be defrayed by the State, as they conceive that no assumpsit of Mr. Jefferson in his public capacity can bind him in his private character" (same; see also TJ to Harrison, 22 Sep. 1782).

From Arthur Campbell

SIR   Richmond Nov. 7th. 1782

Permit me to present to you a large Jaw tooth of an unknown Animal lately found at the Salina in Washington County.

The Salina lyes near that branch of the Cherokee River called North Holstein in a Plain or Meadow ground of about three Miles in circumference surrounded by a number of high round Hills or Knobs: in the center of the Meadow is a Pond of Water, adjoining it is a Marsh except in dry seasons in which Pits are sunk to reach the Veins or Springs of Salt Water. In sinking one of these Pits, several feet under the surface was found Bones of an uncommon size, of which the Jaw Tooth now offered you is one.

I shall hope thro your means at some future day to see in print, some disquisitions on the subject.

Whether it is a bone of same kind of Animal, as those found near the Ohio in Fayette. Whether of the carnivorous Species; or those that feed on Vegetables? Why the Species are extinct; or at least unknown, since the introduction of Europeans into the New World.

Major Alexander Ouitleau, the present director of the Salt Works, sent me the Bone a few days before I set out for this place; any future information you may desire, he will gladly transmit it.

I am Sir with great Respect Your very humble servant,

ARTHUR CAMPBELL

RC (DLC).   MAJOR ALEXANDER OUITLEAU was Major Outlaw of North Carolina (see *N.C. State Records*, Saunders ed., XVIII, 696-700).

From Robert R. Livingston, enclosing Jefferson's Appointment as a Peace Commissioner

SIR   Philadelphia, 13th. Novr. 1782.

I have the honor to transmit a resolution of Congress, appointing you one of their[1] Ministers Plenipotentiary for negociating a peace. I rejoice in this fresh proof of their confidence in your Virtue and abilities. The sacrifices you have heretofore made to the interests of your Country, induce me to hope that you will suffer no personal consideration to prevent their being employed in its service upon this important occasion.

I have the honor to be, Sir With the greatest respect and esteem Your most obedt humble Servt.,   ROBT R. LIVINGSTON

ENCLOSURE

By the United States in Congress Assembled

RESOLVED   November 12th. 1782.

That the appointment of Thomas Jefferson Esquire, as a Minister Plenipotentiary for negotiating peace on the fifteenth day of June 1781. be and the same is hereby renewed, and that on his acceptance thereof, he be invested with all the Powers and be subject to all the Instructions which have been or may be issued by Congress to the Ministers Plenipotentiary for negotiating peace in the same manner as if his original appointment had taken effect.   CHAS. THOMSON Secy.

RC (MHi); in a clerk's hand, signed by Livingston; endorsed by TJ: "Livingston Rob. R. Phila. Nov. 13. 1782 recd Amphthill [*sic*] Nov. 25. 1782. Renewal of Appmt. of June 15. 1781. as Min. Plenipy. for negociating peace." Dft (NHi). Tr (DLC: PCC, No. 119). Enclosure (filed with RC in MHi) in a clerk's hand, signed by Thomson; also endorsed by TJ. The original resolution, in James Madison's hand, is in DLC: PCC, No. 36, I; endorsed by Charles Thomson: "Motion of Mr Madison Passed 12 Novr 1782."

The Journals state that the resolution renewing TJ's appointment (see Huntington to TJ, 15 June 1781, and enclosure) was made on the motion of Madison, seconded by Theodorick Bland, but Madison's "Notes of Debates" add the following details: "The reappointment of Mr. Jefferson as Minister Plenipo: for negotiating peace was agreed to unanimously and without a single adverse remark. The act took place in consequence of its being suggested that the death of Mrs. J. had probably changed the sentiments of Mr. J. with regard to public life, and that all the reasons which led to his original appointment still existed, and indeed, had acquired additional force from the improbability that Mr. Laurens would actually assist in the negotiation" (JCC, XXIII, 720, 848). How correctly TJ's friends in Congress judged his feelings is clear from his immediate and favorable reply to the present letter; see under 26 Nov. 1782, and see also TJ's "Autobiography" (Ford, I, 71-2).

[1] Livingston first wrote, in the draft, the word "Commissioners" and then interlined "Ministers Plenipotentiary."

To Chastellux

Dear Sir   Ampthill Nov. 26. 1782.

I received your friendly letters of[1]   and June 30 but the
latter not till the 17th. of Oct. It found me a little emerging from
that stupor of mind which had rendered me as dead to the world
as she[2] was whose loss occasioned it. Your letter recalled to my
memory, that there were persons still living of much value to me.
If you should have thought me remiss in not testifying to you sooner
how deeply I had been impressed with your worth in the little time
I had the happiness of being with you you will I am sure ascribe
it to it's true cause the state of dreadful suspence in which I had
been kept all the summer and the catastrophe which closed it.
Before that event my scheme of life had been determined. I had
folded myself in the arms of retirement, and rested all prospects of
future happiness on domestic and literary objects. A single event
wiped away all my plans and left me a blank which I had not the
spirits to fill up. In this state of mind an appointment from Congress found me requiring me to cross the Atlantic, and that temptation might be added to duty I was informed at the same time from
his Excy. the Chevalier de la Luzerne that a vessel of force would
be sailing about the middle of Dec. in which you would be passing
to France. I accepted the appointment and my only object now is
so to hasten over those obstacles which would retard my departure
as to be ready to join you in your voiage, fondly measuring your
affections by my own and presuming your consent. It is not certain
that by any exertions I can be in Philadelphia by the middle of
December. The contrary is most probable. But hoping it will not
be much later and counting on those procrastinations which usually
attend the departure of vessels of size I have hopes of being with
you in time. This will give me full Leisure to learn the result of
your observations on the Natural bridge, to communicate to you
my answers to the queries of Monsr. de Marbois, to receive edifica-
tion from you on these and on other subjects of science, considering
chess too as a matter of science. Should I be able to set out in
tolerable time and any extraordinary delays attend the sailing of
the vessel I shall certainly do myself the honour of waiting on his
Excy. Count Rochambeau at his Headquarters and of assuring him
in person of my high respect and esteem for him—an object of
which I have never lost sight. To yourself I am unable to express
the warmth of those sentiments of friendship and attachment with

which I have the honour to be Dr Sir Your most obedt. & mo. hble. servt.

Dft (DLC); written on the cover of a letter addressed to TJ; notation of address at foot of text: "The Chevalr. de Chastellux Marechal de camp Philadelphia." Dft is much corrected, but with one exception the corrections are not noted here, all of them being variations in phraseology only. The RC is presumably in the archives of Château de Chastellux, Chastellux (Yonne), France (communication from Duc de Duras to Howard C. Rice, Jr., 20 May 1950, wherein TJ's letter to Chastellux of this date is described as a "copie").

1 Blank in MS. TJ no doubt refers to Chastellux's letter of 10 June 1782.
2 This word deleted (by error?) in Dft. TJ may have intended to insert it after the word following so that the passage would read, instead, "as was she whose loss occasioned it."

To George Rogers Clark

DEAR SIR   Nov. 26. 1782.

I received in August your favour wherein you give me hopes of your being able to procure for me some of the big bones. I should be unfaithful to my own feelings were I not to express to you how much I am obliged by your attention to the request I made you on that subject. A specimen of each of the several species of bones now to be found is to me the most desireable object in Natural history, and there is no expence of package or of safe transportation which I will not gladly reimburse to procure them safely. Elkhorns of very extraordinary size, petrifactions, or any thing else uncommon would be very acceptable. New London in Bedford, Staunton in Augusta, or Fredericksburg are places from whence I can surely get them. Mr. Steptoe in the first place, Colo. Matthews in the second, Mr. Dick in the third will take care of them for me. You will perhaps hear of my being gone to Europe, but my trip there will be short. I mention this lest you should hesitate in forwarding any curiosities for me. Any observations of your own on the subject of the big bones or their history, or on any thing else in the Western country, will come acceptably to me, because I know you see the works of nature in the great, and not merely in detail. Descriptions of animals, vegetables, minerals, or other curious things, notes as to the Indians, information of the country between the Missisipi and waters of the South sea &c. &c. will strike your mind as worthy being communicated. I wish you had more time to pay attention to them.

I perceive by your letter you are not unapprised that your services to your country have not made due impression on every mind. That you have enemies you must not doubt, when you reflect that

View of the Natural Bridge

Resignation of General Washington, December 23, 1783

you have made yourself eminent. If you meant to escape malice you should have confined yourself within the sleepy line of regular duty. When you transgressed this and enterprized deeds which will hand down your name with honour to future times, you made yourself a mark for malice and envy to shoot at. Of these there is enough both in and out of office. I was not a little surprized however to find one person hostile to you as far as he has personal courage to shew hostility to any man. Who he is you will probably have heard, or may know him by this description as being all tongue without either head or heart.[1] In the variety of his crooked[2] schemes however, his interests may probably veer about so as to put it in your power to be useful to him; in which case he certainly will be your friend again if you want him. That you may long continue a fit object for his enemity and for that of every person of his complexion in the state, which I know can only be by your continuing to do good to your country and honour to yourself is the earnest prayer of one who subscribes himself with great truth & sincerity Dr. Sir Your friend & servt.,   TH: JEFFERSON

RC (WHi); docketed in the hand of Lyman C. Draper. Dft (DLC). Neither copy bears external evidence as to the addressee, but RC is among the Clark Papers in the Draper Collection, and TJ is manifestly replying to Clark's letter of 20 Feb. 1782, received in August. This letter has been printed from Dft by HAW, by Ford, and by L & B as if addressed to "Mr." or "James Steptoe," who is, however, mentioned in the letter itself. Dft shows numerous corrections and varies in small details from RC; one major correction is recorded below.

Both the long deletion indicated below and the embittered characterization of THE ONE PERSON HOSTILE TO YOU in the text above prove that TJ had Patrick Henry in mind. On many other occasions for the next four decades TJ expressed derogatory (and occasionally commendatory) estimates of Henry, but rarely did he exceed the bitterness exhibited in the present letter. This attitude was undoubtedly due to the fact that TJ considered Henry the one who had induced George Nicholas to introduce the resolution in the General Assembly calling for an investigation of the conduct of the Executive and had made TJ the target of a cruel and vindictive but hidden assault (see TJ to Isaac Zane, 24 Dec. 1781; for other characterizations of Henry, see TJ to Madison, 7 May 1783, 8 Dec. 1784, and 18 Mch. 1785; to William Wirt, 12 Apr. 1812; to William Short, 16 Oct. 1792; and to Archibald Stuart, 14 May 1799).

[1] Preceding two sentences read as follows in Dft: "I was not a little surprized however to find one person ⟨your enemy⟩ hostile to you as far as he has personal courage to ⟨be the enemy of⟩ shew hostility to any man. ⟨You will know who I mean by recollecting among those who concerted with you your first great expedition one who is⟩ Who he is you will probably have heard, or may know him by this description as being," &c., as in RC.

[2] By "crooked" TJ meant that the schemes were devious or tortuous, not criminal or dishonest. TJ thought that Henry's capacity for intrigue and manipulation exceeded his indubitable eloquence, but there is no evidence that he ever considered him venal.

To Robert R. Livingston

SIR   Chesterfeild Nov. 26. 1782.

I received yesterday the letter with which you have been pleased to honour me, inclosing the resolution of Congress of the 12th. inst. renewing my appointment as one of their ministers plenipotentiary for negotiating a peace; and beg leave through you to return my sincere thanks to that august body for the confidence they are pleased to repose in me and to tender the same to yourself for the obliging manner in which you have notified it. I will employ in this arduous charge, with diligence and integrity, the best of my poor talents, which I am conscious are far short of what it requires.[1] This I hope will ensure to me from Congress a kind construction of all my transactions, and it gives me no small pleasure that my communications will pass through the hands of a gentleman with whom I have acted in the earlier stages of this contest, and whose discernment and candour I had the good fortune then to prove and esteem. Your letter finds me at a distance from home, attending on my family under inoculation. This will add to the delay which the arrangement of my particular affairs would necessarily occasion. I shall lose no moment however in preparing for my departure, and shall hope to pay my respects to Congress and to yourself at some-time between the twentieth and the last of December. I have the honour to be with very great esteem & respect Sir Your most obedt. & most humble servt.,   TH: JEFFERSON

RC (PHC); endorsed: "29th. [sic] Novr. 1782. From Mr. Jefferson." Dft (DLC); endorsed: "Livingston Robert R"; there are many corrections and alterations in the draft, most of which pertain to choice of phraseology, but one of which is noted below. The date may possibly refer to La Luzerne's letter of 29 Nov.; it could not possibly be the date of receipt. Tr (DLC: PCC, No. 119).

[1] At this point TJ deleted in the draft an expression which reflects his determination, borne out by the record of his mission, to represent the interests of the country as a whole: "But I shall trust that if I pursue the object of my mission with integrity and impartial regard to the good of the whole states, I shall," &c. He no doubt deleted this on the ground that his very appointment subsumed both integrity and impartiality on the part of the minister appointed.

To James Madison

DEAR SIR   Ampthill in Chesterfield Nov. 26. 1782.

Your favour by Colo. Basset is not yet come to hand. The intimation through the Attorney I received the day before Colo. Bland's arrival by whom I am honoured with your's of the 14th inst. It finds me at this place attending my family under inoculation. This will of course retard those arrangements of my domestic affairs which will of themselves take time and cannot be made but at home. I shall lose no time however in preparing for my departure; and from the calculation's I am at present enabled to make I suppose I cannot be in Philadelphia before the 20th. of December, and that possibly it may be the last of that month. Some days I must certainly pass there; as I could not propose to jump into the midst of a negotiation without a single article of previous information. From these data you will be enabled to judge of the chance of availing myself of his Excy. the Chev. de la Luzerne's kind offer to whom I beg you to present my thanks for his friendly attention and to let him know I shall use my best endeavors to be in time for the departure of his frigate. No circumstance of a private nature could induce me to hasten over the several obstacles to my departure more unremittingly than the hope of having the Chevalr. de Chattlux as a companion in my voiage. A previous acquaintance with his worth and abilities had impressed me with an affection for him which under the then prospect of never seeing him again was perhaps imprudent.

I am with very sincere esteem Dr. Sir Your affectionate friend & humble servt.

Dft (DLC); at foot of text: "Hon. James Madison at Congress." Corrections made in composition are not noted here.

Neither Madison's FAVOUR BY COLO. BASSET nor that of THE 14TH INST. has been found. The INTIMATION THROUGH THE ATTORNEY clearly refers to the fact that, before TJ received Livingston's official notification or Madison's (missing) letter of 14 Nov., Edmund Randolph (THE ATTORNEY) had informed him of the news of the reappointment; for Madison had written Randolph on 12 Nov. in which he quoted the resolution that he had introduced and added: "This resolution passed a few minutes ago. I sent you a line for the post but I fear too late. This catches Doctr. Tucker in the street proceeding by the State House. You will let it be known to Mr. J. as quickly as secrecy will admit. An official notification will follow by the first opportunity. This will prepare him for it: It passed unanimously and without a single remark adverse to it. On this subject again by the post next week or by Col: B[land] if earlier" (Madison, *Writings*, ed. Hunt, I, 257). On the 14th Madison again wrote Randolph: "Col. Bland by whom this goes, conveys an official notification from Mr. Livingston under cover to Col. Monroe. As you will probably in consequence of it, if not before have an interview with Mr. [J.], no observations on the subject are necessary. I confide in his acceptance and flatter myself with the pleasure of soon seeing him in Philada." (same, I, 257). It is possible that Theodorick Bland also carried a (missing) letter from LA LUZERNE to TJ informing him of the opportunity to sail on a French vessel (see TJ to Chastellux, this date). Randolph saw TJ on 28 Nov. and found it "unnecessary to add incentives to his acceptance of his plenipotentiary-ship" (Randolph to Madison, 29 Nov. 1782; also 8 Nov. and 13 Dec. 1782; DLC: Madison Papers).

From Arthur Campbell

Richmond Nov. 29. 1782

On my way here I shewed Colo. Preston the tooth I sent you. At first sight, before I told him where it was found, he give it as his opinion that it was of the same animal as those found near the Ohio, a tooth of which he had obtained above 30 years ago and thinks it was sent to England. Doctor Lee says it is the same species, of that sent to England from the Ohio, that being a member, he was present when the subject was discussed, in a meeting of the Royal Society, and that it was satisfactorily demonstrated, that the species was of the carnivorous kind. Perhaps the result of this produced Doctr. Hunters Publication. Several sensible Africans have seen the tooth, particularly a fellow at your neighbour Colo. Lewises, all of whom pronounced it an Elephants. A certain Mr. Stanley was captivated by the Indians, some years ago, near the mouth of the Cherokee River on his way to the Mississippi. I have been told by different persons that since his return, he relates, that after being transfered from one Tribe to another, he was at length carried over Mountains west of the Missouri, to a River that runs Westwardly; that the natives told him there were animals in the Country which from the description he judges to be Elephants. These apparent contradictions still leaves the matter in doubt. I trouble you with the information to assist in your researches.

I hear you are destined for Europe, and am particularly happy you are likely to have a share in forming the ultimatum of our long Struggle. The Western Country I have been afraid, would not be properly attended to. I who have travelled thro it, in different directions from Lake Huron, to the Hiwasee, well know its importance: It will cramp our prospects exceedingly, and be ruinous to the adjacent Country, should Britain retain her Claim to the banks of the Ohio. We had better fight a year or two more than submit to such a Claim. I am told that it was once the view of Congress to insist for our limits, to extend as high as Lat. 45°. I should think we have gained a great point if it would include the Cataract at Niagara, west thro the middle of Lake Erie to the Illinois and down the same. Excuse my freedom. My prayers and best wishes will attend you. With sentiments of the most perfect esteem and respect I am Sir Your most Obedient Servant,

ARTHUR CAMPBELL

P.S. I will not fail in sending other Bones to Mr. Steptoe.

RC (DLC); addressed: "The Honbe. Thomas Jefferson."

DOCTOR LEE: Arthur Lee, who had earned his M.D. at Edinburgh, afterwards settled in London and in 1766 was elected a member of THE ROYAL SOCIETY, at a meeting of which (25 Feb. 1768) the famous anatomist DOCTR. [WILLIAM] HUNTER read a paper on the collection of fossil bones furnished by George Croghan and housed in the Tower of London. In this paper, entitled "Observations on the Bones, Commonly Supposed to Be Elephant's Bones, Which Have Been Found Near the River Ohio, in America" (*Philos. Trans. Royal Soc.*, LVIII [1769], 34-45), Hunter concluded that the bones were those of a carnivorous mammal, not the elephant, which he designated as the "American *incognitum*" and which he believed was extinct. In *Notes on Virginia*, Query VI, TJ agreed with Hunter that the fossil bones found in the Ohio Valley were those of a carnivore and not the elephant, but he denied that the *incognitum* or American mammoth was extinct, citing Indian testimony and also the MR. STANLEY mentioned in the present letter in support of this view (Ford, III, 130ff., 144). On the controversy over the fossil bones, see George Gaylord Simpson, "The Beginnings of Vertebrate Paleontology in North America," Amer. Philos. Soc., *Procs.*, LXXXVI (1942-1943), 148ff. A MS copy of Hunter's paper is to be found among the papers of Thomas Hutchins, PHi.

La Luzerne to Robert Livingston

MONSIEUR   A Philadelphie le 29. Novembre 1782.

J'ai reçu la lettre par laquelle Vous m'apprenés le renouvellement de la Commission de M. Jepherson et la resolution du Congrès dont elle etoit accompagnée; c'est avec peine que j'avois vû ce Ministre decliner de prendre part à la négotiation pour la paix et j'apprends avec un grand plaisir qu'il se dispose à joindre les autres Ministres que le Congrès en a chargés. L'habileté de M. Jepherson et les services importans qu'il a rendus aux Etats unis sont bien connus en Europe et Vous pouvés être persuadé, Monsieur, que tous ceux qui s'interessent à la prosperité et aux avantages de ce pays ci, applaudiront au choix du Congrès.

J'ai l'honneur d'être avec le plus sincere et inviolable attachement Monsieur Votre très humble et très obéissant serviteur,

LE CHR DE LA LUZERNE

RC (DLC: PCC, No. 95, II); in a clerk's hand, signed by La Luzerne. Tr (DLC: PCC, No. 119). An English translation is printed in Wharton, *Dipl. Corr. Amer. Rev.*, VI, 90.

This letter is a reply to Livingston's communication of 26 Nov. 1782 in which he had informed the French minister of TJ's appointment and had voiced the following comment: "Mr. Jefferson's established character, his abilities, and the honorable offices he has sustained with reputation in this country, leave no room to doubt that this appointment will be highly acceptable to your court when you shall have placed them in that favorable point of view in which, I persuade myself, you take a pleasure in representing them" (same, p. 81; Tr in DLC: PCC, No. 119, p. 188-9, in French). La Luzerne's letter seems to assume that Livingston meant TJ had already accepted the appointment, but neither could have learned by 29 Nov. that this was so.

Advertisement

Monticello, December 15, 1782.

THE Subscriber having occasion to be absent from the State for some time, has confided the care of his affairs to Francis Eppes, Esq; of Chesterfield, and Col. Nicholas Lewis, of Albemarle, to whom, therefore, he begs leave to refer all persons having business with him.

THOMAS JEFFERSON.

Printed from Hayes' *Virginia Gazette, or American Advertiser* (Richmond), 28 Dec. 1782.

Jefferson's Contemplated Mission to Europe

I. RESOLUTION OF CONGRESS CONCERNING A COMMERCIAL CLAUSE

II. JEFFERSON'S NOTES RELATING TO FOREIGN AND DOMESTIC AFFAIRS

III. JEFFERSON'S COMMISSION AS A MINISTER PLENIPOTENTIARY FOR NEGOTIATING PEACE

IV. REPORT OF A COMMITTEE TO PREPARE A LIST OF BOOKS FOR CONGRESS

[31 Dec. 1782—24 Jan. 1783]

EDITORIAL NOTE

The documents here grouped together have no special unity beyond the fact that all of them relate to Jefferson's mission to France in 1783 —a mission never carried out because provisional articles of peace between the United States and Great Britain had been signed at Paris on 30 Nov. 1782. They can, however, be advantageously presented as a group in order to show Jefferson's activities during this interesting period when his correspondence was necessarily scanty.

Jefferson's Autobiography (MS in DLC) provides the following very useful summary of events:

"On the 15th. of June 1781. I had been appointed with Mr. Adams, Dr. Franklin, Mr. Jay, and Mr. Laurens a minister plenipotentiary for negociating peace, then expected to be effectd thro' the mediation of the Empress of Russia. The same reasons [*i.e., family responsibilities*] obliged me still to decline; and the negociation was in fact never entered on. But, in the autumn of the next year 1782 Congress recieving assurances that a general peace would be concluded in the winter and spring, they renewed my appointment on the 13th. of Nov. of that year. I had two months before that lost the cherished companion of my life, in whose affections, unabated on both sides, I had lived the last ten years in unchequered happiness. With the public interests, the state of my mind concurred in recommending the change of scene proposed;

and I accepted the appointment, and left Monticello on the 19th. of Dec. 1782. for Philadelphia, where I arrived on the 27th. The Minister of France, Luzerne, offered me a passage in the Romulus frigate, which I accepted. But she was then lying a few miles below Baltimore blocked up in the ice. I remained therefore a month in Philadelphia looking over the papers in the office of State in order to possess myself of the general state of our foreign relations, and then went to Baltimore to await the liberation of the frigate from the ice. After waiting there nearly a month, we recieved information that a Provisional treaty of peace had been signed by our Commissioners on the 3d. of Sep. [*error for 30 Nov.; the Definitive Treaty was signed 3 Sep. 1783*] 1782. to become absolute on the conclusion of peace between France and Great Britain. Considering my proceeding to Europe as now of no utility to the public, I returned to Philadelphia immediately to take the orders of Congress, and was excused by them from further proceeding. I therefore returned home, where I arrived on the 15th. of May 1783."

On 30 Dec. 1782, three days after Jefferson reached Philadelphia, "His Excellency the President having informed Congress that the honorable T. Jefferson was arrived in town: *Ordered*, That Mr. Jefferson have access to the several offices of Congress, in order that he may gain a knowledge of the affairs of the United States, and prepare himself for the execution of the trust reposed in him" (JCC, XIII, 833). The several parts of Document II below result from this order and reveal Jefferson characteristically engaged in studies for his important assignment.

Document I is the single additional instruction to the joint commissioners that Jefferson was to carry to his colleagues. It is doubtless to this instruction relative to a commercial clause that Jefferson refers in his letters to Franklin and Jay of 3 Jan. 1783 "I am told," he wrote the latter, "that a new article of instruction is making out by Congress, but that it is not of a nature to produce difficulty." (For TJ's own statement of "the principal matters confided" to him as commissioner, see postscript in his letter to Madison, 14 Feb. 1783.) Jefferson was of course to bear numerous other papers and letters. Some of these are mentioned in his correspondence with the office of the Secretary for Foreign Affairs printed below; others are recorded only in Robert R. Livingston's "Despatch Book" (DLC: PCC, No. 126), under their several dates, as follows:

(1) 12 Jan. 1783. "Furnished Mr. Jefferson with a copy of a Letter from the Minister of France to Congress, enclosing a communication made by Don Juan de Marillis dated 25th. Novr 1779." See Miralles to La Luzerne, Philadelphia, 25 Nov. 1779, offering Spanish cooperation with American offensives against British posts in Florida and "northeast of Louisiana"; also La Luzerne to Congress, Philadelphia, 23 Nov. 1779, transmitting Miralles' letter and warmly seconding its proposals. Both letters are printed in Wharton, *Dipl. Corr. Amer. Rev.* III, 414-16. They may have been furnished to Jefferson for study rather than for transmission to France.

(2) 18 Jan. 1783. "Delivered the Honourable Mr. Jefferson the following Letters and inclosures for Europe." Seven letters to Franklin, with sundry enclosures, are listed.

(3) 22 Jan. 1783. "Sent by Mr. Jefferson 3plicate of the Letter to Messieurs Wilhelm and Jan Willink and Co.—with 3plicate Copies of the Contracts." These relate to a Dutch loan but have not been identified.

Jefferson's Commission (Document III) speaks for itself.

The Report of the first plan for a congressional library (Document IV) is a Jefferson document merely because James Madison, who drafted it, relied heavily on a book list prepared by his friend and fellow lodger at this time in the home of Samuel House in Philadelphia. Madison's plan was not then carried out, but it is highly appropriate that Jefferson, who was later to have so distinguished a part in developing the Library of Congress, should have had a share in the earliest effort to establish a collection of books for the use of Congress.

I. Resolution of Congress concerning a Commercial Clause

In Congress, 31 Dec. 1782. "On the report of a Committee to whom was referred a letter of the 14th of October last from the Minister plenipotentiary at the Court of Versailles, Resolved" that the American joint commissioners be instructed "to endeavour to obtain for the Citizens and inhabitants of the United States a direct Commerce to all parts of the British dominions and posessions in like manner as all parts of the United States may be opened to a direct Commerce of British subjects, or at least that such direct Commerce be extended to all parts of the British dominions and possessions in Europe and the West Indies."

MS (DLC); 2 p., signed by Charles Thomson. Printed in JCC, XXIII, 838.

Franklin's letter of 14 Oct. evoking this addendum to the instructions is printed in Wharton, *Dipl. Corr. Amer. Rev.*, V, 811-12. The original report to Congress was drawn up by James Madison (JCC, XXIII, 838, note). On this matter, see Vernon G. Setser, *The Commercial Reciprocity Policy of the United States 1774-1829*, Philadelphia, 1937, p. 37ff.

II. Jefferson's Notes relating to Foreign and Domestic Affairs

[*Philadelphia, without date, taken down in Jan. 1783.*] Several series of notes, the order of which is not determinable, from papers principally in the office of the Secretary for Foreign Affairs.

(1) Notes captioned "Journal of Foreign Affairs. Vol. I. they begin Nov. 29. 1775." These were taken by TJ from the "Secret Journal of Foreign Affairs" kept separately by Secretary Thomson from the "Rough Journal" of the proceedings of Congress. They are paragraphed by date of each original entry in the Journal and extend in time from 2 Dec. 1775 to 5 Dec. 1778. Important entries abstract the "plan of treaty" of 17 Sep. 1776; the instructions to commissioners to foreign states, 24 Sep. 1776; appointments of commissioners to Vienna, Russia, Prussia, and Tuscany, Dec. 1776 to Jan. 1777; instructions to Franklin

to inform the French government of a proposed plan for the reduction of Canada, 22 Oct. 1778.

(2) Notes without caption, marginally lettered by paragraphs from "a" to "w." These notes, running from 22 Mch. 1779 to 2 Mch. 1782, were also taken from the "Secret Journal of Foreign Affairs" but include as well abstracts of letters written and received by the Secretary for Foreign Affairs. Most of the notes summarize instructions to Franklin in France, Jay in Spain, Adams in Holland, and the commissioners for negotiating peace with Great Britain.

(3) Miscellaneous notes on various subjects. These include a brief set of notes headed "Williams's hist. of the Northern govmts.," recording data on the revenue, debt, and military and naval establishments of Holland, Denmark, Sweden, and Russia from John Williams, *The Rise, Progress, and Present State of the Northern Governments*, London, 1777. Also abstracts of British diplomatic correspondence relating to the fisheries question in the negotiation of the Treaty of Paris, 1763. Overleaf, without caption or indication of source, is a fairly full abstract of James Madison's highly interesting paper of 1 May 1782 called "Observations Relating to the Influence of Vermont and the Territorial Claims on the Politics of Congress" (original printed in Burnett, *Letters of Members*, VI, No. 494). On a second leaf are notes headed "Observns. of Mr. M—s [Miralles?] on the boundary between the Spaniards and Americans," in the form of arguments for the Americans' claim to all territory east of the Mississippi and Spanish answers to these arguments; also a summary of Francis Dana's letter to Robert R. Livingston, St. Petersburgh, 30 Mch. 1782 (Wharton, *Dipl. Corr. Amer. Rev.*, V, 230-3), and of its statistical enclosures on Russian commerce; also a summary of John Adams' letter to Congress, Amsterdam, 11 June 1781 (same, IV, 487-91).

N (DLC); entirely in TJ's hand. Most of these notes are written in a somewhat abbreviated form, and some are in so condensed a form as to be virtually shorthand. The group here called (1) consists of 4 pages (TJ Papers, 2: 197-8); (2) consists of 6 pages (same, 3: 453; 7: 1136; 4: 574); and (3) consists of 4 pages (same, 9: 1397-8).

III. Jefferson's Commission as a Minister Plenipotentiary for Negotiating Peace

[8 January 1783]

The United States in Congress Assembled
To all who shall see these presents Greeting.
Know Ye that among the Records in our
Secretary's Office there is a Commission in the words following

The United States of America in Congress Assembled to all to whom these presents shall come send Greeting

Whereas these United States from a sincere desire of putting an end to the hostilities between his Most Christian Majesty and these United States on the one part and his Britannic Majesty on the other, and of terminating the same by a peace founded on such solid and equitable principles as reasonably to promise a permanency of the blessings of tranquility did heretofore appoint the honble. John Adams late a Commissioner of the United States at the Court of Versailles, late Delegate in Congress from the State of Massachusetts and Chief Justice of the said State their Minister Plenipotentiary with full powers general and special to act in that quality to confer, treat, agree and conclude with the Ambassadors or Plenipotentiaries of his Most Christian Majesty and of his Britannic Majesty and those of any other Princes or States whom it might concern, relating to the re-establishment of peace and friendship; and whereas the flames of War have since that time been extended and other Nations and States are involved therein: Now know Ye, that we still continuing earnestly desirous as far as depends upon us to put a stop to the effusion of blood and to convince the powers of Europe that we wish for nothing more ardently than to terminate the War by a safe and honorable peace have thought proper to renew the powers formerly given to the said John Adams and to join four other persons in Commission with him, and having full confidence in the integrity, prudence and ability of the honorable Benjamin Franklin our Minister Plenipotentiary at the Court of Versailles, and the honorable John Jay late president of Congress and Chief Justice of the State of New York and our Minister Plenipotentiary at the Court of Madrid, and the honble. Henry Laurens formerly president of Congress and Commissionated and sent as our Agent to the United Provinces of the Low Countries, and the honble. Thomas Jefferson Governor of the Commonwealth of Virginia have nominated, constituted and appointed and by these presents do nominate, constitute and appoint the said Benjamin Franklin, John Jay, Henry Laurens and Thomas Jefferson in addition to the said John Adams, giving and granting to them the said John Adams, Benjamin Franklin, John Jay, Henry Laurens and Thomas Jefferson or the majority of them or of such of them as may assemble or in case of the death, absence, indisposition or other impediment of the others to any one of them full power and authority general and special conjunctly and seperately and general and special command to repair to such place as may be fixed upon for opening negotiations for peace, and there for us, and in our name to confer, treat, agree and conclude with the Ambassadors, Commissioners and Plenipotentiaries of the Princes and States, whom it may concern, vested with equal powers relating to the establishment of peace, and whatsoever shall be agreed and concluded, for us and in our name to sign and thereupon make a treaty or treaties and to transact every thing that may be necessary for compleating securing and strengthening the great work of pacification in as ample form and with the same effect as if we were personally present and acted therein, hereby promising in good faith that we will accept, ratify, fulfil and execute whatever shall be agreed, concluded and signed by our said Ministers Plenipotentiary or a majority of them or of such of them as may assemble or in case of the death, absence, indisposition or other impediment of the others by any one of them, and that we will never act nor suffer any person to act contrary to the same in whole or in any part. In Witness whereof we have caused these presents to be signed by our president and sealed with his Seal.

Done at Philadelphia the fifteenth day of June in the Year of our Lord One thousand seven hundred and Eighty one and in the fifth Year of our Independence, by the United States in Congress Assembled.

And also a Resolution in the words following—
By the United States in Congress Assembled

November 12th. 1782.

Resolved That the appointment of Thomas Jefferson Esquire as a Minister Plenipotentiary for negotiating a Peace made on the fifteenth day of June 1781. be and the same is hereby renewed and that on his acceptance thereof he be invested with all the powers and be subject to all the instructions which have been or may be issued by Congress to the Ministers Plenipotentiary for negotiating peace in the same manner as if his original appointment had taken effect.

All which we have caused to be exemplified by these presents, In Testimony whereof we have caused these our Letters to be made patent and our Seal thereto affixed. Witness His Excellency Elias Boudinot Esquire President of the United States in Congress Assembled the Eighth Day of January in the Year of our Lord one thousand seven hundred and Eighty three, and of our Sovereignty and Independence the Seventh.

CHAS THOMSON secy.

MS (MHi); engrossed by a clerk; star-shaped paper seal in left-hand margin of first page; signed by Elias Boudinot and by Charles Thomson (the original commissions of 15 June 1781 were, of course, signed by Samuel Huntington and Charles Thomson). A copy, from a copy certified by Richard Oswald and obtained by Oswald from John Jay on 1 Oct. 1782, is in MiU-C.

IV. Report of a Committee to Prepare a List of Books for Congress

[*In Congress, 24 Jan. 1783.*] "The Committee instructed on the motion of Col. Bland to report a list of books proper for the use of Congress, recommend that Superintdt. of Finance and the Secy. of Congress be empowered to take order for procuring the books enumerated below; the same when procured to be under the care of the said Secy." The list itself, entirely in James Madison's hand, is headed by the *Encyclopédie Méthodique* and contains more than 300 other titles classed as follows: Law of Nature and Nations, Treaties and Negociations, General History, Chronology, Geography, Particular History (subdivided by nations), Politics, Law, War, Marine, Languages, America. (The last class, consisting of what would today be called Americana, contains by far the greatest number of titles.) Madison's list was largely, but not exclusively, based on a much longer book list compiled by TJ, consisting partly of books he owned and partly of books he intended to procure (Brant, *Madison*, II, 288-90). This "1783 Catalogue" of TJ's (MS in MHi) was presumably drawn up, or at least revised, in preparation for TJ's contemplated mission to Europe; much of the work on it may have been done while he was in Philadelphia in Jan. 1783, and perhaps more on his return to Philadelphia in March of that year, since a preliminary leaf of the list bears the date "1783 Mar. 6." Madison and TJ roomed in the same house during these months and certainly must have discussed both TJ's long personal list and Madison's select list for a proposed congressional library.

MS (DLC: PCC, Miscellany); 3 p. in Madison's hand, with endorsement by Charles Thomson: "No. 27. Report of Comee List of Books to be imported for the use of Congress Read Jany 24. 1783. Question taken to empower Superint: finance & Secy to import them. Passed in the Negative. Comee. Mr. Madison Mr Williamson Mr Mifflin." Printed in JCC, XXIV, 83-92; also by Fulmer Mood in "The Continental Congress and the Plan for a Library of Congress in 1782-1783," PMHB, LXXII (1948), 3-24.

Though he does not notice TJ's collaboration with Madison in compiling this list, Mr. Mood in the article just cited gives an otherwise thorough account of this first proposal of a library for Congress. The motion that a list of books for purchase be drawn up had been made by Theodorick Bland before he left Congress in mid-November 1782; the highly interesting arguments for and against Madison's Report when submitted were recorded by Madison in his "Notes of Debates" (JCC, XXV, 858-9); the economy-minded delegates prevailed, and the proposal was defeated, says Madison, "by a substantial majority." A substitute motion by James Wilson, seconded by Madison, "to confine the purchase to the most essential part of the books" was also negatived.

To Benjamin Franklin

SIR   Philadelphia Jan. 3. 1783.

I arrived at this place a few days ago expecting to have proceeded to Europe in the vessel which carries Count Rochambaud and the

Chevalr. de Chastellux; but it sails before I can be ready. I shall follow however in a very few days, and may possibly be with you as soon as this. Conscious that I can add no good to the commission, it shall be my endeavor to do it no injury. I understand that I am to be the bearer of something new to you, but not of a nature to embarrass your operations. I expect so shortly after your receipt of this to have the pleasure of paying my respects to you in person, that I shall only add those expressions of respect & esteem with which I have the honor to be Sir Your most obedient & most humble servt,

TH: JEFFERSON

RC (PPAP). Dft (DLC).

On 28 Dec. 1782 James Madison wrote to Edmund Randolph: "Mr. [Jefferson] arrived here on friday last, and is industriously arming himself for the field of negociation. The commission issued to Mr. Oswald impresses him with a hope that he may have nothing to do on his arrival but join in the celebrations of victory and peace. [Congress] however anxiously espouse the expediency of his hastening to his destination" (Burnett, *Letters of Members*, VI, No. 722; the words in brackets were written in cipher). On 8 Jan. 1783 Washington, from Newburgh, wrote Livingston: "What office is Mr. Jefferson appointed to, that he has, you say, lately accepted? If it is that of Commissioner of Peace, I hope he will arrive too late to have any hand in it. My best respects to him when he arrives" (FC in DLC: Washington Papers). It was possibly during these days at Philadelphia, where he arrived on 27 Dec., that TJ first met Alexander Hamilton, who was then a member of Congress. The SOMETHING NEW that TJ refers to here was doubtless Document No. I in the preceding series.

To John Jay

SIR   Philadelphia Jan. 3. 1783.

Having arrived here a few days ago in order to proceed to Europe, I had hoped to have been able to accompany the Generals Rochambaud and Chastellux, the latter of whom is so kind as to undertake the delivery of this. But their vessel sails before I can be ready. I shall follow however in a very few days and may perhaps have the pleasure of being with you as soon as this will. Had I joined you at a more early period I am sure I should not have added to the strength of the commission and, coming in at the eleventh hour, I can propose no more than to avoid doing mischeif. I am told that a new article of instruction is making out by Congress, but that it is not of a nature to produce difficulty. I had entertained a thought of so far presuming on our former acquaintance as to have asked the favor of you to engage for me a proper lodging, convenient to yours (Dr. Franklin, I understand, continues at Passy) and perhaps, encouraged by Mr. Izard who is here, I should have proposed the Hotel de Vendosme if there should be spare apartments as being recommended by the additional circumstance of Mrs. Izard's being in it with her family, with whom a little motherless daughter accompanying me might sometimes be permitted to associate. But expecting almost to accompany this letter I cannot resolve to give you the unreasonable trouble of doing for me what I shall so immediately be on the spot to do for myself. We are told here that Mr. Laurens declines acting in the commission and that Mr. Adams continues still at the Hague. I beg you to accept a sincere assurance of the high respect & esteem with which I have the honour to be Sir Your most obedient & most humble servt.,   TH: JEFFERSON

RC (Frank Monaghan, Washington, D.C., 1951); endorsed: "Govr. Jefferson 3 Jany 1783 Recd. 19 March 1783." Dft (DLC); much abbreviated and much corrected, though the corrections are not noted here; written on the address leaf of a letter to James Madison.

To William Livingston

DEAR SIR   Philadelphia Jan. 3. 1782 [1783].

It gives me real concern that I have been here several days and so closely engaged that I have not been able to pay you the respect of a letter and to assure you that I hold among my most estimable acquaintances that which I had the pleasure of contracting with you at this place. I am the more concerned, as expecting to leave this place about Tuesday next, I might have been gratified with the carrying letters from you to Mr. and Mrs. Jay. Perhaps it may not yet be too late. I take the liberty of putting this into the hands of the President as the most likely person to give it immediate conveyance. I beg you to accept my sincere wishes for your happiness, and to beleive me very really Dr. Sir Your most obedt. & most humble friend & servt.,   TH: JEFFERSON

RC (MHi); addressed: "His Excellency Governor Livingston Trenton"; endorsed by Livingston. LETTERS . . . TO MR. AND MRS. JAY: Mrs. Jay was the former Sarah Livingston, daughter of Gov. Livingston (DAB). THE PRESIDENT, of course, was Elias Boudinot.

To George Rogers Clark

DR. SIR   Philadelphia Jan. 6. 1783.

I wrote you a letter from the neighborhood of Richmond during the course of the last month, but as there were no delegates at the assembly from the counties on the Ohio, and the conveiance of that letter may therefore be incertain, I will mention again a part of the subject of it. You were so kind in a former letter as to inform me you had procured for me some teeth and bones of the big buffalo. In the letter abovementioned I took the liberty of asking you to endeavor if possible to procure me one of every species of the bones now remaining, that is of every member or part. This request I again repeat, and that I shall chearfully incur the necessary expences of good package and carriage. New London in Bedford, Staunton in Augusta, or Fredericksburg in Spotsylvania would be safe places of lodgement: so also would Winchester if directed to the particular care of Mr. Isaac Zane. I am here just on my departure for Europe, not to return (from the nature of my appointment) till peace. Yet I hope to return the ensuing summer. Whether in peace or war I wish you every felicity & am with sincere regard Dr. Sir Your most obedt. humble servt,

TH: JEFFERSON

RC (WHi).   TJ's LETTER . . . OF THE LAST MONTH was that of 26 Nov. 1782. Clark's letter about the BONES OF THE BIG BUFFALO (though he did not employ the term) was that of 20 Feb. 1782.

To Francis Eppes

DEAR SIR   Philadelphia, Jan. 14, 1783.

You will hardly expect to receive a letter from me at this place, and of so late a date. Yet I have apprehensions of being here ten days or a fortnight longer, for though ready myself, some time since, the vessel in which I go is not ready. Yesterday's post brought no mail from Virginia. I was not disappointed in this, as I was pretty certain that under expectation of my being gone you did not write. I had entertained some hope of meeting a letter from you on my first arrival here, but suppose the same idea of its not coming in time prevented it, so that at present I have no hope of hearing again, while on this side water, from yourself and family and those dear little ones I have left with you. We have heard nothing since my last from which the length of my absence may be conjectured. The last authentic advices were of the 14th of October, but the affair of Gibraltar happened just then, and the negotiation was in such a state that what had passed between the negotiators was at that time under submission to the British court for their approbation or disavowal. How far this would be influenced by their good fortune at Gibraltar is the question which the next advices must certainly solve. Since I came here there has been sold the Westover copy of Catesby's History of Carolina. It was held near a twelvemonth at twelve guineas, and at last sold for ten. This seems to fix what should be given for Mr. Bolling's copy, if you can induce him to let me have it, which I am very anxious for. Perhaps it would be a temptation to offer that the ten guineas should be paid to Mr. Ross's agent at Nantes, where he could lay them out and send the articles to Mr. Bolling. His draft shall be paid on sight in Paris. Perhaps you had better effect this by making the proposition to Mrs. Bolling. Of this your knowledge of the family will enable you to judge. Be so good as to present me most affectionately to Mrs. Eppes, Mr. and Mrs. Skipwith, and the two families, and believe me to be, with very great sincerity, dear sir, Your friend and servant,   TH: JEFFERSON

MS not located. Text from Randall, *Life*, III, 586, where the letter is printed without indication of source. It is printed also in Ford, III, 296-7, and in L & B, IV, 429-30.

Mark Catesby's *The Natural History of Carolina, Florida, and the Bahama Islands*, originally published in parts (London, 1731-1748), was issued in two folio volumes in London, 1754 (Sabin 11508; see TJ's comments on Catesby in *Notes on Virginia*, Ford, III, 170). The WESTOVER COPY was sold by Robert Bell, who purchased the library of William Byrd III.

To Daniel Hylton

DEAR SIR   Philadelphia, Jan. 20. 1783

I received yesterday your favor of the 9th. inst. and am happy that the sale of Elkhill is at length compleeted. I would at once renew the deed here, but that there exists no such law of Congress as you suppose which could make a record here effectual to pass lands in Virginia. There is I believe some law of Virginia allowing a considerable time for the probat of deeds executed out of the State. Quare whether this would not admit the deed executed here last year to be still recorded? Be this as it may, I shall be in Virginia ere long, and will then do whatever is necessary to compleet the title. Till then also, I would rather you should either keep the bonds and other papers which are in your hands, or deliver them to Mr. T. Randolph whenever you see him, and he will deposit them at Monticello. In the mean time, if the papers I before sent you did not authorize you to deliver possession of the lands to the purchasers, I do it fully by this letter, and further, to remove any tenant who may be on it, except the old woman (if she be living) who has her life in the 50 acres on the back of one of the tracts. I pray you not to fail having the mortgage immediately recorded. With many thanks for the trouble you have had in this business, and with my best respects to Mrs. Hylton I am Dear Sir Your friend & servt.,

THS. JEFFERSON

Tr (ViU); in a 19th-century hand. Date has been corrected from the copyist's erroneous "1788." Hylton's letter of 9 Jan. 1783 has not been found.

Honorary Degree Conferred on Jefferson by the College of William and Mary

The president and professors of the university or College of William and Mary to all to whom these present letters shall come, greetings.

Since academic degrees have been instituted in order that men deserving most highly of learning and the state may be honored by such distinctions, know ye that we by the sole means in our power —the conferring gladly and eagerly of the degree of doctor in the civil law—bear witness to the high opinion we hold of Thomas Jefferson, Virginian, who, having been educated in the bosom of our alma mater, exhibits wonderful good will to this seat of the Muses and bears hence good will not inferior; most skilled both in private and public law; of exceptional love for his country; illustrious not only in other matters but especially in championing American liberty; and so imbued with letters, whether popular or recondite and abstruse, that all the fine arts seem to foregather in one man; these arts are adorned by the greatness of his mind which proposes nothing with regard to ostentation, everything with regard to conscience, and for a deed well done he seeks his reward not from popular acclaim but from the deed itself. Therefore, in a solemn convocation held on the twentieth day of the month of January in the year of the Lord one thousand seven hundred and eighty-three, by the unanimous votes of all, we have elected and appointed this honorable and illustrious man, Thomas Jefferson, doctor in the civil law, and him, by virtue of the present diploma, we have ordered to enjoy and rejoice in, for the sake of the honor, the several rights, privileges, and honors pertaining in any way to this degree. In testimony of this fact we have caused to be affixed to the present document the common seal of the University which we employ in this capacity. Granted in the home of our convocation on the aforesaid year, day, and month.

J: MADISON, Pr.

G. WYTHE, P.L.P.

R. ANDREWS, M.P.P.

C. BELLINI, M.L.P.

MS (MHi); engrossed on parchment, in Latin, with ribbon and seal at foot of page; signed by the Rev. James Madison, president; George Wythe, professor of law and police; Robert Andrews, professor of mathematics and philosophy; and Charles Bellini, professor of modern languages. There can be little doubt that this document, with its high tribute to TJ's sense of public duty, was drafted by his former teacher and legislative colleague, George Wythe. More than any others on the faculty of the College of William and Mary, Wythe had cause to know not only how indefatigably TJ had labored in the "holy cause of liberty" to which they both were so deeply devoted, but also how much his sensitive nature had suffered from the impugning of his conduct as Governor. It may well have been that this tribute from his own college was inspired by the sense of injustice—though belatedly rectified—done him by the legislature in June, 1781, in calling for an investigation. The conjecture that Wythe was the author of the diploma is perhaps supported also by the nature of the Latin text as well as by the thoughts expressed. Professors Allen C. Johnson (emeritus) and John V. A. Fine of the Department of Classics, Princeton University, to whom the editors are indebted for the translation above, are of opinion that the author of the text was not, to say the least, a carefully trained classical scholar. According to tradition, Wythe was largely self-taught in the classics, having been given some instruction in "Latin . . . and the fundamentals of Greek" by his mother (DAB).

To George Washington

SIR   Philadelphia Jan. 22. 1783.

Having lately received a call from Congress to pass the Atlantic in the character of one of their ministers for negotiating peace, I cannot leave the Continent without separating myself for a moment from the general gratitude of my country to offer my individual tribute to your Excellency for all you have suffered and all you have effected for us. Were I to indulge myself in those warm effusions which this subject for ever prompts, they would wear an appearance of adulation very foreign to my nature: for such is become the prostitution of language that sincerity has no longer distinct terms in which to express her own truths. Should you give me occasion, during the short mission on which I go, to render you any service beyond the water, I shall for a proof of my gratitude appeal from language to the zeal with which I shall embrace it. The negotiations to which I am joined may perhaps be protracted beyond our present expectation; in which case, tho' I know you must receive much better intelligence from the gentlemen whose residence there has brought them into a more intimate acquaintance with the characters and views of the European courts, yet I shall certainly presume to add my mite, should it only serve to convince you of the warmth of those sentiments of respect & esteem with which I have the honor to be your Excellency's most obedient & most humble servt.,   TH: JEFFERSON

RC (PHi); addressed by TJ: "His Excellency General Washington Headquarters"; endorsed by Washington: "From The Hon. Ths. Jefferson 22d. Jan. 1783." Dft (DLC); contains minor corrections not noted here.

From Benjamin Rush

Jany 24. 1783 Thursday Evening

Dr. Rush's Compliments to Mr. Jefferson and sends him herewith a packet for Mr. B: Vauhan to whom he has taken the liberty of introducing Mr. Jefferson as a fellow worshipper in the temple of Science. Mr: Vauhan is a gentlemen of knowledge and taste in Science, and possesses a most extensive acquaintance among the literati in London. Dr. Rush wishes Mr. Jefferson a safe voyage, and a continuance of his Usefulness and reputation in the Service of his Country.

RC (DLC: Madison Papers); addressed: "Mr Jefferson." On the cover is a note by Madison: "Mr. Jefferson informed me when he put this into my hands that he should not deliver the letter to Mr. B. Vaughan untill a peace shall be finally concluded; as he understood that he is a Secy to one of the British Ministers. J Madison Jr. Philada. Jany. 25th. 1783."
Vaughan was actually a representative of his friend Lord Shelburne at the peace negotiations; he and Franklin, despite the great disparity in their ages, were warm friends. Vaughan in 1779 had brought out the only edition of Franklin's works to appear during his lifetime, and he was connected by marriage with Henry Laurens. It is not known how or when Rush met him; Vaughan, like Rush, studied medicine in Edinburgh, but many years after Rush had been there.

From William Livingston

DEAR SIR   Trenton 25 January 1783

Being just returned to this place from a Journey to the eastern parts of the State, I find myself honoured with your very kind and obliging Letter of the 3d. instant. My host here having neglected to transmit it to me from his daily expectations of my return, I fear that this letter will not find you in America, and in such case I have desired the President of Congress to do me the favour of directing it accordingly, and of sending it to France by the first opportunity.

And now, my dear Sir, give me leave to assure you, that I am not only extremely sensible of the politeness of your offer to be the bearer of my Letters to Mr. and Mrs. Jay, but that I am particularly flattered by the value you are pleased to set on *the acquaintance you contracted with me*, in Philadelphia: An Acquaintance, which I most earnestly wish to cultivate to my dying day, 'tho' like the rest of the world, that is too much actuated by motives of self-interest, this wish of mine, partakes, I fear, too much of that inglorious passion; as the benefits that will result from an intimacy, (which I pray you to perpetuate by your correspondence) will be altogether on my side.

Heaven grant you a prosperous voyage and a safe return; and be assured, that I am with the greatest sincerity Your most humble Friend & Servant, WIL: LIVINGSTON

RC (CSmH).

Jefferson's Statement of Losses to the British at His Cumberland Plantations in 1781

[27 January 1783]

State of the losses of *Thomas Jefferson* in the county of Cumberland by the British in the year 1781.
Slaves who went off with the British and died
  Hannibal
  Patty
  Prince
  Sam 9. years old
  Sally
  Nanny
  Fanny
  Nancy.
  Flora
  Quomina
Went off with the British and was never more heard of
  Sam.
Went off with the British, returned and died of the camp fever
  Lucy. Black Sall. Jame 10. years old

Lost for want of cultivation by loss of the hands
   about 80 barrels of corn
      130. ℔. of cotton
         7. hogheads of tobacco.
9. head of cattle taken away from Elk island where they happened
   to stray
1. Fearnought filly 2 years old
   1783. January 27. This day Charles Karr[1] overseer for Thomas
Jefferson made oath to the truth of the above state.

HENRY SKIPWITH

Cumberland court 27th. January 1783.

The within state was presented in court and the same having
been proved by the oath of Charles Karr as appears by the certificate there annexed is ordered to be certified to the governor and
council.   Teste   GEO. CARRINGTON jr Clk.

MS (NN: Arents); in TJ's hand, with certifications in the hands of Skipwith and Carrington respectively. Endorsed: "Tho. Jeffersons losses occasioned by the Brittish proved Jan 1783 For Governor."

On TJ's losses see also Archibald Cary to TJ, 19 June 1781; TJ to William Gordon, 16 July 1788; and Farm Journal (MS in MHi), which contains at p. 29 a tabulation of TJ's losses at all his plantations.

[1] Corrected by overwriting from "Carr." The name should be spelled "Kerr." Charles Kerr witnessed a deed of sale for a tract of land in Goochland co. bought by TJ of Reuben and Judith Smith, 19 May 1783 (MS deed owned by Miss Amanda D. Pitts, Elk Hill, Va., 1945).

To James Madison

DEAR SIR   Baltimore Jan. 31. 1783.

A gentleman returning from this place to Philadelphia gives me
an opportunity of sending you a line. We reached Newport the
evening of the day on which we left you. There we were misled by
an assurance that the lower ferry could not be crossed. We therefore directed our course for the Bald friar's: and thence to another
ferry 6 miles above. Between these two we lost two days, in the
most execrable situation in point of accomodation and society
which can be conceived. In short braving all weather and plunging
thro' thick and thin we arrived here last night being the fifth from
Philadelphia. I saw Monsr. de Villa-brun last night and augur him
to be agreeable enough. I learnt (not from him but others) that to
embark their sick &c. will keep us three days. Having nothing
particular to communicate I will give you an *anecdote*[1] which pos-

[225]

sibly you may not have heard and which is related to me by *Major Franks* who had it from *Doctr. Franklin²* himself. I use the only cypher I can now get at using the paginal numbers in order and not as concerted. *Mr. Z. while at Paris had often pressed the Doctor to communicate to him his several negociations with the court of France which the Doctor avoided as decently as he* could. *At length he received from Mr. Z. a very intemperate letter. He folded it up and put it into a pigeon hole. A second, third and so on to a fifth or sixth he received and disposed of in the same way. Finding no answer* could *be obtained by letter Mr. Z. paid him a personal visit and gave a loose to all the warmth of which he is susceptible. The Doctor replied I can no more answer this conversation of yours than the several impatient letters you have written me (taking them down from the pigeon hole). Call on me when you are cool and goodly humoured and I will justify myself to you.* They never saw each other afterwards. As I find no A. in the book erase the B in the first A.B. so that 1.1 may denote A. instead of AB.

I met here the inclosed paper which be so good as to return with my compliments to Miss Kitty. I apprehend she had not got a copy of it, and I retain it in my memory. Be pleased to present me very affectionately to the ladies and gentlemen whose pleasing society I lately had at Mrs. House's and believe me to be Your assured friend,

Th: Jefferson

RC (DLC: Madison Papers); endorsed; partly in cipher. Enclosure not found. Since this letter represents the first appearance in this edition of a letter involving code, a statement concerning method has been given in the foreword to this volume. WE REACHED NEWPORT: TJ had left Philadelphia on Sunday morning, 26 Jan. (Account Book, that date; Burnett, *Letters of Members*, VII, No. 25). He stopped in Newport, Del., the first night; his traveling companion was David Franks (MAJOR FRANKS), who was to proceed to France as TJ's secretary (see TJ to Franks, printed at end of Mch. 1783). MR. Z has been variously identified as John Adams (Ford, III, 299), Arthur Lee (Burnett, *Letters of Members*, VII, No. 45, note 2), and Ralph Izard (Brant, *Madison*, II, 266-7); the last attribution is doubtless the correct one. MISS KITTY: Catherine Floyd, daughter of William Floyd, a veteran member of the New York delegation to Congress; Madison hoped to marry her, but was disappointed (same, ch. xviii). MRS. HOUSE'S: A rooming house at 5th and Market streets, Philadelphia (*Philadelphia Directory* for 1785), conducted by Mrs. Mary House. Here Madison roomed, as did Floyd and his daughters. Among the ladies WHOSE PLEASING SOCIETY TJ enjoyed at Mrs. House's was Eliza Trist, with whom he formed a lifelong friendship; she was the daughter of Mrs. House and the wife of Nicholas Trist (Brant, *Madison*, II, 16-17).

¹ This and subsequent words in italics were written in cipher and partly decoded interlineally by Madison, employing the code designated in TJ Editorial Files as Code No. 1. This code was based on Thomas Nugent's *New Pocket Dictionary of the French and English Languages*, London, 1774. This, together with the fact that TJ and Madison followed pagination in sequence rather than "as concerted," made it possible for the editors to correct Madison's decoding in the present and other letters (see TJ to Madison, 14 Feb. 1783, note 2, for an important

error made by TJ or Madison) in which Code No. 1 was employed. In one or two instances approximations only have been achieved, since no copy of this edition of Nugent's *Dictionary* has been found through the Union Catalogs at DLC or elsewhere. The reading established through the editors' partial reconstruction of Code No. 1 has been followed rather than that given by Madison; see note 2.

2 The cipher for "Franklin" was, under Code No. 1, "352.4" (*frank*) and "483.30" (*line*), which Madison decoded literally as "*Frank Line*." In this and other instances the editors have employed the form that TJ would normally have chosen.

From Lewis R. Morris

SIR   Philadelphia 31st. January 1783.

The packet accompanying this directed to Mr. Adams, contains the Treaty and Convention lately received from him, and this day ratified by Congress, which I have the honor to present for your care to Europe. The great dearth of news in this City deprives me of the pleasure of communicating any information to you, either interesting or entertaining, unless I may be permitted to assure you of the wishes of your Country to see you engaged in the important mission committed to your charge.

Accept Sir, my most ardent wishes for your prosperity and that of Miss Jefferson, and beleive me with great Respect and Esteem Your most obedt. humble servant,   L R MORRIS

RC (DLC). On the enclosures, see below.

Lewis R. Morris was at this time secretary to Robert R. Livingston (Washington, *Writings*, ed. Fitzpatrick, XXVI, 258, note). This communication from him is a little puzzling in two respects. Under the same date in Livingston's "Despatch Book" (DLC: PCC, No. 126) is the entry: "Wrote to Mr. Adams and Mr Jefferson directed to the care of Colo. Samuel Smith at Baltimore." But no letter from Livingston of this date to TJ has been found, and even though TJ on 7 Feb., q.v., acknowledged such a letter, the acknowledgment seems clearly to apply to Morris' letter, for TJ says: "Your letter of the 31st. Ult. came safely to hand *with the packet to Mr. Adams accompanying it*" (italics supplied). The packet for Adams contained the treaty of amity and commerce between the United States and the Netherlands, together with a convention concerning vessels recaptured, which had been transmitted by Adams to Livingston on 8 Oct. 1782 and which was ratified by Congress on 23 [*not 31*] Jan. 1783, according to the Journals of Congress; see JCC, XXIV, 50, 65-82.

To La Luzerne

SIR   Baltimore Feb. 7. 1783.

The Chevalier de Ville Brun was so kind as to communicate to me yesterday your Excy.'s letter to him of Jan. together with the intelligence therein referred to. I feel myself bound to return you my thanks for your orders to the Guadaloupe frigate to receive me if I should think a passage should be hazarded under present circumstances. According to this information (which is the most worthy of credit of any we have received here) it would seem that our capture would be unavoidable were we to go out now. This therefore is a risk to which I cannot think of exposing his majesty's vessel and subjects, however I might be disposed to encounter personal hazards from my anxiety to execute with all the promptitude in my power a service which has been assigned to me. I shall therefore wait with patience the arrival of the moment when the Chevlr. de Ville-brun shall be of opinion that the one or the other of the vessels may venture out without any greater risk than he shall think proportioned to her proper object independantly of mine. It has been suggested to me this evening that perhaps their safe departure might be greatly forwarded by their falling down to York or Hampton there to be ready at a moment's warning to avail themselves of those favourable circumstances which the present season sometimes offers. But of this yourself will be the proper judge.

I cannot close my letter without expressing to you my obligations to the Chevalr. de Villebrun for the particular attention he has shown to my accomodation on board his ship. The apartments he has had constructed for me are ample and commodious and his politeness and merit as an officer are an agreable presage of every thing which shall depend on him.[1]

I have delivered the two large packets you were pleased to put into my hands, and he will dispose of them according to your orders.

I have the honr. to be with the highest sentiments of esteem yr. Excy's mo. obedt. & mo. hble. servt.

Dft (DLC). Tr (DLC: PCC, No. 119); this was made from a (missing) copy of the present letter enclosed to Robert R. Livingston (see the following letter). Date in Dft is corrected, evidently in another hand than TJ's, from "6" to "7" Feb.; and Dft is endorsed in an unidentified hand: "Copy —to His Excelly. the Minister to France Philada. Baltimore 7th. Feby. 1783." Another copy of the present letter, now missing, was enclosed in a letter from TJ to Villebrune, 8 Feb., also missing; see Villebrune to TJ, 12 Feb. 1783.

[1] This paragraph was an afterthought inserted by TJ in margin of Dft.

To Robert R. Livingston

SIR   Baltimore Feb. 7. 1783.

I arrived here on the 30th. of the last month, and had a short interview the same evening with the Chevalr. de Ville-Brun Commander of the Romulus. There appeared at that time little apprehension but that we might sail within a few days; but we were not very particular in our conference as we expected so soon to see each other again. The severity of the cold however which commenced that night obliged the Chevalr. de Villebrun to fall 12 miles below this place and excluded all correspondence with him till yesterday, when I found means to get through the ice on board his ship. He then communicated to me by direction of his Excy. the minister of France intelligence as to the number and force of the cruisers now actually watching the Chesapeak. I must acknolege that they appear such as to render a capture certain were we to hazard it. The minister was pleased at the same time to submit the Guardaloupe to my wishes if I chose to adventure. I take the liberty of troubling you with a copy of my letter to him on that subject. I should certainly be disposed to run very considerable risks myself to effect my passage but I should think it an unfortunate introduction to an ally who has already done so much for us, were I to add to his losses and disbursements that of a valuable ship and crew. I wish that the present delay offered some period less distant than the lassitude of an avaritious enemy to watch for prey. Perhaps you may be able to put me on some more expeditious mode of passage than the one under which I am acquiescing at present. I shall be much pleased to adopt any such which may come recommended from you without regard to personal risk or trouble. In the mean time any intelligence which you can be able to collect and will be pleased to give me as to the state of our coast will be of utility in determining whether and when we shall depart hence.

I have the honor to be with very great esteem and respect Sir Your mo. ob. & mo. hble. servt.

P.S. Your letter of the 31st. Ult. came safely to hand with the packet to Mr. Adams accompanying it.

Dft (DLC); notation of address in margin, and "No. 1" in TJ's hand in upper right corner of text; endorsed in a hand other than TJ's: "Copy, to Mr. Livingston . . . Baltimore 7 Feby. 1783. No. 1." Tr (DLC: PCC, No. 119). The (missing) RC was accompanied by a copy of TJ's letter to La Luzerne of this date, preceding.

An entry in Livingston's "Despatch Book" (PCC, No. 126) under 10 Feb. 1783 reads: "Recieved a Letter from the Honorable Mr Jefferson No. 1—enclosing a copy of his Letter to the Minister of France on the subject of his passage to Europe. Laid the above Letters before Congress." For the action of Congress, see under 14 Feb., below.

To James Madison

I write by this post to the Minister of foreign affairs, but will repeat to you the facts mentioned to him and some others improper for a public letter, and some reflections on them which can only be hazarded to the ear of friendship. The cold weather having set in the evening of the 30th. Ult. (being the same in which I arrived here) the Chevalr. de Ville-brun was obliged to fall down with his ship and the Guardaloupe to about twelve miles below this; and the ice has since cut off all correspondence with him till yesterday, when I got a boat and attempted a passage. There having passed a small boat before us we got about half way with tolerable ease, but the influx of the tide then happening the ice closed on us on every side and became impenetrable to our little vessel, so that we could get neither backwards nor forwards. We were finally relieved from this situation by a sloop which forced it's way down and put us on board the Romulus, where we were obliged to remain all night. The Chevalr. de Ville-brun communicated to me several letters of intelligence which deserves weight; by which we are informed that the enemy having no other employment at New York, have made our little fleet their sole object for some time, and have now cruising for us nothing less than

   1. ship of 64. guns
   4.   50
   2.   40.
  18. frigates from 24 to 30. guns, a most amazing force for such

---

25

an object. The merchants who intended to have sent their vessels out with us, have so far declined it, that two vessels only go with us. But they are unfortunately the greatest sluggards in the world. The Minister has given Ville-brun leave to remain if he thinks it expedient till the *Middle of March*[1] but politely and kindly offered the Guardaloupe for my passage if I chose to run the risk. I find that having laid ten months under water she got perfectly sobbed, insomuch that she sweats almost continually on the inside. In consequence of which her commander and several of the crew are now laid up with rheumatism: but this I should have disregarded had it not appeared that it was giving to the enemy the ship and crew of a friend, and delaying myself in fact by endeavoring at too much haste. I therefore have not made use of the liberty given me by the minister. Ville-brun seems certain he shall not sail till the *first of March* and I confess to you I see no reason to suppose that when that time arrives the same causes will not place our departure as distant as it now seems. What then is to be done? I will mention the several propositions which occur with some reflections on each.

1. To go to Boston and embark thence. Would to God I had done this at first. I might now have been half-way across the Ocean. But it seems very late to undertake a journey of such length, thro' such roads, and such weather: and when I should get there some delay would still necessarily intervene.—Yet I am ready to undertake it if this shall be thought best.

2. To stay here with patience till our enemies shall think proper to clear our coast. There is no certain termination to this object. It may not be till the end of the war.

3. To fall down to York or Hampton and there wait those favourable circumstances of winds and storms which the winter season sometimes presents. This would be speedier than the 2d. but perhaps it may not be approved by the commander for reasons which may be good tho' unknown to me. Should this however be adopted we ought to be furnished by the Marine department with, or authorised to employ one or more swift sailing boats to go out of the capes occasionally and bring us intelligence to York or Hampton wherever we should be.

4. To ask a flag for me from the enemy and charter a vessel here. This would be both quickest and most certain. But perhaps it may be thought injurious to the dignity of the states, or perhaps be thought such a favour as Congress might not chuse to expose themselves to the refusal of. With respect to the last, nothing can be said: as to the first, I suppose, were history sought, many precedents might be found where one of the belligerent powers has received from the other, passports for their plenipotentiaries; and I suppose that Fitzgerald and Oswald got to Paris now under protections of a flag and passport. However these are tender points and I would not wish the sensibility of Congress to be tried on my account, if it would be probably disagreeable.

5. To await a truce. This cannot take place till after preliminaries signed, if then: and tho' these are not definitive, yet it must be evident that new instructions and new or perhaps inconsistent matter would be introduced with difficulty and discredit.

There is an idle report here of peace being actually concluded. This comes by the way of the W. Indies, and must probably be founded on the settlement of preliminaries, if it has any foundation at all.

Should you think that the interference of Congress might expedite my departure in any of the above ways or any other I have suggested these hasty reflections in hopes that you would do in it whatever you think right. I shall acquiesce in any thing, and if nothing further comes to me I shall endeavor to push the third proposition with the Commander, and if I fail in that shall pursue the 2d. I wish to hear from you as often as you have any thing new. I fear I shall be here long enough to receive many letters from you. My situation is not an agreeable one, and the less so as I contrast it with the more pleasing one I left so unnecessarily. Be so good as to present my esteem to the good ladies and gentlemen of your fireside and to accept yourself the warmest assurances of friendship from Dr. Sir Your friend & servt,   TH: JEFFERSON

Feb. 8. The preceding was written the last night. Before I close my letter I will ask the favor of you to write me by the return of post and to let me have your own sentiments (whether any thing be, or be not determined authoritatively) which will have great weight with me. I confess that after another night's reflection the 4th. is the plan which appears to me best on the whole, and that the demand from New York is nothing more than what is made at the close of almost every war, where the one or the other power must have a passport: it is no more than asking a flag to New-York. Should this however be disapproved, the 3d seems the only remaining plan which promises any degree of expedition. Perhaps the minister may have a repugnance to venture the Romulus at York or Hampton, in which case if I could receive his approbation I should be willing to fall down there with the Guardaloupe alone and be in readiness to avail ourselves of a Northwesterly snow-storm or other favourable circumstance.

RC (DLC: Madison Papers); endorsed; partly in cipher.

FITZGERALD: TJ erred in referring to Alleyne Fitzherbert, one of the British commissioners carrying on peace negotiations with the American commissioners. The IDLE REPORT . . . OF PEACE is doubtless that cited in Burnett, *Letters of Members*, VII, No. 36, Note 5, to the effect "that a gentleman in St. Thomas had written to a correspondent in Baltimore that he had copied from a London paper a letter from Secretary Townshend to the directors of the bank of England"; what was said to be a copy of the Townshend letter was published in the *Maryland Journal* of 4 Feb. 1783, where TJ probably saw it. That letter (printed in Burnett), had already appeared in Philadelphia papers.

[1] This and other words below in italics were written in cipher and were decoded interlineally by Madison, employing Code No. 1.

From James Monroe

DEAR SIR   Richmond Feby. 8. 1783.

I fear this will not reach you but I risque it for tis probable you may be detaind a few days at Baltimore. I take the liberty to enclose you a cypher of men and places which will perhaps in some instances form the subject of a correspondence. I beg of you to accept my most sincere acknowledgments for your kind offer. As yet I cannot possibly determine how to act but shall consult Mr. Short. If peace does not shortly take place we will most probably join you. I most sincerely wish you and your family a safe and happy arrival to the destin'd port, & am yr. affec. friend & servant,

JAS. MONROE

RC (DLC). Enclosure (ViU); List of words with numerical equivalents, to be used as a cipher and cipher key in correspondence between Monroe and TJ; there are 99 items in the list, of which examples are: "1. Spain 2. Ld. Shelburne 3. Ct. de Vergennes 4. Dr. Franklin . . . 60. peace 61. western posts 62. committee of the States 63. laws of nations . . . 90. Mr. Howell 91. Trenton 92. Phila. 93. Genl. Washington." It does not appear that this simple cipher device was ever actually used; Monroe had another cipher prepared for use in his correspondence with TJ when the latter was about to depart for Europe in 1784; see Monroe to TJ, 20 May, and Samuel Hardy to TJ, 21 May 1784. This cipher has been designated as Code No. 2.

From George Washington

DEAR SIR   Newburgh 10th. Feby. 1783.

I have been honored with your favor of the 22d. of Jany. from Philadelphia. I feel myself much flattered by your kind remembrance of me in the hour of your departure from this Continent and for the favourable Sentiments you are pleased to entertain of my Services for this our common Country. To merit the approbation of good and virtuous Men is the height of my ambition; and will be a full compensation for all my toils and sufferings in the long and painful contest we have been engaged.

It gave me great pleasure to hear that, the call upon you from Congress, to pass the Atlantic in the Character of one of their Ministers for Negociating Peace, had been repeated. But I hope you will have found the business already done. The speech of his Britainic Majesty is strongly indicative of the Olive branch; and yet, as he observes, unforeseen events may place it out of reach.

At present, the prospect of Peace absorbs, or seems to do so, every other consideration among us; and would, it is to be feared, leave us in a very unprepared state to continue the War if the

Negociation at Paris should terminate otherwise than in a general pacification. But I will hope that it is the dearth of other News that fills the Mouths of every person with Peace, while their Minds are employed in contemplating on the Means for prosecuting the War if necessity should drive us to it.

You will please accept my grateful thanks for your obliging offer of Services during your stay in France. To hear frequently from you, will be an honor and very great satisfaction to Dr Sir, Yr Most Obedt and Most Hble Servt.,   Go: WASHINGTON

RC (DLC), with addressee's name at foot of text. Dft (DLC: Washington Papers); endorsed.

From James Madison

DEAR SIR   Philada. Feby. 11th. 1783.

Your favor of the 31 of Jany. was safely brought me by Mr. Thomson. That of the 7. instant came by yesterdays mail. The anecdote related in the first was new to me; and if there were no other key, would sufficiently decypher the implacability of the party triumphed over. In answer to the second I can only say at this time that I feel deeply for your situation: that I approve of the choice you have made among its difficulties, and that every aid which can depend on me shall be executed to relieve you from them. Before I can take any step with propriety however it will be expedient to feel the sentiments of Congress, and to advise with some of my friends. The first point may possibly be brought about by your letter to the Secy. of F. A. which I suppose came too late yesterday to be laid before Congress, but which will no doubt be handed in this morning.

The time of Congress since you left us has been almost exclusively spent on projects for a valuation of the land, as the federal articles require; and yet I do not find that we have got an inch forward towards the object. The mode of referring the task to the States which had at first the warmest and most numerous support seems to be in a manner abandoned; and nothing determinate is yet offered on the mode of effecting it without their intervention. The greatest misfortune perhaps attending the case, is that a plan of some kind is made an indispensable preliminary to any other essay for the public relief. I much question whether a sufficient number of States will be found in favor of any plan that can be devised, as I am sure that in the present temper of Congress a sufficient number cannot who will agree to tell their Constituents that the law of the Confederation cannot be executed, and to propose an amendment of it. *Congress yesterday received*[1] from *Mr. Adams several letters dated* September not remarkable for any thing unless it be a *display*[2] *of his vanity, his prejudice against* the *French Court* and *his venom against Doctr. Franklin.* Other preparations for the post do not allow me to use more cypher at present.

I have a letter from Randolph dated Feby. 1. confirming the death of his aunt. You are acquainted no doubt with the course the estate is to take. He seems disposed in case he can make a tolerable compromise with his Father's creditors to resign his appointment under the State and go into the Legislature. His zeal for some continental arrangement as essential for the public honor and safety forms at least one of his motives, and I have added all the fuel to it in my power.

My neglect to write to you heretofore has proceeded from a hope that a letter would not find you at Baltimore; and no subject has occurred for one of sufficient importance to follow you. You shall hence forward hear from me as often as an occasion presents, until your departure forbids it. The Ladies and Gentlemen to whom I comunicated your respects, return them with equal sincerity and the former as well as myself very affectionately include Miss Patsy in the object of them.

I am Dr. Sir Yr. Sincere friend,   J. Madison Jr.

RC (DLC: Madison Papers). Dft (Madison Papers); endorsed. Coded passages appear in both.

The letters RECEIVED FROM MR. ADAMS, as acknowledged by Livingston on 13 Feb. 1783, were those "of the 6th, the 7th, the 17th, the 19th, and the 23d of September" (Wharton, *Dipl. Corr. Am. Rev.*, VI, 250; however, letters of Adams of the dates 6, 7, 17 [*bis*], and 23 are printed in same, V, 703-709, 733-4, 735-8, and 750-2, indicating that one of Adams' letters of the 17th was erroneously dated and should have been the 19th). Livingston did not agree with Madison's estimate. In his letter of acknowledgment to Adams he said: "They contain important and useful information; and that particular of the 6th is replete with matter which deserves an attention that I lament not having it in my power to give it at this moment, as the express by which this goes to Baltimore is on

the wing" (same, VI, 250).

[1] This and subsequent words in italics were in code and were decoded interlineally by Madison in both RC and Dft (though less completely in latter), employing Code No. 1.

[2] Madison first wrote "full" before "display" and then struck out the first word. This deletion appears in both RC and Dft. Then, or at a later time, he interlined "fresh" in Dft, making the passage read "a fresh display," &c. But since the interlineal decoding was done in RC by Madison after TJ's death when Madison borrowed his own letters to TJ (failing to return the present one) and since the decoded passages in RC are in pencil, as is the word "fresh," it is clear that this was an afterthought added half a century later by Madison and that TJ read the passage as given above, not as "a fresh display."

From La Villebrune

MONSIEUR   Baltimore Le 12 fevrier 1783.

J'ai Recu La Lettre que Votre Excellence Ma fait L'honneur De M'Ecrire Le 8 De ce mois avec La Copie De Sa Lettre à M. Le Cher. De La Luzerne. Je ne peu asse vous Remercier de L'interet que Vous avés bien Voulu prendre pour faire Terminer L'objet en contestation avec M. Le Gros. J'ai fait Choix de M. Pringle comme arbitre Dans cette affaire, et J'ai Lieu de penser grace a vos bons offices qu'elle Sera Terminé sans Retour.

Je serois bien de L'avis proposé a Votre Excellence d'aller Mouiller a York ou Hampton pour être a portée de profiter Des premiers Vents De Nord Ouest qui me Mettroient Loin de la Cote, Dans La nuit, Surtout Si Je navois pas de convoy à conserver, Mais Des Batiments entrés aujourd'hui Raportent Avoir été Chassés par quatre frégattes Jusque sur Le Cap Charles et avoir vu au Mouillage de Linhaven-Baye, un vaisseau et une frégatte qui ont appareillés et pris un Brieg qui navigoit avec eux; deplus York, Et Hampton, N'ont pas un canon Monté. Si L Ennemy Tres Supérieur Entreprenoit de venir nous y forcer il y auroit peu de Sureté.

Peut etre conviendroit-il autant D'attendre comme Le propose M. De La Luzerne Jusqu'au Mois prochain, Des Nouvelles D'Europe, ou L'arivée D'une Division des Antilles promise par M. De Veaudreuil, Ou bien Encore que L Ennemi fatigué ne fut obligé de Rentrer a Newyork.

Je voi par La Lettre de Votre Excellence a M. Le Cher. de La Luzerne qu'elle aprecie Beaucoup Les Dispositions prises pour son Logement. C'est un Effet de Votre Tres grande indulgence qui ajouteroit Encore S'il Etoit possible au désir de vous Rendre tout ce que Je vous Doit.

Je Suis avec Respect Monsieur Votre tres Humble et tres Obeissant Serviteur,   LA VILLEBRUNE

RC (DLC); in a clerk's hand, signed by Villebrune.

The name of the writer, a *capitaine de vaisseau*, is variously spelled by TJ and is given as Jacques-Aimé Le S. Villèsbrunne in Contenson, *La Société de Cincinnati en France*; but the form followed by the editors is that of his signature. After the reduction of Yorktown, La Villebrune was ordered by De Grasse to remain in Chesapeake in command of the *Romulus*, *Hermione*, and *Diligente*. The letter to which the present one is a reply has not been found; that from TJ to La Luzerne, of which a copy had been enclosed to La Villebrune, is printed under 7 Feb. 1783.

From La Luzerne

MONSIEUR   A Philadelphie le 13. Fevrier 1783.

J'ai reçu la lettre que Vous m'avés fait l'honneur de m'ecrire le 7. de ce mois. J'ai été dans le tems très faché des delais que Vous avés été dans le cas d'eprouver, mais je vois avec bien du plaisir que Vous avés approuvé le parti que nous avons pris de retenir les deux Fregattes. J'ai parlé ce matin à un homme qui etoit à bord du Lion il y a dix jours, il m'a dit que ce Vaisseau avec le Centurion et plusieurs Fregattes etoit en croisière resolu à ne quitter les Caps qu'après le depart des deux Fregattes du Roy et du convoy.

J'ai l'honneur d'adresser à Votre Excellence le discours du Roy d'Angleterre à son Parlement. Il laisse bien peu de doutes touchant la paix et j'espere que Vous approuverés les instructions que j'envoye en consequence à M. de la Villebrune.

J'étois bien persuadé que Vous auriés à Vous louer de cet Officier autant qu'il avoit à se feliciter lui même de l'avantage qu'il avoit de faire la traversée avec vous.

J'ai l'honneur d'être avec une consideration distinguée Monsieur De Votre Excellence le très humble et très obéissant serviteur

LE CHR DE LA LUZERNE

RC (DLC); in a clerk's hand, signed by La Luzerne. Enclosure missing, but see note on the letter immediately following.

LES INSTRUCTIONS QUE J'ENVOYE: These were in turn transmitted to TJ by La Villebrune in a letter of 19 Feb., q.v.

From James Madison

DEAR SIR   Philada. Feby. 13th. 1783.

The Chevr. de la Luzerne having just given me notice that he shall send an Express to the Romulus in ½ an hour I sieze the opportunity of inclosing a copy of the British Kings speech which presages a speedy establishment of peace. What effect this circumstance may have on your mission is at present uncertain. For myself I cannot think that any thing short of a final and authentic ratification ought to be listened to in that view. But I am told that it is the opinion of Mr. Morris that no vessel will sail from any American port whilst the critical uncertainty continues. Whether any and what changes may be produced in the orders to the Romulus will be known from the Commander. Adieu.

J. MADISON JR.

RC (DLC: Madison Papers); endorsed by Madison with his name and the date sent. Enclosure: See below.

THE BRITISH KINGS SPEECH: George III's speech on the opening of Parliament, 5 Dec. 1782, stated that he had pointed all his "views and measures" to "an entire and cordial reconciliation" with the "colonies" and that he had gone so far as to offer "to declare them free and independent states, by an article to be inserted in the treaty of peace. Provisional articles are agreed upon, to take effect whenever terms of peace shall be finally settled with the court of France" (Hansard, *Parl. Hist.*, XXIII, 205-6). Copies of the King's speech reached Congress on 13 Feb. 1783 (see Elias Boudinot to Nathanael Greene, 13 Feb., Burnett, *Letters of Members*, VII, No. 49; Madison, "Notes of Debate," JCC, XXV, 898). Confirmation of the news that a provisional treaty had been signed (an event which had in fact taken place in Paris, 30 Nov. 1782) was "hourly" expected, but Capt. Joshua Barney of the *Washington*, who had been granted a passport by the express order of George III on 10 Dec., did not reach America until a month after copies of the King's speech circulated here; hence the grave uncertainty attending TJ's mission. (The passport is printed in Wharton, *Dipl. Corr. Amer. Rev.*, VI, 137, note.) Meanwhile, on 20 Jan. 1783, provisional articles of peace between Great Britain and France had been signed in Paris, and a declaration of the cessation of hostilities had been signed by the British and American commissioners (same, p. 223-4). This news reached Congress on 24 Mch. "by a French Cutter from Cadiz despatched by Ct. d'Estaing to notify the event to all vessels at sea, and engaged by the zeal of the Marquis de la Fayette to convey it to Congress. This confirmation of peace produced the greater joy, as the preceding delay, the cautions of Mr. Laurens's letter of the 24 of Decr. and the general suspicions of Ld. Shelburne's sincerity had rendered an immediate and general peace extremely problematical in the minds of many" (Madison's "Notes of Debate," JCC, XXV, 940; Laurens' letter from Paris, 24 Dec. 1782, printed in Wharton, VI, 164-5, was apparently received just prior to the news confirming the treaty; see also Lafayette to Robert R. Livingston, Cadiz, 5 Feb. 1783, same, p. 238-40). Not until 24 Mch., then, could TJ be relieved of the last vestige of doubt as to whether he would still have to proceed to France. Congress officially released him from his appointment on 1 Apr.; see the resolution printed under that date and also Livingston to TJ, 4 Apr. 1783.

To Robert R. Livingston

SIR   Baltimore Feb. 14. 1783.

I apprised you in my former letter of the causes which had so long delayed my departure. These still continue. I have this moment received a printed copy of his Britannic majesty's speech to his parliament by which we learn that preliminaries between America and Great Britain, among which is one for the acknolegement of our independence, have been provisionally agreed on to his part, that the negociations with the other powers at war were considerably advanced and that he hoped in a very short time they would end in terms of pacification.

As considerable progress has been made in the negociations for peace since the appointment with which Congress were pleased to honour me, it may have become doubtful whether any communications I could make or any assistance I could yeild to the very able gentlemen in whose hands the business already is, would compensate the expence of prosecuting my voiage to Europe. I therefore beg leave through you Sir, to assure Congress that I desire this question to be as open to them now as it was on the day of my appointment, and that I have not a wish of my own to go, or to stay. They will be pleased to weigh the œconomy of the one measure against the chance which the other may offer of my arriving in such time as that any communications which have been confided to me may produce effect on definitive articles.

I shall continue here for the prosecution of my voiage, under the orders before received: or for it's discontinuance should that be more eligible to Congress and be so signified at any moment before my departure.

I have the honour to be with the highest sentiments of esteem & regard Sir Your most obedt. & most humble servt,

TH: JEFFERSON

RC (PHC); addressed: "The honble. Robert R. Livingston Secretary for foreign affairs Philadelphia"; endorsed: "Mr Jefferson 14th. Feby 1783." Dft (DLC); contains a number of corrections in phrasing not noted here. RC was enclosed in TJ's second letter to Madison of this date, q.v. Livingston's "Despatch Book" (DLC: PCC, No. 126) enters this letter as received 17 Feb.

From Robert R. Livingston, Enclosing a Resolution of Congress

SIR   Philadelphia 14th: February 1783.

I have delayed answering your favor of the 7th Instant until I could obtain the sense of Congress on the matter it contains. I conceive it hardly possible while the british Cruizers retain their present Station for you to elude their vigilance in either of the Ships offered to your choice. This concurring with the late advices from England, has induced Congress to pass the enclosed Resolution. We have reason to conjecture the peace is already concluded, whether it is or not a few days must determine.

I transmit the speech of his Britannick Majesty which with what you already know of the State of our Negotiations will enable you to form your opinion on the same ground that we do. I have the honor to be Sir with great Respect and Esteem your most obedient humble servt,   ROBT. R. LIVINGSTON

ENCLOSURE

By the United States in Congress assembled.

February 14th. 1783.

The Committee consisting of Mr. Jones, Mr. Rutledge and Mr. Wilson, to whom was referred a letter of the 7th. from the Honorable Thomas Jefferson reported thereon, Whereupon on motion of Mr. Gorham seconded by Mr. Wolcott—Ordered,

That the Secretary for Foreign Affairs inform Mr. Jefferson, that it is the pleasure of Congress, considering the advices lately received in America, and the probable situation of Affairs in Europe, that he do not proceed on his intended Voyage until he shall receive their further instructions.   CHAS THOMSON Secy

RC (DLC); in Lewis R. Morris' hand, signed by Livingston. Dft (NHi). Tr (DLC: PCC, No. 119). Enclosure (DLC); also in Morris' hand, signed by Thomson. Dft of enclosure (DLC: PCC, No. 19, III); entirely in Thomson's hand. TJ's letter of 7 Feb. had been referred by Livingston to Congress on the 10th; the original report of the committee to whom it was referred has not been found; Livingston's

"Despatch Book" (DLC: PCC, No. 126) has the following under date of 14 Feb.: "Received from Congress, Letter from Mr. Jefferson to me, with the enclosure that had been laid before them, and a resolution directing Mr. Jefferson not to sail at present. Wrote to Mr. Jefferson enclosing the above mentioned Resolution by this day's Post."

To James Madison

DEAR SIR   Baltimore Feb. 14. 1783.

Patsy putting the inclosed into my hands obliges me to make a separate letter of it, that while I give it the protection of your address I may yet pay it's postage. I suspect by the superscription (which I saw before Majr. Franks amended it) and by what I know of Patsy's hierogliphical writing that Miss Polly must get an interpreter from Egypt. Be so good as to remind the ladies and gentlemen of the house of my affection for them. I am particularly obliged to Mr. Carrol for an introduction to his relation near this, with whom I have been able to pass agreeably some of my heavy hours. I shall write to E. Randolph on the subject of his going into the legislature and use my interest to promote it. I hope you will be there too when you can no longer be in any more important place. I am with sincere esteem Dr Sir Your friend & servt,

TH: JEFFERSON

RC (DLC: Madison Papers). Enclosure (missing): Letter from Martha Jefferson to Polly Floyd (see Madison to TJ, 18 Feb.).

MISS POLLY was the daughter of Wil-

liam Floyd, a member of Congress from New York who had served steadfastly from 1774 with the exception of one year; he had entered the Revolution as a man of wealth, but emerged with his estate in ruin. TJ had known him since 1775 (DAB). MR. CARROL was Daniel Carroll, a member of Congress from Maryland; Carroll's letter of introduction has not been found nor has the relation to whom it was addressed been identified. TJ's promised letter to Randolph is that of 15 Feb. 1783.

To James Madison

DEAR SIR   Baltimore Feb. 14. 1783.

Yours of the 11th. came to hand last night. From[1] what you mention in your letter I suppose the newspapers must be wrong when they say that Mr. Adams, had taken up his abode with Dr. Franklin. I am nearly at a loss to judge how he will act in the negotiation. He hates Franklin, he hates Jay, he hates the French, he hates the English.[2] To whom will he adhere? His vanity is a lineament in his character which had entirely escaped me. His want of taste I had observed. Notwithstanding all this he has a sound head on substantial points, and I think he has integrity. I am glad therefore that he is of the commission and expect he will be useful in it. His dislike of all parties, and all men, by balancing his prejudices, may give the same fair play to his reason as would a general benevolence of temper. At any rate honesty may be extracted even from poisonous weeds.

My stay here has given me opportunities of making some experiments on my amanuensis Franks, perhaps better than I may have in France. He appears to have a good enough heart, an understanding somewhat better than common but too little guard over his lips. I have marked him particularly in the company of women where he loses all power over himself and becomes almost frenzied.[3] His temperature would not be proof against their allurements were such to be employed as engines against him. This is in some measure the vice of his age but it seems to be increased also by his peculiar constitution.

I wrote to the Chevalier de Ville Brun proposing his falling down to York or Hampton which was one of the measures I suggested in my letter to you, and was the most eligible except that of the flag, in my own opinion. His answer, dated Feb. 12. is in these words. 'Je serois bien de l'avis proposé a votre Excellence d'aller mouiller a York ou Hampton pour etre a portee de profiter des premiers vents de Nord Ouest qui me mettroient loin de la côte dans la nuit, sourtout si je n'avois pas de convoy a conserver. Mais des batiments entrès aujourd'hui raportent avoir eté chassés par quatre fregates jusque sur la Cap Charles et avoir vu au mouillage de Linhaven bay un vaisseau et un fregate qui ont appareillés et pris un Brig qui navigoit avec eux. De plus York et Hampton n'ont pas un canon monté, si l'ennemi, tres superieur, entreprenoit de venir nous y forcer, il y auroit peu de sureté.

Peut etre conviendroit-il autant d'attendre, comme le propose M. de la Luzerne, jusqu'au Mois prochain, des nouvelles d'Europe, ou l'arrivée d'une division des Antilles promise par M. de Vaudreuil, ou bien encore quel'ennemi fatigué ne fut obligé de rentrer a New-York.' The last basis is relish and furnishes matter for doubt how far the departure of the Romulus is a decided measure. It seems not unlikely. So for a purpose wherein time is the most pressing circumstance the idea of going in her is to be abandond.⁴ To go to *Boston* would be the most œconomical plan. But it would be *five weeks* from my leaving this place before I could expect to sail from thence. Of course I may from here be *in France* by the time I should be sailing from *Boston*. *Five weeks* in a crisis of *negotiation* may be much. Should I accept of the *Guadaloupe* and she should be lost, it would under present circumstances draw censure. Moreover in this or the former case, besides losing the vessel, what will be my situation? That of a prisoner certainly. From what has been done in Laurence's case⁵ they would not release me; in expectation of a high exchange; or if they did, it would only be on parole, in which case I could neither act nor communicate. This plan would have in it's favour œconomy and a possibility (a bare one) of dispatch. That of the flag still appears best. It is favoured by the circumstances of dispatch, safety, and the preservation of my papers. But when I think of the expence I feel myself annihilated in comparison with it. A vessel may be got here, but I question if for less than *a thousand* or *two thousand* pounds.⁶ Besides can a passport be obtained from New York without naming the vessel, the crew &c.? If not it would take long to furnish these circumstances from hence. The Delaware would be more eligible in that case. Otherwise this place is. If this should be adopted, what would be the extent of the protection of the flag to the papers I should carry? These, so far as this question would affect them, would be of three descriptions. 1. my own commission, instructions and other documents relative to my mission. 2. public letters to the Consuls, ministers and others on other business. 3. private letters. I have no means of satisfying myself on these points here. If therefore this measure should be adopted I should thank you for your opinion on them, as you can, where you are doubtful, make enquiry of others. I am exceedingly fatigued with this place, as indeed I should with any other where I had neither occupation nor amusement. I am very particularly indebted here to the politeness and hospitality of Genl. La Vallette who obliges me to take refuge in his quarters from the tedium of my own, the latter half of every day. You are indebted to him too as I should make my long letters much longer and plague you with more cypher were I confined at home all day. I beg you to be assured of my warmest wishes for your happiness.

Th: Jefferson

Feb. 15.[7] 9. o'clock P.M. After sealing up this letter I received yours of yesterday inclosing the King's speech, for which I thank you much. The essential information conveyed to us by that is that the preliminary for our independance (which we before knew to have been agreed between the plenipotentiaries) has been provisionally ratified by him. I have thought it my duty to write the inclosed letter which after reading you will be so good as to stick a wafer in and deliver. I wish no supposed inclination of mine to stand in the way of a free change of measure if Congress should think the public interest required it. The argument of œconomy is much strengthened by the impossibility (now certain) of going but in an express vessel. The principal matters confided to me were. 1. the new instruction; which perhaps may have been sent by Count Rochambeau, or may yet be sent. 2. the details of the financier's department which Mr. Morris not chusing to trust to paper had communicated verbally. These in the event of peace or truce may safely go in paper. 3. the topics which supp[ort] our right to the fisheries, to the Western country, and the navigation of the Missisipi. The first of these is probably settled: the two latter should only come into discussion in the Spanish negociation, and therefore would only have been the subject of private conversation with Mr. Jay, whose good sense and knolege of the subject will hardly need any suggestions.

I forgot to mention to you in my letter that Mr. Nash arrived here the day before yesterday on his way to N. Carolina, and that Mr. Blunt is not yet arrived, but is weekly expected.[8] I am yours affectionately,

Th: Jefferson

RC (DLC: Madison Papers); endorsed in a hand other than Madison's; partly in code. Enclosure: TJ to Livingston, this date.

The letter that TJ WROTE TO THE CHEVALIER DE VILLE BRUN, dated 8 Feb., is missing.

1 Beginning with this word the remainder of this paragraph and all of the next were written in code and were, in part, decoded interlineally by Madison, employing Code No. 1 (verified by the editors' partial reconstruction of the cipher as indicated in the note to TJ to Madison, 31 Jan. 1783). The word "would," which occurs twice in this passage, was not encoded by TJ.

2 As decoded by Madison and as all texts print it, this sentence reads: "He has F——, he has Jay, he has the French, he has the English." This, of course, is nonsense in the context in which it appears, and a partial reconstruction of the code makes it plain that the reading given above is the correct one. The letter "h" in the 1774, London, edition of Nugent's *Dictionary* begins around page 400 (the word "guard" appears on p. 394); and the code as here employed involves, near these pages, the following: 401.25 (*hate*, as here conjectured), 401.29 (*have* or its variants), 402.1 (*he*), 402.24 (*head*), 403.16 (*heart*), &c. In *all* other instances in this letter and others in which Code No. 1 is employed, the code for "has" is 401.29; in the present sentence only does the code symbol 401.25 appear, and in this sentence it occurs four times, each time being rendered by Madison as "has." It is clear that he miscounted the lines and thus gave a nonsense reading to the passage.

3 The code symbol for this word is 369.9 and was not decoded by Madison. The symbols immediately preceding and following it are: 367.4 (*frank*), 368.7 (*French*), 369.34 (*from*). This narrowly limits the possible readings. Burnett, in his discussion of our Code No. 1 (*Amer. Hist. Rev.*, XXII [1916-1917], 332, note), suggests "frivolous" as the reading, but this scarcely fits the context for "one who loses all power over himself." "Frenetic" is also more plausible than "frivolous" in this context.

4 This and the two preceding sentences were written in code; other words following this point that were written in code are given in italics. The words "basis" and "unlikely" in this passage are conjectural, since Madison did not decode their symbols (80.15 and 895.-17). Preceding and following code symbols for these two words are 60.27 (*balancing*), 89.1 (*be*), 861.3 (*understanding*), and 915.1 (*up*). Madison's punctuation of the passage is also faulty, for he appears to have read it as if there were no period preceding "so" and he capitalized "the" after "circumstance" as if it were the beginning of a new sentence; in doing this he was probably misled by the extra space and by TJ's habit of beginning sentences with lower case letters.

5 The case of Henry Laurens, who was captured by the British in 1780 while on his way to negotiate a loan and a treaty of amity and commerce with Holland. He was confined in the Tower of London until 31 Dec. 1781 (DAB).

6 Not deciphered by Madison, who wrote in the margin, probably at a later date, "See Dictionary F & English." As encoded by TJ, the passage reads: "1.1.819.36 or 843.10.819.36." In Code No. 1 the symbol for "a" is 1.1 and the symbols immediately preceding and following 819.36 are: 818.25 (*third*) and 824.2 (*time*), suggesting clearly that "thousand" is the correct reading for 819.36. This word is repeated in the second pair of symbols, and both the character and the context of the remaining symbol suggest that "two" is the proper reading.

7 An error for "Feb. 14." This postscript was clearly added on the evening of the day when the main body of the letter was written. In the first sentence of the postscript TJ acknowledges a letter from Madison of "yesterday," which was Madison's letter of 13 Feb.; and Madison's letter of 18 Feb. acknowledges "two favors of the 14th" from TJ.

8 Abner Nash and William Blount were members of Congress from North Carolina.

To Francis Eppes

DEAR SIR   Baltimore Feb. 15. 1783.

After writing my letter of this date which is to go by Govr. Nash now here on his way to N. Carolina, I went to his lodgings to chat an hour. He has proposed to me a land party which I think is hopeful and great and which he desires may be entirely secret. I have never adventured in this way in my own country because being concerned in public business I was ever determined to keep my hands clear of every concern which might at any time produce an interference between private interests and public duties. This is with him also the first attempt. He proposes to form a company of twenty shares and on the opening of the land office in North Carolina which will be the next spring, to enter for all the lands within Ld. Granville's Southern boundary between the Missisipi and Cherokee rivers. The breadth from North to South, that is from the Virginia line to Ld. Granville's Southern boundary is one degree, which is 69 miles: and from the Missisipi to the Cherokee river is about the same distance on an average. So that it will contain upwards of two millions of acres, and be more than a hundred thousand acres to a share. He supposes it will cost about ten shillings a hundred. He has admitted me a share, and I have got him to let yourself Mr. Skipwith and Mr. Lewis in for another share if you chuse it. Being incertain at this instant whether I go to Europe or not, I can only say that if I do not I shall be in place to take care of this matter myself; but if I go it will devolve with my other troubles on yourself and Mr. Lewis. Govr. Nash will apprise you by letter when any thing is to be done. Should there be a difficulty in raising the money for my share, rather than miss of it I would wish you to draw on me in Paris at 60. days sight where I will take care to engage some body to pay the money. Possibly I may sell there a small portion of my share for the sum requisite. As I know you have had a desire to engage something of this kind for your family, and you might wish to speak with Governor Nash on this subject, I will take measures for his sending off this express to you from Richmond as soon as he arrives there which will enable you to visit him at Colo. Bannister's where he proposes to stay a day or two. I shall authorize the person engaged as express to call on you for his hire which please to charge to my account. I am Dr. Sir Your affectionate friend, TH: JEFFERSON

RC (ViU); endorsed: "Recd. 20th. March." TJ's LETTER OF THIS DATE has not been found. His yielding to the allurements of western speculation was momentary; see TJ to Nash, 11 Mch. 1783.

From James Madison

DEAR SIR   Philada. Feby. 15th. 1783.

The Committee, to whom was referred your letter to Secretary Livingston, reported to Congress yesterday that they had conferred with Mr. Morris who was of opinion that no vessel would sail from American ports after the arrival of the British King's speech until the suspence produced by it should be removed, and that if your immediate embarkation were still wished by Congress it would be proper to obtain for that purpose a Frigate from the Chevr. de la Luzerne. He informed the Committee that there was a fit vessel in this river which would have sailed for France but for the prospect of peace afforded by the Speech; and which I suppose will still proceed if that prospect should fail. The effect of this information to Congress and of a request from the Committee to be instructed on the subject was, a resolution directing the Secy. of F. A. to acquaint you that it was the pleasure of Congress, considering the present situation of things, that you should suspend your voyage until their further instruction. This resolution will I suppose be forwarded by the post which conveys this. I do not undertake to give any advice as to the steps which may now be proper for you, but I indulge with much pleasure the hope that a return to this place for the present may be the result of your own deliberations.

I am Dear Sir with Sincerity Yr friend & Servt.,

J. MADISON Jr.

RC (DLC: Madison Papers); endorsed at head of text by Madison.

To Edmund Randolph

DEAR SIR   Baltimore Feb. 15. 1783.

You will be surprised to hear I am still in America. The vessel, in which Ct. Rochambeau and Chastlux went, having been destined for Cadix it was thought more adviseable for me to take my passage in the Romulus which was to sail within a few days. This was concluded the rather as at the sailing of the Emeraude I had not got half through the necessary communications. The French fleet having sailed about the time the Emeraude did, and all restraint thereby taken off the cruisers there have been 18. Frigates, 2 forties, 4 fifties and a sixty four cruising ever since from Delaware to Chesapeake: so that after waiting a month for the Romulus I find less probability of her sailing now than at first. In the mean time things are changing appearance. I received last night a copy of the k's speech announcing that preliminaries are agreed between us and them, to be in force on the conclusion of the war with France, that the negotiations with the other powers are considerably ad-

vanced, insomuch that he hopes a speedy pacification. I have therefore written to Mr. Livingston that he may submit to Congress a
suggestion of the small likelihood there is of my arriving at the
scene of negociation in time for any new communications I carry
to make impressions on the definitive treaty, to weigh this chance
against the certain expence and to say whether they think it more
eligible or not for me to discontinue my voiage. Within a week I
shall probably get an answer, and within the same space after your
receiving this I think it probable you will see me at Richmond, as
I shall take that route home to pick up my little family in that
neighborhood. The king seems to part with us with a sigh; he makes
it his earnest and humble prayer to Almighty god that Great Britain may experience no evils on so important a dismemberment of
the empire, and that we may not find in experience as she had done
how necessary *Monarchy* is for the preservation of constitutional
liberty. He prays them to turn their attention to their extensive
Asiatic possessions and seems to consider these as succeeding to
our places. There is much lying and some puffing in the speech.

I hear with very great pleasure thro' Mr. Madison that you have
a thought of qualifying yourself for a seat in the legislature. Indeed
I hear it with as much pleasure as I have seen with depression of
spirit the very low state to which that body has been reduced. I am
satisfied there is in it much good intention, but little knowlege
of the science to which they are called. I only fear you will find the
unremitting drudgery, to which any one man must be exposed who
undertakes to stem the torrent, will be too much for any degree of
perseverance. I sincerely wish you may undertake and persevere
in it. I hope you will be joined e'er long by Madison and Short. I observe the assembly in it's last session led into a declaration of a
doctrine of the most mischeivous tendency. The object of the paper
I allude to was the excluding the return of refugees and insisting
on the escheat of their property; a very tempting bait indeed, and
which would dispose them not to be nice in the preliminary reasoning which was to lead to it. This matter stands on it's best ground
when urged on the reasonableness of a mutual risk in all contests,
on the superior dangers we encountered, and the inequality of our
conditions if we staked every thing and they nothing. But not
content with this they go on to talk of the dissolution of the social
contract on a revolution of government, and much other little stuff
by which I collect their meaning to have been that on changing
the form of our government all our laws were dissolved, and ourselves reduced to a state of nature. This is precisely the Vermont

doctrine against which the other states and Virginia most especially has been strenuously contending. The Vermonteers insist that on the demolition of the regal government all the municipal laws became abrogated, and of course those which had constituted any particular tract of country into one state, that any portion of what had been an integral state had then a right to assume a separate existence, and to govern themselves: and I have no doubt that their next declarations will cite that of the Virginia assembly which is the first authority they have ever had it in their power to cite. For my part, if the term *social contract* is to be forced from theoretical into practical use, I shall apply it to all the laws obligatory on the state, and which may be considered as contracts to which all the individuals are parties. And that whenever it becomes necessary to amend any of these, whether they respect the mode of administering the government or the transmission or regulation of private property, or any other branch of the laws, that any of these may be amended without affecting the residue. If you and I have a contract of six articles and agree to amend two of them, this does not dissolve the remaining four. The former laws had fixed the mode of transmitting the executive powers from one hand to another, the mode of appointing the judges, the mode of making alterations in the laws. These modes were found prejudicial to the state and it became necessary to change the laws which had fixed them. Why should this abrogate another law which had said that on the death of a father his eldest son shall inherit his lands?————
I find also the pride of independance taking deep and dangerous hold on the hearts of individual states. I know no danger so dreadful and so probable as that of internal contests. And I know no remedy so likely to prevent it as the strengthening the band which connects us. We have substituted a Congress of deputies from every state to perform this task: but we have done nothing which would enable them to enforce their decisions. What will be the case? They will not be enforced. The states will go to war with each other in defiance of Congress; one will call in France to her assistance; another Gr. Britain, and so we shall have all the wars of Europe brought to our own doors. Can any man be so puffed up with his little portion of sovereignty as to prefer this calamitous accompaniment to the parting with a little of his sovereign right and placing it in a council from all the states, who being chosen by himself annually, removeable at will, subject in a private capacity to every act of power he does in a public one, cannot possibly do him an injury, or if he does will be subject to be over-

hauled for it? It is very important to unlearn the lessons we have learnt under our former government, to discard the maxims which were the bulwark of that, but would be the ruin of the one we have erected. I feel great comfort on the prospect of getting yourself and two or three others into the legislature. My 'humble and earnest prayer to Almighty god' will be that you may bring into fashion principles suited to the form of government we have adopted, and not of that we have rejected, that you will first lay your shoulders to the strengthening the band of our confederacy and averting those cruel evils to which it's present weakness will expose us, and that you will see the necessity of doing this instantly before we forget the advantages of union, or acquire a degree of ill-temper against each other which will daily increase the obstacles to that good work. You feel by this time the effects of my idleness here and rejoice in the admonition of my paper that it is time to assure you of the sincere esteem with which I am Dr Sir Your friend & servt,

Th: Jefferson

P.S. Since writing the above the k's speech is printed here. I therefore inclose a copy.

RC (William M. Elkins, Philadelphia, 1945); endorsed by Randolph: "T. Jefferson Balt. Feby. 15. 1783," and in a later hand: "found among the letters from J.M. to E.R. returned from the files of the latter to the former."

The DOCTRINE OF THE MOST MISCHEIVOUS TENDENCY to which TJ referred was that set forth in the report of the committee of the whole on 17 Dec. 1782 (JHD, Oct. 1782, 1828 edn., p. 69-70) as follows:

"Whereas, revolutions in States which end in a dissolution of their former government or Constitution, bear no similarity to contests between independent nations, in which the object is the defence and support of their constitutions and governments; inasmuch as in the former, the life, liberty and property of the individual are risked; and in the latter the powers and rights of the whole community in their political capacity are hazarded;

"Resolved therefore, unanimously, That when the former constitution or social compact of this country, and the civil laws which existed under it were dissolved, a majority of the inhabitants had, through necessity, an unquestionable natural right to frame a new social compact, and to admit as parties thereto, those only, who would be bound by the laws of the majority; and consequently as no individual can claim immunities, privileges or property in any community but under the laws of that community, so all those who were members of the former government, which, and its dependant laws have been dissolved, abrogated and made void, cannot have legal claim to any immunity, privilege or property under our present constitution, or those laws which flow from it, if they were not parties to the present social compact originally, or have become parties by the subsequent laws thereof;

"Resolved, unanimously, That the laws of this State, confiscating property held under the laws of the former government (which have been dissolved and made void,) by those who have never been admitted into the present social compact, being founded on legal principles, were strongly dictated by that principle of common justice, which demands, that if virtuous citizens, in defence of their natural and constitutional rights, risk their life, liberty and property on their success, the vicious citizens, who side with tyranny and oppression, or who cloak themselves under the mask of neutrality, should at least hazard their property, and not enjoy the benefits procured by the labors and dangers of those whose destruction they wished;

"*Resolved, unanimously,* That all demands or requests of the British Court for the restitution of property confiscated by this State, being neither supported by law, equity or policy, are wholly inadmissable; and that our delegates in Congress be instructed to move Congress, that they may direct their deputies, who shall represent these States in the General Congress, for adjusting a peace or truce, neither to agree to any such restitution, or submit that the laws made by any independent State of this Union, be subjected to the adjudication of any power or powers on earth."

These resolutions and resultant legislation prohibiting admission of British subjects into Virginia and denying British creditors access to Virginia courts (Hening, XI, 136-8, 176-80) were in part due to the resolutions of Congress of 4 Oct. 1782 strongly recommending to the states adoption of a strict policy of non-intercourse with British subjects and in part to an influx of British merchants who sought to recover debts owed by Virginians (see Harrell, *Loyalism in Virginia*, 123ff.). In pursuance of these laws Governor Harrison issued a proclamation forbidding British subjects to enter or remain in Virginia and the Council revoked special leave it had previously given to John Wormeley and others. Some merchants attempted to land in Virginia under protection of flags of truce, and the Governor and Council made every effort to stop such abuses even before Congress and the legislature had acted. On 24 Jan. 1782 the minutes of Council contain the following: "Mr. Thomas C. Williams Captain of a Brigantine Flag of Truce from New York, now lying at York town having come up to Richmond without permission from the Executive under pretext of applying for leave to remain in this State to settle his accounts for purchases alledged to have been made from his Agents in York under the Capitulation of the 19th of October 1781, The Board advise that Mr. Williams be directed to return immediately to York and there embark without loss of time and return to New York. That if his Vessell shall not depart from York before the 28th Instant she will be seized, and the Master and Crew Committed to Prison. The Board are induced to give this advice as Mr. Williams conduct is a manifest violation of the rights of Flags" (when Williams fell ill the Council extended the time to 4 Feb.; MS Va. Council Jour., 24, 28 Jan. 1782).

From Robert R. Livingston

SIR   Philadelphia 18th. February 1783.

I was yesterday honoured with your favor of the 14th which I shall lay before Congress this morning. As you have by this time received their resolution, which I had the honor to send you by the last Post, and again enclosed, you will be relieved in some measure from your embarrassments, tho' not entirely from your suspence with respect to their final determination. But that cannot be long doubtful, since the negotiations have certainly arrived at such a crisis, as either to terminate soon in a peace, or a total rupture, in the latter case, you will necessarily be obliged to proceed on your voyage, as Congress seem anxious to avail themselves of your abilities and information in the negotiations, unless they are fully assured that a speedy peace will preclude them from that advantage. I enclose a paper which contains all that we have yet received on this interesting subject. It may perhaps be difficult to account for our Ministers having signed before those of France. But if this letter is genuine, it serves when compared with their instructions to prove that the terms of peace are acceptable to us, and not disagreable to France.

I have the honor to be Sir with great Respect and Esteem your most obedt. humble servant,   ROBT R. LIVINGSTON

RC (DLC); in Lewis R. Morris' hand, signed by Livingston. Tr (DLC: PCC, No. 119); also in Morris' hand. Enclosures are missing; one was a copy of Congress' resolution of 14 Feb., enclosed in Livingston's letter of that date, q.v.; the other was doubtless a copy of the *Penna. Packet* for 18 Feb., which printed a letter of Thomas Townshend, one of the British secretaries of state, to the Lord Mayor of London, 3 Dec. 1782, announcing the arrival of an express from Paris bringing news that preliminary articles of peace had been signed by the British and American commissioners at Paris (Burnett, *Letters of Members*, VII, No. 55, note 3).

The journals of Congress contain no reference to TJ's mission on this date, but Madison wrote to Randolph: "In consequence of the prospect of peace the departure of Mr. Jefferson has been suspended" (Madison to Randolph, 18 Feb. 1783; Burnett, same, VII, No. 60).

From James Madison

DEAR SIR   Philada. Feby. 18th. 1783.

Your two favors of the 14th. one of them inclosing a letter to Miss Floyd were received by yesterday's mail.

The last paper from N.Y. as the inclosed will shew you has brought us another token of the approach of peace. It is somewhat mysterious nevertheless that the preliminaries with America should be represented by Secy. Townsend as *actually signed* and those with France as *to be signed*, as also that the signing of the latter would constitute a general peace. I have never been without my apprehensions that some tricks would be tried by the British Court notwithstanding their exterior fairness of late, and these apprehensions have been rendered much more serious by the *tenor*[1] *of some letters* which *you have seen* and particularly by the *intimation of minister of France to Mr. Livingston*. These considerations have made me peculiarly solicitous that your mission should be pursued as long as a possibility remained of *your sharing in* the *object of it.*

Your *portrait of your am[anuensis]* is I conceive drawn to *the life.* For all un*confidential services he is a convenient instrument.*[2] For any*thing farther* ne *sutor ultra* cre*pidam.*[3]

The turn which your case has for the present taken makes it unnecessary to answer particularly the parts of your letter which relate to the expediency of a flag and the extent of its protection. On the first point I am inclined to think that the greatest objection with Congress would have been drawn from the risk of a denial.

On the second I have no precise knowledge, but the principle would seem to extend to every thing appertaining to the mission as well as to the person of the Minister. Nor can I conceive a motive to the latter indulgence which would admit of a refusal of the former.

I am impatient to hear of the plan which is to dispose of you during the suspense in which you are placed. If Philada. as I flatter myself, is to be your abode, your former quarters will await you. I am Dear Sir Yr. Affecte. friend,   J. MADISON Jr.

An answer to Miss Patsy's letter is in the same mail with this.

RC (DLC: Madison Papers); endorsed at head of text by Madison after its return to him; partly in code. Enclosures (missing): Letter from Polly Floyd to Martha Jefferson, and probably a copy of *Penna. Packet*, 18 Feb. 1783 (see note to preceding letter).

[1] This and subsequent words or parts of words in italics were written in code and were decoded in part by TJ and in part by Madison, employing Code No. 1. The text as given here follows the editors' decoding.

[2] TJ decoded this passage as "he be convenient instrument." The code symbols are: 402.1 (*he*) 29.1 (*am, is, &c*) 1.1. (*a*) 194.33 (*convenient*), &c. The verb *be* had the symbol 89.1.

[3] Madison's encoding was more abbreviated than TJ's, since he omitted an article occasionally or permitted such an abbreviation as "am" to stand for "amanuensis." His encoding of the Latin phrase was partial also: the full text, from Pliny, was "ne supra crepidam sutor indicaret" (the cobbler should not go beyond his last).

From La Villebrune

[*Baltimore*,] *19 Feb. 1783.* Appends copy of a letter from La Luzerne to La Villebrune of 13 Feb. which shows that "Les Bruits de paix S'accredittent et que Son Excellence persiste a croire quil convient encore de Différer notre Départ."

RC (DLC); in a clerk's hand, signed by La Villebrune. La Luzerne's letter, copied below that of La Villebrune, had enclosed "un hand bill qui ajoute infiniment aux Esperances que nous avons d'une paix prochaine et qui même nous permêt de croire qu'elle est actuellement conclue." La Luzerne added that he thought under these circumstances La Villebrune ought not "mêttre à La voile avant que nous ayons des nouvelles ulterieures" and asked that he "communiquer Cette Lettre a M. D'yerferson. Il se Loue infiniment de vos intentions."

The handbill was undoubtedly a printing of the King's speech that La Luzerne also sent to TJ on 13 Feb.

To Francis Eppes

DEAR SIR   Philadelphia, March 4, 1783.

In my last, from Baltimore, I informed you that my voyage to Europe was at least suspended till further intelligence should be received. I returned to this place about four or five days ago, that I might be on the spot to act as shall be ultimately concluded by

Congress. Though nothing since has come to us, we consider the event of peace as certain and speedy. The hearing nothing is a proof of this. The French minister, the British at New York, and Congress, are equally uninformed. This would not have been the case had the conferences for peace broken off, as has been pretended, or had they become languid. The packets and dispatch vessels are detained, doubtless, on a daily expectation of sending something more definitive than the signing of preliminaries. Capt. Barney is lying at L'Orient with the Washington, a dispatch vessel of Congress, ready to bring the advices from our plenipotentiaries. From these circumstances, you will judge that I expect every hour to receive permission to return home. I shall be here but a very few days after this shall be received, and expect to be myself the bearer of the first intelligence to you. There is nothing new here. I hope by the next post to receive a letter from you, though after near three months' absence without having ever heard a word of my dear little ones, I shall receive your letter with fear and trembling, lest any accident should have happened. This dread, I hope, will be removed. Patsy is well. I hope Mrs. Eppes has recovered better health. If my prayers would be a medicine, she should have them with more fervor than they were ever offered for myself. Present my love to her and the little ones, and whenever you have an opportunity, be so good as to let Mr. and Mrs. Skipwith know that I remember them with affection. I am, dear sir, Your sincere friend,

Th. Jefferson

MS not located. Text from Randall, *Life*, III, 586-7, where the letter is printed without indication of source; at foot of text: "Francis Eppes, Esq., Eppington, (near Richmond)."

TJ left Baltimore on 24 Feb. and arrived in Philadelphia on 26 Feb. (Account Book, under dates). On 4 Mch. 1783 Madison wrote to Randolph: "Mr. Jefferson is here awaiting further instructions of Congress which [will] be adapted to the first authentic advices from Europe" (Burnett, *Letters of Members*, VII, No. 76).

To Edmund Pendleton

Dear Sir   Philadelphia Mar. 4. 1783.

Had it been predicted to you that you would receive a letter from me of this date you would probably have expected it would be from the other side the Atlantic. I had proceeded to Baltimore to embark on board the Romulus. The number of cruisers then off our capes deterred her from sailing. In the mean time I received a copy of the king's speech, and wrote to submit to Congress a reconsideration of the expediency of my proceeding when it seemed almost certain that peace would either be definitively settled before I could reach the scene of negotiation or at least that preliminaries would be so far settled as to admit little or no alteration from new instructions. I returned to this place and am waiting their pleasure. Not a tittle worthy notice has come to hand since the king's speech. This I think proves that the negotiations are neither broken off as has been pretended by mercantile letterwriters, nor become languid. In either of these cases our Plenipo's would have dispatched Capt. Barney of the Washington who waits at l'Orient to bring us advices. In either case too the French minister, here, and the British in New York would have been informed by their respective courts that they should be prepared for the possibility of a new campaign. Count d'Estaing's not sailing is another good symptom. Where authentic intelligence is wanting, facts are the best grounds for forming a judgment. On a question of such influence on commerce the commercial gentlemen cannot be relied on for intelligence. I am under hourly expectation that something will come to hand which by permitting me to return home will for the first time allow me the happiness of paying my respects to you at your own house. No interesting event having occurred in this quarter and peace engrossing all conversation I am enabled to communicate to you nothing more than the state of suspence in which we are on that subject. Permit me to pay through you my respects to Mrs. Pendleton & be assured of the truth & sincerity with which I am Dr Sir Your friend & servt,   TH: JEFFERSON

RC (NN); addressed: "The honble. Edmund Pendleton Caroline county Virginia"; endorsed: "Thos. Jefferson Esq [MS torn by seal] Mar. 4th. 1783"; postmarked.

From La Valette

A Baltimore ce 5. mars 1783.

C'est a moy, Monsieur, a vous faire des remerciments de m'avoir favorisé de votre bonne et agreable compagnie, pendant votre sejour a Baltimore; elle a fait mon agrément et mon bonheur: je me rappellerai toujours avec plaisir ce tems heureux, il me donne infiniment de regrets de la préference que vous venés de donner a philadelphie mais il faut scavoir faire des sacrifices aux personnes qu'on aime. Lesperance que vous me donnés de vous revoir a votre passage ici me console et me fait desirer que ce retour soit prochain et que vous me dédomagiés de ce que vous m'avés fait perdre; Soyés assuré du plaisir que jaurai a rechercher votre connoissance et de mon empressement a saisir Les occasions de vous prouver Les Sentiments dattachement aussi sinceres que Respectueux avec lesquels j'ai L'honneur d'etre Monsieur Votre tres humble et tres Obeissant Serviteur,   LE CH: DE LA VALETTE

RC (MHi).

This letter was manifestly written in response to a (missing) letter from TJ to La Valette thanking him for his hospitality. Charles-François Chandéon, Chevalier de La Valette, had a brilliant record at Yorktown (Contenson, *La Société des Cincinnati de France*, p. 211).

To Abner Nash

DEAR SIR   Philadelphia Mar. 11. 1783

Since I had the pleasure of seeing you at Baltimore I have further reflected on the proposition you were so kind as to make me there of entering into a partnership for the purpose of purchasing some of the escheated territory in your state. I consider it as one of those fair opportunities of bettering my situation which in private prudence I ought to adopt, and which were I to consider myself merely as a private man I should adopt without condition or hesitation. But I find it is the opinion of some gentlemen that the interests of land companies may by possibility be brought on the carpet of negotiation in Europe.[1] Whether I may or may not participate in those negotiations remains still as incertain as it was in the moment of our conversation on this subject. However I having hitherto while concerned in the direction of public affairs made it a rule to avoid engaging in any of those enterprizes which on becoming the subjects of public deliberation might lay my judgment under bias or oblige me for fear of that to withdraw from the decision altogether, I would wish still to pursue that line of conduct.[2] Indeed I feel the obligation to do it the stronger in proportion to the magnitude of the trust at present confided to me. If my mission to Europe be still pursued I would chuse for my own satisfaction as well as for that of Congress to have not a single interest which in any point of the negotiation might separate me from the great bulk of my countrymen, or expose me to a suspicion of having any object to pursue which might lead me astray from the general. You will therefore be sensible that my situation does not leave me an equal liberty with the other gentlemen of availing myself of this opportunity of repairing some of my losses; on the contrary that it calls for this in addition to the sacrifices I have already made. I therefore make it; begging leave at the same time to tender you my sincerest acknowledgements for this proof of your friendship. A return to a private character and determination to continue in it may yet perhaps restore me the liberty enjoyed by the mass of my fellow citizens of doing something for myself.[3] In this event it is not improbable that I may trouble you with an application for readmission to this proposition if it should not be too far advanced to admit it, which in such case I shall do with all the freedom your former friendship has encouraged me to use. We are still as I before mentioned to you uninformed what is likely to be the issue of the present negotiations. While circumstances in general seem to portend a happy conclusion some have arisen which bear a more doubtful aspect. The common cry is that we cannot possibly be left much longer in suspence. Should the gentleman who furnishes me with a conveiance of this letter be on the road, you may possibly hear the great event before you receive this. Whether I may be disposed of on this or the other side the water I shall always be happy to hear from you and to avail myself of every opportunity of assuring you of the sincer[e] esteem with which I have the honour to be Dr Sir Your friend & servt.

Dft (DLC); endorsed: "Nash, Govr. 83. Mar. 11." Dft was heavily corrected in the course of composition, revealing the difficulties TJ experienced in the effort to withdraw from his first tentative engagement in land speculation. Some of the corrections are noted below.

When TJ wrote this letter, he was convinced that he would not be sent to Europe and would soon return to Virginia (see his letters to Eppes and Pendleton of 4 Mch. 1783). The question at once arises: why, if this was so, did he feel it necessary to withdraw from a scheme that a return to private life would leave him free to pursue? The answer may lie hidden in the labored attempt to phrase the declaration of his intention to retire from public life. As shown in note 3, every attempt at phrasing this intent was qualified by such words as "at present," "I think," and, as finally expressed, "may yet perhaps." This is very different indeed from the categorical assertions to be found in letters of preceding months (e.g., TJ to Monroe, 20 May 1782). In view of this, it is difficult to escape the conclusion that TJ at this time began to think of entering Congress again, where the interests of land companies would certainly be brought on the carpet. Madison must have had much to do with persuading TJ to arrive at this conclusion, for, as TJ later

remarked, the matter of his going into Congress was "sometimes the subject of our conversation" during this interval in Philadelphia (TJ to Madison, 7 May 1783).

[1] TJ deleted at this point: "a very strange subject . . . without doubt for foreign nations."

[2] TJ first wrote: "which might on any question whatever separate my interests from those of the bulk of the people or coming before me in a public character might leave my judgment under bias" and then altered the passage to read as above.

[3] TJ made several false starts at this point and deleted the following: "and have only to entreat of your goodness and friendship that my becoming or not becoming an adventurer may . . . [depend?] on the issue of my going or not going to Europe in a public character. If I go, be pleased to consider me as declining it altogether. If I do not, as I am at present resolved against any further intermeddling in public affairs in any other character I shall hold myself indebted to you for this opportunity of doing something for myself. The suspension of this question cannot be long: should it however be longer than is convenient for you to wait consistent with the formation of your company, and a determination whether I be a member

or not become necessary"; then he began again: "Should conclusion of peace progress &c. . . . and permit me again to retire to that private situation from which I think I shall not emerge, I shall very probably"; and finally he altered the passage to read as above.

To Robert R. Livingston

SIR   Pha. Mar. 13. 1783.

Supposing the dispatches received by the Washington may have enabled Congress to decide on the expediency of continuing or of countermanding my mission to Europe, I take the liberty of expressing to you the satisfaction it will give me to receive their ultimate will so soon as other business will permit them to advert to this subject.

I have the honour to be with very great respect & esteem Sir Your most obedt. & most humble servt,   TH: JEFFERSON

RC (DLC: PCC, No. 79, III); addressed: "The honourable Robert R. Livingston Minister for Foreign affairs"; endorsed: "Letter from the honble. T. Jefferson to the Secy for foreign Affairs March 13th 1783." Dft (DLC). This letter was transmitted by Livingston to Congress with a covering letter of same date (DLC: PCC, No. 79, III); for Congress' resolution see under 1 Apr. 1783.

The dispatches RECEIVED BY THE WASHINGTON: Captain Joshua Barney, commander of the *Washington*, left L'Orient on 17 Jan. 1783 and arrived at Philadelphia on the morning of 12 Mch. He brought dispatches from the American ministers dated as late as 25 Dec. 1782 and copies of the preliminary peace treaty signed on 30 Nov.; Elias Boudinot sent this information to Washington at "3 O'Clock P.M." the same day (Burnett, *Letters of Members*, VII, No. 86). "The arrival of this intelligence," Madison reported to Randolph, "will probably procure from Congress some final decision with respect to Mr. Jefferson" (same, No. 92).

To Robert R. Livingston

[*Philadelphia, 27 Mch. 1783*. Stan V. Henkels' sale catalogue No. 683 (5-6 Apr. 1892) records as lot 378 a Jefferson A.L.S., 1 p., 4to, of this date, and prints the following extract from it: "I think with you clearly that the three months after notice of recall could only be intended for gentlemen actually in Europe in the execution of their commissions, and that in a case like mine the appointments should end either with the dispensation of further services or at the utmost with an allowance of only a reasonable time for return home." No copy of this letter has been found. The letter is manifestly a reply to an inquiry from Livingston, also missing, regarding TJ's expectations of payment for his period of service as a peace commissioner; see the exchange of letters between TJ and Livingston, 4 Apr. 1783.]

To David S. Franks

[March or April 1783]

Mr. Jefferson's compliments to Colo. Franks and begs the favor of him during his stay in Paris to call on Mr. Pancouck publisher of the Encyclopedie Methodique and endeavor to get him entered as a subscriber for that work. As soon as Mr. Jefferson is informed of the number of volumes ready to be delivered and their price he will instantly remit the sum and will then expect to receive those volumes, and will afterwards from time to time remit such other sums as may keep beforehand with the deliveries so as to authorize him to receive every volume as soon as published.

He would suggest to Mr. Pancoucke the expediency of appointing some agent in Philadelphia who may open a subscription for this work, deliver the copies to the subscribers and receive the money from them. Mr. Jefferson could himself carry in to such an agent a respectable number of subscriptions. Our distance and the obstacles of the war put it out of our power to subscribe in Paris within the time limited for European subscribers. It would therefore be just as well as grateful to the Americans to have an opportunity laid open to them also of contributing to bring forward this valuable depository of science.

Dft (MHi); endorsed: "Franks Davd. S."

It is probable that this letter, of which Dft is undated and no RC has been found, was written soon after TJ knew he was not going to Paris. Though he was not formally released from his appointment until 1 Apr., it was increasingly clear from 12 Mch. on that he would not be required to go. Franks himself did not return to Europe at this time, though it was his intention to do so and he was currently active in soliciting recommendations for a consular post; see an autobiographical sketch in *Amer.-Jewish Hist. Soc., Publs.*, x (1902), 101-105; and Hersch L. Zitt, "David Salisbury Franks, Revolutionary Patriot (c. 1740-1793)," *Penna. Hist.*, xvi (1949), 77-95. Since TJ left Philadelphia on 12 Apr., this letter was almost certainly written after 12 Mch. and before 12 Apr. 1783. Franks sailed for Europe, finally, on 17 Feb. 1784, bearing a copy of the ratification of the Definitive Treaty.

Meanwhile, delivery of the copy of the *Encyclopédie Méthodique* that TJ had caused to be ordered for the public use (see Fitzgerald to TJ, 3 Oct. 1780; TJ to Fitzgerald, 27 Feb. and 1 Apr. 1781) had apparently been delayed because of the military situation in Virginia in 1781. On 14 Dec. 1781 the Governor and Council took the following action: "Colonel Fitzgerald is desired to deliver to the order of Mr. Jefferson the Encyclopedia purchased for this state, he having promised to send for the same." It is obvious from this that the authorization of the Council was taken at TJ's request (he was then in Richmond). It is also clear that TJ obtained the encyclopedia from Fitzgerald and apparently became absorbed in it, for seven months later the Council adopted the following resolution: "The Commercial Agent is desired to take measures for getting from Mr. Jefferson the Encyclopaedia belonging to the public" (5 July 1782; see also 13 Dec. 1782, MS Va. Council Jour., Vi). The "measures," whatever they were, were doubtless effective and TJ therefore endeavored to obtain a copy of the encyclopedia for his own use.

Resolution of Congress Releasing Jefferson from His Commission to Negotiate Peace

By the United States in Congress Assembled

April 1st. 1783.

Resolved that the Secretary for foreign affairs inform the Hon'ble T. Jefferson in Answer to his Letter of the 13th. of March that Congress consider the Object of his Appointment so far advanced as to render it unnecessary for him to pursue his Voyage, and that Congress are well satisfied with the readiness he has shewn in undertaking a Service which, from the present Situation Affairs, they apprehend can be dispensed with.

Extract from the Minutes.   CHAS THOMSON Secy

MS (DLC); in a clerk's hand, signed by Thomson. Another copy, entirely in Thomson's hand, together with a tabulation of the vote, is in PCC, No. 25, II, 191.

TJ's letter to Livingston of 13 Mch. was laid before Congress by Livingston on the same date (Livingston's letter of transmittal is in PCC, No. 79, III, 29). Five days later Madison reported to Randolph that TJ "is still left *in dubio* as to his destination" (Madison to Randolph, 18 Mch. 1783, Burnett, *Letters of Members*, VII, No. 103). The committee to whom TJ's letter of 13 Mch. had been referred (along with letters from Adams, Dana, and Laurens respecting their resigning their commissions as ministers) reported on 1 Apr. (JCC, XXIV, 225-6); the vote on this particular resolution is recorded and is printed in same, p. 226,

note; Theodorick Bland was one of five who voted against releasing TJ from his appointment. On 24 Mch. Livingston noted in his "Despatch Book" (PCC, No. 126, under date) the receipt of a letter from Lafayette of the 5th of Feb. announcing that the preliminaries for a general peace had been signed at Paris on 20 Jan. This appears to have been the first word received, and Livingston at once sent the letter to Congress, an express to Washington, and a circular letter to the governors announcing the fact. This news was decisive in determining Congress to cancel TJ's commission. "The mission of Mr. Jefferson," Madison wrote to Randolph, "has entirely superceded by the latest advices. He will set out in a few days for Virga." (8 Apr. 1783; Burnett, *Letters of Members*, VII, No. 140).

From Robert R. Livingston

SIR   Philadelphia 4th. April. 1783.

I have the honor to inform you by the direction of Congress in answer to your Letter of the 13th. March "that they consider the object of your appointment as so far advanced, as to render it unnecessary for you to pursue your Voyage; And that Congress are well satisfied with the readiness you have shewn in undertaking a Service which from the present situation of Affairs they apprehend can be dispensed with."

I have caused your Account to be settled to the first of April, and hope to be able to send you the warrant for the amount to morrow. If you please I will apply for such farther sum as you may think proper to charge for the time that may be necessary to carry you home, as I think that within the Spirit of the Resolution of Congress I have the honor to be, Sir, with great Respect & Esteem your most obedt humble servt,

ROBT. R. LIVINGSTON

Tr (DLC: PCC, No. 119).

In the Calendar of Jefferson Correspondence in Bulletin of the Bureau of Rolls and Library of the Department of State, No. 8, Washington, 1894, p. 528, there is a summary of a letter (of which no other record exists) from Charles Thomson to TJ, Philadelphia, 1 Apr. 1783, reading: "In answer to his letter of March 13, states that Congress decides that it is unnecessary for him to pursue his voyage from the present condition of affairs." This entry has every appearance of authenticity, but the experience of the editors in using this Calendar has made them skeptical of all entries in it that are not otherwise verified. Undoubtedly, an error confusing the resolution of 1 Apr. with the present letter of Livingston must have been made. Consequently, no separate entry for the supposed letter from Thomson is made in the present edition.

To Robert R. Livingston

SIR   April 4. 1783.

I am much obliged by the receipt of your favor of to-day and thankful for the honor Congress do me in expressing so kindly their satisfaction with what was no more than duty in me.

I beg leave also to acknowlege your goodness in the trouble you have taken with my account. It is perfectly agreeable, settled as you mention it, and I would wish nothing further to be proposed for any time I may spend on my return. The sum allowed will liberally reimburse my expences and I never wished any thing more.

Permit me to express to you my sensibility of the kindness and attentions you have shown me and to subscribe myself with very great sincerity & esteem Sir Your most obedient friend & servt,

TH: JEFFERSON

RC (Morristown National Historical Park, N.J.); endorsed: "From Mr. Jefferson 4th. April 1783." A fragment of Dft of this letter is on verso of Dft of TJ's letter to John Jay, 11 Apr. 1783.

To John Jay

DR SIR   Philadelphia Apr. 11. 1783.

In a letter which I did myself the honor of writing you by the Chevalr. de Chastellux I informed you of my being at this place with an intention of joining you in Paris. But the uncommon vigilance of the enemy's cruisers immediately after the departure of the French fleet deterred every vessel from attempting to go out. The arrival of the preliminaries soon after shewed the impropriety of my proceeding, and I am just now setting out on my return to Virga. I cannot however take my departure without paying to yourself and your worthy collegues my homage for the good work you have completed for us, and congratulating you on the singular happiness of having borne so distinguished a part both in the earliest and latest transactions of this revolution.[1] The terms obtained for us are indeed great, and are so deemed by your country, a few ill designing debtors excepted. I am in hopes you will continue at some one of the European courts most agreeable to yourself that we may still have the benefit of your talents. I took the liberty in my letter of suggesting a wish that you would be so kind as to engage lodgings for me. Should you have given yourself this trouble, I beg leave to return you my thanks and to ask the favour of you to communicate the amount of their hire to Mr. Rob. Morris of this city who will immediately remit it to you as I lodge money in his hands for this purpose. Accept my warmest wishes for your happiness and be assured of the sincerity with which I have the honor to be Dr Sir Your mo. ob. & mo. hble. servt. I beg to be affectionately remembered to Dr. F[ranklin]. and Mr. A[dams]. if they be still with you.

Dft (DLC); contains several corrections, of which one is noted below. On verso is the beginning of Dft of TJ's letter to Livingston, 4 Apr. 1783.
A LETTER . . . BY THE CHEVALR. DE CHASTELLUX: TJ to Jay, 3 Jan. 1783.

[1] Deleted in Dft is the following additional clause: "which ⟨will⟩ may possibly in time change the face of the globe."

To James Madison

DEAR SIR   Susquehanna Apr. 14. 1783.

Meeting at our quarters with a Mr. Levi going to Philadelphia and having no other employment, I write by him just to say that all is well, and that having made our stages regularly and in time we hope to make better way than Mr. Nash did. The Carolina letter bearer is here also. We pass one another two or three times a day. I never saw Mr. Ingles to speak to him about my books. Will you be so obliging as to make my acknowledgements to him for his undertaking and to ask him to send them to Richmond to the care of James Buchanan. Be pleased to make my compliments affectionately to the gentlemen and ladies.

I desire them to Miss Kitty particularly. Do you know that the raillery you sometimes experienced from our family strengthened by my own observation, gave me hopes there was some foundation for it. I wished it would be so as it would give me a neighbor whose worth I rate high, and as I know it will render me happier than you can possibly be in a single state. I often made it the subject of conversation, more exhortation, with her and was able to convince myself that she possessed every sentiment in your favor which you could wish. But of this no more without your leave.[1]

I am with much affection Dr. Sir Your sincere friend,

TH: JEFFERSON

RC (DLC: Madison Papers); endorsed in a hand other than Madison's: "Ths. Jefferson Apl. 14. 1783"; partly in code, as indicated below. Madison in his reply of 22 Apr. 1783 mentions "the several letters inclosed" in the present letter, but these have not been found.

For an account of Madison's romance with MISS KITTY—Catherine Floyd—see Brant, *Madison*, II, 283-7, where appears the first transliteration of the coded passage in this letter, but which differs in some particulars from the decoded passage given above. It was in 1783 that Madison and Catherine Floyd exchanged miniatures of each other; for a reproduction of the one of Madison by Peale that he gave to her, see above, Vol. 3: 3. OUR FAMILY: That is, the Floyds, the Trists, and others who resided at the home of Mrs. House on the corner of Fifth and Market streets.

[1] This paragraph (though not indented separately as a paragraph in RC) was written entirely in cipher and has been decoded by the editors, employing Code No. 3. This was the first use of Code No. 3, which TJ and Madison had evidently devised sometime between 26 Feb. and 12 Apr. as a substitute for the one based on Nugent's *Dictionary*, obviously because that one required such labor in encoding and decoding.

From James Madison

DEAR SIR   Philada. Apl. 22. 1783.

Your favor of the 14. inst: written in the Susquehanna with the several letters inclosed were safely delivered to me. I did not fail to present as you desired your particular compliments to Miss K. Your inference on that subject was not groundless. Before you left us I had sufficiently ascertained her sentiments. Since your departure the affair has been pursued. Most preliminary arrangements, although definitive, will be postponed untill the end of the year in Congress. At some period of the interval I shall probably make a visit to Virginia. The interest which your friendship takes on this occasion in my happiness is a pleasing proof that the dispositions which I feel are reciprocal.[1]

The report on funds &c. passed Congress on Saturday last with the dissent of R. Island and the division of N. York only. The latter vote was lost by the rigid adherence of Mr. Hamilton to a plan which he supposed more perfect. The clause providing for unauthorized expenditures, could not be reinstated, and consequently no attempt was made to link all the parts of the act inseparably together. As it now stands it has I fear no bait for Virga. which is not particularly interested either in the object or mode of the revenues recommended, nor in the territorial cessions, nor in the change of the constitutional rule of dividing the public burdens. A respect for justice, good faith and national honor is the only consideration which can obtain her compliance.

We have received no intelligence from abroad which deserves to be noted, since your departure. The interval between the preliminary and definitive Treaties, has produced several nice and interesting questions. One is whether laws prohibiting commerce with British Ports during the war, have expired with the cessation of Hostilities. A similar one is whether the soldiers enlisted for the war are entitled to a discharge. At least half of the army under Genl. Washington are under this description and are urgent for such a construction of their engagements. A third question is whether the preliminary treaty between F. and G.B. has given such effect to the provisional articles between the latter and the U.S. as to require an execution of the stipulations in the 6 and 7 articles or whether a definitive Treaty only can produce this effect.

The system for foreign affairs is not yet digested: and I apprehend will be long on the anvil, unless the actual return of our Ministers from Europe should stimulate Congress on the subject.

I am charged with many compliments from the whole family for yourself and Miss Patsy, which you will accept with an assurance of sincere friendship from Yr Obt. & Hbl Servt.,

J. MADISON Jr.

RC (DLC: Madison Papers); endorsed; partly in cipher.

It seems not to have been particularly noted that, on this matter of THE REPORT ON FUNDS &c. and the political conflicts engendered by it, TJ found himself supporting the idea of an assumption of state debts by the United States (see TJ to Madison, 7 May), whereas Alexander Hamilton opposed in 1783 what he so ardently advocated in 1790. Both, however, along with Madison, took the position they did in 1783 in order to strengthen the bonds of union. Following the defeat of the impost of 1781 because of the intransigence of David Howell and other extremist states' rights delegates from Rhode Island, a committee consisting of Nathaniel Gorham, Alexander Hamilton, James Madison, Thomas Fitz-Simons, and John Rutledge who had been appointed "to consider the means of restoring and supporting public credit and of obtaining from the States substantial funds for funding the whole debt of the United States" reported on 6 Mch. 1783 (JCC, XXIV, 170-4). The report was printed as a resolution and debated for the next few weeks (a copy of this printed report—obviously made subsequent to 6 Mch., though P. L. Ford assigns it the date 18 Apr. and Hunt gives it the date of 6 Mch. when the committee reported [same, XXV, 983-4]—is in DLC: TJ Papers, 9: 1458, bearing marginal notations in the hand of Madison). There was included at this stage of the Report the following paragraph PROVIDING FOR UNAUTHORIZED EXPENDITURES: "That conformably to the liberal principles on which these recommendations are founded, and with a view to a more amicable, complete adjustment of all accounts between the united states and individual states, all reasonable expences which shall have been incurred by the states without the sanction of congress, in their defence against, or attacks upon British or Savage enemies, either by sea or by land, and which shall be supported by satisfactory proofs, shall be considered as part of the common charges incident to the present war, and be allowed as such" (JCC, XXIV, 172-3). This was the "conversion of state into federal debts" that TJ believed to be "one palatable ingredient at least in the pill *we* were to swallow" (TJ to Madison, 7 May 1783). When TJ left Philadelphia on 12 Apr. he thought "This proposition . . . hopeful" but between 18 Mch. and 18 Apr. the "palatable ingredient" was deleted (JCC, XXIV, 195-8, 257-60; a copy of the printed resolution in broadside form as it existed after 18 Mch. and before 18 Apr., though headed by the former date and so described by Hunt, same, p. 984, is in DLC: TJ Papers, 9: 1446 and was probably given by Madison to TJ before he left Philadelphia; it did not contain the clause for conversion of state debts, but TJ and Madison both seemed to have thought that it would be possible for it to be "reinstated," a hope which the present letter shows was groundless).

The PLAN WHICH . . . [HAMILTON] SUPPOSED MORE PERFECT was the alternative plan that he submitted on 18 Mch.; it took away the 25-year limitation on the impost and proposed both a land tax and a house tax (though revenues from the latter were to be credited to the states in which they arose), but there was nothing in his plan providing for the assumption of state debts. Thus when the REPORT ON FUNDS &c. came up for final vote on 18 Apr., the roll-call listing of noes and ayes showed that Alexander Hamilton was the only member of Congress voting with the states' rights delegation from Rhode Island which, though intransigent in the extreme, had at least been thoroughly consistent in its opposition to the nationalist position in matters of finance. Though Madison agreed with TJ about the deletion of the "palatable ingredient" and for the same reasons, he was the one who wrote the eloquent address to the states with which the REPORT was accompanied (26 Apr. 1783; JCC, XXIV, 277-83). For an excellent account of this and other aspects of "The Politics of Demobilization," see Merrill Jensen, *The New Nation*, 1950, p. 73ff. and 411-21.

1 Most of this paragraph, beginning with "Miss K.," was written in cipher, except for "the" (twice). Almost half a century later Madison obliterated the passage and then wrote in the margin: "Undecypherable" (see reproduction in Brant, *Madison*, II, p. 223 and p. 284, where the passage was first decoded for publication). The code employed was our Code No. 3; the decoding by the editors differs slightly from that by Brant.

From James Madison

DEAR SIR   Philada. May 6. 1783.

Your favor of the 21. Ult. written at Col: Pendleton's was brought to hand by the post of last week. Col: Floyd's family did not set out untill the day after it was received. I accompanied them as far as Brunswick, about 60 Miles from this, and returned hither on friday evening. Mr. Jones will attend the Assembly, and proposes to begin his journey this afternoon, if the present rain should cease. Mr. Lee also means to set out for the same purpose in a few days.

Congress have received a long and curious epistle from Mr. Adams[1] dated in February addressed to the president not to the secretary for foreign affairs. He animadverts on the revocation of his commission for a treaty of commerce with Great Britain, presses the appointment of a minister to that court with such a commission, draws the picture of a fit character in which his own likeness is ridiculously and palpably studied, finally praising and recommending Mr. Jay for the appointment, *provided* injustice must be done an older servant.[2]

Letters from the Marquis de la Fayette and Mr. Carmichael shew that the Court of Spain has become pretty tractable since the acknowledgment of our Independence by G.B. The latter has been treated with due respect. And the Court has agreed to accede to the territorial limit fixed for W. Florida in the provisional Articles. The navigation of the Mississippi remains to be settled.

My absence from Congress for the past week disables me from giving you exact information of their latest proceedings. I am told that in consequence of Mr. A's[1] letter the secretary of foreign affairs has been instructed to project a treaty of commerce with Great Britain which will probably bring the attention of Congress to the general department of foreign affairs.[3]

Under the same cover with this are two letters for Miss Patsy, one from Mrs. Trist, the other from Miss Floyd with the copy of a song. I beg that my compliments may be accepted along with them.

I am Dear Sir Your sincere friend,   J. MADISON Jr.

RC (DLC: Madison Papers) endorsed by Madison after its return to him with his name and date of letter; two passages in cipher, decoded by TJ on a separate leaf endorsed by Madison: "decypher of letter May 6. 1783." Enclosures missing.

TJ's letter of 21 Apr. 1783 written from Edmund Pendleton's in Caroline county has not been found.

[1] Name crossed out in TJ's decoding; probably done by Madison after the letter was returned to him. Adams'

letter was that of 5 Feb. 1783, printed in Adams' *Works*, VIII, 33-40, and in Wharton, *Dipl. Corr. Amer. Rev.*, VI, 242-7; by both editors it was captioned as if addressed to Secretary Livingston.

[2] This entire paragraph was written in cipher and was decoded by TJ, employing Code No. 3, and verified by the editors.

[3] Except for the words "which will," that part of this sentence beginning with the words "Mr. A's letter" was written in cipher and was decoded by TJ and verified by the editors.

To James Madison

DEAR SIR   Tuckahoe May 7. 1783.

I received your favor of Apr. 22. and am not a little concerned at the alterations which took place in the Report on the impost &c. after I left you. The article which bound the whole together I fear was essential to get the whole passed; as that which proposed the conversion of state into federal debts was one palatable ingredient at least in the pill *we* were to swallow. This proposition being then hopeful, I never consulted you whether the paiment of our Western expenditures, annexed as a condition to our passing the articles recommended, would not be acceded to by Congress, more especially when one of those articles is the cession of that very territory for the acquisition and defence of which these expenditures have been incurred. If I recollect rightly, Congress offered this in their first proposition for a cession. I beg your sentiments however on this subject by return of the first post. Notwithstanding the unpromising form of these articles I have waited a fortnight in the neighborhood of Richmond that I might see some of the members. I passed yesterday *in*[1] *associating and conversing with as* many of them *as I could. The Attorney* has *cooperated* in this work. This is the view I form at present of *the leaders. Dr. Lee, R. H. Lee M. Page, Taylor* will be *against* them. So will *Thruston and White if elected*, and even an *A. Campbell* is thought *worthy of being named* with these as having some *influence in the S. Western* quarter. In their *favour will probably be Tyler Tazewell, Genl. Nelson, W. Nelson, Nicholas* and a *Mr. Stewart*[2] *a young man* of *good talents* from the *Westward. Henry* as usual is *involved in mystery:* should the *popular tide run strongly* in either *direction, he* will fall *in with it.* Should it *not*, he will have a *struggle between his enmity to the Lees, and his enmity* to every*thing which may give influence to* Congs.[3] *T. Mason* is a *meteor* whose *path cannot* be *calculated.* All the powers of *his mind* seem at present *concentrated* on one *single object*, the *producing* a *Convention* to *new model* the *Constitution.* This *is a subject* much *agitated*, and seems the *only one* they will have to *amuse themselves* with *till* they shall *receive* your *propositions. These should* be *hastened; as* I think the session will be short.

I have seen Mr. Wythe. He has none of his amendments or notes on the Confederation.

Mr. Short has desired me to suggest *his name* as that of a *person willing* to become a *legatine secretary* should these *offices be continued. I have apprised him of* the possibility that they may not. You know *my high opinion of his abilities and merits*. I will therefore only add that a *peculiar talent* for *prying into facts* seems to mark *his character as proper for* such a *business. He is young* and little *experienced in business* tho well *prepared for it.* These defects will *lessen daily*. Should *persons* be *proposed less proper* on the whole you *would* on motives of public good, *knowing his willingness* to *serve, give him* a *nomination* and do justice to *his character*.[4]

I rejoice at the information that *Miss K.*[5] *and yourself concur* in *sentiments. I rejoice* as it will *render you happier* and will give *to me a neighbor on whom I shall set high value. You* will be continued in *your* delegation[6] till the end of three years from the completion[7] of the Confederation. *You* will therefore *model your measures accordingly*. You say nothing of the time when you shall pay your visit to *Virginia:* I hope you will *let me know* of your *arrival* as soon as *it happens*. Should the *call* be made *on me*, which was sometimes the subject of *our conversation*, and be *so timed with your* visit *as that you may* be the *bearer of* it *I shall* with great pleasure accomodate *my movements to yours* so as to *accompany you on your return to Philadelphia*.

I set out this morning for Monticello. My affectionate compliments to the ladies & gentlemen of the house, and sincere friendship to yourself. Adieu.

RC (DLC: Madison Papers); unsigned; endorsed by Madison: "From Ths. J-son to J.M. May 5. 1783." Dft (DLC); endorsed: "Madison James. 1783. May 7." Partly in cipher in RC, partly decoded by Madison on a separate leaf now with RC. A fragment of Dft is missing.
THE ATTORNEY: Edmund Randolph. This must have been pleasing to Madison, for when TJ's mission to Europe was cancelled, Madison had written to Randolph: "As his services are not required, at least for the present, in Europe, it is to be most devoutly wished that they could be engaged at the present crisis at home" (8 Apr. 1783; Burnett, *Letters of Members*, VII, No. 140) and TJ's consultation with members of the legislature must have encouraged Madison to believe that TJ would soon emerge in public life once more. On the CONVERSION OF STATE INTO FEDERAL DEBTS (see Madison to TJ 22 Apr. 1783). SHOULD THE CALL BE MADE ON ME: That is, TJ's election as a member of Congress, a topic "sometimes the subject of . . . conversation" between the two during the preceding winter; see TJ to Nash, 11 Mch. 1783. On 28 June 1783 Randolph wrote Madison: "Mr. Jefferson was placed at the head of the delegation not without his approbation, as I have been informed" (DLC: Madison Papers).

[1] This and subsequent words in italics were in cipher in RC and most of them were underscored in Dft. Because Madison obliterated part of the coded passages in RC, Dft has been employed for the coded parts. Where Dft is mutilated, however, and in one or two other places, the editors have decoded the passage themselves, employing Code No. 3. In one or two instances words underscored in Dft were not put in code in RC, and some not underlined in Dft were coded in RC.
[2] Archibald Stuart.
[3] All of the words in cipher in this sentence have been decoded by the editors, since Dft is mutilated. At this point in Dft TJ first wrote and then deleted: "The Attorney thinks T. M. [Thomas Mason]."
[4] The passage decoded on a separate sheet by Madison ends at this point; at the bottom of the first page of RC Madison wrote, next to a symbol subjoined to the beginning of the coded passage: "See the paper decyphering what is in [ ]s."
[5] The name is left blank in Dft, but written in code in RC and decoded by the editors.
[6] From the beginning of this paragraph to this point, Madison heavily scored out the passage. Madison decoded interlineally only the words "I rejoice."
[7] TJ first wrote "signing" and then deleted it.

From James Madison

Marbois lately took occasion in our family to complain of ungenerous proceedings of the British against individuals as well as against their enemies at large and *finally signified that* he was no stranger to the letter transmited to Congress which he roundly avered to be spurious. *His* information came from Boston *where* the incident is said to be no secret, *but* whether [it] be the echo of letters from Philada. or has transpired from the correspondence of Mr. Adams to his private friends is *uncertain. This* conversation passed during my absence in New Jersey, but was related to me by Mr. Carrol.

A project for a treaty of commerce with Britain has been reported by Secretary foreign affairs and is now in the hands of a committee. The objects most at heart are first a direct trade between this country and the West Indies. Second a right of carrying between the later and other parts of the British empire. Third*ly* the right of carrying from West Indies to all other parts of the world. As the price of these *advantages* it is proposed that we shall ad[mit] British subjects to equal privileges with our own citizens. As to the 1st object it may be observed that the bill lately brought in British parliament renders it probable that it may be obtained without such a cession. *As to the* second that it concerns eastern states *cheifly and as* to the third that it concerns them alone. *Whilst the* privilege to be ceded *will cheifly if not alone* affect the southern states. *The interest of these* seems to require that they should retain at least the faculty of giving any *encouragement* to their own merchants ships or mariners which may be necessary to prevent relapse under scotch monopoly *or* to *acquire* a maritime importance. *The* Eastern states need no such precaution.[1]

Genl. Washington and Genl. Carlton have had an interview on the subject of arrangements for executing the provisional Treaty. It was interrupted by the sudden indisposition of the latter. In the conversation which took place he professed intentions of evacuating New York and all the posts in the U.S. held by British Garrisons as soon as possible, but did not authorize any determinate or speedy expectations. He confessed that a number of Negroes had gone off with the Refugees since the arrival of the Treaty, and undertook to justify the permission by a palpable and scandalous misconstruction of the Treaty, and by the necessity of adhering to the proclamations under the faith of which the Negroes had eloped into their service. He said that if the Treaty should be otherwise explained, compensation would be made to the owners and to make this the more easy, a register had been and would be kept of all Negroes leaving N.Y. before the surrender of it by the British Garrison. This information has been referred by Congress to a Committee. But the progress already made in the discharge of the prisoners, the only convenient pledge by which fair dealing on the other side could be enforced, makes it probable that no remedy will be applied to the evil.

I have sent Mr. Randolph a pamphlet comprehending all the papers which are to be laid before the States relative to the National debt &c., and have desired him to let you have the reading it. The fewness of the copies made it impossible for me to get one for each of you.

I am Dr Sir your sincere friend　　　　　J. MADISON Jr.

RC (DLC: Madison Papers); addressed to TJ (without place) and franked by Madison; endorsed by Madison after its return to him; partly in cipher.

The LETTER TRANSMITTED TO CONGRESS was doubtless that from Adams referred to in Madison's letter to TJ of 6 May 1783. The COMMITTEE to whom the project of a treaty of commerce was referred reported on 19 June (see JCC, XXIV, 404-405). Washington's INTERVIEW with Sir Guy Carleton took place on 6 May 1783. A clerk's copy of an "Extract from the Substance of the Conference between General Washington and Sir Guy Carleton at an Interview at Orange Town 6th May 1783," together with a press copy made from it, is in DLC: TJ Papers, 9: 1470-2, 1473-8. There are also in DLC: TJ Papers clerk's copies of the following pertaining to this same general subject: (1) a report in the hand of William Stephen Smith concerning protests made to Carleton against the removal of slaves from New York City, undated; (2) Carleton and Robert Digby to Washington, 19 Mch. 1783; (3) Carleton to Livingston, 26 Mch. 1783; (4) Digby to Livingston, 27 Mch. 1783; (4) Carleton to Washington, 6 Apr. 1783; (5) Carleton to Livingston, 14 Apr. 1783; (5) an extract from Carleton's general orders of 15 Apr. 1783

giving force to the 7th Article of the preliminary treaty which included a clause forbidding the carrying away of slaves. The PAMPHLET that Madison sent to Randolph was Address and Recommendations to The States, by The United States in Congress assembled, Philadelphia, 1783 (see JCC, XXV, 986). Joseph Jones later reported to Madison that "many [members of the Assembly] now say the reading the pamphlet of Congress determined them against the measure, and Randolph, writing "with a despondency," said that "by some unaccountable revolution the zealous patrons have cooled" and gave, later, the information that General Washington's circular letter on the 5 per cent impost may have been a contributing factor: "The murmur is free and general against what is called the unsollicited intrusion of his advice" (Randolph to Madison, 14, 28 June; Jones to Madison, 14 June 1783, Madison Papers, DLC).

¹ Except for the italicized words and parts of words, this and the preceding paragraph were written in code and were decoded by TJ on a separate sheet preserved with RC, on which Madison wrote: "Decypher of May 13. 1783." Code No. 3 was employed and TJ's decoding has been verified by the editors.

To Simon Nathan

SIR   Monticello May 18. 1783.

On my arrival at home I turned my attention to the transaction between us for wine, which was the subject of your letter of Jan. 16. I was to pay for the two quarter casks by our original agreement 3000 ℔. of tobacco or it's price. The current price of tobo. in Philadelphia at the date of your draft on me was 60£ continental or 200 Doll. the hundred. So that the 3000 ℔. of tobo. was then worth 6000 Dollars. For this sum precisely you drew in favour of Mr. Rose (as indeed there could be no reason for your drawing for less than your whole demand) and I paid the draught on sight. No time intervened between the date of your draught and my paiment, but while it was on the road from Philadelphia to Richmond, and if, during that, another month happened to enter, it is not sufficient ground for opening the account again. The difference of exchange in Virginia from July to Aug. 1781. was that of 65. and 70. for one. So that on the whole the balance appearing due in your account is the result of a double error; first the charging me 3000£ Continental instead of £1800 for the wine; and secondly the extending the debit at one exchange and the credit at another. I hope that on revising the matter you will find the state of it contained in this and my letter of Jan. 18. to be satisfactory, and that at the time of furnishing the wine you drew for the whole sum; which was paid. I am sir Your very humble servt.,   TH: JEFFERSON

RC (MHi); addressed by TJ: "Mr. Simon Nathan Merchant in Philadelphia"; endorsed by TJ: "Nathan Simon." This letter is written out fair, has no corrections, and is addressed, so that in all respects it appears to be a recipient's copy, though it remains among TJ's papers. It is of course possible that it was never sent.

But the coldness of TJ's manner is obvious; rarely can there be found in TJ's letters the formal close: "I am sir Your very humble servt."; and "the extending the debit at one exchange and the credit at another" was a matter that TJ had reason to suspect Nathan had indulged in earlier (see TJ to Harrison, 18 Sep. 1782). Neither Nathan's LETTER OF JAN. 16 nor TJ's reply of JAN. 18 has been found; there is no reference to this transaction in TJ's Account Books for 1783.

From James Madison

DEAR SIR   Philada. May 20. 1783.

In obedience to your request I am to answer by this post your favor of the 7. inst. received yesterday. My brevity will therefore be excused.

For the tenor of the conditions on which Congress were formerly willing to accept the Cession of Virga. I beg leave to refer to their resolutions of the 6 of Sepr. and 10 of Oct. 1780. I take it for granted you have their Journals. The expunging of the article relative to State expences was a subject of no less regret with me than it is with you and for the same reason. But I acknowledge that considering the probable defect of vouchers in Virga. and the ardor with which the clause was supported from some other quarters, mine was much diminished in the course of the discussion. On the last trial there were but two or three states besides Virga. that favored it. *S. Carolina*'s opposition to it had great weight. After this clause was expunged it was thought improper to retain the connective clause as Virga. will now be at liberty to confine her accession to the revenue part of the plan, without enlarging her territorial cession or being deprived of the opportunity of annexing any conditions she may think fit. The connective clause however could not have been carried I believe either before or after the mutilation of the plan. Notwithstanding this disappointment I adhere to my wishes not only that the revenue may be established, but that the fœderal rule of dividing the burdens may be changed, and the territorial disputes accomodated. The more I revolve the latter subject, the less inducement I can discover to a pertinacity on the part of Virga. and the more interesting it appears to the Union.

I am sorry your departure from Richmond became necessary before more of the members were assembled. I make no doubt that useful impressions have been left with those who were so and were susceptible of them. I shall keep in mind the intimation relative to Mr. Short. The idea of adding the fraction of a year to my Congressial service is totally new, and even if it should prevail, will not as far as I can now see, coincide with my private conveniency.

Since my last I have been able to procure for you a copy of pamphlet which I herewith enclose. If in consequence of the provisional steps I before took it should prove a duplicate I shall thank you to forward one of them to my father. The ladies & gentlemen join me in complimts. to Miss Patsy and to yourself. Adieu.

RC (DLC: Madison Papers); unsigned; endorsed by Madison with his own name at head of text after this letter was returned to him. For the enclosure (missing), see note on Madison's earlier letter to TJ, 13 May 1783.

From Wakelin Welch, Sr., with Jefferson's Account with Robert Cary & Co.

S<small>R</small>   London 31st. May 1783.

Permit me to congratulate You on the happy Restoration of Peace which I flatter myself will be permanent and Satisfactory to all Parties. During the national Misfortunes I have had the Unhappiness to lose both my Partners Cary and Moorey. The Business for many Years was chiefly under my Management and which I flatter myself was so conducted as to meet the Approbation of You and the rest of our Friends: in order to continue the same and to establish my Son in the Trade I have taken him into Partnership which from his known good Character I believe will be found no ways exceptionable.

It was my Intention to forward some Vessels for the particular Accomodation of our Friends, but so many are going on Speculation that there can be no want of freight, and perhaps it may be obtained much cheaper in the Country than the Merchants here can charter: as to our own Ships, them we sold on the Commencement of the Difference, we being determined to follow no Calling that might give Umbrage to our Connexions with our Friends in Virginia; and ever since I have been out of all Trade; indeed were it not for my Son, I should have totally declined it but for his Sake I embrace the Opportunity of asking the Continuance of your Friendship assuring all honest Endeavours shall not be wanting to render You every Satisfaction You can wish. All intercourse being so long Stop'd I have had no Opportunity of transmitting your Account before. The Ballance £115.18.4 believe you will find right, and as Opportunity offers hope you will favour me with a remittance—in the interim being Yr most humble Servt,

W<small>AKE</small>. W<small>ELCH</small>

E N C L O S U R E

Dr. Mr Thomas Jefferson of Virginia in Acct Currt with Robert Cary & Co. of London

1774 Novr. 17th	To Goods per the Active	87. 4
1783 Feby. 22	To 7 Yrs 3 Mo 5 Dys Interest on £85. from 17th Novr 1775 to this day	30.17. 4
		£118. 1. 4

Cr.

1777. June 11th	By Cash for 86 lb Old Pewter sold by Capt. Power	2. 3
1783 Feby 22	By Ballance due to us	115.18. 4
		£118. 1. 4

London 22nd February 1783
Errors Excepted
Wake. Welch Surviving Partner to Cary &
    Moorey both Deceased

RC (MoSHi). Enclosure is in MoSHi. See the following letter, from Wakelin Welch, Jr., and also a summary of TJ's (missing) reply to the present communication, under 24 July 1784.

From Wakelin Welch, Jr.

London, 31 May 1783. Announcing that he has taken been taken into partnership by his father; solicits TJ's custom.

RC (MoSHi); 1 p.; signed "Wake. Welch Junr."

To James Madison

DEAR SIR   Monticello June 1. 1783.

The receipt of your letter of May 6. remains unacknoleged. I am also told that Colo. Monroe has letters for me by post tho' I have not yet received them. I hear but little from our assembly. Mr. Henry has declared in favour of the impost. This will ensure it. How he is as to the other questions of importance I do not learn.

On opening my papers when I came home I found among them the inclosed cyphers which I had received from either Mr. Morris's or Mr. Livingston's office. Will you be so good as to return them for me? The confusion into which my papers had got going to and from Baltimore and left there for some time will I hope apologize for my having overlooked them when I returned the other papers. I send you inclosed the debates in Congress on the subjects of Independance, Voting in Congress, and the Quotas of money to be required from the states. I found on looking that I had taken no others save only in one trifling case. As you were desirous of having a copy of the original of the declaration of Independance I have inserted it at full length distinguishing the alterations it underwent.

Patsy increases the bundle inclosed with her correspondence. My compliments attend my acquaintances of the family. Patsy's letter to Miss Floyd will need a safe more than speedy conveyance for which she trusts to your goodness. Our friendship for that family as well as your interest in it will always render any news of them agreeable. I am with the sincerest esteem Dr. Sir Your affectionate friend,

Th: Jefferson

P.S. I inclose for your perusal the account of the Pain de singe which I mentioned. Be so good as to communicate it to Dr. Shippen who had not heard of it. My compliments attend him.

RC (DLC: Madison Papers); endorsed in a hand other than Madison's. Of the numerous enclosures mentioned only one is clearly identifiable, namely TJ's notes of proceedings in Congress, 7 June to 1 Aug. 1776, including a copy of the Declaration of Independence showing the changes it underwent between the time it was drafted and adopted; this document is printed above, Vol. 1: 309-29. Another enclosure must have consisted of printed forms for preparing and reading diplomatic ciphers; bearing numbers from 1 to 1700, these were given by R. R. Livingston to American diplomats going abroad (see E. C. Burnett, "Ciphers of the Revolutionary Period," *Amer. Hist. Rev.*, XXII [1916-1917], 332); there are examples of these in TJ Files from ViU, one of them blank and one filled in. "Patsy's letter" was no doubt that of 28 May to Maria Floyd, acknowledged by the latter on 11 Jan. 1784 (DLC: TJ Papers, 9: 1626) who added a postscript: "please to present this paper to your Papa my Love. It's an answer to his exercise." Neither the exercise nor its answer has been found.

I FOUND ON LOOKING THAT I HAD TAKEN NO OTHERS SAVE ONLY IN ONE TRIFLING CASE: It is possible that TJ here refers to his notes taken on 12 Aug. 1776 at the hearing held before Congress to determine the charges against Commodore Esek Hopkins for having violated his orders (JCC, V, 648). This interesting document, consisting of four pages of TJ's extremely abbreviated notes, should have been included in Vol. 1 of the present edition (and will be included in the supplementary volume for documents discovered too late to be inserted in proper chronological order). It is in DLC: TJ Papers, 9: 1525-6 and bears at its top, in TJ's hand, the date "Aug. 12. 1783." It was, quite naturally, catalogued under that date and the MS inserted in TJ Papers among documents for 1783. But the error was TJ's. It is obvious that when he went over his early Revolutionary papers in the spring of 1783 to obtain for Madison the notes that he had promised, TJ found the notes bearing on Commodore Hopkins' hearing of 12 Aug. 1776; it must have been undated and, referring to his copy of the *Journal* of Congress, TJ established the proper date of day and month and then, from force of habit, wrote the year "1783."

From James Madison

My dear Sir   Philada. 10. June 1783.

Congress have received two letters from Mr. *Laurens*[1] dated one the *fifteenth of March* the *other fifth of April.* In the former *persists in* the *jealousy* expressed in *his letter of* the *thirtieth*[2] *of December of the British Councils. He* says *that Shelburne had boasted of his success* in *gaining the provisional treaty without the concurrence of France and of the good effect he expected to draw from that advantage. Mr. L.'s remark was that admitting the fact which he did not* altho' it *might disgrace* and even *prove fatal to the Ameri-*

can Ministers, It *could have no such effects on the United States.* His *second letter* expresses more *confidence in the D. of Portland and Mr. Fox.* These *ministers have*[3] withdrawn the subject of Commerce with the U.S. from Parliament and mean to open negociations for a Treaty with their Ministers in Europe. Mr. Fox asked Mr. L. whether these had powers for that purpose: his answer was that he believed so. That he had seen a revocation of Mr. Adams' commission noticed in the Gazettes but that he considered the paragraph as spurious. From this it would seem that *Mr. A. had never communicated this* diminution of *his power to his colleagues.* These letters leave us in the suspence in which they found us as to the definitive Treaty. Mr. L. thinks that no such event could have been relied on under Shelburnes Administration. He was on the 5th. of Apl. setting out for Paris with Mr. David Hartley successor to Mr. Oswald, from which he should proceed to America unless a definitive Treaty was near being concluded. Notwithstand the daily arrivals from every quarter we get not a line on the subject from our Ministers at Versailles.

Mr. Dumas has inclosed to Congress sundry papers from which it appears that the *Dutch indulge a* violent animosity *against the French court* for *abandoning their interests and the* liberty of *navigation by a premature concluding of the preliminaries.* Complaints on this head are *made through Dumas to Mr. Adams* with *enquiries whether the American ministers had powers to* concert engagements *with the United Provinces, His Most Christian Majesty, and His Catholic Majesty for maintaining the rights asserted by the neutral confederation* or if the two last *decline with United Provinces alone. The answer of Mr. A. is not included, but references to it import it was satisfactory and* that *negociations were to be opened accordingly.* It is certain notwithstanding that no *powers equal to such a transaction* were *ever given generally to the ministers* and that as far as they were given they were *superceded by the commission to Mr. Dana.* This correspondence commenced in Jany. and is brought down to late in March and yet no *intimation whatever* concerning it has been *received from the ministers themselves.*

Congress have lately sent instructions to the Ministers in Europe to *contend* in *the final treaty for such* amendment of the *article relating to British debts* as will *suspend payment for three years after the war and expressly*[4] *exclude interest during the war.*

Mr. Livingston has taken his final leave of the department of Foreign Affairs. He would have remained if such an augmentation of his Salary had been made as would have secured him against future expence. But besides the disinclination of several members to augment salaries, there was no prospect of a competent number of States for an appropriation of money, until he must have lost the option of the Chancellorship of N.Y. No successor has been yet nominated, altho' the day for a choice has passed. I am utterly at a loss to guess on whom the choice will ultimately fall. *A.L.* will be *started* if the *defection⁵ of a* respectable *competitor* should be *likely to force votes upon him.* No such has yet *been a subject of conversation in my particular presence.*

The general arrangement of the foreign system has been suspended by the thinness of Congress in part, and partly by the desire of further information from Europe. I fear much the delay will be exceedingly protracted. Nothing but final resignation of the Ministers abroad and the arrival of Foreign Ministers here, will effectually stimulate Congress into activity and decision on the subject. How far and at what time the first cause will operate is precarious. The second seems less so. Mr. Van Berkel has sent directions for proper provisions for his reception in the next month. A Sweedish Gentleman recommended by Dr. Franklin as a Philosopher, and by the Ct. de Vergennes as an intended Minister has been here for some time. From the temper of Spain, a mission from that Court also is not improbable.

The Treaty of Comerce with G.B. is another business suspended by the same cause. The Assembly have instructed us to reserve to Congress a revisal after it shall have been settled in Europe. This will give force to the doctrine of caution hitherto maintained by us. The time of my setting out for Virga. continues to be uncertain, but cannot now be very distant. The prospect of seeing you, I need not assure you, enters much into the pleasure I promise myself from the visit. Mrs. House and Mrs. Trist charge me with their very sincere and respectful compliments to you and beg that they may be remembered very affectionately to Miss Patsy. I am Dear Sir Your sincere friend,   J. MADISON Jr.

RC (DLC: Madison Papers); endorsed by Madison with his name at head of text after the letter was returned to him; partly in code. TJ's transcription of the paragraphs containing coded passages is in DLC: TJ Papers, 10: 1597-8.

The letters of Henry LAURENS here discussed are printed from PCC in Wharton, *Dipl. Corr. Amer. Rev.*, VI, 303-5, 360-1.

¹ This and subsequent words in italics were written in code and were decoded by TJ on a separate paper, employing Code No. 3. TJ's decoding has been verified and corrected by the editors.

² TJ decoded this as "thirty six of December," but did not bother to make a correction.

³ The word "have" is written out and is also in code.

⁴ The code symbol for "expressly" is underlined, though the decoded word was not underlined by TJ.

[5] TJ decoded this by using its first meaning for the symbol 763: "defect." This decoding was followed in *Madison Papers*, ed. Gilpin, I, 544-7; copied from that source by Wharton in *Dipl. Corr. Amer. Rev.*, VI, 479; and in turn followed by Burnett, *Letters of Members*, VII, No. 217. But the symbol 763 also meant "defection," which is the obvious meaning here and which TJ no doubt understood but did not bother —as was sometimes the case with him and with Madison—to alter an erroneous decoding. The "respectable competitor" may have been Laurens. John Armstrong, Jr. made the following comment on the day preceding the present letter: "There are many in nomination—some of them have pretensions— but there are objections to all. Old Laurens has been mentioned and is by far the most unexceptionable, but I don't imagine He will serve, and if he would, He is not now here" (Armstrong to Morris, 9 June 1783, Burnett, *Letters of Members*, VII, No. 217, note 5).

To James Madison

DEAR SIR   Monticello June 17. 1783.

Your favours of the 13th. and 20th. Ult. came to hand about a week ago. I am informed the assembly determined against the capacity of reelection in those gentlemen of the delegation who could not serve a complete year. I do not know on what this decision could be founded. My hopes of the success of the Congressional propositions here have lessened exceedingly. Mr. Henry had declared in favor of the impost: but when the question came on he was utterly silent. I understand it will certainly be lost if it be not already. Instead of ceding more lands to the U.S. a proposition is made to revoke the former cession. Mr. Henry is for bounding our state reasonably enough, but instead of ceding the parts lopped off he is for laying them off into small republics. What further his plan is I do not hear. However you get the parliamentary news so much more directly from Richmond that it is idle for me to give it you from hence.

A Convention for the amendment of our Constitution having been much the topic of conversation for some time, I have turned my thoughts to the amendments necessary. The result I inclose to you. You will have opportunities during your stay in Philadelphia of enquiring into the success of some of the parts of it which tho' new to us have been tried in other states. I shall only except against your communicating it to any one of my own country, as I have found prejudices frequently produced against propositions handed to the world without explanation or support. I trust that you will either now or in some future situation turn your attention to this subject in time to give your aid when it shall be finally discussed. The paper inclosed may serve as a basis for your amendment, or may suggest amendments to a better groundwork. I further learn that the assembly are excluding members of Congress from among them. Whether the information they may derive from their presence, or their being marked by the confidence of the people, is the cause of this exclusion I cannot tell.

Be pleased to present me with affection to my acquaintances of the house and to receive yourself the sincerest assurances of the esteem with which I am Dr. Sir Your friend & servt,

TH: JEFFERSON

P.S. I will take the first opportunity of forwarding the pamphlet to your father.

RC (DLC: Madison Papers); endorsed in part: "June 17. 1783. ideas of Constitution." Enclosure: TJ's draft of a Constitution for Virginia (see following documents).

Jefferson's Proposed Revision of the Virginia Constitution

I. ALBEMARLE COUNTY INSTRUCTIONS CONCERNING THE VIRGINIA CONSTITUTION [ca. SEP.-OCT. 1776]

II. ADDITIONAL INSTRUCTIONS FROM THE INHABITANTS OF ALBEMARLE [ca. SEP.-OCT. 1776]

III. JEFFERSON'S DRAFT OF A CONSTITUTION FOR VIRGINIA [MAY-JUNE 1783]

IV. MADISON'S OBSERVATIONS ON JEFFERSON'S DRAFT OF A CONSTITUTION FOR VIRGINIA [OCT. 1788]

EDITORIAL NOTE

When Jefferson stopped off in Richmond in May on his way back to Monticello, his discussions with various political figures led him to the conclusion that a convention to revise the Virginia Constitution was imminent. No doubt remembering his experience in 1776 when his earlier draft of a fundamental law arrived almost too late, he lost no time in drafting a text for a new constitution. He arrived at Monticello on 15 May 1783 and in the next four weeks had completed the text of Document III in the present series which he enclosed in his letter to Madison of 17 June. Though his impact upon the American constitutional experience was one of Jefferson's most significant contributions, this was an indirect consequence of his principles rather than a direct effect of his attempts at constitution-drafting: his effort of 1783 produced even less concrete results than had that of 1776. The agitation for revision continued for years, but the Virginia Constitution of 1776 was not replaced until 1830. Nevertheless, Jefferson's draft of 1783 is a significant document. With some violation of strict chronology, the editors have decided to present in one sequence the draft of a constitution itself and two other related documents.

For Jefferson's objections to the Constitution of Virginia of 1776, see Vol. 1: 330, 373, 530ff. and, especially, his comments in *Notes on the State of Virginia* prefaced by the following remarks: "This constitution was formed when we were new and unexperienced in the science of government. It was the first, too, which was formed in the whole United States. No wonder then that time and trial have discovered very capital defects in it" (Ford, III, 222-235). Among these the chief one that disturbed Jefferson was that all powers—legislative, executive, and judicial—were controlled by one body which, having power to alter the Constitution at will, caused Virginia polity to be "precisely the definition of despotic government." From his point of view it made no difference that this power was vested in many hands that were elected rather than in one that was hereditary: this was "An *elective despotism*" and was not "the government we fought for." Hence he thought it essential to form a new government "on free principles . . . in which the powers of government should be so divided and balanced among several bodies of magistracy, as that no one could transcend their legal limits, without being effectually checked and restrained by the others"; he conceded that the Convention of 1776 had approved the principle of separation of powers, but thought that no checks and balances providing effective barriers to a violation of the principle had been set up. It was equally essential, he felt, to protect these principles by a constitution that would precisely and unequivocally distinguish between fundamental and statute law, making the ordinary legislature competent for the latter only.

The Constitution of 1776 was indeed a mere ordinance, as was the accompanying Declaration of Rights. Jefferson had in many instances demonstrated his concern over this anomaly, but it particularly disturbed him that the Act for Establishing Religious Freedom, which touched "the natural rights of mankind," could only be enacted as a statute and not as part of a fundamental law. To declare that Act irrevocable, he knew, would be of no effect in law; "yet we are free to declare," he asserted, "and do declare, that . . . if any act shall be hereafter passed to repeal the present or to narrow its operation, such act will be an infringement of natural right" (Vol. 2: 546-7).

But this objection to the Constitution of 1776 rested largely on a legal distinction. Regardless of the manner of its adoption, that Constitution in actual practice was treated as a fundamental law, different in character and superior in authority to ordinary legislation. This was made plain in many ordinary acts of the legislative, executive, and judicial authority, both by implication and by expressly recognized derivation of powers. It was categorically affirmed in George Wythe's famous *obiter dictum* in the case of Commonwealth *v.* Caton (4 Call 5-51). And more than once a similar affirmation was made by the Council while John Marshall was a member (1782-1784), though this fact was not noted in Beveridge's *Life of John Marshall* in which Marshall's very active, though brief, career as a Councillor was almost casually dismissed. On one occasion, for example, the Council was asked to remove from office one John Price Posey, a magistrate of New Kent county, on the ground that he "had been guilty of diverse gross misdemeanors, disgraceful to the Character which should be preserved by a Justice of the Peace." In an opinion signed by Marshall and two other members of the Council, the Executive declared that "the Law authorizing the Executive to enquire into the Conduct of a Magistrate and determine whether he has or has not committed a certain act is repugnant to the Act of Government, contrary to the fundamental principles of our constitution, and directly opposite to the general tenor of our Laws." In consequence, the Council refused to consider the complaint against Posey "unless the facts are found in a Court of justice" (MS Va. Council Jour., 20 Feb. 1783, Vi; but Posey was convicted of a misdemeanor in General Court on 10 Dec. 1783 and was therefore removed from the commission "pursuant to powers in such cases vested in the Executive by law"; same, 25 Oct. 1784).

Indeed, Jefferson admitted that, to a limited extent, the Virginia Constitution was regarded as a fundamental law. Though he felt that "a great proportion of the legislature consider the constitution but as other acts of legislation" and that in consequence "laws have been frequently passed which controuled it's effect," he was willing to concede that "there is a part of the state which considers the act for organising their government as a constitution and are content to let it remain." He asserted nevertheless that "There is another part which considers it only as an ordinary act of the legislature, who therefore wish to form a real constitution, amending some defects which have been observed in the act now in force. Most of the young people as they come into office arrange themselves on this side, and I think they will prevail ere long. But there are no heats on this account" (TJ to Démeunier, 24 Jan., 1786).

Jefferson's desire to "form a real constitution" was genuine enough, but his legislative and executive experience had strengthened and amplified his objections to the substance of the Constitution of 1776 as well as to its source of authority. A comparison of the present text with that proposed by Jefferson in 1776 (third draft, Vol. 1: 356-64) suggests the extent to which his ideas had been altered in the light of experience. The principle of separation of powers is made far more emphatic in phraseology, but departed from in such concrete provisions as those calling for a council of revision and for a court of impeachments. In respect to suffrage and number of representatives there was little alteration, but Jefferson's hostility to the inequality of representation which gave to the Tidewater a disproportionate share in government, whereby "every man in Warwick has as much influence . . . as 17 men in Loudon," was reflected in the provision that the number of representatives should be kept proportionate to the number of qualified electors. The district system for the election of senators was retained, but the manner of their election was taken from the House of Delegates and transferred to the electorate operating through senatorial electors. Elections were to be held triennially instead of annually. In the House of Delegates the number required for a quorum was reduced from two-thirds to a simple majority. No doubt recalling his experience in May

1781 when he had had to issue a special and extra-legal appeal to members of surrounding counties so that a sufficient number could be brought together to effect an adjournment to a safer place than Richmond, Jefferson provided that the Governor, with the advice of the Council, could call the legislature at a different time or place in case of danger "from an enemy or from infection." Members' pay was provided for in commodity values. The list of persons ineligible to election as members of the legislature was extended and made more specific. There was no bill of rights specifically designated as such, but the Declaration of Rights of 1776 would have presumably remained unrepealed under his 1783 constitution. In addition, the right of habeas corpus was affirmed and the legislature was specifically forbidden to pass certain laws. These included bills of attainder, with no such distinction as Jefferson attempted later in order to justify his own bill of attainder against Josiah Phillips (see Vol. 2: 189-93). They also included the essence but not the phraseology of the Bill for Establishing Religious Freedom. *Ex post facto* laws were forbidden, the slave trade was abolished, and gradual emancipation of slaves was provided for. Though his 1776 draft had included a proviso giving the lower house exclusive right in originating and amending bills "levying money" (Vol. 1: 359), Jefferson's experience in the case of Thomas Johnson, wherein he defended the provisions of the Constitution of 1776 forbidding the Senate to alter such bills, no doubt caused him to anticipate the Constitution of 1830 by omitting such a restriction from his 1783 draft (see Vol. 2: 44). Probably because of his experience with Greene, Steuben, and other military commanders, TJ provided that the Governor should have direction of the militia and also state regulars and that the military should be subordinate to the civil power. The judiciary remained substantially the same, but the provision for a court of impeachments, in which the three branches of government were intermingled in function, was new. But it was in respect to the executive branch that Jefferson's own experience was most evidently reflected. The term of office was extended from one to five years, and an interim ineligibility was made permanent. A broad delegation to the governor of "those powers . . . necessary to carry into execution the laws" and not by nature legislative or judicial was stipulated, some limitations being removed and the application of this general principle "left to reason." The governor was still not vested with a veto power, but what amounted to such was placed in the hands of the council of revision. Jefferson's experience was also strikingly reflected in the provisions concerning the functions of the council of state. No doubt recalling that in effect he alone had been held responsible for alleged faults of an administration in which the Governor and Council shared almost equally in the executive power, he reduced the Council virtually to the status of an advisory board, by implication thereby fixing both authority and responsibility in the single hands of the Governor. He must also have had in mind, as he drafted the proviso penalizing members of the Council for non-attendance, the dark days of the spring of 1781 when some members of Council resigned and almost none attended.

The legislature, of course, was denied "the power to infringe this constitution," and in order to make certain that this was not attempted, Jefferson borrowed from the New York Constitution of 1777 with its Council of Revision. There is in DLC: TJ Papers: 233: 41791 a copy in Jefferson's hand of that part of the New York Constitution providing that the governor, chancellor, and judges of the supreme court should constitute "a Council to revise all bills about to be passed into laws by the legislature" in order that "laws inconsistent with the spirit of this constitution, or with the public good" might not be "hastily and unadvisedly passed." On the verso of this MS Jefferson outlined what was apparently an earlier adaptation of this device than the one he finally incorporated in the present text: "The Governour [and] two of the Chancellors, two of the [judges of the] General court, one of the [judges of the] Admiralty, to be chosen from among the rest by the Council of state." The list of judges is bracketed in the MS while the governor is not, indicating that, following New York precedent, Jefferson intended that the quorum should always include that officer. To this notation he added the following which did not become a part of his final text: "each member intitled to assign his objections separately." In the matter of the council of revision Jefferson followed the New York Constitution in substance though not in phraseology, the constituency of the council being the principal difference.

Another document that Jefferson must have had before him in drawing up the present text is to be found in DLC: TJ Papers, 10: 1569-71, presented here as Documents I and II. This set of instructions from the inhabitants of Albemarle was drawn up, as shown in the notes accompanying Document I, sometime during the late summer or autumn of 1776. Jefferson himself may possibly have participated in its drafting, as he did on at least one other occasion when he wrote but did not sign a petition from the Albemarle inhabitants (see under 24 Dec. 1798). Certainly there are striking similarities between the instructions and his draft of 1783, as for example the insistence in the former that "the fundamental Pillars of the Constitution should be comprised in one Act or Instrument, which should never be subject to alteration but with consent of the people at large." In making no distinction as between the powers of the two houses of the legislature, Jefferson's draft also is closer to the instructions than to his own proposed constitution of 1776. In respect to the appointment of county officers and in provisions safeguarding the freedom of the press, Jefferson's draft differed from the instructions. Though there are phrases here and there in the instructions that have a Jeffersonian ring, the style for the most part is not his. In all likelihood his own draft constitution of 1783 was influenced by these views of the Albemarle inhabitants, but there is no evidence for regarding him as a co-author of the instructions.

Madison acknowledged receipt of Jefferson's draft in his letter of 17 July 1783, but without comment. On 15 May 1784 he wrote that he expected to make use of Jefferson's ideas in what he hoped was an imminent revision of the Constitution of 1776. This hope grew out of an agitation that continued from 1783 through 1785 and manifested itself in June 1784 in a petition from Augusta county that "touched on a Reform of the Government" (Madison to TJ, 3 July 1784). The members of the House of Delegates favoring revision seized this opportunity to bring the matter up for debate, but Patrick Henry opposed the move and nothing came of it (JHD, May 1784, 1828 edn., p. 55; Madison, *Writings*, ed. Hunt, II, p. 54, 57-8, 65; Rives, *Madison*, I, 557-9). Several "Petitions from the Western side of the Blue ridge" later in 1784 called for revision of the Constitution, and Madison thought that the "friends of the undertaking seem to be multiplying rather than decreasing" (Madison to TJ, 9 Jan. 1785). Madison, however, did not make active use of Jefferson's draft until 1788. By then the text drawn up in the 1783 draft had been printed as an Appendix to *Notes on the State of Virginia* and Madison's "Observations" (Document IV) were based upon that printing rather than upon the MS version presented here. John Brown of Kentucky had shared quarters with Madison while in Congress and Madison may possibly have handed him the manuscript draft at that time (John Mason Brown, *Political Beginnings of Kentucky*, p. 149; Brown errs, however, in thinking that Jefferson's draft was for a new constitution for Kentucky; same, p. 195, note). On 26 Aug. 1788 Brown wrote to Madison: "I will thank you . . . also (if your leisure will permit) for some remarks upon Jefferson's plan of Govt. denoting such alterations as would render it more applicable to the District of Kentucky. These might be of the greatest consequence to that Country and if sent by Post will certainly reach me" (DLC: Madison Papers). Madison promised "forthwith [to] execute the request contained in your letter from Fort Pitt, and forward the remarks on Mr. Jefferson's draft by the next mail" (Madison to Brown, 18 Oct. 1788, typescript copy in DLC: Madison Papers). No further correspondence between Brown and Madison appears on this subject, but it is clear that the "Observations" were made in 1788 and that they apply to the text of 1783, not, as stated by Hunt, to that of 1776 (Madison, *Writings*, ed. Hunt, v, 284-94).

In consequence, Madison's comments should be viewed in the context of the later date and in the light of his purpose, which was to assist in the forming of the Kentucky constitution. He was therefore much more critical and in general less approving of Jefferson's innovations than would have been likely if these comments had been drafted prior to Shays' Rebellion, to the great debates of the Federal Convention of 1787, and to his participation in the authorship of *The Federalist*. A more contemporaneous comment by Madison on the Virginia Constitution of 1776 seems to show a greater degree of agreement with Jefferson and perhaps even a reliance on the present draft. This is to be found in his "Notes of Speech on Proposed Amendment to the Constitution of Virginia, June, 1784," in which he pointed out the following objections to the Constitution which are also reflected in Jefferson's draft: (1) the Convention of 1776 which drew it was "without due power from the people" and therefore the Constitution was like "other ordinances of same Session deemed alterable" by the legislature; (2) there was in it "a Union of powers which is tyranny"; (3) the Senate was "badly constituted and improperly barred of the originating of laws"; (4) "equality of representation [was] not provided for"; (5)

"Impeachments [were] of great moment and on bad footing"; (6) "Habeas Corpus [was] omitted"; and (7) there was "no mode of expounding constitution and of course no check to Genl. Assembly" (Madison, *Writings*, ed. Hunt, II, 54). The last objection seems to suggest that in 1784 Madison was not as hostile to the idea of review of legislation by the judiciary as he appears to be in the "Observations" of 1788.

Though Jefferson's efforts to revise the Virginia Constitution in 1783 were fruitless, perhaps due to the hostility of Patrick Henry, some traces of his draft are to be found in the first Constitution of Kentucky (see note 10, Document III). But the fundamental law of Kentucky was not adopted until seven years after the publication of Jefferson's text and more than three years after Madison's "Observations" had been sent to John Brown. The intervening time no doubt caused some of Jefferson's innovations to seem even less attractive to Kentuckians than they had to Madison, and none is to be found in the Constitution of 1792—no council of revision, no court of impeachments, no council of state. The Supreme Court, however, was called "the Court of Appeals." But the influence of the Federal Constitution and of the constitutions of other states, particularly the resolutions of various state conventions of 1788 calling for a bill of rights to be added to the former, is more apparent in the Kentucky Constitution than are traces of the proposed Virginia constitution drawn by Jefferson in 1783.

I. Albemarle County Instructions concerning the Virginia Constitution

The Instructions of the Inhabitants and freemen of Albemarle county to their Representatives in General Assembly.

You are desired to signify to the house of Representatives our approbation, and thanks, for their prudent, noble, and spirited conduct from the time of their appointment to that of our happy deliverance from the insidious tyrannical Government of the British king.

They have, during the above mentioned period, conducted our affairs as well as it could be expected in so unsettled a situation; they have been exposed to a greater danger than the other members of the Community, as it is notorious that, had our enemies carried their point, they would have fallen a sacrifice, to their barbarous resentment. We set a full value upon all that; we esteem them; we respect them; we are determined to stand by them, and defend them to the last drop of our blood. We scorn the flattering hypocritical perfidious hints of our enemies, who affect to entertain the most favourable opinion of the people at large, and endeavour to insinuate that we have been mislead by our directors. God forbid we should be succumbent! We would rather, than accept any conditions from our inveterate inhuman enemies, imitate the most noble Saguntines, who preferred throwing their property and themselves into the flames, to the wretched ignominious life offered them by their proud ambitious Conquerors. We cannot pay too much regard to the zeal of the worthy Representatives, who to the honor of this State went foremost in the glorious declaration of Independence.

But in order, that so good and so necessary an understanding, amongst all the members of this now free Community, may be maintained and transmitted to our posterity, we think it the duty of every body to deliver their sentiments in regard to the new Constitution, or form of Government, and the new Code of laws, which are the most noble, most important, and most difficult works, that occupy at present the attention of our Representatives.

Such an assistance from all the Counties in the State, must be of infinite service to that respectable body, now almost overwhelmed by the greatest variety of affairs (greater than perhaps any assembly of men ever had at one time) and every one of the utmost importance, to the defence, happiness, and prosperity of our Country.

For this reason we highly approve the prudent Ordinance, for continuing in force such of the old laws, as are requisite to avoid disorder in the State, untill a new Code may be compiled after a mature and well digested consideration.

We admire the Bill of Rights, as truly a master piece. There is in few words, according to our opinion, every thing comprehended for instituting the most free, and of consequence the most perfect Government: such as was ever wished, and never before obtained on Earth.

With rapture of joy we see so near the happy period, when the most spirited men now labouring under the oppression of Tyranny in other Countries, will fly to this free land to partake with us, and our posterity, all those blessings that must be the ensuing consequence of a Government founded upon such principles, as to be admired by all good men, and true Philosophers of all nations and Religions.

And 'tho many of us cannot expect to enjoy for a long time the phisical advantag[es] of it, yet the glory of having been the founders will afford such a gratification to our hearts as to over balance all the inconveniences and labours attending it.

Our Bill of Rights will be an honorable monument to the memory of its Compilers.

But as we find, that the true sense of it is not generally understood; for which reason a great many still remain ignorant of their rights, and others infer from it certain wrong notions inclinable to destroy the necessary subordination, and to bring on anarchy and confusion, we must desire, that in the new form of Government every point may be so clearly and explicitly digested, as to be easy to the comprehension of every individual.

We wish, that a proper and clear line may be drawn between the powers necessary to be conferred by the Constituents to their Delegates, and what ought prudently to remain in their hands.

That a regular method may be pointed out for the whole Community to assemble, whenever it should be thought necessary to delibrate about some considerable alteration in Government, agreeable to the 3d. paragraph of the bill of Rights.

That agreeable to the 2d. paragraph, an easy way may be shewn to the people how to call to account any body of magistrates, if they should ever be reasonably suspected to have been partial in favour of some of their own body, or to have abused their trust in any other instance.

That, agreeable to the 5th. paragraph, a plan may be determined upon to reduce our Representatives to a private station at fixed periods, and to consider whether it would not be proper they should then be ineligible for one, or two years, as it will be thought best, and that our Delegates in Congress may not be continued in that high office longer than two years consecutively.

We think, that according to that salutary sentiment in the 15th. paragraph, (that no Government can be preserved but by a firm adherence to justice, and frequent recurrences to fundamental principles) that no man should be allowed to vote but once in a general Election; no freeman should be deprived, without cause, of the right of voting and offering as a Candidate to any office; and that the number of Representatives in the Legislature ought to be as proportionate as possible to the number of Electors, and then at all times agreeable to their increase or diminution.

We wish, that not a single point may be subject to the least ambiguity, and that as soon as the whole plan has been maturely digested, a sufficient number of copies may be printed and sent to every County to be distributed among the Electors for them to consider it, after which to meet at their respective Court-houses to approve, or disapprove, its contents, as they shall think proper, and their determination entered on their several records; the majority of the Electors of a County to be the sense of that County, the majority of the Counties the sense of the Community.

We recommend most earnestly, that the present confidence we repose in each other, may not make us negligent in our duty at this grand juncture; since the least deficiency in legality, or even solemnity, may in future times be productive of such dreadfull consequence as to make our Posterity lament our existence.

It is our opinion, that among the rights, of which men cannot deprive, or divest their Posterity, the most important is that of approving, or disapproving, their own laws; which power ought forever to remain with the whole body of the people.

And if the exercise of this should be thought inconvenient in a Country of so great extent, that then the fundamental Pillars of the Constitution should be comprised in one act or instrument, which should never be subject to alteration, but with consent of the people at large, and that all laws for enlarging the prerogatives or emoluments of the Members of either branch of Legislature should in like manner receive the previous assent of the people.

It is incontestable, that the freedom of a Community is reduced in proportion to the power conferred to a small number of its Members, and that such reduction of freedom is a necessary evil in an extensive Country, where all the people cannot meet at one place to transact their public concerns. Therefore it would be inconsistent with prudence, and with the justice due to our Posterity, to delegate any more than what is absolutely necessary to the good Government of a free State.

We wish, that the institution of the Senate may not be continued on its present plan, as it appears to us totally unnecessary; and we even apprehend from it several great inconveniencies, if the people should ever happen not to make choice of their very best, most sensible, and most able men; and in case they should be such, it appears to us, that from a defect in their powers, they would be so many valuable Members almost entirely lost to the Community. We wish, that their number should be increased, their Election put upon a different method, and they should be invested with the same powers entirely as the other members of the Legislature. They would then be in fact two houses of Representatives, every one endeavouring to promote what they would think advantageous to the Community; and there can be no reason for granting less power to one, than the other, none of them being hereditary, and both having the same concerns at stake.

We think, that the Election of whoever should be proved to have solicited for votes, either directly or indirectly, ought to be void, and he rendered incapable of holding any office for a certain space of time; that in case the severity of the weather, or other accidents, should prevent a general meeting of the Electors on the day of the Election, they should be allowed to vote at some other time appointed by the Legislature, and that in an affair of such importance, it should not be in the breast of the Sheriff, or any other person, or persons, to act according to his, or their opinion, or pleasure.

And in order, that the Electors should not become negligent in the greatest of their duties, those who do not attend the Election, unless prevented by the weather, sickness or being out of the County, should be compellable by more effectual means, than the present, which in consequence of their nature are not put in execution.

In regard to the freedom of the press, which certainly is, as mentioned in the Bill of Rights, one of the great bulwarks of Liberty, we think that the Printers should never be liable for any thing they print, provided they may give up authors, who are responsible, but on the contrary that they should print nothing without. Many good people have been lately mislead by the artifices of ingenious, but malicious, interested and corrupt writers. Had their names been published, their Characters would have been the antidote to their own poison. We are convinced, that by such a regulation many inconveniencies may be avoided, and whether the objections to it are of greater weight we submit to the consideration of our Representatives.

We dont think it necessary to enumerate to you all the remains of despotism and barbarism, still existing in the English Constitution (piercing thorns, from which hope to be soon delivered!) We are convinced, that the Wisdom of our Delegates will not suffer one to remain, and that they will adopt from other Governments nothing but what may serve to bring ours as near perfection as possible. We shall only mention among the antient laws a few of the most obnoxious; as for example the iniquitous entails, so prejudicial to Communities, and so unjust to individuals, every thing that is comprehended under the meaning of that most tyrannical word *Prerogative*, and those most partial laws in favour of the Episcopal Church.

And as the apprehension of having these last renewed, disturbs the minds of a great proportion of our Community, we must desire of you, that this may be one of the first matters you will go upon, in order that they may be made sensible by some prudent and decent method, as soon as possible, that their suspicion is groundless.

I. ALBEMARLE INSTRUCTIONS

We hope that no one Member in that respectable body, will incline to the renewal of such laws; but in case you should find any propensity to it, we desire you to do your utmost endeavours to shew that it would be contradictory to what is said in the 16th paragraph of the Bill of Rights; that we could not be said to enjoy an equal share of freedom in religious matters, if the people of one persuasion were obliged, besides maintaining their own Ministers, to contribute to the maintenance of the Ministers of another, the members of which were only to contribute to maintain their own; that unless every body was obliged to be of that Church (which would immediately destroy the liberty of Religion) such laws would signify, that those who by the dictates of conscience are called to another persuasion, ought to have no Ministers, or if they would have them, they ought not to maintain them, which way of reasoning could not be heard with any degree of patience.

You might even ask, what would be the consequence, if the Presbiterians, who are supposed to form already more than one third of our Community, or the Annabaptists, or the people of any other denomination, were to become more numerous than any other in the State, were to have a majority in the Legislative body, and should think of obliging those of the Episcopal Church to contribute to the maintenance of their own Ministers.

Such a question must make every one withdraw from the thought of promoting so bad, and so dangerous a president; a president diametrically opposite to Liberty; to that liberty, which we are bound to one another to maintain unstained, to that dear liberty, for which we now submit ourselves and families to so many heavy inconveniencies; to that sacred liberty, to whose Alter we are now making a sacrifice of our lives and fortunes; to that blessing, without which there can be no enjoyment in life, and which the whole World cannot take from us, provided we continue in perfect unanimity.

We recommend to your endeavours the having the descent of lands from persons dying intestate, put on a more just footing; that all their children, or other Representatives, may inherit that equal portion of the property of their Ancestors, which they may be presumed to have possessed in his Affection.

We recommend that Grandjury courts should be holden more frequently, and that fixed times may be appointed for Courts of Claims, Propositions, and Grievances, that so the people may know the stated periods, at which they may apply for the liquidation of their accounts against the Public, for redress of their grievances, and amendment of the laws.

We are so convinced, that the blessing of Liberty cannot be maintained without frugality, as it is expressed in the 15th. paragraph of the Bill of rights, that we most heartily recommend the establishment of effectual sumptuary laws, without which no free Government upon Earth can have a long duration.

To reduce our wishes to one point, we recommend, that this grand work may be calculated to rule mankind considered in their natural state, free from all prejudices of custom, as the only means to ensure happiness to our Posterity, as far as it lies in the power of men, under a just and lasting Government.

Edmund Cobbs
                his
Henry   X   Ford
                mark
John Watkins
Natl. Morris
                his
James   X   Nimmo
                mark
                his
Wm.   X   Raynolds Junr.
                mark
                his
Harry   X   Kirby
                mark
Thomas West
                his
William   X   Hays
                Mark
William Ball
Michael Thomas
James Martain
John Jopling
Harrison Thomas
John Stricker
Robertson Bailey
William Jordan
Thomas Hughs
John Eads
Richd Farrar
Stephen Hunter
Jacob Morris
William Martin
Thomas Hewes
Matthew Phillips
Robert Davis
Joseph Upton
William Aron

David New
John Jones
Wm. Tuley
Thomas Watt
Ralph Thomas
Cutbut Webb
John Steven
Jesse Martin
Jas. Bailey
Abram Eads
Cammel Good
David Weaver
Daniel Jopling
Thomas Upton
Ralph Jopling
James Jopling
John Garrot
Owen Lewis
William Bowman
William Miles
Benjn. Jordan
John Childress
Wm. Cox
Thomas Stevens
Joseph Thomas
Benjn. Miles
Saml. Sorrer
Wm. Hughes.
John Snead
Richard Thomas
Charles Kerr
Thomas McDaniel
Chas. Patrick
Alexdr. Craig
Robt. Field
Wm. Williams
John Epperson

MS (DLC); in an unidentified hand; undated, except for a pencilled date "[1783]" at the top of the first page, but this was clearly affixed much later. The reference in the opening paragraph to "our happy deliverance from the insidious tyrannical Government of the British king" would seem to indicate that the instructions were drawn up at the close of the war. But the deliverance referred to must have been the assertion rather than the achievement of independence, for other internal evidence removes all doubt that the document was drawn up in 1776. It certainly cannot have been drawn up much later than the date of enactment of the Act abolishing entails (14 Oct. 1776; see Vol. 1: 560), since it calls for the repeal of all obnoxious laws comprising "the remains of despotism and barbarism, still existing in the British Constitution . . . as for example the iniquitous entails, so prejudicial to Communities, and so unjust to individuals." The instructions also refer to "the prudent Ordinance, for continuing in force such of the old laws, as are requisite to avoid disorder in the State" (May 1776; Hening, IX, 126-8), a reference that would scarcely have been made after 1776. The allusions to the Declaration of Rights, to the Virginia Constitution, and to the Declaration of Independence prove that the document could not have been drawn up before the end of July 1776. Since Document II in this series, which was a sort of afterthought, expresses regret that the two sets of instructions could not have been "joined . . . and sent under one together," it seems clear that both documents must have been *sent* to the delegates in General Assembly after they had departed for Williamsburg, rather than handed to them prior to their going. Hence it is plausible to conclude that the instructions were drawn up in September or October (the session for Oct. 1776 opened 7 Oct. and was adjourned 21 Dec.).

II. Additional Instructions from the Inhabitants of Albemarle

The Instructions of the Inhabitants and freemen of Albemarle County to their Representatives in General Assembly.

We are sorry, that we did not think of the following Instructions sooner, so that they might have been joined with the Instructions drawn up in another paper, and sent under one together. We hope that every attempt of this nature, will meet with a kind reception from our worthy Representatives, whom we so highly esteem, and whose virtues and noble conduct, since our glorious strugle for Liberty began, speak louder than the pen of any celebrated scriber.

You are desired to signify, that we wish, that part of the Ordinance respecting Civil Magistrates may not be continued on the same footing that it now is; as we look upon it productive of many evils, and attended with many bad consequences to the Commonwealth. We desire they may be chosen by the people at the term of every two, or three years as our Representatives shall think proper.

We apprehend, that as all power is radically in the people, they should neither give up, nor suffer any of it to be taken out of their hands, which they could mannage with equal advantage to the public, and conveniency to themselves, and this we apprehend to be the GREAT GOLDEN LINE between the Rulers and the Ruled. The question might be asked, who have a better opportunity to know those, who are proper for Magistrates, than the people among whom they live? If the people have a right to chuse Representatives and Senators, whom every one must confess to be in higher lengths than the Civil Magistrates belonging to their particular counties; certainly they ought to retain the power of choosing the later as well as the former, and not have the power of it taken from them, when they can perform the one as conveniently as the other. It must also be allowed, that the bulk of the people always aim at the public good, prefering it to any sinister end whatever; but we cannot suppose that this will always be the aim of a small number of Magistrates, where, we may suppose a part to be of bad moral, and others biassed, that they will not act for the public good, but rather through favour and interest in the recommendation of others for that important office who may be unfit; we say important; because, the safety, the peace, and the prosperity of the Commonwealth depend upon this faithful discharge of their office both by precept and example. From the shrewd and glaring conduct of many (of which, we wish there were not so many instances daily before our eyes) we may without breach of charity suspect this will be the case in many places, should the appointment of Magistrates depend upon the recommendation of those who are in trust. Let the laws be ever so pure and just, it will avail nothing, if the Magistrate, who is to execute them, is unfaithful to the great charge and trust committed to him. For these reasons and many more that might be laid down, we infer the power of choosing the Magistracy ought to remain in the hands of the people, which will give an opportunity of still continuing those in place who are faithful, and of deposing those who act out of character. Therefore we desire that not only the laws may be just; but a plan laid down if possible to choose Magistrates, such as may be inflexible.

We recommend to you, that the power of choosing the high Sheriffs of each county may be put into the hands of the people; that their continuence at one time, may not exceed two years, and that they shall from that period be ineligible for the term of two, four, or six years as our Representatives shall think fit; so that others may have an opportunity of serving their county in that lucrative office as well as they.

With regard to the militia officers, we could wish that the method of appointing them may be put on plan more agreeable to the principles of Liberty and the minds of the people; that at least it might be upon some such plan as this; that the several companies of each county from this time, when any officer is wanting, shall choose by a majority of votes the said officer, and when chosen he shall be sworn in, if agreeable, if not, he who is not though[t] fit by the court-martial, or any other judicature in whose hands this power may be lodged, shall have a negative power of refusing him; and the said company to which he belonged shall choose another in his place: that the Colonels and Major of each county may after the same manner be chosen by the people collected at their county court-house, by a majority of votes, or by a majority of votes of the captains and subaltren officers collected together for that purpose.

We could wish that there was some such plan as this laid down in the regular army; and that when any officer of a company should happen to be killed in battle or displaced thro bad conduct, or any other circumstance, that there should be another chosen in his place by a majority of votes of that very company to which he belonged; and also in like manner when a Colonels, or Majors place was to be filled. We look upon this to be the only plan, that we should always go upon, and that which leaves an open door for men of virtue and valour to use, and no ways partial, but founded on principles of Liberty.

Upon the whole, we wish that every thing may be done as agreeable, as possible to the real principles of Liberty, that we may transmit Liberty and religion to our Posterity, and that they may be handed down inviolate to the latest generations, and that this happy land may be an Asylum for all destressed sons of Liberty, to which they may flee.

Thos. Maxwell	Edm. Boyd
Saml. Murrell	Thomas Tadlock
Pleasant Martin	Jacob Moon
Webb Kidd	George Murrell
Saml. Dillen	John Richardson
John Doglass	Thos. Appling Jr.
Joseph Laurance	Jno. Tharman
Thomas James	Guttredge Tharman
Bezl. Maxwell	his
William Morans	Stephen X Moor
William Goolsly	mark
Bezl. Maxwell	David Lane
Joel Appling	his
David Crawford	Pete X Chetam
William Hilton	mark
Jacob Fariss	Geo. Martin
John Tuggle	Daniel White

William Maxwell
Mask Leak
John Mathews
Peter Lyon
George Savage
John Martin
John McCue Junr.
Edwd. Crawford
Alexandr Blane Sr.
Samuel Blane
John Blane
George Blane
Ephraim Blane
Richd. Farrar
Thomas Appling
Roge Casay
Robert Page
Thomas Gay
Jesse Morriss
John Reid
      his
Geo.   X   Maxwell
     mark
James Mozt
James Laurence
William Leak
John Massie
Jas. Reid
James Stephenson

Willim. Bonnel
Alexander Ramsey
John Black
William Dollains
John Black
William Black
David Graves
Jules Weeb
John M. William
Alxder. Intwell
Willm. McCord
John Rozel
William Branham
James Epperson
Joseph Wallace
William Raglan
John Davis
John Wallace
William Kare
John Alexander
David Allan
John Bailey
James Woods
John Anderson
Claudius Buster
Samuel Stockton
William Woods
John Jameson
Samll. Jameson

MS (DLC); in an unidentified hand, different from that in Document I in this series.

III. Jefferson's Draft of a Constitution for Virginia[1]

To the citizens of the Commonwealth of Virginia, and all others whom it may concern, the Delegates of the said Commonwealth[2] send greeting.

It is known to you and to the world that the government of Great Britain, with which the American states were not long since connected, assumed over them an authority which to some of them appeared[3] unwarrantable and oppressive; that they endeavoured to enforce this authority by arms, and that the states of New Hampshire, Massachusets, Rhode island, Connecticut, New York, New Jersey, Pennsylvania, Delaware, Maryland, Virginia, North Carolina, South Carolina and Georgia, considering resistance, with all it's train of horrors, as a lesser evil than abject submission, closed in the appeal to arms. It hath pleased the sovereign disposer of all human events, to give to this appeal an issue favourable to the rights of these states, to enable them to reject for ever all dependance on a government which had shewn itself so capable of abusing the trusts reposed in it, and to obtain from that government a solemn and explicit acknowlegement that we are free, sovereign and independant states. During the progress of that war through which we had to labour for the establishment of our rights, the legislature of the commonwealth of Virginia found it necessary to establish a form of government[4] for preventing anarchy and pointing our efforts to the two important objects of war against our invaders and peace and happiness among ourselves. But this, like all other their acts of legislation, being subject to be changed[5] by subsequent legislatures, possessing equal powers with themselves, it has been thought expedient that it should receive those amendments which time and trial have suggested, and be rendered permanent by a power superior to that of the ordinary legislature. The General assembly therefore of this state recommended it to the good people thereof to chuse delegates to meet in General convention with powers to form a constitution of government for them,[6] to which all laws present and future shall be subordinate; and in compliance with this recommendation they have thought proper to make choice of us, and to vest us with powers for this purpose.

We therefore the Delegates chosen by the said good people of this state for the purpose aforesaid, and now assembled in General convention do, in execution of the authority with which we are invested, establish the following Constitution[7] of government for the said state of Virginia.[8]

The said state shall hereafter for ever[9] be governed as a Commonwealth.

The LEGISLATIVE, EXECUTIVE, and JUDICIARY departments shall be separate and distinct, so that no person, or collection of persons of any one of them shall exercise any power properly belonging to either of the others, except in the instances hereinafter expressly permitted.[10]

The LEGISLATURE shall consist of two distinct branches, the concurrence of both of which expressed on three several readings, shall be necessary to the passage of a law. One of these branches

LEGISLATURE.

shall be called the House of Delegates, the other the Senate, and both together the General Assembly.[11]

H. OF DELE-
GATES.[12]   Delegates for the General assembly shall be chosen on the Monday preceding the 25th. day of December which shall be in the year 178 and thenceforwards triennially.[13] But if an election cannot be concluded on that day, it may be adjourned from day to day till it can be concluded.

The number of delegates shall be so proportioned to the number of qualified electors in the whole state[14] that they shall never exceed 300. nor be fewer than 100. ⟨For the⟩ Whenever such excess or deficiency shall take place, the house of delegates so deficient or excessive, shall, notwithstanding this continue in being during it's legal term; but they shall during that term, re-adjust the proportion so as to bring their number within the limits beforementioned at the ensuing election. If any county be reduced in it's qualified electors below the number necessary[15] to send one delegate, let it be annexed to some adjoining county.[16]

SENATE.   For the election of Senators, let the several counties be allotted by the ⟨legislature⟩ Senate from time to time into such and so many districts as they shall find best, and let each county at the time of electing it's delegates chuse Senatorial electors, qualified as themselves are, and four in number for each delegate their county is entitled to send, who shall convene and conduct themselves in such manner as the legislature shall direct with the Senatorial electors from the other counties of their district, and then chuse by ballot one Senator for every six delegates which their district is entitled to chuse. Let the Senatorial districts be divided into two classes, one of which shall be dissolved[17] at the first ensuing general election of Delegates, the other at the next and so on alternately for ever.

All free male citizens of full age and sane mind, who for one year before shall have been resident in the county, or shall through the whole of that time have possessed therein real property of the value of   or shall for the same time have been enrolled in the militia, and no others, shall have right to vote for delegates for the said county, ⟨and persons of the same description qualified by the like residence, property, or military condition within the district shall have right to vote for Senatorial⟩ and for Senatorial electors for the district. They shall give in their votes personally and by balot.[19]

GENERAL
ASSEMBLY[18]   The General assembly shall meet at the place to which they shall have last adjourned themselves on the 14th. day after the day of

the election of Delegates, ⟨*and so annually on that day till the period of their dissolution. The Governor shall have pow*⟩ and thenceforward at any other time or place on their own adjournment.[20] But if they shall at any time adjourn for more than one year,[21] such adjournment shall be void and they shall meet on that day twelvemonth. Neither house without the concurrence of the other shall adjourn for more than one week, nor to any other place than the one at which they are sitting. The Governor shall also have power, with the advice of the council of state, to call them at any other time to the same place, or to a different one where[22] that shall have become since the last adjournment, dangerous from an enemy or from infection.

A majority of either house shall be a Quorum[23] and shall be requisite for doing business: but any smaller numbers which from time to time shall be thought expedient by the respective houses, shall be sufficient to call for and to punish their non-attending members and to adjourn themselves for any time not exceeding one week.

The members[24] during their attendance on General assembly and for so long a time before and after as shall be necessary for travelling to and from the same shall be privileged from all personal restraint and assault, and shall have no other privilege whatsoever. They shall receive during the same time daily wages in gold or silver equal to the value of two bushels of wheat. This value shall be deemed one dollar by the bushel till the year 1790. in which and in every tenth year thereafter the General court at their first sessions in the year shall cause a special jury of the most respectable merchants and farmers to be summoned to declare what shall have been the averaged value of wheat during the last ten years; which averaged value shall be the measure of wages for the ten subsequent years.

Of this General assembly[25] the Treasurer, Attorney General, Register, Ministers of the Gospel, officers of the regular armies of this state or of the United states, persons receiving salaries or emoluments from any power foreign to our Confederacy, ⟨*persons*⟩ those who ⟨*shall*⟩ are not resident in the counties for which they are chosen Delegates or districts for which they are chosen Senators,[26] persons who shall[27] have committed treason, felony or such other crime as would subject them to infamous punishment or who shall have been convicted by due course of law of bribery or corruption in endeavouring to procure an election to the said assembly, shall be incapable of being members. All others not herein elsewhere excluded who may elect, shall be capable of being elected thereto, and none else.[28]

Any member of the said assembly accepting any office of profit under this state, or the United states, or any of them shall thereby vacate his seat, but shall be capable of being re-elected.

Vacancies[29] occasioned by such disqualifications, by death, or otherwise, shall be supplied by the electors on a writ from the Speaker of the respective house.

The General assembly[30] shall not have power to infringe this constitution; to abridge the civil rights of any person on account of his religious belief; to restrain him from professing and supporting that belief, or to compel him to contributions, other than those he shall himself have stipulated, for the support of that or any other: to ordain death for any crime but treason or murder, or offences in the military line:[31] to pardon or give a power of pardoning persons duly convicted of treason or felony, but instead thereof they may substitute one or two new trials and no more:[32] to pass laws for punishing actions done before the existence of such laws: to pass any bill of attainder, ⟨or other law declaring any person guilty⟩ of treason or felony: to prescribe torture in any case:[33] nor to permit the introduction of any more slaves to reside in this state, or the continuance of slavery beyond the generation which shall be living on the 31st. day of December 1800; all persons born after that day being hereby declared free.

The General assembly shall have power to sever from this state all of any part of it's territory Westward of the Ohio or of the meridian of the mouth of the Great Kanhaway, and to cede to Congress 100 square miles in any other part of this state, exempted from the jurisdiction and government of this state so long as Congress shall hold their sessions therein or in any territory adjacent thereto which may be ceded to them by any other state.

They shall have power to appoint the Speakers of their respective houses, Treasurer, Auditors, Attorney general, Register [all General officers of the military][34] their own clerks, and serjeants ⟨and doorkeep⟩ and no other officers, except where in other parts of this constitution such appointment is expressly given them.

EXECUTIVE GOVERNOR   The EXECUTIVE powers shall be exercised by a Governor who shall be chosen by joint balot of both houses of assembly, and when chosen shall remain in office five[35] years, and be ineligible a second time. During his term he shall hold no other office or emolument under this state or any other state or power whatsoever. By Executive powers we mean no reference to those powers exercised under our former government by the crown as of it's prerogative; nor that these shall be the standard of what may or may not be deemed the rightful powers of the Governor. We give him those powers only which are necessary to carry into execution the laws,[36] and which are not in their nature [either legislative or][34] Judiciary. The application of this idea must be left to reason. We do however expressly deny him the praerogative powers of erecting courts, offices, boroughs, corporations, fairs, markets, ports, beacons, lighthouses, and seamarks; of laying embargoes, of establishing precedence, of retaining within the state or recalling to it any citizen thereof, and of making denizens, except so far as he may be authorized from time to time by the legislature to exercise any of these powers. The powers of declaring war and concluding[37] peace, of contracting alliances, of issuing letters of marque and reprisal, of raising or introducing armed forces, of building armed vessels, forts or strongholds, of coining money or regulating it's value, of regulating weights and measures, ⟨so far as they are or may be⟩ we leave to be exercised under the authority of the Confederation; but in all cases respecting them which are out of the said confederation, they shall be exercised by the Governor under the regulation of such laws as the legislature may think it expedient to pass.

The whole military of the state, whether regular or militia, shall be subject to his directions; but he shall leave the execution of those directions to the General officers [appointed by the legislature.][34]

His salary shall be fixed by the legislature at the session of assembly in which he shall be appointed, and before such appointment be made; or if it be not then fixed, it shall be the same which his next predecessor in office was entitled to. In either case he may demand it quarterly out of any money which shall be in the public treasury, and it shall not be in the power of the legislature to give him less or more, either during his continuance in office, or after he shall have gone out of it. The lands, houses, and other things appropriated to the use of the Governor, shall remain to his use, during his continuance in office.

A COUNCIL OF STATE shall be chosen by joint balot of both houses of assembly, who shall hold their offices [during good behavior, 7. years and be ineligible a second time,][38] and who, while they shall be of the said council shall hold no other office or emolument under this state or any other state or power whatsoever. Their duty shall be to attend and advise the Governor when called on by him, and their advice in any case shall be a sanction to him. They shall also have power and it shall be their duty to meet at their

COUNCIL OF STATE.

own will and to give their advice, tho' not required by the Governor, in cases where they shall think the public good calls for it. Their advice and proceedings shall be entered in books to be kept for that purpose and shall be signed as approved or disapproved by the members present. These books shall be laid before either house of assembly when called for by them. The said council shall consist of eight members for the present: but their numbers may be increased or ⟨diminished⟩ reduced by the legislature whenever they shall think it necessary; provided such reduction be made only as the appointments become vacant by death, resignation, disqualification, or regular deprivation. A majority of their actual number ⟨shall be a Quorum⟩ and not fewer shall be a Quorum. They shall be allowed for the present 500.£[39] each by the year, paiable quarterly out of any money which shall be in the public treasury. Their salary however may be increased or abated from time to time at the discretion of the legislature; provided such increase or abatement shall not by any ways or means be made to affect either then or at any future time any one of those then actually in office. At the end of each quarter their salary shall be divided into equal portions by the number of days on which during that quarter a council has been held, or required by the governor or their own adjournment, and one[37] of those portions shall be withheld from each member for every of the said days which without cause allowed good by the board[40] he failed to attend, or departed before adjournment without their[37] leave ⟨of the board⟩. If no board should have been held during the quarter there shall be no deduction.

PRESIDENT. They shall annually chuse a President who shall preside in council in the absence of the governor, and who in case of his ⟨death⟩ office becoming vacant by death or otherwise shall have authority to exercise all his functions, till a new appointment be made, as he shall also in any interval during which the Governor shall declare himself unable to attend to the duties of his office.

JUDICIARY. The Judiciary powers shall be exercised by County courts and such other inferior courts as the legislature shall think proper[41] to erect, and by four Superior courts, to wit, a court of Admiralty, a General court of common law, a High court of Chancery and court of Appeals.

The judges of the HIGH COURT OF CHANCERY, GENERAL COURT and COURT OF ADMIRALTY shall be four in number each, to be appointed by joint balot of both houses of assembly, and to hold their offices during good behavior. While they continue judges they shall hold no other office or emolument under this state or any other state or power whatsoever, except that they may be delegated to Congress, receiving no additional allowance.

These judges assembled together shall constitute the COURT OF APPEALS.[42]

A majority of the members of either of these courts, and not fewer, shall be a Quorum; but in the court of Appeals nine members shall be necessary to do business. Any smaller numbers however may be authorized by the legislature to adjourn their respective courts.

They shall be allowed for the present 500.£[39] each by the year, paiable quarterly out of any money which shall be in the public treasury. Their salaries however may be increased or abated from time to time at the discretion of the legislature: provided such increase or abatement shall not by any ways or means be made to affect,[43] either then or at any future time, any one of those then actually in office. At the end of each quarter their salary shall be divided into equal portions by the number of days on which during that quarter their respective courts sat, or should have sat, and one of these portions shall be withheld from each member for every of the said days ⟨he failed to attend⟩ which without cause allowed good by his court, he failed to attend or departed before adjournment without their leave. If no court should have been held during the quarter there shall be no deduction.

There shall moreover be a court of IMPEACHMENTS to consist of three members of the Council of state, one of each of the Superior courts of Chancery, Common law, and Admiralty, two members of the House of Delegates and one of the Senate, to be chosen by the body respectively of which they are. Before this court any ⟨one⟩ member of the three branches ⟨of government may impeach any member of the other two for any cause sufficient to remove him from his office; and the only sentence they shall have authority to give⟩ of government, that is to say, the Governor, any member of the Council, of the two houses of legislature or of the Superior courts may be impeached by the Governor the Council, or either of the said houses or courts[44] for ⟨any sufficient⟩ such misbehavior in office as would be sufficient to remove him therefrom: and the only sentence they shall have authority to pass shall be that of deprivation and future incapacity of office. Seven members shall be requisite to make a court and two thirds of those present must concur in the sentence. The offences cognisable by this court shall be cognisable by no other, and they shall be judges of fact as well as law.[45]

The Justices or judges of the inferior courts already erected, or hereafter to be erected shall be appointed by the Governor on advice of the Council of state, and shall hold their offices during good behavior or the existence of their court. For breach of the good behavior they shall be tried according to the laws of the land before the court of Appeals, who shall be judges of the fact as well as of the law. The only sentence they shall have authority to pass shall be that of deprivation and future incapacity of office, and two thirds of the members present must concur in the[46] sentence.

All courts shall appoint their own clerks, who shall hold their offices during good behavior or the existence of their court: they shall also appoint all other their attending[37] officers to continue during their pleasure. Clerks appointed by[47] the Superior courts shall be removeable by their respective courts: those to be appointed by other courts shall have been previously examined and certified to be duly qualified by some two members of the General court and shall be removeable for breach of the good behavior by the court of Appeals only, who shall be judges of the fact as well as of the law, [and] two thirds of the members present must concur in the sentence.[48]

The justices or judges of the inferior courts may be members of the legislature.

The judgment of no inferior court shall be final in any civil case of greater value than 50. bushels of wheat as last rated in the General court for settling the allowance to the members of the General assembly, nor in any case of treason, felony, or other crime which would subject the party to infamous punishment.

In all ⟨courts except that of Impeachment and that of Appeals in the particular cases before specified⟩ causes depending before any court, other than those of Impeachments, of Appeals and Military courts facts [put in issue][34] shall be tried by jury, and ⟨the⟩ in all courts whatever[49] witnesses shall give their testimony vivâ voce in open court wherever their attendance can be procured; and all parties shall be allowed Counsel and compulsory process for their witnesses.

Fines, amercements and terms of imprisonment left indefinite by the law other than for Contempts[49] shall be fixed by the jury triers of the offence.

COUNCIL OF REVISION. The Governor, two Counsellors of state, and a judge from each of the Superior courts of Chancery, Common law and Admiralty, shall be a council to revise all bills which shall have passed both houses of assembly; in which council the Governor, when present, shall preside. Every bill, before it becomes law, shall be presented to this council, who shall have a right to advise it's rejection, returning the ⟨same⟩ bill with their advice and reasons in writing to the house in which ⟨said bill⟩ it originated, who shall proceed to reconsider the said bill. But if after such reconsideration two thirds of the house shall be of opinion the bill should pass finally, they shall pass and send it with the advice and written reasons of the said council of revision to the other house, wherein if two thirds also shall be of opinion it should pass finally, it shall thereupon become law: otherwise it shall not.

⟨A bill rejected on advice of the Council of revision may again be brought in during the same session of Assembly with such alterations as will render it conformable to their advice.⟩

If any bill presented to the said Council be not within one week (exclusive of the day of presenting it) returned by them with their advice of rejection and reasons to the house wherein it originated, or to the clerk of the said house in case of it's adjournment over the expiration of the week, it shall be law from the ⟨time of such⟩ expiration[50] of the week and shall then be demandeable by the clerk of the house of Delegates to be filed of record in his office.

The bills which they approve, ⟨or on which they omit to decide within the week before limited,⟩ shall become law from the time of such approbation ⟨or week's omission,⟩ and shall then be returned to or[32] demandeable by the clerk of the House of Delegates to be filed of record in his office.

A bill rejected on advice of the Council of revision may again be ⟨brought on⟩ proposed during the same session of Assembly with such alterations as will render it conformable to their advice.

The members of the said Council of revision shall be appointed from time to time by the board or court of which they respectively are. Two of the Executive and two of the Judiciary members shall be requisite to do business. And to prevent the evils of non-attendance, the board and courts may at any time name all or so many as they will of their members in the particular order in which they would chuse the duty of attendance to devolve from preceding to subsequent members, the preceding failing to attend. They shall have additionally for their services in this council the same allowance as members of assembly have.[51]

The Confederation is made a part of this constitution, subject to such future alterations as shall be agreed to by the legislature of this[53] and by all the other confederating states. The DELEGATES TO CONGRESS shall be five in number.[54] They shall be appointed by

DELEGATES TO CONGRESS[52]

joint balot of both houses ⟨*of assembly and shall hold this office till revoked by the joint will of both the said houses, or until their incapacitation under the Confederation*⟩ of assembly for any term not exceeding one year, subject to be recalled at any time within the term by joint vote of both the said houses. They may at the same time be members of the Legislative or Judiciary departments.[55]

HAB. CORP.[56] ⟨*Every citizen*⟩ The benefits of the writ of Habeas corpus shall be extended by the legislature to every person within this state and without fee, and shall be so facilitated that no person may be detained in prison more than ten days after he shall have demanded and been refused such writ by the judge appointed by law, or if none be appointed, then by any judge of a superior court; nor more than ten days after such writ shall have been served on the person detaining him and no order given on due examination for his remandment or discharge.

MILITARY. The MILITARY shall be subordinate to the civil power.

PRINTING. PRINTING PRESSES shall be subject to no other restraint than liableness to legal prosecution for false⟨hoods⟩ facts printed and published.

CONVENTION Any two of the three branches of government concurring in opinion, each by the voices of two thirds of their whole existing[37] number, that a Convention is necessary for altering this Constitution or correcting breaches of it, they shall be authorized to issue writs to every county for the election of so many delegates as they are authorized to send to the General assembly, which elections shall be held and writs returned as the laws shall have provided in the cases[57] of elections of Delegates to assembly, mutatis mutandis, and the said delegates shall meet at the usual place of holding assemblies three months after the date of such writs, and shall be acknoleged to have equal powers with this present Convention. The said writs shall be signed by all the members approving of the same.

To INTRODUCE THIS GOVERNMENT the following special and temporary provision is made.

This Convention having been ⟨assemb⟩ authorized[58] only to amend those laws which constituted the form of government, no general dissolution of the whole system of laws can be supposed to have taken place; but all laws in force at the meeting of this Convention and not inconsistent with this Constitution, remain in full force, subject ⟨however⟩ to alterations by the ordinary legislature.

The present General assembly shall continue till the Monday

preceding the 25th. day of December in this present year. The several counties shall then, by their electors[59] qualified as provided by this constitution, elect delegates which for the present shall be in number one for every   militia of the said county according to the latest returns in possession of the Governor, and shall also chuse Senatorial electors in proportion thereto, which Senatorial electors shall meet on the 7th.[60] day after the day of their election at the court house of that county of their present district which would stand first in an Alphabetical arrangement of their counties, and shall chuse Senators in the proportion fixed by this Constitution.

The elections and returns shall be conducted in all circumstances not hereby particularly prescribed by the same persons and under the same form and circumstances[61] as prescribed by the present laws in elections of Senators and Delegates of assembly. The said Senators and Delegates shall constitute the first General assembly of the new government, and shall specially apply themselves to the procuring an exact return from every county of the number of it's qualified electors, and to the settlement of the number of Delegates to be elected for the ensuing General assembly.

The present governor shall continue in office to the end of the term for which he was elected.

All other officers of every kind shall continue in office as they would have done had their appointment been under this constitution, and new ones, where new are hereby called for, shall be appointed by the authority to which such appointment is referred. One of the present judges of the General court, he consenting thereto, shall by joint ballot of both houses of assembly at their first meeting be transferred to the High court of Chancery.[62]

MS (DLC: Rives Papers); 10 p.; endorsed by William C. Rives: "Constitution of Virginia 1784," and additionally, by Rives or another: "Drawn by Mr Jefferson." (This MS is hereafter referred to as the Rives MS.) MS (MHi); 11 p.; bound with MS of TJ's Notes on the State of Virginia, but having its own separate pagination. (This MS is hereafter referred to as the MHi MS.) Fragmentary Dft (DLC: TJ Papers, vol. 10, between p. 1597 and p. 1598); see note 62 below. There are also two early printed texts that should be mentioned: (1) *Draught of a Fundamental Constitution of Virginia*, a 14-page appendix in the first or private edition of *Notes on the State of Virginia*, Paris [1785]; "Paper is similar to that of the text [of this edition of *Notes*] but the type is different" (Coolie Verner, *A Further Checklist of the Separate Editions of Jefferson's Notes on the State of Virginia*, Charlottesville, 1950, p. 5); (2) "[Appendix] No. II" in the London edition (Stockdale, 1787) of *Notes on the State of Virginia*, p. [356]-382 (see note 1 below).

The relationship of the MSS and early printed texts has been established by collating all of them successively with the MS here employed as the master text, namely the Rives MS. The Rives MS was sent as an enclosure to Madison in TJ's letter of 17 June 1783. It was certainly composed between TJ's conversation with members of the General Assembly in Richmond early in

May (see TJ to Madison, 7 May 1783) and 17 June 1783. Even if no telltale fragment of an early draft of this paper had been found, the characteristics of the Rives MS would make it clear that this is not a composition draft. Despite numerous deletions and substitutions (all of them recorded here either in the text or in footnotes), the strikingly handsome calligraphy and the occasional insertion of passages that could have been omitted only in the process of copying (see, e.g., note 43, below) indicate that TJ was copying, with occasional alterations and expansions, from an earlier draft.

That the MHi MS was copied from the Rives MS (or from a missing copy intervening between it and MHi MS) is certain from the fact that it incorporates all the alterations made in the latter and includes others that must have been made after TJ sent it to Madison; (see, for example, notes 8, 16, 43, and 55, below). All variations between the two MSS have been recorded in the footnotes below; they are numerous, and some of them are important. Either the MHi MS or a copy taken from it served as printer's copy for the first printed text, Paris [1785]. Apart from punctuation, spelling, and capitalization, the variations between the MHi MS and the earliest printing on the one hand, and between the Paris [1785] and the London, 1787, printings on the other hand, are so minute as to be negligible. When, therefore, a variant reading in the MHi MS is recorded in the notes below, it is to be assumed that the printed texts incorporate this reading.

1 MHi MS has the following title in the margin: "Draught of a Fundamental Constitution for the Commonwealth of Virginia"; a similar title in the Paris [1785] appendix to *Notes on Virginia* is recorded above. The London, 1787, appendix is without caption except "No. II," but has the following introductory note not found elsewhere: "*In the Summer of the Year 1783, it was expected, that the* ASSEMBLY OF VIRGINIA *would call a* CONVENTION *for the Establishment of a* CONSTITUTION. *The following* DRAUGHT *of a* FUNDAMENTAL CONSTITUTION *for the* COMMONWEALTH OF VIRGINIA *was then prepared, with a Design of being proposed to such Convention, had it taken place.*"

2 MHi MS adds at this point: "in Convention assembled."

3 MHi MS omits preceding six words.

4 MHi reads: "make a temporary organization of government."

5 MHi MS reads: "subject to change."

6 MHi MS adds at this point: "and to declare those Fundamentals."

7 MHi MS adds at this point: "and Fundamentals."

8 In Rives MS this paragraph is written in the margin, with an indication that it is to be inserted in its present position. It appears in its proper place in MHi (and of course in the printed texts), corroborating the view advanced above that the Rives MS precedes the MHi MS.

9 MHi MS reads: "for ever hereafter."

10 In MHi MS this paragraph reads as follows: "The powers of government shall be divided into three distinct departments, each of them to be confided to a separate body of magistracy: to wit, those which are legislative to one, those which are judiciary to another, and those which are executive to another. No person or collection of persons being of one of these departments, shall exercise any power properly belonging to either of the others, except in the instances hereinafter expressly permitted"; the corresponding passage in the Kentucky Constitution of 1792 follows the text here quoted almost literally (B. H. Young, *History and Texts of the Three Constitutions of Kentucky*, p. 16).

11 In MHi MS this paragraph reads as follows: "The Legislature shall consist of two branches, the one to be called the House of Delegates, the other the Senate, and both together the General assembly. The concurrence of both of them, expressed on three several readings, shall be necessary to the passage of a law."

12 In MHi MS the gloss at this point is "Election"; beside the following paragraph is the gloss "Delegates."

13 In MHi MS this sentence reads: "Delegates for the General assembly shall be chosen on the last Monday of November in every year."

14 In MHi MS this sentence, up to this point, reads: "The number of Delegates which each county may send shall be in proportion to the number of it's qualified electors, and the whole number of Delegates for the state shall be so proportioned to the whole number of qualified electors in it."

15 MHi MS reads: "authorized."

16 In Rives MS this sentence is an interlined afterthought, but it appears

in its proper place in MHi MS and the printed texts.

17 MHi MS reads: "two classes and let the members elected by one of them be dissolved," &c.

18 In MHi MS the gloss at this point is "Electors."

19 MHi MS deletes preceding three words and substitutes "and vivâ voce."

20 In MHi MS this sentence has been altered to read: "The General assembly shall meet at the place to which the last adjournment was on the 42d day after the day of election of delegates, and thenceforward at any other time or place on their own adjournment till their office expires which shall be on the day preceding that appointed for the meeting of the next General assembly."

21 In MHi MS the remainder of this sentence reads: "it shall be as if they had adjourned for one year precisely."

22 MHi MS: "if."

23 In MHi MS this word also appears as a marginal gloss beside this paragraph.

24 In MHi MS the marginal gloss "Privileges" appears beside this paragraph.

25 In MHi MS the marginal gloss "Exclusions" appears beside this paragraph.

26 MHi MS adds at this point: "those who are not qualified as electors."

27 In the Rives MS, from the phrase "those who are not resident" to this point, this is an interlineation.

28 In MHi MS the preceding three words are deleted.

29 In MHi MS this word also appears as a marginal gloss beside this paragraph.

30 In MHi MS the marginal gloss "Limits of power" appears beside this paragraph.

31 MHi MS reads: "or military offences."

32 In Rives MS the preceding three words are interlined.

33 MHi MS adds at this point: "whatever."

34 The brackets are in Rives MS; the words enclosed therein appear in MHi MS (and in the printed texts) without brackets.

35 The number is bracketed in MHi MS, with another number written above it which was later deleted and is now illegible. Rives MS and printed texts read "five" without brackets. (This is the single instance found where the printed texts follow Rives MS rather than MHi MS.)

36 MHi MS reads: "to execute the laws (and administer the government)."

37 In Rives MS this word is interlined.

38 Brackets in both Rives and MHi MSS. TJ is here offering alternatives for the councillors' terms of office. In the printed texts he settled on the seven-year term rather than "good behavior."

39 MHi MS has a blank instead of a sum.

40 In Rives MS the preceding eight words are interlined.

41 In MHi MS, from this point on, this sentence reads: "to continue or to erect by three Superior courts, to wit, a court of Admiralty, a General court of Common law and a High court of Chancery, and by one supreme court to be called the court of Appeals."

42 MHi MS adds at this point: "whose business shall be to receive and determine appeals from the three superior courts; but to receive no original causes except in the cases expressly permitted herein."

43 In Rives MS the preceding four words are interlined. This omission of a passage essential to sense and syntax strongly suggests that TJ was copying rather than composing when he prepared this MS.

44 MHi MS adds at this point: "and by no other."

45 MHi MS reads: "and they shall be triers of the fact as well as judges of the law."

46 MHi MS: "this."

47 MHi MS adds at this point: "the Supreme or."

48 In Rives MS this sentence is an interlined afterthought.

49 In Rives MS the preceding four words are interlined.

50 In Rives MS the remainder of this sentence is interlined.

51 In Rives MS this sentence was altered from the following: "They shall have no additional allowance for their services in this council."

52 In MHi MS the gloss at this point is "Confederacy," and the present gloss is moved down beside the following sentence, which begins a new paragraph.

53 MHi MS adds at this point the word "state."

54 MHi MS adds at this point: "any three of whom, and no fewer, may be a representation."

55 In Rives MS this sentence is interlined. In MHi MS it has the following

addition at the end: "but not of the Executive."

56 In Rives MS this marginal gloss is substituted for another that was deleted and is now illegible.

57 MHi MS: "case."

58 MHi MS: "This Convention being authorized."

59 In MHi MS this paragraph is altered to read, up to this point, as follows: "The present General assembly shall continue till the 42d day after the last Monday of November in this present year. On the said last Monday of November in this present year the several counties shall, by their electors," &c.

60 MHi MS: "14th."

61 In MHi MS the preceding two words are deleted.

62 TJ's fragment of a composition draft of this document, mentioned in the descriptive note above, covers in abridged form and with numerous corrections most of the last three paragraphs. One passage, for example, reads: "All other officers of every kind shall continue in office as they would have done had their appmt. been under this constn, and new ones (*shall be appd where new are*) where new are called for by this constn. shall be appd by the authority to which such apptmt. is referred."

IV. Madison's Observations

on Jefferson's Draft of a Constitution for Virginia

Senate. The term of two years is too short. Six years are not more than sufficient. A Senate is to withstand the occasional impetuosities of the more numerous branch. The members ought therefore to derive a firmness from the tenure of their places. It ought to supply the defect of knowledge and experience incident to the other branch. There ought to be time given therefore for attaining the qualifications necessary for that purpose. It ought finally to maintain that system and steadiness in public affairs without which no Government can prosper or be respectable. This cannot be done by a body undergoing a frequent change of its members. A Senate for six years will not be dangerous to liberty. On the contrary it will be one of its best guardians. By correcting the infirmities of popular Government, it will prevent that disgust against that form which may otherwise produce a sudden transition to some very different one. It is no secret to any attentive and dispassionate observer of the political situation of the U.S. that the real danger to republican liberty has lurked in that cause.[1]

The appointment of Senators by districts seems to be objectionable. A spirit of *locality* is inseparable from that mode. The evil is fully displayed in the County representations, the members of which are everywhere observed to lose sight of the aggregate interests of the Community, and even to sacrifice them to the interests or prejudices of their respective constituents. In general these local interests are miscalculated. But it is not impossible for a measure to be accomodated to the particular interests of every county or district, when considered by itself, and not so, when considered in relation to each other and to the whole State; in the same manner as the interests of individuals may be very different in a State of nature and in a Political Union. The most effectual remedy for the local biass is to impress on the minds of the Senators an attention to the interest of the whole Society by making them the choice of the whole Society, each citizen voting for every Senator. The objection here is that the fittest characters would not be sufficiently known to the people at large. But in free Governments, merit and notoriety of character are rarely separated, and such a regulation would connect them more and more together. Should this mode of election be on the whole not approved, that established in Maryland presents a valuable alternative. The latter affords perhaps a greater security for the selection of merit. The inconveniences chargeable on it are two: first that the Council of electors favors[2] cabal. Against this the shortness of its existence is a good antidote. Secondly that in a large State the meeting of the Electors must be expensive if they be paid or badly attended if the service be onerous. To this it may be answered that in a case of such vast importance, the expence which could not be great ought to be disregarded. Whichever of these modes may be preferred, it cannot be amiss so far to admit the plan of districts as to restrain the choice to persons residing in different parts of the State. Such a regulation will produce a diffusive confidence in the Body, which is not less necessary than the other means of rendering it useful. In a State having large towns which can easily unite their votes the precaution would be essential to an immediate choice by the people at large. In Maryland no regard is paid to residence. And what is remarkable vacancies are filled by the Senate itself. This last is an obnoxious expedient and cannot in any point of view have much effect. It was probably meant to obviate the trouble of occasional meetings of the Electors. But the purpose might have been otherwise answered by allowing the unsuccessful candidates to supply vacancies according to the order of their standing on the list of votes, or by requiring provisional appointments to be made along with the positive ones. If an election by districts be unavoidable and the ideas here suggested be sound, the evil will be diminished in proportion to the extent given to the districts, taking two or more Senators from each district.

The first question arising here is how far property ought to be made a qualification. There is a middle way to be taken which corresponds at once with the Theory of free Government and the lessons of experience. A freehold or equivalent of a certain value *Electors.*

may be annexed to the right of voting for Senators, and the right left more at large in the election of the other House.[3] Examples of this distinction may be found in the Constitutions of several States, particularly if I mistake not, of North Carolina and N. York.[4] This middle mode reconciles and secures the two cardinal objects of Government, the rights of persons, and the rights of property.[5] The former will be sufficiently guarded by one branch, the latter more particularly by the other. Give all power to property, and the indigent will be oppressed. Give it to the latter and the effect may be transposed. Give a defensive share to each and each will be secure. The necessity of thus guarding the rights of property was for obvious reasons unattended to in the commencement of the Revolution. In all the Governments which were considered as beacons to republican patriots and lawgivers, the rights of persons were subjected to those of property. The poor were sacrificed to the rich. In the existing state of American population and American property, the two classes of rights were so little discriminated that a provision for the rights of persons was supposed to include of itself those of property, and it was natural to infer from the tendency of republican laws that these different interests would be more and more identified. Experience and investigation[6] have however produced more correct ideas on this subject. It is now observed that in all populous countries, the smaller part[7] only can be interested in preserving the rights of property. It must be foreseen that America and Kentucky itself will by degrees arrive at this State of Society; that in some parts of the Union a very great advance is already made towards it. It is well understood that interest leads to injustice as well when the opportunity is presented to bodies of men as to individuals; to an interested majority in a republic, as to the interested minority in any other form of Government. The time to guard against this danger is at the first forming of the Constitution and in the present State of population when the bulk of the people have a sufficient interest in possession or in prospect to be attached to the rights of property, without being insufficiently attached to the rights of persons—Liberty not less than justice pleads for the policy here recommended. If *all* power be suffered to slide into hands not interested in the rights of property which must be the case whenever a majority fall under that description, one of two things cannot fail to happen; either they will unite against the other description and become the dupes and instruments of ambition, or their poverty and dependence will render them the mercenary instruments of wealth. In either case liberty will be subverted; in the first by a despotism growing out of anarchy, in the second, by an oligarchy founded on corruption.

The Second question under this head is whether the ballot be not a better mode than that of voting viva voce. The comparative experience of the States pursuing the different modes is[8] in favor of the first. It is found less difficult to guard against fraud in that than against bribery in the other.

Does not the exclusion of Ministers of the Gospel as such violate a fundamental principle of liberty by punishing a religious profession with the privation of a civil right? Does it not violate another article of the plan itself which exempts religion from the cognizance of Civil power? Does it not violate justice by at once taking away a right and prohibiting a compensation for it? And does it not in fine violate impartiality by shutting the door against the Ministers of one religion and leaving it open for those of every other? *Exclusions.*

The re-elegibility of members after accepting offices of[9] profit is so much opposed to the present way of thinking in America that any discussion of the subject would probably be a waste of time.

It is at least questionable whether death ought to be confined to "Treason and murder." It would not therefore be prudent to tie the hands of Government in the manner here proposed. The prohibition of pardon, however specious in theory would have practical consequences which render it inadmissible. A single instance is a sufficient proof. The crime of treason is generally shared by a number and often a very great number. It would be politically if not morally wrong to take away the lives of all, even if every individual were equally guilty. What name would be given to a severity which made no distinction between the legal and the moral offence, between the deluded multitude, and their wicked leaders. A second trial would not avoid the difficulty because the oaths of the jury would not permit them to hearken to any voice but the inexorable voice of the law. *Limits of power.*

The power of the Legislature to appoint any other than their own officers departs too far from the Theory which requires a separation of the great Departments of Government. One of the best securities against the creation of unnecessary offices or tyrannical powers is an exclusion of the authors from all share in filling the one, or influence in the execution of the other. The proper mode of appointing to offices will fall under another head.

An election by the Legislature is liable to insuperable objections. It not only tends to faction intrigue and corruption, but leaves the Executive under the influence of an improper obligation to that *Executive Governour.*

department. An election by the people at large, as in this[10] and several other States, or by Electors as in the appointment of the Senate in Maryland or indeed by the people through any other channel than their legislative representatives, seems to be far preferable. The inelegibility a second time, though not perhaps without advantages, is also liable to a variety of strong objections. It takes away one powerful motive to a faithful and useful administration, the desire of acquiring that title to a re-appointment. By rendering a periodical change of men necessary, it discourages beneficial undertakings which require perseverence and system, or, as frequently happened in the Roman Consulate, either precipitates or prevents the execution of them. It may inspire desperate enterprises for the attainment of what is not attainable by legitimate means. It fetters the judgment and inclination of the Community; and in critical moments would either produce a violation of the Constitution, or exclude a choice which might be essential to the public Safety. Add to the whole, that by putting the Executive Magistrate in the situation of the tenant of an unrenewable lease, it would tempt him to neglect the constitutional rights of his department, and to connive at usurpations by the Legislative department, with which he may connect his future ambition or interest.

The clause restraining the first magistrate from the immediate command of the military forces would be made better by excepting cases in which he should receive the sanction of the two branches of the Legislature.

Council of State. The following variations are suggested: 1. The election to be made by the people immediately, or thro' some other medium than the Legislature. 2. A distributive choice should perhaps be secured as in the case of the Senate. 3. Instead of an ineligibility a second time, a rotation as in the federal Senate, with an abridgement of the term to be substituted.

The appointment to offices is, of all the functions of Republican and perhaps every other form of Government, the most difficult to guard against abuse. Give it to a numerous body, and you at once destroy all responsibility, and create a perpetual source of faction and corruption. Give it to the Executive wholly, and it may be made an engine of improper influence and favoritism. Suppose the power were divided thus: let the Executive alone make all the subordinate appointments; and the Governor and Senate, as in the Federal Constitution, those of the superior order. It seems particularly fit that the Judges, who are to form a distinct department, should owe their offices partly to each of the other departments rather than wholly to either.

Much detail ought to [be] avoided in the constitutional regula- *Judiciary.* tion of this department that there may be room for changes which may be demanded by the progressive changes in the State of our population. It is at least doubtful whether the number of courts, the number of Judges, or even the boundaries of Jurisdiction ought to be made unalterable but by a revisal of the Constitution. The precaution seems no otherwise necessary than as it may prevent sudden modification of the establishment, or addition of obsequious Judges, for the purpose of evading the checks of the Constitution and giving effect to some sinister policy of the Legislature. But might not the same object be otherwise attained? By prohibiting, for example, any innovations in those particulars without the consent of that department; or without the annual sanction of two or three successive assemblies, over and above the other pre-requisites to the passage of a law.

The model here proposed for a Court of appeals is not recommended by experience. It is found as might well be presumed that the members are always warped in their appellate decisions by an attachment to the principles and jurisdiction of their respective Courts and still more so by the previous decision on the case removed by appeal. The only effectual cure for the evil, is to form a Court of Appeals, of distinct and select Judges. The expence ought not be admitted as an objection. 1. Because the proper administration of Justice is of too essential a nature to be sacrificed to that consideration. 2. The number of inferior Judges might in that case be lessened. 3. The whole department may be made to support itself by a judicious tax on law proceedings.

The excuse for non-attendance would be a more proper subject of enquiry some where else than in the Court to which the party belonged. Delicacy, mutual convenience &c. would soon reduce the regulation to mere form; or if not, it might become a disagreeable source of little irritations among the members. A certificate from the local Court or some other local authority where the party might reside or happen to be detained from his duty, expressing the cause of absence as well as that it was judged to be satisfactory, might be safely substituted. Few Judges would improperly claim their wages, if such a formality stood in the way. These observations are applicable to the Council of State.

A Court of Impeachments is among the most puzzling articles of a republican Constitution, and it is far more easy to point out defects in any plan, than to supply a cure for them. The diversified expedients adopted in the Constitutions of the several States prove how much the compilers were embarrassed on this subject. The plan here proposed varies from all of them; and is perhaps not less than any a proof of the difficulties which pressed the ingenuity of its author. The remarks arising on it are 1. That it seems not to square with reason that the right to impeach should be united to that of trying the impeachment, and consequently in a proportional degree, to that of sharing in the appointment of, or influence on the Tribunal to which the trial may belong.[11] 2. As the Executive and Judiciary would form a majority of the Court, and either have a right to impeach, too much might depend on a combination of these departments. This objection would be still stronger, if the members of the Assembly were capable as proposed of holding offices, and were amenable in that capacity to the Court. 3. The House of Delegates and either of those departments could appoint a majority of the Court. Here is another danger of combination, and the more to be apprehended as that branch of the Legislature would also have the right to impeach, a right in their hands of itself sufficiently weighty; and as the power of the Court would extend to the head of the Executive by whose independence the constitutional rights of that department are to be secured against Legislative usurpations. 4. The dangers in the two last cases would be still more formidable; as the power extends not only to deprivation, but to future incapacity of office. In the case of all officers of sufficient importance to be objects of factious persecution, the latter branch of power is in every view of a delicate nature. In that of the Chief Magistrate it seems inadmissible, if he be chosen by the Legislature; and much more so, if immediately by the people themselves. A temporary incapacitation is the most that could be properly authorised.

The 2 great desiderata in a Court of impeachments are 1. impartiality. 2. respectability. The first in order to a right, the second in order to a satisfactory decision.[12] These characteristics are aimed at in the following modification. Let the Senate be denied the right to impeach. Let ⅓ of the members be struck out, by alternate nominations of the prosecutors and party impeached; the remaining ⅔ to be the *Stamen* of the Court. When the House of Delegates impeach let the Judges or a certain proportion of them and the Council of State be associated in the trial. When the Governor or Council impeaches, let the Judges only be associated: When the Judges impeach let the Council only be associated. But if the party impeached by the House of Delegates be a member of the Executive or Judiciary let that of which he is a member not be associated. If the party impeached belong to one and be impeached by the other of these branches, let neither of them be associated, the decision being in this case left with the Senate alone or if that be thought exceptionable, a few members might be added by the House of Delegates. ⅔ of the Court should in all cases be necessary to a conviction and the chief Magistrate *at least* should be exempt from a sentence of perpetual if not of temporary incapacity. It is extremely probable that a critical discussion of this outline may discover objections which do not occur. Some do occur; but appear not to be greater than are incident to any different modification of the Tribunal.

The establishment of trials by Jury and viva voce testimony in *all* cases and in *all* Courts, is to say the least a delicate experiment; and would most probably be either violated, or be found inconvenient.[13]

A revisionary power is meant as a check to precipitate, to unjust, and to unconstitutional laws. These important ends would it is conceded be more effectually secured, without disarming the Legislature of its requisite authority, by requiring bills to be separately communicated to the Executive and Judiciary departments. If either of these object, let ⅔, if both ¾ of each House be necessary to overrule the objection; and if either or both protest against a bill as violating the Constitution, let it moreover be suspended notwithstanding the overruling proportion of the Assembly, until there shall have been a subsequent election of the House of Delegates and a repassage of the bill by ⅔ or ¾ of both Houses, as the case may be. It should not be allowed the Judges or the Executive to pronounce a law thus enacted unconstitutional and invalid. *Council of Revision.*

In the State Constitutions and indeed in the Federal one also, no provision is made for the case of a disagreement in expounding them; and as the Courts are generally the last in making their decisions, it results to them[14] by refusing or not refusing to execute a law, to stamp it with its final character. This makes the Judiciary Department paramount in fact to the Legislature, which was never intended[15] and can never be proper.

The extension of the Habeas Corpus to the cases in which it has been usually suspended, merits consideration at least. If there be emergencies which call for such a suspension, it can have no effect to prohibit it, because the prohibition will assuredly give way to the impulse of the moment; or rather it will have the bad effect of facilitating other violations that may be less necessary. The Exemption of the press from liability in every case for *true facts*[16] is also an innovation and as such ought to be well considered. This essential branch of liberty is perhaps in more danger of being interrupted by local tumults, or the silent awe of a predominant party, than by any[17] direct attacks of Power.

Dft (DLC: Madison Papers); endorsed by Madison: "Remarks on Mr Jeffersons draught of a Constitution—sent from N. York to Mr. Brown Ocr. 1788—see his letters to J. M. on the subject"; and again by Madison: "Brown Jno (Kenty. Augt. 23 1785) Copd.," followed by the date "Oct. 1788" in a darker ink. Madison's draft is headed by the caption: "Observations on the 'Draught of a Constitution for Virginia' "; from this and other internal evidences it is clear that, as noted in Madison's *Letters and Other Writings* (Phila., 1865), I, 185-95, this commentary was based on TJ's draft of a constitution as printed in *Notes on the State of Virginia*. There is in ICU a three-page transcript of the first part of Madison's observations, as indicated below, captioned: "Extract from a letter of Ocr. 1788 to J. Brown Esqr. containing observations on the 'Draught of a Constitution' annexed to Mr. Jefferson's Notes on Virginia." This copy is in Madison's hand; it differs from the draft in a few minor particulars, two instances of which have been indicated below. How far the fair copy that Madison transmitted to Brown differed from the text as here presented cannot be known in the absence of such a copy. (See note 15 below for a possible variation; if Madison did omit or greatly modify the expressions contained in the paragraph of the draft concerning the power of the judiciary over legislation, that fact would be significant.) Madison made many deletions and alterations in the course of composing the "Observations." The more important of these are also indicated, though neither the printing of the "Observations" in Madison's *Letters and Other Writings* (as cited above) nor that in *Writings*, ed. Hunt, V, 284-94, presents these deletions.

1 Madison first wrote and then deleted: "The experience of every State in the Union proves that the real danger to liberty lurks in a mistaken zeal for too much liberty."

2 Madison first wrote "generates" and then deleted it.

3 Madison first wrote: "A freehold of moderate value may be annexed to the right of voting for Senators, and property of considerable value to a Seat in the Senate, whilst the right of suffrage and of representation may be left on a broader foundation for the other branch of the Legislature" and then altered the passage to read as above. Even then, however, Madison made minor changes, for the extract (ICU) reads: "A freehold or an equivalent property may confer the right of voting for Senators," &c.

4 Madison deleted the following at this point: "It is of more importance to annex the qualification of property to the elector than to the Senator, if not annexed to both, for several reasons. 1. Because it is more easy for the latter than for any considerable portion of the former to evade the rule. The practice in England is a sufficient proof of this. 2. Because the electors in that case will generally prefer men of property. 3. Because in all great and interesting questions the sense of the constituents will be sure to predominate in the vote of the Representatives."

5 The extract (ICU) reads: "the rights of things."

6 Madison first wrote "reflection."

7 The extract (ICU) reads "number."

8 The word "clearly" was deleted at this point. On the mode of voting, the Rives MS (Document III) provided that votes should be given "personally and by balot"; this was altered in the later version (MS, MHi) to read "personally and vivâ voce." The latter, of course, was the reading that appeared in *Notes on the State of Virginia*, which was the text that Madison employed for his "Observations" (see note 19, Document III).

9 The extract (ICU) ends here at the bottom of its fourth page; there was obviously more to the extract, but how much is not known.

10 At this point, perhaps at a much

later date, Madison subjoined the following: "N. York where these remarks were penned."

[11] At this point Madison wrote and then deleted the following: "2. The liability of the members of the Legislature for their conduct in office, to any others than their respective Houses and Constituents. This would be a serious innovation on an established doctrine of liberty. It might hold the Parliamentary leaders in a very improper and dangerous awe of the other branches of Government. A Combination of the Executive and Judiciary—of the Senate and the latter."

[12] Madison first wrote: "the first in order to a just decision, the second in order to inspire the requisite confidence and acquiescence in the decision. Perhaps these qualities may be found in an adequate degree in a Court thus modified"; and then altered the passage to read as above.

[13] Madison was mistaken in thinking that jury trial of the facts was provided for in *all* cases in TJ's constitution; courts of "Impeachments, of Appeals and Military courts" were specifically excepted (see Document III).

[14] Madison first wrote, and then deleted: "depends on them, whether."

[15] Madison deleted at this point: "nor ought to be"; the entire paragraph is marked by a vertical line in the margin and the letter "N." This may possibly indicate that Madison deleted the passage before making a fair copy for Brown, but more likely it was a mark made at a later date by someone impressed by Madison's vigorous denial of the doctrine of judicial review.

[16] Madison deleted at this point: "tending to unnecessary provocations &c."

[17] Madison first wrote: ". . . by local tumults, or the fear of offending silent influence of a predominant faction, than by any regular invasions of Government direct and deliberate."

To Isaac Zane

DEAR SIR   Monticello June 17. 1783.

I received your kind letter of the 7th inst. I have long intended myself the pleasure of visiting you, but fortune has as long been contriving obstacles to it. The appointment with which you inform me I am honoured will oblige me to stay pretty closely at home for some time to get my affairs into such a state as that they may be left. It at the same time perhaps offers me an opportunity of fulfilling my wish with respect to you by taking you in my route to Philadelphia which I shall endeavor to do. Nothing will deter me from it unless I should learn that the roads are too rough for a light carriage, a circumstance of which I am as yet uninformed. I shall be happy to hear from you while in Richmond by every opportunity. Parliamentary news is interesting and I hear little or nothing of it. What have you done? What are you doing? What are the manoeuvres of your leaders? Who are they? What the dispositions of the two houses? &c. You see you may easily fill a letter to me while I have nothing to communicate to you but what you have long known that I am with great esteem Dr. Sir Your friend & servt.,

                                        TH: JEFFERSON

RC (Mrs. Aubrey Huston, Villanova, Penna., 1949); docketed in a later hand: "Found among the papers of the late Isaac Zane, Esq. member of the house of Delegates &ca."

Zane's letter to TJ of 7 June 1783

has not been found. The APPOINTMENT to which TJ alluded was his election on 6 June as a delegate to Congress, along with Samuel Hardy, John Francis Mercer, Arthur Lee, and James Monroe (JHD, May 1783, 1828 edn., p. 36, 39; a copy of the credentials of these delegates is in PCC, No. 179, I; the credentials were presented at Princeton on 3 Nov. 1783 by Mercer and Lee—TJ did not attend until the next day—and are printed in JCC, XXV, 797-9).

From John Adams

[*Paris, 23 June 1783.* There is recorded in SJL, under date of 16 Apr. 1784, the receipt of a letter from "J. Adams. Paris. June 23. by Mazzei." Mazzei landed at Hampton, Virginia, in Nov. 1783, but he did not forward Adams' letter for some months; see Mazzei to TJ, 4 Apr. 1784, and Mazzei, *Memoirs*, p. 274. Adams' letter to TJ has not been found.]

From James Madison

DEAR SIR   Philada. July 17th. 1783.

Your two favors of the 1 and 17 of June, with the debates of Congress and the letter for Miss Floyd and the Cyphers inclosed in the former, and your amendments to the Constitution inclosed in the latter, have been duly received. The latter came by yesterdays mail. I feel too sensibly the value of these communications to omit my particular acknowledgments for them.

The usual reserve of our Ministers has kept us in entire suspence since my last with regard to the definitive Treaty and every thing else in Europe. The only incident produced in this interval has been that which removed Congress from this City to Princeton. I have selected the Newspaper which contains the Report of a Committee on that subject, from which you will collect the material information. Soon after the removal of Congress the Mutineers surrendered their arms and impeached some of their officers, the two principal of whom have escaped to sea. Genl. Howe with a detachment of Eastern troops is here and is instituting an enquiry into the whole plot, the object and scheme of which are as yet both involved in darkness. The Citizens of this place seem to disavow the alledged indisposition to exert force against insults offered to Congress, and are uniting in an address rehearsing the proofs which they [have] given of attachment to the fœderal authority, professing a continuance of that attachment, and declaring the utmost readiness on every occasion, to support the dignity and privileges of Congress if they should deem this place the fittest for transacting the public business until their permanent residence shall be fixed. What effect this address backed by the scanty accomodations of Princeton will have on Congress is uncertain. The prevailing disposition seemed to be that a return to their former residence as soon as the way should be decently opened would be prudent in order to prevent any inferences abroad of disaffection in the mass of so important a state to the revolution or the fœderal Government. Others suppose that a freer choice among the seats offered to Congress could be made here than in a place where the necessity of a speedy removal would give an undue advantage to the seat happening to be in greatest readiness to receive them. The advocates for Anapolis appear to be sensible of the force of this consideration, and probably will if they can, detain Congress in Princeton until a final choice be made. N. Jersey will probably be tempted to concur in the plan by the advantage expected from actual possession. Other Members are extremely averse to a return to Philada. for various reasons.

I have been here during the week past engaged partly in some writing which, my papers being all here could not be so well done elsewhere, partly in some preparations for leaving Congress. The time of my setting out depends on some circumstances which in point of time are contingent. Mr. Lee arrived here two days ago and proceeds today to Princeton. Mr. Mercer is gone to the Seaboard in N. Jersey for his health. I shall probably return to Princeton next week, or sooner if I should have notice of any subject of consequence being taken up by Congress. Subjects of consequence, particularly a ratification of the Treaty with Sweden have been long waiting on their table for 9. states.

I am Dr. Sir Yr. sincere friend,   J. MADISON Jr.

RC (DLC: Madison Papers); endorsed by Madison, after the return of the letter, with his name and the date. Enclosure missing.

For the best account of the mutiny that REMOVED CONGRESS FROM THIS CITY TO PRINCETON, see V. L. Collins' *The Continental Congress at Princeton*; see also, Burnett, *Letters of Members*, VII, 215ff.; Brant, *Madison*, II, 293-5; Butterfield, *Letters of Benjamin Rush*, I, 301-303. The REPORT OF A COMMITTEE ON THAT SUBJECT is printed in JCC, XXIV, 413-21.

To Edmund Randolph

DEAR SIR   Monticello July 18. 1783.

I am sorry you have been at the trouble of sending an express to me for information as to the transactions between the Executive and Nathan as I am satisfied I do not recollect a single fact that you are not already possessed of. In the winter of 1779. 1780. Mr. Nathen presented us some bills drawn by Genl. Clarke, Colo. Todd and perhaps others, which he said he had taken up at New Orleans or the Havanna and paid a hard dollar for every one named in the bill. At that time I think we had been made to beleive that depreciation had not reached Kaskaskia, and the bills appearing fair, we considered them in the nature of many others taken up by Pollock, and wrote acceptances on the greatest part of them undertaking to pay them in tobacco at 4⅙ dollars the hundred. I beleive we rejected some of them, perhaps as drawn by subordinate officers, till we could write to Genl. Clarke and Colo. Todd. We wrote to them and desired a description of the bills we were to pay fully, and the rates of depreciation if depreciation had affected any. They sent us a description of the hard money bills, to wit all drawn on N. Orleans, and a table of depreciation for the others. This shewed we had wrote acceptances for hard money on some bills whereon depreciation should have been allowed. We laid the case before Mr. Pendleton and Wythe intending if they thought us bound by our erroneous acceptances that we would pay them. They differed in opinion. We then informed Nathan of Clarke and Todd's marks to distinguish the bills, that this had proved we had accepted some in hard money on which depreciation should have been allowed, told him as it was a case in which every man in the state was interested we did not wish to be judges in it ourselves, nor to refer it to any persons within the state but we would refer it to lawyers in Philadelphia whither we knew he was going, and therefore that it would be convenient for him to have it decided there, as it would to us our delegates being on the spot to act for us. He agreed to it. I wrote a state of the case, read it to him at the Council board, he agreed every article was right, we inclosed it to our delegates and that is the last part of the transaction which happened within my knowlege. Our delegates have told me since that he tergiversated a little there, disputing facts, declining the reference &c. but that he had finally come to. But of this they can give more certain information. In every part of the transaction with us he acted candidly enough as far as we could see; and we should certainly have thought ourselves bound to pay the money agreeable to the award.

There was another transaction with him. Colo. Gibson (I beleive it was) came for clothing for the troops at Fort Pitt. We were distressed how to procure them. Nathan offered to go with Gibson to Baltimore, and buy them, and to wait a considerable time for the money. Perhaps he might name a year or some such term. We agreed. He went, bought them and drew on us immediately for the money which we did not like.

I am persuaded there is nothing above but what you know from more certain hands, for indeed my recollection is too faint to be trusted even as to what I have said. Some parts I recollect positively enough, others very faintly or perhaps conjecture steps in the place of memory. I should really be afraid to affirm them positively. If there be however any particular circumstances which you would wish to have sworn to I will endeavor to recollect them with more certainty and send them to you. There is never a day scarcely but Mr. Short, Colo. Monroe, or J. Buchanan can send me a letter, and I can as speedily return an answer. Be pleased to present my compliments to Mrs. Randolph & beleive me to be with much affection Dr. Sir your friend & servt,

Th: Jefferson

RC (Vi); addressed: "Edmund Randolph esq. Atty. General"; endorsed by Randolph: "No. 3. Mr. Jefferson's letter and Mr. Nathan's case." (Ford, III, 335-7, gives the name of the addressee as Gov. Benjamin Harrison.)

If the EXPRESS that Randolph sent to Monticello bore a letter to TJ from the attorney general, it has not been found. The long and complicated TRANSACTIONS BETWEEN THE EXECUTIVE AND NATHAN have never been satisfactorily set forth. That Nathan was engaged in part in furnishing supplies and in part in speculating in bills of exchange is very likely, but his claims against Virginia should be considered in the context of several other complicating factors—his ownership of 300 shares in the Indiana Company (CVSP, VI, 2, 17, 34); the fact that purchases for the public in the Illinois country were extraordinarily subject to inflation and fraud—Gov. Harrison thought that "Mr. Nathan's transactions may be very fair for what I know but so many frauds have been practic'd in that quarter that I am led to doubt every Thing" (Harrison to the Virginia delegates, 2 Nov. 1782, Official Letters, III, 362) and even the commissioners appointed to investigate western accounts reported, after stating at length their investigations of Nathan's activities, that they would have to decline expressing an opinion as to the validity of his claim since they had not "fully examined the affair" (commissioners to Harrison, 17 Feb. 1783, CVSP, III, 436); the claims of George Rogers Clark, Oliver Pollock, and others against the state, &c.

A thorough study of such claims and of the extent of speculation in bills of exchange during the Revolution in Virginia is much needed. Even so, a few facts concerning the Nathan case are clear. TJ had accepted each of the bills of exchange, endorsing them: "March 1780, accepted, to be discharged in tobacco at twenty-five shillings the hundred, by advice of Council. Thomas Jefferson" (JHD, May 1783, 1828 edn., p. 74; see also TJ to Board of Trade, 18 Mch. 1780; TJ to the judges of the High Court of Chancery, 5 Mch. 1781; Pendleton to TJ, 7 Mch. 1781; Wythe to TJ, 9 Mch. 1781; TJ to Harrison, 22 Sep. 1782; Harrison to TJ, 3 Oct. 1782). The list of bills and their value taken up by Nathan was stated in "an accurate account . . . by Governor Jefferson," but this was probably not (though it may have been included in) the STATE OF THE CASE that TJ drew up, read to Nathan in Council, and enclosed in his letter to the Virginia delegates on 15 Mch. 1781 (JHD, May 1783, 1828 edn., p. 73). In accordance with these acceptances, warrants for payment to Nathan totaling more than 200,000 pounds of tobacco were issued on 8 June 1780 (same, p. 74). But TJ's acceptances proved premature, and, according to his own admission, in part mistaken. According to the report of a committee of the legislature, George Rogers Clark and John Todd informed the Governor and Council that the bills drawn on them and on the treasurer of Virginia "were negotiated as paper dollars according to their depreciation at the time of drawing the bills, and that government had received value for them at that rate only" (JHD, May 1783, 1828 edn., p. 74; the scale of depreciation regarded by Clark and Todd as fair is printed at p. 73). TJ and the Council, "finding that they had too hastily assumed the payment of the bills, and supposing that Mr. Nathan could not stand on a better footing than the original holders of the bills," informed Nathan that they did not consider him as "entitled to more than the hard money value of the bills at the time of their being drawn." Nathan, on the contrary, asserted that he "took up these bills at the Havanna and New Orleans . . . at the rate of a silver dollar for every paper dollar, without knowing that they had been drawn at a depreciated rate" (same, p. 74; Governor Harrison later quoted him as having "absolutely denied" that the scale of depreciation applied, *Official Letters*, III, 368). He insisted on the legal obligation arising from TJ's acceptances. TJ and the Council then proposed arbitration, to which Nathan agreed. TJ laid his state of the case before the delegates in Congress and they immediately set about having the matter arbitrated (TJ to the delegates in Congress, 15 Mch. 1781; Virginia delegates to TJ, 27 Mch. and 3 Apr. 1781).

But Nathan evidently "tergiversated" and the effort at arbitration failed. During the summer of 1781 he also made the mistake of attempting to attach supplies in Philadelphia belonging to Virginia that were needed for the military campaign (David Ross to Gov. Nelson, CVSP, II, 230). Thus, when Thomas Smith, Nathan's attorney, applied early in 1782 in behalf of his client, the Council advised that "as Mr. Nathans accounts have been once liquidated and warrants given and the money received they cannot again enter into another settlement of them" (MS Va. Council Jour., 4 Feb. 1782, Vi). This apparently referred to warrants for tobacco issued in June 1780, as noted above, and in consequence Nathan threatened suit against TJ personally; but when Harrison laid TJ's letter of 22 Sep. 1782 before Council, that body authorized assurances to TJ that the state would sustain all expences in the trial of such a suit or in damages recovered as a result of it (same, 2 Oct. 1782, Vi). Smith then applied to Council in what was a virtual admission of Nathan's obstruction of earlier proceedings: "Notwithstanding his former imprudence," Smith expressed the hope that the Council would "throw aside the prejudices against this unfortunate man, altho' a Jew, and afford him relief, for the sake of his innocent family &c." (30 Nov. 1782, CVSP, III, 370). This was in support of a memorial that Nathan had sent to the Governor and Council through the delegates in Congress (22 Oct. 1782; same, 352). On these proceedings, Harrison commented: "if Mr. Nathan had not formerly put a Stop to a similar proposition of his for a reference his balance would have been long since paid"; he admitted that TJ had given acceptances for the bills "to be discharged in hard money" but he added "we have every reason to think it never was intended by Gen: Clarke that they should be paid in it as he Expressly tells us that all his Bills drawn [on] the Treasurer or Governor . . . were for paper money, and to be accounted for and paid in it according to a scale of depreciation which he sent us" (Harrison to the Virginia delegates, 2 Nov. 1782, *Official Letters*, III, 362). At the same time Harrison advised the commissioners appointed to study western accounts to investigate the whole matter: "there is just cause to suspect the goods were bought for depreciated money, and that some Advantage has been taken of the drawers either thro' Ignorance of the method of drawing Bills or from some other cause not known to us. . . . Nathan is so extremely pressing that I think he is conscious of the unjustness of his demand and hopes to worry me into payment before your report reaches me" (4 Nov. 1782, same, III, 368).

Nathan appeared in Richmond in Dec. 1782 to press his memorial (Burnett, *Letters of Members*, VI, No. 695, note 5) and the Governor and Council decided to offer "the same Terms of arbitration . . . that were formerly proposed by our Delegates in Congress, which are that you [Nathan] shall make choice of a Gentleman learned in the law, and the Executive of another, to settle the dispute and if they can not agree that they shall chuse an umpire" (Harrison to Nathan, 24 Dec. 1782, *Official Letters*, III, 411). Again Nathan agreed. Harrison informed the delegates in Congress and asked them to proceed, otherwise "the acceptance of the Bills will . . . be looked on as binding the State which from what I have heard will not be doing it Justice" (Harrison to the Virginia delegates, 4 Jan. 1783, same, III, 421). A week later he forwarded "such papers as are necessary respecting the arbitration with Mr. Nathan. I have no other directions to give but to request you to persue the same methods for having the Matter adjusted as were proposed by Governor Jefferson" (Harrison to the Virginia delegates, 11 Jan. 1783, same, III, 425). These communications were received later that month and arbitration proceedings were begun. Unhappily, Harrison's letter transmitting the necessary papers had made one crucial omission: the clerk of Council left out an authenticated copy of the statement by Todd and Clark concerning the scale of depreciation. Harrison did not discover the omission for a month. He then sent it off to the delegates in haste, hoping that it would arrive "in Time to prevent his [Nathan's] obtaining an award in his favor which appears to me manifestly unjust. Surely the arbitrators will never proceed to a final settlement without a Paper of such Consequence which they are assured is being and will soon be sent them" (Harrison to the Virginia delegates, 15 Feb. 1783, same, III, 451). But it was too late. The delegates and Nathan had referred the matter to Joseph Reed and William Bradford, Jr., agreeing that the award should be final and binding on both parties. Nathan had entered into bond in the amount of £30,000, but the delegates refused to do this "on their part, thinking the faith of the State, plighted by them, a sufficient security." And on 17 Feb. 1783, before the letter from Harrison with the missing document had got fairly on its way, the arbitrators made their award. They found that the bills drawn on the Governor or treasurer of Virginia "were negotiated at New Orleans, at specie value . . . that none (as far as we can learn) were negotiated at that place at a depreciated value"; and that "the acceptance of the bills, is binding both in law and equity on the Executive . . . and that they ought to be discharged accordingly" (text of award, dated Philadelphia, 17 Feb. 1783, in JHD, May 1783, 1828 edn., p. 75).

Despite the terms of the award, Nathan endeavored to collect his balance through the Virginia delegates. "It appears to me astonishing that Nathan should give you so much trouble," Harrison wrote the delegates on 19 Apr. 1783, "when he must know his

Debt can be paid no where but at this Place. This his Agent has been told, and that there are no funds as yet established for that Purpose. I shall lay the Award of the Arbitrators before the next Assembly, who will no doubt provide for the payment" (Executive Letter Book, Vi). This Harrison did in a letter to the Speaker of the House on 5 May 1783, giving a history of the affair and explaining why the matter had been submitted for arbitration. The Executive, he said, "to give him [Nathan] as little Trouble as possible, and to avoid all complaints of partiality . . . proposed the Arbitrators should be chosen in Philadelphia, which Nathan at first refused, but seeing he could obtain Payment no other way, he at length came into the Proposal and the dispute was settled accordingly, tho' I can not say to my satisfaction, as the award turned on the Governor's acceptance and the deposition of Mr. Oliver Pollock, who swore that his Bills that were of a similar nature were paid by the Assembly for the Honor of the State. Tho' I am dissatisfied with the Award yet I think we are now bound to pay it" (Harrison to Speaker, 5 May 1783, Executive Letter Book, Vi; Harrison had told the delegates in his letter of 19 Apr. 1783 that he regarded Pollock as "at least the most imprudent Man in the world" since he had continued to take up bills of exchange after Todd had warned him they were drawn by adventurers for private purposes; the letter from the commissioners appointed to settle western debts on which this observation was based was transmitted by Harrison in his letter to the Speaker of 5 May 1783). The House of Delegates appointed a committee to consider the entire matter; the list of bills and values made by TJ, the scale of depreciation set by Todd and Clark, the opinions of Pendleton and Wythe, and the award of Reed and Bradford were all reviewed and set forth in the committee's report; and the committee recommended that the balance due Nathan ought to be paid with interest at 6 per cent from 8 June 1780 "agreeably to the resolution of the Executive of this State" (JHD, May 1783, 1828 edn., p. 75). This recommendation was rejected by the House. Instead a resolution was adopted calling for another arbitration by "any two gentlemen in the State of Maryland" who were to have power to make a final determination "according to the principles of law and equity"; Nathan was required to enter into bond in the sum of £15,000 to abide by the award (same, p. 82). James Madison, who had helped arrange the arbitration, thought that this reversal of the award might "be just in itself," but told Randolph that "it will require all your eloquence I fear to shield the honor of the State from its effects. The Agency which the Delegation had in the affair will impart no small share of the mortification to them. I suppose the feelings of Mr. Jefferson and Mr. Harrison also will not be much delighted by it" (Madison to Randolph, 8 July 1783; *Writings*, ed. Hunt, II, 1). Randolph looked upon his assignment as one "to prop the reputation of Virginia for good faith and to submit to hear just and copious reproaches thrown upon her." After the first argument, he admitted that TJ's "assumpsit and the subsequent delay [in renouncing the assumpsit] are indeed thorns in the path," but concluded that "if right could be made to prevail" he should expect an award in favor of the state. He also informed Madison that Nathan's accounts had "been the subject of much vehemence in the Assembly" (Randolph to Madison, 28 June, 23 Aug. 1783, Madison Papers, DLC).

Though Harrison had agreed with the opinion expressed by TJ in the present letter that the award of the arbitrators was binding, he acted with his usual promptness by laying the resolution of 24 June before Council as soon as it was approved by the Senate. The Council named Daniel Dulany of Annapolis to act for the state, and Harrison invited him to serve, setting the time and place for the arbitration at Baltimore on 10 Aug. 1783 (MS Va. Council Jour., 27 June 1783, Vi; Harrison to Dulany, 9 July 1783, Executive Letter Book, Vi). Randolph, who was required to attend the meeting of the arbitrators, sent off his express to TJ for additional evidence; presumably the present letter was introduced in evidence at the meeting in Baltimore.

That meeting, however, did not suffice to conclude the business and the arbitrators adjourned to meet in Alexandria in December (MS Va. Council Jour., 22 Oct. and 11 Dec. 1783, Vi). Apparently the second meeting was no more fruitful. Nor is the ultimate outcome known. Five years later Leighton Wood, solicitor, asked Gov. Randolph for directions about a bill of exchange for 10,000 livres not previously accounted for by Nathan in his claims against the public, stating that in the absence of such instructions he would have to place this bill "to the Debit of Mr. Nathan's claim against the Commonwealth for sundry Western accepted bills" (Wood to Randolph, 30 Sep. 1788, CVSP, IV, 492), a statement indicating that the claims were still outstanding. In at least one respect Nathan's claim seems to have been valid: one of the drafts given Nathan on Penet & Co. in 1780 (see Vol. 3:322-3) for 15,000 livres was paid over to John Donaldson; it was then protested and Donaldson brought suit against Nathan, in which he was given judgment and "received full satisfaction"; in 1791 the agent of the creditors of Nathan petitioned the Governor and Council for the principal, with costs, damages, and interest (8 Feb. 1791, William Alexander to Governor and Council, CVSP, v, 259). The remark made by Gov. Harrison in connection with the case of the unfortunate Oliver Pollock is equally applicable to the history of the Nathan affair: "a difficulty arises as no part of a note can with security be paid till the Assembly shall please to determine whether the Notes shall be taken up according to the tenor of them, or at a depreciation. If the latter should be thought right, a general system should be formed, that the holders of the Notes may have equal justice done them" (Harrison to the Speaker of the House, 18 Oct. 1784, Executive Letter Book, Vi; same, 24 July 1783, 20 Oct. 1783, 29 May 1784).

To Philip Turpin

DEAR SIR   Monticello July 29. 1783

I have considered the circumstances of your present situation as stated in the papers you have been pleased to communicate to me and will proceed to give you my thoughts on them as clearly as I am able.[1] I shall take the following facts as the ground of my opinion. That previous to the present revolution you had gone to Gr. Britain to qualify yourself for the exercise of the medical profession in your own country: that before you had compleated your course of studies, hostilities were commenced between the two nations: that having visited and attended the medical institutions at Paris[2] you returned to London in the spring of 1776 in order to procure a passage to Virga.: that in the mean time all remittances from hence having been cut off, you retired into the country and lived on the charity of your friends 15 months in daily hopes of receiving some supply which might enable you to pay your debts and to defray your passage to your own country: that this hope failing you went again to London in the fall of 1777. to sollicit some merchants there acquainted with yourself and your connections for as much money as would bring you over: that such were their doubts of American affairs that they would give you no assistance: that in this situation, destitute of every resource but that of your profession from the known difficulties which a young hand and a stranger encounters in getting into Medical business on shore, you were constrained to take a birth in one of the enemy's ships, not only for the purpose of present subsistence but that also of saving something to pay your passage home: that to render this act as innocent as possible, you took your stand on board a stationed ship: that having continued in the exercise of your profession there till you thought you had saved money enough to bring you home, you resigned your employment and repaired to London to procure your passage: that having waited there six months,[3] and being prevented getting a passage by the embargoes which took place on the rupture with Spain, your savings being nearly expended you found it necessary to return again to your birth on board ship, where you continued till the ensuing spring: that you then went to London again and got a passage to N. York on board a transport on condition of serving to that port as surgeon of the ship: that the ship deviated from her course and went to Chas. T. [Charleston] where as soon as you were landed you endeavored by advertisement in the public papers and otherwise to procure a surgeon as a substitute to perform your engagements to the port of N.Y. meaning to ask permission to come on directly to your own country: that being unable to procure a substitute you attended your ship to N.Y. and took the 1st opportunity that occured of coming from thence to Virga.:[4] that this was in July 1781 on board of a store ship and immediately on your arrival in Virga. by yourself and your friends you sollicited of Ld. Cornwallis leave to pass his lines, he being with his army then in this state, and American affairs in a more desperate condition than they had been since the winter of 1776: that you were refused such leave and being unable otherwise to get quarters or to draw subsistence you undertook to assist in the hospital department, in which situation you were when that army surrendered: that you immediately communicated your case to Govr. Nelson, who satisfied with what you had done, and that you were not to be considered as a subject of exchange, gave you a passport to return to your friends: that during the whole course of these transactions you manifested repeatedly and uniformly your firm attachment to the cause of your country, your desire to rejoin it and that it was solely to effect this that you took the preceding measures. These are the facts which are either proved by your papers or rendered probable by your known situation, and to my mind certain by your own assertions. I find in the whole train of them but a single one capable of bearing a hostile construction, that is your undertaking to act in the military hospitals of the enemy. As it is the intention alone which constitutes the criminality of any act, the question is simplified into this form by the Law, viz. Quo animo did you undertake that office? Forster 202. 208. Was it with a criminal purpose, with hostile views of subjugating your own country, or only under the urgency of absolute necessity, when you had no other resource to procure present subsistence, no other means of paving the way for regaining your own country? This question is answered by the facts previously stated, every one of which was bottomed on a desire to get home again. Many are the circumstances of necessity, moral as well as physical, which excuse in law an act otherwise criminal. Force or fear will justify the furnishing an enemy with provisions, with money, with arms, ammunition &c. This has been the predicament of a great part of the citizens of America. They will in like manner justify the joining an enemy and bearing arms against one's country. Forster 216. This was the case of our citizens taken captive on the high seas. The peculiarities in the late war have produced many new and trying cases which cannot possibly be solved by reference to others exactly similar, nor otherwise than by a liberal extension of former principles and of the reasons on which these principles were founded. Thus the law having decided the foregoing exculpations expressly on the principle that the will must be criminal as well as the act, that the act is culpable only so far as it is a means to effectuate some wicked purpose of the heart (Forster 203) we are safe in bringing under the protection of this principle every case where the *act* and the *purpose* did not concur. We may then consistently with the reason of the law lay down another rule that it is justifiable to deceive an enemy by appearing to take sides with him in order to obtain an opportunity of escaping to our friends. It is only necessary in this case that the first safe opportunity be embraced and every demonstration given of our real[5] purpose which circumstances will admit. This was the predicament of our soldiers taken in Ft. Washington, on Long isld., in Chastown &c. They enlisted very generally with the enemy purposing it as a means of procuring their escape. They actually bore arms against us on many occasions before an opportunity of escape occurred. Many of those taken at Ft. Washington and on other occasions early in the war having been kept either on board ships or in Long Isld. or Staten isld. could not get from the enemy till they came to Virginia with Genl. Arnold. Upwards of 200 of these then deserted. They told their cases honestly,[6] were received into the bosom of their country and are enjoying in tranquillity the advantages of the revolution in common with their fellow citizens. But must the garrisons of Ft. Washington, of Chas. t. &c. be now driven from their country? I consider your case as more nearly parallel with theirs than with any other which has come within my knolege. You like them were a captive; that is you were within the power of the enemy and effectually imprisoned by not having the means of crossing that barrier which nature had placed between them and us, and if you could have crossed that, then without the power of getting out of the lines of their armies here. Thus we know that Mr. Griffin who had money to bring him across the sea, was detained in N. York 4. months before he could get leave to come out and yourself, after having got across the sea were absolutely refused that leave altogether.[5] It is true you were not confined to particular limits within the island of Grt. Britain as the souldiers were in those places where they were held in captivity; but then you had not like them the advantage of a present subsistence from the enemy, and a right to call on your country for an exchange in your turn. You were to get back as you could, or never to get back. They received from the enemy bounty money, pay, clothing and subsistence, bore arms, did guard duty, and often were in action against us; whereas your office was only that of administering medecine to sick and wounded individuals; an office as inoffensive as any one you could have exercised with them, and of much less hostile appearance than that of arraying yourself in arms with the enemies of your country. If therefore the necessities which drove you to this measure should appear less pungent to some than those which operated on the poor souldiers, it should be taken into account also that the measure you adopted was less injurious, less hostile, more innocent: that your plan of escape was by saving the lives of enemies while theirs was that of taking away the lives of their countrymen. The office of surgeon has been considered as on a footing with that of chaplain, and the administering of medecine to be as inoffensive as giving religious instruction to those with whom we are contending. Had any of our surgeons in Chs. town dressed the wounds of those of our enemies who were carried from the Cowpens or the Utaws no liberal mind would have censured them. Instances are not wanting of medical relief and refreshments for the sick sent to an enemy's camp. Yet this was never considered, in the officer who sent it, as an act of infidelity to his country: but rather of magnanimity. In the MSS. records of Congress is a letter from Sr. G. Carlton to Genl. Washington stating that the practice which had prevailed in the American war of considering Chaplains and Surgeons as prisoners of war was against the modern usage of nations and proposing it should be discontinued. To which proposition Genl. Washington answered that the matter had been remedied as to chaplains at a former conference and that as to Surgeons it should be treated of at the interview they were then proposing. What was the result I did not learn. But I mention it to shew the inoffensive light in which the office of a surgeon is viewed, and that his duties like those of the chaplain are rather religious than military, rather of humanity than hostility. On the principles of general law then I think your conduct was justifiable: nor do I find any act of assembly previous to Oct. 1782 which has changed the law as to this point. It is suggested that an act which passed then may perhaps have affected your case. I have not seen the act, as those laws have never yet reached this part of the country. But as the Governor's proclamation of the 2d. inst. is probably founded on that act I will venture to suppose it has adopted its descriptions precisely. Now these descriptions are 1. of Voluntary refugees since Apr. 1775. 2. Exiles since the same period. 3. Natives who have at any time borne arms with the enemy against this Commonwealth. The latter[7] description, if any can, must be applied to you. But I apprehend that cannot, because it must certainly mean a criminal and not an innocent bearing of arms. It must mean to describe the case of those natives who, preferring the cause of the enemy to that of their country, took arms on the other side with the nefarious purpose of subjugating it, those in other words in whom as the law expresses it both the overt act and the purpose concurred, for the purpose must concur to render the act criminal. Neither the law nor the proclamation could wish to comprehend and banish the souldiers already mentioned because tho' they bore arms it was not with the wicked purpose of subduing their country, but with the justifiable one of procuring an opportunity to rejoin it. Still less can it be intended for you, because while your purpose was equally with theirs to rejoin your country, you did not like them actually bear arms against it. Should the expression 'bearing arms' be extended not only to those who literally bore arms tho' with an innocent intention as was the case of those souldiers but by construction to those also who with equal innocence rendered any other service, it must sweep off a number of our very good citizens who under the operation of their fears furnished the enemy while here with provisions, transported their baggage, their ammunition, their sick &c., served them as guides, and did many other acts of service to them. I must conclude then that it cannot involve you. I have the more confidence in my opinion because it is not recently formed but was the result of enquiry and consultation on a former occasion when the parties concerned were merely indifferent and no principles of private friendship were operating to warp my judgment. It was formed at a time when I could not possibly foresee that I should have occasion to apply it to the case of one whose talents and merit I respect and who standing acquitted in my mind of ever having entertained an unfriendly wish to a cause which I have loved and fostered from it's earliest to it's latest day I feel myself justified in unreserved professions of that sincere esteem with which I have the honour to be Dr. Sir your affte frd & servt.

P.S. I have closed my letter a little too hastily having omitted to apply the treaty of peace to this case. By the 6th. article of the treaty we have stipulated 'that no prosecutions should be commenced against any person for the part they have taken in the present war and that no person shall on that account suffer any future loss or damage either in his person liberty or property' &c. But loss or damage in every one of these points must ensue this proclamation if applied to you. To your property if you obey it, and to your person and liberty if you disobey it. This treaty is made in pursuance of powers given to our Commissioners by Congress; these powers were given by Congress in pursuance of authorities vested in them by the Confederation; the Confederation is a convention between all the states, not liable to be altered or repealed by any one of them but by such act as would in itself be a declaration of war, and of course it is of superior authority to any act of assembly. If it be objected that the treaty is only provisional, and not yet obligatory, it may be answered that the obligatory instrument may be expected every hour, that it would be beneath the dignity of a state to order out persons who may the next day return in defiance of it; and that when the articles of a compact are settled and ratified between two nations and nothing but the ceremonial of signature wanting, to be proceeding in direct contradiction to them, is neither consistent with the faith of an honest individual nor favourable to the character of a nation which has that character to establish, or (I wish I were not obliged to say) to retrieve.

Dft (DLC); written on four sheets of paper of varying size, some of which contain other writing; much corrected and interlined. Tr (photostat furnished by the late Dr. Maude Woodfin of Richmond, from an original whose location is unknown); this was evidently a contemporary copy and must have been made from the now missing RC. Tr has been useful in confirming illegible and semi-legible readings in Dft; it varies only slightly from Dft as corrected except that it lacks the postscript. A few of the deleted passages in Dft are recorded in the notes below.

On Philip Turpin see note to TJ to Thomas Turpin, 2 Feb. 1769, where it is erroneously stated that Philip Turpin went to Edinburgh to study law; as the present letter shows, his object was to study medicine (Turpin's petition, referred to below, states "that when your petitioner was of a tender age and previous to the revolution he was sent by his father to Great Britain to finish his education and qualify himself for the exercise of the medical profession in his native country"). He is included as M.D., 1774, in Lewis' "List of the American Graduates in Medicine in the University of Edinburgh," *New Engl. Hist. & Geneal. Reg.*, XLII (1888), 160. The ACT OF . . . OCT. 1782 was "to prohibit intercourse with, and the admission of British subjects into this state" (Hening, XI, 136-8); the GOVERNOR'S PROCLAMATION was issued as a result of the suspension of hostilities and "an abuse of . . . indulgences . . . [by] many evil disposed persons still obnoxious to the laws of this Commonwealth" (MS Va. Council Jour., 2 July 1783, Vi; a copy is in DLC: TJ Papers,

9: 1499-1503). At the surrender of Yorktown some thirty-six individuals were taken, "there being just cause to suspect that all . . . are disaffected to the Independence of the American states and attached to their enemies"; among these were such well-known Loyalists as William Skinner and Joseph Shoemaker. They were turned over to the public jailer at Yorktown by Gov. Nelson; Turpin was not among them (for the list of names of those taken and proceedings against them, see MS Va. Council Jour., 4 and 17 Dec. 1781; 11 Jan. 1782; 1 Mch. 1782).

THE PAPERS that Turpin showed TJ may have included testimonials that were prepared for presentation to the Governor and Council. These included: (1) a letter to Turpin from John Harris, London, 8 May 1783, who had been with Turpin at the surrender of Yorktown and who was "uneasy on Account of the Singular Predicament You was in when we were taken Prisoners"; Harris assured Turpin that he himself had taken every opportunity in Virginia to inform men of rank that "You came to Virginia a warm Friend to Your Country and with an Anxious Expectation of immediately returning to your Friends, and that you accepted of a Place in the Hospital only till such time as you should be able to get up the Country"; (2) a letter from Charles Scott to Gov. Harrison, Powhatan, 11 July 1783; as one taken prisoner at the fall of Charleston on 12 May 1780, Scott was there when Turpin, "some time in the Spring 81 . . . Came a Shore to my Quarters with Every Mark of Joy and Satisfaction that he had once more Put his foot on the American

Shore"; Scott testified that Turpin was extremely anxious to accompany him to Virginia but that he could "by no means get Discharged from the Ship that he had come over in . . . untill he had procured a person to fill his office"; that one of the reasons actuating Turpin was his disinclination to part with his medical books which he felt he could never replace, though he said that he would give them up rather than lose the opportunity to return to Virginia; and that he had carried several letters from Turpin to friends in Virginia in which he had so warmly expressed his loyalty to America that Scott felt it necessary to advise him to be more discreet; (3) a letter from Peterfield Trent to Gov. Harrison, dated at Weir Hall, 12 July 1783, in which Trent affirmed that he had been asked by Turpin to appear at the Council meeting on 14 July 1783 since Turpin had stated that the Governor regarded him as being comprehended under the proclamation of 2 July; that he had received some "15 or 20 Letters" written by Turpin from England throughout the war in which he had urged "Americans not to give up their Rights and not to have any Divisions in their Councills"; that he knew Turpin had remained in England because of debts contracted there; that Turpin had written him from Charleston (presumably one of the letters carried back by Gen. Scott) saying "he was detained by the Enemy, but would leave them when in his power"; and that when Trent was "detained in York" before the surrender he had roomed with Turpin and heard him "enter into Arguments in favor of America with such warmth that some other Doctors said he was as great a Rebel as myself, or any other American" (this letter was sworn to before George Woodson, justice of the peace for Chesterfield, 13 July 1783); and (4) an undated letter from Alexander Trent, Jr., to Gov. Harrison stating that he had parted from Turpin in England in 1778; that Turpin had assured him he was "acting as Surgeon on board a ship for present subsistence, and with a view of acquiring by this means wherewith to support him to America"; and that his "situation on board appear'd very distressing as he was considered as a Reble and frequently call'd by that Epithet" (all of the foregoing are in Vi; the Trents are thought to have been related to the

Turpins and Jeffersons, VMHB, XXXIV [1926], p. 367.

There is nothing in the journal of the Council to show that Turpin appeared on 14 July 1783 or subsequently. But his petition to the "Speaker and Gentlemen of the House of Delegates" was read in the House on 5 Dec. 1783 and referred to the committee on propositions and grievances (JHD, Oct. 1783, 1828 edn., p. 48). This petition is in an unidentified hand, but it is, with some exceptions, a literal copy of that part of TJ's present letter which consists of a statement of the facts in the case. Among these exceptions were the following: (1) the statement about Turpin's having lived off the "charity of . . . friends 15 months" was altered to "a considerable time"; (2) the passage about returning to London in "the fall of 1777" and soliciting merchants was omitted; (3) the assertion that he took a berth in "one of the enemy's ships" was changed to "a ship bound for New York on condition of serving to that post as surgeon but the ship deviating from her course went to Charles Town," this elliptical statement omitting all of the matter in the corresponding passage of the present letter; (4) the statement that, on Cornwallis' refusing a pass, Turpin "undertook to assist in the hospital department" was changed to show that the pass "was refused and your petitioner compelled to serve in the hospital department"; and (5) that part following an account of Nelson's issuing a passport contained the additional passage: "he remained in quiet until it was suggested to him (to his very great astonishment) that he came within the description of the Governour's Proclamation." The petition concluded with the hope that, since Turpin could prove a "steady attachment to the liberty and independence of his native country," the legislature would admit him to the full enjoyment of citizenship (Vi).

There are no serious contradictions in the documents here involved, but it is equally certain that less information was presented in the petition than had been gathered for presentation to the Governor and Council. The most conspicuous difference between the petition and the other documents (including the present letter from TJ) is that the former is so vague about dates and so careful to eliminate all specific references to dates or to periods of time elapsed as to suggest that this was purposeful. The same is true of the deletions in TJ's rough draft, though to a lesser extent (see note 3, for example). This, together with the obvious fact of TJ's unusual care in drafting the letter to Turpin, leads to the conclusion that TJ was engaged in making a case for his kinsman that the situation may not have warranted in a strict legal sense, in spite of Turpin's evident loyalty. For, on a reconstruction of the chronology from various documents involved, the following is apparent: Turpin finished his studies in Edinburgh, went to Paris, and returned to London by the spring of 1776. For fifteen months, until the fall of 1777, he lived in the country with friends. He then took a berth on the stationed ship and served until April 1779. Next he went to London to procure passage, remaining there for six months (or until Sep. 1779). Then he returned to the stationed ship and served until the spring of 1780. Then he returned to London again "and got a passage to N. York on board a transport" but the "ship deviated" and went to Charleston instead. The last statement, which probably explains why TJ deleted the time sequence noted below (note 3), overlooks a stay of almost a year in London, from the spring of 1780 to the spring of 1781.

Several questions occur: (1) why, in 1776, when it was obvious that the difficulties between England and the colonies had already led to open hostilities, should Turpin have returned from Paris to London in order to obtain passage home? Remittances that were due could have reached him in Paris perhaps more readily than in London. (2) If Alexander Trent, a brother of Peterfield Trent who was obligated to send these remittances, could have left England in 1778, why could not Turpin have done so (Alexander Trent's testimonial, cited above, begins: "Previous to my leaving England in 78 I frequently saw and convers'd with Dr. Turpin on the Affairs of America")? (3) Why should Turpin have failed to point out in his petition that he had spent six months in London in 1779 and a whole year from 1780 to 1781 when he was *not* serving on the ship "bound for New York"? The conclusion is inescapable that, if Turpin had not had some other reason for remaining in London, these obviously purposeful omissions in chronology would not have been apparent in the various documents. That other rea-

son, whatever it was, must not have touched his political views toward his native land; but it is equally apparent that if he had been as intent on returning as were Alexander Trent and others of his countrymen, he could have done so. At all events, the evidence of Turpin's loyalty to America was persuasive and the committee reported favorably on 13 Dec. 1783. An Act granting him, John Wormeley, and Presley Thornton full citizenship was passed (JHD, Oct. 1783, 1828 edn., p. 59-60; Hening, XI, 316). That part of the Act respecting Wormeley was qualified. He was born in Virginia but he had served in the British army during the war and had informed Council of his arrival in the state in May; that body, though conceding that he was "not literally a traitor," yet thought he stood "in a higher degree of criminality than the subjects of England in general do," and forbade his being admitted until authorized by law (MS Va. Council Jour., 17 May 1783; copy and press copy from it are in DLC: TJ Papers, 9: 1482-4). On 23 May the Council reconsidered and granted Wormeley permission to remain " 'till further orders"; this permission, however, was canceled on 2 July when the Council received letters from a number of British subjects "announcing their arrival . . . and intention of remaining for the purpose of carrying on trade, and collecting their debts before the War" (MS Va. Council Jour., 23 May and 2 July 1783; copy and press copy of each are in DLC: TJ Papers, 9: 1485, 1496). The status of CHAPLAINS AND SURGEONS was discussed in Sir Guy Carleton's letter of 7 July 1782 to Washington and in Washington's reply of 18 Aug. 1782 (Washington, *Writings*, ed. Fitzpatrick, XXV, 38).

TJ's argument on the treaty had the concurrence of Attorney General Edmund Randolph, who expressed the opinion to Madison that the proclamation of 2 July "carries the disagreeable idea, that the executive have adopted the spirit of the resolutions of the committees to the northward, who act as if the treaty were within their power of appeal" (Randolph to Madison, 12 July 1783, DLC: Madison Papers). Randolph also pointed out that the proclamation "draws forth every hour men, who seemed to have fixed themselves in all the rights of citizenship, to supplicate a little time, until they can arrange their domestic affairs. Among these is a doctor Turpin, the possessor of the most valuable lots for the purposes of government within the city. He is a native, was taken at York with a medical commission, as I am told, in his pocket, and has been suffered to remain here without interruption ever since. . . . But much toleration is due to those, who merely to avoid famine, to the danger of which they have been subjected by the prosecution of their studies, and to gain a fair opportunity of coming to his native country, have submitted to enter into the british service" (same to same, 18 July 1783, DLC: Madison Papers). A month later Randolph reported: "The governors proclamation expelling the obnoxious adherents to British interests, continues to give great disquiet to the friends of those, who fall within that description. Mr. Jefferson has taken Dr. Turpin by the hand, and in a long letter to him attempted to shew, that his case belongs not to the offensive class. . . . From these facts [as set forth in TJ's letter respecting Turpin's case], Tenderness is due Turpin. But I cannot admit, that the necessities of that gentleman would protect him from the operation of the law as it now stands; because they do not seem to have been incapable of being supplied thro channels which were not hostile. Mr. J. doubts whether surgeons ought to be ranked among the instruments of hostility, and refers to a proposition from Carlton to consider them as exempt from the rights of war. But I believe that he might find more examples than one of a surgeon being executed for treason in joining the king's enemies" (same to same, 23 Aug. 1783, DLC: Madison Papers).

[1] The following passage is deleted in Dft: "In doing this I shall be obliged to hazard something because not being possessed of a complete collection of the acts and resolutions of assembly, some of these may escape me which should have their weight. These laws too are in a state of much confusion, the first passed on the subject having been amended from time to time and this not on a general and comprehensive view of the subject, but merely to remedy particular cases as these happened to arise."

[2] Deleted in Dft: "for the same purpose of qualifying yourself as a Physician."

[3] Deleted in Dft: "from April to Sep. 1779."

[4] Deleted in Dft: "that you landed at Norfolk."

[5] Preceding three words supplied from Tr.

[6] Deleted in Dft: "to the executive, who far from conceiving them as unfaithful to their country gave them."

[7] Tr reads, more correctly: "last."

From James Madison

My dear Sir   Philada. Aug. 11th. 1783.

At the date of my letter in April I expected to have had the pleasure by this time of being with you in Virginia. My disappointment has proceeded from several dilatory circumstances on which I had not calculated. [One[1] of them was the uncertain state into which the object I was then pursuing has been brought by one of those incidents to which such affairs are liable. The result has rendered the time [of] my return to Virga. less material, as the necessity of my visiting the State of N.Jy:[2] no longer exists. It would be improper by this communication to send particular explanations, and perhaps needless to [trou]ble you with them at any time. An [. . .] is in general [. . .] impediment of [. . .][3] for a profession of indifference at what has happened [. . .] by some more propitious turn of fate.] My journey to Virga. tho' still somewhat contingent in point of time cannot now be very long postponed. I need not I trust renew my assurances that it will not finally stop on this side of Monticello.

The reserve of our foreign ministers still leaves us the sport of misinformations concerning the definitive Treaty. We all thought a little time ago that it had certainly arrived at N. York. This opinion however has become extinct, and we are thrown back on the newspaper evidence which as usual is full of contradictions. The probability seems to be that the delay arises from discussions with the Dutch. Mr. Dana has been sorely disappointed in the event of his announcing himself to the Court of Russia.[4] His written communications obtain verbal answers only and these hold up the Mediation to which the Empress with the Emperor of G——y have been invited as a bar to any overt transaction with the U.S. and even suggest the necessity of new powers from the latter of a date subsequent to the acknowledgment of their sovereignty by G.B. Having not seen the letters from Mr. Dana myself, I give this idea of them at second hand, remarking at the same time that it has been taken from such passages only as were not in Cypher; the latter being not yet translated. Congress remain at Princeton utterly undecided both as to their ultimate seat and their intermediate residence. Very little business of moment has been yet done at the new metropolis, except a ratification of the Treaty with Sweden. In particular nothing been done as to a foreign establishment. With regard to an internal peace establishment, though it has been treated with less inattention, it has undergone little discussion. The Commander-in-chief has been invited to Princeton with a view to obtain his advice and sanction to the military branches of it, and is every day expected [t]here. The Budget of Congress is likely to have the fate of many of their other propositions to the States. Delaware is the only one among those which have bestowed a consideration on it that has acceded in toto. Several Legislatures have adjourned without giving even that mark of their [co]ndescension. In the Southern States a jealousy of Congressional usurpations is likely to be the bane of the system: in the Eastern an aversion to the half pay provided for by it. New Jersey and Maryland have adopted the impost, the other funds recommended being passed for one year only by one of these States, and postponed by the other. Pa. has hitherto been friendly to liberal and fœderal ideas and will continue so, unless the late jar with Congress should give a wrong bias of which there is some danger. Massts. has in the election of Delegates for the ensuing year stigmatized the concurrence of those now in place, in the provision for half-pay, by sub-stituting a new representation; and has sent a Memorial to Con-gress which I am told is pregnant with the most penurious ideas not only on that subject but on several others which concern the national honor and dignity. This picture of our affairs is not a flattering one; but we have been witnesses of so many cases in which evils and errors have been the parents of their own remedy, that we cannot but view it with the consolations of hope. Remind Miss Patsy of my affection for her and be assured that I am Dr Sir Yr. Sincere friend,   J. MADISON Jr.

RC (DLC: Madison Papers); en-dorsed by Madison with his name and date after the letter was returned to him. The text was deliberately muti-lated by him in old age in order to ob-scure the reference to Catherine Floyd.

1 The passage within brackets (sup-plied) was heavily scored out by Madi-son. For an account of the failure of Madison's romance, see Brant, *Madi-son*, II, 283-7, with a facsimile of the page containing the present passage. Catherine Floyd married William Clark-son in 1785.

2 Brant, who gives a partial reading for this passage, construes this to be "New York" (same, II, 286) on the obvious ground that the Floyds lived on Long Island; but the initials seem clearly "N.Jy:" and Madison may have intended only to go thus far, as he did on other occasions.

3 About three lines are missing here.

4 "Russia" was obviously written in by Madison after the letter was re-turned to him, the original reading be-ing "Court of —."

To James Madison

DEAR SIR   Monticello Aug. 31. 1783.

Your favor of July 17. which came to hand long ago remains still unacknoleged, as from the time of it's receipt I had constant hope that you would be on the road for Virginia before an answer could reach you. That of the 11th. inst. I received yesterday, and leaves the time of your visit as unfixed as ever, and excites some fear that I shall miss of you. I propose to set out for Congress about the middle of October, unless they should be returned to Phila-delphia in which case I shall take at home the week I meant other-wise to pass at Philadelphia on my way to Congress. I wish it had been possible for your journey to have been so timed as that your return could have been when I go: for I still suppose you mean to pass the winter there as you told me at a time when it seemed to have no object but that of prosecuting your studies more at leisure. I sincerely lament the misadventure which has happened from whatever cause it may have happened. Should it be final however, the world still presents the same and many other resources of hap-piness, and you possess many within yourself. Firmness of mind and unintermitting occupations will not long leave you in pain. No event has been more contrary to my expectations, and these were founded on what I thought a good knowlege of the ground. But of all machines ours is the most complicated and inexplicable.—Either here or in Philadelphia I must ask a perusal of your Congressional notes with leave to take notes from them, as they will better than any thing else possess me of the business I am to enter on. What is become of the mutineers? What of the Secretaryship of foreign affairs? What of the commercial treaty with Gr. Britain? These and many other questions I hope for the pleasure of having answered by you at Monticello. Be so good as to present my compliments to Mrs. House and Mrs. Trist and to ask whether the pleasure of lodging in their house may be counted among the circumstances which will render Philadelphia agreeable to me in case of the return of Congress thither. Should Congress not return thither, would it be possible for you to engage me a tolerable birth wherever they are? A room to myself, if it be but a barrack, is indispensable. In either event of my being or not being in Philadelphia I propose to place Patsy there; and will ask the favor of Mrs. Trist to think for me on that subject, and to advise me as to the person with whom she may be trusted. Some boarding school of course, tho' I am not without objections to her passing more than the day in such a one.—The want of public occurrences worth detailing has filled my letter you find with private and unimportant subjects. I wish you every possible felicity and am with sincere esteem Dr. Sir Your friend & servt.,   TH: JEFFERSON

RC (DLC: Madison Papers); addressed: "The honble. James Madison of the Virginia delegation in Congress"; endorsed in two or three later hands.

THE SECRETARYSHIP OF FOREIGN AFFAIRS: When Robert R. Livingston determined to resign, late in 1782, he approached Madison and asked him whether he thought TJ would "prefer the vacancy to his foreign appointment"; Madison "answered him in the negative" (Madison to Randolph, 3 Dec. 1782; Burnett, *Letters of Members*, VI, No. 695).

From James Madison

DEAR SIR   Princeton Sepr. 20. 1783.

Your favor of the 31 ult: came to hand yesterday. As the reason which chiefly urged my departure for Virga. has ceased I have been led to protract my attendance on Congress by the interest I felt in some measures on foot, and the particular interest which my Constituents have in them. Two of these were the territorial cession and the permanent seat of Congress. The former was a few days ago put into a form which I hope will meet the ultimatum of Virginia. The first Monday in next month is fixed for a decision of the latter; after which it may still be necessary to choose a temporary residence untill the permanent one can be made ready. I am utterly unable to foretell how either of these points will be determined. It is not impossible that an effective vote may be found attainable on neither; in which case the Winter must be spent in this village where the public business can neither be conveniently done, the members of Congress decently provided for, nor those connected with Congress provided for at all. I shall lose no time in looking out for quarters for you and entering into provisional engagements in your favor. Your other request relative to Miss Patsy shall be equally attended to as soon as I go to Philada. which will probably be towards the end of next week.

It will give me real concern if we should miss one another altogether in the journies before us; and yet I foresee the danger of it. Mr. Jones and myself will probably be on the road by the middle of next month or a few days later. This is the time about which you expect to commence your journey. Unless therefore we travel the same road a disappointment of even an interview will be unavoidable. At present our plan is to proceed thro' Baltimore Alexandria and Fredericksbg. and we may possibly be at the races of the second place. I am at a loss by what regulation I can obey your wishes with regard to the notes I have on hand; having not yet made any copy of them, having no time now for that purpose, and being unwilling for several reasons to leave them all behind me. A disappointment however will be of the less consequence, as they have been much briefer and more interrupted since the period at which you[1] run them over, and have been altogether discontinued since the arrival of Congress here.

My plan of spending this winter in Philada. in close reading was not entirely abandoned untill Congress left that City and shewed an utter disinclination to returning to it. The prospect of agreeable and even instructive society was an original consideration with me; and the subsequent one of having yours added to it would have confirmed my intention after the abortive issue of another plan, had not the solicitude of a tender and infirm parent exacted a visit to Virga. and an uncertainty of returning been thereby incurred. Even at present if Congress should make Philada. their seat this winter and I can decline a visit to Virga. or speedily get away from it my anxiety on the subject will be renewed.

Our last information from Europe is dated the 27th. July.

France and Spain were then ready for the definitive signing of the Peace. Holland was on the point of being so. The American Plenipos. had done nothing on the subject and in case of emergency could only sign the provisional Treaty as final. Their negociations had been spent chiefly on commercial stipulations from which G.B. after very different professions and appearances, altogether drew back. The ready admission she found into our commerce without paying any price for it has suggested the policy of aiming at the entire benefit of it, and at the same time saving the carriage of the W. India trade the price she at first bid for it. The supposed contrariety of interests among the states and the impotence of the fœderal Government are urged by the ministerial pamphleteers as a safeguard against retaliation. The other nations of Europe seem to have more honorable views towards our commerce, sundry advances having been made to our Ministers on that subject.

Congress have come to no decision even as yet on any of the great branches of the peace establishment. The military branch is supported and quickened by the presence of the Commander in chief but without any prospect of a hasty issue. The department of foreign affairs both internal and external remains as it has long done. The election of a Secretary has been an order of the day for many months without a vote being taken. The importance of the marine department has been diminished by the sale of almost all the Vessels belonging to the U.S. The department of Finance is an object of almost daily attack and will be reduced to its crisis on the final resignation of Mr. M. [Morris] which will take place in a few months. The War office is connected with the Military establishment and will be regulated I suppose in conformity to what that may be. Among other subjects which divide Congress, their Constitutional authority touching such an establishment in time of peace is one. Another still more puzzling is the precise jurisdiction proper for Congress within the limits of their permanent seat. As these points may possibly remain undecided till Novr. I mention them particularly that your aid may be prepared. The investigation of the Mutiny ended in the condemnation of several Sergeants who were stimulated to the measure without being apprised of the object by the two officers who escaped. They have all received a pardon from Congress. The real plan and object of the mutiny lies in profound darkness. I have written this in hopes that it may get to Monticello before you leave it. It might have been made more interesting if I had brought the Cypher from Philada. tho' my present situation required a great effort to accomplish as much as

I have. I am obliged to write in a position that scarcely admits the use of any of my limbs: Mr. Jones and myself being lodged in a room not 10 feet square and without a single accommodation for writing.

I am Dear Sir Your sincere friend & obt servt.,

J. MADISON Jr.

RC (DLC: Madison Papers); endorsed with date by Madison at top of last page of text.

A ROOM NOT TEN FEET SQUARE: Madison, a graduate of Princeton, several times mentioned in letters at this period that he and Jones were obliged to share a single bed in extremely cramped quarters; on this date he wrote a brief note to Randolph that "the circumstances which produced brevity in my last [lack of space] as strongly recommended it at present" (Madison, Writings, ed. Hunt, II, 18). Madison's complaint was not unique; for a general description of difficulties encountered in finding space for members of Congress, see V. Lansing Collins, The Continental Congress at Princeton, Princeton, 1908, p. 41-59, 113-36. There is also in DLC: PCC a document dated 13 Oct. 1783, in which the inhabitants of Princeton and vicinity, "desirous to testify their Respect for the supreme Legislature of America and their Wishes for their honouring New Jersey with their Residence, have agreed to furnish the best [accommodations] in their Power . . . for One Year"; the tabulation is headed by the name of President John Witherspoon of the College of New Jersey, who agreed to supply three "Rooms with Fire Places," an equal number of beds, bedding, breakfasts, and tea, and accommodations for "any number" of horses. Some of the inhabitants did "not propose to take Members of Congress but can accommodate Attendants." It was also stipulated that "Mr. Lawrence and Coll. Morgan [of Prospect] will undertake to supply the best of Wines at the most reasonable Rates" (photostat in NjP).

¹ As originally phrased, this passage read: "at which you left Philadelphia."

To Thomas Walker

DEAR SIR   Monticello Sep. 25. 1783.

The inclosed are part of some papers I wrote in answer to certain queries sent me by Monsr. de Marbois in 1781. Another foreigner of my acquaintance, now beyond the water, having asked a copy of them, I undertook to revise and correct them in some degree. There are still a great number of facts defective and some probably not to be depended on. Knowing nobody so able as yourself to set me right in them I take the liberty of sending you that part of the answers which I am most anxious to have as accurate as possible, and of asking the favour of you to peruse them with a pen in your hand, noting on a peice of paper as you proceed what facts and observations you think may be corrected, or added to, or should be withdrawn altogether. That part particularly which relates to the positions of Monsr. de Buffon I would wish to have very correct in matters of fact. You will observe in the table of

[339]

animals that the American columns are almost entirely blank. I think you can better furnish me than any body else with the heaviest weights of our animals which I would ask the favour of you to do from the mouse to the mammoth as far as you have known them actually weighed, and where not weighed, you can probably conjecture pretty nearly. It is of no consequence how loose and rough your notes are, as I shall be able to incorporate them into the work and would wish to give you as little trouble as possible. If you could be as pointed as possible as to those circumstances relating to the Indians I should be much obliged to you: as I think it may happen that this may be the subject of further discussions. I fear you will think me too free in giving you trouble and more especially when I further ask the favour of you to get through them by the 4th. of the next month when I shall be returned from a journey I am now setting out on, and shall be preparing for my departure to Philadelphia. I know not what apology to make you unless my necessity be one, and my knowing no body else who can give me equal information on all the points. I am with very great esteem Dr. Sir Your most obedt. humble servt.,

TH: JEFFERSON

RC (DLC: Rives Papers); addressed: Dr. Thomas Walker Castlehill"; endorsed: "Sept. 25 83. Thos. Jefferson [*and in a later hand:*] T. W. Papers to be exd." The enclosure (not found) was, of course, some part of TJ's MS of *Notes on the State of Virginia*.

Walker's reply, if it was a formal letter, has not been found. He may have replied merely by furnishing memoranda. Among the loose notes and memoranda with the MS (MHi) of

Notes on the State of Virginia are notations of the weights of various American animals marked "Dr. Walker" and "W." One of these, in Walker's hand, reads: "I saw certificates in the hand of several reputable officers that a Buck was killed near Presque Isle weighing 273. I have observed Deer near Pittsburg are much larger than they are here and further south are much less." The other FOREIGNER was Chastellux.

Bond to James Currie

Know all men by these presents that I Thomas Jefferson of Albemarle in Virginia am bound unto Dr. James Currie of Richmond in the same state in the full sum of four hundred and thirty one pounds fifteen shillings current money of Virginia to be paid to the said James, his attorney, his executors administrators or assigns: to which paiment I bind myself, my heirs, executors and administrators by these presents, sealed with my seal and dated this 30th. day of September one thousand seven hundred and eighty three.

The Condition of the above obligation is such that, if the above bound Thomas shall pay to the said James, his attorney, his executors, administrators or assigns the sum of two hundred and fifteen pounds seventeen shillings and six pence of like current money as aforesaid whenever the same shall be demanded then the above obligation to be void, or else to remain in full force and virtue.

Sealed & delivered
in presence of
W Short

TH: JEFFERSON

"215-17-6
2
———
431-15."

MS (MHi); entirely in TJ's hand, signed by him, and signed by William Short as witness; endorsed in an unidentified hand: "[B]ond Col. [Thoma]s Jefferson £21[5. 17]. 6. 30th. Septr. 1783"; there is also another endorsement in a different hand. In the margin near the beginning of the text TJ made the following calculation:

TJ's Account Book contains the following entry under this date: "executd. bond to Dr. Currie for £215-17-6 paiable on demand for medical services." On Dr. James Currie of Richmond, see Blanton, *Medicine in Va. in the 18th Cent.*, p. 335-6.

From James Madison

DEAR SIR   Philada. Sepr. 30. 1783.

My last was written on the supposition that Mr. Jones and myself would be on our way to Virga. by the middle of Ocr. and that my best chance of an interview with you might be at Alexandria at the time of the races. On further thought I fear that you may be led by that suggestion to suspend your setting out longer than you proposed, and that I may not find it practicable to leave this place finally before it will be practicable for you to reach it by pursuing your own plan. One circumstance which increases the uncertainty of my movements is a melancholy event in Mr. Jones family which may [a]ffect his plans, to which I shall as far as necessary make mine su[bservi]ent. It will rather therefore be my wish that you should ha[sten] than retard your journey, if it be a matter of indifference to y[o]u tho' not that you should do either if it be not so.

I have laid a train at Princeton which I hope will provide as commodious quarters as could be expected. If these should become necessary in Philada. Mrs. House's disposition towards you will be a sure resource. Mrs. Trist concurs in your idea of a boarding school; that it may be expedient for Miss Patsey for hours of instruction but no farther. She will enquire and think for you on the subject as far as her preparations for a voyage to the Mississippi will admit. She and Mrs. House make a tender of their respectful regards for yourself and Miss Patsey. I have nothing to add to my last on public subjects, nor to the above any thing but that I am Dr. Sir Yr. sincere friend & obt. Servt.,   J. MADISON Jr.

As the latest papers are very barren I inclose a former one containing No. 1. of N. American, leaving the Author to your conjectures.

RC (DLC: Madison Papers); endorsed by TJ: "Madison James of Orange." There is a small tear in MS affecting the text. Enclosure missing.

NO. 1 OF N. AMERICAN: Two papers signed "North American" appeared in the *Pa. Journal, and Weekly Advertiser* for 17 Sep. and 8 Oct. 1783. On the basis of Madison's remark in the present letter to TJ, both Burnett (tentatively) and Brant (positively) ascribe the authorship to Madison himself (Burnett, *Letters of Members*, VII, No. 374, note 3; Brant, *Madison*, II, 302-305). The two articles were reprinted in WMQ, 3rd ser., III (1946), p. 569-587. In general the views coincide with the national sentiments entertained by both Madison and TJ, but the style at times borders on hyperbole and is, as Mr. Brant acknowledges, both declamatory and akin to the "poetic fervor of his early days in the American Whig Society" (*Madison*, II, 302). The editors think an equally good argument could be made for attributing these essays to someone from one of the eastern commercial states (a Philadelphian or a New Yorker) or to someone from one of the small states having no western land claims (Maryland or New Jersey). They feel that the reference in the present letter cannot be accepted unqualifiedly as sufficient basis for establishing Madison's claim to authorship. If Madison was the author, one wonders why he did not enclose North American No. 1 in his letter of 20 Sep. or why he made no reference in the present letter to a forthcoming North American No. 2. The purpose of the author, whoever he was, was "deliberately to investigate and to expose with freedom, the real situation of these States, and in anticipating evil and misfortune, to suggest their remedy."

From Archibald Cary

DEAR SIR   Tuckahoe 12th of October 1783.

I received yours by Doctor Currie but to late to send to Mr. Eppes. I am sorry I have not been more attentive to the Waights of Many Wild Anamals for except a Ber; an elk and several Bucks I never waighd any. I saw in England a Panther sayd to be from the Cost of Gania, and a Wolf sayd to be from Germany both full Grown, and I Can assure you I have seen of both Kinds in Virginia much larger; I Killd a bear, not fat which waighed 410 ℔ after he was Quartered, and have seen much larger but had no opportunaty of Trying their Waight. My largest Elk a doe of 4 Years old waigh'd 83 pr Quarter. The largest buck say Dear[1] I ever Killd waighed 42 pr Quarter, it was in August. They are not Full fatt before November and it was thought had he lived to be so he would have reach'd 48 or 50. He was the largest I ever saw Killd. But I have been Told by Col: Gist he has Killd them about Pittsburg that have waigh'd Upwards of 200, I think one 220.

The same Gentleman Informs me, for I let him see Your letter this last Week, he has seen Elks which he Judged to be 14½ hands high, and one that waighd nigh 600. He waigh'd a Bull Buffalo far from being Fat 1150, has Killd much larger but no oppartunaty of finding their waight.

Our Foxes are not so large as the European, nor do I think [them] the same Anamal, as I am sure our Hair [Hare] is very [. . .]² kitens than once in the summer. When Pursued like the Rabbet of whose Kindred she is takes the First hole she Can find for shelter. She is less than the English hair and of the same sise of their wild Rabbit.

Raccoons and Possams I never heard they had of Either in Europe. The Former is about the sise of their badger and not much unlike him.

I Killd in England a Mink. Ours are in sise and shape the same.

Our Ratts and mice do not differ from the European. We have two Kind of the Former. One a Native, he is Black and smaler. The other Kind have not made their way far from Navigation, but abound nigh where the shiping Come, are Calld the Norway Ratt, and are full as large as Ever I saw in England.

I once saw what is Calld a Hedge hog. It was Killd by one of my Overseers. It resembled in part the English hedg hog but much larger. I am told they are Frequently seen in the Mountains.

We have a small anamal about the sise of our Fox Calld a Moonack. I have killd several, but believe they have none in England. They burrow in the Earth, are rather darker than a Raccoon, and fight very Fierce.

You must have seen the Pole cat.

As to Domestick Anamals, I am fully satisfied we have as large as any to be found, but of the Horse and Ox I wish you to apply to the Northward where being better Farmers they are larger than with us [. . . .] I Imported about 25 Years Agone [. . .] Lancaster Long hornd breed. I have many now Much larger than any Either of the Imported ones but I never had one that reachd 1000, by 20 pound. I have seen as large dogs and Catts as I Ever saw in England and have raisd hounds much larger than I Ever saw there.

The heaviest hog I Ever saw reached 900 but Col: Tucker Killd one the Net weight above 1000.

I have seen several Mules very nigh 15 hands. Sons of Midas. I have a Jack 3 Years old of his Geting which is upwards of 13 hands and will be larger than his Father.

They have in Kent and about the Fens in Linconshire very large sheep much larger than any in Virginia. The heaviest I Ever saw here was 103 fit for Markit. I have frequently Killd them above 90. Have seen Many Imported Rams and have my self raisd larger than any Imported one. But our sheep are in General with the little Care we take much larger than in the North of England, where I have seen Many Thousands, In their Markets that would not waigh above 50.

You observe that our Elk is Taken for the Fallow dear. They are almost as unlike as the Monkey and Fox. Their horns are Totally dissimalar. Their sha[pe] different the Elk much larger. He has [a white?] spot as large almost as a Common hat on his buttock, the Center of which is at the root of his Tail. This is universal amongst them. I have seen a pair of Elks horns 12 points on a beam the Extreem points of which measured 4 Feet from one point to the other and were very nigh five feet in Length. I have heard of Larger.

I do not recollect the ratling of the joints you Mention but you are Exact in Your discription.

You Know General Green. He lately at Ampthill told me he saw an ox of 3 Years old of 1400 wt. I think I have Mensiond all the anamals I am acquainted with and have Given as just an Account of them as I [have] in my Power.

It proceeds from Vanaty in the European Gentlemen who not only think our anamals Less than theirs but assume as Great a superiority to their Minds as they do to the sise of their anamals. Would to heaven we had the same oppartunaty of Cultivating the Mind as they have and I veryly believe we should Exceed them as much as the People of Attaca did those of Beotia. I am Confident, that those of Europe of the Lower Clas are as much Inferior in point of Understanding to the Americans of the same rank as Ever those of Thebes were to the Athenians.

RC (MHi); a fragment at foot of the 4-page folded sheet is torn away, removing bits of the text and the signature. The author has been identified by his handwriting, by his allusion to Ampthill and other internal evidence, and by the fact that TJ cites some of the figures in this letter as Col. Cary's in his rough memoranda for *Notes on Virginia*, among which the letter itself has been preserved. (The identification was first made by Mr. William H. Gaines, Jr., of the Alderman Library, University of Virginia.)

TJ's letter to Cary has not been found. It was probably written about the same time that he wrote to Walker (25 Sep. 1783) on the same subject

and may have been handed to DOCTOR
CURRIE when TJ saw him in Richmond
on 30 Sep. The MOONACK was a
groundhog or woodchuck (OED), called
by TJ "monax" (Ford, III, 140).

1 The preceding two words are interlined.
2 Several words missing or only partly legible.

Benjamin Harrison to the Virginia Delegates in Congress

GENTLEMEN   Octo: 25th. 1783.

I am much disappointed in not receiving a letter from you by
the last post, as we are all anxious to know where Congress means
to fix its permanent residence, reports say it is to be in the woods
near Princeton or on the delaware a little below Trenton. I think
it impossible that either can be true. If I should be mistaken it will
fix this state in an opinion that there is a decided majority against
the southern states, and that they are not to expect that justice
they are entitled to when the interest of the other states shall induce
a deviation from it. Tho' great offers were made Congress to
remove to us yet I never expected a compliance nor would I have
voted for it if not Commanded so to do, as the common principles
of honor would have forbidden it. Maryland is the central state
and there it ought to have been fixed, no great matter in what part
of it tho' George town was certainly the most proper. A sufficient
of members are not yet met to hold the assembly nor do I think
we shall have one before the middle of next week.

I am &c.

FC (Vi); caption reads: "The Virginia Delegates in Congress."
Harrison's "disappointment in not receiving a letter . . . by the last post"
reflects a dissatisfaction that he occasionally voiced, especially with regard
to John F. Mercer's failures as a correspondent. On one occasion he chided
Mercer bluntly and on another, when
the proceedings in Congress on the Virginia cession of western territory were
laid by him before the House of Delegates, he pointedly stated that the
document "this moment came to hand
in a blank cover from Mr. Mercer"
(Harrison to Speaker of the House, 11
Dec. 1783, Executive Letter Book, Vi).
There is no doubt but that Harrison
placed much more value upon TJ's
communications from Congress and
that he approved the plan of regular
correspondence that TJ devised (see

TJ to Harrison, 17 Dec. 1783). GREAT
OFFERS WERE MADE CONGRESS TO RE-
MOVE TO US: On 28 June 1783, the
last day of the session, the General Assembly unanimously adopted resolutions
offering a "fixed place of residence for
Congress" in the following terms: (1)
that if Williamsburg should prove "a
fit Place," the General Assembly would
present "the Palace the Capitol and all
the public buildings and three hundred
acres of land adjoining the . . . city
together with a Sum of money not exceeding one hundred thousand pounds
this States Currency to be paid at five
annual Installments and to be expended
in erecting thirteen Hotels for the Use
of the Delegates in Congress"; (2) that
the General Assembly would cede a
district adjoining Williamsburg not
over "five miles square with such exempt Jurisdiction . . . as the inhabit-

ants residing therein shall consent to yield to Congress"; (3) that if Congress preferred "any place on the River Patowmack within this Commonwealth," the General Assembly would offer similar terms governing any place that should be selected, plus the additional purchase of 100 acres of land for erecting such public buildings as Congress might direct to be built; and (4) that if the legislature of Maryland should be willing to join in a cession of territory on the Patomac, the General Assembly would make a cession opposite to that ceded by Maryland, "freely leaving it with Congress to fix their residence on either Side of the said River as they may see proper," but if Congress decided in this event to locate on the north side of the river, then Virginia would "contribute forty thousand pounds for the aforesaid Purposes in full confidence that the State of Maryland will supply the Deficiency" (attested copy of joint resolution in DLC: PCC No. 46, f. 55; endorsed in part by Thomson: "Read July 16. 1783. Copies to be made out and sent to the several states"; see JCC, XXIV, 438, note; JHD, May 1783, 1828 edn., p. 97, 98).

These resolutions also required that the "Governor with Advice of Council . . . make application to the . . . Citizens [of the district five miles square adjoining Williamsburg] and report their assent" to the Virginia delegates in Congress. This Harrison promptly did, apparently without consulting the Council (no reference to this matter appears in MS Va. Council Jour., Vi) by writing to the mayor of Williamsburg to "fall on some mode for obtaining" the sentiments of the inhabitants on the matter of yielding jurisdiction." He added that "the sooner it is done the better as I am convinced from a late Circumstance Congress will not remain long where they now are. The Advantages that will derive to the Inhabitants of the City are so great that I doubt not their giving as ample Jurisdiction as Congress could wish" (Harrison to the mayor of Williamsburg, 4 July 1783, Executive Letter Book, Vi). On the same day Harrison sent the resolutions forward to the delegates in Congress, and exhibited evidence that the offer of Williamsburg was not expected to be accepted, but was apparently made to place Virginia and the Southern states in an advantageous bargaining position: he thought the legisla-

ture's "offers are liberal, and I should think if consider'd impartially the latter [i.e., the last] would be accepted, as it will certainly be more central on either side of the Patowmack than at any of the other places proposed" (Harrison to Virginia delegates, 4 July 1783, same). But Harrison's confidence that the inhabitants of Williamsburg would grant "ample Jurisdiction" encountered a reluctance not without parallel in the twentieth century when the permanent site of the United Nations was being selected. At a meeting of the citizens of Williamsburg, "together with those residing within five miles thereof," the resolutions of the General Assembly and Harrison's covering letter were discussed, with George Wythe presiding. The inhabitants stated that they were "fully sensible of the great Advantages which will redound to the state in general, as well as to the said district in particular" if Congress should decide to accept the offer and, if this should happen, they were "fully determined to exert their best endeavours to make the place agreeable, by promoting harmony and good order, that the members of that august body may never have reason to resent their choice." But, they added, "this meeting are not authentically advised, what extent of jurisdiction would be satisfactory to Congress, and they find themselves upon that account at a loss to define with precision the cession they might be willing to make in that respect and can only deal in generals, until they can have an opportunity of seeing the expectations of the honorable Congress drawn more to a point." In consequence, they concluded, "this meeting are willing to submit to any such jurisdiction as may be compatible with their political welfare, and worthy of generous minds either to demand or yield" (clerk's copy of proceedings, DLC: PCC, No. 46, f. 89, endorsed: "Proceedings of the Inhabitants of Williamsburg . . . Read July 23. 1783. Referred to Mr. Duane Mr. Wilson Mr. Reed Mr. McHenry Mr. Madison"; JCC, XXIV, 444, note).

"I now fulfil my Promise [to forward the account of the Williamsburg proceedings]," Gov. Harrison wryly informed the Virginia delegates, ". . . tho' you will collect nothing from it, but that they are still jealous of our Liberty and are unwilling to give up any part of it even to Congress. However when your desires on the subject are made known which I wish to be as speedily as possible I doubt not but they will by their Moderation remove the apprehensions the Inhabitants of the District may be under of a loss of any part of their Liberty, and perhaps quiet some of the grave ones, on the score of the Luxury your Attendants will probably introduce" (Harrison to Virginia delegates, 12 July 1783, Executive Letter Book, Vi). But in the bitter contests that were developing over the permanent location of Congress, such cautious dealing "only . . . in generals" was not calculated to have any weight in the decision; two days before the present letter was written Elias Boudinot expressed the fear that "the late maneuvres relating to our erratic residence . . . [would lay] a solid Founda-

tion for future divisions. It [the decision of Congress to have two residences, one at or near Trenton on the Delaware and the other at or near Georgetown on the Patomac; JCC, XXV, 697-715] was not obtained in the most candid and generous way, and was finally accomplished by the most heterogenous Coalition that was in the power of Congress to Form" (Boudinot to Robert Morris, 23 Oct. 1783, Burnett, *Letters of Members*, VII, No. 410).

On the offers of Maryland, New Jersey, and New York, see same, VII, No. 215, note 2; these offers, along with that from Virginia, were transmitted to the governors of the various states on 22 July 1783 (same, VII, No. 272).

Benjamin Harrison to the Virginia Delegates in Congress

GENTLEMEN   In Council Octo: 30th. 1783.

The two last posts brought no letters from you which I am really sorry for as a full account of the proceedings of Congress on the place of their permanent residence was expected.

There are not yet a sufficient number of members to proceed to business.

I am &c.

FC (Vi); caption reads: "Delegates in Congress."

To Isaac Zane

DEAR SIR   Philadelphia Nov. 8. 1783.

By Colo. Bland who is returning to Virginia in a carriage I send you a thermometer, the only one to be had in Philadelphia. It appears to be a good one. You must do me the favour to accept of it from me. The following are the observations which I would trouble you to make and transmit to me.

The temperature of the cave at different distances from the mouth.

The temperature of your ice house.

That of a good spring.

That of a good well if you have one.

The observations in the cave should be at every foot or two when you first enter, till you find it's temperature become nearly uniform which will probably be at about 20 feet. The most convenient way of doing this will be to let it down by a string to different depths as far as the whole goes down nearly perpendicular; letting the glass remain till you think it is settled at it's due point and then drawing it up hastily.

Before this reaches you you will have heard that the definitive treaty is signed. I can give you no Congressional news having been so little with them. Being engaged in some necessary matters at this place, and knowing the first day of Congress would be spent in chusing a president and other matters of form I did not go till the second day: and in the evening of that they adjourned to Annapolis. Pennsylvania, Rhode island and N. Carolina being the only states which were entitled on the plan of rotation to offer candidates for the presidentship, the choice fell unanimously on Mifflin. His state being displeased with the departure of Congress it was thought this choice would be soothing to them.—I send you also the ball and screw of your theodolite. The pistol is not yet ready. I have put it into very good hands by the advice of Mr. Nancarro, but I am afraid they will be tedious, and it does not appear very certain to me that I shall not be obliged to leave it here.—After leaving your house a construction for a water wheel (such as yours) occurred to me which I think preferable. It differs from yours only in the manner of fixing the buckets. They are suspended each on a pin which being fixed in the side of the wheel then passes

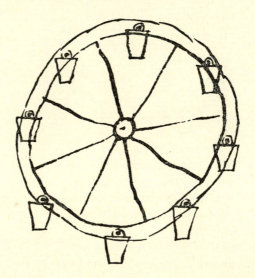

through the two ear-holes of the bucket. They always hang perpendicular, and of course lose no water. When the bucket gets to the top it strikes the edge of the cistern which tilts it up and empties every drop into the cistern. The buckets are somewhat narrower at bottom than top for a reason which will readily occur to you, as will all the minutiae both of the theory and execution. I am with much esteem Dr. Sir Your friend & servt.,   TH: JEFFERSON

RC (Andre deCoppet, New York City); endorsed below signature: "recd. the 6th of Jany. at Night." Sketch in TJ's hand is at foot of text. Recipient identified from substance of TJ's later letter to Isaac Zane, 17 Mch. 1784, q.v.

TJ's Account Book shows that he "left Monticello for Congress" on 16 Oct.; arrived at Philadelphia 29 Oct.; stopped overnight at Trenton on 3 Nov.; paid a "barber at Princeton 1/6" and took his seat in Congress on 4 Nov.; again stopped overnight at Trenton on

5 Nov.; and arrived at Philadelphia 6 Nov. where he stayed until 22 Nov. (Account Book under dates given; JCC, XXV, 803-7). He arrived in Annapolis on 25 Nov.; Congress convened the next day, but so few members were in attendance that it adjourned from day to day without doing business until 13 Dec. (same, XXV, 809-10; Edith R. Evans, "Thomas Jefferson in Annapolis," *Md. Hist. Mag.*, XLI [1946], p. 115-24 includes the Account Books in full for this period).

To Francis Eppes

DEAR SIR   Philadelphia Nov. 10. 1783.

I arrived at this place, not hearing till I had almost reached it that Congress had determined to remove for a time to Annapolis. Being engaged in some necessary business and knowing that the first day of the new Congress at Princetown would be emploied in chusing their president and other formalities of no public consequence, I did not join them there till the second day, and that evening they adjourned from that place: so that I have had and shall have the trouble of travelling near 400 miles more than would have been necessary. The rule of rotation had reduced the choice of a President to Pennsylvania, Rhode island and N. Carolina. The choice fell pretty unanimously on General Mifflin. You will have seen the votes for dividing the residence of Congress between Trenton and Annapolis till accomodations can be provided at Georgetown which is then to be substituted for Annapolis. This however is not to be considered as an ultimate determination. Trenton alone had been fixed on. The Southern delegates, extremely dissatisfied with this, contrived after an interval of many days to get a vote for Georgetown in the terms you have seen. I rather view this as unsettling the point which had been previously determined
[   ]
whole matter open for discussi[on   ]

I have not yet been a[ble   ]
am under great anxieties [pro-]
vide good tutors than a [   ]
Mrs. Eppes that there [   ]
place so shaped and [neces-][1]

sary among our countrywomen. The high head is made as flat as
a flounder. Instead of the burthen of lawn, ribbon, false hair &c.
the head is covered with a plain chip hat with only a ribbon round
the crown. The shoulders are where the chin used to be, and the
hips have succeeded to the place of the shoulders. The circumference of the waste is the span of the lady's own hands in order
to preserve due proportion. All the residue of the figure is resigned
to the possession of a hoop which at each angle before projects like
two bastions of a fort. I am impatient to see whether our married
ladies will be able to reduce and keep themselves to this form.
For this communication of the mode and putting it in Mrs. Eppes's
power to take herself up in time I charge her the delivering for
me half a dozen kisses to dear Poll and letting her know I have
not been able yet to get a ship to send with the babies, and to
deliver the same salutation to little Lu[cy]. I wish her, yourself &
family every happiness and am with much esteem Dr Sir Your
affectionate hble. servt,   TH: JEFFERSON

P.S. You doubtless will have heard that the definitive treaties were
signed on the 3d of Sep. and the ratifications exchanged by the
European powers on the [. . . .]

RC (CtY); large fragment of text torn away at lower right-hand corner.
Recipient's name assigned on the basis of internal evidence and the fact that a
letter to Eppes is recorded in SJL under date of 11 Nov. 1783.
[1] MS torn as indicated by space in square brackets (supplied).

From Joseph Reed

SIR   3d. Street Monday Morning [10? Nov. 1783]

The Esteem of the wise and virtuous is the most desirable
Acquisition in human Life, but the wise and virtuous as well as
weak and vicious are liable to Imposition and Mistake. Considering the active Industry of the Partizans of this City I should not
wonder if the many Slanders propagated against me should sometimes have made Impressions.

Under this Idea I was induced to publish a small Pamphlet

taking Notice of the most material and annexing some Letters from a few of the first Characters of America.

Permit me Sir to crave your Acceptance and Perusal of one of them. An Answer to that Part which respected Genl. Cadwallader was attempted, supported by very contemptible Testimony but none was ever offered to the other.

Your amiable and respectable Character has induced me to take this Liberty which I shall not enlarge farther than to request you to believe me with much Respect Sir Your most Obed & very Hble. Servt.,

JOS. REED

RC (ViWC); endorsed by TJ: "Reed Presidt."

This letter was evidently written in 1783 and it must have been sent while TJ was in "this City." Reed's SMALL PAMPHLET (*Remarks on a Late Address to the People of Pennsylvania, on the Many Libels and Slanders Which Have Lately Appeared against the Author*, Philadelphia, 1783) appeared very early in the year, since a second edition was advertised in the *Pa. Gazette* for 25 Feb. 1783 (Hildeburn, *The Issues of the Press in Pennsylvania, 1685-1784*, No. 4355). But Reed's letter cannot have been written as early as 26 Feb. to 12 Apr. 1783 (the period of 1783 when TJ was first in Philadelphia), for the ANSWER TO THAT PART WHICH RESPECTED GENL. CADWALLADER (*A Reply to General Joseph Reed's Remarks on a Late Publication in the Independent Gazetteer, with Some Observations on his Address to the People of Pennsylvania*) was announced in the *Pa. Journal* 24 May 1783 as "This Day . . . Published, and to be Sold by T. Bradford, in Front street, the fourth Door below the Coffee-House." The letter, therefore, must have been written on 10 or 17 Nov., the only other Mondays in 1783 when TJ was in Philadelphia. It is possible, of course, but not very likely, that the letter was written on 17 or 24 May 1784 when TJ was in Philadelphia just prior to sailing for France. The pamphlets referred to in this letter supplied some of the materials for "The War of the Grandfathers" in the mid-nineteenth century; see Ellsworth Eliot, *The Patriotism of Joseph Reed*, New Haven, 1943, for a résumé and bibliography of this controversy, though one of the crucial documents therein presented for the first time—a British protection form issued early in 1777 to "Joseph Reed" and bearing the endorsement indicating that he had sworn allegiance to the crown on 21 Feb. 1777—has been convincingly challenged as pertaining not to Joseph Reed of Pennsylvania but probably to an obscure person of that name residing in Newtown, Long Island (John F. Roche, "Was Joseph Reed Disloyal?" WMQ, 3rd ser., VIII [1951], p. 407-17).

To Benjamin Harrison

SIR   Philadelphia Nov. 11. 1783.

Your Excellency's letter of the 25th. Ult. on the determination of Congress as to their future residence has been duly received. You would doubtless soon after have heard of their subsequent determination on the same subject. As all this had taken place before my arrival I can give you an account only from the information of others. Congress, it seems, thought it best to generalize their first determination by putting questions on the several rivers on which it had been proposed that they should fix their residence. Hudson's river, the Delaware and Patowmac were accordingly offered to the vote. The first obtained scarcely any voices; the Delaware obtained seven. This of course put Patowmac out of the way: and the Delaware being once determined on there was scarcely any difference of opinion as to the particular spot. The falls met the approbation of all the states present except Pennsylvania, which was for Germantown, and Delaware which was for Wilmington. As to the latter it appeared that she had been induced to vote for the Delaware on the single idea of getting Congress to Wilmington, and that being disappointed in this, they would not wish them on that river at all, but would prefer Georgetown or any other place. This being discovered, the southern delegates at a subsequent day brought on a reconsideration of the question, and obtained a determination that Congress should set one half their time at Georgetown and that till accomodations should be provided there, Annapolis should be substituted in it's place. This was considered by some as a compromise; by others as only unhinging the first determination and leaving the whole matter open for discussion at some future day. It was in fact a rally, and making a drawn battle of what had at first appeared to be decided against us. What will be it's final decision can only be conjectured. I take the following to be the disposition of the several states.

The four Eastern states are for any place in preference to Philadelphia. The more Northern it is however the more agreeable to them.

New York, and New Jersey are for the falls of Delaware.

Pennsylvania is for Germantown first, and next for the falls of Delaware. It is to be noted that Philadelphia had no attention as a permanent seat.

Delaware is for Wilmington: but for Georgetown in preference to the falls of Delaware or any other situation which would attract the trade of their river.

Maryland is for Annapolis, and to the smallest hope for this will sacrifice a certainty for Georgetown.

Virginia. Every place Southward of Patowmac being disregarded by the states as every place North of the Delaware was it would be useless to consider her interests as to more Southern positions. The falls of Patowmac will probably therefore unite the wishes of the whole state. If this fails, Annapolis and the falls of Delaware are then the Candidates. Were the convenience of the

Delegates alone to be considered, or the general convenience to government in their transaction of business with Congress, Annapolis would be preferred without hesitation. But those who respect commercial advantages more than the convenience of individuals will probably think that every position on the bay of Chesapeak or any of it's waters is to be dreaded by Virginia as it may attract the trade of that bay and make us with respect to Maryland what Delaware state is to Pennsylvania. Considering the residence of Congress therefore as it may influence trade, if we cannot obtain it on the Patowmac it seems to be our interest to bring it past all the waters of Chesapeak bay.
The three Southern states are for the most Southern situation.

It should be noted that N. Hampshire and Georgia were absent on the decisions of these questions, but considering their interests would be directly opposite, it was thought their joint presence or absence would not change the result. From the preceding state of the views of the several members of our union your Excellency will be enabled to judge what will be the probable determination on any future revision of the present plan; the establishment of new states will be friendly or adverse to Georgetown according to their situation. If a state be first laid off on the lakes it will add a vote to the Northern scale, if on the Ohio it will add one to the Southern. I had the happiness of seeing Genl. Washington the other day after an interval of 7. years. He has more health in his countenance than I ever saw in it before. Among other political conversations he entered earnestly into one respecting the Western cession of Virginia, and the late vote of Congress accepting it. He thinks the conditions annexed by Virginia and not acceded to by Congress altogether unimportant, at least much less important than the consequences which would result from the state's adhering to these conditions. He thinks that a friendly and immediate settling of the matter can alone give us that political happiness and quiet which we must all wish for: and that besides other disagreeable consequences the land will be lost to both as a source of revenue by the settlement of adventurers on it who will not pay anything. It is now become evident that the nine states North of Patowmac have made up their minds on these questions and will act together.

I have the honour to be with very great respect your Excellency's most obedt. & most humble servt,   TH: JEFFERSON

RC (PHi); endorsed: "Mr. Jeffersons Letter." Addressee not indicated, but an entry in SJL for this date reads: "to the Governour."

To John Key

[*Philadelphia, 11 Nov. 1783*. Entry in SJL reads: "J.Key. to provide clothing and blankets." Not found. On Key see Account Book under date of 24 Sep. 1783: "Agreed with John Key to serve me as steward another year for £80."]

Benjamin Harrison to the Virginia Delegates in Congress

GENTLEMEN   In Council November 14th 1783

I have at last received a letter from you which with its important enclosures were immediately laid before the Assembly. They came in the most critical time, the subject of the impost being then under consideration. Mr. Adams's letter silenced the opposition and I have now no doubt of its obtaining.

I earnestly wish Congress had entered into some general recommendations for counteracting the British regulations of trade. Our resentments are high at present and I think the Assembly disposed to adopt any measures that the other states may be willing to come into to bring down the British pride and force them into measures that may be reciprocally advantageous or oblige them to take our produce from the neutral ports of other nations or pay for them in cash alone in our own. Perhaps it would not be amiss to prohibit the importation of their manufactures altogether 'till they open their ports to us. Our wants if not our luxuries may be supplyed amply from other countries. This they are not willing to believe and I confess it to be the touchstone of our virtue. I hope however we have still enough left to induce us to forego everything that may interfere with the general good of America.

We had received information of the treaty's being signed before your favor came to hand. We now anxiously wait for the treaty at large, as it may be useful in the formation of some of our laws. I am &c.   B.H.

FC (Vi); caption reads: "The honorable Virginia delegates in Congress."

Harrison sent to the Speaker of the House, on 13 Nov., "two letters from our delegates in Congress with sundry other papers of consequence"; he added that "The letter from Mr. Adams being of a confidential nature seems not calculated for the ear of the public; if you should coincide with me in opinion you will take measures to keep its contents a secret" (Harrison to Speaker, 13 Nov. 1783, Executive Letter Book, Vi). One of the letters transmitted by Harrison was certainly that from the delegates of 1 Nov. 1783 (Burnett, *Letters of Members*, VII, No. 436, where the letter from Adams is tentatively identified as that of 18 July 1783).

From William Jones

[*Bristol* [*England*], *18 Nov. 1783.* Entry under 10 Apr. 1784 in
SJL reads: "received W. Jones.' Bristol. Nov.18.1783. Richd. Hanson
will bring a letter." Not found.]

To James Monroe

DEAR SIR   Philadelphia Nov. 18. 1783.

Your favor of the 9th. came to hand yesterday and relieved us
from the fear that sickness or some other accident had detained you.
I am very particularly obliged to you for the attention you have
been so good as to pay to my accomodation; several circumstances
had prevented my taking measures for this purpose so early as I
wished. I had ultimately relied on Mr. Carrol, who left this place
two days ago. I will therefore be obliged to you to releive him
from the trouble I had given him, as he has many commissions of
the same kind on his hand. As you have been so kind as to procure
alternatives for me it ensures me a comfortable situation. I leave
Patsy here, having had it in my power to procure for her the best
tutors in French, dancing, music and drawing. Mr. Carrol was so
kind as to undertake to procure for me a stable for five horses. This
I shall still wish for. Mr. Mercer talks of setting out tomorrow.
Mr. Madison and myself shall leave this place certainly on the
21st. so as to be in Annapolis on the 24th. The President does not
set out till the 23d. Dr. Lee did not engage the house for the delegation, not having been desired to do so, nor having ever informed
them he had done so. I rather suppose it is for some particular set
of gentlemen with whom he means to join.[1] Be so good as to present my compliments to Mr. Hardy, and assure yourself of the
esteem with which I am Dr. Sir Your affectionate friend & servt.,

TH: JEFFERSON

RC (DLC: Madison Papers); addressed: "The honourable James Monroe of the Virginia delegation at Annapolis"; stamped with postmark: "18
NO" in a circle; endorsed: "1783.
Novr. 18."
Monroe's FAVOR OF THE 9TH has not
been found. TJ did not leave Philadelphia until 22 Nov., arriving in Annapolis on the 25th (see Account Book
and also his letter to Marbois, 5 Dec.
1783).

[1] Ford, III, 344, prints only that part
of the letter preceding this point which
begins with the statement: "Mr. Mercer talks of setting out tomorrow." To
this Ford subjoins a note saying: "This
is merely an extract of a letter, on a
sheet used by Jefferson later for another purpose." The extract to which he
refers, cited as being in DLC: TJ Papers, has not been found.

Oliver Pollock to the Virginia Delegates in Congress

SIRS   Havana Novr. 20th. 1783

The Inclosed Copy has no less Astonished than Chagrined me. Indeed it has been almost more than I could support and has required the whole of my fortitude and resolution particularly when received at the time I am surrounded by my Creditors as you will find by the sequal.

The only consolation that I have now left is that (thank Heaven) I have all the orriginal Bills at new Orleans, where I have wrote for them and expect them up the latter end of next month. Those Bills if necessary I shall go to the Trouble and Expence to lay before the State in hopes of redress or at least they will prove my demands to be Justly due to all impartial judges.

Mr. Clark whom has been waiting at your State upon this Bussiness about three years who's patience I am afraid is wore out, and I expect him now to come upon me for his Fortune, as also many others of the Mississippi whom has already applied to that Government to stop my families passage from that place untill they are paid. They have also applied to this Government to sue me and I don't know the moment I may be Arrested here as I was in Philada. for my drafts on Messrs. Penette Dacosta freres & Co., as also for 13,000 Dolls. I borrow'd from Dr. Bernardo de Otter's Comptroller General at New Orleans to take up some of those Bills that come out Protested before I left that place, which that Gentleman lent me to save me from a Goal and is now obliged to send my Obligation to his friend Ignasio Penelvere Treasurer of this place to sue me for recovery.

All which the inclosed Copies of Letters I have lately received which I have taken the liberty to inclose for your perusal but two well confirms.

I shall endeavour to prevail upon Government here for a further. Indulgence untill you Answer their Letters on that Subject wherein I hope you will point out the mode of payment that I and my family may not be totally ruined in this place and detained here Prisoners where we have nothing to expect but Insults untill those debts are paid, and in fine I expect as the representatives of your State and friends to your Country, that you'll exert your power and Influence to bring me about Justice, that I may be at least relieved from my present disagreeable situation. In the mean time honor me with an answer, and let me Know what I have to depend on to appease my Creditors; Creditors which I have made to serve your state in time of distress.

I have the honor to be with all due Submission and respect Gentn. Your most Obedient and Very Hum: Servt:,

OLR. POLLOCK

RC (Vi); at foot of text: "The Honble. The Delegates representing the Common Wealth of Virginia in Congress." Enclosures not identified, but the one that called forth the whole of Pollock's fortitude and resolution was no doubt a copy of the resolution adopted by the House of Delegates on 25 June 1783 as a result of a review of Pollock's accounts: "That the auditors . . . be directed to issue no more warrants in favor of the said Oliver Pollock; and that the treasurer . . . be directed to make no further payments on those already issued, until further orders from the General Assembly" (JHD, May 1783, 1828 edn., p. 83, 85). This letter and its enclosures were sent by the delegates to Gov. Harrison in their letter of 23 Jan. 1784 (see also their reply to Pollock, same date).

From Benjamin Harrison

DEAR SIR   In Council November 21st. 1783.

I am much obliged to you for your favor of the 11th. instant. It very fully explains the views and interests of the several states as to the future residence of Congress, tho' it is to be lamented that either should have any weight against the justice due to the whole confederation, which calls on them to fix on the most central place that can be made convenient which is certainly at or near the falls of Potowmac.

I cannot agree in opinion with those gentleman who think it impolitic to fix on any other of the waters of the Chesapeak; if we cannot be gratified in all our wishes let us come as near them as we can. The fears entertained of Annapolis's drawing to it the trade of this state I think are groundless. Nature never intended it for a great town and it is in vain to attempt altering what she has determined against. It has no back trade to support it but what must come by Alexandria or Baltimore where it will certainly stop. A little of our trade has been carried to the latter and it will be the case till we have more opulent merchants settled amongst us, but I think it never will increase so much as to be detrimental to us in any great degree, yet if I should be mistaken in this I am certain that tho' Congress should fix at Annapolis both towns will not take more of it than would go to Baltimore alone. Let us now take a short view of the advantages that would arise to this country by Congress's fixing there rather than on the Delaware. Every part of the lower country would be benefited by it as from it they might supply all kinds of provisions and grain. Lumber for building and even hay might be furnished from the low lands of Gloster and the shores of the bay. Our back country would supply horses black cattle sheep and hogs nearly on the same terms they could sell them at, at the falls of Potowmac, and what is as much to be considered as any thing else our merchants and the public would have as quick intelligence from thence as they could have in Philadelphia and might avail themselves of it from their vicinity to the sea much quicker than they could from thence or perhaps from Baltimore. Experience has proved to us that every one of these advantages would be lost to us by fixing on the Delaware. Philadelphia has been a continual drain to us and will continue to be so if the residence of Congress is either in it or its neighborhood. It is a vortex that swallows up our wealth and leaves us no prospect of recovering a single shilling. These are my sentiments. Their weight you will judge of.

Our house of delegates has passed a bill postponing the tax till March next and gives a liberty of paying one half of it in produce. What such frequent changes in our councils will end in time will discover. To me they hold up but a gloomy prospect.

I am &c.   B. H.

FC (Vi); caption reads: "The honorable Thomas Jefferson Annapolis."

To John Key

[*Annapolis, 26 Nov. 1783*. Entry in sJL reads: "J.Key to sell grey horses for £50. and give me notice. Use of books to Mr. Madison." Not found.]

To Jacquelin Ambler

[*Annapolis, 27 Nov. 1783*. Entry in sJL reads: "Jaquel. Ambler. Mad's bill—impost—cession—meeting and separation of Congr." Not found.]

To Mann Page

[*Annapolis, 27 Nov. 1783*. Entry in sJL reads: "M. Page. Meeting and separation of Congr.—cession without alterations." Not found.]

To William Short

[*Annapolis*, *27 Nov. 1783*. Entry in SJL reads: "W. Short. Foreign arrangement—Shelton's affairs—Martin—Western cession—importance of establishing interest in Congress—residence of Congress—instructions on that head—Patsy's situation." Not found.]

To John Tyler

[*Annapolis*, *27 Nov. 1783*. Entry in SJL reads: "Speaker H. D. Impost. Western cession. Seat of Congress. Instructions to require cession from others." Not found.]

Francis Hopkinson to Robert Bremner

Philadelphia, *28 Nov. 1783*. "Mr. Jefferson of Virginia" having consulted Hopkinson "respecting the Importation of a Harpsichord for his Daughter," the matter is referred to Bremner's judgment and care. "He wishes to have an Instrument of the very best kind—a double Harpsichord with Merlin's forte-piano Stop and such other modern Improvements as you may think advantageous . . . also all necessary Apparatus viz. a Set of Strings, a tuning Hammer, a tuning fork &c. &c. as you shall judge proper. Mr. Jefferson will write to you himself on the Subject giving directions how the Case shall be address'd," &c. "You will oblige me much by your attention in seeing that Mr. Jefferson is well served on this Occasion."

RC (MHi); addressed: "Mr. Robert Bremner Opposite to Sommerset House in the Strand *London*." This letter was no doubt sent to TJ (perhaps as an enclosure in an unidentified letter from Hopkinson) to be forwarded in one of his own to Bremner; but it was evidently never forwarded to London. TJ acknowledged receipt of it in his to Hopkinson of 23 Dec. 1783.

To Martha Jefferson

MY DEAR PATSY   Annapolis Nov. 28. 1783.

After four days journey I arrived here without any accident and in as good health as when I left Philadelphia. The conviction that you would be more improved in the situation I have placed you than if still with me, has solaced me on my parting with you, which my love for you has rendered a difficult thing. The acquirements which I hope you will make under the tutors I have provided for you will render you more worthy of my love, and if they cannot increase it they will prevent it's diminution. Consider the good lady who has taken you under her roof, who has undertaken to see that you perform all your exercises, and to admonish you in all those wanderings from what is right or what is clever to which your inexperience would expose you, consider her I say as your mother, as the only person to whom, since the loss with which heaven has been pleased to afflict you, you can now look up; and that her displeasure or disapprobation on any occasion will be an immense misfortune which should you be so unhappy as to incur by any unguarded act, think no concession too much to regain her good will. With respect to the distribution of your time the following is what I should approve.

from 8. to 10 o'clock practise music.
from 10. to 1. dance one day and draw another
from 1. to 2. draw on the day you dance, and write a letter the next day.
from 3. to 4. read French.
from 4. to 5. exercise yourself in music.
from 5. till bedtime read English, write &c.

Communicate this plan to Mrs. Hopkinson and if she approves of it pursue it. As long as Mrs. Trist remains in Philadelphia cultivate her affections. She has been a valuable friend to you and her good sense and good heart make her valued by all who know her and by nobody on earth more than by me. I expect you will write to me by every post. Inform me what books you read, what tunes you learn, and inclose me your best copy of every lesson in drawing. Write also one letter every week either to your aunt Eppes, your aunt Skipwith, your aunt Carr, or the little lady from whom I now inclose a letter, and always put the letter you so write under cover to me. Take care that you never spell a word wrong. Always before you write a word consider how it is spelt, and if you do not remember it, turn to a dictionary. It produces great praise to a lady to spell well. I have placed my happiness on seeing you good and accomplished, and no distress which this world can now bring on me could equal that of your disappointing my hopes. If you love me then, strive to be good under every situation and to all living creatures, and to acquire those accomplishments which I have put in your power, and which will go far towards ensuring you the warmest love of your affectionate father,   TH: JEFFERSON

P.S. keep my letters and read them at times that you may always have present in your mind those things which will endear you to me.

RC (John A. Sutro, San Francisco, California, 1952). Entry in SJL reads: "Patsy. 8 to 10. music—10. to 1. dance one day, draw another.—1 to 2 draw the day she dances, write a letter the other —3 to 4. French.—4 to 5 Music—5 to bedtime read English, write &c." Sarah N. Randolph, TJ's great-granddaughter, writing in 1871, stated that this letter "is now in the possession of the Queen of England. Mr. Aaron Vail, when Chargé d'Affaires of the United States at the Court of St. James, being requested by Princess Victoria to procure her an autograph of Jefferson, applied to a member of Mr. Jefferson's family, who sent him this letter for the princess" (*Domestic Life*, p. 68-9). (For another Jefferson letter said to have been in Queen Victoria's collection, see TJ to Martha Jefferson Randolph, 28 Apr. 1793.) Vail was chargé d'affaires at London from 1832 to 1836; hence the present letter was given to Princess Victoria when she was not much older than Martha, who was eleven. Enclosure not found.

THE GOOD LADY WHO HAS TAKEN YOU UNDER HER ROOF was Mrs. Thomas Hopkinson, the widowed mother of Francis Hopkinson (see Hastings, *Hopkinson*, p. 331-5). THE LITTLE LADY FROM WHOM I NOW INCLOSE A LETTER: Probably Polly Floyd.

Documents concerning the Residence of Congress

I. NOTES BY MADISON [OCT. 1783]
II. NOTES AND CALCULATIONS BY JEFFERSON [NOV.? 1783]
III. ANALYSIS OF VOTES OF 7 OCTOBER 1783 [NOV. 1783]
IV. COMPARATIVE TABLE OF DISTANCES [NOV.-DEC.? 1783]
V. JEFFERSON'S DRAFT RESOLUTION AUTHORIZING ERECTION OF PUBLIC BUILDINGS FOR USE OF CONGRESS [1783?]
VI. RESOLUTION ON THE PRIVILEGES AND IMMUNITIES OF CONGRESS

[ca. Nov.-Dec. 1783]

EDITORIAL NOTE

Except for Document III in this series, all of the notes and memoranda pertaining to the embittered question of finding a permanent seat for Congress were printed by Ford, III, 458-62, as if they proceeded entirely from Jefferson's hand, and were assigned the conjectural date of 13 Apr. 1784 on the belief that they were drafted at the time of the renewed discussion of the question. But most if not all of these documents belong to the earlier maneuvers in Congress of Oct.-Nov. 1783. Madison's notes, now first printed as his, summarize the sentiment in Congress reflected in the votes of 6-8 and 17-21 Oct. before Jefferson took his seat (see JCC, XXV, 647-60, 711-14). Madison himself left Congress soon afterward (his last recorded vote was on 22 Oct.), and he probably set down this information for the guidance of Jefferson. The further inquiries that Jefferson himself made were no doubt inspired in part at least by Governor Harrison's inquiry of 25 Oct., to which Jefferson replied on 11 Nov. 1783 presenting some of the observations gained from Madison. On the background of the offer by Virginia of a place of residence for Congress, referred to in the concluding observation of Document II, see notes to Harrison to Jefferson, 25 Oct. 1783. Jefferson's belief that nothing would come of this offer led him to make a bold proposal that Virginia join with Maryland in what was nothing more nor less than a gamble—to erect public buildings in the hope that, once available, Congress might decide to use them. This he put in the form of a draft resolution which he intended to have introduced in the General Assembly. If he had matured such a plan by 11 Nov. 1783, he doubtless would have mentioned it to Harrison in his letter of that date. Since he did not do so, it is safe to assume that the proposed resolution was drawn up later. It is possible that he enclosed a copy of it in his letter to Archibald Cary, Speaker of the Senate, 19 Dec. 1783, and that it was the basis of the "proposition on G. town to Delegates of Maryld" mentioned in the sJL entry which constitutes the only available information about the contents of that letter. It is also possible, of course, that Document V was drawn up considerably later than the other documents here presented, and that it may belong to the period of the votes of Congress of 14 and 26 Apr. 1784 which showed that sentiment in Congress was running strongly against a site on the Potomac (see JCC, XXVI, 223-4). But it is most probable that TJ drew up his bold proposal around Nov.-Dec. 1783.

I. Notes by Madison

[Oct. 1783]

Permanent seat of Congress

North River—recommended for the permanent seat of Congress chiefly by its security against foreign danger.

Falls of Potowmac—By 1. geographical centrality—2. proximity to western Country already ceded—3. inducement to further Cessions from N.C. S.C. and Georgia. 4. remoteness from the influence of any overgrown commercial city.

Falls of Delaware—By 1. centrality with regard to number of inhabitants. 2. centrality as to number of States and of Delegates. 3 facility of obtaining intelligence from sea.

Temporary Seat of Congress

Princeton—in favor of it, 1. its neighbourhood to the Permanent [se]at, 2. inconveniency of a removal. 3. beneficial effort of a fruga[l] situation of Congress on their popularity throughout the States. 4. the risque in case of removal from Princeton of returning under the commercial and corrupt influence of Philada. —Against it. 1. unfitness for transacting the public business.

2. deficiency of accomodation, exposing the attending members to the danger of indignities and extortions, discouraging perhaps the fitest men from undertaking the service, and amounting to a probitition of such as had families from which they would not part.

Trenton. Arguments in favor and against it similar to those respecting Princeton. It was particularly remarked that when the option lay with the President and committee between Trenton and Princeton the latter was preferred as least unfit to receive Congress on their removal from Philada.

Philada. In favor of it. 1. its unrivalled conveniency for transacting the public business, and accomodating Congress. 2. its being the only place where all the public offices, particularly that of Finance could be kept under the inspection and controul of, and proper intercourse with Congress. 3. its conveniency for F[oreign] Ministers, to which, caeteris paribus, some regard would be expected. 4. the circumstances which produced a removal from Philada. which rendered a return as soon as the insult had been expiated, expedient for supporting in the eyes of foreign nations the appearance of internal harmony, and preventing an appearance of resentment in Congress against the State of Pa: or City of Philada. an appearance which was very much strengthened by some of their proceedings at Princeton—particularly by an unnecessary and irregular declaration not to return to Phi. In addition to these overt reasons, it was concluded by sundry of the members who were most anxious to fix Congress permanently at[1] the falls of Potowmac that a temporary residence in Philada. would be most likely to prepare a sufficient number of votes for that place in preference to the Falls of Delaware,[2] and to produce a reconsideration of the vote in favor of the latter.—against Philada. were alledged. 1. The difficulty and uncertainty of getting away from it at the time limited. 2. The influence of a large commercial and wealthy city on the public councils. In addition to these objections, the hatred against Mr. M. [Robert Morris] and hope of accelerating his final r[esigna]tion were latent motives with some, as perhaps envy of the prospe[rity of] Philada. and dislike of the support of Pa. to obnoxious recomendations of Congress were with others.

Annapolis—in favor of it, 1st. its capacity for accomodating Congress and its conveniences for the public business. 2. the soothing tendency of so Southern a position on the temper of the S.

States.—Against it, 1st. the preposterousness of taking a temporary station so distant from the permanent seat fixed on, especially as better accomodations were to be passed by at Philada. which was less than ⅘ths of the distance from the Permanent Seat. 2d. the peculiar force such a step would give to the charge against Congress of being swayed by improper motives. Besides these considerations it was the opinion of some that a removal of Congress to Annapolis would inspire Maryland with hopes that would prevent a cooperation in favor of George town, and favor the commerce of that State at the expence of Virginia.

MS (DLC: TJ Papers, 10: 1561); entirely in Madison's hand.

1 "Georgeto[wn]" deleted in MS.
2 The words "for the permanent" deleted in MS.

II. Notes and Calculations by Jefferson

[Nov.? 1783]

1. It requires 9. states to appropriate money, and only 7 to adjourn. There cannot therefore be buildings erected at Georgetown without the concurrence of 9 states, a number [whic]h I fear we shall never obtain. Yet if the buildings were erected, 7 could adjourn us there, and this number is within [hope], but not within certainty.

Obj. it is then but a speculation by which the state may throw away 15000 Dollars.

Answ. True, but this is the extent of their loss.

Their possible advantages will be

Common to all the states

1. The firmness and tone which will be given to the federal government by fixing it's administration more nearly central.
2. The placing the federal council within reach of the Western states and thereby cementing them to it's Eastern part.
3. Securing the seat of federal government from sudden enterprize without expensive works or establishments.
4. Adjacence to two states from the one or the other of which a protection may generally be expected.

Common to Southern states

1. Drawing the federal fleets into the bay of Chesapeak.
2. Bringing the federal administration nearer to the Southern states.
3. Rendering an attendance in Congress more convenient to Southern members, and by removing obstacles, increase the chances for inducing the best men into the office.

Common to Virga. and Maryland

1. Attracting foreigners manufacturers and settlers to the two states of Virga. and Maryland.
2. Attracting commerce to them.
3. Throwing a very large sum of money annually into circulation which will be divided between them.
4. Preferment of their citizens to[1] the federal administration.
5. The advantages of a favourable biass in the Executive officers.

Peculiar to Virga.

1. The establishment of Alexandria on a par with Baltimore as a secondary place of commerce.
2. Leaving Norfolk in possession of all the advantages of a primary emporium.

Add[2] to these that the £100,000 offered by Virginia will never be accepted.

MS (DLC: TJ Papers, 10: 1563); entirely in TJ's hand. The conjectured date is confirmed by TJ's letter to Clark, 4 Dec. 1783 (note second argument in first category above concerning western states).

[1] The following deleted at this point: "posts of honor—profit and power."
[2] A word, illegible, was written just above this word and was then apparently erased.

III. Analysis of Votes of 7 October 1783

Absent N. Hampshire and Georgia

N. Hampshire
Massachusets
Rhodeisland
Connecticut
} for any place in preference to Philadelphia. the further North however the more agreeable to them.

New York. for the most Northern situation

New Jersey. the same.

Pennsylvania. for Germantown, next Lamberton[1]

Delaware. for Wilmington. but for Georgetown in preference to Lamberton or any other situation which would attract the trade of their river.[2]

Maryland. for Annapolis. to the smallest hope for this she will sacrifice a certainty of George T.

Virginia. for George T. she ought to prefer Philadelphia or Lamberton to Annapolis or any other situation North of Patowmack which would attract the trade of Chesapeak.

N. Carolina ⎫
S. Carolina. ⎬ for the most Southern situation
Georgia ⎭

When the question was put on the several rivers.

Hudson's river.   N. York alone

Delaware river   4. E.S. [Eastern States] *N.Y. NJ. P. D.*

Patowmac.   5. S.S. [Southern States][3]

MS (DLC: TJ Papers, 10: 1560); entirely in TJ's hand. This document of the present series not printed by Ford. It agrees in substance and in large part in phraseology with the analysis in TJ to Harrison, 11 Nov. 1783, which TJ admitted was based on information furnished by others.

[1] This passage was corrected from the following: "Pennsylvania. for Philadelphia, next the falls of the Delaware."

[2] This passage was corrected from the following: "Delaware. for Philadelphia, but for Georgetown in preference to the falls of Delaware or any other situation," &c.

[3] Following these notes, on the same page, is a table in TJ's hand showing the population of the thirteen states with their respective proportions of the national expenses (JCC, XXIV, 231, 259).

IV. Comparative Table of Distances

[Nov.-Dec.? 1783]

	Phila		Trenton		George Town. 146 from P.
N. Hampshire	429		399		575
Massachusets	365		335		511
Rhode island	317		287		463
Connecticut	245		215		391
N. York	97		67		243
N. Jersey	30		0	1303	176
				2805	
Pennsylva.	0	1483	30		146
		2595			

Delaware	30	60	116		
Maryland	144	174	0	2621	784
				1837	
Virginia	280	310	134		
N. Carola.	427	457	281		
S. Carola.	797	827	651		
Georgia	917	947	771		

MS (DLC: TJ Papers, 10: 1564); entirely in TJ's hand.

V. Jefferson's Draft Resolution Authorizing Erection of Public Buildings for Use of Congress

[1783?]

Resolved that the Governor be desired to propose to the state of Maryland to concur with this Commonwealth in erecting buildings for the immediate accomodation of the Congress of the United states on the lands on Patowmac offered to be ceded to them by these two states, and particularly on such parts of them as they shall have reason to beleive will be most agreeable to the Congress, the expence of which buildings with the purchase of the ground shall not exceed thirty thousand dollars to be advanced from time to time, as it shall be wanting, by the said states in equal portions: which advances on the part of this commonwealth the Treasurer is hereby authorized and required to make on warrants from the Auditors according to the established forms of his office.

Resolved that three Commissioners be appointed by joint balot of both houses of assembly to act with Commissioners or other persons appointed or to be appointed on the part of the state of Maryland, who shall have powers to purchase sufficient ground, to agree on the buildings necessary to be erected, to have them erected without delay, to call for and to apply monies by way of paiment or of advance for the same, and to tender the said buildings to Congress for the sole purpose of their general and of their personal accomodation.

Resolved that to prevent any difficulties or delays which might be produced by doubts in what manner the said Commissioners when assembled shall vote, it be proposed to the state of Maryland that they shall proceed to business always with an equal number (not less than two) from each state, that, so constituted, they shall be considered as forming one Committee, every member whereof shall have one vote and no more, and that if at any time they shall be divided on any question which may be likely to delay the said work, they shall state the same in writing to the delegates of the two states in Congress who concurring by a majority of their respective members present, shall decide the same.

MS (DLC: TJ Papers, 10: 1562); entirely in TJ's hand; printed by Ford, III, 462, as a separate document under the assigned date 13 Apr. 1784.

VI. Resolution on the Privileges and Immunities of Congress

[ca. Nov.-Dec. 1783]

1. Resolved that the object of the several states in appointing delegates to meet in General Congress being that they may therein transact for the good of the Union in general and their State in particular[1] those matters which the Confederation has submitted to the direction of Congress, the said delegates ought to be invested in the place where they may be sitting with such privileges and immunities[2] as will cover them from molestation and disturbance, and leave them in freedom and tranquillity to apply their whole time and attention to the objects of their delegation.

2. That territory and exclusive jurisdiction in and about the place of their session is not necessary to attain these ends and would subject them to avocations from their proper objects.

3. That long experience has led the civilized nations of Europe[3] to an ascertainment of those privileges and immunities which may enable the representatives of an independant nation exercising high functions within another to do the same unawed and undisturbed and that therefore the privileges and immunities annexed by the law and usage of nations to such characters should be allowed to the Congress of the united states collectively and to their members individually by the laws of the states in and adjacent to which they may be sitting and should be secured in their continuance by sufficient sanction.

4. That legal provision should also be made for protecting and vindicating those privileges and immunities to which foreign ministers and others attending on Congress are entitled by the law of nations.

5. That Congress will rely on the honour and affection of the states in and adjacent to which they may be sitting as a security that measures shall be provided for preventing violations of the rights[4] before stated in general and duly punishing them when arising too suddenly for prevention.

6. That the United States should be made capable of acquiring and holding in perpetuum such grounds and buildings in and about the place of the session of Congress as may be necessary for the transaction of business by their own body, their committees and officers, that each state should be made capable of acquiring and holding in perpetuum such grounds and buildings as they may at any time think proper to acquire and erect for the personal accomodation of their delegates: and that the grounds and buildings beforementioned so long as Congress or a Committee of the states shall be resident at such place should[5] be exempt from taxation.[6]

7. That as in time of war the enemies of these states might employ emissaries and spies to discover the views and proceedings of Congress, that body should have authority within a certain distance of the place of their session to arrest and deal with as they shall think proper all persons, not being citizens of these states nor entitled to their protection, whom they shall have cause to suspect to be spies.

8. That as the United states in Congress assembled represent the sovereignty of the whole Union, their body collectively and their President individually should on all occasions have precedence of all other bodies and persons.

9. That during the recess of Congress the Committee of the states being left to pursue the same objects and under the same circumstances their body, their members, and their President should respectively be placed on the same footing with the body, the members and the President of Congress.

MS (DLC); entirely in TJ's hand, with a number of deletions and corrections, of which the more important are noted below. At foot of page 2 TJ made the following note: "contempts Congr. and states made capable of holding lands. Qu. if free from taxes?" Immediately above this is the following: "Resolved that Congress, in the place where they may be sitting, need no powers or privileges, other than these"; this corresponds with what became paragraph 2 and its position on the page (upside-down in relation to the note just quoted) indicates that TJ originally intended this as the opening paragraph. Despite these notes and the numerous alterations, this MS has every appearance of being a copy of some preceding draft. There is no record in the Journals that this resolution was read in Congress, nor is there any indication on the MS or elsewhere of the date of composition. Ford, III, 463, prints it (with indications of alterations) under the conjectured date of 14 Apr. 1784; Burnett, *Letters of Members*, VII, No. 519, note 7, prints it as a note to TJ to Madison, 20 Feb. 1784 on the ground that it "seems more probable . . . that the resolution was prepared about this time." The editors reject both dates as less probable than the period Nov.-Dec. 1783 during which TJ is known to have been at work on related documents as shown in the present series; it is certainly implausible to suggest that he may have drafted this resolution around 20 Feb. 1784 when, in the letter to Madison of that date, TJ remarked: "Georgetown languishes. The smile is hardly covered now when the federal towns are spoken of."

The question of jurisdiction was brought to the fore with Benjamin Hawkins' motion of 8 July 1783 for the appointment of a committee to "consider and define the jurisdiction proper to be established by Congress within the bounds of the district that may be allotted to them by the State in which they may choose to fix their permanent residence." Madison became a member of the committee on 23 July; a report was handed in 5 Sep. 1783 to the effect that Congress "ought to enjoy an exclusive jurisdiction over the District which may be ceded and accepted" and that this district should be not less than three nor more than six miles square. This report was debated 22 Sep. and then, or at some other date, Madison and Arthur Lee offered resolutions that were clearly drafted with the Williamsburg proceedings in view; both resolutions agreed that Congress should have exclusive jurisdiction, but where Madison thought the government of the district ought to be "concerted between Congress and the inhabitants," Lee felt that Congress should appoint judges and executive officers, and that the inhabitants should have the privilege of trial by jury and should be governed by "Laws made by Representatives of their own election." These motions and the report of the committee were not acted upon, and in the debates of 7 and 18-21 Oct. on a place of residence, the issue was left indeterminate by the use of such a proviso as the following: "that the right of soil and an exclusive or such other jurisdiction as Congress may direct, shall be vested in the United States" (JCC, XXIV, 428; XXV, 603, 604, 654, 656, 657, 698, 707, 712, 714). TJ's resolution, of course, differed from all of these by applying usages of the law of nations to the problem of protecting the delegates in their functions and by rejecting as unnecessary the idea of an exclusive jurisdiction within the district. When the unfinished business of Congress was reviewed in May 1784 the "Report on Jurisdiction proper for Congress . . . together with proceedings of inhabitants of Williamsburg relative to that subject" was referred to the next meeting of Congress (same, XXVII, 403).

1 TJ first wrote: "of their several states and of the Union in general" and then altered the passage to read as above.

2 This word interlined in substitution for "exemptions," deleted.

3 This passage originally read: "the legations which have been practised among the civilized nations of Europe have led by a long course of experience," and was then altered to read as above.

4 The words "when forewarn[ed]" are deleted at this point.

5 "Shall" is deleted at this point.

6 This paragraph was written on a separate slip attached by wafer to the MS; paragraph 4 is written in the margin. Since the numbering of the paragraphs shows no erasures or overwriting, it is clear that this was done after the additions represented in this and paragraph 4 had been made.

To Martha Jefferson Carr

[*Annapolis, 4 Dec. 1783*. Entry in SJL reads: "Mrs. Carr. A.S.J. Pats. [i.e., Anna Scott Jefferson, TJ's sister, and Patsy, his daughter]." Not found.]

To George Rogers Clark

DEAR SIR   Annapolis Dec. 4. 1783.

I received here about a week ago your obliging letter of Oct. 12. 1783. with the shells and seeds for which I return you many thanks. You are also so kind as to keep alive the hope of getting for me as many of the different species of bones, teeth and tusks of the *Mammoth* as can now be found. This will be most acceptable. Pittsburg and Philadelphia or Winchester will be the surest channel of conveyance. I find they have subscribed a very large sum of money in England for exploring the country from the Missisipi to California. They pretend it is only to promote knolege. I am afraid they have thoughts of colonising into that quarter. Some of us have been talking here in a feeble way of making the attempt to search that country. But I doubt whether we have enough of that kind of spirit to raise the money. How would you like to lead such a party? Tho I am afraid our prospect is not worth asking the question. The definitive treaty of peace is at length arrived. It is not altered from the preliminaries. The cession of the territory West of Ohio to the United states has been at length accepted by Congress with some small alterations of the conditions. We are in daily expectation of receiving it with the final approbation of Virginia. Congress have been lately agitated by questions where they should fix their residence. They first resolved on Trentown. The Southern states however contrived to get a vote that they would give half their time to Georgetown at the Falls of Patowmac. Still we consider the matter as undecided between the Delaware and Patowmac. We urge the latter as the only point of union which can cement us to our Western friends when they shall be formed into separate states. I shall always be happy to hear from you and am with very particular esteem Dr. Sir Your friend & humble servt.,   TH: JEFFERSON

RC (WHi); addressed: "Genl. George Rogers Clarke"; endorsed in several hands, including Lyman C. Draper's. Entry in SJL reads: "Genl. Clarke. Bones. Expedition towards Califa."

Clark's letter of 12 Oct. 1783 has not been found. The DEFINITIVE TREATY . . . IS AT LENGTH ARRIVED: The *Pa.* *Journal* for 3 Dec. 1783 spread the text of the treaty on its first page with the announcement that it had arrived "By the Lord Hyde Packet, from Falmouth." The treaty was not as yet officially before Congress, since a quorum could not be mustered until 13 Dec. (JCC, XXV, 809).

To Elizabeth Wayles Eppes

[*Annapolis, 4 Dec. 1783.* Entry in SJL reads: "Mrs. E. Pats.—Bets." Not found.]

To Francis Eppes

[*Annapolis, 4 Dec. 1783.* Entry in SJL reads: "Mr. E. State of Congr.—Rise of tobo. in Engld.—Martin." Not found.]

To Samuel Coleman

[*Annapolis, 5 Dec. 1783.* Entry in SJL reads: "Saml. Coleman. About tobacco due him." Not found.]

To James Currie

[*Annapolis, 5 Dec. 1783.* Entry in SJL reads: "Dr. Currie. Study of law.—Settlement in Alb[emarle].—Health." Not found.]

Benjamin Harrison to the Virginia Delegates in Congress

GENTLEMEN   In Council December 5th. 1783.

The last post brought no letter from you which I am really sorry for as the definitive treaty which we hear is certainly arrived is much wanted by the assembly and would perhaps prevent some steps being taken that may be contrary to it. Do Congress mean to take no measures to counteract the designs of the British respecting our trade? If they do it must be immediately to have any effect here as the assembly will rise in a fortnight. Our taxes are again postponed 'till the first of february and one half are to be commuted for. I fear this fluctuation in our Councils will be attended with the worst of consequences, our credit was low before and this will probably totally destroy it.

I am &c.

FC (Vi); caption reads: "The Virginia delegates in Congress."

Harrison was much concerned here and in other communications about the DESIGNS OF THE BRITISH RESPECTING OUR TRADE. On 3 Oct. 1783 he had written the delegates (before TJ had left Virginia): "The determinations of

[372]

the French and English respecting our trade is really alarming and in the end will prove ruinous to us if not counteracted by some spirited conduct on our part. I think the way is plain and easy with the latter, but with the former little can be done as trade has never been an object with the french court tho' the want of it has been severely felt by the nation at large and frequently brought the Kingdom to the brink of ruin. Great Britain knows its intrinsic value and if we prohibit the use of their manufactures or west india commodities except when brought by our own vessels or by those of other nations and thereby oblige them to make their purchases in cash, they will very soon come to a compromise. How far the powers of Congress may be competent to bring about this or any other regulation that will better answer the end is not for me to say, but surely they should at least take up the matter and recommend some general regulation to the States. Unfortunately for us the subject is not well understood here nor is that attention paid to it that its importance requires: yet we are sometimes reasonable people and can understand things if we please to give them due consideration. It will be your parts therefore to smooth the way by a plain and pointed state of the advantages that will derive to the Union by a spirited opposition to the measures of the British ministry" (Executive Letter Book, Vi). See also Harrison to the Delegates, 26 Dec. 1783.

To Samuel House

[Annapolis, 5 Dec. 1783. Entry in sjl reads: "Mr. Hou. enq. pri. copg. mach." Expanded, this probably means "enquiring the price of a copying machine." Since this is the earliest allusion to TJ's interest in mechanical copying devices, it is most unfortunate that the letter has not been found. Samuel House, son of the Mrs. House with whom TJ lodged in Philadelphia in 1782 and 1783, and brother of his much-admired friend Mrs. Eliza House Trist, was a merchant who kept a shop on Chestnut Street between Second and Third (*Philadelphia Directory* for 1785; letters of House to TJ in 1784-1785). House may have imported, or planned to import, some English copying presses of the kind recently patented by James Watt. The result of TJ's inquiry of House is not known, but among the Franklin Papers (PPAP) is a letter from the London firm of Herries & Co. to William Temple Franklin, 13 Apr. 1784, acknowledging an order forwarded by Franklin on 3 Apr. from Robert Morris for a "Copying Machine with Paper &c. for Mr. Jefferson," to be sent "by the first Opportunity to Virginia."]

To Gabriel Jones

[Annapolis, 5 Dec. 1783. Entry in sjl reads: "G. Jones. Money." Not found, but see TJ to Gabriel Jones, 29 Apr. 1779.]

To Marbois

SIR   Annapolis Dec. 5. 1783.

Your very obliging letter of Nov. 22. was put into my hands just in the moment of my departure from Philadelphia, which put it out of my power to acknolege in the same instant my obligations for the charge you were so kind as to undertake of presenting a French tutor to my daughter and for the very friendly dispositions and attentions you flatter me with. The same cause prevented my procuring her the books you were so kind as to recommend, but this shall be supplied by orders from hence. I had left with her a Gil Blas, and Don Quichotte which are among the best books of their class as far as I am acquainted with them. The plan of reading which I have formed for her is considerably different from what I think would be most proper for her sex in any other country than America. I am obliged in it to extend my views beyond herself, and consider her as possibly at the head of a little family of her own. The chance that in marriage she will draw a blockhead I calculate at about fourteen to one, and of course that the education of her family will probably rest on her own ideas and direction without assistance. With the best poets and prosewriters I shall therefore combine a certain extent of reading in the graver sciences. However I scarcely expect to enter her on this till she returns to me. Her time in Philadelphia will be chiefly occupied in acquiring a little taste and execution in such of the fine arts as she could not prosecute to equal advantage in a more retired situation.—We have yet but four states in Congress. I think when we are assembled we shall propose to dispatch the most urging and important business, and, putting by what may wait, separate and return to our respective states, leaving only a Committee of the states. The constant session of Congress can not be necessary in time of peace, and their separation will destroy the strange idea of their being a permanent body, which has unaccountably taken possession of the heads of their constituents, and occasions jealousies injurious to the public good.

I have the honour of being with very perfect esteem & respect Sir Your most obedient & most humble servt., TH: JEFFERSON

RC (Bibl. Nat., Paris); addressed and franked: "Monsr. de Marbois Secretaire d'Ambassade Philadelphia. free Th: Jefferson." Entry in sjl reads: "Monsr. de Marb. Thanks for offer—

will get the books—general idea of my plan reading Pats."
Marbois' letter of 22 Nov. 1783 has not been found.

To Archibald Stuart

[*Annapolis, 5 Dec. 1783*. Entry in sjl reads: "Arch. Stewart.—Convention—secretary to delegation—state of Congr." Not found. See TJ to Madison, 7 May 1783.]

To Eliza House Trist

[*Annapolis*, 5 *Dec. 1783*. Entry in SJL reads: "Mrs. Tr.—Mad[ison]. —Annap.—Mr. Tr [presumably Nicholas Trist, Mrs. Trist's husband, who is listed in Ford, *British Officers*, as a lieutenant in 1775]. Mr. Hou.—Browse [Mrs. Trist's son, Hore Browse Trist]." Not found. There are no further entries in SJL between this date and 11 Dec.]

From Eliza House Trist

[ca. 8 December? 1783]

I am greatly indebted to worthy Mr. Jefferson for his polite and friendly letter. I wish I cou'd express my greatful feelings in language suitable to what my mind suggests. I can and will say that you are incapable of esteeming me more than I do you. I cou'd give as many reasons were I to enumerate your Virtues as wou'd fill a Volume folio. Your caracter was great in my estamation long before I had the pleasure of your acquaintance personally for I allways understood your Country was greatly benefited by your councels; and I value you now because I know you are good. The favor conferd on me by an assurance of your esteem shall be ever rememberd. Very little merit on my part has gain'd your good opinion and I will endeavour not to forfiet it. We were anxious to hear from you one and all and expected Mr. Madison wou'd have wrote a few lines but I believe he dont feel as much at Parting as we do. Indeed he has not the same reason. I cant help thinking he might have said a few words by way of comfort to his old friends. Mr. Mercer too not a line from him. I am determined to write only to those who first writes to me.

Mama pines exceedingly; she has sustaind a heavy loss. It is not likly she will ever have so agreeable a family again for I have not the most distant hope that Congress will ever return to this city. Mr. Harrison and Lady (he is a banished tory from N York) and old Smith who is grown intollarable are all that at present encircles our board. I realy am obliged to be silent and bite my tongue fear of Quarreling I wou'd rather live among Hornets then be obliged to live with Mr. Smith. His manners are very disagreeable to me. It reminds us of our former happiness. They must be exceeding clever who can be considerd tolarable after those Gentlemen that we have been accustomd to live with.

Tell Mr. Mercer I shall never abuse congress while I live. I even feel an affection for those I formerly disliked and I allways thought highly of my congressinal friend but now I think I did not so much as I ought. I was happier than I deserved

> I prized every hour that went by
> Beyond all that had pleased me before
> But now they are gone and I sigh
> And I grieve that I prized them no more.

I have been again disapointed in my Passage but am now determined to go by Pittsburg. A very good opportunity offers the first breaking up of the winter down to Orleans and Mr. Fowler a friend of mine is now in the city and intends setting out in a few days. I have sent off my baggage in a Waggon and have purchased a Horse for my self to ride and have equiped my self for the expedition. Unless something unforeseen happens I shall very soon proceed on my journey. It is a very great undertaking for me who never experiencd any hardships to ride over the Mountains this season of the year. I expect to suffer a little but this I am certain the fatigues of the Body can not be worse than that of the mind which I have experiencd in the extreem. I can not return so soon as you advise but I may venture to promise I will meet you here for it will be a long time before the Bob reaches this city. The needle dont Point this way. The kindness and attention of the inhabitants of Maryland so far exceeds that of Pennsylvania that I dont Expect your *August* Body will ever leave that State.

RC (MHi); without place, date, salutation, signature, or endorsement; it is possible that a final page or pages is missing, though the present text is very likely the whole. The date is conjectural. Mrs. Trist was replying to TJ's letter of 5 Dec. 1783. He seems to have had that reply in hand when he wrote Madison on 11 Dec. and also when he wrote the "postscript" letter to Mrs. Trist which all evidence indicates could only have been written on the same date. Nevertheless, when he knew that she intended leaving Philadelphia about 18 Dec. (see TJ to Madison, 1 Jan. 1784), why did he wait until 22 Dec. to write her urging that she postpone her trip to Pittsburgh? This interval can best be explained by the supposition that, on Mrs. Trist's receiving the "postscript" letter around 15 Dec., she wrote another (and missing) reply stating that she intended to depart about 18 Dec., to which TJ responded on 22 Dec. Another possibility is that TJ's reference in his to Madison of 11 Dec. to the effect that "Our news from the good family we left is not agreeable" was based on a letter from someone else to him or to another member of the Virginia delegation; that the "postscript" letter had reference in part to this information from another source; and that, therefore, the present letter may have been written around 15-18 Dec., TJ's letter of 22 Dec. being an immediate reply to it. The terms "Our news" and "We hear" in the letter to Madison, together with the statement that "the *ladies . . .* propose soon to depart," may lend plausibility to this supposition. But the editors incline to the former interpretation—that Mrs. Trist wrote TJ twice between 5 and 22 Dec. and that, therefore, the present letter must have been written about 8 Dec.

THE BOB: This was an allusion to a designation given by Francis Hopkinson to Congress in one of his satirical essays. Under the caption "Intelligence Extraordinary," there appeared in the

Penna. Gazette for 29 Oct. 1783 an announcement of a new discovery: "The Americans having observed the great irregularities to which the political systems of Europe are liable, have invented a method of regulating the affairs of their empire by ACTUAL MECHANISM. For this purpose an immense pendulum hath been constructed, of which the point of suspension is fixed somewhere in the orbit of the planet *Mars*, and the *Bob* is composed of certain heterogeneous matter of great specific gravity, called the *American Congress*. This miraculous pendulum is to vibrate between Annapolis, on the Chesapeak, and Trenton, on the Delaware; a range of about 180 miles" (quoted in Hastings, *Hopkinson*, p. 382).

From James Madison

DEAR SIR   Orange Decemr. 10th. 1783.

My journey from Annapolis was so much retarded by rains and their effect on the water courses that I did not complete it till the ninth day after I left you. I took *Col. Mason*[1] in my *way and had an evening's conversation with him. I found him much less opposed to the general impost than I had expected.* Indeed *he disclaimed all opposition to the measure itself but had taken up a vague* apprehension that *if adopted at this crisis it might embarrass* the *defence of our trade against British machinations. He seemed* upon the whole to *acquiesce in the territorial cession* but *dwelt much on the* expediency of the *guaranty. On the article of a convention* for *revising our form of government he was sound and ripe and I think would not decline a* participation *in the work. His heterodoxy lay chiefly in being too little impressed with* either the *necessity* or the *proper means of preserving the* confederacy.

The situation of the commerce of this country as far as I can learn is even more deplorable than I had conceived. It can not pay less to Philada. and Baltimore if one may judge from a comparison of prices here and in Europe, than 30 or 40 Per Ct. on all the exports and imports, a tribute which if paid into the treasury of the State would yield a surplus above all its wants. If the Assembly should take any steps towards its emancipation you will no doubt be apprized of them as well as of their other proceedings from Richmond.

I am not yet settled in the course of law reading with which I have tasked myself and find it will be impossible to guard it against frequent interruptions. I deputed one of my brothers to Monticello with the draught on your library, but Capt. Key was down at Richmond. As soon as he returns I propose to send again. My Trunk with Buffon &c. has come safe to Fredg. so that I shall be well furnished with materials for collateral reading. In conversing on this author's Theory of Central heat I recollect that we touched upon, as the best means for trying its validity, the comparative distances from the Earths center of the summits of the highest mountains and their bases or the level of the sea.[2] Does not the oblate figure of the earth present a much more extensive and perhaps adequate field for experiments? According to the calculations of Martin grounded on the data of Maupertius &c.

The Equatorial diameter of the Earth is 7942.2. Eng: Miles
The polar diam: 7852.4. E.M.
difference between Eq: and pol: diameter   89.8. E.M.

The difference then of the semidiameters is 44.9 E. Miles, that is $\frac{1}{87.94}$ of the mean semidiameter, calling this difference in round numbers 45 Miles, and disregarding the small variations produced by the elliptical form of the Earth, the radii will be shortened ½ of a mile by each degree from the Equator to the poles. It would seem therefore that the difference of distance from the center at the Equator and at the highest latitude that may [be] visited must be sufficient to produce a discoverable difference in the degrees of any heat emitted equally in every direction from the center: and the experiments might be sufficiently diversified to guard against illusion from any difference which might be supposed in the intermediate density of different parts of the earth. The distance even between the Equator and the polar circle produces a difference of no less than 33⅙ miles i.e. $\frac{1}{119}$ of the mean distance from the center; so that if the curiosity of the two setts of French Philosophers employed in ascertaining the figure of the earth, had been directed to this question, a very little additional trouble and expence might perhaps have finally solved it. Nay the extent of the U.S. computing from the 31°. of lat: to the 45°. only makes a difference of 7 miles in the distance from the center of the Earth; a greater difference I suppose than is afforded by the highest mountains or the deepest mines or both put together.

On my delivering you the draught on Mr. Ambler I remember you put into my hands a note which I never looked into, supposing it to relate to that circumstance. In examining my papers I perceive that I have lost it and mention it to put you on your guard in case the note should fall into bad hands and be capable of being abused. Present my respects to Mr. Mercer and the other Gentlemen of the Delegation and be assured that I am Yrs Sincerely,

J. MADISON Jr.

You will be so good as to give the inclosed a safe conveyance to Mrs. House.

RC (DLC: Madison Papers); en-dorsed with date by Madison after it had been returned to him; partly in code. Enclosure not found.

Madison's discussion with George Mason on the subject of A CONVEN-TION FOR REVISING OUR FORM OF GOV-ERNMENT referred, of course, to the Virginia Constitution (see under 17 June 1783). YOU PUT INTO MY HANDS A NOTE: This was a promissory note to Madison given in exchange for a

draft on Jacquelin Ambler by Madison that TJ had borrowed (see TJ to Am-bler, 27 Nov. 1783; TJ to Madison, 1 Jan. 1784).

1 This and subsequent words were written in code and were decoded inter-lineally by TJ, employing Code No. 3.

2 In the margin of this passage, Madison added, at a much later date, a reference to his letter to TJ of 17 Feb. 1784.

To Peter Carr

DEAR PETER   Annapolis Dec. 11. 1783

In inclose for you under cover to Mr. Madison a copy of Homer. I am anxious to hear from you, to know how your time is employed, and what books you read. You are now old enough to know how very important to your future life will be the manner in which you employ your present time. I hope therefore you will never waste a moment of it. You may be assured that nothing shall be wanting on my part which may contribute to your improvement and future happiness. I hope you have restored yourself perfectly to the esteem of Mr. Maury. I have so much confidence in his justice and pru-dence as to be satisfied he will always make your good the object of what he does. Were it to happen however that in the exercise of that strict discipline which a large school requires, that he should be harsher with you than you suppose to be necessary, yet you must have resolution enough to bear it, and to bear it with resigna-tion. You will find it contribute to your happiness in the end. Do not be misled by others into an opinion that to oppose a tutor and to set him at defiance is shewing a laudable spirit, on the con-trary nothing can be more blameable, and nothing will discredit you more in the opinion of sensible men. If you doubt this, look abroad into the world and see whether there be one single instance of a man of learning and influence in his country, who spent his youth in warfare with his tutors. I wish you to be particularly attentive to Mrs. Maury. Nothing can be more unmanly than to treat a lady supercilious[ly]. It is in her power to make your time more comfortable, and should you be sick from whom else are you to expect assistance? Besides that it is proper for you now to begin to learn those attentions and that complaisance which the world requires should be shewn to every lady. The earlier you begin the practice of this, the sooner it will become habitual, and with the more ease to yourself will you enter on the public stage of life, and conduct yourself through it. You will find that on rendering yourself agreeable to that sex will depend a great part of the happiness of your life: and the way to do it is to practice to every one all those civilities which a favourite one might require. If you can find means to attract the notice and acquaintance of my friend Mr. Madison lately returned to your neighborhood from Congress he will be a most valuable patron to you. His judgment is so sound and his heart so good that I would wish you to respect every advice he would be so kind as to give you, equally as if it came from me.

I am Dr. Peter Yours affectionately,   TH: JEFFERSON

RC (Gabriel Wells, New York City, 1946). Entry in SJL reads merely: "P. Carr."

To Martha Jefferson

MY DEAR PATSY   Annapolis Dec. 11. 1783

I wrote you by the post this day fortnight, since which I have received two letters from you. I am afraid that you may not have sent to the post office and therefore that my letter may be still lying there. Tho' my business here may not let me write to you every week yet it will not be amiss for you to enquire at the office every week. I wrote to Mr. House by the last post. Perhaps his letter may still be in the office. I hope you will have good sense enough to disregard those foolish predictions that the world is to be at an end soon. The almighty has never made known to any body at what time he created it, nor will he tell any body when he means to put an end to it, if ever he means to do it. As to preparations for that event, the best way is for you to be always prepared for it. The only way to be so is never to do nor say a bad thing. If ever you are about to say any thing amiss or to do any thing wrong, consider before hand. You will feel something within you which will tell you it is wrong and ought not to be said or done: this is your conscience, and be sure to obey it. Our maker has given us all, this faithful internal Monitor, and if you always obey it, you will always be prepared for the end of the world: or for a much more certain event which is death. This must happen to all: it puts an end to the world as to us, and the way to be ready for it is never to do a wrong act. I am glad you are proceeding regularly under your tutors. You must not let the sickness of your French master interrupt your reading French, because you are able to do that with the help of your dictionary. Remember I desired you to send me the best copy you should make of every lesson Mr. Cimitiere should set you. In this I hope you will be punctual, because it will let me see how you are going on. Always let me know too what tunes you play. Present my compliments to Mrs. Hopkinson, Mrs. House and Mrs. Trist. I had a letter from your uncle Eppes last week informing me that Polly is very well, and Lucy recovered from an indisposition. I am my dear Patsy Your affectionate father, TH: JEFFERSON

RC (DLC). For a presumed postscript to this letter, see TJ to Mrs. Trist, this date. Entry in sjl merely refers to "Patsy" and does not mention postscript.

The TWO LETTERS FROM Patsy to TJ have not been found, nor has that FROM YOUR UNCLE [Francis] EPPES.

To James Madison

DEAR SIR   Annapolis Dec. 11. 1783.

Your determination to avail yourself of the fine weather proved I fear a very unfortunate one. I pitied your probable situation in the tempestuous season which immediately succeeded your departure. It is now above a fortnight since we should have met, and six states only appear. We have some hopes of Rhodeisland coming in to-day, but when two more will be added seems as insusceptible of calculation as when the next earthquake will happen. We have at length received the Definitive treaty with a joint letter from all our Commissioners. Not a tittle is changed in the treaty but the preamble and some small things which were of course. The Commissioners write that the riot of Philadelphia and departure of Congress thence made the most serious impressions in Europe, and have excited great doubts of the stability of our confederacy, and in what we shall end. The accounts were greatly exaggerated, and it is suspected that Gr. Br. wished to sign no treaty.

You have seen G.M. [George Mason] I hope and had much conversation with him. What are his sentiments as to the amendment of our constitution? What amendments would he approve? Is he determined to sleep on, or will he rouze and be active? I wish to hear from you on this subject, and at all times on any others which occupy your thoughts. I see Bradford advertises Smith's history of N. York. As I mean to write for one for myself, and think I heard you say you had it not, I shall add one for you. Our news from the good family we left is not agreeable. Mrs. Trist is much agitated by the doubts and difficulties which hang over her and impede her reunion with Mr. Trist. They are without lodgers except those we left there, and the ladies we left there propose soon to depart. We hear some circumstances of rudeness in Mr. S. inconsistent with the inoffensiveness of character we had given him credit for. I wish you much happiness and am with the sincerest esteem Dr. Sir, Your friend & servt,   TH: JEFFERSON

P.S. I have taken the liberty of putting under cover to you a book for my nephew Peter Carr who is at Mr. Maury's in your neighborhood.

RC (DLC: Madison Papers); addressed: "James Madison junr. esq. Orange. to the care of Mr. Jas. Maury Fredericksburg"; endorsed in a later hand. Entry in SJL reads: "Jas. Madison. No Congress—definitive treaty—G. Mas.—Mrs. H's family—Homer to P.C."

To James Maury

[*Annapolis, 11 Dec. 1783*. Entry in SJL reads: "Jas. Maury. What ports [posts?] would prefer—whether like the footing." Not found.]

To Philip Mazzei

[*Annapolis, 11 Dec. 1783*. Entry in SJL reads: "P. Mazzei. Account of my transactions for him—how my own time filled up in his absence." Not found.]

To Eliza House Trist

TH: J. TO MRS. TRIST   [Annapolis, 11 December 1783?]

Availing myself of the place in P's letter where a postscript should be, I take the liberty of adding my wishes for your health and happiness, and assurances that I feel myself much interested in those events which may affect either. I hope the day is near when Mr. Trist's return will make amends for the crosses and disappointments you complain of, and render the current of life as smooth and placid as you can wish. In the mean time you are supported by a certainty that you are again to meet. If you wish to know the value of this circumstance, ask it of the many wretched from whom that consolation is cut off. They will tell you it is from heaven you are looking down on them. It is not easy to reconcile ourselves to the many useless miseries to which Providence seems to expose us. But his justice affords a prospect that we shall all be made even some day. To be less serious—I think you will be a distinguished creditor if you pursue your wild Missisipi scheme. If you chuse to live in the woods you may find them nearer. I have much to say in favour of those of my own country, and particularly of that part of it in which I live. But as this panegyric would make my postscript too long for it's letter I will postpone it till I shall have the pleasure of seeing you, and in the mean while will be looking out for some of the tallest and most recluse I can find. I have now in my eye a mountain where nothing but the eagle can visit you which I think would suit your present taste for retirement. It looks down on mine as a giant does on a dwarf. It wants but one circumstance to render it perfect, which is that it should be placed within a dozen miles of Philadelphia, or rather Philadelphia within a dozen miles of it. Be so good as to present my compliments to Browse with the little tale inclosed, which if he will repeat by heart whenever we meet again, I will give him half a dozen of the best Barton's knives in Philadelphia and he may commence merchant.

FC (MHi); in TJ's hand but without date or signature; endorsed by him: "Trist mrs." The message was written as a postscript to one of TJ's letters to Martha Jefferson at about this time. TJ's earliest letter to Mrs. Trist is clearly that of 5 Dec., and she set out on her journey down the Mississippi on 21 Dec.; the only letter to Martha to which this might have been a postscript is therefore that dated 11 Dec., for on the same day on which TJ next wrote Martha (22 Dec.) he wrote a separate letter to Mrs. Trist, the summary of which in SJL does not correspond with the present message. From the circumstance that TJ very seldom kept copies of his outgoing letters at this time, it might be thought that the message was written but not sent; but Mrs. Trist seems unquestionably to allude to it in a letter she wrote TJ from "Accadian Coast Mississippi," 25 Dec. 1784, q.v. The LITTLE TALE INCLOSED for Browse Trist, her son, has not been found or identified.

To Benjamin Harrison

[*Annapolis*, 12 Dec. 1783. Entry in SJL reads: "Governor. Definitive treaty—British proclamation on commerce." Not found.]

To Joseph Jones

[*Annapolis*, 12 Dec. 1783. Entry in SJL reads: "Jos. Jones. No Congr. Definitive treaty. Western cession." Not found.]

Report on the Definitive Treaty of Peace and the Letter from the American Commissioners

[16 December 1783]

The committee to whom were referred the Definitive treaty of peace between the United states of America and his Britannic majesty, and the joint letter from Mr. Adams, Mr. Franklin and Mr. Jay, have agreed to the following report.

Resolved that it is the opinion of this committee that the said Definitive treaty ought to be ratified by the United states in Congress assembled.[1]

That a Proclamation should be immediately issued notifying the said definitive treaty and ratification to the several states of the Union, and requiring their observance thereof.[2]

That Congress should immediately and earnestly recommend to the legislatures of the respective states, to provide for the restitution of all estates, rights and properties, which have been confiscated, belonging to real British subjects; and also of the estates, rights, and properties of persons resident in districts which were in possession of his Britannic majesty's arms at any time between the 30th. day of November 1782. and the   day of December 1783[3] and who have not borne arms against the said United states and that persons of any other description shall have free liberty to go to any part or parts of any of the thirteen United states, and therein to remain twelvemonths unmolested in their endeavors to obtain the restitution of such of their estates, rights and properties as may have been confiscated; and that Congress should also immediately and earnestly recommend to the several states a reconsideration and revision of all acts or laws regarding the premises, so as to render the said laws or acts perfectly consistent not only with justice and equity, but with that spirit of conciliation, which, on the return of the blessings of peace, should universally prevail: and that Congress should also immediately and earnestly recommend to the several states, that the estates, rights and properties of such last mentioned persons, should be restored to them, they refunding to any persons, who may be now in possession, the bonâ fide price (where any has been given) which such persons may have paid on purchasing any of the said lands, rights or properties since the confiscation.

MS (DLC: PCC, No. 29); endorsed by Charles Thomson: "Report of Mr Jefferson &c On Definitive treaty Delivered 16 Decr. 1783 Read.—Entd. Passed Jany 14. 1784." With the exceptions noted below, the MS is entirely in TJ's hand. According to Committee Book (PCC, No. 186), the committee on the Definitive Treaty and the joint letter from the American ministers in Paris (dated 10 Sep. 1783 and printed in Wharton, *Dipl. Corr. Amer. Rev.*, VI, 687-91) was appointed on 13 Dec. and consisted of TJ, Gerry, Ellery, Read, and Hawkins. Read on 16 Dec., the Report was adopted in an altered form on 14 Jan. 1784; see under that date.

On the subject of confiscated property and admission of "persons of any other description" to any part of the United States, one of the Virginia delegates wrote the following on 10 Dec. to a member of the General Assembly: "Your taking up the subject of the Citizen Bill, was, in my judgment, premature, before the recommendations of Congress, on that subject had come forth. I am, myself, principled against refugees and British debts. I think the former will *make wretched Republicans*; and *to the latter*, in my opinion, all *just title* has been *forfeited*. But let us see what the faith of America as a caution, and her interest as a people, require, and leaving all prejudice against those people aside, act in conformity thereto. Our conduct, or rather the conduct of some very wild and unthinking people, scattered throughout the United States, has hurt us much in the eyes of all Europe, where that article in favor of refugees is considered as very humiliating to Great-Britain, and such as our honor and interest call on us to explain and adhere to liberty" (*Pa. Journal*, 3 Jan. 1784, entitled: "Richmond [Virginia] Dec. 20. Extract of a letter from a Member of Congress, to his correspondent in this City, a gentleman in the General Assembly, dated Annapolis, December 10th, 1783"). This letter was probably written by Hardy, Lee, Mercer, or Monroe; the sentiments expressed about debts and the fact that it is not recorded in SJL make it certain that TJ was not the author. On TJ's later connection with the recommendation here made to the states concerning confiscated property and Loyalists, see an excellent summary in Malone, *Jefferson*, II, 414-17.

[1] This paragraph was corrected by deletions and interlineations in Charles Thomson's hand to read: "Resolved that the said Definitive treaty be ratified by the United states in Congress assembled."

[2] Opposite this paragraph, also in Thomson's hand, is the word "Agreed."

[3] Corrected in Thomson's hand to read: "the 14th day of Jany 1784."

To Edmund Pendleton

DEAR SIR   Annapolis Dec. 16. 1783.

I received your favor of the 8th inst. with great satisfaction as it anticipated a proposition I want to make you of interchanging communications sometimes. The termination of the war will render what I can send you less interesting perhaps, while your intelligence will retain it's value. It is very essential to us to obtain information of facts, of opinions, and of wishes from our own country: with this view I have been writing by every post to my acquaintances in the General assembly but never yet have been able to provoke one scrip of a pen from any person of that honourable body.

On the day before yesterday we for the first time had seven states. The Definitive treaty had been received by the President some time, and a joint letter from our Ministers. This gave us an account of the various propositions and steps taken on both sides in the negociation which preceded the Definitive treaty. Mr. Hartley was the British negotiator with America. He was well disposed but his zeal for systems friendly to us constantly exceeded his powers to agree to them. Our ministers proposed a free intercourse between every part of the British dominions and the U.S. saving the rights of their chartered companies. Mr. H. approved of it, but his court declined assenting. He then[1] proposed that the *unmanufactured produce* of the U.S. should be admitted into G.B. and the *manufactures* of G.B. into the U.S. and that we should be allowed to carry our own produce to the W. Indies. On being questioned however he had no authority to conclude upon these articles even if agreable to us. News then arrived in France that our ports were thrown open to British vessels unconditionally. This stopped the negotations till he should communicate the intelligence to his court and receive their instructions. They immediately drew back; no further instructions were sent, till the other powers were ready to sign their definitive treaties when the British court ordered Hartley to sign the provisional articles as definitive. While they were expecting his instructions for the commercial treaty our Ministers went on with discussions for the definitive pacification. They proposed that we should be allowed to stay execution on judgments for British debts 3 years from the signature of the treaty, and that no interest should be demanded but from the time of the signature: that instead of recommending a restitution of confiscated property, a valuation of all destructions of property on both sides should be made and the balance only be paid by the party which had suffered least: that the Lakes, the Missisipi and St. Laurence with all the carrying places should be common to both. No answer could ever be obtained from the British court on any of these points. After signing definitively Hartley went to England expecting to return and settle the Commercial system; but they think it very incertain whether he will return. They press in the warmest terms the execution of the articles in favor of the tories. They say that the introduction of committees and town-meetings when we have a regular government established, the situation of the army, our reluctance to pay taxes, and the circumstances under which Congress left Philadelphia have reduced our new establishments much in the eyes of the European nations: that if England can be prevailed on to establish a liberal system of commerce, other nations will do so too; but probably not otherwise: that were it certain we could be brought to act as one united nation she would make extensive concessions, but under present appearances she has no inducement to this as she is not afraid of retaliation: and conclude by observing that if in our commercial system we do not act collectedly 'we shall soon find ourselves in the situation in which all Europe wishes to see us, viz. as unimportant consumers of her manufactures and productions, and [as]² useful labourers to furnish her with raw materials.' We have no certain prospect of nine states in Congress and cannot ratify the treaty with fewer. Yet the ratifications are to be exchanged by the 3d of March.

We have received a copy of the Dutch preliminaries. G.B. keeps Nagapatnam, and restores all other places taken. The Dutch are still to pay them the usual salute at sea.

There being at present nothing else worthy a communication to you, I subscribe myself with great esteem Dr. Sir Your friend & servt.,   TH: JEFFERSON

RC (NN); endorsed by Pendleton. Entry in SJL reads: "E.P. 7 states— Definitive treaty—joint letter of ministers—general view of negotations— their thoughts on tories, committees, situation of army, reluctance of taxes, departure of Congress. They are not acting as one nation in matters of commerce—Dutch treaty."

Pendleton's FAVOR OF THE 8TH INST. has not been found, nor have the letters that TJ evidently wrote BY EVERY POST TO . . . ACQUAINTANCES IN THE GENERAL ASSEMBLY (see note to preceding document), though entries in SJL appear for letters to such members of the legislature as David Ross, Mann Page, John Tyler, Gabriel Jones, Archibald Stuart, and Joseph Jones (see under dates of 27 Nov., 5 and 12 Dec. 1783). Other acquaintances in the General Assembly to whom he might have written were Izaac Zane, Thomas Mann Randolph, John Page, and Thomas Nelson, Jr. David Hartley's ZEAL FOR SYSTEMS FRIENDLY TO US appears in a copy of a MS in DLC: TJ Papers, 9: 1489-94, commenting on the American Commissioners' proposal "for an universal and unlimited reciprocity of Intercourse and Commerce between Great Britain and the . . . United States." Hartley found this proposal "fertile in future Prospects to Great Britain" and thought that "America also may wisely see in it a solid foundation for herself." His conclusion exhibited a statesmanlike vision too far-seeing to gain acceptance: "The Independance of the American states being established, their first Considera-

tion ought to be, to determine with what Friendships and Alliances they will enter into the new World of Nations. They will look round them, and cast about for some natural, powerful, and permanent Ally, with whom they may interchange all cementing Reciprocities, both commercial and political. If such an Ally is to be found anywhere for them, it is still in Great Britain. . . . [She] is undoubtedly the first of European Nations in Riches, Credit, Faculties, Industry, Commerce, Manufactures, internal Consumption and foreign Export; together with Civil Liberty, which is the source of all, and Naval Power, which is the Support of all. The Dominions appertaining to the Crown of Great Britain are large and fertile, its Colonies still extensive and in close Vicinity to the American States; Great Britain being herself an American as well as an European Power and all her Empire connected by her Naval Force. The Territories of the American States, from the Atlantic Ocean to the Mississippi, contain an inexhaustible Source of Riches, Industry and future Power. These will be the Foundations of great Events in the new Page of Life. Infinite Good or infinite Evil may arise according to the Principles upon which the Intercourse between Great Britain and the American States shall be arranged in its Foundation. Great Britain and the United States must be still inseparable, either as Friends or Foes. This is an awful and important Truth. These are considerations not to be thought slightly of, not to be prejudged in Passion, nor the Arrangements of them to be hastily foreclosed. Time given for Consideration may have excellent Effects on both sides. The Pause of Peace, with friendly Intercourse, returning Affection and dispassionate Inquiry can alone decide these important Events, or do justice to the anxious Expectations of Great Britain or America" (dated 1 June 1783; endorsed by TJ: "Commerce. Notes &c. on treaty of by D. Hartley").

1 At this point TJ deleted the following: "probably by their instructions."
2 TJ omitted "as" in the quotation from the Commissioners' letter of 10 Sep. 1783 (Wharton, *Dipl. Corr. Amer. Rev.*, VI, 687-91).

To Benjamin Harrison

SIR   Annapolis Decemb. 17. 1783.

I had the honour of writing to your Excellency on the 12th. instant on the subject of the Definitive treaty. On the day following we made up a Congress of seven states, but nine being requisite to ratify the treaty, we have been unable to get this done; and of course till it be ratified Congress can make no communications on the subject to the states. I am sorry to say that I see no immediate prospect of making up nine states, so careless are either the states or their delegates to their particular interests as well as the general good which would require that they be all constantly and fully represented in Congress.

Several letters from our foreign ministers have been read in the course of the past week. A joint one accompanying the treaty informs us that they were proceeding in negociations on the subject of commerce with Mr. Hartley the British minister, giving and receiving propositions, when a vessel arrived in France from Philadelphia bringing intelligence that all our ports were thrown open to British vessels. Mr. Hartley on this informed them he could take no other steps till he should communicate this intelligence to his court and receive their instructions. He communicated it, and from that moment they were locked up in impenetrable reserve, and he unable to extort an answer of any kind from them. While expecting this answer, the ministers proceeded to exchange propositions for a definitive pacification. Ours proposed a three years suspension of executions on judgments for British debts, and that no interest should be allowed from the commencement of the war till the definitive signing: that accounts should be taken of all wanton waste of property on both sides and confiscations, and the balance be paid in money by the party suffering least: that the St. Laurence, the water boundary between us, and the Missisipi with the carrying places on whatever side, should be common to both. But it was now become impossible to get an answer of any sort from the court of London: and when the negotiations between the other belligerent powers were matured for signing, Mr. Hartley received orders to sign the preliminary articles as definitive, which was done. Mr. Hartley, who wished to establish a liberal system of commerce with us, then went to London hoping to return shortly and renew the commercial discussions. But our ministers think it doubtful whether he will return at all. I take the liberty of inclosing you an extract from their letter expressing their sentiments on some subjects of importance, supposing it will be neither unpleasant nor unprofitable to know how we are viewed on the general scale of nations. I am sure it would be unnecessary even to hint to your Excellency that no part of this extract should be permitted to fall into the indiscreet hands of any printer. It seems possible that Great Britain may continue on the reserve till the present crisis in Europe shall have taken it's direction. The two Empires have formed an alliance defensive against all Christian powers, and offensive against the Turks. When announced by the Empress to the K. of Prussia he answered 'that he was very sensible upon this communication as one is on the communication of things of great importance,'[1] thus avoiding a declaration and reserving himself at liberty to take any side or no side. The Court of France took it up in a higher tone, and expressed her astonishment at the objects of the alliance. She immediately began the work of putting her army on the war establishment. Yet it is said there is a division in their councils. The present minister cannot retire from his declarations, which are for opposing the dangerous accession of power to Austria and Russia should they, as they propose, drive the Turks out of Europe and divide the territories they should abandon. The continuance or removal of the present minister is suggested as an index of the ultimate determination of France. If he goes out, they mean to be pacific; and to be active if he is retained. Yet it is doubted whether France can venture into the war without the aid of Prussia. Great Britain it is suspected will lie dormant to avail herself of the distresses of her neighbor. Happy for us that we have got into port just as this storm is rising. Propositions for treaties of commerce have come to Dr. Franklin from several European courts, and others are ready to treat. Denmark, Portugal, Sardinia, the Emperor of Morocco have made overtures. The last is so well disposed that he has issued orders to his armed vessels to molest no American, and has sent a person to Paris to attend any[2] person delegated from us to his court. Great Britain will send no minister to America till she receives one from thence. The Emperor of Germany cannot from the custom of his court. Our Minister Mr. Dana is on the return from Petersburg: nothing being done there, tho' probably their dispositions were become favourable at the time it was thought necessary by his recall to shew we should no longer be suppliants any where. It is to be noted that the observation of our ministers in the inclosed extract 'that the present aspect of our affairs has somewhat abated the ardor of the European nations to form connections with us' is posterior in time to the state given above. I recollect nothing important enough to be added to this sketch of our affairs in Europe and of those of Europe itself.

The former method of correspondence by joint letters from the delegates to the Executive has been liable to some difficulties. The same object does not always make the same impression on different eyes. Of consequence it might happen that by pursuing the method of joint representation, much must be kept back because all had not formed the same ideas of it. Being sensible that frequent and full communications are for the public good, we have agreed to adopt the following plan of official correspondency with your Excellency if it shall meet with your approbation. Resolutions of Congress and other solemn things which call for authentic notification we will communicate jointly. But all other matters which admit differences of opinion we propose shall be communicated weekly by some one gentleman of the delegation, having previously shewn his letter to his collegues. If they think he has omitted any thing or represented it differently from their own view of it, they reserve a private and separate right of writing to your Excellency their separate sentiments. In this way we think you will receive fuller informations and that you may judge for yourself where you find a difference of opinion. The duty of correspondence is made mine for the present month, and will be taken up by my collegues successively in the order of their nomination, each exercising it a month.

I have the honour to be with sentiments of the most profound esteem & respect Your Excellency's Most obedient & most humble servt. TH: JEFFERSON

RC (PHi); endorsed. Enclosure is missing, but that part of the ministers' letter of 10 Sep. 1783 that TJ sent may have been in part the same as that for which a press copy exists in DLC: TJ Papers, 9: 1535. This extract reads as follows: "Permit us to observe, that in our opinion the Recommendation of Congress, promised in the 5th Article, should immediately be made in the terms of it and published; and that the states should be requested to take it into consideration as soon as the evacuation by the enemy shall be completed. It is also much to be wished that the Legislatures may not involve all the Tories in banishment and ruin, but that such discrimination may be made, as to entitle the decisions to the approbation of disinterested men, and dispassionate posterity" (extract in clerk's hand). For TJ's inclusion of the ministers' advice in the report of the committee on the Definitive Treaty, see under 16 Dec. 1783. As soon as this report was acted on by Congress on 14 Jan. 1784, that part of it containing the recommendation to the state legislatures was printed and TJ enclosed a copy thereof in his letter to Gov. Harrison of 17 Jan. 1784 (see notes to both letters of that date). But because he knew that the Virginia General Assembly had already taken up the questions of British debts and the admission of British subjects, TJ here gave advance information to Harrison and on 18 and 19 Dec. he also sent other copies of the extract from the ministers' letter to the Speakers of both houses (see under dates given). But the extract must also have contained those paragraphs of the ministers' letter concerning the "unseasonable and unnecessary resolves of various towns on this subject, the actual expulsion of tories from some places, and the avowed implacability of almost all who have published their sentiments"; these popular assemblies and

their proceedings on matters within the cognizance of the different legislatures, the ministers asserted, had "exceedingly lessened the dignity of the states in the eyes of these nations"; and "the situation of the army, the reluctance of the people to pay taxes, and the circumstances under which Congress removed from Philadelphia" had also served to diminish "the admiration in which the people of America were held among the nations of Europe" (Wharton, *Dipl. Corr. Amer. Rev.*, VI, 689-90).

The plan of correspondence by the delegates IN THE ORDER OF THEIR NOMINATION called for this sequence of rotation: TJ, Samuel Hardy, John Francis Mercer, Arthur Lee, and James Monroe. See TJ to Harrison, 17 Jan. and 3 Mch. 1784, for comments on the working of the plan.

1 TJ deleted the following at this point: "answered that it affected him strongly as the communication of great events must affect reflecting minds."

2 TJ deleted the following at this point: "American minister that may be appointed."

To Speaker of the House of Delegates

[*Annapolis*, 18 Dec. 1783. Entry in SJL reads: "Sp. H. Del. European intelligence.—extract from letter of Ministers." Letter and enclosure not found, but see preceding document and note.]

To Martha Jefferson Carr

[*Annapolis*, 19 Dec. 1783. Entry in SJL reads: "Mrs. Carr. My request of W. S. [William Short] and orders to Key—ill health—heard only once from P. and L. [Polly and Lucy]. Not found.]

To Speaker of the Senate

[*Annapolis*, 19 Dec. 1783. Entry in SJL reads: "Sp. Sen. European intelligence—extract from letter of Ministers—proposition on G. town to Del. of Maryld." Letter and enclosure not found, but see TJ's letter to Benjamin Harrison, 17 Dec. 1783, and note. The phrase "proposition on G. town" (i.e., Georgetown) clearly refers to a proposal TJ, presumably with other members of the Virginia delegation, must have made to the Maryland delegates in Congress; nothing further is known of this, but it probably involved TJ's resolution for joint action by Virginia and Maryland to fix the seat of Congress on the Potomac (see Document v in Notes and Memoranda by Madison and TJ, printed above at end of Nov. 1783).]

From Benjamin Harrison

SIR   Council Chamber Decr. 19th. 1783.

I send you an act of our assembly by which you will see their willingness to join the other states in any plan that Congress and they may think necessary to force Great Britain into a generous commercial treaty with us. Great expectations are entertained here of the efficacy of the measure, tho' I confess I expect nothing from it. The jaring interests of the States will ever prevent their delegating as much power to Congress as will be adequate to the purpose. I sent your favor of the 12th. to the Assembly and suggested a measure that pleases me better than the present one which is to recommend to the several states the appointment of a deputy to meet at Philadelphia to settle a general plan of opposition for the whole united States. To this I think none can object as it will remove their fears, by the appointments being only temporary and for a particular purpose. Whether the proposal will be adopted or not, I know not, as they are resolved to rise tomorrow and are as usual all hurry and confusion.

The impost bill has passed both houses and differs as I am told but in two instances from the recommendations of Congress; the first is the appointment of collectors which is given to the executive, the other postpones the time of its taking place till the other states shall pass similar acts which will probably never happen.

I am &c.

FC (Vi); caption reads: "The honorable Thomas Jefferson."

On 18 Dec. Harrison sent TJ's FAVOR OF THE 12TH. TO THE ASSEMBLY with the following comment: "The enclosed letters from Mr. Jefferson and Mr. Mercer are just come to hand. As they throw some light on the situation of our trade I suppose they will be acceptable to the Assembly and therefore request the favor of You to communicate their contents to them. I am fearful from what Mr. Jefferson says of the opinions of many gentlemen in Congress that nothing effectual will be done by that body, and that the methods we are pursuing will not answer our expectations even if they should enter on the business, as it is much to be doubted whether the different states will give them power to act with vigor. Should this be the case and the present moment lost, we shall feel the ill effects of it a great length of time. If it should not be thought going beyond my line I would suggest the appointment of some gentleman of abilities acquainted with the subject to meet a deputy from each of the other states at Philadelphia to consult with them one general plan of conduct for the whole united States which would take off the objection, in which there is some weight, of putting the regulation of our commerce into the hands of Congress. I am the more confirmed in my opinion that the mode adopted will not answer the desirable end proposed from a perfect recollection of the arguments used when the subject was under consideration at the æra of the general confederation, a great majority of the states appearing then to revolt at the idea of delegating such a power" (Harrison to Speaker of the House, 18 Dec. 1783, Executive Letter Book, Vi). For action by the General Assembly on this recommendation, see Harrison to the Virginia delegates, 26 Dec. 1783.

To William Short

[*Annapolis, 19 Dec. 1783.* Entry in SJL reads: "W. Short. 1st. hope desperate—2d doubtful—to dispose of P. C. [Peter Carr]—call on Key for money and conveiance." Not found.]

Report on Letters from the American Ministers in Europe

[20 December 1783]

The committee consisting of Mr. Jefferson, Mr. Gerry and Mr. Williamson to whom were referred the letters of the Ministers for the U.S. in Europe have agreed to the following report.

They find that instructions bearing date the 29 of Octr. 1783 were sent to the Ministers plenipotentiary of the U S of America at the court of Versailles empowered to negotiate a peace or to any one or more of them for concerting draughts or propositions for treaties of Amity or commerce with the commercial powers of Europe but that their powers will not extend to the actual signature of any such treaty nor to negotiate with any state or power out of Europe.

They do not find that any commission consonant with these instructions has been issued to the said Ministers.

They are of opinion it will be advantageous to these United States to conclude such treaties with Russia, ⟨*Germany*⟩ the Court of Vienna, Prussia, Denmark, the Elector of Saxony, Hamburg, Great Britain, Spain, Portugal, Genoa, Tuscany, Rome, Naples, Venice, Sardinia and the Ottoman porte ⟨*for its possessions in Europe and Asia and Africa*⟩.[1]

That in the formation of these treaties the following points be carefully stipulated.

1. That each party shall have a right to carry their own produce, manufactures and merchandize in their own bottoms to the ports

of the other and thence to take the produce and merchandize of the other paying in both cases such duties only as are paid by the most favoured nation, freely where it is freely granted to such nation, or paying the compensation where such nation does the same.

2. That with the nations holding territorial possessions in America a direct and similar intercourse be admitted between the U.S. and such possessions or if this cannot be obtained then a direct and similar intercourse between the U S and certain free ports within such possessions. That if this neither can be obtained permission be stipulated to bring from such possessions in their own bottoms the produce and merchandize to these states directly and for these states to carry in their own bottoms their produce and merchandize to such possessions directly ⟨*or lastly a permission to the inhabitants of such possessions to carry their produce and merchandize in their own bottoms to the free ports of other nations, and thence to take back directly the produce and merchandise of these states*⟩.[2]

3. That these U S ⟨*being by their constitution consolidated into one fœderal republic they*⟩ be considered in all such treaties and in every case arising under them as one nation upon the principles of the fœderal Constitution.[3]

4. That it be proposed, though not indispensibly required that if war should hereafter arise between the two contracting parties, the merchants of either country then residing in the other shall be allowed to remain 9 months to collect their debts and settle their affairs and may depart freely carrying off all their effects without molestation or hindrance and all fishermen, all cultivators of the earth and all artizans or manufacturers unarmed and inhabiting unfortified towns villages or places who labour for the common subsistance and benefit of mankind and peaceably following their respective employments shall be allowed to continue the same and shall not be molested by the armed force of the enemy in whose power by the events of war they may happen to fall; but if any thing is necessary to be taken from them for the use of such armed force the same shall be paid for at a reasonable price and all merchants and traders exchanging the products of different places and thereby rendering the necessaries, conveniences and comforts of human life more easy to obtain and more general shall be allowed to pass free and unmolested and neither of the contracting powers shall grant or issue any commission to any private armed vessel, empowering them to take or destroy such trading ships or interrupt such commerce.

5. And in case either of the contracting parties shall happen to

be engaged in war with any other nation it be farther agreed in
order to prevent all the difficulties and misunderstandings that
usually arise respecting the merchandize heretofore called contraband such as arms ammunition and military stores of all kinds that
no such articles carrying by the ships or subjects of one of the
parties to the enemies of the other shall on any account be deemed
contraband so as to induce confiscation and a loss of property to
individuals. Nevertheless it shall be lawful to stop such ships and
detain them for such length of time as the captor may think necessary to prevent the inconvenience or damage that might ensue from
their proceeding on their voyage[4] paying however a reasonable
compensation for the loss such arrest shall occasion to the proprietors. And it shall farther be allowed to use in the service of the
captors the whole or any part of the military stores so detained,
paying the owners the full value of the same, to be ascertained by
the current price at the place of it's destination. But if the other
contracting party will not consent to discontinue the confiscation
of contraband goods then that it be stipulated that if the master of
the vessel stopped will deliver out the goods charged to be contraband he shall be admitted to do it and the vessel shall not in that
case be carried into any port but shall be allowed to proceed on her
voiage.

6. That in the same case where either of the contracting parties
shall happen to be engaged in war with any other power, all goods
not contraband belonging to the subjects of that other power and
shipped in the bottoms of the party hereto not engaged in the war
shall be entirely free. And that to ascertain what shall constitute
the blockade of any place or port, it shall be understood in such
predicament, when the assailing power shall have taken such a
station as to expose to eminent danger any ship or ships that would
attempt to sail in or out of the said ports. And that no vessel of the
party who is not engaged in the said war shall be stopped without
material and well grounded cause: and in such cases justice shall
be done, and an indemnification given without loss of time to the
persons aggrieved and thus stopped without sufficient cause.

7. That no rights be stipulated for aliens to hold ⟨lands⟩ real
⟨estate⟩[5] property within these States this being utterly inadmissible
under their several laws and policy.[6] But where on the death of
any person holding real estate within the territories of one of the
contracting parties such real estate would by their laws descend
on a subject or citizen of the other were he not disqualified by
alienage, then he shall be allowed a reasonable time ⟨to qualify

himself for holding it by changing his country and allegiance⟩ to dispose of the same, and withdraw the proceeds without molestation.

8. ⟨*And*⟩ That such treaties be ⟨*limited to the*⟩ made for a term ⟨*of*⟩ not exceeding 10 years from the exchange of ratifications.

9.[7] That these instructions be considered as supplementary to those of Oct. 1783. and not as revoking except where they contradict them. ⟨*That our ministers be informed that such articles as may be disagreeable to the other party and are indifferent to us in point of interest we mean not that they should insist on indispensably.*⟩ That where, in treaty with a particular nation, they can procure particular advantages, to the specification of which we have been unable to descend, our object in these instructions having been to form outlines only and general principles of treaty with many nations, it is our expectation that they will procure them, tho' not pointed out in these instructions.[8] And where they may be able to form Treaties on ⟨*general*⟩ principles which in their judgement will be more beneficial to the United States, than those herein dictated to be made their basis, they are ⟨*notwithstanding any thing herein*⟩ permitted to adopt ⟨*such and agree to*⟩ such principles:[8] That as to the duration of the treaties tho' we have proposed to restrain them to the period of 10. years yet they are at liberty to extend the same as far as 15[9] years with any nation which may pertinaciously insist thereon: and that it will be agreeable to us to have supplementary treaties with France, the United Netherlands and Sweden, which may bring the treaties we have entered into with them as nearly as may be to the principles of those now directed: but that this be not pressed if the proposal should be found disagreeable.

That treaties of Amity or[10] of Amity and commerce be entered into with Morocco and the ⟨*other states on the coast of Barbary*⟩ and the Regencies of Algiers Tanis and Tripoly to continue for the same term of 10. years or for a term as much longer as can be procured.[11]

That our Ministers to be commissioned for treating with foreign nations make known to the Emperor of Morocco the great satisfaction which Congress feel from the amicable disposition he has shewn towards these states and his readiness to enter into alliance with them. That the occupations of the war and distance of situation have prevented our meeting his friendship so early as we wished; but that powers are now delegated to them for entering into treaty with him, in the execution of which they are ready to proceed: and that as to the expences of his Minister they do therein what is for the honor and interest of the United States ⟨and conformable to the practice of other nations⟩.

That a commission be issued to Mr. Adams, Mr. Franklin and ⟨Mr. Jay⟩ Mr. Jefferson[12] giving powers to them or the greater part of them to make and receive propositions for such treaties of amity and commerce and to negotiate and ⟨conclude⟩ ⟨agree to⟩ sign[13] the same transmitting them to Congress for their final ratification and that[13] such commission be in force for a Term not exceeding two years and no longer.[14]

⟨That the said Ministers be instructed to the powers with whom they may negotiate the great value at which these states will esteem their friendship and consideration and that it will be their constant endeavour to promote a good understanding and harmony with them and to prevent every thing which might interrupt it by every means in their power, but the heavy debts which they have contracted during the late war and the state of desolation and depopulation in which every part of these states were left by it[15] has rendered it inconvenient at present for them to keep ministers resident at the courts of Europe and they hope that this deviation from the practice of friendly nations may be ascribed to its true cause and not to any want of respect to their friends or of attachment to treaties to the faithful observation of which they shall at all times pay the most earnest attention.⟩

⟨That the said ministers be instructed in their negotiations with the [foreig]n court to urge with perseverance the necessity of a reasonable forbearance in the levy of debts due within these states to British subjects, the establishment of the idea of these states that all Demands for Interest accruing During the War would be highly inequitable and unjust;[16] and the expediency of settling this by precise stipulation, in order to avoid those mutual complaints and altercations which may disturb the harmony of the two nations.⟩[17]

That the said Ministers to be commissioned for treating with foreign nations be referred to the Instructions of the thirtieth day of May 1783 relative to British Debts the objects of which they are hereby directed to urge with perseverance.[18]

That they require with firmness and decision full satisfaction for all slaves and other property belonging to citizens of these states taken and carried away in violation of the preliminary and definitive articles of peace: and to enable them to do this on precise grounds Congress will furnish them with necessary facts and documents.[19]

That Consuls be appointed for the ports of

And consuls general established at[20]

That Doct. Franklin be desired to notify to the Apostolical Nuncio at Versailles that Congress will always be pleased to testify their respect to his sovereign and state but that the subject of his application to Doct. Franklin being purely spiritual it is without the jurisdiction and powers of Congress, who have no authority to permit or refuse it, these powers being reserved to the several states individually.

That Doct. Franklin be instructed to express to the court of France the constant desire of Congress to meet their wishes; that these states are about to form a general system of commerce by treaties with other nations ⟨and by internal regulations⟩; that at this time we cannot foresee what claims might be given to those nations by the explanatory propositions from the Count de Vergennes on the 2 and 3 articles of our treaty of Amity and commerce with his M. C. M.; but that he may be assured it will be our constant care to place no people on more advantageous ground than the subjects of his Majesty.

That the papers containing the claims of the five Forsters, brothers, for the prize of their vessel the three friends made by Capt. Landais of the alliance frigate, which papers were communicated by the Count de Vergennes to Doct. Franklin to the end he might apply to Congress for an indemnification of the said Forsters be remitted to the said ministers with a copy of the fourth clause of the instructions to them of Oct.   1783 and the following extract from Doct. Franklins letter of July 22. 1783 to the Secretary for foreign Affairs viz. "Mr. Barclay has in his hands the affair of the Alliance and Bon homme Richard. I will afford him all the assistance in my power, but it is a very perplexed business. That expedition though for particular reasons under American commissions and colours was carried on at the Kings expence and under his orders. Mr. de Chaumont was the agent appointed by the minister of the marine to make the outfit. He was also chose by all the captains of the squadron as appears by an instrument under their hands, to be their agent, receive, sell and divide prizes &c. The crown bought two of them at public sale and the money I understand is lodged in the hands of a responsible person at L'Orient. Mr. D Chaumont says he has given in his accounts to the

Marine and that he has no more to do with the affair except to receive a ballance due to him. That account however is I believe unsettled and the absence of some of the captains is said to make another difficulty which retards the completion of the business. I never paid nor received any thing relating to that expedition nor had any other concern in it than barely ordering the alliance to join the Squadron at M. de Sartine's request." From which extract there is reason to believe the United States of America had no concern in the expedition but that it was carried on wholly under the authority and for the advantage of his Most Christian Majesty; that if this fact should not be so apparent as to give full satisfaction to his Majesty's Ministers, they then take such measures as in their discretion shall be thought most conducive to an amicable and equitable adjustment thereof on the best evidence they shall be able to procure.

That the claim of the Sr. Bayard against these United States for the sum of 255.236 dollars continental Money is not founded in justice ⟨in the Opinion of your committee⟩ from the circumstances of the case as stated by himself, which are that a vessel and cargo in which he was interested sailing in May 1779 from Charles town for France was taken by an english armed vessel and retaken by an American frigate called the Boston, that she was carried to Boston and there sold as french property by Mr. de Valnais consul for France at that port: that he unfaithfully and irregularly as is suggested endeavoured to have the whole adjudged to the recaptors but that the sentence was that they were only entitled to one eighth, and the Sr. Bayard's correspondents obliged Mr. de Valnais to deposit with the consul of France in Philadelphia 255.236 dollars continental money in part of the proceeds with a reserve to the Sieur Bayard against Mr. de Valnais of every right of redress for his irregular conduct; that no injurious intermeddling by the U.S. or any of them or by any of their citizens is here complained of; that the money was constantly in the hands of the Sieur Bayard's correspondents or of the consul for his nation; that he may indeed have suffered by its depreciation as many others have suffered, both foreigners and citizens but the latter in ⟨an infinite proportion to⟩ a much ⟨greater⟩ higher Degree than the former; that this depreciation was not effected by any arbitrary change by Congress in the value or denomination of the money (which yet has been frequently practised by european states who never have thought themselves bound to make good the losses thereby incurred, either by their own citizens or by foreigners) but ensured against the will and the unremitting endeavours of Congress; that in this case too it might have been lessened if not prevented by investing ⟨it⟩ the Money immediately in gold and silver or in other commodities. Your committee therefore are of opinion that these states are not bound to make good the loss by depreciation, ⟨and that the doing it would bring on an infinitude of other cases with endless investigations and unfairness and would require greater funds than we are prepared with⟩.

That as to the residue of the claims of the Sr. Bayard if founded in truth and Right they lie only against the state of Georgia, to the governor whereof it will be proper for Congress to transmit copies of the papers expressing our confidence that that state will cause to be done in it what justice and the respect due between friendly nations require; and that the Sr. Bayard be referred to them.

That the friendly services rendered by the Sr. John Baptist Pequet agent for the french nation at Lisbon to great numbers of American sailors carried prisoners into that port during the late war and his sufferings on that account merit the sincere acknowledgments of Congress and that it be referred to the said ministers to deliver him these in honorable terms and to make him such gratification as may indemnify his losses and properly reward his zeal.[21]

MS (DLC: PCC, No. 25, II); 7 p. and 5 insertions on separate slips of paper; principally in Charles Thomson's hand, but with major insertions by TJ and lesser ones by others as indicated in the notes below. Endorsed by Thomson: "Report of Mr Jefferson Mr Gerry Mr Williamson On the letters from the Ministers of the U. S. at Paris.—Delivered Decr. 20. 1783.—Read and entd. 22.—Jany 22. 1784 Recommitted.—Reported again March 4. 1784 Entd. Read.—Monday next assigned for Consideration. No copies to be made out.—Secret—Ent. Reported 14 April 1784 Order for Thursday 15."

Thomson's endorsement tells in condensed form, with some gaps, the long legislative history of this important Report which TJ helped prepare and which eventually guided his own conduct as one of the ministers empowered to negotiate treaties of amity and commerce with foreign powers. On 15 Dec. 1783, TJ, Elbridge Gerry, and Hugh Williamson were appointed a committee to report on letters received from Adams, Franklin, Dana, Dumas, and Barclay (JCC, XXV, 813, note; 814,

note). The committee delivered in a report on 20 Dec. which was read two days later (JCC, XXV, 821-8). Though the Journal does not say so, the Report was debated on 22 Jan. 1784 and recommitted (see the endorsement). At this point, very likely, Charles Thomson made the copy from which the present text and that in JCC (cited just above) are taken. The authorship of the report is obviously composite; as occasionally happened, Thomson may have put together the various parts of the committee report, copying part and having various members of the committee make their own insertions. At any rate, this appears to be the only version of the report as submitted on 20 Dec. and the extent of TJ's contribution can only be estimated by the parts in his hand, as noted below. On 4 Mch. 1784 the committee brought in an amended report, and on 26 Mch. it was debated, when an alteration was made in the third numbered instruction (see note 3). It was again debated on 1 and 2 Apr., and on the latter date was recommitted a second time (JCC, XXVI, 176-7, 180-5). On 12 Apr. an amended version was debated and re-committed for the third and last time, two new members (Richard Dobbs Spaight and Ephraim Paine) being added to the committee. According to Thomson's endorsement, this enlarged committee reported two days later, and there was an "Order for Thursday 15 [Apr.]." The Journal records no action on either 14 or 15 Apr., but on 7 May 1784 the report was in large part embodied in the instructions to the ministers to negotiate treaties of commerce, and on the same day TJ was elected one of these ministers in the place of John Jay, who was elected secretary for foreign affairs (see JCC, XXVI, 355-6; Charles Thomson to TJ, 16 May 1784, and its enclosures). On 11 May the remainder of the Report was adopted (though see note 20 below), completing the Instructions (JCC, XXVII, 368-72).

1 There is a beginning square bracket before "Rome" in MS, but no closing bracket, which should doubtless be placed at the point where the superscript numeral appears. The deleted words "Europe and" (which were interlined) are in TJ's hand. Opposite the deletion is this notation: "Postponed from [."

2 Preceding 13 words in the deletion were added in TJ's hand. On the verso of the first separate insertion by TJ is the following in Thomson's hand which is part of this paragraph: "own bottoms the produce and merchandize thereof to these states directly and," a phrase repeated in lines 1 and 2 of page 2 of MS, indicating that Thomson was copying perhaps from a rough draft of the Committee report.

3 Preceding 7 words in Hugh Williamson's hand; JCC, XXV, 822, note. The alteration in this instruction was adopted on 26 Mch. 1784; same, XXVI, 169. The Rhode Island and Connecticut delegates voted to strike out the whole of this instruction, but were defeated.

4 From this point to the end of paragraph 6 the text is an addition in TJ's hand, the first line of which was written at the bottom of Thomson's second page and the remainder on recto of the separate leaf mentioned in note 2. The paragraphs following this insertion, originally numbered 6, 7, and 8 were, of course, changed correspondingly to 7, 8, and 9.

5 TJ deleted "lands," interlined "real estate," and then struck out "estate" and substituted "property."

6 From this point to the end of the paragraph the text is in TJ's hand. The present paragraphs 7 and 8 were, before this addition, a single paragraph bearing the number 6. After TJ's insertion, the conjunction "And" was deleted, the part following the insertion was numbered separately, and both numbers (6 and 7) were altered subsequently in consequence of the change indicated in note 4. This insertion is written in the margin of Thomson's copy. On the subject treated in this paragraph, see TJ's notes on British and American alienage, printed at end of 1783.

7 The present paragraph, with the exceptions indicated in notes 8 and 9, is an insertion in TJ's hand on a separate slip of paper. This insertion was made prior to that described in note 4, for it originally was numbered 8 and altered to 9 in consequence of TJ's addition of a large part of paragraph 5 and all of paragraph 6 as indicated.

8 The preceding part of this sentence is an insertion within TJ's insertion (see note 7). It is on a separate slip of paper and is said by JCC, XXV, 824, note, to be in the hand of John Francis Mercer (who is, however, not known to have been a member of the committee that prepared this report).

9 TJ left a blank for the number of years; this was subsequently filled up in another hand.

10 Preceding 3 words interlined in TJ's hand.

11 Preceding 20 words interlined in TJ's hand.

12 This correction shows that the present MS was used to the end of Congress' proceedings on this topic, for TJ was not elected a minister until 7 May 1784; his name is interlined in an unknown hand.

13 This word interlined in TJ's hand.

14 The concluding words of this paragraph originally read: ". . . be in force and no longer." Then the words "for a Term not exceeding two years" were interlined after the word "force," and the concluding words "and no longer," which were located after the blank in the middle of the next line, were obviously intended to be deleted but were not. On 7 May 1784 Congress agreed to all the foregoing instructions as amended (JCC, XXVI, 357-62).

15 Preceding 18 words had been de-

leted before the whole paragraph was struck out.

[16] Preceding 14 words substituted in Thomson's hand for the following in TJ's hand: "no interest during the war is due on these debts."

[17] This paragraph, with one exception, was in TJ's hand and represented an insertion written on a separate slip. It was struck out by Congress on 11 May (JCC, XXVII, 367-8).

[18] This paragraph was evidently substituted for the part deleted as indicated in note 16. It is on still another separate slip but is keyed by the symbol "O" for insertion at this point. According to JCC, XXV, 825, note, this insertion is in the hand of Jacob Read (who was not a member of the committee). It was agreed to, along with all the rest of this Report as amended

(with the exception indicated in note 20) on 11 May (JCC, XXVII, 368-72).

[19] This paragraph is also in TJ's hand, being the concluding portion of his insertion as described in note 18.

[20] Blanks are in MS. This paragraph was discussed in Congress on 11 May and postponed "to Saturday next" (15 May), but no further action appears to have been taken on it, and it does not appear among the Instructions transmitted by Thomson to TJ, 16 May.

[21] The Report as finally adopted on 11 May as Instructions to the ministers to negotiate treaties of amity and commerce contains an additional paragraph at the end relating to the North Carolina owned schooner *Nancy*, Capt. Gladden, detained in England (JCC, XXVII, 372).

George Washington's Resignation as Commander-in-Chief

I. REPORT OF A COMMITTEE ON ARRANGEMENTS FOR THE PUBLIC AUDIENCE

II. JEFFERSON TO ELBRIDGE GERRY AND JAMES McHENRY

III. WASHINGTON'S ADDRESS TO CONGRESS RESIGNING HIS COMMISSION

IV. REPORT OF A COMMITTEE ON THE RESPONSE BY THE PRESIDENT OF CONGRESS

[20-23 December 1783]

EDITORIAL NOTE

Washington's surrender of his commission at a formal audience granted by Congress was a symbolic event of the highest significance. The documents presented in the present series are evidence enough that Congress as well as the Commander-in-Chief fully appreciated the nature of the occasion. Nevertheless, though this event at Annapolis on 23 Dec. 1783 has not received the attention accorded Washington's address to the officers at Newburgh or his Farewell Orders to the Army at Princeton, it gave dramatic emphasis to his wise utterances on those two occasions. In the former, setting himself firmly against any incipient "dangerous combinations" in the army for the purpose of establishing military dictatorship, Washington urged his officers to "rely on the plighted faith of your Country, and place a full confidence in the purity of the intentions of Congress. . . . And let me conjure you, in the name of our common Country, as you value your own sacred honor, as you respect the rights of humanity, and as you regard the Military and

National character of America, to express your utmost horror and detestation of the Man who wishes, under any specious pretences, to overturn the liberties of our Country, and who wickedly attempts to open the flood Gates of Civil discord, and deluge our rising Empire in blood. By thus determining, and thus acting, you . . . will, by the dignity of your Conduct, afford occasion for Posterity to say, when speaking of the glorious example you have exhibited to Mankind, 'had this day been wanting, the World had never seen the last stage of perfection to which human nature is capable of attaining'" (15 Mch. 1783; *Writings*, ed. Fitzpatrick, xxvi, 226-7). At Princeton Washington had recurred to this theme in his farewell advice to the soldiers who were about "to change the military character into that of the Citizen": "And, altho the General has so frequently given it as his opinion, in the most public and explicit manner, that, unless the principles of the federal government were properly supported and the powers of the union increased, the honour, dignity, and justice of the nation would be lost forever. Yet he cannot help repeating, on this occasion, so interesting a sentiment, and leaving it as his last injunction to every Officer and every Soldier, who may view the subject in the same serious point of light, to add his best endeavours to those of his worthy fellow Citizens towards effecting these great and valuable purposes on which our very existence as a nation so materially depends" (2 Nov. 1783; same, xxvii, 226).

But Washington must have sensed the need of a formal, dramatic incident to underscore these words. Thus the commander who had it in his power and who some thought aspired to be a Caesar came to Congress voluntarily to yield up his authority in a conscious gesture calculated to demonstrate before the world the subordination of the military to the civil authority. The unusual preparations by Congress and the extreme attention to small ceremonial details (see Document i) show that the delegates fully understood the unprecedented importance of the event.

Washington arrived in Annapolis on 19 Dec. and the next day wrote the president of Congress stating his intention to resign his commission and asking in what manner it would be "most proper . . . whether in writing, or at an Audience" (same, xxvii, 278). Congress immediately resolved that "his Excellency the Commander in Chief be admitted to a public audience, on Tuesday next [23 Dec.], at twelve o'clock" (jcc, xxv, 818). At the same time, it was resolved that "a public entertainment be given to the Commander in Chief on Monday next," but action on this was postponed until it was decided, on a roll-call vote that was all but unanimous, that "seven states in Congress assembled are competent to receive the resignation of a Commander in Chief" (same, xxv, 818-19).

The entertainment (public dinner) was held on Monday, 22 Dec., in the ballroom of Mann's tavern, "where every thing was provided by Mr. Mann, in the most elegant and profuse style." That night the Maryland General Assembly gave a ball, which Washington opened with Mrs. James Maccubbin. (For these proceedings and the addresses accompanying them, see David Ridgely, *Annals of Annapolis* [1841], p. 208-11; Washington, *Writings*, ed. Fitzpatrick, xxvii, 281-2; Burnett,

Letters of Members, VII, No. 465, esp. note 8 concerning Mann's bill; and James Tilton to Gunning Bedford, 25 Dec. 1783, quoted in full below.)

On the same day, in Congress, "the report of a committee consisting of Mr. Jefferson, Mr. Gerry and Mr. McHenry appointed [*on 20 Dec. but not noted in the Journals of Congress; see PCC: No. 186*] to make the necessary arrangements for the public audience of General Washington" was adopted (JCC, XXV, 820). Clearly this report (Document I) had been drawn up over the week-end. It is probable that the same committee was charged on 20 Dec. with the task of preparing a response to the address by Washington that would be inevitably called for. The one drafting the response had to know what he was responding to: hence, in accordance with custom, a copy of Washington's address was made available to the committee. With a great public dinner and a brilliant ball planned in his honor and scheduled for the day preceding his appearance before Congress, Washington must have consulted with Jefferson immediately after Congress had acted on his letter on 20 Dec. Probably he had his address ready, for he had come to Annapolis for a specific purpose which could have been put in writing in advance. Certainly his address must have been available to the committee by Sunday, 21 Dec., and Jefferson must have spent a part of that day in drafting the response intended to be delivered on Tuesday by President Thomas Mifflin. A hitherto unpublished Jefferson letter (Document II) throws some light on the committee's deliberations and also reveals the fact that Jefferson produced both a composition draft and what he had "intended for a fair copy." Curiously, neither of these drafts is known to be in existence. This fact has led to the supposition that James McHenry, another member of the committee, was the author of the address that was delivered on 23 Dec., since the text employed in the report of the committee (Document IV) is in his hand.

In the absence of either of Jefferson's drafts of this significant document, it cannot be precisely determined how far the text of the committee report followed his own words. He had in fact authorized his colleagues on the committee to take his draft and "handle it roughly and freely and make it what it should be" (Document II). Unquestionably those parts of Jefferson's "sketch" referring to "actions which redound to General Washington's particular credit"—the campaigns of Trenton and Yorktown—were omitted. But it cannot be known whether the omission was made by Jefferson's colleagues, or by Jefferson, or by all three in consultation, though Jefferson's feeling that his draft was "Perhaps . . . too short" even before the omission was made seems to indicate that the suggestion for making it still shorter must have come from Gerry or McHenry. Yet it is almost certain that the text was Jefferson's composition (with minor exceptions indicated in notes to Document IV) and that the final form differed from his original text chiefly in the omission noted. This, of course, is conjectural, but the reasons supporting it are weighty.

First, it is clear that the work of the committee was distributed by allocating the matter of protocol to Gerry and that of drafting the response to Jefferson. Jefferson had been far from well since arriving in Annapolis, as his letters of this period indicate; he may have been experiencing one of his periodic headaches over this week-end. A fact not previously noted in connection with the printing of the McHenry copy of the response (JCC, XXV, 838-9) is that it bears a caption in Jefferson's hand: "The Committee to whom were referred &c. have agreed to the following report." This fact at once indicates that, after Gerry and McHenry had returned the "intended . . . fair copy" of the response, probably with a suggestion that parts be omitted and perhaps with other recommended alterations, Jefferson began another fair copy of the committee report. Having written the caption, he then may have turned the matter of transcribing over to McHenry, perhaps because he himself was ill, perhaps because McHenry had been spared any serious share of the committee's responsibility.

Second, this supposition is supported not only by the otherwise inexplicable fact that the caption is in Jefferson's hand and the text in McHenry's, but also by McHenry's own contemporary testimony. At this time McHenry was deeply in love with the beautiful Margaret Caldwell of Philadelphia, to whom he was married on 8 Jan. 1784. In mid-December, by his own admission he was and had been for some days "on a rack of suspense" because he had not heard from his fiancée. Indeed, his suffering on this account was such that he thought he should "become mad" and he told Margaret Caldwell that he was "nearly so at this instant." Then, as further evidence of his concern, he made this statement: "I was to assist in writing our answer to General Washington's resignation—but I am unfit for this purpose" (Steiner, *McHenry*, p. 68). This is fairly conclusive as evidence that McHenry was only the copyist of Jefferson's amended "fair copy" and not the composer of the text that appears in his hand. A further significance attaches to his letter to Miss Caldwell: it was dated 22 Dec. 1783, but it must have been written on Sunday the 21st, for in it he stated that he had been supposed "to have spent the evening with some ladies but . . . sent an excuse" instead. This could scarcely have been on Monday evening, for McHenry must have attended the ball at that time. If this assumption is correct, then McHenry's remarks are evidence also that the committee appointed to make the arrangements was already engaged over the week-end at the task of preparing the response, in which McHenry was supposed "to assist." An agitated lover's letter is not the most accurate or dependable historical evidence ("I am now become reasonable," McHenry wrote Miss Caldwell on 23 Dec.; same, p. 69), but, taken in connection with other evidences, there seems no reason to doubt his own assertion that he was unable even to assist in writing the response. His agitation, real as it was, would not have been so great in all probability as to keep him from performing the function of copying what someone else had written.

Third, there is the testimony of James Madison. Writing to Samuel A. Smith on 4 Nov. 1826, Madison, in enumerating Jefferson's important literary compositions, said: "His services at Annapolis will appear in the Journal of Congress of that date. The answer of Congress to the resignation of the Commander in Chief, an important document, attracts attention by the shining traces of his pen" (DLC: Madison Papers, 76: 85).

Finally, the style of the response—what Madison so felicitously expressed as "the shining traces of his pen"—removes doubt as to the authorship. The opening sentence, in cadence and in expression, is one of the strikingly Jeffersonian sentences in the composition. As originally phrased, it read: "The U.S. in congress assembled receive with emotions too affecting for utterance this solemn deposit of the authorities under which you have led us with safety and triumph through a long, a perilous, and a doubtful war." The final paragraph, with its appeal to God, was less characteristic of Jefferson's state papers, but it is to be remembered that the author was here responding to sentiments expressed by Washington and to have failed to take note of the climactic expressions of the address of the Commander-in-Chief would have been unthinkable on such an occasion.

Yet, in the absence of Jefferson's composition draft and his "intended . . . fair copy," the extent of changes made by Gerry and perhaps even by McHenry cannot be determined. Some changes were made by Jefferson himself even after McHenry had returned the text to him as chairman of the committee. The text almost certainly was read and discussed in Congress on 22 Dec., though the Journals make no mention of the fact, for there are some alterations (see notes to Document iv) in the hand of Charles Thomson that must have represented amendments offered in Congress.

For the ceremonial of Washington's resignation, besides the bare account in JCC, xxv, 837-9, there are available two excellent descriptions by eye-witnesses. The first is part of a letter written by McHenry to Margaret Caldwell on the day itself and reads as follows:

"To day my love the General at a public audience made a deposit of his commission and in a very pathetic manner took leave of Congress. It was a solemn and affecting spectacle; such an one as history does not present. The spectators all wept, and there was hardly a member of Congress who did not drop tears. The General's hand which held the address shook as he read it. When he spoke of the officers who had composed his family, and recommended those who had continued in it to the present moment to the favorable notice of Congress he was obliged to support the paper with both hands. But when he commended the interests of his dearest country to almighty God, and those who had the superintendence of them to his holy keeping, his voice faultered and sunk, and the whole house felt his agitations. After the pause which was necessary for him to recover himself, he proceeded to say in the most penetrating manner, 'Having now finished the work assigned me I retire from the great theatre of action, and bidding an affectionate farewell to this august body under whose orders I have so long acted I here offer my commission and take my leave of all the employments of public life.' So saying he drew out from his bosom his commission and delivered it up to the president of Congress. He then returned to his station, when the president read the reply that had been prepared—but I thought without any shew of feeling, tho' with much dignity.

"This is only a sketch of the scene. But, were I to write you a long letter I could not convey to you the whole. So many circumstances crowded into view and gave rise to so many affecting emotions. The events of the revolution just accomplished—the new situation into which it had thrown the affairs of the world—the great man who had borne so conspicuous a figure in it, in the act of relinquishing all public employments to return to private life—the past—the present—the future—the manner—the occasion—all conspired to render it a spectacle inexpressibly solemn and affecting." (Steiner, *McHenry*, p. 69-70.)

The other account is in a letter from Dr. James Tilton to Gunning Bedford, written from Annapolis on Christmas Day:

"The General came to town last friday, and announced his arrival, by a letter to congress, requesting to know, in what manner they chused he should resign his authority; whether by private letter or public audience? The latter was preferred without hesitation. Some etiquette being settled on saturday, a public dinner was ordered on monday and the audience to be on tuesday. The feast on monday was the most extraordinary I ever attended. Between 2 and 3 hundred Gentn: dined together in the *ball-room*. The number of cheerful voices, with the clangor of knives and forks made a din of a very extraordinary nature and most delightful influence. Every man seemed to be in heaven or so absorbed in the pleasures of imagination, as to neglect the more sordid appetites, for not a soul got drunk, though there was wine in plenty and the usual number of 13 toasts drank, besides one given afterwards by the General which you ought to be acquainted with: it is as follows. 'Competent powers to congress for general purposes.'

"In the evening of the same day, the Governor gave a ball at the State House. To light the rooms every window was illuminated. Here the company was equally numerous, and more brilliant, consisting of ladies and Gentn: Such was my villanous awkwardness, that I could not venture to dance on this occasion, you must therefore annex to it a cleverer Idea, than is to be expected from such a mortified whelp as I am. The General danced every set, that all the ladies might have the pleasure of dancing with him, or as it has since been handsomely expressed, *get a touch of him.*

"Tuesday morning, Congress met, and took their seats in order, all covered. At twelve o'clock the General was introduced by the Secretary, and seated opposite to the president, until the throng, that filled all the avenues, were so disposed of so as to behold the solemnity. The ladies occupied the gallery as full as it would hold, the Gentn: crouded below stairs. Silence ordered, by the Secretary, the Genl. rose and bowed to congress, who uncovered, but did not bow. He then delivered his speech, and at the close of it drew his commission from his bosom and handed it to the president. The president replied in a set speech, the General bowed again to Congress, they uncovered and the General retired. After a little pause until the company withdrew, Congress adjourned. The General then stepped into the room again, bid every member farewell and rode off from the door, intent upon eating his Christmas dinner at home. Many of the spectators, particularly the fair ones shed tears, on this solemn and affecting occasion. Sir Robert Eden and Mr. William Harford attended very respectfully. They were also at the public dinner and the dance" (25 Dec. 1783; Washington, *Writings*, ed. Fitzpatrick, XXVII, 285, note; from a MS owned by Guy Stonestreet, New York City).

A month after this stirring event, Washington wrote Charles Thomson: "If my Commission is not necessary for the files of Congress, I should be glad to have it deposited amongst my own Papers. It may serve *my Grand Children* some fifty or a hundd. years hence for a theme to ruminate upon, *if they should be* contemplatively disposed" (22 Jan. 1784, same, XXVII, 312). This called for something more impressive in dignity than a mere enclosure from the secretary of Congress, universally admired though he was. It was not even customary for general officers to yield up their actual commissions when resigning them; the President of Congress himself had resigned his commission as major general in August 1778 by merely writing a letter (Mifflin to Jay, 25 Feb. 1779, DLC: PCC, No. 19, II). But Washington's commission had been delivered up formally by request of Congress and formality was required in its return. Thomson no doubt mentioned Washington's letter to members of Congress and on 29 Jan. 1784 Hugh Williamson introduced the following resolution: "*Resolved*, That his late Commission be returned to General Washington in a neat gold box to be preserved among the archives of his family" (JCC, XXVI, 54; the motion is in the hand of Williamson and is in DLC: PCC, No. 36, II). This motion was adopted and referred to Jefferson, Williamson, and Howell (DLC: PCC, No. 186). A few days afterward Thomson replied to Washington that "it had been in agitation among the members to have an Order passed for returning it to you in a gold box. A motion has accordingly been made to that effect, which was received with general approbation, and referred to a committee to be drawn up in proper terms. The committee have not yet reported. But I have not the least doubt of its being returned to you in a way that will be satisfactory and I heartily wish, that this sacred deposit may be preserved by your *children* and children's children to the latest posterity and may prove an incentive to them to emulate the virtues of their worthy and great progenitor" (7 Feb. 1784; Washington, *Writings*, ed. Fitzpatrick, XXVII, 312, note). From this it seems clear that Jefferson was appointed chairman of the committee in order that the resolution transmitting the commission in a gold box should "be drawn up in proper terms." But Charles Thomson's manuscript recording the dates of appointment and reports of committees of Congress has only a blank in the column for dates of reports opposite the names of the committee to whom was referred the "motion of Mr. Williamson to return to Genl. Washington his commission in a gold box" (DLC: PCC, No. 186). Considering the fact that Jefferson was chairman of the committee; that he was prompt and conscientious in discharging all duties assigned to him in committee; and that Thomson informed Washington what was being done, the failure of the committee to report at all is very puzzling. The only satisfactory explanation seems to be that Washington himself must have put a stop to such a handsome gesture, though there is no documentary evidence for this conjecture. Whether this is correct or not, there is henceforth only silence on this subject in the papers of Congress, the correspondence of its members, and the writings of the Commander-in-Chief. The commission remained among the papers of the Continental Congress and is today in the Library of Congress. Washington had been jocose in referring to his grandchildren, but, whether the cause was due to some inexplicable failure of Jefferson to draw up the report "in proper terms" or to Washington's modest declination of the honor, it seems nevertheless that all who were concerned achieved the most fitting answer by allowing the commission, perhaps unintentionally, to rest among the records of the nation rather than among the "archives of his family."

I. Report of a Committee on Arrangements for the Public Audience

[22 December 1783]

Order for a publick Audience of General Washington.

1st. The president and Members are to be seated and covered, and the Secretary to be standing by the Side of the president.

2dly. The Arrival of the General is to be announced by the Messenger to the Secretary, who is thereupon to introduce the General attended by his Aids to the Hall of Congress.

3dly. The General being conducted to the Chair by the Secretary, is to be seated with an Aid on each side, standing, and the Secretary is to resume his place.

4thly. After a proper Time for the Arrangement of Spectators, Silence is to be ordered by the Secretary if necessary, and the president is to address the General in the following Words *"Congress sir are prepared to receive your Communications"*[1] Whereupon the General is to rise and address Congress, after which[2] he is to deliver his commission and a Copy of his Address to the president.[3]

5thly. The General[4] having resumed his place,[5] the president[6] is to deliver the Answer of Congress,[7] which the General is to receive standing.

6thly. The president having finished, the Secretary is to deliver the General a Copy of the Answer[8] from the president, and the General[9] is then to take his Leave.

N. B. When the General rises to make his Address, and also when he retires, he is to bow to Congress, which they are to return by uncovering without bowing.

MS (DLC: PCC, No. 19, vi, f. 467-70); in Elbridge Gerry's hand with the exceptions noted below; endorsed: "Report of a Comee passed Decr. 22. 1783 [*and in another hand:*] Audience of Genl Washington." Ford, iii, 363-4, prints this report as if it were entirely written by TJ; the text is also in jcc, xxv, 820; both repeat the same errors, being somewhat less accurate than these sources usually are. Among other things, the caption is omitted. A copy of the text as finally approved by Congress, in Charles Thomson's hand, is in DLC: Washington Papers; this, no doubt, was the copy furnished to Washington before the ceremony; it is printed in Washington, *Writings*, ed. Ford, x (1891), 337.

[1] The words within quotation marks are underscored and a crossed circle placed in the margin, indicating that an amendment was offered in Congress. That amendment appears, in Thomson's hand, on the verso: "Sir, The U.S. in Congress Assembled are prepared to receive your Communications." The first words of this amendment brought the passage into line with the phraseology of the first words of the President's response (see Document IV). Ford, III, 364, and JCC, XXV, 820, print the amendment as if it were a part of the report, omitting the committee's phraseology entirely.

[2] The words "after which" are interlined in the hand of Thomas Mifflin in substitution for the words "and being seated again," which are deleted. Since the President of Congress was to read the response, it is possible that the committee submitted the report on arrangements to him for approval before handing it in to Congress.

[3] A number of changes were made in this passage that are difficult to disentangle, but an analysis seems to indicate that the first part of the alteration took place in committee and the last by amendment in Congress. As originally phrased the passage read: ". . . after which he is to deliver a Copy of his Address to his Aid to be presented to the Secretary." TJ altered this by interlining the words "with his commission"

after the word "Address"; then, with appropriate additions and deletions, the first part of the passage was inverted to read as above. This alteration probably took place in committee. The words "to his Aid to be presented to the Secretary" are enclosed in parentheses and underscored, indicating that Congress deleted them and substituted therefor the words "to the president." JCC, XXV, 820, contains a note to the effect that the words "his Commission and a" and "to the President" (as well as those changes indicated in notes 2, 4, and 9) are in the hand of Elias Boudinot; but the former are indisputably TJ's and the latter are in the same hand as the alteration in note 2, which is unquestionably Mifflin's. Boudinot was not in Congress at this time.

[4] The word "Aid" was deleted at this point and "General" interlined in the hand of Mifflin.

[5] The words "by the side of the General" were deleted at this point as a part of the alteration indicated in notes 3 and 4.

[6] The words "after a proper interval," in Mifflin's hand, were written in the margin following this point and were then deleted.

[7] This passage was altered by Mifflin from the following: ". . . an Answer, which," &c.

[8] The word "Address" is deleted at this point and "Answer" interlined in Mifflin's hand.

[9] The words "and the General" are interlined in TJ's hand. Preceding this point, the following words, enclosed in parentheses and underscored, were deleted (no doubt by Congress): "and receive the Commission from the General, who."

II. To Elbridge Gerry and James McHenry

[21? December 1783]

TH: JEFFERSON TO MESSRS. GHERRY & McHENRY

I send you the sketch, which I have been obliged to obliterate and blot after making what I intended for a fair copy. You will observe my plan was to make a short review in very general terms of those actions which redound to the General's particular credit, viz. the discouraging circumstances under which he accepted the command—his steadiness and perservance when obliged to retire across the Delaware and our affairs then at their lowest point of depression—his revival of our hopes by recrossing the Delaware—and finally the capture of Cornwallis which undoubtedly made the peace. I have noted these events in the margin opposite to the passages alluding to them, and have drawn lines under other expressions taken from the General's address. Perhaps this answer is too short; perhaps it is too warm. A want of time must apologize for the one, and an exalted esteem for the other faults. Be so good as to handle it roughly and freely and make it what it should be.

RC (PHi); without date, but probably written on 21 Dec. as suggested in editorial note at head of this series of documents; not recorded in SJL. A fragmentary address remains: "Messrs. Gh[. . .]"; this is on the verso of the letter, the text of which is covered with blots as if made by offset from a preceding page. These facts suggest that TJ's "intended . . . fair copy" must have occupied the first and second pages of the MS, the third page of which carried the present letter; for, had the text of the "sketch" been an ordinary enclosure, the letter would doubtless have begun on page one. Also it is clear that, from the position of the fragmentary address on the verso, another leaf had to precede that on which the letter is written in order to form a cover for the letter alone, to say nothing of a possible enclosure. If this conjecture is correct, then a 19th century collector may have been responsible for the separation of TJ's "intended . . . fair copy" from the letter to which it was attached, for the verso also bears this endorsement in the hand of the well-known Baltimore autograph collector who signed it: "Given to me in 1860 by Daniel McHenry, Secretary of War under John Adams R. Gilmor." From this it is also certain that, along with the first draft of Washington's address, McHenry retained TJ's "intended . . . fair copy" of the response.

III. Washington's Address to Congress Resigning his Commission

MR. PRESIDENT   [23 Dec. 1783]

The great events on which my resignation depended having at length taken place; I have now the honor of offering my sincere Congratulations to Congress and of presenting myself before them to surrender into their hands the trust committed to me, and to claim the indulgence of retiring from the Service of my Country.

Happy in the confirmation of our Independence and Sovereignty, and pleased with the opportunity afforded the United States of becoming a respectable Nation, I resign with satisfaction the Appointment I accepted with diffidence. A diffidence in my abilities to accomplish so arduous a task, which however was superseded by a confidence in the rectitude of our Cause, the support of the Supreme Power of the Union, and the patronage of Heaven.

The Successful termination of the War has verified the most sanguine expectations, and my gratitude for the interposition of

Providence, and the assistance I have received from my Country-men, encreases with every review of the momentous Contest.

While I repeat my obligations to the Army in general, I should do injustice to my own feelings not to acknowledge in this place the peculiar Services and distinguished merits of the Gentlemen who have been attached to my person during the War. It was impossible the choice of confidential Officers to compose my family should have been more fortunate. Permit me Sir, to recommend in particular those, who have continued in Service to the present moment, as worthy of the favorable notice and patronage of Congress.

I consider it an indispensable duty to close this last solemn act of my Official life, by commending the Interests of our dearest Country to the protection of Almighty God, and those who have the superintendence of them, to his holy keeping.

Having now finished the work assigned me, I retire from the great theatre of Action; and bidding an Affectionate farewell to this August body under whose orders I have so long acted, I here offer my Commission, and take my leave of all the employments of public life.

Text from Washington's *Writings*, ed. Fitzpatrick, XXVII, 284-5, from a photostat of the original draft in his hand that Washington presented to McHenry (DLC: McHenry Photostats). Steiner, writing in 1907, said that this "original draft . . . was given to Mc-Henry and has been preserved by his descendants to this day" (Steiner, *Mc-Henry*, p. 68). A facsimile was published in the *Magazine of American History*, VII (1881), p. 106. This was doubtless the copy made available to the committee engaged in framing a response; it may not have been actually presented to McHenry by Washington, but may have been retained by him as a member of the committee, its presence among his papers leading Steiner and others to assume that it was a more formal gift. A fair copy (and doubtless the copy that Washington employed in his appearance before Congress), in David Humphreys' hand and signed by Washington, is in DLC: Washington Papers; it was the text employed in Washington's *Writings*, ed. Ford, x (1891), p. 338.

IV. Report of a Committee on the Response by the President of Congress

[22 December 1783]

The Committee to whom were referred &c.
have agreed to the following report.[1]

SIR

The U.S. in congress assembled receive with emotions too affecting for utterance this solemn Resignation[2] of the authorities[3] under which you have led their[4] troops with Success[5] through a perilous and a doubtful war. Called by your country to defend its invaded rights you accepted the sacred charge before it[6] had formed alliances, and whilst it[7] was without funds or a government to support you. You have conducted the great military contest with wisdom and fortitude invariably regarding the rights of the civil power[8] through all disasters and changes. You have by the love and confidence of your fellow citizens enabled them to display their martial genius and transmit their fame to posterity. You have persevered till these united States, aided by a magnanimous king and nation have been enabled under a just providence to close the war in freedom safety and independence, on which happy event we sincerely join you in congratulations.[9]

Having defended[10] the standard of liberty in this new world: having taught a lesson useful to those who inflict and to those who feel oppression, you *retire from the great theatre of action*[11] with the blessings of your fellow citizens—but the glory of your virtues will not terminate with your military Command.[12] It will continue to animate remotest ages.[13]

We feel with you *our obligations to the army in general*, and will particularly charge ourselves with the interests of *those confidential officers* who have attended your person to this affecting[14] moment.

We join you in *commending the interests of our dearest country to the protection of almighty god*, beseeching him to dispose the hearts and minds of its citizens to improve *the opportunity afforded*[15] *them of becoming a happy and respectable nation*: And for you we address to him our warmest prayers, that a life so beloved may be fostered with all his care; that your days may be happy as they have been illustrious, and that he will finally give you that reward which this world cannot give.

MS (DLC: PCC, No. 19, vi, f. 461-4); in James McHenry's hand with the exceptions noted below; endorsed: "Report of a Committee Decr. 23d. 1783. Answer of Congress to Genl. Washington." A fair copy of the text of the response as finally approved is in DLC: Washington Papers; it is in Thomson's hand. Only the more important of the alterations in the text are noted below. Those parts in italics are (as they were in TJ's "fair copy") "expressions taken from the General's address." But these borrowings were not exact. Where Washington spoke of "my obligations to the army in general," the present text reads "our obligations"; also, Washington spoke of the "opportunity afforded the United States of becoming a respectable Nation" and the committee made it read "a happy and respectable nation" (Washington's original draft, however, had added at this point, and then deleted, the following: "as well as in the contemplation of our national happiness"; *Writings*, ed. Ford, x, 339, note 2).

[1] The caption is in TJ's hand; for the significance of this, see editorial note at head of this series of documents. A vertical line was drawn through the two-line caption, probably by Thomson before making his fair copy for Washington.

[2] The word "Resignation" is interlined in substitution for "deposit."

[3] This word is underlined as if an

amendment had been moved but not adopted.

4 The report originally read "us"; this was changed by TJ who interlined the words "our troops"; the word "our" was then deleted and "their" substituted, apparently by Gerry.

5 This word was interlined in substitution for "safety and triumph."

6 The MS originally read "we"; this was deleted and "they" interlined in Gerry's hand; this, in turn, was deleted for "it," a change probably made by Congress, since "it" is in Thomson's hand.

7 The same change that took place as indicated in note 6 was made here, "were" being changed in consequence to "was."

8 This word is interlined in substitution for "government."

9 The preceding ten words are interlined in TJ's hand.

10 This word is interlined in substitution for "planted," an alteration probably made by Congress.

11 The word "loaded" is deleted at this point.

12 This passage was involved in many minor changes, most of them probably being made in committee; the words "military Command" are interlined in substitution for "official life," which in turn was a substitution for "public life."

13 This passage was altered from the following: ". . . remotest posterity and this last act will not be among the least conspicuous."

14 This word is interlined in substitution for "interesting."

15 This word is interlined by TJ in substitution for "offered."

From Joseph Jones

DR. SIR   Richmond 21st Decr. 1783

I have your favor by the Post this week and have the satisfaction to inform you the Assembly have passed a law granting the impost to Congress, also that a bill has passed the Delegates and [is] now before the Sennate, accepting the terms stipulated by Congress respecting the western lands, and authorising the Delegates to convey the claim of this State to the united States. I have no doubt of its Passing the Sennate, tho' I fear they will attempt to restore a clause which in the third reading was struck out by the Delegates whereby a further condition was annexed that a quantity of land sufficient to comply with the resolves of the two Houses granting lands to certain persons should be reserved. The Delegates upon reflection thought it better to put a finishing hand to this business than hazard further altercation and perhaps the final settlement of so important an object and therefore parted from the clause. That the Sennate, some of whom are much attracted to those for whom the clause provided, might not restore it by amendment, I have mentioned to a few of them as a better and less exceptional mode the instructing our Delegates to move in Congress for such an allowance of land out of that ceded as may enable the State to fullfill their engagements. This course will probably be taken. We had passed a law empowering the Congress to prohibit if they thought fit the entry of British vessels into our ports or to adopt any other mode they preferred to counteract the designs of Great

Britain on our Commerce, so long as they should adhere to their present system. Your letter to the governor intimates your apprehensions the business will not be speedily done by Congress as they can only recommend. We meant in publishing our resolutions on the subject to call the immediate attention of the States to it, that similar measures might be taken by them. The plan of counteracting the British policy I could wish should proceed from Congress in consequence of powers to be communicated for that purpose to exhibit to that Nation an instance that the states are not so jealous of that Body as to withhold powers that are necessary whenever the general welfare presents the occasion and to convince them of their error that we cannot in this business act in concert. The transmission of our act to the Executives of the several States with request that their attention may be immediately called to this great object may produce similar acts on their part and expedite the plan of opposition. We expected to rise today but think at present we shall not accomplish it. I am Yr aff Servt,   Jos: Jones

NB. Mr. H—y who at first proposed to instruct the Delegates to press for cessions from other States at length relinquished the design for the reason you mention—the disagreeable predicament in which we should place our Delegates.

RC (DLC).   On the law passed to COUNTERACT THE DESIGNS OF GREAT BRITAIN ON OUR COMMERCE, see Harrison to the Virginia delegates, 26 Dec. 1783. MR. H—Y was, of course, Patrick Henry.

From Francis Eppes

Dr Sir   Eppington Decbr. 22d. 1783

Your letters of Novbr. 10th. and Decbr. 11th came both together a few days ago and reliev'd us from the anxiety we had for some time been under least some indisposition might have prevented your writing. I am happy to inform you that you[r] children continue very well. Polly often mentions you and Patsy, she desires her love to you both, and begs you will make haste home, for she longs to see you. Betsy was relieved of her burthen on the seventh of last month by the birth of a fine Girl, she going about tho' by no means well she has fever more frequently than formerly in the same situations. I am much pleasd to hear that Virginia Tobacco sells so high in England, as it must of course raise the price from the low ebb to which it has been reduc'd for some time in this country, wou'd you believe it has sold as low as eighteen? Twenty has been the current price and then we were oblig'd to take one half goods at a very extravagant price. I am oblig'd to ask your opinion on a subject which concerns you as well as myself, I mean Col. Richard Randolphs account with Mr. Wayles's Estate. Nothing but the necessity of having a final settlement with that wou'd induce me at this time to add in the smallest degree to your business being well convinc'd you have your hands full will [with] publick affairs, but I hope when you recollect the advanc'd age and infirmities of Colo. Randolph it will sufficiently excuse my intruding on your moment either of business or recration; he has charg'd the Estate near four hundred pounds on account of the Guineaman. He pretends to be very anxious to have the matter settled and wishes to have it referd to any court whose determination may be binding on all concern'd. Your directions in this matter will be very pleasing to me. Mr. Maury has remov'd his School from Orange to Williamsburg, your Sister Carr desirs you will inform whether she is to send her son there. Jack is at present quite unfix'd as to a school. Mr. Maurys fickle disposition deters me from having any thing farther to do with him, for if we judge of the time to come by his past conduct we can hardly expect his School in Wmsburg will continue more than one year. As great an objection as I have to keeping Jack at home I wou'd at present do it provided I cou'd git a man who cou'd be depended on and wou'd give generous wages to such a one who wou'd undertake him and half a dozen others. Betsy's eyes are so weak she begs you will excuse her writing at present but will most certainly do it by the next opportunity. With our best wishes for yours and Patseys health & happiness. Dr Sir Your sincear Friend, FRANS. EPPES

RC (ViU); endorsed: "Eppes Fras." Not recorded in SJL.

YOUR LETTERS OF NOVBR. 10TH. AND DECBR. 11TH.: The former appears under its date, but the latter has not been found. None is recorded in SJL under that date; Eppes may have misread "4"

for "11," for TJ did write to him on 4 Dec. 1783 (see entry under that date). POLLY was Maria Jefferson, who later married JACK (John Wayles Eppes), son of Francis and Elizabeth Wayles Eppes. On the matter of MR. WAYLES'S ESTATE, see Malone, *Jefferson*, I, 441-5.

To Martha Jefferson

MY DEAR PATSY   Annapolis Dec. 22. 1783

I hoped before this to have received letters from you regularly and weekly by the post, and also to have had a letter to forward from you to one of your aunts as I desired in my letter of November 27th. I am afraid you do not comply with my desires expressed in that letter. Your not writing to me every week is one instance, and your having never sent me any of your copies of Mr. Simitiere's lessons is another. I shall be very much mortified and disappointed if you become inattentive to my wishes and particularly to the directions of that letter which I meant for your principal guide. I omitted in that to advise you on the subject of dress, which I know you are a little apt to neglect. I do not wish you to be gayly clothed at this time of life, but that what you wear should be fine of it's kind; but above all things, and at all times let your clothes be clean, whole, and properly put on. Do not fancy you must wear them till the dirt is visible to the eye. You will be the last who will be sensible of this. Some ladies think they may under the privileges of the dishabille be loose and negligent of their dress in the morning. But be you from the moment you rise till you go to bed as cleanly and properly dressed as at the hours of dinner or tea. A lady who has been seen as a sloven or slut in the morning, will never efface the impression she then made with all the dress and pageantry she can afterwards involve herself in. Nothing is so disgusting to our sex as a want of cleanliness and delicacy in yours. I hope therefore the moment you rise from bed, your first work will be to dress yourself in such a stile as that you may be seen by any gentleman without his being able to discover a pin amiss, or any other circumstance of neatness wanting.

By a letter from Mr. Short I learn that your sisters are well. I hope I shall soon receive a letter from you informing me you are so. I wrote a letter to Polly lately, which I supposed her aunt would read to her. I dare say it pleased her, as would a letter from you. I am sorry Mrs. Trist has determined to go at so inclement a season, as I fear she will suffer much more than she expects. Present my compliments to her and the good family there, as also very particularly to Mrs. Hopkinson whose health and happiness I have much at heart. I hope you are obedient and respectful to her in every circumstance and that your manners will be such as to engage her affections. I am my Dear Patsy Yours sincerely & affectionately,

TH: JEFFERSON

RC (DLC); endorsed with date in a hand other than TJ's. Entry in SJL under 21 Dec. reads: "Patsy—not writing to me—not sending drawings—dress."
The letter FROM MR. SHORT has not been found, nor has TJ's LETTER TO POLLY.

To Eliza House Trist

[*Annapolis, 22 Dec. 1783*. Entry in SJL reads: "Mrs. Trist—dissuading immediate departure. Pittsbg till Mar. or Apr.—Smith—Browse's alienage." Not found. Mrs. Trist had left Philadelphia on 21 Dec.; see her acknowledgment of the present letter from Pittsburgh, 8 Apr. 1784. On Browse's alienage, see TJ's notes on British and American alienage, printed at the end of 1783.]

To Jacquelin Ambler

[*Annapolis, 23 Dec. 1783*. Entry in SJL reads: "J. Ambler to set apart my dividends and give me notice—will not draw till then—go through £200—far advanced in 3d." Not found.]

To Francis Hopkinson

[*Annapolis, 23 Dec. 1783*. Entry in SJL reads: "F. Hopkinson—letter to Bremner—clavichord—spinette—Buffon's theory—Rittenh's orrery for k. of Fr." Not found, but see Hopkinson to Bremner, 28 Nov. 1783. The reference to Rittenhouse's orrery pertains to a suggestion made by TJ the preceding January at a meeting of the American Philosophical Society. On 3 Jan. 1783 TJ attended his first meeting of the Society "at the University" and presented "in the name of the author, the works of the Abbe Fontana"; two weeks later he also attended and, "On motion by Mr. Jefferson, seconded by Mr. [Joseph] Reed, It was unanimously agreed that an Orrery to be made by Mr. Rittenhouse a citizen of Pennsylvania, be presented by this Society to His Most Christian Majesty"; at the latter meeting the Rev. William White, Hopkinson, and Dr. Shiell were appointed a committee "to devise ways and means to carry the foregoing resolve into execution." The committee reported on 6 Mch. 1783 that they had conferred with Rittenhouse and that he had agreed to make an orrery for £200. This intention of the Society was communicated to La Luzerne, who informed the committee that he had received a communication "intimating his Most Christian Majesty's Approbation of the Society's Design . . . to present him with an Orrery invented and executed by Mr. Rittenhouse; and expressive of his Majesty's Intention by his royal Patronage to excite an Emulation between the literary Societies of France and the United States." The committee were instructed by the Society to inform the French minister "of the high Sense the Society entertain of the Honor done them by his Majesty, and that they flatter themselves with the Hope of seeing the Work speedily completed." Unhappily, this was an illusory hope and TJ's dual intention of showing gratitude to France as an ally and of impressing European scientists with the work of an American whose genius he admired extravagantly came to naught. Two days after TJ's present letter to Hopkinson, La Luzerne wrote to

Vergennes: "M. Rittenhouse, Monseigneur, travaille à son Planetaire, mais avec un peu de lenteur; il est Trésorier de l'Etat de Pensylvanie; il en remplit à regret les fonctions peu analogues a ses talens mais necessaires pour le faire vivre. Il ira peut-être lui-meme en France pour presenter au Roy ce bel ouvrage quand il sera fini. . . ." (minutes of the American Philosophical Society, MS in PPAP, 3, 18 Jan., 6 Mch., 26 Sep. 1783; La Luzerne to Vergennes, 25 Dec. 1783, Arch. Aff. Etr., Corr. Pol., Etats-Unis, XXVI, 252-3—a copy of the last generously contributed by Howard C. Rice, Jr.). Rittenhouse never completed this orrery and never went to France.]

To Benjamin Harrison

SIR   Annapolis Dec. 24. 1783.

The present week affords us nothing new for communication unless it be the affecting scene of yesterday. Genl. Washington then had his last audience of Congress, laid down his commission and bid a final adieu to them and to all public life. His address on the occasion was worthy of him. This you will see in the public papers. I cannot help expressing my extreme anxiety at our present critical situation. The departure of a member two days hence leaves us with only six states and of course stops all business. We have no certain prospect of nine within any given time; chance may bring them in, and chance may keep them back. In the mean time only a little over two months remain for their assembling, ratifying and getting the ratification across the Atlantic to Paris. All that can be said is that it is yet possible. It is well known that Great Britain wished to postpone the conclusion of the treaty. Her reasons we know not. But she certainly knew that a great continental war was kindling, and that France our principal support would be probably deeply engaged in it. It is not impossible then but she might hope for some favourable opportunity of changing the face of the treaty. If the ratifications are not offered by the day she will have too much ground for objection to the validity of the treaty, and to ratify or not as she pleases. As every circumstance of distress will render her the easier on this point, we are pleased with the intelligence of the day which is that she has actually landed twenty one regiments in Ireland. It comes by a ship from London to Baltimore, and from thence here. But Baltimore has not been famed for the truth of it's intelligence.

I have the honour to be with sentiments of the highest esteem and respect Your Excellency's Most obedient & most humble servt.,

TH: JEFFERSON

RC (PHi); addressed and franked: "His Excellency Governor Harrison Richmond. Th: Jefferson"; endorsed. Entry in sjl reads: "Genl. W's audience— only 6 states—report that the British landed 21 regiments in Ireland."

To the Rev. James Madison

[*Annapolis, 24 Dec. 1783*. Entry in sjl reads: "J. Madison of the college—to observe thermometer just before sunrise—Crawford's theory —Rittenh's orrery. Hopkinson's quilling." Not found, but see Madison to TJ, 22 Jan. 1784. Hopkinson's "quilling": on 21 Nov. 1783 TJ attended a meeting of the American Philosophical Society at which Hopkinson presented "a Plan and directions for improving the method of quilling an Harpsichord"; a year later "A paper containing further improvements in quilling a Harpsichord was presented by Mr. Hopkinson" (minutes of the Am. Phil. Soc., 9 Dec. 1784, MS in PPAP; see Hopkinson to TJ, 25 May 1784).

To Charles Carter

[*Annapolis, 26 Dec. 1783*. Entry in sjl reads: "C. Carter. General's audience—European news—danger of not having 9. states for ratification—queries about white neg[roes]." Not found. On "white negroes" see Charles Carter to TJ, 9 Feb. 1784, and *Notes on Virginia*, under Query vi (Ford, iii, 174-5).]

From Benjamin Harrison

DEAR SIR   Council Chamber December 26th. 1783.

I am much obliged to you for your favor of the 17th. It contains many interesting particulars and such as the executive of every State ought to know, tho' I have seldom 'till your arrival in Congress been favored with anything of the kind. The mode of correspondence proposed by you is perfectly agreeable to me, and I think good will result from it. We seem to blunder here more from the want of information than design. I do not mean by what I say that every thing communicated to me, shall be made public, but only that being myself informed, I may be able when necessary to stop the progress of evil, which would have been the case I trust when the citizen bill passed if the European opinions had.[1] I coincide in opinion with our Commissioners and the people of England in reprobating Committees and their late conduct, and will most certainly suppress them in this state and punish all rioters as far as the law will permit me, tho' I hope I shall have no more trouble on this head as the prosecution now carrying on against those in Essex seems to have put a stop to such excuses.

The multiplicity of business now before me in carrying into execution the acts and resolutions of the assembly forces me to conclude sooner than I intended and only allows me time to add that I am &c.

FC (Vi).   ¹ The clerk obviously omitted something here. Harrison no doubt meant to add "been known earlier" or something to this effect.

Benjamin Harrison to the Virginia Delegates in Congress

GENTLEMEN   Council Chamber Decr. 26th. 1783.

You have enclosed the copy of an act of the general assembly to authorise the united States in Congress to adopt certain regulations respecting the british trade, also the acts empowering Congress to levy an impost, and empowering the delegates to convey to Congress the claim of this State to the country north westward of the river Ohio, which several acts you will please to lay before Congress. I also send you ten copies of the act for admission of emigrants and declaring their rights to Citizenship which I beg the favor of you to forward by any vessel that may be going to France to Mr. Thomas Barclay at Nantz who acts as our agent. The Letter to him is open for your perusal, from which you will learn the intention of sending them, and which may perhaps suggest to you some more certain mode of having it promulgated in the several kingdoms and states in Europe in which case you will oblige me by altering the destination of one half of them.

If I can obtain a copy of the other act declaring who shall be deemed citizens I will send that also for your information and wish you may be able to reconcile the two acts to each other, which from the cursory view I have had of them I confess I am not able to do.

The assembly fled from this place on Monday last to their Christmas dinners with as much haste as they did when Arnold paid us a visit and of course have left much of the public business of consequence undone.

I am &c.

FC (Vi); caption reads: "The honorable Virginia delegates in Congress." Enclosures missing; a copy of the Act authorizing cession of the northwestern territory is in DLC: PCC, No. 75; see under 1 Mch. 1784.

The ACT . . . RESPECTING THE BRITISH TRADE was adopted in retaliation for the British order in council of 2 July 1783 prohibiting the produce of the United States "from being carried to any of the British West India Islands, by any other than British subjects, in British built ships, owned by British subjects, and navigated according to the laws of that kingdom." The General Assembly regarded this, though a temporary expedient, as "repugnant to the principles of reciprocal interest and convenience, which are found by experience to form the only permanent foundation of friendly intercourse between states," and therefore authorized Congress to prohibit the importation of West Indian produce or to adopt any other method of counteracting this restrictive British policy so long as it continued (Hening, XI, 313-14). The Act required that all other states would have to join in a similar authorization before it became effective. While the General Assembly did not direct Harrison to do so, he immediately wrote to the governors of other states enclosing copies of the Act and impressing upon them "the necessity of a vigorous opposition to the measures . . . to destroy the American trade" in order "to force that still haughty nation" to come to mutually advantageous commercial relations. "The proposed plan," concluded the Governor, ". . . appears to me the only one that will prove efficaceous or blast the expectations of the British who build all their hopes of enforcing their regulations on the want of power in Congress to form one general system for the whole union and the aversion of the several states to invest them with such a power." Harrison also enclosed in this letter "an interesting paragraph of a letter from our ambassadors to Congress this moment received which places our situation at present in such a light that I think it impossible for the states to hesitate a moment in investing Congress with sufficient powers to make effectual opposition not only to the plans of Great Britain but to all other European nations who may be inclined to follow their example"; the enclosure that Harrison sent with this letter was no doubt a part of the extract from the letter written by the American Commissioners on 10 Sep. 1783 that TJ enclosed in his to Harrison of 17 Dec. 1783, q.v. (Harrison to the "Governors of Several States," 26 Dec. 1783, Executive Letter Book, Vi). On the same day that Harrison wrote the present letter and his urgent communication to the American governors, the British ministry in Whitehall brought together into a single order in council the various measures that had alarmed American commercial interests; the advocacy by David Hartley and others of principles of free trade between the two countries was smothered under the movement led by the Earl of Sheffield to defend the principle of the Navigation Acts. Sheffield's *Observations on the Commerce of the American States*, which appeared in 1783, was the best-known exposition of the point of view of the British shipowners and shipbuilders that had led to the adoption of the restrictive orders in council. For an excellent summary of the political and economic background of British attitudes toward trade following the war, see Merrill Jensen, *The New Nation: A History of the United States During the Confederation, 1781-1789*, p. 157-66 and references cited there, particularly Gerald S. Graham, *Sea Power and British North America, 1783-1802* (Harvard Historical Studies, XLVI); however, these share the common historical view that the major protests to British policy came from New England commercial interests and from West Indian planters and overlook such a vigorous example of protest originating in the Southern states as is provided by Harrison's recommendation to the General Assembly and that body's immediate compliance with his suggestion.

The Acts on the impost, the cession of northwestern territory, and the admission of immigrants are found in Hening, XI, 322-4, 326-8, and 350-2. The letter TO MR. THOMAS BARCLAY that Harrison enclosed related to claims arising out of the agency of Peter Penet, whose commission was issued by Patrick Henry on 22 May 1779 and confirmed by TJ on 15 July 1779 (see Vol. 3: 36); Harrison also enclosed to Barclay copies of the Act for encouraging immigration and requested him "to take measures for having it published in the several states and kingdoms of Europe from whence emigrants may be expected" (Harrison to Barclay, 26 Dec. 1783, Executive Letter Book, Vi). The OTHER ACT DECLARING WHO SHALL BE DEEMED CITIZENS was the Act of May 1779 (Hening, X, 129-30), which was repealed by the Act of Oct. 1783 "for the admission of emigrants and declaring their right to citizenship" (same, XI, 323).

To Henry Skipwith

[*Annapolis, 26 Dec. 1783.* Entry in sjl reads: "H. Skipw. Genl's audience—European news—danger of not having 9 states—Queries about white negroes. Patsy well disposed of—my ill health." Not found, but see Skipwith's reply, 20 Jan. 1784.]

Resolution Providing for Three Vessels to Transmit Definitive Treaty When Ratified

[26 December 1783]

Resolved that the Agent of Marine be directed[1] to have immediately three proper[2] vessels ready, viz. one at this Port one at New York, and one at some Port to the Eastward[3] to receive and convey to some port in France copies of the ratification of the Definitive treaty of peace between these states and his Britannic majesty when the same shall be completed, leaving to his discretion to engage such merchant vessels as may be ready to sail for Europe, paying the expences of their further detention, if he shall find that mode most eligible on the whole.

MS (DLC: PCC, No. 36, IV); in TJ's hand, with additions by Hugh Williamson as noted below; endorsed by clerk: "Motion that the Agent of Marine to have three Vessels ready to convey in some port of France Copies of the Ratification of the definitive Treaty of peace." The resolution bears no date and no reference to it appears in JCC (for reasons explained in note to TJ's resolutions introduced on 27 Dec. 1783, q.v.), but TJ himself stated that he moved this resolution "on the 26th. to save time" (same).

This resolution touched off an acrimonious discussion in Congress: "the debates ran high," Edward Hand wrote to Jasper Yeates; the Pennsylvania delegates wrote for instructions on this "Question of great Importance . . . Whether Seven States in Congress Assembled are competent to a Ratification of the Definitive Treaty"; and, after a brief lull following the first skirmish in which TJ was able to block the move to ratify by seven states, a compromise

was brought forward by him (Hand to Yeates, 30 Dec. 1783; Penna. Delegates to President Dickinson, 30 Dec. 1783; Burnett, *Letters of Members*, VII, Nos. 470-1; see following resolutions by TJ and notes there).

[1] This word interlined in Williamson's hand in substitution for "desired," deleted.
[2] This word interlined by TJ in substitution for "fast sailing," deleted.
[3] The preceding fifteen words interlined in Williamson's hand. These were in substitution for what TJ had written, which was, first: "one in the port of New York, one in the lowest safe port of the Delaware, and one at this place [Annapolis]." This was then changed by TJ to: "one in the port of Boston, one in the port of New-York, and one at this place." When Williamson in turn altered this reading, he failed to delete the final words "and one at this" though "place" is marked out.

Resolution Opposing Ratification of the Definitive Treaty by Less than Nine States

[27 December 1783]

Resolved that however earnestly and anxiously Congress wish to proceed to the ratification of the Definitive treaty, yet[1] ⟨*Resolved that Congress*⟩ consisting at present of seven states only they ought not to undertake ⟨*the*⟩ that ratification ⟨*of the Definitive treaty*⟩ without proper explanations.

⟨*1. Because the 9th. article of Confederation takes from them the power, by declaring that Congress shall not 'enter into any treaty unless nine states assent to the same.'*⟩

1. Because by the usage of modern nations it is now established that the ratification of a treaty by the sovereign power is the essential act which gives it validity; the signature of the ministers, notwithstanding their plenipotentiary commission, being understood as placing it, according to the phrase of the writers on this subject, sub spe rati, only, and as leaving to each sovereign an acknoleged right of rejection.

⟨*2. Because it would be a precedent replete with danger to these states as under that on future occasions seven states in opposition to six may ratify treaties entered into by ministers in direct opposition to their instructions though such instructions should have had the concurrence of nine states.*⟩

2. Because ratification being an act of so much energy and substance, the authority to perform it is reserved to nine states by those words in the ninth article of Confederation which declare that Congress 'shall not enter into any treaty, unless nine states assent to the same.'

3. Because by the terms 'enter into a treaty' the Confederation must have intended that the assent of nine states should be necessary to ⟨*the*⟩ it's completion as well as to ⟨*the*⟩ it's commencement ⟨*of a treaty*⟩; ⟨*it's*⟩ the object having been to guard the rights of the Union in all those important cases wherein it has required the assent of nine states ⟨*is required*⟩: whereas by admitting the contrary construction, seven states containing less than one third of the citizens of the Union in opposition to six containing more than two thirds may fasten on them a treaty, commenced indeed under ⟨*the instr*⟩ commission and instructions from nine states, but concluded ⟨*by the ministers*⟩ in express contradiction to such instructions and in direct sacrifice of the⟨*ir*⟩ interests of so great a majority.

4. Because if 7. states be incompetent generally to the ratification of a treaty they are not made competent in this particular instance by the circumstances of the ratification of the provisional articles by nine states ⟨and ins⟩, the instructions to our ministers to form a definitive one by them and their actual agreement in substance: for either these circumstances are in themselves a ratification, or are not: if they are, nothing further is requisite than to give attested copies of them in exchange for the British ratification; if they are not, then ⟨seven states have no authority to assume any circumstances where they are themselves⟩ we remain where we are, without a ratification by 9. states and incompetent to ratify ourselves.[2]

5. Because the seven states now present in Congress saw this question in the same point of view only 4 days ago when by their unanimous[3] resolution they declared that the assent of nine states was requisite to ratify this treaty and urged this as a reason to hasten forward the absent states.

6. Because such a ratification would be rejected by the other contracting party as null and unauthorized, or, if attested to them by the seal of the states without apprising them that it has been expedited by order of seven states only, it will be a breach of faith in us, a prostitution of our seal, and a future ground, when that circumstance shall become known, of denying the validity of a ratification into which they shall have been so surprised.

7. Because there being still 67. days before the exchange of ratifications is requisite, ⟨we may yet hope the presence of 9. states in time⟩ and two[4] states only wanting to render us competent, we have the strongest presumptions that the measures taken by Congress will bring them forward in time for ratification and for it's passage across the Atlantic.

And 8 because should we be disappointed in this hope, the ratification will yet be placed on more honourable and defensible ground if made by 9. states as soon as so many shall be present, and then sent for exchange, urging in it's support the small importance of an exchange of ratifications, a few days sooner or later, the actual impossibility of an earlier compliance, and that failures produced by circumstances not under the controul of the parties, ⟨and⟩ either in points so immaterial ⟨can never affect the validity of a treaty⟩, as to call for no compensation, or in those which are material and admit of compensation, can never affect the validity of the treaty itself.

MS (DLC). Despite numerous alterations, noted below, this was obviously not a composition draft but a copy made by TJ from an earlier text. MS

(DLC: Rives Papers). Both are entirely in TJ's hand. MS in Rives Papers is a fair copy that is nearly identical with MS (DLC) as corrected, though see notes 2-4 below. It is the copy that TJ enclosed in his letter to Madison of 20 Feb. 1784. Neither MS bears a date, but the time of composition is precisely ascertainable: in paragraph 5 TJ unquestionably refers to a motion made by Williamson and seconded by him, 23 Dec. 1783, as having been agreed to four days earlier (JCC, XXV, 836-7). In paragraph 7 he states that the time left before ratifications must be exchanged is 67 days. The deadline was 3 Mch. 1784 (six months from the date of signing on 3 Sep. 1783), which was 67 days from 27 Dec. 1783.

This resolution, though never introduced in Congress, is evidence that TJ was unwilling to compromise the integrity of the seal of the United States despite his great anxiety to have the Treaty ratified. It was drafted because of a movement among some of the delegates "to ratify the Definitive treaty by seven states only, and to impose this under the sanction of our seal (without letting our actual state appear) on the British court"; TJ informed Madison that "[Jacob] Reade, [Hugh] Williamson and [Arthur] Lee were violent for this, and gave notice that when the question should be put they would call the yeas and nays, and shew by whose fault the ratification of this important instrument should fail, if it should fail" (Madison to TJ, 20 Feb. 1784). In his "Autobiography" he gave a more detailed account of this rather bitter legislative skirmishing. He stated that, after the resolution of 23 Dec. had been adopted, urging the governors of various states to "press on their delegates the necessity of their immediate attendance" so that the requisite nine states could ratify, he had on 26 Dec. moved a resolution to direct the "Agent of Marine (Robert Morris) . . . to have ready a vessel at this place [Annapolis], at N. York, and at some Eastern port" so that the Treaty could be sent forward with all possible speed the moment ratification took place. This was opposed by Arthur Lee on the ground of expense, and, instead, Jacob Read brought forward a motion to ratify by seven states and send the Treaty on at once, whereupon "those in opposition prepared a resolution expressing pointedly the reasons of the dissent from his motion. It appearing however that his

proposition could not be carried, it was thought better to make no entry at all. Massachusetts alone would have been for it; Rhode Island, Pennsylvania and Virginia against it. Delaware, Maryland, and N. Carolina would have been divided" (Ford, I, 77-81). In his letter to Madison of 20 Feb. 1784, however, TJ stated that he himself had "prepared the . . . resolution" and that he had "informed them [Read and others] I would place that also on the journals with the yeas and nays, as a justification of those who oppose the proposition." In these debates of 26 and 27 Dec. 1783, TJ was clearly the leader of the successful move to thwart the efforts of Read, Lee, and others, though in his "Autobiography" he stated that opposition to Read's motion was "argued by Monroe, Gerry, Howel, Ellery and myself" (Ford, I, 79). The present resolution and its background, therefore, provide an excellent example of TJ's skill as a legislator: defending a principle, he was unyielding and at the same time successful in his tactics. Having won, he was ready to meet "on middle ground" those who had become "very restless under the loss of their motion"; hence on 3 Jan. 1784 he proposed a compromise motion that would protect the good faith of the nation and at the same time send forward a tentative "ratification" by seven states (see under that date). In these maneuvers he found himself linked with strange allies: David Howell and William Ellery of Rhode Island, who were as consistent in defending the rights of the individual states as TJ was in upholding the strength of the Confederation.

[1] This introductory paragraph was an afterthought, and the alterations in what appears here as the second paragraph were made after it was prefixed to the MS.
[2] This paragraph was also an afterthought and was written in the margin; the numbers of the succeeding paragraphs were accordingly changed in the MS by overwriting. MS in Rives Papers shows a slight modification in phrasing at this point, reading: "if they are not, then we remain where we were, without a ratification by nine states, or a competency to ratify by seven."
[3] This word is underscored in MS in Rives Papers.
[4] Blank in MS (DLC); number supplied from MS in Rives Papers.

To Elizabeth Wayles Eppes

[*Annapolis*, *27 Dec. 1783*. Entry in SJL reads: "Mrs. Eppes. She to write every 1st. Sund. and Mr. E. every 3d.—European news, state of Congr. Ratification. Want of money—[sent?] P. J. [Polly Jefferson] 2 sashes." Not found.]

To James Currie

[*Annapolis*, *28 Dec. 1783*. Entry in SJL reads: "Dr. Currie. Crawford's theory—his ivory book not read—cypher." Not found.]

To Benjamin Hawkins

[*Annapolis*, *28 Dec. 1783*. Entry in SJL reads: "Mr. Hawkins. Vocabulary—Buffon's character of Indians." Not found.]

To Thomas Hutchins

[*Annapolis*, *29 Dec. 1783*. Entry in SJL reads: "Capt Hutchins. Vocabulary for any Indian tribes." Not found.]

Report on Gerry's Motion respecting Papers in the Office of Foreign Affairs

[29 December 1783]

The Committee to whom was referred the motion of Mr. Gherry for procuring access to the papers of the office for foreign affairs have agreed to the following ⟨resolution⟩

Resolved that a deputy Secretary for foreign affairs should be appointed at some early day.

MS (DLC: PCC, No. 25, II); in TJ's hand. Endorsed by Thomson: "Report of Mr Jefferson Mr Osgood Mr Lee On Motion of Mr Gerry respectg papers of forn Affairs. Delivered Decr. 29. 1783. Entd. Read Jany. 26. 1784 Referred to Mr Sherman Mr Osgood Mr Read."

Gerry's motion, 24 Dec., proposed that the books and documents of the late secretary for foreign affairs (R. R. Livingston) be deposited in the office of the secretary of Congress and be made available for the perusal of members of Congress (PCC, No. 25, II; not in JCC). The present Report was evidently not discussed until 26 Jan. 1784, when it was referred to another committee of which TJ was not a member (see endorsement as quoted above, and JCC, XXVI, 49-50).

From Joseph Jones

Dr. Sr.   Fredericksburg 29th. Decr. 1783

I have the satisfaction to inform you the Senate contrary to my expectation passed the act authorising the Delegates in Congress to convey the claim of Virginia to the territory northwestward of the ohio to the united States without amendment and it will be transmitted you without the instruction heretofore intimated. The mode adopted for transfering our right was in pursuance and in conformity to the precedent established by N. York on her cession. Perhaps an act vesting the claim of this State in the united states might have been more proper and less troublesome but as there was a precedent it was thought better to [pursue] *that* than adopt a contrary method. Some of the learned Judges not of the Chancery doubted the efficacy of such Deed of conveyance as the Congress not being a corporate Body could not take a title by conveyance. I am so little used to law proceedings of late and so incompetent a judge of difficult cases without recuring to books, that the objection had not struck me and I do not now feel, so strongly as they appeared to do, the force of the objection; conceiving as I do the cession to be a conventional act between sovereign and independent States and not to be scanned by the rules of municipal law. I mention this circumstance that if you think there is weight in it the necessary precaution may be observed. I think I before informed you we had granted the impost duties with some conditions similar to those of Massachusetts. Another perhaps would have been proper and had it occurred in time would probably have been inserted in the act for determining questions of seizures for small value in the County Courts rather then compelling persons in all cases to defend themselves in the Court of Admiralty in Williamsburg. Should this in practice be found oppressive as it reaches not the substance I presume it may be redressed. The compleating the cession and granting the impost may not improperly be called sacrifices by this State to the common good of the union and will it is to be hoped lessen, if not wholly suspend those illiberal censures heretofore cast upon us. Add to these the unanimity and spirit [with] which the legislature passed an Act to empower Congress to concert measures to counteract the designs of Great Britain on our commerce—all of them calculated to produce harmony and strengthen the hands of the federal Government. The impost I assure you was with some a bitter pill, but finding it must be swallowed, they ceased at length to make opposition. Altho' we could not doubt the signing of the

definitive treaty in terms almost the same as the provisional articles,
yet as the same was not ratified and regularly communicated, it
w[as] thought proper to continue the lien law as it is called for
four months and from thence to the end of the next session of assembly. It was strongly contended this would be deemed an infraction
of the Treaty, but a great majority appeared in favor of continuing
the law, from an opinion we were under no obligation to put into a
train of execution what was not properly before us. Pray inform me
at your leisure whether any thing and what has been done respecting the Negros carryed away from New York by the British? What
about the British debts or the interest of them as I think some instructions were given our Commissioners on the subject particularly
the interest. Have any steps been taken or proposed to be taken to
obtain information of the amount of the claim of the British Creditors on these States or will it be left to the respective States to pursue their own measures. If it be true that three millions of pounds
sterl. the lowest calculation I have heard of, be due from the Citizens of America to the subjects of Great Britain, and probably a
much larger sum; is it within their ability encumbered as they are
with other demands, equally just and pressing, to make prompt
payment. If not, should not some negociation be opened under the
authority of Congress, or the respective States to gain knowledge
of the amount of the debt, and at what periods by installment the
Creditors are content to receive payment. This will be an embarrassing business the next Session of Assembly and is rendered the
more so as it involves the payments under the law made into the
Treasury during the continuance of the act and draws into consequence all transactions under the tender laws. Were you in the
Assembly when the confiscation act passed (I am told you were
the draftsman) by which it appears to me the property meant to
be confiscated was by the law vested in the Commonwealth and
altho not yet sold may still be so without infringing the Treaty as I
conceive the proceeding to compleat or take inquisitions for the
purpose of designating the property cannot be deemed such in any
future confiscations, and I learn there is much property at this time
in the predicament I mention. In short I foresee we shall have great
and perplexing questions agitated the next Session of Assembly,
such as call for moderation and wisdom to discuss and settle, and
the prospect of the Bodys possessing abilities equal to the Trust
not so promising as [I could] wish. Madisons aid I think we may
depend on [and] perhaps old Mr. G. Mason's as the Business of the
land Office requires [revision] and his apprehensions on that sub-

ject, [if nothing else, may draw] him from his retirement. Upon these or any other subjects that may fall under our [consideration] I shall thank you for your sentiments so far as you think it either proper or prudent to convey them. Very respectfully I am Dr Sr yr aff hum Servt,

JOS: JONES

RC (DLC). The text being faded and in some places illegible, the editors have taken some readings (enclosed in square brackets) from W. C. Ford's text in *Letters of Joseph Jones*, Washington, 1889, p. 135-8.

On the PRECEDENT ESTABLISHED BY N. YORK: New York's claim was not based on royal grant or charter, but on extremely insubstantial titles derived from the Six Nations of Indians. For whatever it amounted to, the New York claim was ceded to the United States by an Act of 1780, and a deed of cession was executed by the delegates of that state on 1 Mch. 1781 (Clarence E. Carter, *The Territorial Papers of the United States*, II, 3-5). The LIEN LAW (or stay law) AS IT IS CALLED: This was the Act of Oct. 1782 prohibiting the recovery of British debts. It expired on 1 Dec. 1783 and the Act "to revive and continue the several acts of Assembly for suspending the issuing of executions on certain judgments" extended it for "four months and from thence to the end of next session of assembly" (Hening, XI, 349; Harrell, *Loyalism in Virginia*, p. 144). The text of the Treaty, the fourth article of which provided that there should be no impediment to the recovery of British debts, was known to the Virginia legislators in provisional form at least; Gov. Harrison had also on 13 Dec. written to the Speaker of the House: "The enclosed notification of the definitive treaty came to my hands last night which I beg the favor of you to lay before the assembly. I with pleasure embrace the opportunity of congratulating both you and the assembly on this great and glorious event" (Executive Letter Book, Vi). On the CONFISCATION ACT, which Jones had been properly informed was drawn by TJ, see Vol. 1: 170, and on the question of interest on debts during the war, see the report on letters from American ministers in Europe, 20 Dec. 1783; also Vol. 1: 171-2.

WHAT HAS BEEN DONE RESPECTING THE NEGROS CARRYED AWAY FROM NEW YORK BY THE BRITISH?: This was a question dominant in the minds of many Virginians at the time. A part of the answer is to be found in TJ's additions to the report on letters from the American ministers in Europe, paragraph 9 (see above under 20 Dec. 1783). A part also is to be found in a letter from Gov. Harrison to Gov. Clinton of New York, which reads in part as follows: "The predatory war carried on by the British has fallen very heavily on many of our most valuable citizens. Some indeed it has brought to the brink of ruin. Tho' the treaty stipulates that the negroes carried away shall be returned, yet I well know it is intended by General Carleton to evade this part of it if he can and that for this purpose he has sent to the frozen regions of Nova Scotia as many of the poor wretches as could be induced to go there. Such as are left behind and I hear they are not a few are certainly the property of their owners, and I request the favor of you to give your kind assistance for the recovery of them . . ." (Harrison to George Clinton, 19 Dec. 1783, Executive Letter Book, Vi). This situation provides background for another measure proposed by the forthright governor. Three months earlier Harrison had written to Col. Charles Dabney saying he had received information that there had been in Dabney's legion "several negroes who were placed in it by their masters as substitutes and that since it has been disbanded they have in several instances been claimed by them and forced again into slavery; this appears so contrary to the common principles of justice and humanity that I am determined to lay the matter before the Assembly, not doubting but they will pass an act giving to those unhappy creatures that liberty which they have been in some measure instrumental in securing to us, and that I may have it in my power to point them out, I beg the favor of you to transmit to me their names and those of their masters by the first opportunity." Harrison was so outraged over this matter that he did not wait for Dabney to furnish the names of the planters involved, but laid the subject before the Assembly on the first day of its session (Harrison to Dabney, 7 Oct. 1783; Harrison to Speaker of the House, 20 Oct. 1783; both in Executive Letter Book, Vi). The General Assembly responded by passing an Act "directing the emancipation of certain slaves who have served as soldiers in this state," by which it was provided that those Negroes who had served in the Virginia forces and had "thereby of course contributed towards the establishment of American liberty and independence, should enjoy the blessings of freedom as a reward for their toils and labours" (Hening, XI, 308-9). The motives that led Harrison to propose and the legislators to adopt this just Act gain lustre from the fact that he himself, as he informed Governor Clinton, had been "one of the greatest sufferers, having lost thirty of my finest slaves" and that they included among their number and their connections many who had also had slaves carried away by the British.

To Bernard Moore

[*Annapolis*, *29 Dec. 1783*. Entry in SJL reads: "Bernard Moore vocabulary and queries for the Mattaponies and Pamunkies." Not found. Moore lived at West Point, between the Mattaponi and Pamunkey rivers whose names were derived from the Indian tribes inhabiting the region.]

To William Short

[*Annapolis*, *29 Dec. 1783*. Entry in SJL under this date, immediately following entry for preceding letter to Bernard Moore, reads: "W. Short. do. for the Nottoways." Not found.]

To Edmund Randolph

[*Annapolis*, *30 Dec. 1783*. Entry in SJL reads: "E. Rand. European news. Dutch commotions—but 7. states—not fault of delegates but want of money." Not found.]

To Edward Fox

[*Annapolis*, *31 Dec. 1783*. Entry in SJL reads: "Edwd. Fox. On Gilmer's accounts. Not found.]

To Benjamin Harrison

SIR   Annapolis, Dec. 31, 1783.

Letters from Holland from the middle to the last of September inform us that the citizens of the Dutch states are all in commotion.

The conduct of the Prince of Orange having been such as greatly to strengthen the republican party, they are now pressing in the firmest tone a restoration of their constitutional rights. Friesland, as usual, leads the way. They have demanded of the sovereign assembly of the states that the power of the Stadtholder to change or reinforce the garrisons be limited or taken away, and that themselves be authorized to exercise in arms for the defence of their country: of 80000 men able to bear arms among them it is believed scarcely any will refuse to sign this demand. The Hollanders have referred to a Committee in their last assembly the examination of the power by which the prince undertakes to appoint flag officers of their fleet, and that he be desired to abstain from the exercise of it. There happens to be vacant the place of admiral. The other states seem to be in the same temper, and are now regularly exercising themselves in arms under the ensigns of their respective towns. Tho each state is to chuse their Stadtholder out of the Orange family they consider themselves not bound to chuse the eldest, and of course that they may chuse different ones. The state of Europe at present seems favorable to the republican party, as the powers who might aid the prince are either fatigued with the late war, or likely to be engaged in the ensuing one.

We have yet but seven states, and no more certain prospects of nine than at any time heretofore. We hope that the letters sent to the absent states will bring them forward.

MS not located. Text from Ford, III, 368-9, where the letter is printed, without signature, from a MS said to be in Vi. This letter is entered in SJL under 30 Dec., as follows: "[Dec.] 30. the Govr. Dutch commotions—but 7. states yet." See Harrison's reply, 30 Jan. 1784.

To Wilson Cary Nicholas

DEAR SIR   Annapolis Dec. 31. 1783.

Just before I left Albemarle a proposition was started for establishing there a grammar school. You were so kind as to tell me you would write me the progress of the proposition: on my part I was to enquire for a tutor. To this I have not been inattentive. I enquired at Princetown of Dr. Witherspoon. But he informed me that that college was but just getting together again, and that no such person could of course be had there. I enquired in Philadelphia for some literary character of the Irish nation in that city. There was none such: and in the course of my enquiries I was informed that learning is but little cultivated there and that few persons have ever been known to come from that nation as tutors. I concluded on the whole then, if the scheme should be carried on and fixed on so firm a basis as that we might on it's faith venture to bring a man from his own country, it would be best for me to interest some person in Scotland to engage a good one. From that country we are surest of having sober attentive men. However this must await your information.

We learn with certainty that a war in Europe is unavoidable. The two empires on one side and the Turks on the other. It is probable France and Prussia will aid the Turks. Gr. Britain is likely to be employed by Ireland. The Dutch are engaging in civil commotions the object of which is the reduction of the powers of the Stadtholder. We have yet but 7. states in Congress, and 9. are requisite to ratify the treaty. As the ratifications should be exchanged in Paris by the 3d of March this gives us great uneasiness. I am with much esteem Dr. Sir Your friend & servt,

TH: JEFFERSON

RC (MHi). Addressee identified from a summary in SJL, which reads: "Wilson Nicholas. No tutor to be had from Pr. town nor probably Ireld.—best to send to Scotld.—will wait his information—European news—state of Congress and ratification."

Notes on British and American Alienage

[1783]

Qu. 1. Can an American citizen, adult, now inherit lands in England?

Natural subjects can inherit. Aliens cannot.

There is no middle character. Every man must be the one or the other of these.

A Natural subject is one born within the king's allegiance and still owing allegiance. No instance can be produced in the English law, nor can it admit the idea of a person's being a natural subject and yet not owing allegiance.

An alien is the subject or citizen of a foreign power.

The treaty of peace acknowleges we are no longer to owe allegiance to the king of G.B. It acknowleges us no longer as Natural subjects then.

It makes us citizens of independent states; it makes us aliens then.

A treaty with a foreign nation where the king's powers are

competent to it as in this which is a case of peace and war, supersedes all law.

If the king's powers were not competent before, the act of parliament of 1782 has made them so. An American citizen adult cannot inherit then.

Qu. 2. The father a British subject; the son in America, adult, and within the description of an American citizen, according to their laws. Can the son inherit?

He owes no allegiance to Great B. The treaty acknowleges he does not. But allegiance is the test of a natural subject. Were he to do an act here which would be treason in a British subject he could not be punished should he happen to go there.

He owes allegiance to the states. He is an alien then and cannot inherit.

[Obj.¹ The state of the father draws to it that of the son.

Ans. In Villenage it does, but in no other case at the Common law. Thus a Natural subject having a son born in a foreign state; the son was an alien at the Common law. The stat. 25.E.3. st.2. first naturalized him if *both* parents were, at the time of his birth, natural subjects; and 7.Ann.c.5. and 4.G.2.c.21. where the father alone was. So an Alien in England having a child born there, that child is a natural subject. A denizen purchases land. His children born *before* denization cannot inherit, but those born *after* may. The state of the father then does not draw to it that of the child, at the Common law.

But does it by the statutes? No, for here are statutes first making the son born abroad a natural subject, owing allegiance. Then comes a treaty of peace wherein the king absolves him from his allegiance and declares him an Alien. This then supersedes the authority of the statute. It is said 2.P.W.124. 1.Bl.357. that natural allegiance cannot be cancelled but by act of parliament. But surely national treaties supersede acts of parliament. The oath of allegiance took it's origin from the feudal oath of fealty. But as the fealty of the vassal could be relinquished by the lord, so can the allegiance of the subject by the king. If he withdraws his protection allegiance is gone: but he can withdraw his protection without consulting parliament.

Qu. Were the king's subjects in France aliens?

>If they were not, did they not become so when given up?

>Must they not of course become so when taken from him by a superior power?]

Qu. 3. The father a British subject. The son as in Qu. 2. but an infant. Can he inherit?

1st. by the Common law.

>We have seen before that the state of the father does not draw to it as an accessory that of the son where he is an adult.

>But by the common law

Denization may be 1. by parliament 2. by letters patent. 3. by Conquest. As if the king and his subjects conquer a kingdom, they become denizens of kingdom conquered. Calvin's ca. 6.a.

If an alien have issue born within the *king's obedience*, the issue is a natural only: ib. This excludes enemies possessing a town &c. ib.

Abjuratur still owes allegiance because he may be restored. 9.b. So an outlaw. ib. 14.a.

The law of nature is part of the law of Engld. 12.b.

If a noble of another country come to Engld., he sues by his proper name, not by that of his nobility, because on a plea in abatement that he is not noble, it is not tried by jury but by the record of parliament. 15.a.

Ambassadors having children born in foreign nation, they are natural subjects by the common law. 18.a.

While the kings of Engld. had possessions in France, those born during such possession were natural subjects of Engld. 19.a. So is it now of Ireland, Jersey, Guernsey, Man, Alderney, &c.

If a woman alien marrieth a subject she shall not be endowed. 25.a. An alien cannot be ten[ant] by the courtesy. ib.

If Engld. and Scotld. should by descent be divided and governed by several kings, those born under one sovereign while the realms were united would remain natural subjects and not aliens. 27.b.

He cannot be a subject born of one kingdom that was born under the ligiance of a king of another kingdom. 18.a.

MS (DLC); endorsed by TJ: "Alien. British & American." In all likelihood these notes were set down in Dec. 1783. The treaty then about to be ratified is mentioned; the expression "the states" for the United States, current at just this time in TJ's reports as a member of Congress, is used; and TJ had a particular interest in the question of alienage at this moment because Mrs. Trist had consulted him about the status of her son Browse, whose father was a British officer (see TJ to Mrs. Trist, 22 Dec. 1783).

TENANT BY THE COURTESY: Under the *curtesy of England* the husband who survived a wife possessed of lands and having issue able to inherit enjoyed a life tenure in the lands.

1 The passage in brackets (supplied) was written at the bottom of the first and top of the second page and was marked by a vertical line along the margin to indicate that it was to be inserted at the point following the preceding sentence ("He is an alien then and cannot inherit"), where TJ, after making this amplification, inserted the words to which this passage was keyed: "Obj. the state &c."

To James Madison

DEAR SIR   Annapolis Jan. 1. 1784.

Your favour of the 10th. Dec. came to hand about a fortnight after it's date. It has occasioned me to reflect a little more attentively on Buffon's central heat than I did in the moment of our conversation and to form an opinion different from what I then expressed. The term 'central heat' does of itself give us a false idea of Buffon's hypothesis. If it meant a heat lodged in the center of the earth and diffusing it's warmth from thence to the extremities, then certainly it would be less in proportion to the distance from that center, and of course less under the equator than the poles, on high mountains than in deep vallies. But Buffon's theory is that this earth was once in a state of hot fusion, and that it has been, and still continues to be, cooling. What is the course of this process? A heated body being surrounded by a colder one whether solid or fluid, the heat, which is itself a fluid, flows into the colder body equally from every point of the hotter. Hence if a heated spheriod of iron cools to a given degree, in a given space of time, an inch deep from it's surface, in one point, it has in the same time done the same in any and every other point. In a given time more, it will be cooled all round to double that depth, so that it will always be equally cooled at equal depths from the surface. This would be the case of Buffon's earth if it were a smooth figure without unevennesses. But it has mountains and vallies. The tops of mountains will cool to greater depths in the same time than the sides of mountains and than plains in proportion as the line a. b. is longer than a.c. or d.e. or f. g. In the valley the line h.i. or depth of the same temperature will be the same as on a plain. This however is very

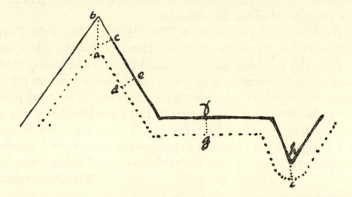

different from Buffon's opinion. He sais that the earth being thinnest at the poles will cool sooner there than under the equator where it is thicker. If my idea of the process of cooling be right his is wrong and his whole theory in the Epochs of nature is overset.

The note which I delivered you contained an acknowlegement of my having borrowed from you a draught for 333⅓ dollars and a promise to repay it on demand. This was exclusive of what I had borrowed in Philadelphia.

We have never yet had more than 7. states, and very seldom that, as Maryland is scarcely ever present, and we are now without a hope of it's attending till February. Consequently having six states only, we do nothing. Expresses and letters are gone forth to hasten on the absent states that we may have 9. for a ratification of the definitive treaty. Jersey perhaps may come in, and if Beresford will not come to Congress, Congress must go to him to do this one act. Even now it is full late. The critical situation in which we are like to be gave birth to an idea that 7. might ratify. But it could not be supported. I will give you a further account of this when it shall be finally settled.

The letters of our ministers inform us that the two empires have formed a league defensive against Christian powers and offensive against the Turks. When announced by the Empress to the K. of Prussia he answered that he was very sensible on it as one is when informed of important things. France answered in a higher tone and offered to mediate. If Prussia will join France perhaps it may prevent the war: if he does not, it will be bold for France alone to take the aid of the Turks on herself. Ireland is likely to find employment for England. The United Netherlands are in high fermentation. The people now marshall themselves in arms and exercise regularly under the banners of their towns. Their object is to reduce the powers of the Stadtholder.

I have forwarded your letter to Mrs. House. Mrs. Trist I expect left Philadelphia about the 18th. of Dec. for Pittsburgh. I had a letter from her in which she complained of your not having written and desired me to mention it to you. I made your excuse on the good grounds of the delays you must have experienced on your journey and your distance from the post road: but I am afraid she was gone before my letter reached Philadelphia. I have had very ill health since I have been here and am getting rather lower than otherwise. I wish you every felicity and am with sincere affection Your friend & servt.,   TH: JEFFERSON

RC (DLC: Madison Papers); endorsed.

From Benjamin Harrison

SIR   Council Chamber Jany 2d. 1784

I have nothing to communicate to you either interesting or entertaining, the bad weather having cut off all communication with the country.

Your favor of the 24th. ultimo really alarms me. Your fears of great britains taking advantage of any slip or neglect of ours are just, and what is still more to be dreaded than their resentment is the falling off of our allies in Europe who will never enter into a war again to defend a people who will appear altogether unworthy of support and that will not give up a little of their domestic pleasures for the greatest national concerns. I wish you very many happy years and am with great truth your most obt. &c.   B.H.

FC (Vi); at head of text: "The honorable Mr. Jefferson."

Report of Committee to Revise the Files of Reports

[2 January 1784]

The committee appointed to revise the files of reports and appointment of Committees and to report what matters will require the attention of Congress previous to an adjournment have revised the files of reports digested them under five heads and agreed to the following report thereon.

The first head comprehends important reports requiring the assent of 9. states. These relate to the ratification of the definitive treaty, the military arrangements in time of peace, the civil arrangements foreign and domestic, the territories on our Western border, and the definition of the powers proper for a Committee of the states: which several matters are thought essential for the consideration of Congress before their adjournment.

The second head comprehends reports which also require the assent of 9. states. They relate to matters of account, and particular claims for money, which may probably be dispatched in those short intervals or portions of the day in which it may not be convenient to discuss the first great subjects. Many of them however are such as ought not to detain Congress whenever they shall be ready for adjournment.

The third head comprehends reports which may be acted on by 7. states and which therefore may be taken up by Congress immediately.

The fourth comprehends those which should be postponed to another session, some of them being not at all pressing and others not yet matured for determination.

The fifth comprehends those reports which having been rendered useless by subsequent events may be postponed generally.

The Committee having not had time yet to revise the appointment of Committees, and to arrange their objects under the same heads beg leave to report again when they shall have made further progress.

MS (DLC: PCC, No. 23); entirely in TJ's hand; docketed by Charles Thomson: "Report of Mr Jefferson Mr Gerry Mr Williamson to revise the files and report the Matters that will require the attention of Congress previous to an adjournmt. Entd.—Read."

On 19 Dec. 1783 TJ, Gerry, and Williamson were appointed as a committee to "report what matters will require the Attention of Congress previous to an adjournment and to revise the files of reports and appointment of Committees" (Committee Book, DLC: PCC, No. 186). The committee "Report in part and discharged" on 2 Jan. 1784 (same; JCC, XXVI, 2-3).

Jefferson's Compromise Motion
concerning Ratification of the Definitive Treaty

[2 January 1784]

Whereas it is stipulated in the definitive treaty of peace between the United states and his Britannic majesty that the ratifications of the said treaty shall be exchanged on or before the 3d. day of

March next and there now remains before that period little more time than is requisite for the passage of the said ratification across the Atlantic; And Congress consisting at present but of 7. states, these differ in opinion, some of them considering 9. as requisite under the Confederation to the establishment of every treaty while others are of opinion that nine having ratified the Provisional treaty, and instructed their ministers to enter into a definitive one conformable thereto which is accordingly done seven may under these particular circumstances ratify what has been so declared by nine to have their approbation; and those of the former opinion being equally desirous with the latter that no power which it may be supposed they possess should remain unexercised for the final ratification of this instrument[1] provided it may be done with the preservation of good faith towards the other contracting party and without being supposed to convey any opinion of Congress that such ratification is authoritative, which supposition would be contrary to truth:

Resolved therefore that the states now present in Congress do declare their approbation and ratification[2] of the said treaty; that the same be duly attested under the seal of the states: and transmitted to our ministers:[3] that so soon as nine states shall be present in Congress, the said treaty shall be submitted to them and their ratification when obtained shall be transmitted to our ministers also in hope of it's reaching them by the stipulated time, in which case this shall be used and the former cancelled; that [if] however they do not receive the ratification by nine states before the time for exchange they then produce[4] the act of the seven states,[5] offering it to the acceptance of the other party in exchange for theirs with assurance that it will be followed by another expedited by nine states which shall be delivered to them also;[6] and at the same time explaining (if they find it necessary for the preservation of our good faith) the differences of opinion which exist as to the compe[tence][7] of seven states to this act; or if it be more eligible to the other pa[rty] that then they agree on a further day for the exchange of ratifications.

MS (DLC: PCC, No. 29); entirely in TJ's hand, with numerous deletions and corrections, the more important of which are noted below; endorsed by Thomson: "No. 9. Motion of Mr. Jefferson Jany. 2. 1784 Referred to Mr Jefferson Mr Williamson Mr Read Mr Gerry Mr Howell of ratification of def. treaty [and, at a later date, in the same hand:] Jany 14 1784 Rendered Useless by the ratification this day by 9 states. to be filed." Committee Book (DLC: PCC, No. 186) records the appointment of the committee on 2 Jan. and the fact that it reported the following day. Ford, III, 372-5, prints the present and the following document as if they are, respectively, the rough draft and the fair copy of the same text. But this is misleading. The present MS seems indeed to be a rough draft and it also bears close resemblance to the document following, but it is more proper to designate it as TJ's *motion* of 2 Jan., whereas the document following is the *report* handed in by the committee of five on 3 Jan.; this is clearly shown by the endorsements on the two and by the record in Committee Book. Since both documents underwent numerous changes that would be difficult to represent if their text should be considered as one, they are here presented separately (in accord with their true nature) despite their duplication in part.

For the earlier debates in Congress that led to the present compromise proposed by TJ, see note to resolution printed above under date of 27 Dec. 1783. The fact that the Journals of Congress contain no reference to this motion or to the report of the committee is explained there. In his Autobiography TJ states that the report "was debated on the 3d. and 4th. and on the 5th. a vessel being to sail for England from this port [Annapolis] the House directed the President to write to our ministers accordingly" (Ford, I, 82-3; see also Burnett, *Letters of Members*, VII, No. 476). There is no evidence that Mifflin wrote such a letter to the ministers.

1 Preceding five words interlined in substitution for "establishment of peace," deleted.

2 TJ first wrote: "approbation of and [. . .] to this" and then over-wrote "and ratification" so as to render one word illegible.

3 The following passage is deleted at this point: "with instructions not to make use of it till the last point of time."

4 This word interlined in substitution for "tender," deleted.

5 Following this point, this passage was deleted and the reading as given above substituted: "expressing at the same time the doubts which Congress themselves entertained of its validity, and proposing that that shall be accepted and shall," &c.

6 Following this point, this passage was deleted: "and that they agree on a further day for the exchange of ratifications at their option."

7 Part of this word obscured; it was probably abbreviated by TJ as "competc." Ford, III, 375, gives it as "compliance" as if the word were completely legible; but it is not, and the reading, which is conjectural, is erroneous: there was never any question of the "compliance" of seven states in the ratification, but only of their competence to ratify.

Report of the Committee
on Jefferson's Compromise Motion concerning Ratification

[3 January 1784]

Whereas it is stipulated in the definitive treaty of peace between the United states of America and his Britannic majesty that the ratifications of the said treaty shall be exchanged on or before the 3d. day of March next, and there now remains before that period little more time than is requisite for the passage of the said ratification across the Atlantic; And Congress consisting at present but of 7. states, these differ in opinion; some of them considering 9. as requisite under the Confederation to the establishment of every treaty, while others are of opinion that 9. having ratified the Provisional treaty and instructed their ministers to enter into a definitive one conformable thereto, which is accordingly done, seven may under these particular circumstances ratify what has been so declared by 9 to have their approbation; and those of the former opinion being equally desirous with the latter that no power which it may be supposed they possess should remain unexercised for the final ratification of this instrument, provided it may be done with the preservation of good faith towards the other contracting party, and without importing that Congress has given any Express[1] opinion that the said ratification is authorized by the Confederation:[2]

Resolved therefore that the states now present in Congress do declare their approbation and, so far as they have power, their ratification of the said treaty: that the Ratification in the usual Form[3] be duly attested under the seal of the states and transmitted to our ministers with instructions to keep the same uncommunicated and to propose to the other contracting party a convention extending the time for the exchange of ratifications 3. months further: that the said ministers be informed that so soon as 9 states shall be present in Congress the said treaty shall be submitted to them and their ratification when obtained shall be transmitted also: that if they should receive the ratification by 9. states before the ultimate point of time allowed for exchange this alone be used and the former cancelled: that if it should not be received in time, they then produce the act of the 7. states and give the same in Exchange[4] *informing the other contracting party that the said treaty came to hand when Congress was not in session,*[5] that 7. states only had yet assembled; that this ratification has been expedited with their unanimous consent and offering it in exchange for theirs.[6]

MS (DLC: PCC, No. 29); in TJ's hand, with several interlineations in the hand of Hugh Williamson; endorsed by Thomson: "Report of Mr. Jefferson &c. relative to ratification of def. treaty. Entd. Read Jany 3. 1784." See notes to preceding document.

[1] This word interlined in Williamson's hand.
[2] TJ originally wrote: "whether the said ratification be or be not authorized," &c. and then altered the passage to read as above.
[3] Preceding five words interlined in the hand of Williamson and the word "same" encircled, probably to indicate that it was deleted and the interlineation substituted for it.

[4] Preceding six words interlined in the hand of Williamson.
[5] This passage in italics was underlined, perhaps by Thomson and no doubt indicating that, during the debate in Congress, it was pointed out that the statement was truthful only in a technical sense, for the treaty had arrived during the interval between Congress' adjournment from Princeton to Annapolis.
[6] The following was deleted at this point: "With an assurance that it will be followed by another expedited in all it's forms by nine states so soon as they shall be assembled which shall be delivered to them also."

From Francis Hopkinson,
with "A Literary Christmas Gambol"

DEAR FRIEND   Philada. Jany. 4th. 1784

I heartily thank you for your favour of the 23d. Decr. last and for the Pains you have taken to abridge Monsr. Buffon's System of Astronomy. However you may think your Time lost in reading his two whimsical volumes, the little Time you took to give me a summary of his Scheme was certainly not spent in vain. Your Letter found me very un-well and in a great deal of Pain; it drew my attention so, as to smother a dozen Groans at least; a Proof that the Laceration of any Part of the Body does not necessarily produce Pain. The extreme Attention with which the Soul watches every Circumstance that concerns the Body occasions the Sense of Pain. If in the very moment of Torture any external object should present, more interesting to the mind than even the Care of the Body, the Soul will bend all her Powers to this new Object; and the Sense of Pain will cease. This is daily experienc'd in small un-interesting Afflictions, such as a slight Tooth-Ach, a trifling Burn &c. When I was in England, I had an excruciating Boil, which was at the Height of Inflamation and Tension; I went, nevertheless to a public Place and heard the Oratorio of the Messiah performed to Admiration. I felt no more the Pain of the Boil. It even broke whilst I was there without my perceiving it. Had I been in my Chamber, I should have cried out with Anguish. May not the Firmness of Martyrs be accounted for on the same Principle? But as to Mr. Buffon. I like his Performance very much. I see your Error. You have read him as some good People read the Revelations of St. John taking every thing in the literal Sense; and I, like some learned Expositors of the said Revelations, will endeavour to give you the true mystical Sense of Monsr. Buffon's work.

This great Philosopher has represented the Court of Great Britain by the Sun and that of France by a Comet. France in the Excentricity of her political movements hath at length struck forcibly against Britain and, by the Collision, struck off a Part of her Body, which, being ballanced by the counteracti[ng] Powers of centrifugal and centripetal Force, hath found an Orbit of it's own, and rolls a new Planet in the System, called the American Empire. The Analogy is obvious. The Sun being in a fluid State it's Surface is much agitated and influenced by the Appearance of a Comet; this points at the Insurrections, mobs and internal Confusion that disturbed England when France formed an alliance with America.

The Fragment which the Comet strikes off from the Sun, takes with it a Portion of his atmosphere. So, America, tho' independent of G. Britain, has taken with her, her Laws, Customs, Language, Religion &c. which is undoubtedly very figurative of an atmosphere: being an assemblage of heterogenus Particles, expansive, variable, fluctuating and of little Solidity. All this is easily accommodated. The Parallel is striking, but the most difficult Passage is yet to be explained. I mean that respecting the Elephant Travelling Southward as the new Planet cools. But an ingenious Commentator surmounts all Difficulties. I analogize it thus—The Heat or Fire of true Patriotism flowed in the United States of America in the Year 1776, when the Declaration of Independence took place— or in Monsr. Buffon's words, when we were struck off from Great Britain. This Heat however, begins gradually to evaporate, the Body cools, especially towards the North-East. The more equatorial Parts containing more matter retain this Heat longer. By the Elephant, which is the greatest of all Beasts, is intended the American Congress, which is the greatest of all political Bodies. Politicians have in vain sought for Reasons sufficient to justify the late movement of Congress to the Southward: Here we see Monsr. Buffon has accounted for this Phænomenon upon demonstrable Principles; with the Eye of a Prophet and the Precision of a Philosopher, he has develop'd the whole mystery: nothing was wanting but my Commentary, to make the whole obvious to every intelligent mind. I have only sketch'd a general Out-line of Exposition; but having put the Clue into your Hand, your Ingenuity will easily investigate the whole, and apply the most minute Parts of Monsr. Buffon's solar System to the American Revolution.

Your Daughter was with me on Wednesday Evening last and danced out the old Year in Company with Mr. Rittenhouse's Daughters and my Children. A Forte Piano served for a *Fidle* and I for a Fidler. I was much indisposed the whole Evening, but their mirth alleviated my Pains. I have the Pleasure to inform you that your Girl comes on finely in her Education; but Mr. Simitiere has, with great Sagacity, discovered that she has no Genius, and declares he will leave her at the End of the Month. If he should, I have advised my mother not to pay him the Guinea he will demand; but to tell him that, as you had paid him a Guinea Entrance, with an Expectation that he would instruct your Daughter in Drawing, if he shall think fit to break off the Instruction in the short Time of one Month, without any real Cause for so doing, she cannot think herself justifiable in paying another Guinea without your express

A Sample of good Writing

"An Author who wishes to ~~rise~~ of Excellence in good Writing,
must ~~condescend~~ to call in mechanical Propriety to his Aid.
He cannot be all at once ~~sublime~~ but gradually descending to the profound,
should as gradually rise to Elegance, unavoidably forming that serpentine
Line, in which according to Hogarth true Beauty is alone to be found.

And whether he writes in plain Prose
Or would in Verse his Thoughts convey
His rhiming Talent to display
a strick Conformity should ever prevail and the Diction
run parallel, pleasing as well the Eye as the Ear, and the Sense.

Some have a happy Talent of expressing themselves
whereby, they compensate the want of Sentiment by the Melody
of their Style: their Language ever flowing like a wave of the Sea, &
every Period closing in such musical Cadence that the Ear is fascinated by the
magic of Sound & the mind lull'd in a pleasing deshore ─ ─ ─ ─ ─

Others, without giving to Grammar Rules offence
shall arrange, so unskilfully, their Words, breaking, as it were
& interrupting the Sense (or rather Nonsense) they mean to
convey, by frequent (& oft-times un-necessary) Parentheses,
that the Ear stumbles over their rugged Paragraphs, as
one would stumble in scrambling thro' a Street where
the pavement had been broken up: Stones and Bricks mixed
and posts together confusedly.

The Mind is fa ─ ti ─ gu ─ ed more, by travelling
over a Paragraph so ill constructed, than it would or
could be in gliding thro' a whole Page of smooth Phra-
-seology. ─ Your learned Grammarians are most
apt to write in this Style: thinking they have well
acquitted themselves, if the Rules of Syntax are, in
no Instance violated ─ The Labourer who mixes the
mortar, & he who carries the Hod may as well pretend
to Skill in Architecture, as those Haberdashers of
moods & Tenses may pretend to Taste & Elegance
in Writing.

Francis Hopkinson, "A Sample of good Writing," page 1

Loftiness

others again affect a   of Expression; scorning the
simplicity of vulgar Diction.   It is an indubitable *low*
verity that their Phrases are collated from the most
approved Authors, & applied with the most becoming
Aptitude, even to the very Point of Precision in Propriety,
and every Period is polished & rounded off

Whilst others scorn the O R N A M E N T S
of Language — deal in Demonstration;   *and write*

            roundly &c

By the above Sample it is obvious that not
only an Authors Sentiments may be more forcibly
impressed on the Mind in reading, but the Readers mem-
-ory be also mechanically assisted: should any thing
so written happen to be worth remembering.
Another Advantage is that such Performances may
be with great Ease reduced to short hand — Take
for Instance the same Example in short hand &
it will stand thus.

I have been much tormented with the Gout
since I wrote my Letter on Sunday last — it is now Wednes-
-day & am just able to sit by the Fire & with the
above on my knee — this is the Reason it is so
badly written — Once more Adieu

                        F. H.

P.S. I have just heard that the Physicians have so
persuaded Dr Martin about his Cancer Medicine & his
want of Learning, that he has actually run crazy—
swearing out that there is Plot against his Life &c

Order. He says he is no *School-Master*, and not obliged to go thro' the Drudgery of teaching those who have no Capacity. You will not be disappointed at this, as you know the Man. Your Daughter is well and now here to dine with me. She desires her dutiful Love. My mother also desires her affectionate Regards.

I enclose for your Amusement a Christmas Gambol, in the Literary way.

I shall be happy in corresponding with you if you give me any Encouragement. My Fancy suggests a Thousand whims which die for want of Communication, nor would I communicate them but to one who has Discernment to conceive my Humour and Candour with respect to my Faults and Peculiarities. Such a Friend I believe you to be.

Remember me kindly to Mr. and Mrs. Thompson and to all my friends in Congress, if my unlucky Talents have left me any there.

I am Dear sir Your affectionate friend & very humble servant,

FRAS HOPKINSON

ENCLOSURE

A Literary Christmas Gambol

Some Account of a new discovered and most commodious Method of Writing; whereby an Author of little or no Genius may be enabled to express himself with mechanical Force and Propriety. Invented and now first made known A.D. 1783 by F———— H———— Esqr.

Genius is the Gift of Heaven, and displays itself in Emanations altogether unexpected and surprising. It's Powers are not to be attained by Application and Study, but they may be assisted by art. When Genius hath been delivered, Art takes up and nurses the Child, and carefully consulting it's Features, deduces Rules for a happy Conception. Genius produces an epic Poem, Art analyses the work and forms Rules for writing epic Poetry. Such being the intimate Connection between Genius and Art, it is but reasonable that a mutual Intercourse of good offices should subsist between them. For my own Part I must confess that Nature hath not been very bountiful to me with Respect to Genius, but am willing to employ the little her Ladyship hath allowed in favour of those who may have as little or less of Genius than myself. For this Purpose I have devised a Method of writing on any subject, in which not only the Sound may seem an Echo to the Sense—if haply any Sense there be—but the Eye also shall be gratified with a mechanical Elegance and Propriety—the only Elegance perhaps to which such writers can attain. By this Scheme the Construction of a Paragraph, the Progress of a Line, of an artful Disposition or Words shall all contribute, to enforce the Idea intended.

It would be a tedious Task to reduce this new Method of writing, to regular Rules, or to give a Description at length of my useful Device. One Example will fully explain the whole, so as to enable an author of any tolerable Capacity to comprehend the Design; and a little Practice will make it familiar to him.

A Sample of good Writing

"An Author who wishes to rise to the Height of Excellence in good Writing must condescend to call in mechanical Propriety to his Aid. He cannot be all at once sublime but gradually descending to the profound should as gradually rise to Elegance, unavoidably forming that serpentine Line, in which according to Hogarth true Beauty is alone to be found.

And whether he writes in plain Prose Or would in Verse his Thoughts convey His rhiming Talent to display a strict Conformity should ever prevail and the Diction and the Sense run parallel pleasing as well the Eye as the Ear.

Some have a happy Talent of expressing themselves whereby they compensate the want of Sentiment by the melody of their Style; their Language ever flowing like a wave of the Sea, and every Period closing in such musical Cadence that the Ear is fascinated by the magic of Sound and the mind lull'd in a pleasing Repose.

Others, without giving to Grammar Rules offence, shall arrange, so unskilfully their Words, breaking, as it were, and interrupting the Sense (or rather Nonsense) they mean to convey, by frequent (and oft times un-necessary) Parentheses, that the Ear stumbles over their rugged Paragraphs, as one would stumble in scrambling thro' a Street when pavement had been broken up over Stones Bricks and posts mixed together confusedly.

The Mind is fatigued more by travelling over a Paragraph so ill constructed, than it would or could be in gliding thro' a whole Page of smooth Phraseology. Your learned Grammarians are most apt to write it this Style; thinking they have well acquitted themselves, if the Rules of Syntax are in no Instance violated. The Labourer who mixes the mortar, and he who carries the Hod may as well pretend to Skill in Architecture, as those Haberdashers of moods and Tenses may pretend to Taste and Elegance in Writing.

Others again affect a Loftiness of Expression; scorning the simplicity of vulgar Diction. It is an indubitable low verity that their Phrases are collated from the most approved Authors, and applied with the most becoming Aptitude, even to the very Point of Precision in Propriety, and every Period is polished and rounded off as round as a Robin is round and a round aye!

Whilst others scorn the ornaments of Language, deal in Demonstration and act and write ever on the Square.

By the Above Sample it is obvious that not only an Author's Sentiments may be more forcibly impress'd on the Mind in reading, but the Reader's Memory be also mechanically assisted; should any thing so written happen to be worth remembering.

Another advantage is that such Performances may be with great Ease reduced to short hand. Take for Instance the same Example in short hand and it will stand thus."

[7 Jan. 1784]

I have been much tormented with the Gout since I wrote my Letter on Sunday last. It is now Wednesday and am just able to set by the

Fire and write the above on my knee. This is the Reason it is so badly written. Once more Adieu. F H

P.S. I have just heard that the Physicians have so persecuted Dr. Martin about his Cancer Medecine and his want of Learning, that he has actually run crazy, crying out that this is [a] Plot against his Life, &c. &c.

RC (DLC). Enclosure (DLC). That part of the enclosure entitled "A Sample of good Writing" has been printed here without any attempt to follow the whimsical form in which it was written; such an attempt was made with conspicuous lack of success when the piece was first printed in Hopkinson's *Miscellaneous Essays*, I, 245-51. There is only one means of accurately conveying Hopkinson's playful mood and that is by employing facsimile; hence these two pages of the MS are reproduced among the illustrations of this volume.

From John Sullivan,
with Petition of John Penhallow

SIR   Annapolis Jany 6th 1784

I have selected the papers you were pleased to mention, have numbred them from one to Thirty and noted their Contents in the enclosed Minutes. In my state of objections which I beg you will peruse I omitted to mention that the Claimants have upon obtaining the Decree brought Trover for the vessel and Cargoe and attached the Cargoe of goods to a very great amount which are now held to respond the Judgment, and must wait the decision of Congress on the remonstrance from the Legislature of New Hampshire. This alone seems to furnish a powerful argument in favor of a speedy Decision. I confess myself unable To discover the necessity of giving notice to the Court of Appeals. The Confederation is before the Committee and Congress will put their own Construction upon the Articles whatever may be the opinion of the Court of appeals. The Laws of New Hampshire are before the Committee and the proceedings of the several Courts are obvious; That an appeal was not granted is indubitable; and that by the Laws of New Hampshire no appeal could be granted is beyond controversy: And that the Court of Appeals have taken up and passed upon a matter thus circumstanced cannot be denied.

The first Question, therefore is whether by the Articles of confederation that Court could be vested with such power and 2dly whether if they had such authority by way of appeal they could possibly exercise it without any appeal being had. Surely both these Questions may and ought to be determined by Congress without the voice of the Judges of that Court. When writs of prohibition, Certiorari or mandamus Issue I know of no Instance of the Judges of the Inferior Jurisdiction being called upon to Account for their Conduct and I think it Less necessary in the present than in either of the Cases before mentioned: should it be suggested That by the ratification of the confederation in 1781 it would bear a Retrospective Construction to the time of its formation it may be well to consider the difficulty of fixing the period of its operation. The time of its signing by the members was not at the same time but many months different. Whether Each was bound by the signing of its own Members or all by the signature of the first will become an important Question and as Congress did not act agreably to the Rules Laid Down by the articles of Confederation untill the accession of Maryland it may become a Question no less important whether the proceedings of that honorable Body from 1778 to 1781 are not a mere nullity. All mony grants without nine states and all determinations where less than seven agreed may upon that principle be with propriety disputed. I flatter myself therefore that the view of these and many other difficulties which might be mentioned As naturally arising from that Construction will induce the Committee to confine the operation of the Articles of union to the Day of their ratification; I have the honor to be very respectfully sir your most obedt servt, JNO SULLIVAN

ENCLOSURE

Portsmouth October 20. 1783.

The Petition and Memorial of John Penhallow, Joshua Wentworth, Ammi R. Cutler, Nathaniel Folsom, Samuel Sherburne, Jacob Treadwell, Thomas Martin, Moses Woodward, Neal McIntyer, Nathaniel Sherburne in behalf of Daniel Sherburne deceased Keith Spence, George Turner, Richard Champney, Elizabeth Dalling in behalf of Thomas Dalling deceased and Robert Furness all of Portsmouth in the County of Rockingham and State aforesaid, Humbly sheweth. That your Memorialists in the year 1777 were owners of a Brigantine called the McClary being a private armed vessel duly authorized and commissioned to cruise against the enemies of the United States of America, which Brigantine so authorized sailed from Portsmouth, and soon after on the high seas in the month of November in the same year, captured and brought into the port of Piscatagua the Brigantine Lusanna with her cargo and appurtenances which they caused to be libelled in the maritime Court for said State, agreeably to the laws thereof, as British property, as being in the service of the enemy and then carrying supplies to the British fleet and garrison at Hallifax. At the same time in the same Court the principal part of said property was claimed by Elisha Doane and Isaiah Doane of wellfleet in the Commonwealth of Massachusetts, and one James Shepherd an American but at that time in Great Britain. The said Elisha Doane claiming the vessel and the largest part of her cargo. After a full and fair hearing, the Jury gave verdict for the condemnation of the vessel and the whole of her cargo and the Court proceeded to decree thereon agreeably to said verdict; from which decree the said claimants demanded an appeal to the Continental Congress; but the Court on examining the laws of this state found that they allowed of appeals to Congress only in cases where the prizes were taken by vessels fitted out at the charge of the United States, and in every other instance directed that the appeal should be to the superior Court of Judicature for this State. The Court therefore refused the claimants an appeal to Congress, but granted them at their request an appeal to said superior Court, where in September following, at Exeter, the cause was again tried, and after the fullest and most candid hearing thereof by a Jury approved by both parties, they gave a verdict confirming that of the Court below; and the Court proceeded to the definitive sentence agreeably thereto, from which last decree the claimants again demanded an appeal to Congress, which the said superior Court unanimously refused as directly contrary to law; and then proceeded to issue a precept to the sheriff as the law directed, requiring him to sell the said vessel and effects at public vendue, and make distribution among the Captors and others concerned according to law; and the Sheriff made the sale and distribution accordingly with a due return to said Court of his doings therein.

Here we flattered ourselves this very troublesome cause ended, when to our great surprize in May 1779 your Memorialists received a very short notification from some persons at Philadelphia (who it seems were appointed a Court of Commissioners in all maritime causes) acquainting them that the same cause (already twice tried, and by the laws of this State completely ended) was brought before them by Col. Doane & al: by way of complaint and would be again tried on the 21st. day of June then next, at Philadelphia. Notwithstanding the surprize of your memorialists at so unexpected a summons, they proceeded with the greatest caution and prudence. They consulted Counsel thereon, and were by them advised to send a person to appear in their behalf at Philadelphia on the day appointed for the trial, there to plead to the jurisdiction of the Court, deny their authority to take cognizance of this cause, and strenuously urge as a principal reason for such a plea. That such an authority was directly repugnant to, and a violation of the laws of this State, by which your memorialists held their lives and all that is dear to them, and which very laws were made in consequence of a Resolve of Congress, in which they particularly recommended the trial by Jury which this new constructed Court entirely took away. This plea was made and enforced by Counsel which your memorialists engaged in their behalf at Philadelphia, but with no other effect than to produce a suspension of a trial on the merits 'till the matter could be laid before the Legislature of this State, in order that they might be prevailed upon to rescind and wholly disannul that law of this state upon which the whole process was bottomed. This the Legislature utterly refused to do. But passed an act giving an appeal to Congress in cases where foreigners were claimants, and in that alone and even this did not retrospect but only related to future causes. This act with the determinations of the General Assembly for this State was seasonably transmitted to Philadelphia to be laid before a new Court of appeals, the first being abolished; together with instructions to your Memorialists Counsel to renew the plea to the jurisdiction of the Court (in case they should presume to try the cause) and should this fail, to intreat a continuance of the cause until your memorialists should receive some material evidence from Great Britain, which they had already sent for, relative to the payment of the insurance on this property. They were also at the expense of again sending a person on purpose to attend the Court at Philadelphia, and instruct the Counsel. But to his and their great astonishment, before he arrived there the cause was brought on, the plea to the jurisdiction was over ruled, the laws of this State were treated with the utmost redicule. The plea for the continuance was wholly disregarded, and the said Agent arrived there just in season to hear the decree of the Court, which reversed the sentences of our Superior and Inferior maritime Courts, and ordered a restoration of the property to the claimants.

In this manner a cause so essentially affecting the Sovereignty and Independence of this State, as well as the rights and property of your memorialists, was decided, without their being cited by the Court of Appeals to appear, or even informed by advertisement in any Gazette of the time or place of the setting of the Court.

Since these very extraordinary, extra-judicial proceedings your memorialists have been threatened on their refusal to comply with the said sentence with being dragg'd to Philadelphia, and there put to bail, or imprisoned until they shall restore the said property or pay a sum amounting to   many times the prime cost thereof, both of which are utterly impossible. The goods having many years since been distributed among a thousand hands, and now entirely consumed. And as to the money, they conceive that justice and the laws of the State will protect them from being obliged to pay   Besides the illegal and assumed authority of this extraordinary Court of Appeals in this case, and their very extraordinary conduct preceding their final decree, there is something if possible, still more astonishing in the decree itself.

The evidence which was laid before them at the trial on the merits was the same that appeared at our Courts, and is in substance as follows. It was clearly and incontestably proved by the papers found on board the vessel (which is the evidence pointed out, as well by the resolves of Congress, as by the laws of the State) that the vessel was bound to Halifax, and it was proved by witnesses then lately arrived from thence, that there were then at that place a British fleet and garrison. That her cargo was to be delivered at Halifax, part of which was manifestly designed for the use of the army and navy there. The supercargo thereof (one Shearjashub Bourne) a Son in law to Elisha Doane, was strongly recommended to several of the principal governmental officers at Halifax, as a zealous friend of the British Government, as having several other vessels which he would gladly get into *their* service, and whose design was to purchase prize vessels at Halifax to be employed in that way. It appeared from his own memorial to the Lords of trade, that he fled from america, from persecution, as he called it, from his Countrymen whom he modestly stiled Rebels, that he employed Governor Hutchinson to assist him in that business, that he had employed the same vessel but the voyage before in carrying Ordnance Stores to Gibraltar, and caused her to wear British Ordnance Colours, that he had uniformly in all his letters to London, Bristol &c. called her *his* and at the Custom house took out a register, swearing that he was the sole owner thereof. The invoice of the goods was marked with the initial letters of his name. They were not charged at the cash price but higher; which would not have been the case, had they been the property of Elisha Doane, who they proved had then money in the hands of the gentlemen who shipped them. The vessel was insured at a high premium in London. The greatest part of which was expressly against American Privateers and she sailed with a British convoy. These are some of the circumstances that fully appeared at the trials here, and at Philadelphia. In addition to all which, it can now be proved by the confession of said Bourne and Shepherd that the Insurance on this property has since been paid, over and above all this, Elisha Doane died long before this trial, so that the decree is principally in favor of a dead man.

Thus we have stated the principal facts and circumstances of this very extraordinary and all important cause and having done this, we look up to your honors as the guardians of our rights and the vindicators of your own laws, and the Independency of this State, for your counsel and assistance; which we do with the greater boldness as we feel a consciousness that we have in no respect been remiss in our duty, but in every instance, have strictly and religiously adhered to the laws of the State, of which we are subjects.

We conceive the authority by which our property has lately been tried, to be assumed and arbitrary to an extreme, by no means justified by the confederation, even if that had been completed at the time of the trials in this State, infinitely less so, as it was not until long after the sentence of our supreme judicial Court within the State, and finally had the authority been just, the exercise of it as manifested by the decree, is as unjust, and iniquitous as the consequences (should it be carried into effect) are ruinous to the interests of your Memorialists, and the peace, dignity and happiness of this State.

One thing more we would suggest, which is, that by the final decree of the Court within this State, one half of the property was adjudged to the Captors, with which we had no concern, who have since been dispersed, or died, excepting four or five widows and Orphans who are in great poverty and distress, and therefore utterly unable to pay any proportion with your Memorialists, who must be wholly accountable if the aforementioned decree of the said Court of Appeals should be carried into effect.

To conclude. It is in the honor, justice, wisdom and authority of the Supreme Legislature of this State that we now wholly confide. The dispute between individuals is ended; and it is now with your honors to say, whether we, who have at such vast expence and trouble endeavored to support and vindicate the laws of this state, shall in turn receive support from them. Or whether your honors will see your laws trampled on, your authority derided, and a number of faithful subjects utterly ruined. Those subjects who have ever stood the foremost to defend those laws, and that State, against the rapacious attempts of a foreign enemy.

John Penhallow
Josh Wentworth
Ammi Ruhamah Cutler
Nathl. Folsom
Samll. Sherburne
Jacob Treadwell
Tho. Martin

Moses Woodward
Neil McIntire
Nathl. Sherburne
Keith Spence
Geo. Turner
Richard Champney
Robt. Furniss
Elizabeth Dalling

A true copy Examined by

C. THOMSON Secy.

RC (DLC: PCC, No. 44): at foot of text: "Governor Jefferson." The "enclosed Minutes" of the thirty documents referred to by Sullivan have not been identified, though all of the documents pertained to the case of the brigantine *Lusanna* and some are filed with Sullivan's letter in DLC: PCC. The petition of John Penhallow and others, a key document in the dossier considered by the committee of which TJ was a member, is taken from the text attested by TJ as Secretary of State, 15 Feb. 1793, as "a true copy from the records of the Department of State" and also by Joseph Pearson, Secretary of State for New Hampshire, 22 Oct. 1793, as "a true copy [*except for two minor errors silently corrected in text printed above*] of an original petition and memorial . . . now in my office"; MS now in McGill University Library, Montreal, Canada.

On 26 Dec. 1783, Abiel Foster, delegate from New Hampshire, received from President Meshech Weare of that state a letter of 10 Nov. enclosing one from the legislature of 6 Nov. (in

DLC: PCC, No. 44) pertaining to the case of the brig *Lusanna*; these were handed to Foster by Sullivan, who had come to defend the interests of the libellants (Foster to Weare, 26 Dec. 1783, Burnett, *Letters of Members*, VII, No. 467). These communications, together with one from Sullivan of 30 Dec. 1783, were laid before Congress on 2 Jan. 1784 and were referred to a committee of five, including TJ, "respecting the powers of court of appeals" (Committee Book, DLC: PCC, No. 186, under date of 2 Jan. 1784). Sullivan's present letter was obviously written as a result of a request made by TJ when Sullivan attended meetings of the committee (see report of the committee, 8 Jan. 1784). IN MY STATE OF OBJECTIONS: This may have been Sullivan's letter of 30 Dec. 1783 (same). Sullivan had also come to Congress to press his own claim for depreciation pay and his memorial on that subject was laid before the same committee, but TJ and Lee did not join in the report (Committee Book, DLC: PCC, No. 186; JCC, XXVI, 14).

Report on the Case of the Brig *Lusanna*

[8 January 1784]

Your Committee find that by a resolution of Congress of Nov. 25. 1775. it was recommended to the legislatures of the several states to erect courts for determining the cases of captures from the enemy on the High seas, and it was declared that in all cases an appeal should be allowed to Congress or such persons as they should appoint for the trial of appeals.

That this resolution was complied with by the several states, some of them ceding appeals to Congress on a larger and some on a more contracted scale; and New Hampshire particularly by their act of assembly of 1776 allowing them only in cases of captures by armed vessels fitted out at the charge of the United states, and reserving the appeal in all other cases to the Supreme court of their own state.

That the course of Congress was to appoint a Committee for the trial of every special appeal till the 30th. day of Jan. 1777. when a standing Committee was appointed to hear and determine appeals from the courts of admiralty in the respective states.

That the brigantine McClary a private armed vessel owned by John Penhallow and others, citizens of N. Hampshire, captured on the high seas in the month of Nov. 1777. the brigantine Lusanna, the subject of the present question, carried her into Piscataqua in the state of N. Hampshire and libelled her before the Maritime court of the said state, whereon the said vessel and cargo were by the said court condemned.

That the claimants Elisha Doane and others prayed an appeal to Congress which being refused, they appealed to the Superior court of N. Hampshire where the sentence being confirmed they again prayed an appeal to Congress which was refused, and the sentence carried into effect by a sale and distribution of the vessel and cargoe.

That on the 9th. day of Octob. 1778. the said Elisha Doane petitioned Congress for a revision of the said sentence, which petition being referred to the Committee of Appeals they in May 1779. summoned the libellants to appear before them in defence of their right.[1]

That on the 22d of the same month Congress resolved that certain resolutions of theirs of Mar. 6. 1779. relative to their controul over all jurisdiction in cases of capture on the high seas should be transmitted to the several states[2] and they be respectively requested to take effectual measures for conforming therewith.

That they were accordingly transmitted to the state of New Hampshire the legislature whereof by their act of Nov. 1779. extended the license of appeal to Congress to every case[3] wherein any subject of any foreign nation in amity with the U.S. should be interested in the dispute, and allowed it no further.

That in May 1780. a court of appeals was established by Congress with jurisdiction over all matters respecting appeals in cases of capture then depending before Congress or the Commissioners of appeals consisting of members of Congress.

That all these transactions were prior to the completion of the Confederation which took place on the 1st. day of Mar. 1781.

That on the 17th. of September 1783. the Court of appeals proceeded to consider the case of the said Elisha Doane and others against the brig Lusanna, John Penhallow libellant and to reverse the said sentences passed by the Inferior and Superior courts of N. Hampshire.

Whereupon your committee have come to the following resolution.

Resolved that the said capture having been made by citizens of N. Hampshire and carried in and submitted to the jurisdiction of that state before the completion of the confederation, while appeals to Congress in such cases were absolutely refused by their legislature, neither Congress nor any persons deriving authority from them had jurisdiction in the said case.

MS (DLC: PCC, No. 44); entirely in TJ's hand, with deletions and corrections, only the more important of which are noted below; endorsed by Charles Thomson: "Report Mr Ellery Mr Hand Mr Spaight Mr Jefferson Mr Lee On letter 6 Novr from Legislature of New Hampshire. Ent. read Jany 12. 1784." The Journals do not mention such a report either on 9 or 12 Jan. 1784, but Committee Book (DLC: PCC, No. 186) contains this entry: "Report Jany 9."

Actually, the report was completed and handed in on 8 Jan. 1784 but not read until the 12th owing to TJ's illness; on the former date Abiel Foster wrote Meshech Weare that the "Committee . . . this morning laid on the Table a Report respecting that affair. The Secretary informed me that Mr. Jefferson, who drew up the report, had sent it in; but desired it might not be read till he could attend, which the state of his Health did not permit to do on this day." Foster went on to describe Sullivan's interest in the case: "Genl. Sullivan in a Letter to Congress, and which was presented at the same time with your Hon'rs, has particularly and in my opinion in a convincing manner, stated the objections against the proceedings of the Court of Appeals in this Cause; he hath also attended the Committee and taken every possible precaution to obtain speedy and just decision. The Committee consisted of five members, and I am informed were unanimous in their report. However, no more than seven States are present, so

that one disenting Voice may reject the report: should there appear to be a danger of this I shall move to postpone the affair till a larger number of States are convened, which I hope will soon be the case. Whatever is in my power shall be done to set aside a judgment, which I conceive to be highly derogatory to souvereignty of the State I have the Hon'r to represent, and injurious to a respectable Number of its Citizens" (Burnett, *Letters of Members*, VII, No. 477). The report, as Foster feared, was debated and postponed on 13 Jan.; surprisingly, when it was brought up again on 21 Jan. and a motion made that it be postponed until New Hampshire should be fully represented Foster voted against postponement (TJ voted for it). The report was again under consideration and postponed on 19, 23, 24, and 30 Mch. 1784 (JCC, XXVI, 17-20, 38-41, 151, 156, 163, 174-5).

It is understandable that it should have received such opposition, for the case, which dragged on for many years, involved at least three important constitutional issues, to say nothing of private and political questions: (1) the date at which the Articles of Confederation became operative; (2) the jurisdiction of the court of appeals set up by Congress under Article IX whereby Congress was given the right of establishing courts "for receiving and determining finally, appeals in all cases of captures"; and (3) the right of Congress "in any way to reverse or controul the decisions, judgments or decrees of such court of appeals" (same, xxvi, 174). When, on 30 Mch. 1784, a motion was made to postpone consideration of the report in order to consider a motion that it would be "improper" for Congress to reverse or control the decisions of the court of appeals in any way, TJ voted against it. The motion was lost, and immediately afterward another to approve the report was also defeated because the Virginia delegation was evenly divided, TJ and Mercer voting in favor of the report and Hardy and Monroe against it (same, xxvi, 175). TJ was thus spared the embarrassment of having to vote on the specific question of Congress' right to reverse or set aside the decisions of a court established by it for "finally determining" cases involving capture.

1 The following was deleted at this point: "which they accordingly did by their counsel and the said Committee on a hearing of both parties reported to Congress that."
2 The following was deleted at this point: "whereupon Congress by their resolution of May 22. 1779."
3 TJ first wrote "all cases" and then altered it to read as above.

Report of the Committee on a Letter of Nathanael Greene

[13 January 1784]

The Committee consisting of Mr. Williamson Mr. Jefferson and Mr. Read to whom was refer'd a Letter of the 3rd of Novr. 1783 from Majr. Genl. Green to the President of Congress beg leave to report

That it appears to your Committee that Genl. Green, during his command in the Southern Department, besides the sume of 38,591^{6}⁄₉₀ Dlrs. which had been advanced to him of the old paper Emissions, has expended in travelling and for the support of his family the Sum of 10,017^{36}⁄₉₀ Dlrs.

That the sum allowed him by the US for his extra Expences during that Period as commanding in a separate Department was 5972^{2}⁄₉₀ Dlrs.: hence it appears that his Expences have exceeded his Allowance by the sume of 4045^{1}⁄₉₀ Dlrs. besides the Paper money refer'd to which at the then current state of Depretiation was of small Value. On which your Committee submit the following Resolve.

That in consideration of the high Price of all the necessaries of Life in the southern States, while Majr. Genl. Green commanded in that Department, his Account be credited with the sum of four Thousand and fourty five Dlrs. and sixteen ninetieth of a Dlr. together with the Sum of Thirty eight Thousand five hundred and ninety one Dlrs and sixty ninetieths of a Dlr. of the old Paper Emissions as an allowance for Extra Expences above the Sums to which he was entitled as a Majr. Genl. commanding in a separate department.

MS (DLC: PCC, No. 19, II); in the hand of Hugh Williamson; endorsed: "No. 42 Report of a Committee on Genl. Green's Accots: [*And, in Charles Thomson's hand:*] Delivered Jany 13. 1784. Entd. Read. Passed April 6. 1784."

This was the first committee to which TJ was appointed. JCC, XXV, 809, note, makes the erroneous statement that Greene's letter of 3 Nov. 1783 (in DLC: PCC, No. 155) was referred to the committee consisting of Williamson, TJ, and Read on 13 Dec. 1783 at Annapolis; actually the reference was made at Princeton on 4 Nov. 1783, though the Journals contain no mention of the fact (see Committee Book,

DLC: PCC, No. 186). Greene was then in Princeton (JCC, XXV, 788); TJ must have seen him, as he did Washington, but his letters contain no reference to such a meeting. As the endorsement indicates, the report of the committee was approved by Congress 6 Apr. 1784, with the addition of a paragraph reimbursing Greene to the extent of £329 6s. 3d. Virginia currency, "which appears by the affidavit of Major William Pierce, late aid-de-camp to General Greene, to have been stolen from the trunk of Major Pierce, while the public money was in his custody" (same, XXVI, 198-9).

Ratification of the Definitive Treaty of Peace[1]

[14 Jan. 1784]

The United States in Congress Assembled,

To all persons to whom these presents shall come greeting:

Whereas definitive articles of peace and friendship between the United States of America and his Britannic majesty, were concluded and signed at Paris on the 3d day of September, 1783, by the plenipotentiaries[2] of the said United States, and of his said Britannic Majesty, duly and respectively authorized for that purpose; which definitive articles are in the words following:[3]

In the name of the most holy and undivided Trinity.

It having pleased the Divine Providence to dispose the hearts of the most serene and most potent prince, George, the third, by the grace of God, king of Great Britain, France and Ireland, defender of the faith, duke of Brunswick and Lunenburg, archtreasurer and prince elector of the holy Roman empire, &c. and of the United States of America, to forget all past misunderstandings and differences that have unhappily interrupted the good correspondence and friendship which they mutually wish to restore, and to establish such a beneficial and satisfactory intercourse between the two countries, upon the ground of reciprocal adavntages and mutual convenience, as may promote and secure to both perpetual peace and harmony; and having for this desirable end, already laid the foundation of peace and reconciliation, by the provisional articles, signed at Paris on the 30th of November, 1782, by the commissioners empowered on each part, which articles were agreed to be inserted in and to constitute the treaty of peace proposed to be concluded between the crown of Great Britain and the said

United States, but which treaty was not to be concluded until terms of peace should be agreed upon between Great Britain and France, and his Britannic majesty should be ready to conclude such treaty accordingly; and the treaty between Great Britain and France having since been concluded, his Britannic majesty and the United States of America, in order to carry into full effect the provisional articles above mentioned, according to the tenor thereof, have constituted and appointed, that is to say, his Britannic majesty on his part, David Hartley, Esquire, member of the parliament of Great Britain; and the said United States on their part, John Adams, Esquire, late a commissioner of the United States of America, at the court of Versailles, late delegate in Congress from the state of Massachusetts, and chief justice of the said state, and minister plenipotentiary of the said United States to their high mightinesses the states general of the United Netherlands; Benjamin Franklin, Esquire, late delegate in Congress from the state of Pensylvania, president of the convention of the said state, and minister plenipotentiary from the United States of America at the court of Versailles; John Jay, Esquire, late president of Congress, and chief justice of the state of New York, and minister plenipotentiary from the said United States, at the court of Madrid, to be the plenipotentiaries for the concluding and signing the present definitive treaty: who, after having reciprocally communicated their respective full powers, have agreed upon and confirmed the following articles:

Article 1st. His Britannic majesty acknowledges the said United States, viz. New-Hampshire, Massachusetts-Bay, Rhode-Island and Providence Plantations, Connecticut, New-York, New-Jersey, Pensylvania, Delaware, Maryland, Virginia, North-Carolina, South-Carolina and Georgia, to be free, sovereign and independent states: that he treats with them as such, and for himself, his heirs and successors, relinquishes all claims to the government, propriety and territorial rights of the same, and every part thereof.

Article 2d. And that all disputes which might arise in future on the subject of the boundaries of the said United States may be prevented, it is hereby agreed and declared, that the following are and shall be their boundaries, viz. from the north-west angle of Nova Scotia, viz. that angle which is formed by a line drawn due north from the source of Saint Croix river to the Highlands; along the said Highlands which divide those rivers that empty themselves into the river Saint Lawrence from those which fall into the Atlantic Ocean, to the north-westernmost head of Connecticut river, thence down along the middle of that river to the forty fifth degree of north latitude; from thence by a line due west on said latitude, until it strikes the river Iroquois or Cataraquy, thence along the middle of said river into lake Ontario, through the middle of said lake until it strikes the communication by water between that lake and lake Erie; thence along the middle of said communication into lake Erie, through the middle of said [lake,] until it arrives at the water communication between that lake and lake Huron; thence along the middle of said water communication into the lake Huron, thence through the middle of said lake to the water communication between that lake and lake Superior; thence through lake Superior northward of the isles Royal and Philipeaux, to the long lake; thence through the middle of said long lake and the water communication between it and the lake of the Woods, to the said lake of the Woods, thence through the said lake to the most northwestern point thereof, and from thence on a due west course to the river Mississippi, thence by a line to be drawn along the middle of the said river Mississippi, until it shall intersect the northernmost part of the thirty first degree of north latitude. South by a line to be drawn due east from the determination of the line last mentioned, in the latitude of thirty one degrees north of the equator, to the middle of the river Apalachicola or Catahouche; thence along the middle thereof to its junction with the Flint river; thence straight to the head of Saint Mary's river, and thence down along the middle of Saint Mary's river to the Atlantic ocean. East by a line to be drawn along the middle of the river Saint Croix, from its mouth in the bay of Fundy to its source, and from its source directly north to the aforesaid Highlands which divide the rivers that fall into the Atlantic ocean from those which fall into the river Saint Lawrence: comprehending all islands within twenty leagues of any part of the shores of the United States, and lying between lines to be drawn due east from the points where the aforesaid boundaries between Nova-Scotia on the one part, and East Florida on the other, shall respectively touch the Bay of Fundy and the Atlantic ocean, excepting such islands as now are or heretofore have been within the limits of the said province of Nova-Scotia.

Article 3d. It is agreed, that the people of the United States shall continue to enjoy unmolested the right to take fish of every kind on the Grand Bank and on all the other banks of Newfoundland; also in gulph of Saint Lawrence, and at all other places in the sea, where the inhabitants of both countries used at any time heretofore to fish; and also, that the inhabitants of the United States shall have liberty to take fish of every kind on such part of the coast of Newfoundland as British fishermen shall use, (but not to dry or cure the same on that island) and also on the coasts, bays and creeks of all other of his Britannic majesty's dominions in America; and that the American fishermen shall have liberty to dry and cure fish in any of the unsettled bays, harbours and creeks of Nova Scotia, Magdalen islands, and Labradore, so long as the same shall remain unsettled, but so soon as the same or either of them shall be settled, it shall not be lawful for the said fishermen to dry or cure fish at such settlement, without a previous agreement for that purpose with the inhabitants, proprietors or possessors of the ground.

Article 4th. It is agreed that creditors on either side shall meet with no lawful impediment to the recovery of the full value in sterling money, of all bona fide debts heretofore contracted.

Article 5th. It is agreed that the Congress shall earnestly recommend it to the legislatures of the respective states, to provide for the restitution of all estates, rights and properties, which have been confiscated, belonging to real British subjects, and also of the estates, rights and properties of persons resident in districts in the possession of his majesty's arms, and who have not borne arms against the said United States. And that persons of any other description shall have free liberty to go to any part or parts of any of the thirteen United States, and therein to remain twelve months unmolested in their endeavours to obtain the restitution of such of their estates, rights and properties, as may have been confiscated; and that Congress shall also earnestly recommend to the several states a reconsideration and revision of all acts or laws regarding the premises, so as to render the said laws or acts perfectly consistent, not only with justice and equity, but with that spirit of conciliation, which on the return of the blessings of peace should universally prevail. And that Congress shall also earnestly recommend to the several states, that the estates, rights and properties of such last mentioned persons shall be restored to them, they refunding to any persons who may be now in possession of the bona fide price (where any has been given) which such persons may have paid on purchasing any of the said lands, rights or properties since the confiscation. And it is agreed that all persons who have any interest in confiscated lands, either by debts, marriage settlements, or otherwise, shall meet with no lawful impediment in the prosecution of their just rights.

Article 6th. That there shall be no future confiscations made, nor any prosecutions commenced against any person or persons for or by reason of the part which he or they may have taken in the present war; and that no person shall on that account, suffer any future loss or damage, either in his person, liberty or property, and that those who may be in confinement on such charges, at the time of the ratification of the treaty in America, shall be immediately set at liberty, and the prosecutions so commenced be discontinued.

Article 7th. There shall be a firm and perpetual peace between his Britannic majesty and the said states, and between the subjects of the one, and the citizens of the other, wherefore all hostilities both by sea and land, shall from henceforth cease; all prisoners on both sides shall be set at liberty, and his Britannic majesty shall with all convenient speed, and without causing any destruction, or carrying away any negroes or other property of the American inhabitants, withdraw all his armies, garrisons and fleets from the said United States, and from every post, place and harbour within the same; leaving in all fortifications the American artillery that may be therein, and shall also order and cause all archives, records, deeds and papers, belonging to any of the said states, or their citizens, which in the course of the war may have fallen into the hands of his officers, to be forthwith restored and delivered to the proper states and persons to whom they belong.

Article 8th. The navigation of the river Mississippi, from its source to the ocean, shall forever remain free and open to the subjects of Great Britain, and the citizens of the United States.

Article 9th. In case it should so happen, that any place or territory belonging to Great Britain or to the United States, should have been conquered by the arms of either from the other, before the arrival of the said provisional articles in America, it is agreed, that the same shall be restored without difficulty, and without requiring any compensation.

Article 10th. The solemn ratification of the present treaty, expedited in good and due form, shall be exchanged between the contracting parties in the space of six months, or sooner if possible, to be computed from the day of the signature of the present treaty. In witness whereof, we, the undersigned their ministers plenipotentiary, have in their name, and in virtue of full powers, signed with our hands the present definitive treaty, and caused the seals of our arms to be affixed thereto.

Done at Paris, this third day of September, in the year of our Lord, one thousand seven hundred and eighty-three.

(L.S.) D. HARTLEY,

(L.S.) JOHN ADAMS,

(L.S.) B. FRANKLIN,

(L.S.) JOHN JAY.

Now know ye that we the United States in Congress assembled having seen and considered the definitive articles aforesaid have approved, ratified and confirmed and by these presents do approve, ratify and confirm the said articles and every part and clause thereof, engaging and promising, that we will sincerely and faithfully perform and observe the same, and never suffer them to be violated by any one or transgressed in any manner, as far as lies in our power.

In testimony whereof, we have caused the seal of the United States[4] to be hereunto affixed.

Witness his Excellency Thomas Mifflin, president, this[5] fourteenth day of January in the year of our Lord one thousand seven hundred and eighty four and in the eighth year of the sovereignty and independence of the United States of America.

Text from JCC, XXVI, 23-8, where it is printed from "the copy in the writing of Benjamin Bankson, in Secret Journal, Foreign Affairs, No. 5." MS (DLC: PCC, No. 29); entirely in TJ's hand except as noted below. Significant differences between the two texts are indicated in notes.

On 13 Jan. 1784 the delegates from Connecticut and New Jersey presented their credentials. On the following day, nine states being present, Congress took up the report of the committee consisting of TJ, Gerry, Ellery, Read, and Hawkins that had been appointed 13 Dec. 1783 and to whom were referred the "Joint letter of Ministers at Paris 10 Sept. 1783 and definitive treaty signed 3 Sept. To prepare a form of ratification" (Committee Book, DLC: PCC, No. 186). The committee had reported on 16 Dec.; hence TJ's draft of the resolution and form of ratification were drawn up between 13 and 16 Dec. 1783 (same; the Journals do not record the appointment of the committee or the date of report).

As indicated in note 1, Col. Josiah Harmar was immediately designated to carry the Treaty to Europe. Next day it was moved "that a triplicate of the ratification" be sent by Lt. Col. David S. Franks, "who is authorized and directed to take passage in the first vessel which shall sail from any port eastward of Philadelphia, for France or any port in the channel, in which neither of the instruments of the ratification, already forwarded, may be sent, provided such vessel shall sail before the 3 day of February next"; the resolution also provided that "the Superintendant of finance furnish Lieutenant Colonel D. S. Franks, with money to defray his necessary expences in going and returning" (JCC, XXVI, 34-5). But this motion was lost, and another, moved by Gerry and seconded by TJ, to refer to a committee the question of considering "the most expeditious mode of sending a triplicate" was referred to the three delegates (Wadsworth, McComb, and Lee) who had voted against the motion to send Franks. They reported at once that "it having been signified to the house that Major [sic] David S. Franks is desirous of going to France on his own affairs, he be requested to take into his care the ratification of the D.T. and deliver it to our Ministers at

Paris" and that he be supplied "with one hundred guineas for his extraordinary expense in so doing." This report was written by Lee, and was adopted, though another, evidently introduced by Samuel Osgood to provide for Franks' "necessary expences," was evidently offered as a substitute, as still another by James Monroe providing for 200 guineas to enable Franks "to bear his expences"; Arthur Lee also apparently introduced a resolution requiring that certified copies of the ratification be sent by express to the governors of Massachusetts, Connecticut, and Rhode Island with the request that they "forward the same by the first vessel sailing from any port in their respective states" (JCC, XXVI, 36). Franks and Harmar were delayed by the severity of the winter; Franks arrived in London on 7 April and the next day set off for Paris. The exchange of ratifications took place on 13 May 1784 (*Va. Gaz.* [N & P], 12 June 1784).

1 The form of ratification was, of course, embodied in a resolution. There is in DLC: PCC, No. 36, II, in TJ's hand a rough draft of the resolution, probably handed in on 16 Dec. 1783 along with the committee report. This reads: "Resolved that the ratification be ⟨immediately expedited⟩ in ⟨good and due form under the seal⟩ the following form to wit [here insert the ratification] and be transmitted to our ministers plenipotentiary ⟨commissioned to negociate the said treaty⟩ by whom the said treaty was negotiated and signed" (brackets in MS). This resolution as adopted 14 Jan. 1784 was altered to read: "*Resolved, unanimously,* nine

states being present, that the said definitive treaty be, and the same is hereby ratified by the United States in Congress assembled, in the form following:" (JCC, XXVI, 23). That part of TJ's draft resolution which was deleted became two as adopted on 14 Jan. 1784: that the "ratification be transmitted with all possible despatch, under the care of a faithful person, to our ministers in France, who have negotiated the treaty, to be exchanged" and that "Colonel Josiah Harmar be appointed to carry the said ratification" (same, p. 29; both resolutions, as revised, are in DLC: PCC, No. 36, II, and are stated in JCC, XXVI, 29, note, to be in the hand of Hugh Williamson, though Williamson was not a member of the committee).

2 This word interlined by TJ in MS in substitution for "Commissioners," deleted.

3 MS reads: "[here insert them]" (brackets in MS), and does not include the text of the treaty. For official texts of the Provisional Treaty of 30 Nov. 1782, of the Armistice of 20 Jan. 1783, and of the Definitive Treaty, see W. M. Malloy, *Treaties*, 1910, p. 580-90.

4 The words "of the United States" are interlined in MS.

5 The following is deleted in MS at this point: "   Day of December in the year of our lord 1783 and of the sovereignty and independance of the United States the eighth" (the phrase "of the United States" was altered by TJ from "of these states"). This deletion was made in Congress and words substituted therefor (that is, from this point to the end of the text) were written in Thomson's hand on TJ's MS.

Proclamation Announcing Ratification of Definitive Treaty[1]

By the United states[2] in Congress assembled.
A Proclamation.

Whereas Definitive articles of peace and friendship between the[3] United states of America[4] and his Britannic majesty were concluded and signed at Paris on the third day of September 1783. by the plenipotentiaries[5] of the said United states and of his said Britannic majesty duly and respectively authorized for that purpose which definitive articles are in these words following [here insert them.][6]

And we the United states in Congress assembled having seen and duly considered the definitive articles aforesaid did by a certain act under the seal of the United states bearing date this 14 day of Jany 1784[7] approve, ratify and confirm the same and every part and clause thereof, engaging and promising that we would sincerely and faithfully perform and observe the same, and never suffer them to be violated by any one, or transgressed in any manner, as far as should be in our power.

And being sincerely disposed to carry the said articles into execution truly, honestly and with good faith according to the intent and meaning thereof we have thought proper by these presents to notify the premises to all the good citizens of these states, hereby requiring[8] and enjoining all[9] bodies of magistracy Legislative Executive and Judiciary, all persons bearing office civil or military of whatever rank, degree, or powers and all others the good citizens of these states of every vocation and[10] condition[11] that reverencing those stipulations entered into on their behalf under the authority of that federal bond by which their existence as an independant people is bound up together, and is known and acknowleged by the nations of the world; and with that good faith which is every man's surest guide, within their several offices, jurisdictions and vocations, they carry into effect the said Definitive articles and every clause and sentence thereof sincerely, strictly and completely. Given under the seal of the United states. Witness his Excellency Thomas Mifflin our President at Annapolis this 14 day of Jany 1784[12] and of the sovereignty and independance of the United states of America[13] the eighth.

MS (DLC: PCC, No. 29); entirely in TJ's hand, but with amendments made in Congress inserted in the hand of Charles Thomson. The more important alterations made by TJ are indicated in the notes below.

Although the committee appointed on 13 Dec. 1783 was directed only "To prepare a form of ratification" of the Definitive Treaty, it is obvious that TJ drew up the present text of a proclamation at the same time and no doubt handed it in on 16 Dec. along with the draft of the text of ratification (see notes to that document). It is a singular fact that TJ was the author both of the document of 1776 that announced the decision to assert independence and of that of 1783 that proclaimed its achievement. Aside from having the same author, both documents also have in common the fact that they were announcements of acts already performed, not the acts themselves. Thus the present document bears the same relation to the resolution of ratification of 14 Jan. 1784 that the Declaration of Independence does to the resolution of independence of 2 July 1776—that is, it proclaimed to the world what Congress had already done. In still another sense both documents enjoy a common distinction: they were presented to the world in broadside form by John Dunlap, whose typographical presentation in both instances was remarkably similar, perhaps consciously so.

Having ratified the Treaty and authorized the issuance of a proclamation, Congress then took up the third recommendation of the committee that had reported on 16 Dec. 1783—that is, that Congress recommend to the states to provide for the restitution of estates of bona fide British subjects that had been confiscated (see report of the committee under date). This final part of the committee's report was adopted the same day, 14 Jan. 1784, and it was "*Ordered*, that a copy of the proclamation of this date, together with the recommendation, be transmitted to the several states by the secretary" (JCC, XXVI, 31). TJ, knowing what a burden of paper work lay on Charles Thomson, took no chances of delay and so sent under his own frank a copy of the proclamation and of the recommendation to Gov. Harrison on 17 Jan. (see both letters of that date).

Thereupon, having dispatched this important business, Congress resolved on the following Wednesday to "celebrate the final ratification" by means of another public entertainment; Read, Howell, and Williamson were appointed a committee to see that this was done (same, p. 31; Committee Book, DLC: PCC, No. 186). Pennsylvania had already taken the lead in preparing for a celebration. The *Penna. Journal* for 31 Dec. 1783 announced: "We are well informed that the public demonstrations of joy, by authority of the state, on the definitive treaty, will be exhibited in this city, about the 20th of January. . . . It is expected that this exhibition will be the most magnificent that has ever been made in America. It will consist of a triumphal arch, 50 feet wide and 40 feet high, exactly in the stile of the triumphal arches among the Romans. It is to be built in Market street, between Sixth and Seventh streets. The appearance of this kind of building is extremely noble; but that now to be erected will be rendered uncommonly grand and beautiful, by its being illuminated. It will also be enriched with a number of emblems and inscriptions suitable to the occasion, disposed in the frize, pannels, ballustrade, and pedestals. . . . The ingenious Capt. Peale is now preparing the paintings; and those figures that are finished have afforded the highest satisfaction to all persons who have seen them. Among them is a striking likeness of our justly beloved Commander in Chief. As the illuminations will continue for many hours, the spectators will have an opportunity of examining the whole work at leisure. From the ballustrade will be thrown up a constant succession of fine fire works." Unfortunately, the "great crowds of spectators" who assembled on Thursday, 22 Jan. 1784, to witness the lighting of the triumphal arch did not have an opportunity to examine the work at leisure, but they did get an even more spectacular exhibit than had been promised. The *Penna. Journal* announced on 24 Jan. 1784 that "by some unlucky accident, the paintings took fire, and were almost instantly consumed; this set fire to a great number of rockets which were on the stage, when a sergeant Stewart, of the artillery, was killed, by one of the rockets entering his head, and four or five persons were hurt." This disaster did not stop the indefatigable artist; Peale at once began repainting the pictures at his own expense, but sympathetic Philadelphians took up a public purse as a testimonial of "their regard for his particular merit on this occasion." By mid-March the work was almost complete again and this time it was announced that there "is to be no display of rockets or other fire-works" (same, 28 Jan. and 13 Mch. 1784).

In Virginia the General Assembly had been even more forehanded, if less spectacular, by giving a ball "to celebrate the arrival of the Definitive Treaty" and when the ratification arrived, the Council advised Gov. Harrison to take measures for having it proclaimed with "the usual solemnity" (same, 31 Dec. 1783, under dateline of Richmond, 20 Dec.; 3 Feb. 1784, MS Va. Council Jour., Vi). But Harrison had already acted by directing the sheriff of Henrico to proclaim the Treaty "with all the solemnity in your power on Thursday next, at the courthouse, in the market place, and the capitol. I shall give orders to the officer commanding here to fire an American salute after each proclamation of which you will please to give him notice by signal" (Harrison to Prosser, 2 Feb. 1784, Executive Letter Book, Vi).

[1] TJ was no doubt the author of the resolution introducing the text of the proclamation, as he was of that embodying the form of ratification which immediately preceded it, but no MS of this resolution appears to have survived. But, in accord with the report of the committee headed by TJ (see under

16 Dec. 1783), Congress forthwith "*Resolved*, That a proclamation be immediately issued, notifying the said definitive treaty and ratification to the several states of the union, and requiring their observance thereof in the form following": it will be noticed that the phraseology closely parallels that of TJ's resolution introducing the ratification (JCC, XXVI, 29).

2 The words "of America" are deleted here. The deletion mark is the same kind of heavy line employed by Thomson for alterations that were clearly made by Congress; hence this also was probably made by amendment on 14 Jan. rather than by TJ.

3 This word interlined by Thomson in substitution for "these," deleted.

4 TJ had written "of America" and then deleted it; Thomson interlined these two words, probably as a part of the amendment in Congress indicated in note 2.

5 This word interlined in substitution for "Commissioners," deleted; TJ made a similar alteration in the text of the ratification.

6 Brackets are in MS.

7 TJ originally wrote: "bearing date the   day of December 1783" which Thomson altered by interlining, over-

writing, and filling in the blank to read as above.

8 This word interlined in the hand of William Ellery, who was a member of the committee appointed 13 Dec. 1783 to "prepare a form of ratification," a fact which lends support to the assumption that that committee considered the matter of a proclamation also.

9 TJ deleted the words "persons and" at this point.

10 TJ first wrote "whatever vocation or" and then altered the phrase to read as above.

11 At this point TJ deleted the following three lines: "in obedience to those delegations, moral, political, and legal whereby they are called to the observance of stipulations duly and regularly derived from their several laws and constitutions, and with that good faith which is every honest man's best comfort, that within their" and then wisely substituted for them the corresponding passage given above.

12 TJ originally wrote: "this   day of Dec. 1783" which Thomson altered by interlining, overwriting, and filling in the blank to read as above.

13 Two preceding words interlined by Thomson.

To Martha Jefferson

MY DEAR PATSY   Annapolis Jan. 15. 1784.

Your letter by the post is not yet come to hand, that by Mr. Beresford I received this morning. Your long silence had induced me almost to suspect you had forgotten me and the more so as I had desired you to write to me every week. I am anxious to know what books you read, what tunes you can play, and to receive specimens of your drawing. With respect to your meeting Mr. Simitiere at Mr. Rittenhouse's, nothing could give me more pleasure than your being much with that worthy family wherein you will see the best examples of rational life and learn to esteem and copy them. But I should be very tender of obtruding you on the family as it might perhaps be not always convenient to them for you to be there at your hours of attending Mr. Simitiere. I can only say then that if it has been desired by Mr. and Mrs. Rittenhouse in such a way as that Mrs. Hopkinson shall be satisfied they will not consider it as inconvenient, I would have you thankfully accept it and conduct yourself with so much attention to the family as that they may never feel themselves incommoded by it. I hope Mrs. Hopkinson will be so good as to act for you in this matter with that delicacy and prudence of which she is so capable. I have so much at heart your learning to draw, and should be uneasy at your losing this opportunity which probably is your last. But I remind you to inclose me every week a copy of all your lessons in drawing that I may judge how you come on. I have had very ill health since I came here. I have been just able to attend my duty in the state house, but not to go out on any other occasion. I am however considerably better. Present my highest esteem to Mrs. Hopkinson and accept yourself assurances of the sincere love with which I am my dear Patsy, Yours affectionately,   TH: JEFFERSON

RC (NNP); endorsed in an unidentified hand: "Jan. 13. 84." Still another date is provided by the entry in SJL, which appears under 14 Jan. and which must refer to the present letter.   Neither Martha's LETTER BY THE POST, nor THAT BY MR. BERESFORD has been found.

To Chastellux

DEAR SIR   Annapolis Jan. 16. 1784.

Lt. Colo. Franks being appointed to carry to Paris one of the copies of our ratification of the Definitive treaty, and being to depart in the instant of his appointment furnishes me a hasty opportunity of obtruding myself on your recollection. Should this prove troublesome you must take the blame as having exposed yourself to my esteem by letting me become acquainted with your merit. Our transactions on this side the water must now have become uninteresting to the rest of the world. We are busy however among ourselves endeavouring to get our new governments into regular and concerted motion. For this purpose I beleive we shall find some additions requisite to our Confederation. As yet every thing has gone smoothly since the war. We are diverted with the European accounts of the anarchy and opposition to government in America.[1] Nothing can be more untrue than these relations. There was indeed some disatisfaction in the army at not being paid off before they were disbanded, and a very trifling mutiny[2] of 200 souldiers in Philadelphia. On the latter occasion, Congress left that place disgusted with the pusillanimity of the government and not from any want of security to their own persons. The indignation which the other states felt at this insult to their delegates has enlisted them more warmly in support of Congress; and the people, the legislature and the Executive themselves of Pennsva. have made the most satisfactory atonements. Some people also of warm blood undertook to resolve as committees for proscribing the refugees. But they were few, scattered here and there through the several states, were absolutely unnoticed by those both in and out of power, and never expressed an idea of not acquiescing ultimately under the decisions of their governments. The greatest difficulty we find is to get money from them. The reason is not founded in their unwillingness, but in their real inability. You were a witness to the total destruction of our commerce, devastation of our country, and absence of the precious metals. It cannot be expected that these should flow in but through the channels of commerce, or that these channels can be opened in the first instant of peace. Time is requisite to avail ourselves of the productions of the earth, and the first of these will[3] be applied to renew our stock of those necessaries of which we had been totally exhausted. But enough of America it's politics and poverty.—Science I suppose is going on with you rapidly as usual. I am in daily hopes of seeing something from your pen which may portray us to ourselves. Aware of the bias of self love and prejudice in myself and that your pictures will be faithful I am determined to annihilate my own opinions and give full credit to yours. I must caution you to distrust information from my answers to Monsr. de Marbois' queries. I have lately had a little leisure to revise them. I found some things should be omitted, many corrected, and more supplied and enlarged. They are swelled nearly to treble bulk. Being now too much for M.S. copies, I think the ensuing spring to print a dozen or 20 copies to be given to my friends, not suffering another to go out. As I have presumed to place you in that number I shall take the liberty of sending you a copy as a testimony of the sincere esteem and affection with which I have the honour to be Dr Sir Your mo. ob. & mo. hbl servt.

Dft (MoSHi); endorsed: "Chastellux, Marquis de." Not recorded in SJL. RC owned by Duc de Duras, Château Chastellux, Chastellux (Yonne), France. Dft is much corrected; some of the more important alterations are noted below.

This letter is reminiscent of others written by TJ at the opening of the Revolution in which he endeavored by private communications to influence opinion of America abroad; see for example his letters to Small and Randolph, Vol. 1: 165, 240, 268. See also TJ's letters to Gov. Harrison, to the Speaker of the House, and to the Speaker of the Senate, transmitting extracts from the American ministers' letter (under dates of 17, 18, and 19 Dec. 1783). In those and other communications TJ was far from being DIVERTED WITH THE EUROPEAN ACCOUNTS OF THE ANARCHY AND OPPOSITION TO GOVERNMENT IN AMERICA.

[1] At this point TJ deleted: "There has not been a shadow for these assertions except."

[2] TJ first wrote: "a little mutiny."

[3] This word interlined in substitution for "must," deleted.

To Benjamin Harrison

SIR   Annapolis Jan 17. 1784.

No post having arrived here from the Southward during the present month till this day, and being to return in a few minutes I am obliged without an opportunity of asking the concurrence of my collegues to inclose you a copy of the proclamation of the Definitive treaty and of it's ratification which happily took place on the 14th. instant. Two officers were immediately dispatched to seek passages by different vessels to France with this important instrument. I expect one of them would reach the French packet at New York which is to sail from thence on the 20th. I have the honor to be with very high esteem & regard Your Excellency's most obedt. & most humble servt,   TH: JEFFERSON

RC (PHi); addressed and franked by TJ: "His Excellency Governor Harrison Richmond"; endorsed in part "Jany. 17. 84." Date at head of letter was changed from 16 to 17 Jan. and it is recorded in SJL under latter date: see note to following letter. The enclosure, probably a copy of the broadside of the proclamation printed by John Dunlap, has not been found. Though not men-tioned in the text, there was another enclosure—a copy of the recommendation of Congress to the states concerning confiscated estates (see notes to following letter for entry in SJL; to the proclamation of the Definitive Treaty, 14 Jan. 1784; and to the report of the committee on these subjects, 16 Dec. 1783; CVSP, III, 554).

To Benjamin Harrison

SIR   Annapolis Jan. 16. [17] 1784.

The Southern post, which had not come in for three weeks past, surprised us by his arrival to-day. Being to return in half an hour I could only, after perusal of my letters, hastily inclose to your excellency a copy of the proclamation announcing the ratification of the peace, which we were enabled to expedite on the 14th. inst. that being the first day on which nine states have attended during the present Congress. This irregularity in the post will account for your having received no letter from Mr. Hardy, the corresponding member for the month. An indisposition at present puts it out of his power to write, in which case, according to our arrangement, the duty devolves on the next member in the nomination. The right of individual correspondence however still remaining to us I take the liberty of communicating the occurrences of the time.

The important subjects now before Congress are

1. authorizing our Foreign ministers to enter into treaties of alli-

ance and commerce with the several nations who have desired it.

2. arranging the Domestic administration.

3. establishing Arsenals within the states, and posts on our Frontier.

4. Disposing of the Western territory.

5. treaties of peace and purchase with the Indians.

6. Money.

Your Excellency will perceive that these are questions of such difficulty as must produce differences of opinion, and of such importance as forbid a sacrifice of judgment to one another. We have but nine states present, seven of which are represented by only two members each. There are 14. gentlemen then, any one of which differing from the rest, stops our proceeding, for all these questions require the concurrence of nine states. We shall proceed in a day or two to take them up, and it is my expectation that after having tried several of them successively and finding it impossible to obtain a single determination, Congress will find it necessary to adjourn till the spring, first informing the states that they adjourn because from the inattendance of members their business cannot be done, recommending to them to instruct and *enable* their members to come on at the day appointed, and that they constantly keep three at the least with Congress while it shall be setting. I beleive if we had thirteen states present represented by three members each we could clear off our business in two or three months, and that hereafter a session of two or three months in the year would suffice.

The manifesto of the Empress of Russia against the Turks is come to hand. It is as flimsy and groundless as that of the Turks is strong substantial and masterly.

I have the honor to be with very great esteem & respect Your Excellency's Most obedient & most humble servt,

TH: JEFFERSON

RC (CtY); franked and addressed by TJ: "His Excellency Governor Harrison Richmond"; endorsed in part: "Jany. 16. 83." This letter was obviously written after TJ had finished the preceding one, which was first dated 16 Jan. and then altered to 17 Jan. Both letters are recorded in SJL as follows: "[1784 Jan.] 17. Govr. Matters before Congress—state of Congress — probability of adjournment — Russian and Turkish manifestos. Do. Another [letter] inclosing proclamation of treaty and recommendation about tories." It is clear from this that TJ wrote both letters on the 17th, corrected the date of the first, and failed to correct that of the second.

TJ did not need to inform Harrison who THE NEXT MEMBER IN THE NOMINATION was or to comment on the reason that led him under the circumstances to make use of the RIGHT OF INDIVIDUAL CORRESPONDENCE, for the delegate following the ailing Hardy was John Francis Mercer, whose delinquencies as a correspondent had long since aroused Gov. Harrison.

To Martha Jefferson Carr

[*Annapolis*, *18 Jan. 1784*. Entry in SJL reads: "Mrs. Carr. Not send P. C. [Peter Carr] to Maury. Where is A. S. J. [Anna Scott Jefferson]. My health better." Not found.]

To Elizabeth Wayles Eppes

[*Annapolis*, *18 Jan. 1784*. Entry in SJL reads: "Mrs. E. Betsy—Congratulations on daughter—P. A. on marriage—health better—hair-powder." Not found.]

To Francis Eppes

[*Annapolis*, *18 Jan. 1784*. Entry in SJL reads: "Mr. E. Authorising him to have R. Rand's affair settled and all others of Mr. W's estate—that I will contribute my quota of expenses of agents, and of paiments when become indispensable—letter from Welch—ratification of Treaty —affairs of Europe—disposition of P. C." Not found.]

To Anna Scott Jefferson

[*Annapolis*, *18 Jan. 1784*. Entry in SJL reads: "A. S. J. My health better—send what she wants, I will get in Phil. whither shall go in spring." Not found.]

To Edmund Pendleton

DEAR SIR   Annapolis Jan. 18. 1784.

Your letter of the 12th. inst. came to hand yesterday. I have the happiness of informing you that on the 14th. inst. we had nine states on the floor and ratified the definitive treaty. Two copies were immediately dispatched by different officers who were to embark in the first vessels they could find going to France. They had 48 days left for it's timely delivery. The important business now before Congress is as follows.

Foreign civil arrangement, and foreign treaties.

Domestic civil arrangement.

Domestic peace establishment of arsenals and posts.

Western territory.

Indian affairs.

Money.

None of these subjects can be transacted but with the concurrence of 9. states. Of the 9. now present 7 are represented by two members each. There are 14. gentlemen then, any one of whom differing from the rest, can stop any vote. The questions are important and difficult, and such as the best and wisest men would divide on. I am satisfied therefore that we cannot get 9. states to concur in a single one of the above subjects. We shall begin tomorrow to bring them on. A few experiments will I expect evince the truth of my conjecture, and the necessity of our adjourning till the spring, informing the states that we adjourn because their business cannot be done in so thin a house, and urging them to instruct and to *enable* their delegates to come punctually to the day of adjournment, and never to be represented by less than three members. The true reason that the delegates do not attend is that their states do not furnish them with money, and if they advance them some to get them here they are then left in the lurch and obliged either to make mean shifts or to go home. Spirited members prefer the latter and thus we are kept with a house incompetent to business. I think if we had a full house, that is, 13 states with three members from each so that no votes might be lost by division we might clear our docket in two or three months, and that an annual session of two months will hereafter suffice. A committee of the states must be left to transact ordinary business.

The Russian manifesto is come to hand. It is as flimsy and barefaced as that of the Turk is nervous, substantial and masterly. This is an extract from the latter. 'What Northern power has the Porte offended? Whose territories have the Ottoman troops invaded? In the country of what prince is the Turkish standard displayed? Content with the boundaries of empire assigned by god and his prophet the wishes of the Porte are for peace. But if the court of Russia be determined in her claims, and will not recede without an acquisition of territory which does not belong to her, appealing to the world for the justice of the proceeding, the sublime Porte must prepare for war, relying on the decrees of heaven, and confident of the interposition of the prophet of prophets who will protect his faithful followers in the hour of every difficulty.' I fear France will be drawn into this war; hope Prussia will, and think Great Br. will reserve herself for Ireland and perhaps for us. A wanton insult lately, which I do not think myself at liberty to particularize, has discovered a sulleness a rancour and a mysterious reserve which is fitted to generate new troubles. A new war on us while France is otherwise engaged would be a calamity of unknown extent. Tho' we possess resources to a certain degree, experience shews that they are utterly inaccessible to any existing power. And we cannot avail ourselves of the prompt resource of paper money with which we began the last war. I wish you a great deal of happiness and am with sincere esteem Dr. Sir Your friend & servt, TH: JEFFERSON

P.S. Where should I direct your letters to be left?

RC (Nathaniel W. Pendleton, Wythe-ville, Va.); franked and addressed by TJ to "The honble Edmund Pendleton Caroline"; endorsed. On the address-leaf are two columns of calculations in Pendleton's hand, part of which pertain to interest computations between 1766 and 1768, leading to the surmise that these figures must relate to accounts of Virginians who were indebted to John Robinson, treasurer of the colony. En-try in SJL reads: "E.P. Ratification—questions before Congress—state of Con-gress — probability of adjournment — European news."

Pendleton's LETTER OF THE 12TH INST. has not been found. The WANTON INSULT to which TJ referred may pos-sibly have been that which formed the subject of the report on the letter of John Allen, q.v. under 26 Jan. 1784.

To William Short

[*Annapolis, 18 Jan. 1784.* Entry in SJL reads: "Short. P. C. [Peter Carr] disapproving Wmsbg—approving Jmscy [James City] but query as to healthfulness—refer to him—subject in cypher—Nicholas—health better." Not found. TJ evidently enclosed in this letter a cipher based on the word "Nicholas," a cipher he used in subsequent letters to Short. In an undated extract of his letter of 30 Apr. 1784, he sent Short another copy of the same code. See also TJ to Short, 1 Mch. 1784.]

From Henry Skipwith

DEAR SIR   Hors du Monde January 20th 1784.

Your favor reached me last evening, preceeding the most tre-mendous Snow storm this country has ever experienced since my rememberance. It commenced about seven at night, and never ceased until the evening of the present day about four OClock. It is impossible to say what the depth of the snow is, since from the wind it is exceedingly irregular, in some places scarcely any in others dangerously deep; its surface is a beautiful representation of a troubled water; Prior to this we have had for four weeks a severe frost, variegated with all the snows, hails rains &c. incident to such a season, so that the industrious of this country begin almost to despond, and those whose crops of grain were short absolutely to dispair. We were exceedingly happy to be told by yourself that you were still in existence; but as all sublunary bliss is imbittered by some sinister circumstance, we feel ourselves sensibly affected at yours being so taxed with disease: however we hope shortly to hear that your prudence and your temperance have induced a return of your accustomed health. Nancy, who greets you most affectionately, is pleased indeed to hear little Pat is accomodated in Philidelphia so much to your satisfaction; her vanity must tell you, she has the finest little girl almost in the world, that her name is to be Martha, and that she shall take the liberty of having a sponsor appointed for you at her baptism. Your political paragraph is truly alarming. Good God! Should the final ratification of peace be prevented or even postponed by a want of representation in Congress, what punishment must be due to those who have withdrawn themselves at so important a period?

Previous to my answering (which I do with pleasure) your queries relative to my White negroes I must premise, that exclusive of mine I knew a very stout robust white negroe slave, the pro[perty] of Captain John Butler near Petersburg, who had issue (by a black man) a daughter of the jet hue, about fourteen years of age very handsome. Also that there is now in existence an elderley, tall, stout, white negro *man* slave in the county of Cumberland, about six miles from me, the property of Charles Lee; as this is the only male I ever knew or heard of, I shall postpone sending this letter until the Snow permits me to see Mr. Lee and give you also a particular history of this Phænomenon. In the mean time you have subjoined answers to your Queries, to wit.

I had three female white Negro slaves.

Full sisters.

Their parents have had three whites and two blacks.

Their parents were very healthy.

Their parents are of the ordinary color of blacks (not jet).

The skin of these white negroes is a disagreeable chalky white, their hair perfectly similar to short Sheeps wool, curled like a common negroe.

They have no coloured seams or spots about them.

They are exceedingly well formed, very healthy, strong, and active.

They hear well.

Their eye sight is not strong, their eyes are much affected by the rays of the Sun, and perpetually quiver in their sockets.

Their senses are remarkably perfect, they are very shrewd and quick at repartee.

I know of no instance of this species generating together. Two of mine have generated with black's and each had issue female children of the ordinary complexion of light coloured negroes. The eldest of the three died in childbed with her second child, at about the age of twenty seven years. The youngest was destroyed at the age of twelve years by lightning from Heaven. The middle one is now alive and well.

Since writing the above I have seen Mr. Lee. He tells me his White Negro man slave was generated between a couple of negro's of the ordinary colour and that he in every respect (the sex excepted) is like my own.

With every sentiment of regard I remain Dear Sir Your afft. friend & Sevt., HENRY SKIPWITH

We request our love may be sent to Patsey by your next letter to her.

RC (ViWC); endorsed by TJ: "Skipwith Henry." YOUR FAVOR: This was TJ's missing letter of 26 Dec. 1783; see record entry under that date.

The Connecticut-Pennsylvania Territorial Dispute

[1782-1784]

I. NOTES CONCERNING BOUNDARIES

II. ARGUMENTS BY JAMES WILSON AND WILLIAM SAMUEL JOHNSON BEFORE THE COURT OF COMMISSIONERS

III. PETITION OF ZEBULON BUTLER AND OTHERS

IV. FIRST REPORT ON PETITION OF ZEBULON BUTLER

V. SECOND REPORT ON PETITION OF ZEBULON BUTLER

VI. ON THE SETTLEMENT OF DISPUTES BETWEEN STATES BY JUDICIAL MEANS

EDITORIAL NOTE

The far-reaching dispute between Connecticut and Pennsylvania over their conflicting charter claims was one that Jefferson became acquainted with on first entering Congress in 1775 (see Vol. 1: 248). The reports that he drew up eight years later came at a climactic moment of the controversy. These reports and related documents printed in the present group require particular comment for several reasons. First, it was believed by responsible individuals at the time and by reputable historians since that, to put it in soft terms, an accommodation of interests was effected in Congress whereby Connecticut's acquiescence in the adverse outcome of the litigation was purchased at the cost to the national domain of a rich and valuable stretch of territory later known as the Western Reserve. Second, though never precisely designated as to time, place, and persons involved, this "deal" is generally regarded as having been managed if not conceived by Roger Sherman of Connecticut and as having included the members of the Court of Commissioners of 1782 who were arbitrators of the controversy. Third, the texts of the reports drawn up by Jefferson in January 1784 may throw some light upon this traditional belief. This has not been possible hitherto because Ford, III, 382-7, printed both reports as if they were rough draft and fair copy of the same document, an error compounded by his inclusion in the former, as if it were an integral part of it, of a true rough draft of part of the latter and by the omission altogether of another revealing (though incomplete) rough draft on its verso. This unfortunate confusion of the texts was accepted without question by Burnett, *Letters of Members*, VII, No. 493, note 2, thus helping to perpetuate the veil of obscurity thrown over the nature of two of Jefferson's separate and quite different reports.

Quite aside from these factors, attention needs to be called to the case of Pennsylvania v. Connecticut because it was the only litigation between two states carried out under the terms stipulated in Article IX of the Articles of Confederation and because its importance as a landmark in our constitutional development has been neglected and thrown into undeserved shadow by the allegations of collusion. At the conclusion of the trial, President John Dickinson of Pennsylvania declared the outcome to be a test of the strength of the union, reflecting honor upon the Confederation and giving proof of its political energy. Robert R. Livingston, perhaps a more disinterested observer, wrote to Lafayette on 10 Jan. 1783: "The great cause between Connecticut and Pennsylvania has been decided. . . . It is a singular event. There are few instances of independent states submitting their cause to a court of justice. The day will come, when all disputes in the great republic of Europe will be tried in the same way, and America be quoted to exemplify the wisdom of the measure" (texts in Wyoming Historical and Geological Society in collection cited below).

Even this important trial between two states, however, was but one episode in a half-century course of events that began about 1750 and in consequence of which British imperial relations were endangered, the management of Indian affairs complicated, the people of two colonies brought several times into armed conflict on a sizable scale, the formation of the American union placed in jeopardy, and post-Revolutionary animosities engendered in such a way as to threaten one of the strongest bonds of union—the national domain—and to endanger it from the separate interests of individual states and of groups controlling the great land-speculating companies. The documentation of the whole is immense. Much of value has been published in the *Pennsylvania Colonial Records* and the *Pennsylvania Archives*, especially Volume XVIII of the second series; four volumes of records covering the first twenty years of the subject have been printed in *The Susquehannah Company Papers*, ed. Julian P. Boyd (Wilkes-Barré, Penna., 1930-

1933); and some 20,000 manuscripts, photostats, and transcripts of all discoverable documents in archives and libraries in America and abroad relating to all aspects of the history of this Connecticut westering movement and of its many ramifying controversies are in the Wyoming Historical and Geological Society awaiting publication or study; a brief account of the whole subject is to be found in "Connecticut's Experiment in Expansion: The Susquehannah Company, 1753-1803," *Jour. of Economic and Business Hist.*, IV (1931), p. 38-69. Only the briefest outline of the subject can be given here by way of background for Jefferson's reports.

The Connecticut expansion into Pennsylvania began about 1750 with the organization of various land companies, of which the Susquehannah Company soon became the leader and absorbed or dominated all others. It was not until 1771 that Connecticut, after allowing her charter claim to lie dormant for more than a century during which she acquiesced or explicitly sanctioned the New York-Connecticut line as her western boundary, gave formal support to the claim to lands west of New York. Governor Jonathan Trumbull, who was a proprietor in the Susquehannah Company and who in 1773 was granted 500 acres as "the one particular Gentleman in this Colony . . . that has done Sundry Services for this Company," identified his political fortunes with this issue; and, though there was an armed expedition from Pennsylvania against the Connecticut inhabitants at Wyoming in 1775 under the guise of a *posse comitatus*, the controversy was more or less suspended during the Revolution. Connecticut law ran in the region, the voters were represented in the Connecticut legislature, and militia and troops for the Connecticut line were recruited there.

Soon after the ratification of the Articles of Confederation in 1781, the Pennsylvania claimants to lands in the same area petitioned Congress to appoint commissioners to arbitrate the dispute according to the provisions of Article IX. Congress acquiesced, and Pennsylvania appointed William Bradford, Jr., Joseph Reed, James Wilson, and Jonathan Dickinson Sergeant as counselors and agents, with Henry Osborne as solicitor; Connecticut designated Eliphalet Dyer, William Samuel Johnson, and Jesse Root to represent her interests (JCC, XXII, 345-7). The legal counsel were not only distinguished, but included on both sides men who were political figures and land speculators. James Wilson was closely identified with Robert Morris, Tench Coxe, Samuel Hodgdon, and other Philadelphia operators in land holdings in the Wyoming region, was president of the Illinois-Wabash Company, and was a member of Congress who actively advocated the theory that the inherent powers of the federal government authorized the taking over as a national domain the northwest territory claimed by Virginia (Merrill Jensen, "The Creation of the National Domain, 1781-1784," MVHR, XXVI [1939], 323-42). Dyer was a member of Congress and had been identified with the Susquehannah Company for three decades, arguing its cause in Connecticut and London; Johnson was not a member of the Company, though he had represented it in London before the Revolution, and in 1773-1774 he had vigorously and unsuccessfully opposed Connecticut's yielding to pressure by Dyer, Trumbull, and other members of the Company to induce the colony to take up the western claim officially. Root was also a member of Congress and was interested in the Company. Though some of the counsel on both sides were interested parties, they included in Wilson and Johnson two of the best legal minds in America.

The opposing agents met before Congress in June 1782 to undergo the arduous and complicated process of agreeing upon the members of the Court of Commissioners. It was at once moved by the Massachusetts delegates that in all disputes between two or more states the delegates ought not to sit as judges in any question to be decided; only Connecticut voted with Massachusetts against this motion, nine other states favoring it. The Connecticut delegates then produced an instruction from the legislature of their state requiring them to move the postponement of the appointment of commissioners "because . . . sundry papers of importance in the case are in the hands of counsel in England, and cannot be procured during the war: nor is it convenient for the states to divert their attention from the great objects of the war to attend to private controversies." But the Connecticut delegates' motion itself was postponed by a vote of ten states to one, only Dyer and Huntington of Connecticut voting in the negative. Root and Dyer as the Connecticut agents then challenged the credentials of the Pennsylvania agents and of the power of the executive council of Pennsylvania to grant them; Root and Dyer as the Connecticut delegates in Congress voted consistently but unsuccessfully to give effect to this and other delaying tactics they had employed as agents. On the crucial vote declaring the Pennsylvania agents' powers adequate, Root and Dyer were the only members to vote nay.

At last, after three weeks had been spent in such maneuvers by the Connecticut agent-delegates, Congress was able on 16 July to direct the counsel of both states to proceed to the appointment by joint consent of the "commissioners or judges to constitute a court for hearing and determining the matter in question" (JCC, XXII, 351-2, 354, 355-6, 389-92). This was done by a highly complicated process of having each side compile lists of names drawn from all states, by exchanging these lists, and then by challenge and agreement reducing the whole to a mutually acceptable remnant. On 8 Aug. 1782 the two groups of agents were able to reach agreement on William Whipple of New Hampshire, Nathanael Greene of Rhode Island, David Brearley and William Churchill Houston of New Jersey, Cyrus Griffin and Joseph Jones of Virginia, and John Rutledge of South Carolina. They also requested Congress to determine how much the commissioners should be paid for their services and in what manner and by whom they should be paid.

The Articles of Confederation were silent on these questions and the committee to whom the matter was referred (including James Madison and John Witherspoon) were emphatically of opinion that "no award of costs can by the law of the land be made by any Judicatory in any cause whatsoever unless provision be made for the purpose by some express and positive law"; that an award of costs in private practice, as it implied, on the one hand, a recompense for injury and, on the other, a penalty for litigiousness, could not be followed because to do so would be "inconsistent with the dignity of Sovereign and Independent States"; and that all that could be done would be to recommend to the two litigant states to fall back upon colonial experience and have the contending parties bear all expenses equally. This recommendation was followed. But while Pennsylvania drew her costs—well over £1000 —from the public treasury, Connecticut, ostensibly engaged in defending a public claim to a vast territory extending far beyond the narrow purchases claimed by the Susquehannah and other companies, revealed the true nature of the issue by passing on the costs to the shareholders of these companies. In addition to bearing this expense, the Susquehannah Company gave one share each to Dyer, Johnson, and Root "as a gratuity" (*Penna. Archives*, 2d ser., XVIII, 103; JCC, XXIII, 466-8).

Of the seven commissioners agreed upon, the agents reported on 23 Aug. that Rutledge declined to serve and Greene could not, being on a military command in the south; they therefore dropped both names and substituted that of Thomas Nelson of Virginia. A general commission was made out for all, but Jones and Nelson declined, and the court as ultimately constituted included only Whipple, Arnold, Brearley, Houston, and Griffin. The commission, reciting the terms of Article IX which provided that no state should be deprived of territory for the benefit of the United States, directed the members of the court or any five or more of them to meet in Trenton, New Jersey, on 12 Nov. 1782 to hear arguments and, if a majority agreed, "finally determine the controversy . . . and if any of the parties shall refuse to submit to the authority of the . . . court, or to appear or defend their claim or cause, the . . . court shall nevertheless proceed to pronounce sentence or judgment, and the judgment or sentence . . . shall be final and conclusive" (JCC, XXIII, 528-9; 533-6). In informing the members of their appointment, President John Hanson gave a solemn warning that "the peace of two states and consequently of the Whole Union depends upon an amicable and final settlement of this dispute." It is worth noting that Dyer, without question the most ardent defender of the Susquehannah Company's interests, told Trumbull that he thought the members of the court bore "a good carracter for Candor and Impartiallity, [but] the local situation of four of them are not so agreeable as we could wish." These four were obviously the two from New England and two from New Jersey—all from states having no charter claims to western lands; what Dyer wished to see was a good representation on the court from a state like Virginia.

Connecticut's agents again played a delaying game when the Court of Commissioners finally became organized on 18 Nov. 1782. They moved that Pennsylvania's petition to Congress asking that a court be established be produced and read. This was over-ruled. They then moved that, as there were several thousand persons living on the Susquehanna river and claiming title to lands under Connecticut or Pennsylvania, proceedings be suspended until these claimants could be "duly cited in some proper and reasonable manner" to appear and defend their interests. Since the Court of Commissioners was enabled to try only the question of jurisdiction and not the private right of soil, this was obviously an attempt to delay. The Court, after argument, decided that a proper construction of its powers under Article IX and the commission they held would not authorize the admission of the Connecticut motion. The agents of Pennsylvania, "apprehending that the agents of Connecticut design to move the court to postpone or put off the determination of the cause now depending before them," then gave formal notice in the presence of the court that they would oppose any such motion if it came after arguments were opened or the cause entered upon and expressed their willingness, if the Connecticut agents had any such intent, "that time be given them for that purpose." To this the Connecticut agents responded that they did not wish to give any unnecessary delay, but that Pennsylvania had "not . . . yet filed any declaration or state of their claim . . . whereby the agents of Connecticut can know what the demands of Pennsylvania are, or what they have to answer to"; they asserted further that they lacked "a certain original deed from the Indians" that had been left in England before the Revolution, as well as "other necessary evidence and proofs," but they were nevertheless willing to proceed to the trial "reserving . . . the right of moving in any stage . . . to have the same postponed, as the nature and exigencies of the case may require." The Pennsylvania agents replied that they were ready to present their claim, and had been for some time, but that they thought the Court should not hear any motion to postpone after the trial was begun. The Court ordered both motions to be filed, and the litigants then stated their claims. Finally, on 25 Nov., arguments got under way. "The merits of the Controversy," James Madison wrote, "are like to be brought under trial of the Court at Trenton, the Agents for Connecticut having been foiled in every plea for an adjournment. But I do not hear that any progress is made from which the issue can be presumed" (Madison to Randolph, 3 Dec. 1782; Burnett, *Letters of Members*, VII, No. 695).

The proceedings of the Court of Commissioners do not contain the arguments of opposing counsel. Fragmentary notes have been printed in "Documents Relating to the Connecticut Settlement in the Wyoming Valley," *Penna. Archives*, 2d ser., XVIII (1893), p. 621-9, but the arguments of the two outstanding figures, James Wilson and William Samuel Johnson, have never been published. An outline of their arguments as taken down by Cyrus Griffin during the trial is in DLC: TJ Papers and is here published for the first time (Document II). Jefferson no doubt obtained this from Griffin and, probably about the same time, he acquired an authenticated copy of the proceedings of the Court of Commissioners. Obviously he could not have obtained either Griffin's notes or the transcript of the proceedings for the purpose of preparing his report on the petition of Zebulon Butler, for there would not have been sufficient time to write to Virginia for the former (only five days intervened between the presentation of the petition and the handing in of the report) and, having at that time ready access to the archives of Congress, he would have had no need to ask for an authenticated copy of the latter. It is plausible, therefore, to assume that Jefferson must have obtained these two important documents during 1783 for some other purpose. Since, as Appendix III in this Volume makes clear, he was engaged in investigating colonial charters and other bases of claims to western territory in order to assist in stating Virginia's claim, it is very likely that he acquired these documents for that purpose in Jan. 1783; he was in Philadelphia then and must have seen Griffin when the latter passed through on his return to Virginia. Other evidence for this is presented in notes to Document VI in the present series. (The transcript of the proceedings of the Court of Commissioners is in DLC: TJ Papers, 9: 1404-22; it is in a clerk's hand and is signed by Thomson as an "Extract from the Journal of Congress," 2 Jan. 1783; the original record, signed by the five Commissioners, is in PCC: No. 77, p. 246-85, and is printed in JCC, XXIV, 6-32).

On 30 Dec. 1782, after more than a month of hearing arguments, the Court of Commissioners handed down a decision which contained no opinions or assessment of the issues involved. They merely announced as a unanimous decision that "the State of Connecticut has no right to the lands in controversy" and that "the jurisdiction and preemption of all the territory lying within the charter boundary of Pennsylvania, and now claimed by the State of Connecticut, do of right belong to the State of Pennsylvania."

This brief outline of the case of Pennsylvania v. Connecticut and of its background is sufficient to show the extreme unlikelihood that the Court of Commissioners were involved in any "agreement" which predetermined the outcome. The delaying and obstructionist tactics of the Connecticut counsel in the selection of the members of the Court, their similar tactics in their roles as Connecticut delegates in Congress, the repetition of these efforts to block the proceedings when the trial began—all point inescapably to the conclusion that Connecticut's counsel viewed their legal position as weak, not that a decision had been prearranged. Madison's statement during the trial and William Samuel Johnson's argument (see Document II) against the impropriety of injecting questions of policy into a trial of a question of legal right also support the view that the proceedings were conducted fairly. The subsequent course of events relating to the private right of soil confirms this view. (See also Document IV and notes.)

The Court of Commissioners wrote to President John Dickinson of Pennsylvania that the conflicting claims of those holding titles under Connecticut or Pennsylvania to the same lands could not properly come before them. They urged that conciliatory measures be adopted with respect to the Connecticut settlers in the Wyoming Valley, and that matters be continued in "the present peaceable posture until proper steps can be taken to decide the controversy respecting the private right of soil in the mode prescribed by the confederation" (31 Dec. 1782; *Penna. Archives*, 2d ser., XVIII [1893], 629-30). At Hartford, on 21 May 1783, the Susquehannah Company voted to apply to Congress for the appointment of another court to try the private right of soil (same, p. 104-105), and the Connecticut General Assembly at its Oct. 1783 session adopted several measures related to this effort. One declared that "this state has the undoubted and exclusive Right of Jurisdiction and Præmption to all the Lands lying West of the Western Limits of the State of Pennsylvania, and East of the Mississippi, and extending throughout from the Latitude 41° to Latitude 42° 2′ North"; it also directed Gov. Trumbull to issue a proclamation asserting the claim and forbidding all settlement within the area except under Connecticut authority. Another resolution recited the claims of the Wyoming inhabitants in language very similar to that of the petition here printed (Document III). It also advised the settlers to apply to Congress for a court to try the private right of soil "as the only Remedy left them" and declared that "it will be the Duty of this State to countenance and patronize them in such application." At the same time the Connecticut delegates in Congress were directed "to give them all necessary Aid therein" and Gov. Trumbull was ordered to "address a full state of their Claims and Sufferings to Congress, and solicit the protection of that Honorable Body until a final adjudication of the Cause shall be had." A third resolution declared that since the trial at Trenton information had been received "of some Evidence, Material to the Cause, then concealed and suppressed from the knowledge of this State or its Agents" and that "there is a probability of ascertaining other facts on which to ground a revision of said Cause." In view of this, the resolution directed Dyer, Johnson, and Root to be continued as agents for the state and directed them "to pursue their Enquiries after Evidence." This last resolution was obviously intended as a threat to reopen the matter as an issue between two states.

These interrelated measures can only be interpreted as intended to lay a foundation for future claims in respect to territory west of Pennsylvania. Roger Sherman, a dominant figure in Connecticut politics, had been present at the General Assembly that adopted these resolutions and there can be little doubt that, if he did not originate the strategy which they reflected, he must have had a powerful influence in its formulation. On 13 Jan. 1784 Sherman arrived at Annapolis, took his seat in Congress, and presented a letter from Gov. Trumbull to the president of Congress which enclosed authenticated copies of the Connecticut measures, together with the proclamation asserting claim to lands between Pennsylvania and the Mississippi (JCC, XXVI, 15, 21; all of the documents referred to are in PCC: No. 66, II, 256-64). The letter from Trumbull to Mifflin underscored the hidden threat in the Assembly's resolution: "The Decision in the case of the disputed Territory between this State and that of Pennsylvania, was not only very unexpected to the Legislature of this State, but, from some circumstances, appears to them very singular indeed;—and such as calls for their further prosecution; and in which they hope to produce such Documents as shall obtain the further interposition of Congress." He did not state the case of the sufferings of the Wyoming people (which were real) as he had been directed by the Assembly to do, for the Connecticut delegates had been present when the matter was discussed and were, he declared, "fully possessed of the subject" (same, II, 256-8).

Trumbull's letter and accompanying documents were read in Congress on 13 Jan. 1784 and referred the same day to a committee composed of Jefferson, Lee, and Williamson. There is no mention in the Journals either of the reading or the commitment, but Thomson's journal of committee assignments under that date shows that the committee were charged with reporting on the following: "Letter Novr. 1 W. Williams Speaker and Address of Assembly of Connecticut respecting commutation for half pay. Novr. 15. Govr Trumbull and Act and resolution of Assembly respecting claim to western territory and the decision on the dispute between Pensylva. and Connecticut" (Committee Book, PCC: No. 186; that part of the committee report respecting half-pay was written by Arthur Lee and was submitted on 26 Feb.; see JCC, XXVI, 100-103). From evidence in the rough draft of his first report, it appears that Jefferson immediately sat down to compose a report that would effectively repudiate the Connecticut insinuations against the Court of Commissioners and would, at the same time, block the threat implicit in the Connecticut measures of reopening the case of Pennsylvania v. Connecticut (see note 1 to Document IV). On 16 Jan. the petition of Zebulon Butler was received and referred to a committee also composed of Jefferson, Lee, and Williamson (Committee Book, PCC: No. 186, under 16 Jan. 1784). The report was handed in on 21 Jan. after suitable changes had been made in the rough draft and then in the fair copy so as to include a reference to the Wyoming petition, but the emphasis was still primarily upon regarding the question of jurisdiction as finally determined and secondarily upon establishing another court for the trial of the private right of soil. The second report, authorizing the establishment of a court to try the private right of soil, was approved 23 Jan. 1784.

It is plain from the nature of the reports and from the alterations made in them by Jefferson and by Congress that a tug of war was in progress between Jefferson and Sherman. The report submitted on 21 Jan. (Document V) was a strong defense of the Court of Commissioners' conduct in the case of Pennsylvania v. Connecticut; it merely mentioned Trumbull's statement of Connecticut's claim to lands westward of Pennsylvania. In the debate on the report on 22 Jan. Sherman and his colleagues evidently found it politic to disavow the insinuations made by Connecticut against the Court of Commissioners and the threat of reopening the case. For not only did the report slam the door vigorously on such intentions, but the arrival of a delegate from Pennsylvania while the matter was under discussion introduced an individual who was personally involved in the operations and political maneuvers of the Pennsylvania land speculators concerning Wyoming—John Montgomery—and provided a timely ally in support of Jefferson's belief that "it is for the quiet of these states that such determinations should be final and conclusive" (see note 2, Document IV). "I was not in Congrass when the petition of Butler and others and the letter from the Governor of Connecticut were first read," Montgomery reported to President Dickinson, "nor did I arrive untill the Committie to whom they had been referred had made report and Congrass was ready to Come to a decision. Upon first hearing the Bussiness I did not like it and was dissposed to give it all the oposition in my power ess[pe]cially as I p[e]rceived by a part of governor Trumbull's letter that the State of Connecticut was not satisfied with the Judgement given and thire was some expressions which seemed to intimate that they want'd it set asside and a new trail granted. But as the Delegates of that State disavowed such intention and moved for exsepunging that part of the report which referred to the exceptionable part of the letter and only insisted on the right of the petitioners, and as that right was founded on the Articles of Confederation, I acquiesed and left my collegues who had heard the matter from the beginning to give the vote of the State" (Burnett, *Letters of Members*, VII, No. 535).

This debate and the resultant amendment must have taken place on 22 Jan., for it was on that day that Montgomery took his seat in Congress (JCC, XXVI, 44). The report was recommitted and the next day Jefferson submitted a new report which was wholly concerned with the authorization of a court to try the private right of soil and with the setting up of procedures by which this could be accomplished (Document IV). But whereas the first report had merely mentioned the fact that Connecticut had asserted a claim to lands westward of Pennsylvania, the second pleaded lack of time for considering that claim.

The Pennsylvania legislature did not share Montgomery's view of the action taken by Congress on 23 Jan. and on 14 Feb. passed a series of resolutions directing their delegates to move for a reconsideration of the resolution and, failing this, to propose that Congress require the Wyoming inhabitants to "exhibit to Congress schedules particularizing their claims" (JCC, XXVI, 280-1). Accordingly, on 24 Apr. Hand brought forward a motion that, since Article IX of the Articles of Confederation provided for the establishment of a court of commissioners to try the private right of soil only in instances where such right was claimed under different grants of two or more states and since the Wyoming settlers had not proved that they came within this category, the resolution of 23 Jan. be suspended until the petitioners should exhibit to Congress such schedules as had been called for by the Pennsylvania legislature and that the claimants or their agents should not appear before Congress or the committee "until the further determinations of Congress" (JCC, XXVI, 280-2). This motion evidently was debated and another, by Hand, to refer it to a committee was adopted by an overwhelming vote; Sherman and Wadsworth of Connecticut were joined in opposition only by Ellery of Rhode Island and Beatty of New Jersey; Jefferson voted with the remainder of the Virginia delegation to commit (JCC, XXVI, 282). Hand's motion was thereupon referred to a committee of which Jefferson was chairman (Committee Book, PCC: No. 186). Nothing further was heard from this committee, and, after Jefferson had left Congress, Thomson merely noted in his journal of committee assignments that the committee had been "renewed" (same, 28 May 1784).

Meanwhile, faced by ejectment suits brought by Pennsylvania land speculators and by forcible dispossession, the Connecticut settlers drew up another petition on 1 May 1784 which was borne to Annapolis by John Franklin, one of the most remarkable leaders of the American frontier who was now emerging to succeed Zebulon Butler as the dominant figure in the troubled area of the Connecticut settlements along the Susquehanna. Franklin arrived in Annapolis early in May and gave the petition to Sherman, who presented it to Congress on 7 May (JCC, XXVI, 363, note; PCC: No. 42, I, 298-305; Burnett, *Letters of Members*, VII, No. 593). It was referred to the same committee to which the motion of Edward Hand on the Pennsylvania measures had been given on 24 Apr.; Jefferson was chairman of this committee, but he was no longer in Congress (Committee Book, PCC: No. 186; JCC, XXVII, 400). On 2 June the committee brought in a report recommending that the day for appointing a court be postponed from the fourth Monday in June to the first Monday in November and that all persons actually possessed of lands or buildings in the disputed territory prior to the decree of the Court of Commissioners should be quieted in their possessions until "a legal decision can be had on their right" (JCC, XXVII, 526-7). Sherman reported to Zebulon Butler on 15 June that "this report was given in the last day of the session, and there was not time to act upon it, but the Committee of the States can pass upon it if the parties desire it" (Burnett, *Letters of Members*, VII, No. 625). He advised that Butler or an agent of the Wyoming settlers appear at Annapolis on 28 June as stipulated in the resolution of Congress of 23 Jan. On the day fixed, James Wilson and William Bradford appeared for Pennsylvania "and sent in to those of the Com'tee [of the States] then met, (being only five) a paper purporting, that they were ready to join in the appointment of Com'rs, for a Federal Court on the Claim at Wyoming, but no Person appearing on the other side, and the want of members, nothing was . . . done on that Subject. M[ess]rs Bradford, and Wilson, withdrew the same evening" (Jonathan Blanchard to Roger Sherman, 24 July 1784, Burnett, *Letters of Members*, VII, No. 655; also Nos. 634, 635). John Franklin had promised as late as 3 Apr. that the Wyoming settlers would certainly have an agent at Annapolis on the day appointed. But, even while he was presenting the petition of 1 May, the Pennsylvania landholders began a wholesale and brutal dispossession of hundreds of Connecticut men, women, and children, and by 28 June Franklin was laying formal siege to the fort occupied by the Pennsylvania forces. Wyoming was again involved in another and final Pennamite war.

On 21 Sep. 1785 the resolution of 23 Jan. 1784 calling for the establishment of a court to determine the private right of soil was repealed. This was ostensibly done on the ground that the petition of Butler and others had not described with sufficient certainty the tract of land claimed nor "particularly named the private adverse claims under grants from the Commonwealth of Pennsylvania" (JCC, XXIX, 725-31; cf. same, XXVII, 603-605). John Franklin, who was then in New York, presented a petition the next day asking the reasons for this action and requesting protection in their possessions until a petition could be brought in on the whole subject (PCC: No. 41, III, p. 326). This was referred to a committee of which William Samuel Johnson was chairman (JCC, XXIX, 737, note). There is nothing in the Journals of Congress concerning the report of this committee, but Franklin on 28 Sep. 1785 made the following entry in his carefully kept diary of actions taken in Congress concerning the dispute: "This day the committee report in favor of our petition. That the repeal of the resolution of Congress was founded in the insufficiency of the allegations, and defective description of the lands in controversy, and was not intended to foreclose the proprietors, settlers and claimants of lands at and near Wyoming, for the appointment of a Federal court to try their rights of soil . . . when a petition shall be brought describing the land, and naming the adverse claimants with due degree of certainty. . . . The report was disapproved" (Charles Miner, *History of Wyoming*, Philadelphia, 1845, p. 379; photostats in Wyoming Hist. and Geol. Soc.). In brief, though Johnson's report held out a hope that a court would be authorized once a condition difficult if not impossible of realization had been met, Congress rejected even that shadow of a hope.

This was done despite the plain intent of the Articles of Confederation. Article IX provided that all controversies concerning the private right of soil "*shall, on the petition of either party* to the Congress of the United States (italics supplied)" be finally determined in the manner stipulated for determining disputes between different states concerning territorial jurisdiction. The repeal of 1785 was a flat denial to the Wyoming settlers of the machinery provided by the national constitution. It had the effect of handing over the determination of the question of the private right of soil to the Pennsylvania legislature, a body that had demonstrated repeatedly in this matter its subservience to Philadelphia land speculators. A year after the repeal took place, Congress accepted the Connecticut cession of lands to the Mississippi beginning 120 miles westward of the western boundary of Pennsylvania (*The Territorial Papers of the United States*, ed. Clarence E. Carter, II, 22-4). Looking at this sequence of events, the Connecticut inhabitants of the Wyoming region considered that they had been sacrificed to larger and more influential interests.

Their belief is understandable. As James Madison pointed out in the Federal Convention of 1787, the assumption that an understanding had taken place was the only adequate explanation for the inconsistent course followed by Congress. Indeed, he went much beyond this and, in the presence of William Samuel Johnson, flatly charged that a *quid pro quo* had been involved: "Have we not seen the public land dealt out to Con[necticu]t to bribe her acquiescence in the decree constitutionally awarded against her claim on the territory of Pena.? for no other possible motive can account for the policy of Cong's in that measure?" (Farrand, *Records of the Federal Convention*, I, 316). This belief was expressed also by William Grayson of Virginia when the Connecticut cession came up for debate in 1786: "It appeared to the Virginia delegation," he wrote, "that the only proper claim [to the territory ceded by Connecticut] was already vested in Congress by the cession of our state and that their cession was nothing but a State juggle contrived by old Roger Sherman to get a side wind confirmation to a thing they had no right to" (Grayson to Madison, 28 May 1786, DLC: Madison Papers; Burnett, *Letters of Members*, VIII, No. 407; cf. David Howell's opinion that the Kentucky petition of 1784 was only a Virginia move "to establish their jurisdiction over that Country by a side wind, as the phrase is"; same, VII, No. 521).

However, as indicated above, there is no reason to accept the view that this accommodation of interests involved the Court of Commissioners who decided the matter of jurisdiction (Charles Miner, *History of Wyoming*, Philadelphia, 1845, p. 309-10, 379). Nor is there reason to believe that the "deal" took place in the spring of 1784 when the national domain came into existence with the acceptance of Virginia's cession. The Act of cession was in Jefferson's hand at the time he was involved in the drafting of reports on the Butler petition; it was finally presented to Congress on 11 Feb. 1784, referred to a committee of which Sherman was chairman, and favorably reported upon by Sherman himself (JCC, XXVI, 89-90; see notes to documents on Virginia cession 1 Mch. 1784). And it was Sherman, evidently, who gained John Montgomery's support for Jefferson's report on the Butler petition by assuring him that Connecticut did not really mean to reopen the case of Pennsylvania v. Connecticut, despite her resolutions of 1783. Montgomery, in turn, was apparently the Pennsylvania delegate by whose single vote the acceptance of the Virginia cession became law (see notes to TJ to Harrison, 3 Mch. 1784). But these coincidences only serve to cloak in deeper mystery the subtle legislative maneuvers of Roger Sherman, who was described by a contemporary who knew him well as being "as cunning as the Devil" in such enterprises (Jeremiah Wadsworth; *Life and Correspondence of Rufus King*, ed. C. R. King, I [1894], 221). For, despite those maneuvers, the essential intent of Jefferson's first report on the Butler petition remained intact when it was recommitted and its text altered. Sherman and Jefferson were no doubt allies in persuading Montgomery and the Pennsylvania delegates to accept a report which established machinery for trying the private right of soil. They were also apparently allied on the question of the Virginia cession. But when Pennsylvania endeavored to upset this machinery with Hand's resolution of 24 Apr. 1784, Jefferson was able to sidetrack the effort by forcing a commitment and by allowing the resolution to slumber in a committee of which he was chairman. As long as he was in Congress, the Connecticut settlers along the Susquehanna were assured of the benefits conferred by his report. The real "State juggle contrived by old Roger Sherman" must have come when Congress repealed this assurance in Sep. 1785. (Sherman was not in Congress at that time, but William Samuel Johnson was there and was of course "fully possessed of the subject," as Trumbull had put it; cf., however, Roger Sherman Boardman, *Roger Sherman*, 1938, p. 160-1.)

But, for a time in 1784, the two strong legislative leaders who were so uncongenial in personality and outlook must have come to some kind of understanding whereby the embarrassing assertion of Connecticut's western claim was left untouched or at least held in suspense ("The Committee having not had time," &c.), the acceptance of Virginia's cession was assured, and the decree in the case of Pennsylvania v. Connecticut confirmed against a possibility of reversal. If this conjecture is correct, John Montgomery must have been a central figure in this temporary alliance of discordant elements. Montgomery's official reason for agreeing to Jefferson's report was this: "it appeared to me that the Court to decide upon the private right of Soil cou'd not be apointed nor have any right to sit or act unless it was taken for granted that the jurisdiction was previously and finally adjudged and Determined" (Montgomery to Dickinson, 7 Mch. 1784; Burnett, *Letters of Members*, VII, No. 535). But this was an explanation that Montgomery did not give until a week after he had cast the deciding vote on the Virginia cession on 1 Mch. 1784, and its interpretation of Article IX of the Articles of Confederation may possibly rest upon a hint that had been supplied him by the one who was the chief architect of the national domain (Jensen, *The New Nation*, p. 353)—and who, like Sherman, was also skilled in legislative maneuvers.

Once the Treaty of Peace had been ratified, Jefferson's major objective in Congress was the establishment of the national domain and the formulation of ordinances for its government. It was in this context that his strategy over the Wyoming matter must be considered. But there was another and even higher context. Document VI, though its precise date is indeterminate, is evidence that Jefferson did not lose sight of universal goals even in the midst of legislative jockeying. The case of Pennsylvania v. Connecticut, like that of Massachusetts v. New York, was to him "such another proof of the empire of reason and right" as the world had not theretofore produced.

Nearly a quarter of a century after these events, Jefferson took notes, while presiding over the Senate, on the bill to accept Connecticut's cession of the territory involved in the Western Reserve (DLC: TJ Papers, 105:17968).

I. Notes concerning Boundaries

[1784?]

Prender of possession, and assumption of boundary, by the Jus gentium of America, gives a right of *preemption* against all nations and individuals but not of *occupation* against the native inhabitants.

Charters from the crown, whether to *proprietors* or *people*, are fundamental rights, vesting in all, and not alterable but by consent of all parties.

Consent of people, expressed by *acquiescence*.

In infant state of settlements the Crown was in the practice of curtailing prior grants by subsequent.

A subsequent grant, extending across the whole of a prior grant and thus cutting off territory tho' not included in 2d grant, implies or is evidence of an intention in the Crown to limit the 1st. state by the 2d. and the 1st. grant is rescinded as to the territory cut off

thus Georgia bounded S. Carola.
       Pensylva. bounded Connecticut

MS (DLC); entirely in TJ's hand. This memorandum is undated, but it presumably represents notes made by TJ during the years 1782-1784 when he was actively investigating the whole question of Virginia's claim. But its context suggests that it may have been set down early in 1784 when the case of Pennsylvania v. Connecticut came into debate in connection with the petition of Zebulon Butler.

II. Arguments by James Wilson and William Samuel Johnson before the Court of Commissioners

W[ILSON]   [14-23 Dec. 1782]

We have the pleasure to meet your honors upon a very important Contest. You are now to decide a territorial controversy, which with other nations would have been decided by the sword. This being a court of the first impression in any part of the Globe and the present subject of litigation being of considerable value, I hope the honorable Court will pardon the tedious discussion I am now to make.

On the part of Pennsylvania I will lay down this first position.

1. "That N. America being discovered by Gabot[1] in 1594, the Crown of England assumed the Right of Granting the property and Jurisdiction thereof to its subjects by letters patent."

I apprehend this position is so evident from the General tenor of history that no contradiction will arise concerning it. However proofs to this purpose may be exhibited in the examination of a second position which I am now to make.

2. "That in 1681 the Crown of England justly considered all the lands in America westward of Delaware River and Northward of lord Baltimore's Grant, as ungranted lands and open to a new Grant."

A Right of *discovery* is common to all nations. The English had not a preference.

A Tittle from discovery was certainly of some force and especially according to the Ideas which prevailed in those early times. In consequence of this we find a Grant from the Pope Alexander the 6th. to his Catholic Majesty in the Year 1493.

2 Harris voyages. 15. 16. 17.

Also a Grant by Henry 7th. of England to the Cabots

2 Harris. 190.

Also a Grant to Monsr. d' Ossions

4 purchas pilgrim. 1609. 1620.

King James the first divided America into two Colonies, South and North Virginia.

The first charters could only extend 100 miles upon the coast and the same distance into the Country.

> 1 Neal history. 17. Stiths history of Virginia. 10

In 1608 Henry Hudson in the service of Holland penetrated so high up the hudson's river as Albany about 43°. N. L.

> Smiths history N. York. 2. 3. 4.
>
> Smith's history N. Jersey. 19.

The dutch settlements in North America were called Nova Belgia or New Netherlands.

The extent of them

> Hielans[1] Cosmography 957.
>
> 2 british Empire in America 237.
>
> 2 Harris 280. 5 atlas Geog. 732.
>
> Ogil. America 168.

The dutch possessions acknowleged as just by England at the Treaty of Breda 1667. and the Treaty of Westminster 1673. From these authorities we have a right to conclude that Nova Belgia or N. Netherlands covered all that Territory at least which is now in dispute.

The Great plymouth patent constituting N. England from 40°. to 48°. N. L. passed in 1620.

This patent we contend could pass no Territory *westward* of N. Netherlands. It was bounded or estopped by the possessions of the first christian prince. 1 Douglas history N. England 114.

> 2 Douglas 391.
>
> Lord Hardwick's opinion in 1 Vezey 451.

The Geography of the Country on this period but little understood and therefore unreasonable and extravagant that Grants should extend to the south seas.

> 3 Purchas 852. 853.
>
> 4 Purchas 1786. Virginia valued—pamphlet

The surrender of this Great patent was in the year 1635.

The Charter to Connecticut was Given in the Year 1662.

New Haven colony united with the Colony of Connecticut 1665.

That charter meant only to *cover* the two Colonies and could never mean to extend *westward* of the Dutch settlements. All Geographers and writers have proceeded upon this Idea—Douglas, Hutchinson, Neal, modern un. history, british Emp. &c. &c.

The Title set up by Connecticut ought to be considered as a *dormant* title. Nothing is mentioned of this *western* Territory from the year 1662 to the year 1754 and not regarded by *Government* untill 1773.

The line drawn by the King's commissioners in 1664 and assented to by Connecticut as a *good issue*, decisive as to the *western* bounds of that Colony.

New York Records. 20.

Connecticut Records. 30.

In 1680 and 1730 Connecticut acknowleges herself bounded *west* by the province of N. York.

Considerations ought to be commensurate with every Grant.

The King was deceived in this Grant to Connecticut as no *exception* was made to the Dutch possessions.

We must discover the *thoughts* of those who make *Contracts*

2 Blacstone 295.

2 Vattel § 270.

2 Hutchinson history Massa. 387.

Interpretation must be *rational*

2 Rutherford—chapter Interpretation.

1 Blacstone 59.

2 Bacon abrid. 661.

The power of explaining charters, &c. must remain with the Crown. 2 Vattel § 282. 287.

Puffendorf 541.

Grotius 365.

Restraining the words of laws, patents &c.

2 Vattel 292. 293.

2 Rutherford. 339.

Puffen. 545. 554.

3. I state as a 3d. position

"That King Charles the second granted to William Penn his heirs and assigns all that Tract of land in America bounded by Delaware River on the East unto the 43°. of N. latitude, the said land to extend westward five degrees in longitude &c."

This position is proved by the charter of Pennsylvania dated 4 March 1681.

4. A fourth position is

"That this charter was considered by the King with *attention* and *caution* and was granted in consideration of *debts due* from the Crown, and also in consideration of the *services* of Sir William Penn the father of the Grantee."

Passed with great caution.

Proceedings of the privy council in
1 Votes assembly 7. 12.

The Grant not *extravagant*.
2 Douglas 306.

The Grant was for *debts* and *services*
2 Harris. 293.
9 Biographical dict. article *Penn*.

Such Grants of the King ought to be construed favorably
4 Bac. ab. 212.

5. A fifth position

"That, to prevent any claim which the duke of York might have upon Pennsylvania, William Penn obtained a *release* from the duke of all such his right, title, and Interest."

This deed of release bears date 21 of August 1682.
2 Douglas 305.

This right, title, or Interest, vested in the duke.

The dutch had the right of *pre-emption* as possessing N. Netherlands. N. Netherlands was cede[d] to England and afterwards granted to the duke.
Colden's history five nations 52. 53. 54. 104.

This makes the foundation of the *cession* made by the state of N. York to the united stats.

6. We state as a sixth position

"That upon the faith of this Grant to Penn Great numbers came from Europe to Pennsylvania, extended the settlements already began, and together with the Proprietor exercised Jurisdiction over all the lands within the bounds of the said patent untill the revolution in 1776."

Many laws of Pennsylvania, the Council Books of Pennsylvania, and Colden's history, page 115. 131. were adduced in proof of this position.

Also a proclamation of the Pennsylvania Government dated 24th. of February 1768. and another dated 10 July 1771.

7. A seventh position is this

"That Penn not content with the Title which the patent gave him to the soil, he and his successors *purchased* the lands from the Natives for a valuable consideration."

The Indian Right to dispose of their lands. Colden. 106.
Also in page 77. 78. 79.
Dummer's defence. 18. 1 Douglas. 5.

Indian deeds and papers exhibited from No. 2 to No. 41.
Treaty of Albany 1754.

Pennsylvania does not mean to *abandon* her *Crown* title by these exhibits. But she means to strengthen her right to the lands in controversy by *combining* her *Indian* title.

8. We advance as the eighth position

"That the Indians of the six Nations in a public and solemn manner conveyed the Right of pre-emption to the proprietors, and covenanted to sell all the lands within the limits of the charter of Pennsylvania to none but to them, their heirs and assigns."

This deed of pre-emption dated 25th of October 1736.

Colden history five nations.

Position 9.

9. "That at a subsequent period a second deed of the same kind was made in the same manner and the former deed recognised."

Deeds of ratification and confirmation in the years 1754. 1758.

Also the great deed at Fort stanwix in the year 1768.

Position 10.

10. "That actual settlements were made by the Inhabitants of Pennsylvania and under rights derived from the proprietors, on the lands in dispute, for more than 20 years, before any claims or settlements on these lands were made by any persons under Connecticut."

To prove this position several exhibits were adduced from letter A to letter G. and also parole testimony.

Position the last.

11. "That by an act of the General assembly, Pennsylvania being a free, sovereign, and Independant state, all the Estate, title, and Interest, of the then proprietors is vested in the Common wealth of Pennsylvania, in consideration whereof the sum of £130,000 sterling money is granted to the said proprietors."

The act in proof of this position is dated 27th. of November in the year 1779.

Not *just* to extend these south sea claims—these unlocated lands ought to be in common as being acquired by the common blood and common Treasury of America.

J[OHNSON]—on the part of Connecticut

I shall state this as my first position.

1. "That by the discovery of the Cabots the Crown of England was vested with a right of colonising from the 25 to the 68°. of N.l. in America, and with the right, property, and pre-emption, to all the lands from sea to sea."

Prince's chronology. 17. 80.

Stiths history of Virginia Appendix 1. 2. 3.

General history and writers upon this subject.

2. A second position I lay down is

"That 1606 King James the first divided the Countries aforesaid into two Colonies South and North Virginia."

Stiths history of Virginia

Douglas—Hutchinson

and Prince.

3. My third position

"That King James the first granted to the Council of Plymouth all the Colony of North Virginia from the 40 to the 48° of
N.l. in longitude from the Atlantic on the East to the south sea on
the west the whole breadth throughout the main land, and gave
it the name of N. England, except only such parts as were actually
in the possession of some other christian prince."

Plymouth patent dated 18th. November 1620.

4. My fourth position

"That many subordinant Grants were made by the Council
of Plymouth, particularly one to the proprietors of the province of
Massachusets Bay, confirmed by King Charles the first in 1629."

Charter prefixed to the laws of Massachusets.

3 Hutchinson, from the beginning.

5. Position.

"That Robert Earl of Warwick president of the Council of
Plymouth conveyed to lord Say and Seal and others all that part
of N. England in America from Narraganset river the space of
40 leagues upon the sea shore, and also all the lands north and
south in latitude and breadth, and in length and longitude of and
within all the breadth aforesaid, throught the main lands there,
from the western ocean to the South Sea."

Patent to Say and Seal dated 19 March 1631.

2 Douglas 90. 160.

2 Hutchinson. 203.

Connecticut records. 57.

6. Position.

"That in 1636 the Colony of Connecticut settled on the said
lands as the associates of Lord Say and Seal &c. and in 1638
formed a constitution of Government extending themselves by
purchases from the Indians to the possessions of the Dutch on
Hudson's river."

Connecticut records. 41.

New-Haven records. 1. 2. 3.

United Colony records. 19. 20. 39.

7. Position.

"That King Charles the 2d. granted the present charter to the Governor and Company of Connecticut. The bounds are All that part of my dominions in New-England bounded East on Narraganset river, on the North by the line of the Massachusetts, and on the south by the sea; and in longitude as the line of the Massachusetts runing from East to West, that is from the said Narraganset on the East to the south sea on the west part."

Petition of the Connecticut assembly to Charles 2d. June 7th. 1661.

Charter 23 of April 1662.

Letter from Charles 2d. to the Governor and Company of Connecticut 23 of April 1664.

8. Position.

"That Charles 2d. gave a patent to his Brother the Duke of York of all that part of New-England from Saint Croise next adjoining to New Scotland, from thence on the sea coast to Pemaquid and up that river to its head as it tendeth northward, and extending from thence to the river Kenebeck and upwards by the shortest course to the river Canada Northward, also Long Island with the Hudsons river, and all the lands from the west side of Connecticut river to the East side of Delaware Bay."

This patent, dated 12th. of March 1664.

9. Position.

"That the Crown of England having granted all the lands from 40°. to 48 N.l. to the Plymouth Company, excepting as is therein excepted, the duke of York's patent took effect by force of the exception and in the settlement of the line with Connecticut the duke's patent was reduced nearly to the dutch possessions on the Hudson's river Eastward."

Connecticut records. 137.

Articles of agreement 29th. of April 1725.

Act of the Connecticut assembly October 4th. 1730.

10. Position.

"That in 1753 the Colony of Connecticut having settled all the lands in the patent east of the line settled with the duke of York—Companies of Adventurers were formed for the purpose of making settlements within the charter on the west of delaware river agreeable to the original Intent thereof and purchased of the

Indians sundry Tracts of land on the Delaware and Susqueh. rivers, and made settlements on the lands in controversy, under the colony of Connecticut, approved by the assembly."

Indian deed 11 July 1754.

Indian deed 29th of october 1756.

Indian recognition. 12th July 1763.

11. Position.

"That in 1773 the Colony of Connecticut did assert their right of Jurisdiction and property and pre-emption in and to the lands in question, and for many years past have actually exercised Jurisdiction over the same."

Act of assembly   October 1773.

Act of assembly   January 1774.

Act of assembly   December 1775.

12. Position—and the last.

"That the Colony of Connecticut at the time of the late Revolution was in fact seised of the right of Jurisdiction of property and preemption in and to all the Territory in their charter and patent including the lands in controversy."

This question upon the whole matter is a very important question and to my Judgment ought to be determined by the *law* which existed at the moment of *acquisition*.

This law had for its basis the great principle or title of *occupancy* and the acknowleged *Right* of the *Prince*.

But America was *inhabited*. Therefore some additional principles were necessary and what were these additional principles? *Preemption*, and actual *purchase*.

But no such purchases could be made unless they were made under the *authority* of the *Prince*, agreeable to the feudal Ideas prevalent at that period.

Hence it followed that the Indian Tittle was subordinate to the Crown Title.

The Indian Title can give no certainty and certainty is necessary in the establishment of property.

We ought to consider the Natives of America as they *were*.

Cultivation or Industry appears to me the only just criterion of property.

Nay property ought to be commensurate with *Civilization*.

We made actual purchases of the Indians but why? That we might purchase *peace* and *quiet*.

All titles in America take their origin from the Crown in the way of Charters and other Grants.

The Crown only could give a right of pre-emption, and that right of pre-emption seems to be admitted by the laws of Nations, consented to by all civilized people and sanctified by prescription.

All the legislatures upon this continent have adopted a language of this sort and therefore ought to be binding upon this court as a fixed determination or law in the American code.

Connecticut had a charter given them in the year 1662 upon valuable considerations.

Charters or Grants are the foundation of all American property and charters or Grants once fairly made should operate eternally.

Connecticut has a legal Title as founded upon *discovery* and subsequent Grant from Charles the second.

Discovery is a right acquiesced in nay ratified by all the nations of Europe and therefore in a national controversy like the present will carry weight with it.

We have no direct proof that the Dutch were in possession of N. Netherlands or any part of N. England *under a title from their sovereign*, untill the year 1621, a year after the Plymouth patent was granted by King James.

Before the year 1620 Governor Argal of Virginia made the Dutch acknowlege the King of England and therefore became Tenants to the Crown of England.

We can consider the Dutch therefore as originally nothing better than *Intruders*.

Then the settlements of the Dutch cannot form a bar or an estoppel to the *western* extension of the Connecticut charter.

It does not appear that King Charles was *deceived* in his Grant to Connecticut. He well knew the extent of that Grant. The Atlantic and Pacific oceans even upon the coasts of them had been explored —latitudes and longitudes pretty accurately determined.

All these Grants or charters extending to the *South Sea* were done so for the purpose of encouragement. They formed a regular system.

At all events, the Instrument itself must determine the Grant.

Every Instrument of this nature should be construed *liberally* and not so *strictly* as to contradict or take away the essential words of it. If the property of these lands in dispute were once *vested*, as we think by the charter of Charles, there is nothing in our opinion to *divest* it.

The reasons, evidence, or documents to the divestiture of property ought to be fully as strong as to the Investiture.

II. ARGUMENTS BY WILSON AND JOHNSON

The settlement of 1664 was only a settlement with the duke of York. In fair construction it can relate to nothing farther than to adjust the bounds of the Dukes patent and the patent of Connecticut as *relative to the Duke.*

If that settlement meant any thing more than I contend it could be only upon the principle of *resumption* by the Crown—the most horrid principle of Tyrannical power—against all *Law* whatever, and what I am certain this Court will never establish in these enlightened times.

In this case the Title of Connecticut cannot be considered as a *dormant* title. *Silence* does not operate against property in the *society* of *nations*. Neither in law or Equity can *nonuses* forfeit the *right* in our situation. Neither Penn or Connecticut made any use of this controverted Territory untill lately. Connecticut took possession and made settlements so soon as her *Eastern* Territory was *populated.*

The acknowlegement of Connecticut as bounded *west* in 1680 and 1730 must be construed *according to the subject matter.* The subject matter was the bounds of the Province of N. York and the bounds of Connecticut as interfering with that province and cannot preclude the *western* extension of Connecticut *beyond* the province of N. York.

Besides if there was a *dereliction* or even such an acknowlegement on the part of Connecticut it cannot operate in favor of the Pennsylvania charter, that being granted to Penn only 19 years after the one to Connecticut.

The *policy* of this great Question has been mentioned. I think improperly. It was meant as an appeal to a majority of this honorable Court who come from the smaller states in the union. But your honors will disregard the policy of this matter if it militates with the right.

However the policy will be found in favor of Connecticut—for at the approaching peace with G. Britain our charters will be the best foundation to stand upon in discussing the subject of the back Territory. We are not entitled to those fine and extensive regions by *Conquest* from Britain nor are we entitled to them by *forfeiture* on the part of Britain. Our charters or Grants from the Kings of England make the only *firm basis* of American claim to those back lands.

MS (DLC: TJ Papers); entirely in the hand of Cyrus Griffin. There is no date on the MS, but Wilson's argu-   ments were presented on 14, 19 and 20 Dec. 1782 and those of Johnson on 21 and 23 Dec. 1782 (JCC, XXIV, 29-

30). As suggested in the editorial note, Griffin may have placed this MS in TJ's hand in Philadelphia in Jan. 1783.

THE POLICY OF THIS GREAT QUESTION HAS BEEN MENTIONED: Johnson is here replying—and with telling force —to an argument that apparently had been advanced by Wilson on 13 Dec. 1782 in which he undertook to "suggest the Advantages or inconv[eniencie]s that are likely to flow from the Decision of this Court" (*Penna. Archives*, 2d ser., XVIII, 622). He may also be referring to the argument that Wilson and other land speculators had advanced in Congress and he repeated here—that "these unlocated lands ought to be in common as being acquired by the common blood and common Treasury of America" ("The Creation of the National Domain," by Merrill Jensen, MVHR, XXVI [1939], 323-42). But there is no doubt of the accuracy of Johnson's observations that at the approaching peace negotiations the sea-to-sea charter claims of the colonies would be one of the main supports of the American contention, and instructions had already been given to that end to the American ministers abroad (JCC, XXIII, 490-516). Nevertheless, policy was doubtless the determining influence in the decision.

[1] Thus in MS. This and other similar errors in MS would seem to indicate that Griffin took down his notes from oral presentation by counsel.

III. The Petition of Zebulon Butler and Others

Wyoming Novr: 11th 1783

To the Honourable The Congress of the United States of America Assembled and Setting at Princetown in the State of New Jersey.

The Petition Remonstrance and Address of Zebulon Butler Nathan Denison, Obadiah Gore, John Franklin, Simon Spaulding and the rest of the Proprietors Setlers and Inhabitants of the Lands lying on the Rivers Delaware and Susquehanah in the Latitude of the Charter granted by King Charles the Second in the Year of our Lord One Thousand Six Hundred and Sixty Two to then Colony Now State of Connecticut West of the River Delaware and within the Charter Boundaries of said State humbly sheweth.

That your Petitioner as Early as the Year AD 1755 made Large Purchases of the Indians, Native Proprietors of said Lands, for good and Valuable considerations paid them, for which they the said Indians made good and Ample Deeds of Large Tracts of Land lying within the description Aforesaid, and in consequence of said Purchases and Deeds your Petitioners Sold their Inheritances and under countenance and with the Approbation of the Government of the then Colony Now State of Connecticut Removed with their Famelies and Seated themselves upon the Lands Aforesaid then in A Wilderness State, Verely beleiveing said Lands were the property off and within the Jurisdiction of then Colony of Connecticut in Virtue of their Charter aforesaid. That they Built Houses and Other Buildings Cleared and Subdued the Rugged Wilderness, Planted Orchards, and made large Improvements thereon to the great Emoluments of the Public as well as themselves, and became An Important barrier to secure the interior parts of the Country from incursions of the Savages: and have waded through the most intollerable sufferings during the late unhapy Warr. Their Houses and Other Buildings have been Burned, and their Lands Laid waste, their Cattle Killed, and Pillaged, Many of their Fathers, Mothers, Wives and Children have been Sacraficed by the relentless fury of A Savage Enemy; Yet through all their Sufferings and distresses they have preserved An Inviolable Attaichment to the Important Cause of America in which many of their nearest and Dearest friends have bled and fallen.

Your Petitioners further Observe that the General Assembly of the Colony of Connecticut by repeated Acts and Resolves (Viz) As Early as the Years of Our Lord 1771. 1772. and 1773 Actualy incorporated your Petitioners into A Town and County by the Name of Westmoreland Erected Courts of Justice Appointed Judges and Other Officers Civil and Millitary and Invested them with pleniary Powers within their respective Jurisdiction in all Matters Civil Criminal and Millitary in Pursuance of the Laws of the Aforesaid Colony of Connecticut and for many Years the said Courts Judges and Other Officers did Actually exercise Jurisdiction there under the Authorety of the Colony of Connecticut.

That in the Year 1782 the State of Pensylvania claiming tittle and Jurisdiction to and Over the Lands aforesaid as being Comprehended within the Patent and Charter of King Charles the Second made to William Penn Esqr. in the Year of Our Lord 1680 about Eighteen Years after the Charter to the Colony of Connecticut, prefered their Petition to your Honourable body praying that A Court might be constituted to hear and determin between them and the State of Connecticut relative to the Jurisdiction of said Lands agreeable to the Ninth Article of the Confederation. Upon which A Court hath been Appointed Constituted and held and A tryal and decision had (to the great surprise of allmost every One) in favour of the State of Pennsylvania against the Claim, right of Preemtion and Jurisdiction of the State of Connecticut yet your Petitioners relying upon the Justice Humanity and good Polity of the Government of the State of Pennsylvania entertained and highest Expectations that upon their recognizeing and submitting to the Jurisdiction of Pennsylvania they should be quieted in all their Justly Acquired property and Possessions Aforesaid but to their great Mortification and greif they are compeled to fly to your Honourable body for Releiff protection and Justice against the Most Bitter and Cruel persecutions from the Citizens of the State of Pennsylvania under Countenance and lycence from the Authorety of said State.

They are driven from their Houses and Settlements with their Helpless Famelies, the fruit of their Industry, the Last Summe is Pileaged from them; and they are turned Adrift att the begining of A Long and inclement Winter, without Covering or the Means of subsistance and have no where to Look for redress and Protection but to your Honourable body in whose Wisdom and Justice your Distressed Petitioners repose the most intire confidence. And thereupon Intreat your Honours to take their distressed Case into your Wise and Equitable consideration and Cause the said State of Pennsylvania and any that may be Concerned to be duly Cited to make Answer to this Petition, And that the Honourable the Congress of these United States would Erect and Constitute A Court Agreeable to the Ninth Article of the Confederation finally to hear and determin relative to the tittle of said Lands between the Petitioners and the State of Pennsylvania or Any of the Citizens thereof Claiming under grants from that State or in some Other way grant releiff to your Petitioners as your Honours in your great Wisdom shall find Expedient and your Petitioners as in duty bound shall ever pray.

MS (DLC: PCC, No. 42, 1); in an unidentified hand, signed by the petitioners; endorsed in clerk's hand: "Petition [*and in the hand of Thomson*:] Zebulun Butler and others. Jany. 16. 1784 Referred to Mr Jefferson Mr Lee Mr Williamson"; signed by Butler, Nathan Denison, Obadiah Gore, John Franklin, John Jenkins, and 84 others. A copy of this petition was sent by Edward Hand to President John Dickinson of Pennsylvania on the day it was presented in Congress: "notwithstanding the irregularity of the form, bad Orthography etca. would at first view lead a person to believe it to be the ofspring of those people [at Wyoming], I apprehend your Excellency will without much difficulty treace it to another Source" (Burnett, *Letters of Members*, VII, No. 493). The other source that Hand had in mind was no doubt Roger Sherman who appeared in Congress on 13 Jan. 1784 with the petition and who had long been associated politically and otherwise with the leaders of the Susquehannah Company. There is no reference in the Journals to the petition as having been presented on 16 Jan. 1784 and referred to the committee as indicated (JCC, XXVI, 37).

IV. First Report on Petition of Zebulon Butler

[21 Jan. 1784]

The Committee to whom were referred the resolutions of the General assembly of Connecticut and the letter and proclamation of Govr. Trumbul desiring a revision of the sentence of the judges formerly appointed to hear and finally determine the controversy between that state and the state of Pennsylvania concerning the boundaries and jurisdiction of the said states on the Western side of the Delaware; also that a court may be instituted for determining the private right of soil within the said territory; and notifying that the said state of Connecticut claims jurisdiction over all the lands between Pennsylvania and the Missisipi from 41°. to 42°-2″ Northern latitude; and the petition of Zebulon Butler and others, inhabitants within the territory late in dispute between the said states complaining that they are disturbed in their private right of soil and praying in like manner the institution of a court for determining the same, have agreed to the following report.[1]

It appears to your Committee that the controversy between the states of Pennsylva and Connecticut for territory on the Western side of Delaware river alledged to be within both their boundaries was originated in Congress so early as the 5th. day of Octob. 1775, and was frequently and much agitated therein from that time to the 3d. day of Nov. 1781.

That the state of Pennsva did then petition Congress that the same might be determined according to the 9th. Article of Confederation.

That Congress did on the 14th. day of the same month direct a notification to the state of Connecticut of the petition from Pennsylvania, and assign a day for proceeding thereon.

That the same was regularly proceeded on according to the 9th. Article of the Confederation, and that the judges met at Trenton on the 12th. day of Nov. 1782 to hear and determine the same.

That a fair, full, and patient hearing of the parties by their agents, was given, and mature consideration had by the said court from the said 12th. day of Nov. day by day without intermission till the 30th. day of Dec. when final sentence was pronounced: that this sentence was with the unanimous concurrence of the said judges.

That no improper biass or conduct in the judges or any of them is suggested or supposed.

That the said 9th. Article of the Confederation declares that the sentence of such a court shall be final and conclusive.

Resolved therefore that the said sentence ought not to be revised.[2]

Resolved that a court should be instituted according to the said 9th. Article of the Confederation for determining the private right of soil so far as the same is by the said article submitted[3] to the determination of such a court.

MS (DLC: TJ Papers, 10: 1627); entirely in TJ's hand; endorsed by Thomson: "Report of Mr Jefferson Mr Lee Mr Williamson. Jany 21. 1784. Entd. Read." Dft of all except the opening two or three lines (i.e., all that precedes the words "concerning the boundaries and jurisdiction of the said states") is in DLC: TJ Papers, 11: 1892. Dft is omitted altogether by Ford, III, 382-7, and is not to be confused with his so-called "rough draft." Important differences between Dft and MS of report are indicated in notes below.

[1] This introductory paragraph is given here as it was written in Dft before the petition of Zebulon Butler was referred to the committee, for the concluding words originally read: ". . . from 41°. to 42°-2″ Northern latitude have agreed to the following resolutions." Then, when the petition of Butler was committed on 16 Jan., TJ struck out the last six words at the end of the opening paragraph of Dft and interlined the following: "and the petition of Zebulon Butler and others inhabitants within the territory late in dispute between the said states praying in like manner the institution of a court for determining their private right of soil, have agreed to the following resolutions." Thus amended, this paragraph was copied in MS. However, this still placed the emphasis upon Connecticut's request for a revision of the decree of the Court of Commissioners, with both Connecticut and the Wyoming inhabitants asking also for a court to try the private right of soil. When John Montgomery of Pennsylvania arrived in Congress on 22 Jan., he opposed the resolutions reported by TJ until the Connecticut delegates "moved for exsepunging that part of the report which referred to the exceptionable part of the letter [from Trumbull] and only insisted on the right of the petitioners, as that right was founded on the Articles of Confederation" (Burnett, *Letters of Members*, VII, No. 535). This change was made and the opening paragraph was altered in MS to read as it does in the second report (Document V) before the adoption of the amendment indicated in note 3 to that report. It is significant that this change was made not by Thomson but by TJ; this may suggest that it was the result of a consultation among TJ, Sherman, and Montgomery rather than (as Montgomery remembered six weeks later) a formal motion in Congress. If this conjecture is right, then the report was recommitted in order that TJ might enlarge it by inserting the date fixed for the appointment of the court and by drafting the form of the notice to the parties concerned, not in order to remove the part to which Montgomery objected; but see note 2 below.

Thomson's entry in Committee Book, PCC: No. 186, under 16 Jan. 1784 reads: "Petition of Zebulon Butler and others praying a court to be established for deciding the title to the lands on which they are settled between them and claimants under the state of Pensylvania." The reference of the letter of Trumbull and resolutions of Connecticut to a committee composed of the same persons (TJ, Lee, Williamson) was made on 13 Jan. (same), but Committee Book, PCC: No. 191 under date of 21 Jan. shows only that a report was handed in "On the pet. Zebulon Butler and others for a court to try the right of property," &c., a fact which further supports the hypothesis that TJ made the alteration noted above *before* the report was submitted to Congress.

The last word in this opening paragraph was changed from "report" to "resolutions" either before or after being submitted.

[2] This and the preceding seven paragraphs were evidently deleted by amendment in Congress, though MS shows a line drawn through the last three only. Article IX provided that a court to try the private right of soil could be granted to those claiming under different grants of two or more states, whose jurisdictions vis-à-vis the lands covered by such grants had been previously "adjusted"; hence, as TJ must have realized and as Montgomery specifically pointed out, the establishment of a court to try the private right of soil was the equivalent of a confirmation of the decree of the Court of Commissioners and therefore no such formal repudiation of the insinuations in the Connecticut resolutions was needed. But the deletion of these paragraphs and the recommitment of the report were obviously not the result of this legal technicality; they were necessary to gain the support of the Pennsylvania delegates, particularly John Montgomery, and they were probably necessary to accommodate various interests respecting western claims of the states. It is significant that, as finally adopted, the second report was completely silent on that part of Connect-

icut's resolutions concerning the Court of Commissioners of 1782 but left in suspense the question of Connecticut's assertion of a claim to lands westward of Pennsylvania. It is difficult to believe that this was not the result of some adjustment of views to which TJ was a party. For in his Dft of this report the part repudiating the Connecticut insinuations was even more vigorous than in the report as submitted. It read in part: ". . . till the 12th day of Nov. 1782 when the said court met, nothing like a surprize on either party can be supposed: that on a fair, full, and patient hearing of ⟨all⟩ the evidence and arguments of both parties and mature consideration of the said court from the said 12th. day of Nov. day by day without any omission to the 30th day of Dec. 1782 during the whole of which no improper biass or conduct in the judges or any of them is suggested, those judges were unanimous in their sentence: that ⟨*they were appointed regularly and agreeable to the said 9th Article of Confederation for which*⟩ the said 9th Article of Confederation declares that the sentence of such judges shall be final and conclusive, and that it is for the quiet of these states that such determinations should be final and conclusive. The sentence of the said judges ought not to be revised or disturbed."

[3] Dft reads "subjected."

V. Second Report on Petition of Zebulon Butler

[23 January 1784]

The Committee to whom were referred the petition of Zebulon Butler and others claiming under the state of Connecticut private right of soil within the territory Westward of the Delaware lately[1] in controversy between the said state and that of Pennsylvania,[2] complaining that they are disturbed in their said right by others claiming under the said state of Pennsylvania and praying that a court may be instituted under the 9th. article of the Confederation for determining the said rights: [also the resolutions of the General assembly of Connecticut and the letter and proclamation of Govr. Trumbul, desiring in like manner the institution of such a court; and further notifying that the said state of Connecticut claims jurisdiction over all the lands between Pennsylvania and the Missisipi from 41°. to 42°-2″ Northern latitude][3] have agreed to the following resolutions.

Resolved that a court be instituted according to the said ninth article of the Confederation for determining the private right of soil within the said territory so far as the same is by the said article submitted to the determination of such a court.[4]

That the 4th. Monday in June next be assigned for the appearance of the parties by their lawful agents before Congress or the Committee of the states wheresoever they shall be then sitting.

That notice of the assignment of the said day be given to the parties in the following form

To the claimants of the private right of soil within the territory Westward of the Delaware heretofore in controversy between the states of Connecticut and Pennsylvania and adjudged [to the latter by the sentence of a federal court pronounced at Trenton on the 30th. day of Decemb. 1782.]

It is hereby made known that sundry individuals claiming private right of soil under the state of Connecticut within the said territory have made application to Congress stating that they have been disturbed in their said right of soil by others claiming under the state of Pennsylvania and praying for the institution of a court for determining the said private right of soil in pursuance of the 9th. article of Confederation: and that the 4th. Monday in June next is assigned for the appearance of the parties by their lawful agents before Congress or a Committee of the states wheresoever they shall be then sitting to proceed in the premises as by the confederation is directed. By order of Congress. Charles Thomson Secretary.

Resolved that the said notice be transmitted by the Secretary to the Executives of the states of Connecticut and Pennsylvania with a request that they take proper measures for having the same on the parties interested under their states respectively.

The Committee having not had time to go through so much of the matters referred to them as relates to the claim of the said state of Connecticut to territory Westward of the state of Pennsylvania beg further time for that purpose.

MS (DLC: PCC, No. 19, I, 477-8); in TJ's hand except as indicated in notes below; endorsed by Thomson: "Report of Mr Jefferson Mr Lee Mr Williamson On the Memorial of Zebulon Butler and others. Entd. Read.

Passed Jany 23 1784." Printed in JCC, XXVI, 45-6, with variations as noted below. Dft of part in DLC as indicated in note 5 below.

[1] This word deleted and "formerly"

interlined in Thomson's hand in substitution therefor; the latter reading
appears in JCC.

² An amendment was offered in Congress to add at this point the following: "and lately determined by a court
constituted and appointed agreeably to
the 9 of the Articles of Confederation
and perpetual union, to be within the
jurisdiction of the state of Pensylvania"; this was interlined and put in
the margin of MS in the hand of Thomson; JCC agrees with the wording as
amended.

³ The words in square brackets (supplied) were deleted by amendment in
Congress; this sentence is shown as
deleted in JCC.

⁴ There is in DLC: TJ Papers, 11:
1892 a rough draft in TJ's hand of all
that follows this point. This passage,
with the important exception of the
final paragraph, is merely an addendum
to the first report fixing the date for
appointment of the court and stating
the form in which the notice was to be
given. The rough draft of this part of
the second report on the Butler petition is printed in Ford, III, 385-7, as if
it were an integral part of the first
report, the whole of which he designated as a "rough draft."

⁵ The words in square brackets (supplied) were deleted by amendment in
Congress and the following (not in
MS but printed in JCC) substituted
therefor: "by the sentence of a court
constituted and appointed agreeably to
the ninth of the Articles of Confederation and perpetual union, to be within
the jurisdiction of the State of Pensylvania." This amendment was obviously
made at the same time as that indicated above in note 2; hence, except for
an interlined "&ca." in Thomson's hand,
there was no need to repeat the full
amendment in the MS. There also was
apparently some objection to TJ's use
of the phrase "federal court" for in the
MS "federal" is struck out and "of
Commissioners" interlined in another
hand after "court"; this amendment is
confused by Ford, III, 385 as "a ⟨fed-
eral⟩ court ⟨of Pennsylva. &c.⟩"

VI. On the Settlement of Disputes between States by Judicial Means

[After June 1784]

The territory of Wioming which had been in dispute between
the states of Connecticut and Pennsylvania having been adjudged
to the latter by a court constituted according to the articles of
confederation, the individuals claiming the private right of soil
under the two states have in pursuance of the same articles asked
from Congress and obtained the appointment of a second federal
court to decide their individual rights.

A federal court is also granted by Congress to decide the claims
on the territory of Vermont which have been so long existing. This
territory is claimed by New Hampshire, Massachusets and New
York and also insists of itself to be adjudged to neither, but to be
erected into a separate state incorporated into the union.

Perhaps history[1] cannot produce such another proof of the
empire of reason and right in any part of the world as these new
states now exhibit. Other nations have only been able to submit
private contests to judiciary determination; but these new states
have gone further. They have set the example of binding a court

for the trial of nations, which submit to the decisions of that court as quietly as[2]

Thus we see these infant states, instead of leaving their national differences to be decided by the sword, the ultima ratio regum, instead of deluging the land with human blood and covering it with human misery upon honest difference of opinion, have by wise and just arrangements submitted the causes of Nations to be weighed in the scales of justice by a tribunal so constituted as to ensure the confidence of all parties and so supported by the rest of the[3] Union as to secure the execution of it's decisions.

MS (DLC: TJ Papers, 11: 1911); entirely in TJ's hand, with a number of deletions and interlineations, some of which are noted below; written on the first of four pages of a folded leaf on which there appears also the text of an article TJ wrote for the *Gazette de Leyde* in Nov. 1784. The present text appears to have been on the leaf before the *Gazette* article was written; hence it was evidently composed prior to 20 Nov. 1784 (see notes to TJ to Dumas, 20 Nov. 1784). It is certain that it was written after 3 June 1784. On 24 Apr. 1784 the New York delegates in Congress submitted the instructions of the New York legislature demanding that Congress make an immediate settlement of the long-standing dispute over the New Hampshire Grants (JCC, XXVI, 283-7). This representation was assigned the same day to a committee of which TJ was chairman and Roger Sherman was a member (PCC: No. 186). No report was made before TJ left Congress and he was obliged to entrust the "papers relating to Vermont" to Blanchard who succeeded him as chairman of the Grand Committee (TJ to Thomson, 21 May 1784). The committee was renewed on 17 May, and when a report was finally submitted on 29 May it was written by Sherman and carried the recommendation that Vermont be admitted to the union under the terms of the Northwest Ordinance (JCC, XXVII, 481-4, 532-6). This report was not approved, but on 3 June 1784, the last day of the session, Congress granted the petition of Massachusetts requesting that a federal court be set up to decide the dispute between that state and New York over the Vermont area (same, XXVII, 547-50). This court never came into existence, but it is clear that TJ could not have written the present text until after the court respecting Vermont had been authorized. He must have learned of this authorization while in Boston in June and, since this text bears the appearance of having been written for publication, he may have intended it for a Boston newspaper. It is more plausible to assume, however, that he wrote it soon after arriving in Europe and that it, like the other text on the same leaf, was aimed at a European audience. It is also possible that TJ intended it as a note to be inserted in *Notes on the State of Virginia*.

But the reflections embodied in these remarks may have been set down earlier. In the issue of the Phila. *Freeman's Journal* for 21 Jan. 1783 there appeared an introductory statement to a summarization of the respective claims of Pennsylvania and Connecticut published in this and subsequent issues. The substance and phraseology of this statement are so closely parallel to certain passages in the present document as to suggest that TJ must have read them and may indeed have been their author. TJ was then in Philadelphia, and Griffin, on his way back to Virginia, must have seen him and presented to him at that time the notes of arguments by Wilson and Johnson. It was at this time, too, that Robert R. Wilson wrote his famous letter to Lafayette commenting upon the significance of the Trenton decision (10 Jan. 1783; see editorial note above). Certainly the decision seems to have stirred the hopes of many leaders in the early days of 1783 and to have inspired renewed confidence in the Confederation. The introductory statement in the *Freeman's Journal* reads in part as follows: "Agreeable to our promise, we present our readers with a short but authentic abstract of the proceedings in the great cause lately decided between this state and Connecticut. . . . This celebrated cause . . . presents to the world a new and extraordinary spectacle: Two powerful and populous states, sovereign and independent (except as members of the federal Union) contending for a tract of country equal in extent to many, and superior to some European kingdoms. Instead of recurring to arms, the *ultima ratio* of kings and states, they submit to the arbitration of judges mutually chosen from indifferent states. The merits of their pretentions are examined by the rules of reason and judgment, framed upon the testimony of records and public documents. . . ." The parallel between these remarks and the present document is obvious; both have a Jeffersonian ring, and it is possible that, during the days that he was awaiting an opportunity to go to France in Jan. 1783, TJ may have written an early version of this memorandum for the editor of *Freeman's Journal*.

[1] This word interlined in substitution for "the world," deleted.

[2] This paragraph has a vertical line drawn through it, indicating—as does the incomplete sentence—that TJ intended to delete it. It is also evident that a break may have come after the word "binding," for the sentence as originally composed read in part: ". . . these new states . . . have been able to establish a court for the trial of nations," &c. This was then altered by the deletion of part but not all of the sentence, thus making it appear that "court" is the object of "binding" when, as originally phrased, it was the object of "establish."

[3] The preceding three words interlined in substitution for "whole," deleted. The emendation is a wry commentary on Connecticut's attitude toward the decision of the Court of Commissioners in the case of Pennsylvania v. Connecticut.

From the Rev. James Madison

DEAR SIR   Jany 22. 1784.

I did not receive your Favour of the 24h Decr. untill last post. I immediately looked out for a Thermometer and obtained one which appears very sensible as to Heat or Cold, tho' it is so constructed that I cannot ascertain the Accuracy of the Division by plunging it in boiling water; This appears of Consequence especially when we keep correspondent Observations. I shall observe the Time you mention, and send at present, as it may be some Gratification, on Account of the Severity of the Season my Morning Observations from the *16*h. untill this Date. Viz. *14*°. 16½. 26°. 38°. 18°. 18°, 25°. In order to observe the greatest Cold, I expose the Thermometer to the Night Air. It either stands out all Night, or lies in an open window. The remainder of the Day it is also as much exposed as it prudently can be, on Account of the Danger of meeting with some Accident—for it is borrowed. I Mention this, because, both ought to be treated in the same Manner. I wish we had [a] Barometer but there is no Possibility of getting one here at present. The British robbed me of my Thermometer and Barometer. We have sent to England and expect a Return by this Spring.

I am much obliged to you for your Goodness in communicating Accounts of such new Books as deserve attention. I have never seen Crawfords, nor indeed heard of it before. But will send for it by the first opportunity. His Theory appears to be altogether new and if well supported by Experiment will introduce philosophical Revolution in that Part of Physics. I think however that Hamilton in his ingenious Treatise on Vapours has led the way to this Doctrine but have not the Book by me to determine at present.

We have availed ourselves of the Informat[ion] you gave concerning the Encyclop. Meth: and have put a Bill of £50 11s. in the Hands of a Merchant so as to have what is already compleated, imported by Spring, and the remainder as soon as finished. I hope to have the best Edition for that Sum.

I think you have adopted an excellent, as well as a very short Method of confuting those Flimsy Theorists, as you justly call them, by sending both Rittenhouse and his Orrery. to Europe.

You have no Doubt observed the Comet which made its Appearance here last Friday Evening for the first Time. The Cloudiness of the Evenings prevented Observations till last Night and the Night before. Its Situation is near, i, in the Piscis Australis. I shall endeavour to trace it's Progress and will send you the Result.

Be pleased to continue your Favours, for which I am really much indebted, and beleive me to be with the greatest Regard Yr. Sevt. & Friend,   JAS MADISON

[Dr. Mc]Clurg, Mr. Bellini and Mr. [Wy]the desire to be affectionately remembered by[1] you.

I doubt whether you received any Answer from me the last Time you were to the Northward. I am no farther concerned, than as I wished to evince my Solicitude for a Continuance of similar Favors.

RC (DLC); MS torn on one margin; the missing words have been supplied from the text printed in WMQ, 2d ser., v (1925), p. 78-80; addressed to TJ at Annapolis; endorsed by TJ: "Madison Revd James."

Some months earlier, Madison's effort to borrow the state's copy of the ENCYCLOPEDIE METHODIQUE for the Virginia philosophical society (see VMHB, XXVI [1918], 308) had met with this response from Gov. Harrison: "I have great pleasure in accomodating your society with the lent of the Encyclopedie. It is at present at Mr. Jeffersons from whence it shall be brought immediately to this place and delivered to any careful person you shall please to appoint to carry it down" (Harrison to Madison, 27 Sep. 1783, Executive Letter Book, Vi).

[1] Thus in MS.

From St. John de Crèvecoeur

SIR   New York 23d. Jany. 1784

Encourag'd by Mr. Le Chevr. de Chastelux whom I Saw Lately in Paris; as well as by Several others French officers, who had the

Honor of Your acquaintance whilst on this Continent, I have been Led to hope you'd not refuse giving an answer to the Question I take the Liberty of Sending you—Give me leave to add that I am commanded to do so by the Minister who is at the head of the Nurseries Established throughout the Kingdom. It has been said in France that in Some of the remotest Settlements of Virginia or Carolina, Brandy has been distilled from Patatoes.

That this Root Contains a Spirit as Strong as that which is obtained from Grain is beyond a Doubt: but the Method of bringing it, in a State of Fermentation is what Puzzles the Learned Chymists, Spite of the Many Tryals they have Made. I shou'd be most Sincerely thankfull, If I cou'd be Informed of the American Méthod, through Your kind assistance. From the Respect with which I have heard Your Name mentioned as well as from your extensive Knowledge and Taste for the Arts and Sciences, I can't but hope you'll be Generous Enough to Communicate me Your thoughts on the Subject, which is More a Matter of Curiosity than of real or usefull Import. I am likewise Commanded to ask you whether the Map of Virginia undertaken by Subscription before the Révolution, has Ever been Engrav'd and where it may be had? Least this Shou'd Miscarry through the Imperfection of Américan Posts, it will be forwarded to you by his Excellency the Chevr. de la Luserne

I have the Honor to be with the Most Sincere Respect & Esteem Sir Your very Humble Servt.,

ST. JOHN
French Consul for the States of
N:Y: N:J: & Connecticut

RC (DLC).

St. John de Crèvecoeur was born in Caen, Normandy, in 1735; his baptismal name was Michel-Guillaume Jean de Crèvecoeur. After serving in the French army in Canada, he arrived in New York and was naturalized in 1765 under the name of John Hector St. John. His *Letters from an American Farmer* (London, 1782) also appeared under the name "J. Hector St. John." On his return to France in 1781-1783 he resumed the family name of Crèvecoeur and subsequently employed several different forms, including St. John, St. Jean de Crèvecoeur, and St. John de Crèvecoeur; American usage follows the form St. John de Crèvecoeur, as in the caption here (DAB; see also H. C. Rice, Jr., *Le cultivateur americain, etude sur l'oeuvre de Saint-John de Crèvecoeur*, Paris, 1933).

Motion to Obtain an Estimate of Current Expenses

[23 January 1784]

That it be an instruction to the Grand committee to prepare and report to Congress an estimate of current expences from the 1st. day of January 1784. to the 1st. day of Jan. 1785.

MS (DLC: PCC, No. 36, II); in TJ's hand.

On 23 Jan. 1784 (according to endorsement on the MS motion in the same volume of PCC), David Howell moved "That the report of 22d. October, 1783 [of Robert Morris, Superintendant of Finance, concerning the foreign and domestic debt of the United States and related matters; see JCC, XXV, 715-16] be referred to a Grand Committee to report a requisition on the States for the payment of interest on the national debt." Among the eleven members named to the Grand Committee was TJ; see JCC, XXVI, 48. Committee Book (DLC: PCC, No. 186)

lists the committee under date of 23 Jan., records the substance of Howell's motion, and contains the following notation: "To sit in the Congress room tomorrow at 10 oclock and proceed on the business"; following this—indicating that the present motion may possibly have been made 24 Jan. or later—is another notation: "The Committee instructed to prepare and report an estimate of current expences from 1 Jany 1784 to 1 Jany 1785"; the reference of this additional instruction was certainly made before 31 Jan. (see Joseph Carleton to TJ, 1 Feb. 1784). The Grand Committee reported on 22 Mch. 1784.

Virginia Delegates in Congress to Benjamin Harrison

SIR   Annapolis Jan 23. 1784

The inclosed papers from Oliver Pollock came to our hands a few days ago. Ignorance of the organization of our government probably led him to make this improper address, on a business so foreign to the line of our duty. We take the liberty, on his behalf, of inclosing them to your Excellency with a copy of our answer to him.

We have the honour to be with the most profound respect & esteem Your Excellencys Most obedient and most humble servants,

TH: JEFFERSON
ARTHUR LEE
JAS. MONROE
S: HARDY

RC (Vi); in TJ's hand, signed by the delegates; endorsed: "Letter from the Virga. Delegates in Congress enclosing one from Mr. Pollock. Jany 23 84." Enclosures: Oliver Pollock to the Virginia Delegates, 20 Nov. 1783 (Vi), q.v.; copy of Virginia Delegates to Pollock (Vi), following; and other unidentified papers.

Virginia Delegates in Congress to Oliver Pollock

Sir   Annapolis Jan 23. 1784

Your letter bearing date at the Havana Nov 20th. 1783 came to our hands a few days ago. The subject of it however is one of those submitted by the constitution of our state to it's Executive power, our duties being such only as respect the confederacy in general. We think it therefore the most likely means of promoting your wishes to inclose the letter with the papers accompanying it to his Excellency the Governor of Virginia which we will immediately do and have no doubt you will receive justice from the state on every well authenticated claim.

We have the honour to be with much respect Sir Your most obedt. & most humble servts.

Tr (Vi); entirely in TJ's hand, enclosed in the Virginia Delegates' letter to Benjamin Harrison, preceding.

Report of Committee on Letter of John Allen

[26 Jan. 1784]

The Committee to whom were referred the letter of John Allen of Dec. 25. 1783 to his Excellency the President of Congress and the papers therein inclosed have agreed to the following resolution.

Resolved that a copy of the said letter be sent to the Governor of Massachusets with a recommendation that he cause enquiry to be made whether the encroachments therein suggested have been actually made on the territories of the state of Massachusets by the subjects of his Britannic majesty from the government of Nova Scotia, and if he shall find any such to have been made, that he send a representation thereof to the British Governor of Nova Scotia with a copy of the Proclamation of the United states of the 14th. inst. (which should be inclosed to the Governor of Massachusets for that purpose) requesting him in a friendly manner and as a proof of that disposition for peace and harmony which should subsist between neighboring states to recall from off the said territory the said subjects of his Britannic majesty so found to have incroached thereon: and that the Governor of Massachusets be requested to inform Congress of his proceedings herein and the result thereof.

MS (DLC: PCC, No. 19, 1); entirely in TJ's hand, with minor deletions and corrections which have not been noted here; endorsed by Charles Thomson: "Report of Mr Jefferson Mr Osgood Mr Williamson On letter 25 Decr. John Allen Delivered 26 Jany Entd. Read Passed 29 Jany 1784."

On 21 Jan. 1784 a letter from John Allan, Boston, 25 Dec. 1783 (in DLC: PCC, No. 58), was read in Congress and referred to TJ, Osgood, and Williamson. According to the above endorsement and Committee Book (DLC: PCC, No. 186), the committee reported on 26 Jan., although there is no mention of the report in JCC under that date. The report was approved by Congress on 29 Jan. (JCC, XXVI, 41, note, 52; Allan's letter is in PCC, No. 58, f. 63).

From Benjamin Harrison

SIR   Council Chamber Jany 30th. 1784

Yesterdays post brought me your favors of the 31st. of last month and 17th. instant which are the only letters received from you for four weeks. The latter enclosing the ratification of the treaty gave me great pleasure as it removed many disagreeable apprehensions of consequences that might flow from its not reaching france by the stipulated time of exchange; if the packet can sail from new York at the expected time she will very probably be in port before the first of March as long passages are very uncommon at this Season of the year.

The weather here has been four weeks a few days excepted as severe as we have known for many years, and we have at present but little prospect of its growing better. The earth being covered with a very deep snow and the wind to the westward great damage has been done to the shiping in every part of the river, five sail of sea vessels that were at Rockets are driven by the ice up Gilly's creek very near the road and it is feared most of them will be lost and Overtons mill is totally destroyed, a few days quick thaw has given us these specimens of the mischeif ice assisted by a current is capable of doing and has filled the inhabitants of the lower town and Rockets with dreadful apprehensions of their houses being over whelmed by it if the weather should break up with another quick thaw.

My son Benjamin has offered to take the money the treasurer has for you and to give a bill for it on Philadelphia at ten days sight which you may be assured may be negotiated at Baltimore or perhaps in Annapolis. I have informed the treasurer of this and suppose he will accept the offer if he cannot find a better mode of doing it. If you and the other gentlemen in the delegation should approve of taking his bills in future at thirty days sight you may command them and I think it will be better than running a risk of being disappointed as you have hitherto been. I am &c.,   B. H.

FC (Vi); at head of text: "The honorable Mr. Jefferson."

From Edmund Randolph

DEAR SIR   Richmond Jany. 30. 1784.

Your friendly overture of a correspondence; altho' written on the 31st. Ulto., did not reach me before the last evening. I pledge myself for furnishing all the intelligence, which the barrenness of this place can supply, fit for your attention.

But for a late occurrence, the executive would languish for employment. A Mr. Geo. Hancock, a citizen of this commonwealth, assaulted and beat a Mr. Jonas Beard, a justice of the peace and member of the legislature, of So. Carolina. About a fortnight ago, the governor of that state, stimulated by the advice of his council, and the application of the chief justice of the general sessions, demanded his body from our governor, under the fourth article of the confederation; charging the assault to be a high misdemeanor. In support of this demand, the affidavit of Mr. Beard was also transmitted, stating the attack to be extravagantly violent, and to have been made "*during the sitting of the court of general sessions.*" Nothing farther was said, to induce a belief, that the injury took place, while Mr. Beard was in the actual exercise of his office of a justice of the peace: nor could I collect from the affidavit or any other communication, what affinity the judiciary system of So. C. had created between Mr. Beard, as a justice and the court of general sessions. Much less could I discover, that legislative privilege was in any manner violated by the assault. I was called upon officially on this occasion. At first sight it seemed difficult to determine, how far our executive ought to be convinced of Hancock's guilt before they could deliver him up. This scruple originated from the 76th. section of Vattel's 2d. book. But the quotation of a practice in Switzerland which deprives the canton, within whose reach an offender may be, from the right of investigating the offence, appeared insufficient to forbid Virginia to exercise her faculties. For that usage is the effect of mere conventional law, and the general law of nations by analogy holds a different language when it permits a state, from which compensation for damages is required, to judge on the propriety of paying them, instead of swallowing any gross quantum, imposed on it. Besides, Virginia and So. C. are as distinct from each other as France and G. Britain, except in the instances, provided for by the confederation. And surely that compact does not destroy the right of previous inquiry.

The next consideration was the definition of a high misdemeanor. But neither in vulgar import, nor in the construction of british law, according to 4th. Black:, is an ordinary assault so stiled. I say an ordinary assault; because not a syllable of the accusation advances the offence to the rank of a high misdemeanor. For "the sitting of the court of general sessions" may mean the term, not the being on the bench: Mr. Beard, tho' a justice of the peace might not be connected with that court: and the phlogiston of governor Guerard's temper, excited as it has been, would have produced expressions, far more decided and inflammatory against Hancock, if this circumstance of aggravation had existed. This criticism on the looseness of the impeachment ought to prevail, when the question is concerning the banishment of a citizen for trial to a foreign tribunal.

If a law of So. C. should proclaim every assault to be a high misdemeanor in the sense of an unequivocal attack on the state, what is to be hereafter done, upon the representation of such a law? I answer with hesitation; but I lean to an opinion, that Hancock ought to be surrendered, howsoever absurd such a law would be. For different states may vary in their policy; and the fourth article of the confederation indulges every state with its own ideas of safety. If Hancock had been apprehended within the limits of So. C., upon the supposition of such a law, he would have suffered as for a high misdemeanor, without the possibility of a murmur from Virginia. Ought his flight to rescue him from the punishment?

But on the other hand if what a state shall choose to call a high misdemeanor, is to rule, there is another desideratum in the information transmitted. Let the real circumstances as they may be in future disclosed even constitute the assault on Mr. Beard a high misdemeanour in common and british interpretation; yet as So. C. may change the nature of the crime, a law should be shewn, manifesting, that its nature is not changed.

I thought it adviseable to point out the mode of arresting the perpetrator of a high misdemeanor in another state, lest the executive should hold sentiments, contrary to mine. In this I was embarrassed. The old act of citizenship repeats the passage of the confederation on this subject. The new act omits it, on purpose to avoid throwing a doubt on the validity of the other parts, not re-enacted. But this omission did not hinder me from viewing the confederation, as a law, howsoever cloathed in the garb of a compact.

My perplexity arose from not knowing, whether the executive should issue a warrant, or a common magistrate. For that this law must be executed, admitted not a doubt; nor yet could it be denied, that the granting of a power by law involves all incidents, necessary for its execution. I therefore recommended, that the executive should in these cases announce that the demand had been made in due form, and require the peace officers to take proper measures for arresting the culprit.

This is the short state of Mr. Hancock's perils. You will perceive that I have paid no attention to another part of the fourth article, respecting full faith and credit &c. I passed it by, as relating to a matter of another sort.

By the severity of the winter our river has been blocked up for some time. The ice came down the other day in such a body as to destroy Overton's mill to its very foundation, and transport five vessels, consisting of brigs and scows, which were lying at Rocket's a considerable distance up the meadow. It was not originally a solid body: but at present appears to be so from the consolidation of several broken pieces drifted from above the falls. The river is again choaked to a more formidable degree: and no underwriter would venture to insure Mr. Mitchell's new house, or Blakey's mill. You know the situation of both.

Can you accommodate me with the Journal of congress for 1782 and 1783.

This letter being already extended beyond my first design, I shall only add, that I am, with the sincerest regard Dr Sir Yr. friend & serv.,   EDM: RANDOLPH.

RC (DLC).

TJ's letter WRITTEN ON THE 31ST. ULTO. was recorded in SJL under date of 30 Dec. 1783, but has not been found. Whether Randolph changed his opinion THAT HANCOCK OUGHT TO BE SURRENDERED or whether he was overruled by the Executive is not known, but the fact is that the Council came to the following decision: "After maturely considering the spirit of the Confederation, and the claim for protection which each individual has on that community of which he is a member—The Board are of Opinion that the act of Confederation does not require, and therefore that the Laws and fundamental principles of the Government of Virginia do not authorize the delivery of a citizen of the State to any power without the same in such cases as his Excellency the Governor of South Carolina has stated this to be. And the Governor is advised not to comply with the requisition for the delivery of the said George Hancock" (MS Va. Council Jour., Vi; 16 Feb. 1784). Article IV of the Articles of Confederation provided that any person guilty of or charged with "treason, felony, or other high misdemeanor" who should flee to another state should, on demand of the governor or executive power from which he fled, "be delivered up and removed to the State having jurisdiction of his offence." The corresponding section of the Federal Constitution was altered to read "treason, felony, or other crime," but in 1861 the United States Supreme Court decided that the word "crime" included every offense forbidden and made punishable by the laws of the state where the offense was committed (Corwin, *The Constitution and What It Means Today*, 1946, p. 133).

Report on the Powers of the Committee of the States

[30 Jan.—ca. 29 Apr. 1784]

EDITORIAL NOTE

In his Autobiography Jefferson gave the following account of the steps leading to the creation of a Committee of the States: "The remissness of Congress, and their permanent session, began to be a subject of uneasiness and even some of the legislatures had recommended to them intermissions, and periodical sessions. As the Confederation had made no provision for a visible head of the government during vacations of Congress, and such a one was necessary to superintend the executive business, to receive and communicate with foreign ministers and nations, and to assemble Congress on sudden and extraordinary emergencies, I proposed early in April the appointment of a committee to be called the Committee of the states, to consist of a member from each state, who should remain in session during the recess of Congress: that the functions of Congress should be divided into Executive and Legislative, the latter to be reserved, and the former, by a general resolution to be delegated to that Committee. This proposition was agreed to; a Committee appointed, who entered on duty on the subsequent adjournment of Congress, quarrelled very soon, split into two parties, abandoned their post, and left the government without any visible head until the next meeting of Congress" (Ford, I, 75-6). This statement is erroneous as to the date and origin of the Committee of the States. It misled Ford into supposing that an amendment offered by Jefferson on 14 Apr. 1784, when an acrimonious debate on the place to which Congress should adjourn occurred, was the proposal referred to in the autobiographical account. But that amendment, which was lost with the motion which it sought to qualify, was merely a proviso that "a committee of the states shall have been . . . constituted" prior to adjournment of Congress (JCC, XXVI, 226). Yet the substance of the proposal as described by Jefferson in the Autobiography is doubtless correct. Further, it provides the only "text" available of the motion made by Jefferson concerning the Committee of the States. As will appear below, this motion was not made in April, but probably on 23 Jan. 1784. Even so, it was far from being the origin of the idea of a committee of the states, as the passage in the Autobiography would seem to indicate.

[516]

Actually Jefferson's connection with such an idea began with his appointment on 13 Dec. 1775 to a committee to draft instructions for the guidance of a committee to sit during the recess of Congress. He drafted the report of that committee on 15 Dec. 1775 (see Vol. 1: 272-3). Although this report of 1775 was not acted upon as such, it was made available to the committee authorized to draft the Articles of Confederation. Thus it became in substance Article XIX of the Articles of Confederation as prepared by John Dickinson and as presented to Congress on 12 July 1776 (JCC, V, 553-4). This relationship between Jefferson's report of 1775 and the corresponding part of Dickinson's draft is not noted above (Vol. 1: 273), where it is also erroneously implied that no action was taken on the report because "Congress did not adjourn for the holiday." The instructions drawn up in 1775 to guide a committee during recess of Congress were, of course, designed to apply to all interims between sessions, not merely to a particular holiday recess. It is important to make this correction and to note the relationship of Jefferson's report of 1775 to the Articles of Confederation since it has been assumed that the rudiments of an executive agency originated with the Dickinson draft.

Indeed, Franklin's proposed Articles of Confederation of 1775 had provided for an "executive council" to be appointed by Congress. Franklin intended this council "in the Recess of the Congress . . . to execute what shall have been enjoined thereby, to manage the general Continental business and interests, to receive applications from foreign countries, to prepare matters for the consideration of the Congress; to fill up pro tempore Continental offices that fall vacant; and to draw on the general Treasurer for such monies as may be necessary for general services and appropriated by the congress to such services" (see Vol. 1: 178). Franklin's delegation of executive powers to the council was obviously employed by Jefferson in drawing up his report of 1775, though the latter report was not only greatly enlarged, but more specific and more detailed in its definition of powers to be employed by the interim body. In the same manner that he had used Franklin's draft, so his report of 1775 was employed by Dickinson, for Article XIX of the Dickinson draft was in many respects a verbatim copy of Jefferson's 1775 report. With one exception, it did not in any important respect go beyond the limits of executive power sought for the committee by Jefferson in 1775. This exception was that which would have granted power "To superintend and controul or suspend all Officers civil and military, acting under the Authority of the United States." In some respects—such as the provisions impowering the interim committee to raise recruits, to direct the keeping and accommodation of prisoners of war, and to take charge of all military stores and procure such others "as may probably be wanted"—the Jefferson report went much further in delegating executive power than did the Dickinson draft. Moreover, the Dickinson draft specifically prohibited the making of "any Engagements that shall be binding on the United States," a severe limitation on the executive power that Jefferson's report of 1775 did not propose.

In the Dickinson draft of the Articles of Confederation the interim committee contemplated by Jefferson's report of 1775 became a Council of State. However, there is no basis for the assumption that this "Council of State was apparently designed as the beginning of an executive organization, a permanent bureaucratic staff of the central government . . . to be appointed annually and . . . to be a permanent body functioning whether Congress was in session or not" (Jensen, *The Articles of Confederation*, 178). On the contrary, Article xviii of the Dickinson draft provided that "The United States assembled shall have the sole and exclusive Right and Power of . . . Appointing a Council of State, and such Committees and civil Officers as may be necessary for managing the general Affairs of the United States, under their Direction while assembled, and in their Recess, of the Council of State" (JCC, v, 550-1). This, together with the nature of the powers delegated in Article xix to the Council of State, clearly meant that the Council was to function only in the interim between sessions of Congress. The corresponding passage in the Articles as finally approved made it unmistakable that this was the intent, for Congress was given authority "to appoint a committee to sit in the recess of Congress, to be denominated 'a Committee of the States,' and to consist of one delegate from each State, and to appoint such other committees and civil officers as may be necessary for managing the general affairs of the United States" (JCC, ix, 919-20). But Jefferson's detailed statement of executive powers to be delegated to the interim body, as adapted in the Dickinson draft, was deleted from the Articles. Instead, Article x merely provided in general terms that "The committee of the States, or any nine of them, shall be authorized to execute, in the recess of Congress, such of the powers of Congress as the United States, in Congress assembled, by the consent of nine states, shall, from time to time, think expedient to vest them with; provided, that no power be delegated to the said committee, for the exercise of which, by the articles of confederation, the voice of nine states, in the Congress of the United States assembled, is requisite" (same, ix, 923-4).

With the coming of peace, the question of establishing a "visible head of the government during vacations of Congress" became a matter of some urgency. This meant that the general terms of the grant and limitation of powers of a committee of the states as set forth in Article x would have to be defined, and a committee headed by James Duane of New York was appointed "to consider and devise the Powers with which a Committee of the States shall be vested during a Recess of Congress." This committee reported at Princeton on 17 Sep. 1783, but its report did little more than beg the question. It merely recommended that the committee to be appointed should be authorized "to perform and exercise, in the Recess of Congress, all such Powers and Duties as may be lawfully exercised by the United States in Congress assembled," except, of course, those powers that Congress was forbidden by Article x to delegate (PCC: No. 23; the report is in the hand of James Duane and is printed in JCC, xxvi, 47). This meant that the Committee of the States would have those executive powers possessed by Congress that did not require the vote of nine states and that Duane's committee "devised" for the Committee of the States merely those powers not prohibited by Article x. Still Congress failed to act by appointing a Committee of the States in pursuance of the authority granted in Article IX, and in the interim of five weeks between the sessions at Princeton and Annapolis there was no "visible head of government."

This obviously disturbed Jefferson and he was determined if possible to prevent its recurrence in future. Even with respect to the constitution from which Congress derived its own authority, Jefferson thought "There should be no vague terms in an instrument of this kind. It's objects should be precisely and determinately fixed" (Vol. 1: 181, note 5). He must therefore have viewed with some concern the rejection of his detailed recommendations of 1775 from the final text of the Articles of Confederation, and he must equally have opposed a general delegation of authority to the Committee of the States as contemplated in the Duane report. On 23 Jan. 1784 that report "and a motion of Mr. Jefferson thereon" were referred to a committee composed of Jefferson, Osgood, and Sherman (Committee Book, PCC: No. 186; also, endorsement by Thomson on report of the Duane committee, showing that it was read 17 Sep. 1783 and referred to the committee of three on 23 Jan. 1784; see also the opening paragraph of Documents II and III). From this it is clear that Jefferson introduced a motion to appoint a committee of the states and define its powers. This motion, very probably, was substantially what he described it to be in his Autobiography: "that the functions of Congress should be divided into Executive and Legislative, the latter to be reserved, and the former, by a general resolution to be delegated to that Committee." Since it was customary with motions requiring reference to commit and, where necessary, to appoint the committee on the day of the motion, it is probable that Jefferson's motion, which he erroneously fixed as "early in April," must have been made on 23 Jan. 1784.

Document I in the present series is a further and explicit categorization of the powers of the committee within the limits imposed by Article X, and must have been drawn up about the time that Jefferson made his motion. Document II represents a more precise and a more extensive delegation of executive power than Jefferson had proposed in 1775. In addition to this it contained a resolution governing the procedure to be observed by the Committee of States. But the report as finally submitted on 30 Jan. 1784 (Document III) was just the reverse of the delegation of authority contemplated in Document II—instead of listing in detail the things that the Committee of the States might do and stating in general terms what it could not do, Document III listed in detail the matters prohibited and stated in general terms what the Committee was authorized to do. In this sense it was a return to the general delegation of authority contemplated in the Duane report.

There is no way to determine the exact chronological sequence of Documents I, II, and III or the causes that gave rise to them; indeed, Ford prints this entire sequence as if it were a single document, Document IV being included as a part of Documents I and II and Document III being printed separately only as a report derived from the "draft" comprising the others (Ford, III, 388-93). Burnett, *Letters of Members*, VII, No. 499, note 4, follows Ford and comments: "The document is of especial interest as showing the development of Jefferson's thought on the subject, but it does not appear to have been presented to Congress in that form." This, except for regarding the various items as a single document, is correct, but Jefferson's thought on this important matter of delegation by Congress of executive power cannot be adequately understood except by a proper separation of the texts and a tracing of their legislative history. Owing to the inadequacy of the Journals and to the absence of committee records, this must be done largely by inference and conjecture.

The first three documents in the present sequence were written, it is obvious, before 30 Jan. 1784 and may have been presented by Jefferson to Osgood and Sherman in the order here printed. Or Document II may have preceded the others. Or Jefferson may have made the analysis represented by Document I and then, at the same time, have drawn up and laid before the committee both Documents II and III as alternative choices. But the most plausible interpretation is that the variety of documents here presented represents the result of a conflict within the committee. If this is the correct interpretation, Document II probably represents Jefferson's own thinking on the subject and the draft of a proposed report that he laid before his colleagues. Finding them opposed —and the evidence would indicate Sherman was particularly so—he then set forth in a detailed analysis the two approaches to the problem as indicated in Document I. The committee chose the course reflected in Document III, and reported the resolutions it contained on 30 Jan. 1784.

This, admittedly, is conjectural, but there are weighty reasons in its support. First, Document II is substantially a derivative of Jefferson's report of 1775. Second, Document III is closer to the Duane report than to the report of 1775, which in turn is close to the generalities of Article X that Jefferson objected to. Finally, when the report of 30 Jan. came up for debate on 26 Apr., an effort to amend the resolutions was made that seems to indicate Jefferson's hand and his dissatisfaction with the report. There were minor amendments to the report (as pointed out in the textual notes to Document III), but the following passages which appear deleted in the Journals on 26 Apr. and are not present in any form in the MS report show a further elaboration of the division of the powers of the Committee of the States into categories:

"II. That they be excluded by Congress from the powers of sending ambassadors, ministers, envoys residents or consuls, establishing rules for deciding what captures on land or water shall be legal and in what manner prizes taken by land or naval forces in the service of the United States shall be divided or appropriated; appointing courts for the trial of piracies and felonies committed on the high seas; establishing courts for receiving and determining finally appeals in cases of captures; instituting courts for deciding disputes and differences arising between two or more states; changing the rate of postage on the papers passing through the post offices established by Congress.

"III. That the said committee exercise the following powers as permitted by the Confederation: of directing the determination of controversies concerning the private right of soil in the cases and according to the mode pointed out by the 9th Article of Confederation; regulating the trade and managing all affairs with the Indians not members of any of the states; regulating the post offices from one State to another throughout all the United States; appointing officers of the land forces in the service of the United States excepting regimental officers; appointing officers of the naval forces; commissioning all officers whatever in the service of the United States; making rules for the government and regulation of the said land and naval forces not inconsistent with the articles of war established by Congress; directing the operations of the said land and naval forces; building, buying and equipping vessels previously agreed by Congress to be built, bought and equipped; and making requisitions from the states for their quotas of men and money proportioned on them by Congress.

"IV. That the said committee exercise also the following powers which are neither expressly given nor refused them by the Confederation, viz: of convoking Congress at an earlier day than that to which they shall stand adjourned, if the public exigencies shall in their opinion require it; superintending all offices appertaining to the United States; supplying all vacancies by new appointments to continue in force only until Congress shall make final appointments; directing and controuling the application of money in the detail according to the general appropriation previously made by Congress; and executing in general the resolutions, orders and ordinances of Congress" (JCC, XXVI, 289-90; see also note 4 to Document III).

These deleted passages were no doubt offered from the floor as an amendment to the committee's reported resolution (see note to Document III). That they represent Jefferson's motion is a conjecture made extremely plausible by the fact that the powers represented in paragraph "IV" as "neither expressly given nor refused . . . by the Confederation" are drawn principally from Jefferson's report of 1775, the first being copied almost verbatim (see Vol. 1: 273). That they were rejected by Congress as they had been by the committee is plainly indicated by their deletion in the Journals.

The debate on the report on 26 Apr. was complicated by Howell's motion of that day to adjourn on 3 June to meet again at Trenton on 30 Oct. and "that a committee of the states shall be appointed to sit in the recess of Congress" (JCC, XXVI, 287-8). McHenry moved to postpone the consideration of Howell's motion in order to take up the report of 30 Jan. This was defeated by a strictly sectional vote, the seven northern states voting solidly against McHenry's motion and the four southern states voting solidly in favor of it (JCC, XXVI, 291). Williamson then moved to amend Howell's motion by adding to it the following: "provided a committee of the states shall first have been appointed to sit in the recess of Congress, and the powers defined with which the said committee shall be vested, according to the tenth of the Articles of Confederation." Again the motion was defeated by a solid sectional vote, Jefferson voting in favor both times. Another motion offered Annapolis as a compromise federal town, but the previous question being called for, Howell's motion prevailed; Jefferson's affirmative vote was one of the two that were cast by delegates from states south of Pennsylvania

(JCC, XXVI, 291; Lord, *Atlas of Congressional Roll Call*, 1943, I, C1134, C1135, C1138).

It was probably about this time that Jefferson endeavored to add to the powers and responsibilities of the Committee of the States by drawing up Document IV of this series. This additional instruction was certainly drawn up after the committee report of 30 Jan. 1784 and before the debates of 26 Apr., for on that same day Jefferson sent a MS of his notes on the establishment of a money unit and a system of coinage for the United States to Robert Morris (TJ to Morris, 26 Apr. 1784 and notes there). But there is no evidence to indicate that this proposed instruction was formally brought before Congress. It probably was not; certainly it was not adopted. The report of 30 Jan. was called for on 27 May and debated fruitlessly; it was again brought up on 29 May and amended in several particulars (see notes to Document III). These alterations restored most of the additions embraced in what was apparently Jefferson's amendment of 26 Apr. Thus amended, the report was finally adopted and a Committee of the States appointed on 29 May 1784 (JCC, XXVII, 474-7).

"The powers of the committee," wrote James Monroe, "are confind so that no injury can be effected. Sherman and Dana will necessarily govern it" (Monroe to TJ, 1 June 1784). The remark possibly gives a clue to the difficulties that Jefferson experienced in his efforts to enlarge the executive powers of the Committee of the States, for Roger Sherman was more distrustful of executive power than most. Even in 1787 in the framing of a federal constitution based squarely upon the doctrine of the separation of powers, he looked upon the "Executive Magistracy as nothing more than an institution for carrying the will of the legislature into effect, and that the person or persons ought to be appointed by and accountable to the legislature only, which was the supreme will of the Society" (Farrand, *Records of the Federal Convention*, I, 65). In 1784 there was no question or possibility of introducing the principle of separation of powers, but Jefferson sought to establish a visible head of government, to enlarge its powers, and, as all evidence indicates, to grant it even that measure of executive authority lying in the undefined twilight zone between what was expressly granted and what was expressly denied by the Articles of Confederation. This was obviously far beyond what Roger Sherman would have approved. It was more than any other member advocated and more than Congress granted. Thus in 1775 and again in 1784 Jefferson fully earned the comment of a careful historian: "It was chiefly through Jefferson's perseverance that the vital need of preserving a visible head of the federal government eventually won the support of a majority in Congress" (Burnett, *The Continental Congress*, 1941, p. 607). But the effort was futile, and during the summer of 1784 the Committee of the States was distinguished by what Thomson called "this invisibility of a fœderal head" (Thomson to TJ, 1 Oct. 1784).

I. Categories of Powers Appropriate to the Committee of the States

Powers from which the Committee of the States are excluded
    Engaging in war
    Granting letters of Marque in time of peace
    Entering into treaties or alliances
    Coining money
    Regulating it's value
    Ascertaining sums necessary for defence or welfare
    Emitting bills
    Borrowing money
    Appropriating money
    Agreeing on number of vessels of war or number of land or sea forces
    Appointing Commander in chief of army or navy

Powers from which they should be excluded
    Sending and receiving Ambassadors
    Establishing rules of decision in cases of captures
    Establishing courts of Appeals in cases of captures
    Deciding disputes between states
    Fixing standard of weights and measures

Powers which they may exercise
    Appointing courts for trial of piracies[1]
    Deciding private rights of soil after decision of the General right
    Regulating Indian trade
    Regulating post office
    Appointing military officers and commissioning them
    Making rules for government of forces
    Directing operations of forces
    Build, buy or equip vessels agreed on by Congress
    Make requisitions on the states for quotas of men

Powers which should be given them
    To Execute whatever Congress has determined on
    To Superintend all the offices
    To apply Definite sums of money to Definite purposes
        e.g. expresses, fuel, paper and other contingencies
    To Supply all vacant offices till meeting of Congress
    To convoke Congress

MS (DLC); entirely in TJ's hand.

1 The first two words of this line have a line drawn through them, indicating possibly that the entire line was intended to be deleted. If this was the intent, then it would suggest that the present document was drawn up in advance of Document II in this series, since the permissible powers listed there do not include "Appointing courts for trial of piracies" and do parallel in sequence the powers named under this and the following category.

II. Proposed Report on Powers of the Committee of the States

[30 January 1784]

The Committee to whom was referred a report on the powers with which [a committee]¹ of the states should be vested during the recess of Congress and a Motion on the same subject have agreed to the following resolutions.

Resolved that the Committee of the states which shall be appointed pursuant to the 9th. article of Confederation to sit in the recess of Congress for conducting the business of the United states shall be invested with the powers of directing the determination of controversies concerning the private right of soil in the cases and according to the mode pointed out by the 9th. article of the Confederation:

regulating the trade and managing all affairs with the Indians not members of any of the states.

regulating the post offices from one state to another throughout all the United states:

appointing officers of the land forces in the service of the United states, except only the commander in chief and regimental officers:

appointing the officers of the naval forces

commissioning all officers whatever in the service of the United states:

making rules for the government and regulation of the said land and naval forces, not inconsistent with the articles of war established by Congress:

directing the operations of the said land and naval forces:

building, buying and equipping vessels previously agreed by Congress to be built, bought and equipped:

making requisitions from the states for their quotas of men and money proportioned on them by Congress:

superintending all offices appurtaining to the United states

directing and controuling the application of money in the detail according to the general appropriation previously made by Congress:

supplying all vacancies by new appointments to continue in force only untill Congress shall make the final appointments:

executing in general the resolutions, orders, and Ordinances of Congress:

[convoking] Congress at an earlier day than that to which they shall stand ad[jour]ned, if the public exigencies shall in their opinion require it:

[Provided] that in none of these instances they repeal or contravene any Ordinance passed by Congress

Resolved that nine members shall be requisite to proceed to business: and that no question, except for adjourning from day to day, shall be determined without the concurrence of seven votes:

that the President of Congress if a member of the said Committee and if not a member, or if absent at any time, then a Chairman to be chosen by themselves shall preside; the President or chairman retaining a right to vote:

that the Secretary and other officers of Congress shall attend on the said Committee

that they shall keep an accurate journal of their proceedings to be laid before Congress:

and that in these journals shall be entered the yeas and nays of the members when any one of them shall have desired it before the question be put.

MS (DLC); entirely in TJ's hand. This is a fair copy and contains only one minor deletion.

III. Report on Powers to be Granted the Committee of the States

[30 Jan. 1784]

The Committee to whom was referred a report on the powers with which a Committee of the states should be vested during the recess of Congress and a motion on the same subject have agreed to the following resolutions.

Resolved that the Committee of the states which shall be appointed pursuant to the 9th. article of Confederation and perpetual union to sit in the recess of Congress for transacting the business of the United states shall possess all the powers which may be exercised by seven states in Congress assembled: except those of Sending Ambassadors, ministers, envoys, residents or consuls:[1]

Establishing rules for deciding what captures on land or water shall be legal and in what manner prizes taken by land or naval forces in the service of the United states shall be divided or appropriated:

Establishing courts for receiving and determining finally appeals in cases of capture:

Constituting courts for deciding disputes and differences arising between two or more states:

Fixing the standard of weight and measures for the United states:

Changing the rate of postage on the papers passing through the post offices established by Congress

and generally[2] of repealing or contravening any Ordinance[3] passed by Congress.[4]

Resolved that nine members shall be requisite to proceed to business.[5]

 that no question except for adjourning from day to day shall be determined without the concurrence of seven[6] votes:

 that [the said President of Congress if a member of the said Committee and if not a member, or if absent at any time then][7] a chairman to be chosen by themselves[8] shall preside; the President or chairman retaining a right to vote:[9]

 that the Secretary and other[10] officers of Congress[11] shall attend on the said Committee:

 that they shall keep an accurate journal[12] of their proceedings to be laid before Congress:

 and that in these journals[13] shall be entered the yeas and nays of the members when any one of them shall have desired it before the question be put.[14]

MS (DLC: PCC); entirely in TJ's hand except as noted below; endorsed by Thomson: "No. 33. Report Mr Jefferson Mr Osgood Mr Sherman On powers of a comee of the states in recess of Congress. Delivered 30 Jany. 1784. Entd. Read. May 27 postponed to 29 May. [and in a clerk's hand:] Pass'd May 29 1784."

It is not possible to tell positively whether the amendments indicated in the notes below were made on 26 Apr., 27 May, or 29 May. It is very likely, however, that only the deletion indicated in note 2 and the attempted addition set forth in note 4 were made on the first date. Except for the introductory paragraph and the deletion shown in note 2, the report as entered in the Journals under 26 Apr. 1784 agrees precisely with the MS report as drawn by TJ before any deletions or additions occurred (JCC, XXVI, 288-9). As recorded in the Journals under 29 May, the report shows all of the amendments noted below except those set forth in notes 2 and 4.

[1] This was amended by deletion and interlineation in the hand of Gerry to read: ". . . residents consuls or Agents to foreign Countries of Courts."

[2] This word deleted by being scored out. It was deleted before report was

incorporated in Journals under 26 Apr., but marking is similar to that usually employed by Thomson; hence deletion must have been made after the committee handed in its report. This is the only respect (except for the omission of the introductory paragraph) in which MS as drawn by TJ differed from the body of report as recorded in Journals under 26 Apr.

3 This was amended by interlineation in the hand of Gerry to read: ". . . Ordinance or Act."

4 Following this point in the Journals for 26 Apr. are the deleted paragraphs numbered II-IV as quoted above in the editorial note; there was also an incomplete fifth paragraph in this deletion reading as follows: "V. That no question except for adjourning from day to day shall be determined in the said committee without the concurrence" (all of these paragraphs are entered in MS Domestic Journal in the hand of a clerk; JCC, XXVI, 289-90). For reasons suggested above, the editors incline to the opinion that these numbered paragraphs were offered by TJ as an amendment to the committee report and in substitution for that part of the report beginning with the words "except those of Sending Ambassadors . . ." and ending with ". . . any Ordinance passed by Congress." Both the form and the nature of these substitute paragraphs suggest that there must have been an accompanying MS from which the Journal entry was made, but no such MS amendment has been found in PCC and it is not a part of the MS report in PCC: No. 23, p. 169-70, which consists of a single leaf.

Also at this point there is a crossed circle on the MS indicating that another amendment was offered. This amendment, having a corresponding symbol, is in PCC: No. 23, p. 167. It is in the hand of Gerry and appears also in the Journals under 29 May. It reads as follows: "or appointing civil or military officers, unless to supply the places of such within the United States as the Committee may suspend for malconduct, or to fill up vacancies which may hereafter happen, by death, resignation, or otherways, within the said states; provided such appointments shall not continue ⟨after the recess of Congress, unless confirmed by them at their next meeting,⟩ more than one month after the assembling of Congress in November next, unless confirmed by them."

5 This sentence deleted in MS, except for word "Resolved."

6 Amended by deletion and interlineation in an unidentified hand to read "Nine." TJ apparently overlooked the fact that the Articles of Confederation stipulated that "The committee of the states, or any nine of them" should exercise whatever powers should be delegated (Article X; italics supplied).

7 Words in square brackets (supplied) deleted.

8 Amended by deletion and interlineation in the hand of Gerry to read: ". . . chosen by the Committee."

9 Preceding nine words deleted.

10 Preceding three words deleted.

11 Amended by interlineation in the hand of Gerry to read: ". . . officers of Congress when required."

12 Amended by deletion and interlineation in the hand of Gerry to read: "that the Committee shall keep a journal."

13 The following words interlined at this point in the hand of Gerry: "which shall be published Monthly, and transmitted to the Executives of the several States."

14 Following this point several amendments were offered and are recorded in the Journals on 29 May. One of them, offered by David Howell, provided that a state might be represented on the Committee of the States by "any one of the delegates of such State or states, and the members of the delegation of any State may relieve each other, in such manner as may be agreed on by themselves, or directed by their State" (see Monroe to TJ, 1 June 1784 for a comment on this). Another, submitted by Hugh Williamson, restored that part of TJ's report (Document II) which gave the Committee the right to convoke Congress prior to the date stipulated in the event "any unexpected and very important business occurs." Another, by Monroe, also restored that part of TJ's report giving the Committee the right to receive communications from foreign ministers, but this was amended by the addition of the proviso that the Committee could transact no business with them unless authorized by "particular acts of Congress." Another, offered by Gerry, may have been inspired in part by TJ's proposed instruction to the Committee to prepare an ordinance on a money unit and coinage, for it authorized and instructed the Committee to prepare an ordinance "for making the necessary arrangements of

the treasury, and for more particularly defining the powers of the Board of Treasury, and also to revise the institutions of the Office for Foreign Affairs." To this was added, by amendment offered by Howell, the requirement that the War Office be included in the "revisions" necessary (JCC, XXVII, 476-7).

IV. An Additional Instruction to the Committee of the States

[ca. 29 Apr. 1784]

That[1] the Committee of the states be authorized and instructed

To appoint proper persons to enquire into the quality of pure silver in[2] the Spanish milled dollars of different dates in circulation with us from the best assays which have been made.[3]

To enquire[4] in like manner into the fineness of all other the coins which may be found in circulation within these states.

To report to the Committee the result of these enquiries[5] by them to be laid before Congress.

To appoint also proper persons to enquire what are the proportions between the values of fine gold and fine silver at the markets of the several countries with which we are or probably may be connected in commerce, and what would be a proper proportion here, having regard to the average of their values at those markets and to other circumstances, and to report the same to the Committee by them to be laid before Congress.

To prepare an Ordinance for establishing the Unit of money within these states, for subdividing it, and for striking coins of gold, silver and copper on the following principles.

That the money Unit of these states shall be equal in value to a Spanish milled dollar containing so much fine silver as the enquiry[6] before directed shall shew to be contained on an average in dollars of the several dates in circulation with us.

That the Unit shall be divided into fractions decimally expressed.[7]

That there shall be a coin of silver of the value of an Unit.

> one other of the same metal of the value of one tenth of an Unit.
> one other of copper of the value of the Hundreth of an Unit.

That there shall be a coin of gold of the value of ten Units, according to the report before directed and the judgment of the committee thereon.

That for the convenience of paiment there shall also be a gold coin of 5. units, and silver coins of ½, ²⁄₁₀ and ⁵⁄₁₀₀ of a [unit].[8]

That the alloy of the said coins of gold and silver shall be equal in weight to one eleventh part of the fine metal.

That there be proper devices for these coins.

That measures be proposed for preventing their diminution and also their currency and that of any others when diminished.

That the several foreign coins be described and classed in the said Ordinance, the fineness of each class stated and it's value by weight estimated in Units and fractions of Units decimally expressed.[9] And that the said draught of an ordinance be reported to Congress at their next meeting for their consideration and determination.

MS (DLC); entirely in TJ's hand; written on verso of an undated invitation from Hardy and Mercer to TJ and Monroe (see at end of Apr. 1784).

While not dated, it is clear that this proposed separate instruction to the Committee of the States was written before 26 Apr. 1784 when TJ enclosed his notes on the establishment of a money unit and coinage system in his letter of that date to Robert Morris. The present text is, except for the alterations noted below, an exact copy of the corresponding part of the notes sent to Morris. These alterations were made *after* TJ had received Morris' reply, as the following comment in an addendum to the notes on a money unit makes clear: "He [Morris] also informs me that the several coins in circulation among us have been already assayed with accuracy, and the result published in a work on that subject. The assay of Sir Isaac Newton had superseded, in my mind, the necessity of this operation as to the older coins which were the subject of his examination. This later work with equal reason may be considered as saving the same trouble as to the latter" (see TJ to Morris, 26 Apr. 1784). It is possible that Morris' missing letter to TJ of 30 Apr. is the reply referred to, for it is apparent that TJ must have received that reply and altered the present MS before he left Congress.

[1] The following deleted at this point: "it be an instruction."
[2] Preceding eight words interlined in substitution for the following: "assay and examine with the utmost accuracy practicable."
[3] Preceding eight words added at end of line.
[4] These two words interlined in substitution for "To assay and examine."
[5] This word interlined in substitution for "assays."
[6] This word interlined in substitution for "assay."
[7] Preceding three words substituted for "tenths and hundredths."
[8] This sentence interlined as an addition; not in MS notes on money unit sent to Morris.
[9] Altered from ". . . estimated in Units and decimal parts of Units" to read as above.

To Boinod & Gaillard

[*Annapolis, 1 Feb. 1784.* Entry in SJL reads: "Boinod & Gaillard. Pfeffel. Hainault. Lignac." Not found. TJ may have ordered these works from a catalogue recently published by Boinod & Gaillard: "This Day is Published (Price One Quarter of a Dollar) A Catalogue of a large and choice Collection of Books, comprehending most branches of literature in the French, Latin, English, German and Dutch Languages, which are offered for Sale by BOINOD AND GAILLARD, Booksellers and Stationers lately from Europe, at their store in Second-street, near Vine-street, to the FREE AMERICANS" (*Penna. Journal*, 17 Jan. 1784).]

From Joseph Carleton, with an Estimate of Expenses of the Military Department

War Office [*Annapolis*], *1 Feb. 1784*. Transmitting general estimate "of the expence of the Military Establishment of the United States for the current year amounting to 219.578 dollars." This estimate was sent in response to orders "of the grand Committee, communicated in your Letter of the 31st. ultimo." Staff estimates not accurate, but "the best that can be made out of the imperfect materials on which they are formed, being chiefly taken from the papers lately transmitted by Major General Knox."

ENCLOSURE

General Estimate of the Expences of the Military
Establishments of the United States for the year 1784

Estimate No. 1	Pay and Subsistence of the Army	145.596$\frac{60}{90}$
2	Paymaster Generals department	12.750
3	Clothier Generals department	29.370
4	Hospital department	4.337$\frac{60}{}$
5	Military Stores department	10.898
6	Quarter Master's department	16.625$\frac{60}{}$

Dollars 219.578

War Office January 1st. 1784

Jos: CARLETON
Secretary

RC and enclosure (DLC: PCC, No. 144); addressed: "The Honl: Thomas Jefferson Esquire in Congress"; endorsed by Thomson: "Letter Feby. 1. 1784 War Office to Grand Comee Estimate of Expence of Military for 1784."

TJ's letter to Carleton of 31 Jan., written for the Grand Committee, has not been found. Joseph Carleton, secretary in the war office, passed through Annapolis before 19 Jan. 1784 and expected to return in a few days (Thomson to Richard Peters, 19 Jan.

1784; Burnett, *Letters of Members*, VII, No. 494). He was no doubt there on 29 Jan. when the report of a committee, of which TJ was a member, on Carleton's letter of 20 Dec. 1783 concerning his authority to issue brevet commissions, &c., was approved by Congress (report is in DLC: PCC, No. 19, II, and is in the hand of Arthur Lee; Committee Book, same, No. 186, under date of 22 Jan. 1784; JCC, XXVI, 44, 51).

To Joseph Crockett

[*Annapolis*, *1 Feb. 1784*. Entry in sJL reads: "Colo Crockett. Enclosed his papers and Carleton's letter." Letter and enclosures not found.]

To Richard Curson

[*Annapolis*, *1 Feb. 1784*. Entry in sJL reads: "Rd. Curson. Returned magazines &c." Not found.]

To Samuel House

[*Annapolis*, *1 Feb. 1784*. Entry in sJL reads: "S. House. Books from B. & G.—probable course of Congress." Not found.]

To John Key

[*Annapolis*, *1 Feb. 1784*. Entry in sJL reads: "J. Key. TMR's phaeton—bill of scantling—tub mill—Watson to be kept—shall be home in spring—sell grey—furnish TMR money to buy horse—Phill break him—Jame garden and do what Giovannini was to do if gone—Anthony to instruct—smokehouse—stocks—Mazzei papers—Anthy. may live at Bellow's—2 or 3 days work of Carps and Geo's.—grass on level—Carr's mare not to horse—settle [balance of?] Hogg's account—Orr's account—how many hogs." Not found.]

To John Moore

[*Annapolis*, *1 Feb. 1784*. Entry in sJL reads: "Jno. Moore. Accounts at barracks to be settled with Turner in Richmond." Not found.]

To Robert Morris

Sir   [1 February 1784]

A grand Committee of Congress is now engaged in preparing estimates of the necessary federal expenses of the present year from the first to the last day of it inclusive and of the articles of interest on the public debts foreign and domestic which call indispensably for immediate provision while the impost proposed ultimately for their discharge shall be on it's passage through the states; these estimates are to lead to a new requisition of money from the states, but the committee have hopes that this new requisition may be lessened if not altogether dispensed with provided a full compliance can be obtained with the former requisitions of November 2. 1781 for 8. millions of dollars and of October 10. 1782 for 2. millions of dollars. They suppose that the requisition of 8. millions was greater than all the objects of it did in event require. They suppose further that some of these objects have been transferred to other funds. Of course there will be a surplus remaining after all the demands[1] paid and paiable out of this fund. In like manner [2]M̶s. having been part of 6 millns. estimated on a war establishment and peace taking place immediately after, they expect a surplus may remain on this also after all payments made and to be made out of it. These surplusses which will be reached by no former appropriation and which are therefore fairly open to be newly appropriated they ask of you to estimate according to the best of your information that they may see how far an enforcement of them will go towards supplying the demands of the current year: but that they may know how to call on the several states to pay up their deficiencies, it will be necessary also for you to inform them what proportion of these requisitions had been paid up by each state to the 1st. day of January 1784.

Another object claimed the attention of the Committee. By a vote of Sep. 4. 1782. 1,200,000 Dollars were required from the states for the special purpose of paying interest, with a permission to them to pay first out of their quotas the interest on loan office certificates and other liquidated debts, loaned or contracted in their own states, so that the balance only was to be remitted to the Continental Treasury. Have any such balances been remitted, or have you any information how far the several states have proceeded to comply with this requisition by payment of interest within their own state?[2]

A former committee had been appointed to revise the civil list and to adapt it to the change of circumstances which peace has induced. They have gone through that work and reported except so far as it relates to the department of Finance, by which I mean to include the establishments in the several offices of the Superintendent, Comptroller, Auditors, Register, Treasurer, and the Commissioners for settling the accounts in the several states, and the accounts of the Staff departments. They hope from your letter in answer to one written you by Dr. Williamson their chairman that you are turning your attention to this subject and that you will be so kind as to inform them whether any of the offices or officers in that department may be dispensed with under present circumstances so as to lessen it's expenses without endangering more substantial loss, a true and laudable œconomy being their object. I take the liberty of mentioning this subject to you only because the Grand Committee under whose instructions I write, will of course be delayed in their estimates till the other committee shall have made a full report on the civil list.

With you I know it is unnecessary to urge as early an answer as is practicable and have therefore only to add assurances of the sincere respect & esteem with which I have the honor to be &c.

Dft (DLC); date assigned from Morris' acknowledgement of 25 Feb. 1784. Not recorded in SJL.

For the report of the COMMITTEE . . . TO REVISE THE CIVIL LIST, see under 5 Mch. 1784.

1 Dft deletes the following at this point: "against this requisition which have been"; Burnett, *Letters of Members*, VII, No. 502, includes this as part of the text, not as a deletion; TJ may have intended it so, but this can be ascertained only if the missing RC should be found.

2 TJ first wrote the latter part of this query as follows, and then altered it to read as above: ". . . paiment of interest to their own citizens on loan office certificates?" To this TJ added, but apparently deleted, the following sentence: "If you have we shall be obliged to you for it." Ford, III, 395, prints this additional sentence as if not deleted and Burnett as if possibly deleted (VII, No. 502), but the former adopts an erroneous and nonsensical reading that is repeated by the latter, as follows: ". . . paiment of interest within their own state? Or loan office certificates? If you have . . ." &c.

To Thomas Mann Randolph

[*Annapolis, 1-14 Feb. 1784.* Entry in SJL under date of 1 Feb. reads: "TMR. Phaeton—buy horse for me—keep eye on two others—give notice to Key to send for him [i.e., the purchased horse]—I will call on him [i.e., Randolph] in Spring—health—[. . .] Judy. P.S. of Feb. 14. health—news." Not found.]

To David Watson

[*Annapolis, 1 Feb. 1784.* Entry in SJL reads: "Watson. TMR's phaeton—list of work—provisions—my return home—will get watch, drawing instruments, clothes when I go to Phila—write to me." Not found.]

To Joseph Jones

[*Annapolis, 2-14 Feb. 1784.* Entry in SJL reads: "Jos. Jones. Efficacy of deed of conveyance to Congress—interest on British debts—

principal—confiscations—slaves carried from N.Y.—want of money."
Not found, but see Jones' reply of 28 Feb. Entry in sJL is prefaced by
the figures "2.14"; Jones acknowledged TJ's letter of 2 Feb., but the
double figure probably means that TJ added a postscript on the 14th
as he did in the case of the letter to Thomas Mann Randolph of 1 Feb.,
q.v.]

From Charles Carter

DEAR SIR   Fredg February 9th 84

My father has only one instance of the white negroe in his
estate. I have been prevented examining her by her being sent
some time since to Amherst. But as she lived many years at Blen-
heim and generally drew the attention of every one who saw her,
I have found little difficulty in collecting answers to your queries.
I feel myself much disposed to see this curiosity and think to visit
Amherst for that purpose this spring. If I should discover any
thing which has escaped the observation of those from whom I
have received my information I will immediately communicate it
to you.

The Parents of this white negroe were brought from Guinea and
were remarkable for their health and longevity. I think they may
be styled dark Mulattoes, of which colour they had three other
children. The colour of this negroe's skin is a sallow white with a
great many dark spots promiscuously scattered over it somewhat
like the freckles on a white person's face but rather larger. It is
disputed whether those spots are natural or acquired, but the blacks
inform me they are natural who I think, from their near connexion
with her, are entitled to the most certain knowledge in this matter.
Her hair is as [thi]ck curled and as coarse as the black negroes but
differs in colour which [. . .] with her skin; she is well shaped,
strong [. . .] enjoys a rich share of health. Her senses are as perfect
as any person's except her sight which fails her very much when
exposed to the sun on which account she is obliged to use a Bon-
nett in summer. Her Eyes are in a continual motion. I am told
she sees much better in the night than day. Indeed I believe better
than we do. She has had a child by a true black, which had the
complexion of the mother. The child lived but a few weeks. Every
Person with whom I have spoke on this subject seems to concur
in this account which I believe a faithfull one tho' I fear, not so
particular as you expected. I was confined in Albermarle a considerable time by the badness of the weather, which I must beg you

will admit as an apology for my not answering your letter sooner. I am Dr Sir with great respect Yrs.,   CHAS CARTER

RC (DLC); endorsed by TJ: "Carter Charles."
This is a reply to TJ's (missing) letter to Charles Carter of 26 Dec. 1783.

From Marbois

Tuesday morning [10? Feb. 1784]

Mr. De Marbois presents his compliments to Mr. Jefferson and begs the favor of a communication of the Constitutions of the thirteen States if Mr. Jefferson has got them.

RC (DLC: PCC, No. 30). TJ's draft of the Virginia deed of cession is on the verso of Marbois' letter. TJ must, therefore, have received this letter sometime before 13 Feb. It may have been written on Tuesday, 10 Feb. 1784; Marbois carried letters to Philadelphia for TJ on 18 Feb. (see TJ to Hopkinson, 18 Feb. 1784; see also Virginia Cession, &c., under 1 Mch. 1784, Document I, notes).

From Thomas Hutchins

SIR   Philadelphia 11th February 1784

Your favor of the 24th of last month I was honored with the 9th instant. I embrace the first opportunity of tendering you my thanks for your friendly communication respecting the error you discovered in my Pamphlet. How to account for so egregious a blunder in calculation, I am really at a loss, as a moments reflection on the subject would have set me right. Should any other mistake appear to you on your further perusal of that small performance, your favouring me with it, will be esteemed an additional mark of your friendship. I am collecting materials to enable me to furnish a more particular account of that valuable country to the Westward, which I purpose doing, by re-publishing the present Pamphlet, after correcting its errors, with the addition of every useful information that I shall be able to acquire; any hints furnished by my friends for the promotion of this work, will be thankfully received. The difficulty of ascertaining, with any degree of precision, the times at which the periodical inundations begin, and end, in the Missisippi, was my reason for not being particular respecting them in the Pamphlet. The difficulty will appear, when we consider that there are some branches which vie with the Missisippi for magnitude, and as these empty into it, some in temperate and others in cold latitudes, their annual floods are consequently in different seasons. The forwardness or backwardness of the spring also contribute to render the fixing of the periodical floods to any determinate time still more difficult. However, I will venture a few thoughts on the subject, which I believe, are not very foreign from the truth, and which, until I am able to transmit you better information, I hope will not prove altogether unsatisfactory. Notwithstanding the sources of the Ohio, Wabache and Illinois Rivers lie nearly in the same parallel of latitude, the longitudinal distance between the branches of the first, and last mentioned of those rivers, occasion so sensible a difference in the temperature of the climate, in favor of the latter, that the periodical flood commence in the Wabache and Illinois about the beginning or middle of February, but seldom sooner in the Ohio, than the beginning, or middle, of March, except when the winter season has been so mild as not to freeze the river across, which is sometimes the case. The Missouri begins to rise early in February, and the upper Missisippi early in March. The continuance of the flood in the Ohio depends much on the sudden or gradual commencement of the spring, but seldom less than Six weeks or more than two months—In the Illinois and Wabache, between five and six weeks—In the Missouri from six to eight weeks—In the upper Missisippi from eight to ten weeks; and in the lower Missisippi, between four and five months, that is, from January to July. As the Cherokee river rises in a mountainous, or hilly country, the water from the melting of the snow in the spring, with which those hills are covered in winter, no doubt, occasion an annual flood, but of what height or continuance, I cannot with certainty determine, but am of opinion, from about three to four weeks. I am entirely unacquainted with the Tanissee more than knowing it to be a branch of the Cherokee—In the spring floods the Missisippi, is very high, and the current so strong, that with difficulty it can be ascended; but that disadvantage is compensated by eddies or counter-currents, which always run in the bends, close to the banks of the river, with nearly equal velocity against the stream, and assist the ascending boats. The current at this season descends at the rate of about five miles an hour. In Autumn, when the waters are low it runs about two miles an hour, but it is rapid in such parts of the river, which have clusters of Islands, shoals and sand-banks. The circumference of many of these shoals being several Miles, the voyage is longer and in some parts more dangerous than in the spring. The Merchandize necessary for the commerce of the upper settlements, on or near the Missisippi, is conveyed in the spring and autumn, in battoes, rowed by 18 or 20 men, and carrying about 40 tons. From New Orleans to the Illinois a distance of 950 miles the voyage is commonly performed in eight or ten weeks. I wish I was able to furnish you with a more satisfactory account, but at present it is out of my power. Health and happiness attend you. I have the honor to be, Sir, your respectful and obedt. hble servant, THO: HUTCHINS

It is more than two weeks since your Box of Books and my Box of Maps left this for Annapolis. I hope they are safe arrived.

RC (MHi); addressed to TJ at Annapolis; postmarked "12 FE" and "Free."

TJ's FAVOUR OF THE 24TH OF LAST MONTH has not been found, nor is it recorded in SJL. THE ERROR . . . IN MY PAMPHLET (probably Hutchins' *Topo-* *graphical Description of Virginia, Penn-* *sylvania*, &c., London, 1778) has not been identified, but in DLC: TJ Papers, 233: 41668-9 there is a draft, together with fair copy, of "errors in the engraved plate" of "Hutchins's Map of Mississippi."

From James Madison

DEAR SIR   Orange Feby. 11. 1784

Your favor of the 11. of Decr. ulto. came safe to hand after a very tedious conveyance. Mr. W. Maury having broken up his school in this Neighbourhood in order to attempt a superior one in Williamsburg and his pupils being dispersed, I have sent the book for Mr. P. Carr into the neighbourhood of Doctr. Walker whence I supposed it would most easily find its way to him. I thank you for the mark of attention afforded by your order for Smith's Hist: of N.Y. for me. If it should be in every respct convenient I could wish a copy of Blairs Lectures to be added to it.

We have had a severer season and particularly a greater quantity of snow than is remembered to have distinguished any preceding winter. The effect of it on the price of grain and other provisions is much dreaded. It has been as yet so far favorable to me that I have pursued my intended course of *law*-reading with fewer interruptions than I had presupposed: but on the other hand it has deprived me entirely of the philosophical books which I had allotted for incidental reading: all my Trunks sent from Philada. both by myself, and by Mr. House after I left it, being still at Fredericksg.

I have been thinking whether the present situation of the Report of the Revisors of the Laws does not render the printing of it for public consideration advisable. Such a step would not only ensure the preservation of the work and gain us credit abroad, but the sanction which it would probably procure to the Legislature might incline them to adopt it the more readily in the gross. If any material objections occur to you, you will be so good as to mention them. I sincerely sympathize with the worthy family left behind us in Philada. but am not without hopes that the vacances produced by our departure were of short duration. If a visit to Miss Patsy should carry you to Philada. I beg you to remember me in the most affectionate terms to the old lady and to Mrs. Trist if the persecutions of fortune should have so long frustrated her meditated voyage. You will also be so good as to tender my respects to Mr. Mercer if he be at Annapolis and to your other Colleagues, and to be assured of my sincerest wishes for your happiness. I am Dr. Sir Your friend & servt.,   J. MADISON Jr.

In the Supplement to the 45. vol. of the Universal Magazine page 373. I find it mentioned by Doctr. Hunter that there are in the British Museum grinders of the Incognitum which were found in Brasil and Lima. If I do not misremember your Hypothesis it supposes no bones of that animal to have been met with to the South.

RC (DLC: Madison Papers).

To Jacquelin Ambler

[*Annapolis, 14 Feb. 1784.* Entry in SJL reads: "Mr. Ambler. Money —6 months if possible." Not found.]

To James Buchanan

[*Annapolis, 14 Feb. 1784.* Entry in SJL reads: "Jas. Buchanan to lay out what money the treasurer spares me in good bills on Baltimore or Philadia." Not found.]

To George Gilmer

[*Annapolis, 14 Feb. 1784.* Entry in SJL reads: "Dr. Gilmer. Inclosed Fox's letter and resolution Congress. I shall be at Mont—ill health—news." TJ's letter to Gilmer and its enclosures have not been found. Fox's letter was evidently one to TJ in reply to TJ's missing letter to Fox of 31 Dec. 1783 concerning Gilmer's accounts. On 22 June 1781 Gilmer had written to Theodorick Bland concerning his accounts (DLC: PCC, No. 78) and his letter was referred on 4 Apr. 1783 to a committee of three; this committee reported on 22 Apr. 1783 to the effect that "the account of Dr. G. Gilmer for pay and rations be settled on the same principles as the accounts of other hospital surgeons of the same rank, according to the time he shall appear to have been employed in the public service; and that the purveyor general return to Dr. George Gilmer a quantity of medicine equal to what he expended out of his private stores, for the use of the continental hospital under his care" (JCC, XXIV, 229, 265). Edward Fox was commissioner for adjusting the accounts of the General Hospital; it is likely, therefore, that the resolution enclosed in TJ's letter to Gilmer was a copy of the one just quoted.]

To James Maury

[*Annapolis, 14 Feb. 1784.* Entry in SJL reads: "Jas. Maury. Acknoleging receipt of his—to bring money from Jones's. News." Neither TJ's present letter to Maury nor Maury's to TJ, thereby acknowledged, has been found, but Maury's was probably in response to TJ's (missing) letter of 11 Dec. 1783.]

James Monroe to Benjamin Harrison

SIR   Annapolis Feby 14, 1784.

Since our late dispatches from Mr. Adams we have received nothing from our ministers in Europe. By these we were informed of his and Mr. Jay's arrival in London, but as Congress hath appointed neither of these Gentlemen to that court, nor directed the scene of negotiation even with that power to be chang'd from Paris, we presume their attendance there is merely on a private visit. As yet no arrangment is form'd in our foreign affairs. Commercial treaties with most of the powers with whom these States will have a commercial intercourse are still to be enter'd into. Whether the gentlemen now in Europe will be jointly commission'd to treat with all these powers or particular courts will be assign'd to each is still to be the subject of discussion. The attention of Congress is engag'd more immediately in our internal arrangments but even in this time nothing is finally determin'd. The States are looking within themselves and calculating their several disbursements during the war and endeavoring to fix the payment on the U. States. Massachuss'ts hath lately demanded the redemption of the old emissions of paper money, the assumpsit of the U.S. to pay the expence of the expedition to Penobscot undertaken by authority of the State alone, together with some allowance for the large bounties given by that State to recruits for the army. To neither of these demands hath an answer as yet been given. How far we shall lose or gain by any general plan adopted here respecting State expenditures we have not sufficient documents to determine by. A great object with us will be to comprehend in any plan of that kind the remainder of our western expenditures which stand precisely on the ground of the expedition to Penobscot. We shall be happy to receive from your Excellency every communication upon this subject that you are possess'd of.

We have it from private but respectable authority that the rupture between the Porte and the two empires will probably be accommodated by concessions on the part of the former without committing their pretensions to the calamitous and uncertain events of war. The diversion which a contest between these powers might have made to the force of our ally, circumstanc'd as we have been with respect to the definitive treaty, hath made the progress of this affair a subject of consequence to us.

I have the honor to be with great respect and esteem your Excellency's most obt servant, JAS MONROE

MS not found; text from Burnett, *Letters of Members*, VII, No. 512, who printed it from a copy "from the original, then in the possession of Mr. Stan V. Henkels of Philadelphia."

From David Ross

SIR   Richmond 14 Feby 1784

I am lately returned from the back Country where I have been for a considerable time in a bad State of health which is the reason I did not reply sooner to your letter.

At present I shall only observe that if you find it Convenient you may draw on me occasionally for such sums as you require and I shall honor your Bills. I am but just come to this Town and Cant tell what Funds the Treasurer may have but I will do it next week and advise you.

If I can in any manner Contribute to your being regularly supplied with money I shall communicate my sentiments to the Treasurer on that Subject.

I Can Write you nothing New, indeed the Weather is now and hath been for some time past so severe, that there has been little doing. I am with great regard Your Most hum Servt,

DAVID ROSS

RC (MHi); endorsed by TJ: "Ross David." YOUR LETTER: This was TJ's (missing) letter to Ross of 18 Nov. 1783, recorded in SJL under that date as follows: "David Ross. On subject of draughts on him."

From James Madison

DEAR SIR   Orange Feby 17th. 1784.

I wrote to you a few days ago by the post acknowledging your favor of the 10th. of Decr. Mr. Maury has since afforded me an opportunity which I cannot omit to acknowledge that of the first of Jany. which has just come to hand, and to express the concern I feel at the account it gives of your ill health. I hope earnestly that this will find it in a better state and that I may soon receive a confirmation of such a favorable change. Your explanation of Buffon's hypothesis has rectified my misconception of it, and I forbear as I ought perhaps formerly to have done making any further remarks on it, at least till I have seen the work itself. I forgot to mention to you in my last that I had received a letter from Mazzei dated at *Richmond*, apprising me of a proposed visit to Orange from whence he meant to proceed to Annapolis. As I wish in a little time to make an effort to import some law-books, and shall probably hereafter extend the plan to other books, particularly from France, I must beg the favor of you to obtain the name and address of a fit Bookseller both in London and Paris if the means of such information should at any time fall in your way. I have committed to Mr. Maury's care another letter to my worthy friend Mrs. House, which in case he should not proceed to Philada. he will put into your hand.

I am my dear Sir with the sincerest wishes for the reestablishment of your health and every other happiness, your Obt. friend & servant,   J. MADISON jr.

RC (DLC: Madison Papers).

To Boinod & Gaillard

[*Annapolis, 18 Feb. 1784.* Entry in SJL reads: "Boinod & Gaillard, to send to Europe for Grot. Paisbas—Wicquefort—De Callieres—Mem. de l'Am.—de la Lande—Barrington's Misc.—Scheele's cheml. observations on air and fire—Le Maitre Cuisinier—Trios of Campioni." Not found; see note to record entry under 1 Feb. 1784.]

To Francis Hopkinson

DEAR SIR   Annapolis Feb. 18. 1784.

Your favour should not have been so long unacknowledged but that I have been in a state of health which permitted me neither to read, write or think. I take advantage now of a small remission in a fever to write you a line of thanks by Monsr. Marbois. You write in a gout (I beleive it was) and I answer in a fever. In truth amidst this eternal surfeit of politics wherein one subject succeeds another like Aesop's feast of tongues a small entremêt of philosophy is releiving. I carried your letter to the printer. He declared it exceeded the typographical art. He observed further that it would be very ill-judged in those capable of writing things of merit in substance, to introduce a merit of form: that it would transfer the whole credit from the writer to the printer, and Bell would become the first genius of America.

What think you of these ballons? They really begin to assume a serious face. The Chevalr. Luzerne communicated to me a letter received from his brother who mentions one which he had seen himself. The persons who ascended in it regulated it's height at about 3000 feet, and passed with the wind about 6 miles in 20 minutes when they chose to let themselves down, tho' they could have travelled triple the distance. This discovery seems to threaten the prostration of fortified works unless they can be closed above, the destruction of fleets and what not. The French may now run over their laces, wines &c. to England duty free. The whole system of British statutes made on the supposition of goods being brought into some port must be revised. Inland countries may now become *maritime* states unless you chuse rather to call them *aerial* ones as their commerce is in future to be carried on through that element. But jesting apart I think this discovery may lead to things useful. For instance there is no longer a difficulty how Congress shall move backwards and forwards, and your bungling scheme of moving houses and moving towns is quite superseded, we shall soar sublime above the clouds. It is happy for us too that this invention happens just as philosophy is taking such a start in our own hemisphere: for I find by the last election of members to the Society there are no less than 21 new philosophers found, every one of whom is superior to my countryman Madison. From philosophy I must pass on to domestic things and thank you for your notice of my little daughter whose education and improvement is my first object now. I am sure your advice and society will forward these works with her. I am sorry Cimetiere thinks her a dull subject in his line. I do not foresee that she will ever have another opportunity of learning to draw, and it is a pleasing accomplishment and a valuable one in many circumstances. As to his pay, I would wish him to receive what he thinks due to him, because I would even purchase his peace at that price. Perhaps I may be able to get him to persevere when I return to Philadelphia which will probably be in the spring —but stop or I shall let out the secret. Much health and happiness to yourself and family, and sincere respects to Mr. and Mrs. Rittenhouse, remaining myself with great sincerity Dr. Sir Your friend & servt,   TH: JEFFERSON

RC (Edward Hopkinson, Jr., Phila.). Not recorded in SJL.

Hopkinson's FAVOUR was that of 4 Jan. 1784. For the BUNGLING SCHEME OF MOVING HOUSES AND . . . TOWNS, see note to Mrs. Trist's letter to TJ under 8 Dec. 1783 and Hastings, *Hopkinson*, p. 336, 358, 427-8. Writing from Passy only a month before this, Franklin had anticipated TJ's vision of the future conquest of the air, taking it as seriously as TJ himself would later: "It appears . . . to be a discovery of great Importance and what may possibly give a new turn to human affairs" (Franklin to Ingenhousz, 16 Jan. 1784, quoted in Jeremiah Milbank, Jr., *The First Century of Flight in America*, 1943, p. 6).

To Samuel House

⟦*Annapolis, 18 Feb. 1784.* Entry in SJL reads: "S. House inclosing Harrison's bill on Holker in favor Monroe for 96. D. to be paid into the bank." Letter and enclosure not found.⟧

To Martha Jefferson

DEAR PATSY   Annapolis Feb. 18. 1784.

I have received two or three letters from you since I wrote last. Indeed my health has been so bad that I have been able scarcely to read, write or do any thing else. Your letters to your aunt and the others shall be forwarded. I hope you will continue to inclose to me every week one for some of your friends in Virginia. I am sorry Mr. Cimetiere cannot attend you, because it is probable you will never have another opportunity of learning to draw, and it is a pretty and pleasing accomplishment. With respect to the paiment of the guinea, I would wish him to receive it, because if there is to be a doubt between him and me, which of us acts rightly, I would chuse to remove it clearly off my own shoulders. You must thank Mrs. Hopkinson for me for the trouble she gave herself in this matter, from which she will be relieved by paying Mr. Cimetiere his demand. Perhaps when the season becomes milder he will consent to attend you. I am sorry your French master cannot be more punctual. I hope you nevertheless read French every day as I advised you. Your letter to me in French gave me great satisfaction and I wish you to exercise yourself in the same way frequently. Your sisters are well. I am in hopes the money I had placed in the bank subject to Mrs. Hopkinson's order had not yet failed. Lest it should have done so, inform her that I have now sent there a further supply. Deliver my most respectful compliments to her & be assured of the love with which I am My dear Patsy Your's affectionately,   TH: JEFFERSON

RC (NNP). TJ's summary in SJL reads: "Patsy. Receipt of letters to Mrs. E. Jud R. and Polly—pay Cimetiere—read Fr. herself—inform Mrs. H. have sent money." Martha's TWO OR THREE LETTERS have not been found; one of these must have been the letter in French.

To Boinod & Gaillard

[*Annapolis, 19 Feb. 1784*. Entry in SJL under this date and immediately below the entry for the letter to Boinod & Gaillard for 18 Feb. reads: "do. Connoissce. des tems pour 1785." TJ's letter of this date, supplementing his order for books of the previous date, has not been found. The volume of *Connaissance des Temps* for 1785 is listed in Library Catalogue, 1815, p. 115.]

To James Madison

DEAR SIR   Annapolis Feb. 20. 1784:

Your favour of the 11th. inst. came to hand this day. I had prepared a multitude of memorandums of subjects whereon to write you, but I will first answer those arising from your letter. By the time my order got to Philadelphia every copy of Smith's history of New York was sold. I shall take care to get Blair's lectures for you as soon as published, and will attend to your presumed wishes whenever I meet with any thing rare and of worth. I wish I knew better what things of this kind you have collected for yourself, as I may often doubt whether you have or have not a thing. I know of no objections to the printing the revisal; on the contrary I think good will result from it. Should this be decided I must make a short trip to Virginia, as from the loss of originals I beleive my copies must often be wanting. I had never met with the particular fact relative to the grinders of the incognitum found in Brasil and Lima and deposited in the British museum which you mention from Dr. Hunter. I know it has been said that in a very few instances such bones have been found in S. America. You will find a collection of these in 2. Buff. Epoq. de la nature 187. but they have

been so illy attested, so loosely and ignorantly described, and so
seldom even pretended to have been seen, that I have supposed their
identity with the Northern bones, and perhaps their existence at
all not sufficiently established. The authority of Hunter is respectable: but if this be the only well attested instance of those bones
brought from S. Amera., they may still be beleived to have been
first carried there either previous to the emigration of the Spaniards
when there was doubtless a communication between the Indns. of
the two continents, or after that emigration when an intercourse
between the Spaniards of N. and S. Amera. took place. It would be
unsafe to deny the fact; but I think it may well be doubted. I wish
you had a thermometer. Mr. Madison of the college and myself are
keeping observations for a comparison of climate. We observe at
Sunrise and at 4. o'clock P.M. which are the coldest and warmest
points of the day. If you could observe at the same time it would
shew the difference between going North and Northwest on this
continent. I suspect it to be colder in Orange or Albemarle than
here.

I think I informed you in my last that an attempt had been made
to ratify the Definitive treaty by seven states only, and to impose
this under the sanction of our seal (without letting our actual state
appear) on the British court. Reade, Williamson and Lee were
violent for this, and gave notice that when the question should be
put they would call the yeas and nays, and shew by whose fault
the ratification of this important instrument should fail, if it should
fail. I prepared the inclosed resolution by way of protest and informed them I would place that also on the journals with the yeas
and nays, as a justification of those who opposed the proposition.
I beleive this put a stop to it. They suffered the question to rest
undecided till the 14th. of Jan. when 9. states appeared and ratified.
Colo. Harmar and Colo. Franks were immediately dispatched to
take passages to Europe with copies of the ratification. But by the
extraordinary severity of the season we know they had not sailed
on the 7th. inst. The ratification will not therefore arrive in time.
Being persuaded I shall be misrepresented within my own state,
if any difficulties should arise, I inclose you a copy of the protest
containing my reasons. Had the question been put there were but
two states who would have voted for a ratification by seven. The
others would have been in the negative or divided. I find Congress
every moment stopped by questions whether the most trifling money
propositions are not above the powers of seven states as being ap-
propriations of money. My idea is that the estimate for the year

and requisition grounded on that, whereon the sums to be allowed to each department are stated, is the general appropriation which requires 9. states, and that the detailing it out provided they do not go beyond these sums may be done by the subordinate officers of the federal government or by a Congress of 7. states. I wish you to think of this and give me your thoughts on the subject. We have as yet no Secretary of Foreign affairs. *Lee*[1] avows himself a candidate. The plan of Foreign affairs likely to take place is to commission Adams, Franklin and Jay to conclude treaties with the several European powers, and then to return, leaving the feild to subordinate characters. Messrs. Adams and Jay have paid a visit to the court of London unordered and uninvited. Their reception has been forbidding. *Luzerne leaves* us in August, whether *recalled* or on *his own request* is not known. This information comes from *himself* tho' is not as yet *spoken* of *publicly*. *Lee* finding no *faction*[2] among *men* here, entered into that among the *women* which rages to a very high degree. A *ball* being appointed by the one party on a certain *night* he undertook to *give* one, and fixed it precisely on the same *night*. This of course has placed him in the midst of the mud. He is *courting Miss Sprig* a *young girl* of *seventeen* and of *thirty thousand pounds* expectation. I have no doubt from some conversations with *him* that there is a design agitating to sever the *Northern Neck* and add it to this *state*. *He* supported in conversation with me the propriety and necessity of such a general measure, to wit of enlarging the *small states* to interest them in the *union*. *He* deserves to be well *watched* in our state. *He* is extremely soured with it and is not cautious in betraying his hostility *against it*. We cannot make up a Congress at all. There are 8. states in town, 6 of which are represented by two members only. Of these two members of different states are confined by the gout so that we cannot make a house. We have not sit above 3. days I beleive in as many weeks. Admonition after admonition has been sent to the states, to no effect. We have sent one to day. If it fails, it seems as well we should all retire. There have never been 9 states on the floor but for the ratification of the treaty and a day or two after. Georgetown languishes. The smile is hardly covered now when the federal towns are spoken of. I fear that our chance is at this time desperate. Our object therefore must be if we fail in an effort to remove to Georgetown, to endeavor then to get to some place off the waters of the Chesapeak where we may be ensured against Congress considering themselves as fixed. My present expectations are, that as soon as we get a Congress to do business, we shall attend to nothing but the most pressing matters, get through them and adjourn, not to meet again till November, leaving a Committee of the states. That Committee will be obliged to go immediately to Philadelphia to examine the offices and of course they will set there till the meeting in November. Whether that meeting will be in Philada. or Trenton will be the question and will in my opinion depend on the vote of *New York*. Did not you once suppose in conversation with me that Congress had no authority to decide any cases between two differing states, except those of disputed territory? I think you did. If I am not mistaken in this I should wish to know your sense of the words which describe those cases which may be submitted to a federal court. They seem to me to comprehend every cause of difference.

We have received the act of our assembly ceding the lands North of Ohio and are about executing a deed for it. I think the territory will be laid out by passing a meridian through the Western cape of the Mouth of the Gr. Kanhaway from the Ohio to L. Erie, and another through the rapids of Ohio from the same river to Michigan and crossing these by the parallels of latitude 37°. 39°. 41°. &c. allowing to each state an extent of 2°. from N. to South. On the Eastern side of the meridian of Kanhaway will still be one new state, to wit, the territory lying between that meridian, Pennsylva., the Ohio and L. Erie. We hope N. Carola. will cede all beyond the same meridian of Kanhaway, and Virginia also. For god's sake push this at the next session of assembly. We have transmitted a copy of a petition from the people of Kentucky to Congress praying to be separated from Virginia. Congress took no notice of it. We sent the copy to the Governor desiring it to be laid before the assembly. Our view was to bring on the question.[3] It is for the interest of Virginia to cede so far immediately; because the people beyond that will separate themselves, because they will be joined by all our settlements beyond the Alleghaney if they are the first movers. Whereas if we draw the line those at Kentucky having their end will not interest themselves for the people of Indiana, Greenbriar &c. who will of course be left to our management, and I can with certainty almost say that Congress would approve of the meridian of the mouth of Kanhaway and consider it as the ultimate point to be desired from Virginia. I form this opinion from conversation with many members. Should we not be the first movers, and the Indianians and Kentuckians take themselves off and claim to the Alleghaney I am afraid Congress would secretly wish them well. Virginia is extremely interested to retain to that meridian:

1. Because the Gr. Kanhaway runs from North to South across our whole country forming by it's waters a belt of fine land, which will be thickly seated and will form a strong barrier for us. 2. Because the country for 180 miles beyond that is an absolute desart, barren and mountainous which can never be inhabited, and will therefore be a fine separation between us and the next state. 3. Because the government of Virginia is more convenient to the people on all the upper parts of Kanhaway than any other which will be laid out. 4. Because our lead mines are in that country. 5. Because the Kanhaway is capable of being made navigable, and therefore gives entrance into the Western waters to every part of our latitude. 6. Because it is not now navigable and can only be made so by expensive works, which require that we should own the soil on both sides. 7. Because the Ohio, and it's branches which head up against the Patowmac affords the shortest water communication by 500. miles of any which can ever be got between the Western waters and Atlantic, and of course promises us almost a monopoly of the Western and Indian trade. I think the opening this navigation is an object on which no time is to be lost. Pennsylva. is attending to the Western commerce. She has had surveys made of the river Susquehanna and of the grounds thro' which a canal must pass to go directly to Philadelphia. It is reported practicable at an expence of £200,000 and they have determined to open it. What an example this is! If we do not push this matter immediately they will be beforehand with us and get possession of the commerce. And it is difficult to turn it from a channel in which it is once established. Could not our assembly be induced to lay a particular tax which should bring in 5. or 10,000£ a year to be applied till the navigation of the Ohio and Patowmac is opened, then James river and so on through the whole successively. Genl. Washington has that of the Patowmac much at heart. The superintendance of it would be a noble amusement in his retirement and leave a monument of him as long as the waters should flow. I am of opinion he would accept of the direction as long as the money should be to be emploied on the Patowmac, and the popularity of his name would carry it thro' the assembly. The portage between Yohogania and the N. branch of Patowmac is of 40 or 50 miles. Cheat river is navigable far up. It's head is within 10 miles of the head of the North branch of Patowmac and I am informed offers the shortest and best portage. I wish in the next election of delegates for Congress, Short could be sent. His talents are great and his weight in our state must ere long become principal. I see the best effects produced by sending

our young statesmen here. They see the affairs of the Confederacy from a high ground; they learn the importance of the Union and befriend federal measures when they return. Those who never come here, see our affairs insulated, pursue a system of jealousy and self interest, and distract the Union as much as they can. Genl. Gates would supply Short's place in the council very well, and would act. He is now here. What will you do with the council? They are expensive, and not constantly nor often necessary; yet to drop them would be wrong. I think you had better require their attendance twice a year to examine the Executive department and see that it be going on rightly, advise on that subject the Governor or inform the legislature as they shall see occasion. Give them 50. guineas each for each trip, fill up only 5 of the places, and let them be always subject to summons on great emergencies by the Governor, on which occasions their expences only should be paid. At an expence of 500 guineas you will thus preserve this member of the constitution always fit for use. Young and ambitious men will leave it and go into the assembly, but the elderly and able who have retired from the legislative feild as too turbulent will accept of the offices. Among other legislative subjects our distresses ask notice. I had been from home four months and had expended 1200 Dollars before I received one farthing. By the last post we received about seven weeks allowance. In the mean time some of us had had the mortification to have our horses turned out of the livery stable for want of money. There is really no standing this. The supply gives us no relief because it was mortgaged. We are trying to get something more effectual from the treasury, having sent an express to inform them of our predicament. I shall endeavour to place as much in the Philadelphia bank as will repay your kindness unless you should alter your mind and chuse to take it in the Virginia treasury. I have hunted out *Chastellux'*⁴ journal and had a reading of it. I had never so falsely estimated the character of a book. There are about six sentences of offensive bagatelles which are all of them publicly known. Because having respected individual characters they were like carrion for the buzzard curiosity. All the rest of the book (and it is a 4to. of 186 pages) is either entertaining, or instructive and would be highly flattering to the Americans. He has visited all the principal feilds of battle, enquired minutely into the detail of the actions, and has given what are probably the best accounts extant of them. He often finds occasion to criticize and to deny the British accounts from an inspection of the ground. I think to write to him, recommend the expunging the few exceptionable passages and publication of the rest. I have had an opportunity here of examining Bynkershoek's works. There are about a fourth part of them which you would like to have. They are the following tracts. Questiones juris publici, de lege Rhodiâ, de dominio maris, du Juge competent des Ambassadeurs, for this last if not the rest has been translated into French with notes by Barbeyrac. I have had from Boinod & Gaillard a copy of Mussenbroeck's cours de Physique. It is certainly the most comprehensive and most accurate body of Natural Philosophy which has been ever published. I would recommend to you to get it, or I will get that and any other books you want from Boinod or elsewhere. I hope you have found access to my library. I beg you to make free use of it. Key, the steward is living there now and of course will be always in the way. Monroe is buying land almost adjoining me. Short will do the same. What would I not give you could fall into the circle. With such a society I could once more venture home and lay myself up for the residue of life, quitting all it's contentions which grow daily more and more insupportable. Think of it. To render it practicable only requires you to think it so. Life is of no value but as it brings us gratifications. Among the most valuable of these is rational society. It informs the mind, sweetens the temper, chears our spirits, and promotes health. There is a little farm of 140 as. adjoining me, and within two miles, all of good land, tho' old, with a small indifferent house on it, the whole worth not more than £250. Such a one might be a farm of experiment and support a little table and houshold. It is on the road to Orange and so much nearer than I am. It is convenient enough for supplementary supplies from thence. Once more think of it, and Adieu.

RC (DLC: Madison Papers); endorsed. Enclosure (DLC: Rives Papers): Resolutions opposing ratification of the Definitive Treaty by less than nine states, q.v., under 27 Dec. 1783. Entry in SJL reads: "[Feb.] 20 Jas. Madison Orge. Appropriation — protest against ratification — Secy. For. affairs — For. Ministr.—Luzerne—jurisdiction federal court—federal towns—Adams and Jay—no representation — L's ball — [. . .] — Northern Neck — Sm's h.N.Y. sold — Blair's lectures—print revisal—incognitum—Harrison—cession to Gr. Kanh.— navigation Ohio and Patowm.—Short to Congress—Gates council—what do with council?—our pay—Chastlux' journal—Bynkershoek—Mussenbroeck." The omitted word appears to be "et.Spr.," which is obviously a reference to the name of the young lady to whom Lee was paying court; Lee was never married.

I HAVE HUNTED OUT CHASTELLUX' JOURNAL: Among the Jefferson Papers in MHi are four closely written pages in TJ's hand containing extracts, with page references, from the extremely rare earliest printing of any part of Chastellux's travel journals, namely, the anonymously issued Voyage de Newport a Philadelphie [sic], Albany, &c. (Newport: Imprimerie Royale de l'Escadre [1781]; Sabin 12225; Evans 17111). The extracts copied by TJ relate to the following subjects (page references are here given to the 1787 edition of the Journals, which included the early journal): sketch of the character and talents of David Rittenhouse (I, 231-2), "un homme tres simple et tres modeste . . . n'est pas assez profond dans les mathematiques pour entendre les livres de M. d'Alembert, mais il en soit assez pour connoitre les mouvemens des corps celestes"; the American habit of drinking healths at the *beginning* of meals, a "usage absurde et vraiment barbare" (I, 185-7); and a summary of a conversation between Chastellux and Samuel Adams on the subject of the new constitution of Massachusetts (I, 269-74). These extracts may have been made earlier or later than 1784. There appears to be no evidence that TJ owned a copy of the 1781 *Voyage*, which was limited to some 25 copies.

[1] This and subsequent words in italics were written in cipher and have been decoded by the editors, employing Code No. 3. These words were partly decoded by Ford, III, 399, but with some serious and misleading errors. TJ first wrote "Lee" and then overwrote the symbols for the name.

[2] TJ first wrote "faction" and then overwrote the symbols for it.

[3] This and the preceding three sentences were interlined by TJ. See letter of this date from the Virginia delegates to Gov. Harrison.

[4] The word was encoded as "Chatlux," which is the way TJ sometimes spelled the marquis' name.

Benjamin Harrison to the Virginia Delegates

GENTLEMEN   Council Chamber Feby 20th. 1784

I received your favor of the 23d. of last month yesterday with Mr. Pollocks letter which I shall lay before the next assembly. Some part of his complaint may be just tho' the last assembly thought more money had been already paid and assumed than he was justly entitled to, and I am of opinion there can be but little more due, tho' they in their hurry at the close of a session had agreed to pay his whole demand, I wish their conduct may not occasion their being censured as it certainly leaves room to suppose they are very unsteady in their proceedings.

The act of cession of the back country to Congress was sent to the post office the 26th. day of December with a long letter from me since which I have forwarded all the acts of the last cession, but lest neither of them should reach You I send duplicates of them both. Would it be amiss to enquire into the delays of the post office? This is not the first time they have been attended with inconvenience to the public.

I am &c.   B. H.

FC (Executive Letter Book, VI); caption at head of text reads: "The Virginia delegates in Congress."

Virginia Delegates in Congress
To Benjamin Harrison,
with Petition from Inhabitants of Kentucky

SIR   Annapolis Feby. 20. 1784.

We have the honor to inclose to your Excellency the copy of a petition from some of the inhabitants of the Kentucky district, lately presented to Congress. It was read when seven States were on the floor and it seem'd to be their disposition to pay no attention to it. Sometime afterwards we mov'd that it might be committed to us to be transmitted to your Excellency and this motion was disagreed to by only one State whose Delegates suggested they did it only upon the principle that the petition should be taken up and rejected by Congress. In this state it still remains nor are we authoriz'd from any circumstance which hath appear'd to us to suppose that it will ever be acted on. We have to desire of your Excellency to lay this before the general assembly. We have the honor to be with great respect your Excellency's most obt. & humble servant,
                                                        TH: JEFFERSON
                                                        ARTHUR LEE
                                                        JAS. MONROE

ENCLOSURE

[2 January 1784]

To his Excellency the President and Honourable delegates of the United States of America in Congress Assembled.

The memorial and petition of a number of Inhabitants of Kentuckey Settlement, westward of the Cumberland mountains on the waters emptying into the river Ohio Humbly sheweth.

That your memorialists have at a great expence and hazard removed themselves to this Country, (and some of us at the expence of our all) with a view and expectation of procuring a sufficiency of land for the support of themselves and families, on which they hoped to settle, and enjoy the remainder of their days in peace and happiness, but they are sorry to be under the disagreeable necessity to complain they are disappointed in their expectations.

Your honors will please to observe that when the State of Virginia opened a land Office for the locating of land on the western waters, there was Commissioners appointed for certain districts in the western territory, to settle and adjust the claimants titles for services done, improvements made on waste unappropriated land in said Country, for which they were entitled to certain quantities of land; whose powers were limited for a certain time, but from unforeseen casualities, the great distance of the way, the Commissioners powers expired before many of us could attend to lay in our claims, and many that did attend

[552]

for want of evidence in time to prove their services and improvements lost the just right; And for reasons unknown to your Memorialists when the Commissioner's powers by act of Assembly were prolonged in the other districts, the Commissioners of Kentuckey district were discontinued to their great loss of our just claims and rights, and others of us being unacquainted with the late law establishing a land office, were in expectation of obtaining a reasonable settlement in waste unappropriated land as formerly, in frontier unsettled Countries, but to their great loss and surprize were disappointed, having sold our little property, the great unavoidable expence in moving such a great distance, the sudden depreciation of the bills of credit and the remoteness of our situation rendered it almost impracticable for us to procure land warrants in time to secure a small quantity of land any way tolerable to live on.

We would further beg leave to observe that while we were struggling with all the difficulties, hardships and dangers of settling a remote new Country, under the disadvantage of a bloody cruel war, protecting and defending our families and all that was dear and near to us (and as might be said at our own expence) from a barbarous, savage enemy, numbers of monied Gentlemen in the settlement, who lived in security and affluence and no ways contributed towards the defence or settling of this Country, monopolized great part of the most valuable lands in their hands to the great discouragement and hindrance of the equitable settlement thereof. It is a well known truth that the riches and strength of a free Country does not consist in property being vested in a few Individuals, but the more general it is distributed, the more it promotes industry, population and frugality, and even morality.

Altho', We with gratitude acknowledge, that several Gentlemen, Inhabitants of this settlement, of fortune and influence, who had engrossed large quantities of land when this Country was invaded by the enemy, generously stepped forth in defence of their Country and some of them nobly fell in the Conflict, whose memory we honor and revere.

That a number of your memorialists from the causes abovesaid and their having heretofore been constrained to live in forts and stations for their own safety and defence, and generally on land claimed by other persons, have spent the most of their little effects they brought with them, which has rendered them unable either to move away or purchase land at the advance price the monopolizers hold it; and now after our long struggle in defending the Country and the land they pretend to hold, at our own expence, with the great loss of blood and Treasure, be forced to give an exorbitant price, or rent the land we have been fighting for, or turn off, we complain of as a great hardship and grievance.

We would further represent, that kind providence has been very bountiful to this remote inland Country in supplying it with a number of salt springs which we humbly conceive ought to be held sacred and for the use of the community in general, but we are sorry to say they are engrossed by Individuals and mostly non-residenters of this settlement, that they have exacted extravagant rents for the privilege of making salt, which has greatly enhanced the price of that most useful, necessary article.

Your memorialists would further beg leave to observe, that from our local situation, Nature placed us at too great a distance from the State of Virginia to be governed by one legislature; the nature of our circumstances differ so materially that it is almost impossible for the legislature of Virginia at such a distance to frame such salutary, wholesome laws that might in all cases answer the weal and interest of this Country; that many salutary laws made for our ease and comfort, from our remote situation, either expires or losses their good intentions before we have timely notice thereof; that from our situation we cannot have that equitable representation we are entitled to; that residenters and Men that has families to take care of and provide for, let them be ever so well qualified, declines the arduous task to represent us in Assembly, unless they have private business of their own to induce them to attend, and be so long absent from their interest and families. That all the public business of this settlement is transacted and governed by the Legislature of Virginia, that most of the profitable Posts and Offices is held by Non-residenters and transacted by their deputies, that all grants and patents for land and other public Offices is transacted and done in Virginia, by which and other means all the little ready specie that can be collected is drained out of this settlement to the great damage and impoverishing thereof, that the salaries and fees of public Offices, levies and taxes raised, are all rated in tobacco which, from its fluctuating price, makes it very uncertain, and this Settlement as yet, raises no tobacco for exportation, it lays the Assessors and Collectors under great difficulties to collect the levies and taxes, and leaves a door open for the public Offices to exact exorbitant fees &ca.

Thus may it please your Honors, We once more make bold to lay before you a few of our many grievances, which we humbly conceive, either from inclination, or want of proper information cannot be so salutarily remedied but by them who has a feeling knowledge thereof.

We therefore your humble Petitioners most earnestly pray that the Honorable Congress will condescend to take under consideration our many grievances and difficulties which we set forth and labor under; and lay off Kentuckey Settlement westward of the Cumberland Mountains in a free, Independent State [reserving to Congress the power and authority as population encreases, for ease and comfort of the Inhabitants, to subdivide the same], and receive us into the fœderal Union, to enable us to enjoy the freedom and blessings of our fellow-Citizens. And We your petitioners on our part do promise and engage to support Civil Government and the Fœderal Union to the uttermost of our power and ability, which from the rapid emigration now taking place, we hope we shall with honor and reputation be able to perform. And grant us such further relief in the premises as to Congress in their Judgement and Wisdom shall think equitable and just; And Your Honor's Petitioners as in duty bound shall ever pray.

RC (Vi); in the hand of James Monroe, signed by TJ, Lee, and Monroe; endorsed: "Letter from Del: in Congress enclosg. Kentucky Memorial for the Assembly Feby. 20. 84." Enclosure (Vi): Tr of the petition of the inhabitants of Kentucky to Congress, with 751 names attached; endorsed: "(Copy) Petition of the Inhabitants of Kentuckey to be erected into a Seperate State, and taken into the Union Read in Congress Jany. 2. 1784 Honble Delegates of Virginia."

According to the endorsement of both the original petition (DLC: PCC, No. 41, V, 101-2) and the above Tr, it was read in Congress on 2 Jan. 1784; but no record of its presentation appears in the Journals, nor is there a record of the motion of the Virginia Delegates, mentioned in the above letter (JCC, XXVI, 3, note). For the debate in Congress on an earlier, similar petition from Kentucky see Burnett, *Letters of Members*, VI, Nos. 604, 607, and references there.

From Derieux

MONSIEUR   Duplicata de Charleston ce 22 fever. 1782. [1784]

Mon epouse m'ayant dit que vous etiés L ami de Mr. Mazzei mon beaupere, Je prends la liberté de vous informer que nous sommes dans ce port depuis le 1er. de ce mois, d'ou nous proposons de faire routte pour la virginie, aussitot que La Santé de ma femme qui est accouchée dans notre traversée de france, nous le permettra. Le desir de faire connoissance avec vous, Monsieur ajoutte beaucoup à mon impatience, d'aller habiter ma nouvelle patrie delection.

Vous m'obligerés beaucoup, Monsieur d'avoir la bonté de me marquer si Mr. Mazzei est arrivé en Virginie, et dans le cas ou il seroit encore a philadelphie de voulloir bien l'instruire que nous attendrons icy de ses nouvelles, il me sera bien agreable de recevoir des votres avant mon depart. J'attends cette satisfaction avec autant d'impatience que je mets d'empressement a vous assurer du profond respect avec lequel je suis, Monsieur, Votre très humble et très obeissant serviteur   DE RIEUX

at Mrs. Sisk queen Street
No. 53. Charleston. South carolina

Ma femme vous prie de voulloir bien agreer Lassurance de ses civilités, et faire ses amitiés à Miss Petty.

Ayant appris que La poste de cette ville, nétoit pas exacte, je vous adresse ce Duplicata par un Vaisseau qui fait voile pour les frontieres de la Virginie.

RC (DLC); 2d copy; endorsed by TJ: "Rieux Monsr. de." Although the date at the head of the text is clearly 1782, this letter was obviously written in 1784. It was received by TJ on 10 Apr. 1784, as indicated by an entry in SJL under that date: "received de Rieux. Chas.town. Feb. 22. 1784."

Mazzei's stepdaughter, Maria Margarita Martin, was married in 1780 to Justin Pierre Plumard de Rieux (later Derieux). They came to America shortly after Mazzei's return from Europe in Nov. 1783 (see Mazzei, *Memoirs*, p. 257, 274, 281-2, for an account of the difficulties that the young couple experienced with their mothers; see also WMQ, 1st ser., XVII [1908-9], 18-20).

To [Daniel?] Dulany

[*Annapolis*, 22 *Feb. 1784*. Entry in SJL reads: "Mr. Dulany to rent house." TJ's letter to Dulany has not been found nor can Dulany be positively identified, though as a famous lawyer, a leading public figure in Maryland, and a friend of TJ (see De la Serre to TJ, 13 May 1786), Daniel Dulany may well have been the landlord involved. On 25 Feb. TJ wrote in his Account Book: "Moved to Mr. Dulany's house." He continued to live there until he left Annapolis in May (Dumbauld, *Jefferson, American Tourist*, p. 56-7; *Md. Hist. Mag.*, XLI [1946], 199).]

From Francis Hopkinson

DEAR SIR   Philada Feby 23d. 1784

I have just now received your favour pr. Mr. Marbois, have not Time to answer in kind, am sorry for your Illness. If your Fever was of the infectious kind you have performed Quarantine. I hope to see you in the Spring. I should not have wrote in such a Hurry, but to inform you that our Philosl. Society is in a promising Way. The Case of Mr. Maddison was this—the Candidates for Election were enter'd on two different pieces of paper. When the Election came on, one of those Papers was missing, in which was Mr. Maddison's Name, with the Names of other worthy Persons. This Paper has never been found. A Debate ensued and it was finally agreed to put the Names on the paper in hand alone to Vote. I have at last Meeting, again enter'd Mr. Maddison as a Candidate. The Election will be in April and I doubt not but every Voter will be glad of such a Member.

Hurried as I am, I must tell you that I have framed a Petition to the House of Assembly, which has been sign'd by many respectable names carried into the House—Leave for a Bill. I drew the Bill on Saturday. It will be presented to Day, and from all Appearances (almost to a Certainty) Mr. Rittenhouse will be turned out of all his offices, having been duly convicted of Astronomical and Philosophical Abilities against the Peace and Dignity of the said Commonwealth, &c., &c., and be appointed Astronomer to the State of Pennsylvania, with a Salary of at least £600, probably £750 pr. An. Adieu your's sincerely,   F: HOPKINSON

Oh! the Congress—the Congress!

RC (DLC).

Benjamin Harrison to James Monroe

SIR   Co. Chamber Feby. 24th. 1784

Immediately on the receipt of your favor of the 14th. of this month I demanded the necessary documents from the Solicitor to give you some general idea of the expenditures of the State for its immediate defence and the conquest of the back country and received such an answer as I expected which I enclose you for your information of the State of Our public accounts. I believe the confusion is without its paralel, and shews plainly that the choice of men to fill those different offices might be placed in better hands than it now is or has been heretofore; the solicitor You know has been long appointed to settle the continental accounts the progress he has made in them may be guessed at from his answer and the difficulties that will arise in bringing them to a conclusion.

I cannot be of your opinion that the Penobscot expedition and those set on foot by this state as they now stand are in the least similar. Clarke was sent out to wrest from the enemy a country evidently within our chartered bounds. He succeeded and we have now given it up to the United States in consideration of their paying the expence of conquering and supporting the country, but before this period we had no claim against Congress for a reimbursement of our expences nor was the demand ever thought of. The Penobscot expedition was a romantic thought of Massachusetts to acquire honor and a country not their own and for themselves. When they give as much as we have done they may make a similar demand and with as good a face but not till then.

If their demand for extra bounties are allowed, I make no doubt but we can balance accounts against them as I think we have been as profuse in that way as any state in the union except South carolina. What the assembly or Congress can do with the forty for one money I really know not. It appears to be a mere job calculated to save individuals at the expence of the united States.

I wish you had been so obliging as to have informed me whether you have received my letter of the 26th. of December covering the act of cession of the back country as I have had some uneasiness at the delay it must have met with on the road.

I am &c.

FC (Executive Letter Book, VI); caption reads: "The honble Colo Monroe in Congress." Enclosure missing.

On 23 Feb. Harrison requested the Solicitor General to furnish, for the use of the Virginia delegates, "as accurate an account of the whole expenditures of the state for its particular defence as can be made out between this and Saturday morning [28 Feb.]" (same).

From Robert Morris,

with Table of Arrears of the States and Jefferson's Notes

SIR   Office of Finance 25th. Febry. 1784.

Your Letter of the first Instant reached me but a few days since and I seize the earliest Moment in my Power of replying to it. I shall reply also in this Letter to that with which I was favored from the honorable Mr. Williamson, and pray both of him and of the Committee that they will excuse it, assuring them that it proceeds from a desire of collecting all I have to say on the Subject under one Point of View.

It was and is my opinion and has frequently been expressed that the Calls of Congress should be confined to the arrears of former Requisitions so long as it can be possible out of such Means to defray the current Expenditures. And altho it has been necessary to comprize a Part of the Expenditures of 1782 and 1783 within that Debt for the Interest whereof permanent Funds have been required I thought it my Duty to oppose any Relinquishment of the existing Requisitions. I will not repeat the Reasons because the grand Committee appear to be of the same opinion. It was evident that if those Requisitions should produce more than the current Expenditure the Surplus could easily be applied towards discharging a Part of the Debt which arose during the Year 1782 and 1783.

Enclosed Sir you will find the required account of Taxes received to the End of the last Year. But since that Period there have been further Receipts and I must observe that among these are some small Sums collected in New Jersey and Pennsylvania on the Requisitions for 1783 but these are nevertheless carried (in the Treasury Books) to account of the unsatisfied Requisitions of 1782. Confining myself to round Numbers because I presume the Committee would rather receive Information materially right in Season than wait for greater Accuracy at the Expence of Moments every one of which must be precious, I take Leave to mention that the Arrearages on the Requisitions of 1782 and 1783 exceed eight Millions and that one of those eight Millions would pay the unfunded Expenditures from the End of 1781 to the Commencement of the current Year by which Term of *unfunded Expenditures* used for want of a better, I mean such Part of the public Debt as arose in that Year and which not having been carried to the Account of the Public Debt but remaining due on my Official Engagements and Anticipations must still be provided for out of the Requisitions. There will remain therefore at best seven Millions for the Service of this Year and Payment of a Part of the former Debt should the

Collections be so rapid as to pay off the required Million beyond the immediate Expences which I confess there is but too little Reason to expect. It will however be useful that pressing applications be made to the States to compleat their Quotas under those Requisitions for if only One hundred thousand Dollars were employed in Payment of our funded Debt before January next, in addition to the Provision for paying the Interest, we might then consider the Independence of our Country as firmly established. I shall dwell no longer [on] this Subject which will I am sure be better matured by the Committee than by any of my Reflections. But I am bound to mention Sir that (from the Slowness and Smallness of the Collections) our Finances are in a more critical Situation than you can easily conceive: Such, that I dare not leave this Place altho I am very desirous of paying my Respects to Congress at Annapolis.

As to the Vote of September 1782 requiring One million two hundred thousand Dollars for Payment of Interest on Loan Office Certificates &c. I have no official Information of what has been done by the States. Some among them have I believe directed the Issue of a certain other Kind of Certificate for Payment of that Interest, but as the Acts do not conform to the Resolution of Congress I cannot know what Conduct the Loan Officers have pursued. It is much to be lamented that the States individually are not sensible how necessary it is to conform to general Regulations. On every Occasion some local Convenience is consulted and a Deviation made which appears to be of little Consequence to the general System and which [is] nevertheless important; and becomes injurious to the very State by which it was made. The Idea of an Officer dependent only on Congress amenable only to them and consequently obedient only to Orders derived from their Authority is disagreable to each State and carries with it the Air of Restraint. Every such Officer therefore finds a Weight of Public Opinion to contend with. But how, in a Continent so extensive, can that Simplicity of Administration which is essential to Order and Œconomy, be introduced; unless such Officers are not only tolerated but aided by the legislative and executive Authorities? I will pursue these Ideas no farther for the present, because I think the Opportunity will arrive in which the Subject must be considered with more diffused Attention.

Enclosed (Sir) I have the Honor to transmit an Account of the Civil Establishment of the United States together with an Account of contingent Expences of the several Offices. Neither of these is as complete as could be wished tho as perfect as they can at present be made. You will doubtless observe that all the Offices are not completely filled and that all the contingent Expences are not brought into the Account. Among the latter Omissions is the contingent Expence of our foreign Ministers which will I am perswaded be far from inconsiderable.

I have thought it proper also to transmit to the Committee an Estimate of the Sums at which our Civil Establishment might be fixed; and on this Estimate I make the following general Observations. 1st That the Articles of Contingencies therein mentioned are carried out on Conjecture and therefore the Sum Total may be somewhat more or less according to Circumstances. 2ly That the Numbers Titles and Salaries of the several Officers being entirely in the Disposition of Congress they will add to or diminish from them as they may think proper wherefore the Totals will doubtless be different from what I have Stated and 3ly. That a very considerable Part of this Expence being occasioned by the old Accounts will cease of itself when those Accounts are settled.

I proceed then to observe more particularly on the Expences of the Presidents Household (I) That the present Mode is certainly objectionable as I have frequently had Occasion to observe and which I now repeat with the more Freedom as Nothing which can be said will bear the least personal Application. My Reasons are 1st. No Person not accountable to the United States should be invested with the Right of drawing at Will on the Public Treasury. 2ly. Every Expenditure ought as far as the Reason and Nature of Things will permit to be ascertained with Precision. 3ly. A fixed Salary being annexed to the Office of President of Congress he will be more effectually Master of his own Household and in Consequence a greater Order and Œconomy may reasonably be expected. On the Expences of the Office of Secretary of Congress (II) I shall say nothing. The Expences, the Duties and the Cares are so immediately under the Eye of Congress themselves that it would be Presumption. But I would observe that to the Account of the Contingencies of this Office ought to be carried the Expence not only of Office Rent Stationary &c. But also Fuel for Congress, Printing of the Journals, Expresses sent by Congress and the like.

The Chaplains of Congress receive at present at the Rate of four hundred Dollars each. If the Office be necessary it ought to be so supported as that the Officers may be entirely attached to Congress and accompany them in their Changes or fix at their permanent Place of Residence which ever of these Modes shall eventually be adopted. I have ventured to state their Salaries at one thousand Dollars each perhaps. I am still under the proper Sum. On the Expence of the Court of Appeals (IV) I can say Nothing because I know not whether the Continuance of it be necessary. But I should suppose that if three Gentlemen well versed in the Law of Nations were from the Tenure of their Offices to be always with Congress (so as to be consulted and employed when the public Service might require it) Such an Establishment would be continued if the Expence did not exceed the Utility.

When all our Accounts shall be settled our Debts either paid or properly funded and Things reduced to a Peace Establishment the Expences of the Office of Finance (V) may perhaps be reduced about two thousand Dollars by taking away the Salaries of the Assistant and one Clerk and adding somewhat to that of the Secretary. Under the present Circumstances I do not think the Number of the Officers can be lessened. The Salary of the Superintendant has often been mentioned as very high. This is a Subject on which I can speak with great Plainness and, but for the disagreable Situation of Things above mentioned, I should speak also without any personal Reference. I humbly conceive that the Object of Congress is what it certainly ought to be an enlightened Œconomy. On the Powers of the Office I will say Nothing here because it would be misplaced. The Expences of it are and ought to be great. Untill we can create new Beings we must take Mankind as they are and not only so but we must take them as they are in our own Country. Now it is evident that a certain Degree of Splendor is necessary to those who are clothed with the higher Offices of the United States. I will venture to say that without it those Officers do not perform one of the Duties which they owe to their Masters. And I can say also from Experience that the Salary of six thousand Dollars does not exceed the Expence of that Office. I speak for my Successor or rather for my Country. Neither the Powers nor the Emoluments of the Office have sufficient Charms to keep me in it one Hour after I can quit it with Consistence and I did Hope that Period would have arived during the next Month. Perhaps it may. If a Man of Fortune chuses to run the Course of Vanity or ambition he will naturally wish the Salaries of Office to be low because it must reduce the Number of honest Competitors. I say honest Competitors because that those who would make a Property of public Trusts will always be indifferent as to the amount of Salary seeing that with such Men it forms the smallest pecuniary Consideration. When a liberal Salary enables a Man not rich to live in a Stile of Splendor without impairing his private Fortune the Show he makes and the Respect attached to him really belong to the Country he serves and are among the necessary Trappings of her Dignity. Now it has always appeared to me that true Œconomy consists in putting proper Men in proper Places; to which Purpose proper Salaries are a previous Requisite. Here I shall pause because the Reflection occurs to my Mind that perhaps this with many other Propositions equally true will never be duly felt untill an opposed Conduct shall lead to disagreable Conviction. If indeed it were my object to enforce this Point I should go no further than the past Experience of Congress and perhaps there might be Room for some Argument on the actual State of the Office of foreign Affairs. The Expences of that Office (VII) as well as of the War Office (VI) require only a Reference to what has been just mentioned. The Expences of the Treasury Office (VIII) cannot be curtailed for before the present Business can be lessened that of our Debt must come forward and there must be some Persons to manage it altho the great Machinery at present employed will be unnecessary.

For Reasons of evident Propriety I say Nothing on the Establishment of our foreign Servants (IX) only recommending that as little as possible be left to the article of Contingencies. Because if on the one Hand it be just to compensate extraordinary and unexpected Expences for the public Service It is proper on the other Hand to reduce within the closest Limits of Certainty which the nature of things can permit the amount of those Burthens which the People must bear. And it ought to be remembered that Contingencies are generally speaking a Kind of Expences which tho justified by necessity are unprovided for by express appropriation and which therefore ought as much as possible to be avoided.

The last article is Expences on Collection of the Revenue (XI) and it is much to be lamented that this is so heavy Not indeed the Sum proposed in the Estimate which is trifling but it will be found on Examination that the Expence of collecting Taxes in this Country is greater than in almost any other—a serious Misfortune and which would certainly be provided against if the Officers of the Collection were nominated by Authority of the United States because then those Principles of Suspicion which have already done so much and spoken so loudly would soon fix upon a Grievance at present overlooked because it forms Part of a System favorable to withholding instead of collecting Taxes. It has already been observed that Officers of the Nature of the Receivers are necessary in several States; it is here repeated and Experience will prove it. At the same Time the Committee will please to take Notice that the Loan Officers are not included in the Estimate the Reason of which is that they can answer no Purpose but the Expence of the appointment and the complicating of a System which ought to be simplified. An Officer whose Duty it is to urge Collections may do good if he performs that Duty but when it is a question of paying Means may be adopted which will be more effectual, less expensive and infinitely less liable to fraud. Not to mention that these means may be such as to avoid long and intricate Accounts. In fact (And I hope Sir you will excuse the Observation) there seems to have existed a Solicitude how to spend Money conveniently and easily but little Care how to obtain it speedily and effectually. The Sums I have proposed as fixed Salaries for these Officers may at first Sight appear large but if the Office is to be at all useful it must be in the Hands of a good Man who can devote to it his whole Time and attention and who will neither by his private Distresses nor by the Scantiness of his Stipend be prompted to betray his Trust or abuse the Confidence reposed in him.

Before I close this letter I will take the Liberty farther to mention to the Committee as a principal means of avoiding many Disagreable Discussions relative to the present Object that the Establishment of a Mint and due Regulations of the Post Office would soon supply the Funds necessary to defray the Expences of our civil Establishment. The former of these is entirely in the Power of Congress and I should suppose that the States could have no reasonable Objection to leave the Revenue which might arise from the second to the Disposition of Congress for that Purpose.

I pray your Excuse Sir for troubling you with so long a letter which I will not add to by making Apologies, But assure you of the Respect with which I have the Honor to be Your most obedient & humble Servant, ROBT MORRIS

ENCLOSURE

Payments and arrears of the several states on the requisition of taxes for 1782. to wit the requisition of October 30, 1781. for 8,000,000 D.

	reqn. & apportnmt. of 8. M. Nov. 1781	Dollars paid	due. Dollars	Requisn. & apportion-ment of 2 M. Oct. 1782	Due on both
N. Hampshire	373,598	3,000	370,598	80,000	450,598
Massachusetts	1,307,596	247,676$\frac{2}{3}$	1,059,919$\frac{1}{3}$	320,000	1,379,919$\frac{1}{3}$
Rhode island	216,684	67,847.86	148,836$\frac{2}{45}$	48,000	196,836$\frac{2}{45}$
Connecticut	747,196	131,577$\frac{5}{4}$	615,618$\frac{1}{8}$	222,000	837,618$\frac{1}{8}$
New York	373,598	39,064$\frac{1}{10}$	334,533$\frac{9}{10}$	90,000	424,533$\frac{9}{10}$
New Jersey	485,699	107,004$\frac{17}{18}$	383,674$\frac{1}{18}$	110,000	493,674$\frac{1}{18}$
Pennsylvania	1,120,794	346,632.89	774,161$\frac{1}{90}$	300,000	1,074,161$\frac{1}{90}$
Delaware	117,085		117,085	28,000	140,085
Maryland	933,996	89,302$\frac{1}{9}$	844,693$\frac{8}{9}$	220,000	1,064,693$\frac{8}{9}$
Virginia	1,307,594	115,103$\frac{24}{45}$	1,192,490$\frac{21}{45}$	290,000	1,482,490$\frac{21}{45}$
N. Carolina	622,677		622,677	148,000	770,677
S. Carolina	373,598	344,301$\frac{25}{45}$	29,296$\frac{19}{45}$	120,000	149,296$\frac{19}{45}$
Georgia	24,905		24,905	24,000	48,905
	8,000,000	1,486,511$\frac{32}{49}$	6,513,488$\frac{13}{45}$	2,000,000	8,513,488$\frac{13}{45}$

Suppose it practicable for the states to raise in one year   4,513,488¹³⁄₄₅
They have paid of the 8 millions   1,486,511³²⁄₄₅

                                                                                                6,000,000

Then they must be required to make up ¾ of their quota of the 8. millions
Let the application of this be as follows.

Balance of interest to end of 1782.	642,764
Interest accruing during the year 1783.	1,272,581
Interest accruing on the foreign debts in 1784.	375,833
Existing debts of the 8. million fund	1,000,000
Expences of the current year	427,525⅓
Deficiencies of collection suppose	794,784⁴³⁄₄₅

                                                                                                4,513,488¹³⁄₄₅

RC (DLC: PCC, No. 137, Appendix); in a clerk's hand, signed by Morris; addressed: "The Honorable Mr. Jefferson Chairman for Grand Committee of Congress Annapolis"; endorsed by Thomson: "Letter 25 feby 1784 Sup: f. to grand Comee enclosing 1. Acct. of taxes recd to end of 1783. 2. Civil Establishmt. 3. An estimate at what the Civil list might be established." The original enclosures have not been located. The first of them, however, was copied off by TJ (DLC: TJ Papers, 233: 41611) and is printed herewith, together with his notes on it. The third enclosure appears to be that which is printed in Wharton, *Dipl. Corr. Amer. Rev.*, VI, 779-80, as "Proposed Expenses of the Civil List."

Benjamin Harrison to James Monroe

SIR   Council Chamber Feby. 27th. 1784

I shall take care to lay the copy of the Kentuckey petition to Congress before the next assembly agreeably to your request.

I have also received your recommendations to the Several States to comply strictly with the articles of the treaty which I much approve and hope they will be generally attended to, but if this is expected by the british are they not under a reciprocal obligation to comply strictly with it in their part? Have they done so with that article which expressly stipulates that our negroes shall be restored to us? No they have not. But on the contrary have shipped them off before our faces and mean to defraud their owners of them at the time when they are calling on them for their debts; to my certain knowledge a great number of the virtuous whigs of this country will be reduced to poverty and distress, by having the remainder of their property taken to pay these very debts if they are not reimbursed for this part of their losses. It certainly therefore behoves Congress to take some decided measures for procuring us redress. If they do not I cannot think this country will ever come into the proposed measures at least till they have made full compensation out of the british debt to those who have been thus deprived of their Slaves. If You and the other gentlemen of the delegation think with me You will no doubt introduce the subject to Congress, who I dare say will take the proper steps either the negroes or full compensation for them.[1] If they do not succeed it will shew to the southern States that they are not inattentive to their interests.

I am &c.

FC (Executive Letter Book, Vi); caption at head of text reads: "The honorable James Monroe in Congress." Though addressed to Monroe, this letter was a reply to the Virginia delegates' letter of 20 Feb. 1784. For the RECOMMENDATIONS TO THE SEVERAL STATES (transmitted by President Mifflin), see notes to the Proclamation of 14 Jan.

[1] The clerk must have omitted a phrase in this sentence. The missing RC may read: "take the proper steps to recover the negroes," &c.

From Joseph Jones

DR. SR.   Spring Hill 28th. Febry 1784

I have yours of the 2d. inst. by Col. Monroes Adam. I lament his not returning accompanied with the means of relief having heretofore experienced the disagreeable as well as disgracefull predicament in which the Gentlemen of the Delegation are placed for want of remittances from the State. It is to be hoped you have received the small supply the Treasurer mentions to me he had lately forwarded and that he will very soon be able to furnish a more ample succour. He has sent me an order for what cash may have been collected by the Sheriffs of Spotsa. [Spotsylvania] and King George of the current Taxes. I will obtain what I can under this order and forward it for your relief. As yet the Sheriffs have done little owing to the severity of the season, which, instead of abating, is to-day and was yesterday as cold as almost any time in the winter, and the River, which had opened a little in particular places, again blocked up.

Knowing that instructions had been given our Commissioners on the subject of British debts and uninformed what had been the issue of the Propositions, I supposed Congress might still have it in contemplation to move in that matter. I apprehended the British claim upon America was more than could be discharged by prompt payment and concluded time for payment indispensably necessary. To judge what time was necessary, a knowledge of the amount of the demand appeared to me a pre-requisite; besides it seemed to me

to be the most proper course to conduct this business by negociation between the Creditors and Debtors or the State in behalf of the
Debtors and that the sooner some steps for this purpose were
adopted the better. In consequence of these reflections I had prepared a motion the last session of assembly to be offered the House
calculated to obtain information as to the debt as well as to feel
the pulse of the B. Creditors as to periodical payments. The departure of some of the principal Members and the thinness of the
House at the close of the session deterred me from offering as it was
a proposition of such importance. I am well satisfied the magnitude
of the debt and the impracticability of speedy payment will authorise ex parte measures without subjecting us to the imputation
of violating the Treaty and perhaps themselves of equal measure
to all our Creditors the most eligible. Yet addition of interest of the
Debt during the war is a great increase of it if we are liable to pay
it. Would not the mode of negociating with the Creditors be the
best to get rid of that difficulty for it is very probable from all I
can hear the Creditors at least many of them would prefer to secure
the principal due when the separation took place than claim interest
during the War. The debts contracted within the State have near
the whole of them been settled and Mortgages and bonds taken by
the factors at the commencement of the contest so that a small
part only rests on simple contract. I thought with you and am yet
inclined to that opinion (tho' I confess I do not openly espouse it)
that the stipulations of the Treaty subjected us to pay the interest.
Inclining as I do to the opinion I yet have my doubts. Could British subjects after the separation claim and recover their debts of
our Citizens? If they could not, how comes it that a dead debt
revived by the Treaty should gather interest during its death or
suspension. I speak not here of the moral obligation to pay. Altho' I
applaud your Sentiments respecting confiscated property and when
I get sufficient information of facts respecting the state of that
business may be disposed to be generous yet at present I own I feel
little propensity to be so. My inquiry respecting the undisposed
confiscations had for its object the more effectually bringing about
an accommodation of the payment of the British debts and is not
intended by me for any other purpose unless circumstances as yet
unknown to me shall alter my Sentiments. I think the information
from our commissioners of the transactions of the negociation gave
us reason to think the British Commissioners expect no fruits from
the recommendation of Congress. Old Franklin overpowered them
on the question by a candid offer to go into a fair settlement of the

account which was declined. As soon as I receive the Treasurers account of the confiscated property I will inform you of it. Your letter to Capt. Keys which went to Buchannan in Richmond is returned by my Servant. I have sent it to Maury to be forwarded to Madison who will take care of it. I fear you will be puzzled to read my bad writing. It is really so cold I can scarcely hold the pen. with much esteem I am Dr Sr. yr. obt Servt.,   Jos: Jones

RC (DLC).

Although TJ's letter OF THE 2D INST. has not been found and the entry in SJL contains but a bare outline of subjects, it is clear from Jones's reply what his stand on the confiscation of property of British subjects and Loyalists had been. His LETTER TO CAPT. KEYS was probably that of 1 Feb. 1784.

To the Speaker of the House of Delegates

[*Annapolis, 28 Feb. 1784.* Entry in SJL reads: "Speakr. H. Del. Accomodation Turks and Russ.—detention of ratification—8. states—importance of Norfolk—propose tax to open Ohio and Patowm.—direction to Gl. Wash." Not found.]

To Edmund Pendleton

Dear Sir   Annapolis Feb. 29. 1784.

Your favor of the 23d. inst. came safely by the last post. Your correspondent of Charlestown who informed you so long ago that an accomodation had taken place between the Russians and Turks was a better prophet than historian. The fact [. . . .]¹ than I beleive, but there are hopes it is so [. . . .]¹ information from our ministers on this [. . . .]¹ tells me he has it from one who has [. . . .]¹ that by the mediation of France and [. . . .]¹ great sacrifices by the Turks, [. . . .]¹ for being so weak and defenc[eless . . . .]cations,¹ tho' the officers [. . . .]¹ by the 20th. of Ja[. . . .]² long blocked up by the [. . . .]³ in time. Yet as we had ratified in good time, and the delay has been produced by accidents not under our controul, it does not furnish a justifiable cause of refusing the exchange. A ninth state appeared yesterday. But eight of the nine being represented by two delegates each, all important questions will require not only an unanimity of states, but of members, for which we have no reason to hope. I very much apprehend we shall be unable to get through even those which seem indispensable. I think it will be prudent immediately to define the powers of a committee of the states, that if we are left in the lurch again as we have been, there may be some power to place at the head of affairs till the states can be made sensible of the necessity of sending on full delegations. I expect we shall execute our deed of cession tomorrow. The Western country, instructions for foreign treaties, and the annual estimates will then be brought forward, to try what we can do on them. I am in hopes[4] therefore my next may tell you what we have done, and not merely what we have to do, which, such is the present barrenness of the times, is really the most copious source of information at this time. Mr. Adams and Mr. Jay have some how or other got themselves over to London. Their reception was not a kind one by any means and they must have [. . . .][1] at this faux pas, as their friends here have been. [. . . .][1] with my materials after wishing you much [. . . .][1] the esteem with which I am Dr Sir [Yo]ur Friend & servt., Th: Jefferson[5]

P.S. Since the writing the above we receive in[for]mation from Philadelphia of the arrival of an English vessel bringing papers which say that Ld. North and Mr. Fox carried their E. India bill triumphantly by ⅔ of the voices through the house of commons, but lost it in the Lords, whereon they resigned and that Mr. Pitt with his friends would come in. The Prince of Wales it is said voted against the bill and was reprimanded by the king. Since writing the above also an appointment of some importance (Commissioner for the Indn. treaty) is conferred by Congress on Genl. Clarke, who is either set out or in the moment of setting out Westwardly. As it is essential he should receive this immediately and I think his father lives near you will you be so good as to send it to him with a desire if the General be set out, but yet within reasonable reach that he will send an express after him.

P.P.S. The president sending an express to Genl. Clarke before the post sets out I have opened the letter and taken out his. It gives me an opportunity of informing you that Congress this day received a letter from the Marqs. Fayette of Dec. 26. confirming the removal of North and Fox, that it was effected by a maneuvre of the King himself and that Pitt and E. Temple would come in, also that the Turks and Russians will be quiet for a while.

RC (Nathaniel W. Pendleton, Wytheville, Va., 1944 and NN); addressed and endorsed. The MS has been torn apart, the upper parts of p. 1 and 2, with date and signature, are in the possession of Mr. Pendleton; the lower parts of these pages, containing a portion of the text of the letter, the two postscripts, and part of the address leaf with Edmund Pendleton's endorsement, are in NN. Both fragments are mutilated and sections of the text are lacking as indicated in the notes below. TJ summarized this letter in SJL under this date as follows: "E. Pend. Accomodation Turks and Russ—delay of ratification—9. states. Ad. & Jay in Lond— their reception." However, the letter could not have been sent, or the postscripts written, before 4 or 5 Mch. On 4 Mch. TJ entered in SJL: "Genl. Clarke. his appmt. as Indn. Commr. Put it under cover to E. P. to send by Express." The portion of the letter in NN is printed in Burnett, *Letters of Members*, VII, No. 527, under an assigned date of 2-4 Mch.

Pendleton's FAVOR OF THE 23D. INST. is missing.

[1] From one-third to two-thirds of a line missing.
[2] The first page of the fragment owned by Mr. Pendleton ends at this point.
[3] Approximately one-half a line missing. The fragment in NN begins with the words "long blocked by the"; there is no loss of text aside from that caused by mutilation, the fragment in NN following immediately after that owned by Mr. Pendleton.
[4] The first page of the fragment in NN ends at this point and the second page of the fragment owned by Mr. Pendleton begins. There is no loss of text between the two.
[5] The text of the fragment owned by Mr. Pendleton ends at this point, the remaining postscripts forming the second page of the fragment in NN.

To William Short

TH: J. TO MR. SHORT   Annapolis Mar. 1. 1784.

I am sorry my letter found you so much indisposed, and still more so that it should have added to your sufferings. But you must learn to bear these things by always calculating on the possibility of a cross as well as pyle and having a plan of reserve to turn to by way of comfort. I can yet add nothing more on the subject. Nine states appeared on the floor to-day. But eight of them are represented by two members only, so that in every important question, as not only an unanimity of states, but an unanimity of members also will be requisite to carry propositions, we must expect to carry none, and that our time will be spent in proposing regulations, hearing one another a week on each, put them to the vote, and see them fall because one or two or more members are against them. We shall immediately try what we can do with the Western country (the deed for which was executed and accepted this day), the foreign arrangement, peace establishment &c. I see no reason yet to doubt the opinion I formerly gave you that there would be no *Ministers*[1] kept *abroad*. You ask an explanation of the ænigma of the book, appendix, and index. For fear you should not understand the cypher, or catch it's key I added that ænigmatical paragraph in hopes it might explain a subject to you who had some hint of it and not to any other who had not. To cure the fever it gave you however I will now observe that the book was a *minister* the appendix a *secretary to the embassy* and the index a *secretary to* the *minister*. There will certainly be no *appendix* and I question if there be a *book*. Of course there can then be no *Index* to it. If there be no *appendix* would *you* be the *Index* to the *book* supposing there should be one. However I still think a *consul* or a *resident* on a *low salary* will be the *highest grade*. Not a word has ever dropt yet from *Monro[e]*.

I thank you for your attentions to P. Carr. I approve of Liberty hall because you do, without knowing what or where it is. Will you inform me on this head? Not that I would detain Peter, for I hope you have sent him there, but that I may write to him, to the master or manager whichever is most proper. Having to my habitual ill health, had lately added an attack of my periodical headach, I am obliged to avoid reading writing and almost thinking. You will excuse me therefore for closing here with an affectionate adieu!

P.S. I wrote by post Dec. 11. to Mr. Mazzei. Knowing that my letters of that date got safe to Richmond I wonder at having received no answer. Will you be so good as to find out and inform me whether my letter came to his hands?

RC (Blumhaven Library, Phila.); endorsed at a later date by Short: "This letter was found among some old papers at my Sister Wilkins in Kentucky in the summer 1803." Entry in SJL reads: "Mar. 1. W. Short. Subject in cypher—explained ænigma—where and what is Liby. hall?—hope he has sent P. C. there—letter Mazz[ei]."

This is the earliest letter known to be extant of the correspondence between TJ and Short. Some of the missing letters from TJ are entered in SJL (see under 27 Nov., 19 and 29 Dec. 1783, and 18 Jan. 1784). TJ's LETTER with the enigma that put Short in a fever must have been that of 18 Jan. 1784. Short's reply to that letter is missing, but it must have been written in Feb. THE SUBJECT must pertain to the question of Short's being employed abroad as secretary to an embassy or secretary to a minister; in his letter of 27 Nov. 1783 TJ had discussed the "foreign arrangement" and in that of 19 Dec. he may have adverted to this subject in the following: "First hope desperate—second doubtful." CROSS AS WELL AS PYLE: the reverse as well as the obverse or "cross" of a coin (OED, under *cross*, sb.21.).

[1] This and subsequent words in italics were written in code. Some of the words were decoded by Short interlineally; these have been verified and all others decoded by the editors, employing Code No. 4 (sent by TJ to Short in his letter of 30 Apr. 1784); see TJ to Short, 30 Apr. and Short to TJ, 8 May 1784.

The Virginia Cession of Territory Northwest of the Ohio

[1 Mch. 1784]

I. PRELIMINARY FORM OF DEED OF CESSION

II. DEED OF CESSION AS EXECUTED

EDITORIAL NOTE

With the acceptance by Congress of the Virginia cession on 1 Mch. 1784, the national domain came into existence. Jefferson, in what was for him a rare disclosure of his methods of guiding an important measure through a legislative body, recounted to Benjamin Harrison the last-minute maneuvers in Congress by which a single vote determined the outcome (TJ to Harrison, 3 Mch. 1784). But this, even as to the final moves, was an understatement. It is apparent that action on Virginia's cession was related somewhat to the matter of Connecticut's western claim as it entered into the discussion of Jefferson's report on the petition of Zebulon Butler (see editorial note to group of documents under 21 Jan. 1784). And the events that Jefferson described to Harrison were only a climax to three years of intense political struggles in Congress that followed Jefferson's transmittal of Virginia's first Act of cession of 2 Jan. 1781 (see TJ to Huntington, 17 Jan. 1781 and note there).

The earlier Act had stipulated several conditions, but the one that produced the difficulty was that all purchases from the Indians and all royal grants within the territory should be "declared absolutely void and of no Effect." The Virginia Constitution of 1776 had forbidden private purchases of land from the Indians (see Vol. 1: 383, 386, note 20), and the Act of cession of 1781 merely sought to continue and make retroactive this prohibition so far as the ceded territory was concerned, "in the same Manner as if the . . . Territory had still remained subject to and part of the Commonwealth of Virginia" (Vol. 4: 388). This reservation was aimed at the Illinois-Wabash, Vandalia, and Indiana companies, whose extensive claims lay within the charter bounds of Virginia. The opposition led by these land companies in the years 1781-1784 was "directed to the sole end of evading the obnoxious conditions attached to the Virginia cession" (Merrill Jensen, "The Creation of the National Domain, 1781-1784," MVHR, XXVI [1939], 323-42—the best short account of the subject; for a more extended study of the complex interrelationships of politics and land interests, see T. P. Abernethy, *Western Lands and the American Revolution*, N.Y., 1937).

The land companies had enough influence in Congress to cause a report to be brought in by a committee of which John Witherspoon was chairman, recommending that Congress reject the cessions of Virginia, New York, and Connecticut because of "the conditions attached to them and other circumstances"; that Congress "take into consideration the western limits beyond which they will not extend their guarantee to the particular States and to ascertain what vacant Territory belongs to the United States in common for the general benefit"; and that, as soon as this western limit was set, a committee be appointed to prepare a plan for dividing and settling the territory and for disposing of it so as to discharge the war debt of the United States (JCC, xx, 704). This recommendation was rejected and a new committee appointed, but the activities of the land companies, the employment of Thomas Paine by Vandalia to write a defense of its claim entitled *Public Good*, and the failure of Congress to act on the Virginia cession caused rumors to spread in such a way as to cause grave doubt as to the eventual outcome. On 5 May 1782 the *Virginia Gazette* (N & P) found it necessary to issue the following ungrammatical but significant reassurance to Virginians: "Notwithstanding the impudent assertions, and false state of facts, which has been held forth to the public, in various paragraphs of the news-papers on this continent, and industriously circulated by the lordly claimants of millions of acres of that western territory, which Virginia has ceded under certain restrictions for the public good, to the United States, and has steadily refused to grant to a few individuals. We can assure the public, that the honourable Congress, as a body, has taken no step to confirm the unfinished grants of the British king to those politic individuals, who at the expence of millions yet unborn, would erect themselves into petty Sovereigns, and defeat the good purpose for which so many brave men have shed their dearest blood in this virtuous struggle for equal liberty. Be not therefore guiled in the purchase or even acceptance of a title which is the shadow of a shade."

Because of this opposition by the land companies, sentiment began to develop in Virginia in support of a "proposition . . . to revoke the former cession" and Patrick Henry avowed himself in favor of laying out the western parts of Virginia into "small republicks" (TJ to Madison, 17 June 1783). Two days before the May 1783 session of the General Assembly was scheduled to open, Gov. Harrison wrote to the Virginia delegates half-seriously: "Please to inform my Friend Charles Thomson that I will send him a Copy of the Cession of the back Country by the next Post and with it a Copy of another resolution repealing it, which may perhaps be a lesson in future not to refuse a good offer when Men are in the Humor for giving" (Harrison to the Virginia delegates, 3 May 1783, Executive Letter Book, VI). The threatened repeal did not materialize.

Virginia's land bounties to officers and troops on the Continental and state establishments, as well as the claims of the land companies, complicated the issue. To satisfy these claims the state had reserved lands on the Cumberland and Tennessee rivers, and the Act of cession of 1781 stipulated that if these should prove inadequate, the deficiency should be made up of good lands between the Scioto and Little Miami. In addition there was a movement among Continental officers from other states to obtain from Congress a colony north of the Ohio to be settled by military men; Washington supported them in this effort (Washington to the President of Congress, 17 June 1783, *Writings*, ed. Fitzpatrick, XXVII, 16-18). The officers of the Virginia line organized, selected a surveyor, and were well represented at the May 1783 session of the General Assembly. Gen. Weedon wrote his old friend Steuben that doubt as to Congress' acceptance of the 1781 Act of cession would delay the officers' claims until autumn, but that, "if in the power of the Assembly they will grant us from Muskingum to the Great Miami which will be a Country Sufficient to lay all our claims in, and is supposed to be [the] finest in the world. . . . [I] have connected your Interest with mine in the Land Business and hope we shall be Neighborly on the Banks of the Scioto. My fish Trap and hunting ground shall be at your Service, but no man except those who can give a good account of himself shall have the same privilege" (Weedon to Steuben, 24 June 1783; Duval to Steuben, 16 May 1783; Steuben to Duval, 20 June 1783, all in NHi).

Fortunately, Virginia's struggles in Congress against the land companies began about this time to point to a more favorable issue. A committee relatively free of influence by the land interests reported on the Virginia Act of cession on 6 June 1783. This report took up each of the eight conditions imposed by Virginia and agreed to most of them, but a categorical annulment of the land companies' claims was avoided and the requirement that Congress should guarantee to Virginia her territories southeast of the Ohio was rejected as being "unnecessary and unreasonable" (JCC, XXV, 559-64). On 13 Sep. 1783 Congress approved the report, and the question of agreeing to this compromise solution was thereupon placed before the General Assembly. Madison expressed the hope that this action would "meet the ultimatum of Virginia" (Madison to TJ, 20 Sep. 1783; also Madison to Randolph, same date, *Writings*, ed. Hunt, II, 18). Gov. Harrison wrote the Virginia delegates: "I shall lay the resolutions of Congress . . . before the Assembly and suppose with you they will approve them as they differ very little from their proposals. The Guaranty required [of territories remaining to Virginia after the cession] was too humiliating for me" (Harrison to Delegates, 26 Sep. 1783; Harrison to Speaker of the House, 20 Oct. 1783, Executive Letter Book, Vi). Jefferson also clearly desired Virginia to accept the solution offered without further stipulations that would delay a final settlement (see entry for TJ to Mann Page, 27 Nov. 1783; and TJ to Harrison, 11 Nov. 1783 and 3 Mch. 1784).

But representatives of the Virginia officers were present and active at the Oct. 1783 session of the legislature. On 8 Dec. the House of Delegates ordered a bill to be brought in authorizing and directing the Virginia delegates in Congress "to convey by proper instrument in writing" the territory northwest of the Ohio according to the terms agreed upon by Congress, but with the single proviso "that lands be reserved out of those . . . to be ceded sufficient to make good the several military bounties agreed to be given to sundry officers . . . the lands hitherto reserved being insufficient for that purpose" (JHD, Oct. 1783, 1828 edn., p. 53). Joseph Jones was the author of the bill; the original MS (Vi) is in his hand and, of course, contains the proviso as a final paragraph. Since Jones, in drawing up the Act, copied the 1781 Act of cession as given in Congress' resolutions of 13 Sep. 1783 instead of going back to the engrossed text in the Virginia archives, he continued the chain of error that had been begun when John Beckley omitted a phrase in the copy of the 1781 Act of cession that Jefferson transmitted to Congress on 17 Jan. 1781 (see Document II, note 1). By this omission, Virginia officers and troops on state establishment would have been wholly neglected, whereas those on Continental establishment would have been provided with grants.

The proviso was struck out on the third reading, but Jones feared that the Senate ("some of whom are much attracted to those for whom the clause provided") might restore it. This fear proved to be groundless (Jones to TJ, 21 Dec. 1783; JHD, Oct. 1783, 1828 edn., p. 62, 65, 70, 79, 81; Hening, XI, 326-8). "The last session of our Assembly," Weedon reported to Steuben, "closed with the officers finally respecting our lands. Everything that could be done for us with propriety was granted, but there were so many Interests to reconcile and some of them of a National Nature that we the Deputation from our line were Oblige[d] to Compromise Matters in the best Manner we could, and by the Laws as they now stand must begin our Surveys on the Cumberland and Tenesee Rivers and go to Scioto for Deficiencies. . . . We were allowed our Own Surveyor and Superintendent from our Own Body to see strict justice done as well to the absent officers as those on the spot, with a Covering party of 100 Men and so many Deputy Surveyors as we might think proper to employ" (Weedon to Steuben, 24 Feb. 1784, NHi).

Thus, both in her own legislature and in Congress, Virginia placed the welfare of the nation above special interests in her effort to create a national domain. A few leaders, such as George Mason, James Madison, Thomas Jefferson, George Washington, Joseph Jones, Benjamin Harrison—some of whom were far from being disinterested themselves —led the three-year fight to yield in the national interest a vast tract of territory for which the state had a more defensible title than most other western claims. When it is considered that land resources constituted an all but irresistible magnet for those inclined toward speculation and acquisitiveness, and that legislatures—including that of Virginia—had known the influence of such pressures even before the Revolution, the Virginia Acts of cession of 1781 and 1783 stand as a monument to the strength of national feeling in the post-Revolutionary period and to the solid accomplishments of the Confederation. There were, as Weedon remarked, "so many Interests to reconcile" in this matter, but it is an enduring tribute to the temper of Virginia's councils that, in accommodating these various interests, the national welfare was placed first. No other state, then or since, ever yielded so great a natural resource to the domain of the whole people.

Harrison forwarded the Act of cession of 1783 to the Virginia delegates along with other measures designed in the national interest. Jefferson had not received it on 1 Feb., though news of its passage was known in Congress as early as 30 Dec. (copy of Act of cession is in PCC: No. 75, 388-91); he laid it before Congress on 13 Feb. 1784. In the early part of Feb., Jefferson drew up a form of conveyance (Document I) which, with the Act of cession of 1783, was presented to Con-

gress and referred to a committee consisting of Sherman, Read, and
Spaight (TJ to Jones, 2-14 Feb. 1784; PCC: No. 186). Sherman
drafted the report which was presented on 23 Feb. and which approved
of the Virginia Act and also of the "form of a deed to be executed by
the delegates . . . for carrying the same into effect" (JCC, XXVI, 90).
But this report was not approved (see TJ to Harrison, 3 Mch. 1784).
On 1 Mch. David Howell moved that "the United States in Congress
assembled, are ready to receive this deed, whenever the delegates of
the State of Virginia are ready to execute the same" (JCC, XXVI, 112-
16; Spaight had evidently attempted a similar motion earlier, but without success; same, 90). Beatty of New Jersey, seconded by Montgomery of Pennsylvania, then moved a proviso that "the acceptance of
the said cession, in manner and form aforesaid, shall not be considered
as implying any opinion or decision of Congress respecting the extent or
validity of the claim of . . . Virginia, to western territory, by charter
or otherwise." But only the New Jersey, Rhode Island, and Pennsylvania delegates voted in favor of the amendment. In the voting on
Howell's motion, only six states supported acceptance, New Jersey was
opposed, and Pennsylvania and South Carolina were divided. But when
the Pennsylvania delegate who stood in opposition asked to change his
vote, the cession was accepted and the national domain came into being
(JCC, XXVI, 116-17; TJ to Harrison, 3 Mch. 1784). All evidence
points to John Montgomery as the delegate whose change of mind
brought about this result, and there is reason to surmise that, in doing
so, he may not have been unmindful of the fact that it was Jefferson
who had drafted a report which had as one of its major objects the
silencing of Connecticut's threat to reopen her claim to lands in Pennsylvania (see notes to documents on the Connecticut-Pennsylvania
dispute, 21 Jan. 1784).

Once this decisive vote was taken, the delegates from Virginia, according to the Journals of Congress, proceeded the same day to sign,
seal, and deliver the Deed of Cession and Congress ordered that it be
"recorded and enrolled among the acts of the United States in Congress
assembled" (JCC, XXVI, 117). But the engrossed copy could not have
been completed on that day; presumably the engrossing clerk required
from two to three weeks for the preparation of the text on parchment
(see Document II, note).

The Virginia delegates transmitted an exemplification of the Deed
of Cession in their letter to Gov. Harrison of 22 Mch. 1784. Harrison
laid it before the House of Delegates and that body on 20 May resolved that it should "be carefully preserved and enrolled by the clerk
of this House among the archives of the General Assembly; and that
as a further security for its preservation, he deliver a copy thereof,
and of this resolution to the Chief Magistrate of this Commonwealth,
to be deposited among the papers of the Executive" (Harrison to
Speaker of the House, 3 May 1784, Executive Letter Book, Vi; JHD,
May 1784, 1828 edn., p. 7, 13-14).

I. Preliminary Form of Deed of Cession

[13 Feb. 1784]

To all who shall see these presents we [here name the delegates] the underwritten, delegates for the Commonwealth of Virginia in the Congress of the United states of America, send greeting.

Whereas the General assembly of the Commonwealth of Virginia at their sessions begun on the 20th. day of Octob. 1783. passed an act intituled 'an act to authorize the delegates &c.[1] in these words following to wit 'Whereas the Congress &c. [reciting the act verbatim][2]

And whereas the said General Assembly by their Resolution of June 6th. 1783. had constituted and appointed us the said A.B.C.&c.[3] delegates to represent the said Commonwealth in Congress for one year from the first Monday in November then next following, which resolution remains in full force[4]

Now therefore know ye that we the said A.B.C.&c. by virtue of the power and authority committed to us by the act of the said General assembly of Virginia before recited, and in the name and for and on behalf of the said Commonwealth do by these presents convey, transfer, assign and make over unto the United states in Congress assembled for the benefit of the said states, Virginia inclusive, all right, title and claim as well of soil as of jurisdiction which the said Commonwealth hath to the territory or tract of country within the limits of the Virginia charter, situate, lying and being to the Northwest of the river Ohio, to and for the uses and purposes and on the conditions of the said recited act.

In testimony whereof we have hereunto subscribed our names and affixed our seals in Congress the   day of   in the year of our lord 1784. and of the independance of the United states the eighth.

Signed, sealed and
delivered in presence of [5]

MS (DLC: PCC, No. 30, p. 575); entirely in TJ's hand; written on address leaf of Marbois to TJ, printed above under date of 10 Feb. 1784. Marbois' letter bears on its face the following in Thomson's hand: "Mr Sherman Mr Read Mr Spaight"; these are the names of the committee to which the Virginia Act and the preliminary form of conveyance were referred. Under date of 13 Feb. 1784 Thomson's journal of committee assignments lists these same names and describes the documents referred as a "Law of Virginia empowering their delegates to convey to the US. the claim of that state to lands NW. of Ohio, agreeably to Act of Congress of Sept 1783.—and a form of Conveyance offered by delegates" (PCC: No. 186). This proves that the present form was drawn up some time before 13 Feb. Another MS (described in notes below as FC), also entirely in TJ's hand, is in DLC: TJ

Papers, 10: 1639; this text differs in some particulars from the present, but it could not have been drawn up before 1 Mch. 1784 and in all probability (see note 5) was not made until after the engrossed copy on parchment had been completed, signed, and witnessed; endorsed:

"Commonw. of ⎫ Copy Deed
Virga. to ⎬ of Cession of
United States ⎭ Western Territory."

1 FC has the following at this point, completing the title: " '. . . convey to the United states in Congress assembled all the right of this Commonwealth to the territory North Westward of the river Ohio.' "

2 FC reads: " '. . . [reciting the act verbatim to the least words]—present in Congress.' " All square brackets here and elsewhere in the text are in MS and FC.

3 In the three places in the text where the names of delegates occur, FC gives the full names in the first instance and initials in the others.

4 TJ first wrote: ". . . remains unrevoked and unexpired" and then altered it to read as above.

5 FC has the date-blanks filled in to read: "the 1st. day of March," gives the sigillated initials of the four signers, and includes the names of the three witnesses. It is obvious, therefore, that this must be a true FC made by TJ after the engrossed copy on parchment had been completed.

II. Deed of Cession as Executed

To all who shall see these presents,

We Thomas Jefferson, Samuel Hardy, Arthur Lee and James Monroe the underwritten, delegates for the Commonwealth of Virginia in the Congress of the United States of America send Greeting

Whereas the General Assembly of the Commonwealth of Virginia at their Sessions begun on the twentieth day of October one thousand seven hundred and eighty three passed an Act entitled "an Act to authorize the Delegates of this State in Congress to convey to the United States in Congress Assembled all the Right of this Commonwealth to the Territory North-Westward of the River Ohio" in these words following to wit

"Whereas the Congress of the United States did by their Act of the sixth day of September in the year one thousand seven hundred and eighty recommend to the several States in the Union having claims to waste and unappropriated Lands in the Western Country a liberal Cession to the United States of a portion of their respective Claims for the common Benefit of the Union; And Whereas this Commonwealth did on the second day of January in the Year one thousand seven hundred and Eighty one yield to the Congress of the United States for the Benefit of the said States all right, Title and Claim which the said Commonwealth had to the Territory North-West of the River Ohio subject to the Conditions annexed to the said Act of Cession; And Whereas the United States in Congress Assembled have by their Act of the

[577]

thirteenth of September last stipulated the Terms on which they agree to accept the Cession of this State should the Legislature approve thereof which Terms although they do not come fully up to the propositions of this Commonwealth are conceived on the whole to approach so nearly to them as to induce this State to accept thereof in full confidence that Congress will in justice to this State for the liberal Cession she hath made earnestly press upon the other States claiming large Tracts of waste and uncultivated Territory the propriety of making Cessions equally liberal for the common Benefit and support of the Union. BE IT ENACTED by the General Assembly that it shall and may be lawful for the delegates of this State to the Congress of the United States or such of them as shall be assembled in Congress and the said delegates or such of them so assembled are hereby fully authorized and empowered for and on behalf of this State by proper deeds or Instrument in writing under their Hands and Seals to convey, transfer, assign and make over unto the United States in Congress Assembled for the Benefit of the said States all right title and claim as well of soil as jurisdiction which this Commonwealth hath to the Territory or Tract of Country within the limits of the Virginia Charter situate lying and being to the North-West of the River Ohio subject to the Terms and Conditions contained in the before recited Act of Congress of the thirteenth day of September last that is to say upon condition that the Territory so ceded shall be laid out and formed into States containing a suitable extent of Territory not less than one hundred nor more than one hundred and fifty miles square or as near thereto as circumstances will admit and that the States so formed shall be distinct Republican States and admitted members of the Fœderal Union, having the same rights of Sovereignty, Freedom and Independence as the other States[1]—That the necessary and reasonable expences incurred by this State in subduing any British Posts or in maintaining Forts or Garrisons within and for the defence or in acquiring any part of the Territory so ceded or relinquished shall be fully reimbursed by the United States and that one Commissioner shall be appointed by Congress one by this Commonwealth and another by those two Commissioners who or a majority of them shall be authorized and empowered to adjust and liquidate the account of the necessary and reasonable expences incurred by this State which they shall judge to be comprized within the intent and meaning of the Act of Congress of the tenth of October one thousand seven hundred and Eighty respecting such expences—That the French and Canadian Inhabitants and other Settlers of the Kaskaskies, St. Vincents and the neighbouring Villages who have professed themselves Citizens of Virginia shall have their possessions and Titles confirmed to them and be protected in the enjoyment of their rights and liberties—That a quantity not exceeding one hundred and fifty thousand Acres of Land promised by this State shall be allowed and granted to the then Colonel now General George Rogers Clarke and to the Officers and Soldiers of his Regiment who marched with him when the Posts of Kaskaskies and St. Vincents were reduced and to the Officers and Soldiers that have been since incorporated into the said Regiment to be laid off in one Tract the length of which not to exceed double the breadth in such place on the North-West side of the Ohio as a Majority of the Officers shall choose and to be afterwards divided among the said Officers and Soldiers in due proportion according to the Laws of Virginia. That in case the quantity of good Lands on the South-East side of the Ohio upon the Waters of Cumberland River and between the Green River and Tenessee river which have been reserved by Law for the Virginia Troops upon Continental establishment[2] should from the North Carolina Line bearing in further upon the Cumberland Lands than was expected prove insufficient for their legal Bounties the deficiency should be made up to the said Troops in good Lands to be laid off between the Rivers Scioto and little Miami on the North-West side of the River Ohio in such proportions as have been engaged to them by the Laws of Virginia—That all the Lands within the Territory so Ceded to the United States and not reserved for or appropriated to any of the beforementioned purposes or disposed of in Bounties to the Officers and Soldiers of the American Army shall be considered as a common fund for the use and benefit of such of the United States as have become or shall become Members of the Confederation or Fœderal Alliance of the said States Virginia inclusive according to their usual respective proportions in the general charge and expenditure and shall be faithfully and bona fide disposed of for that purpose and for no other use or purpose whatsoever. PROVIDED that the Trust hereby reposed in the delegates of this State shall not be executed unless three of them at least are present in Congress." AND WHEREAS the said General Assembly by their Resolution of June sixth one thousand seven hundred and Eighty three had constituted and appointed us the said Thomas Jefferson, Samuel Hardy, Arthur Lee and James Monroe delegates to represent the said Commonwealth in Congress for one Year from the first Monday in November then next following, which resolution remains in full force Now THEREFORE KNOW YE that we the said Thomas Jefferson, Samuel Hardy, Arthur Lee and James Monroe by virtue of the power and authority committed to us by the Act of the said General Assembly of Virginia before recited, and in the name and for and on behalf of the said Commonwealth do by these presents convey, transfer, assign and make over unto the United States in Congress Assembled for the Benefit of the said States Virginia inclusive all right, title and claim as well of soil as of jurisdiction which the said Commonwealth hath to the Territory or tract of Country within the limits of the Virginia Charter, situate, lying and being to the North-West of the River Ohio, to and for the uses and purposes and on the Conditions of the said recited Act. IN TESTIMONY whereof we have hereunto subscribed our names and affixed our Seals in Congress the first day of March in the Year of our Lord one thousand seven hundred and Eighty four and of the Independence of the United States the Eighth.

Sign'd, Sealed and Delivered
in presence of

CHAS THOMSON

HENRY REMSEN JR.

BENJN. BANKSON JUNR.

TH: JEFFERSON

S. HARDY

ARTHUR LEE

JAS. MONROE

MS on parchment (DLC: PCC Miscellany); signed by delegates, with wax seals affixed (though that of TJ has become detached); endorsed: "Virginia Cession of Western Territory executed by Delegates of that State March 1st. 1784," [*and in another hand:*] "Recorded page 7"; measures 14.75 by 56.75 inches. Another MS (Vi); seal impressed on paper over wax, with ribbon attached; engrossed on paper and authenticated by Thomson as follows: "To all to Whom these presents shall come, Know Ye, that among the Archives of the United States in Congress Assembled is lodged a Deed or Instrument in the words following [*here follows a verbatim copy of the Deed of Cession as given above*] . . . In Testimony whereof the United States have caused their Great Seal to be affixed to this exemplification—Witness Charles Thomson Esquire their Secretary and Keeper of their Great Seal. Chas. Thomson." This exemplification of the Deed of Cession was enclosed in the delegates' letter to Gov. Harrison of

22 Mch. 1784. It may be presumed that the signing of the Deed of Cession took place shortly before the delegates sent the authenticated copy to Harrison—that is, on or just before 22 Mch. Hence it appears that the engrossing clerk required from two to three weeks to prepare the parchment copy. MS of the exemplification is in Vi and is printed in Hening, XI, 571-5.

[1] This condition was altered by Virginia in 1788 in consequence of its inconvenience and the passage of the Northwest Ordinance of 1787 (*Territorial Papers of the United States*, ed. Clarence E. Carter, II, 172-3).

[2] Actually the Act of Cession should have read: ". . . upon Continental establishment *and upon their own State Establishment.*" For an explanation of the clerical error that led to the omission of the phrase in italics (supplied) and to the repetition of this error in all texts employed after 1781, see Vol. 4: 390, note 4.

Plan for Government of the Western Territory

[3 Feb.-23 Apr. 1784]

EDITORIAL NOTE

On 1 Mch. 1784, immediately after the acceptance of the Virginia Deed of Cession, Jefferson presented his report of a plan for the government of the territory embraced by the newly created national domain and by other territories that would be ceded. But this report, the foundation stone of American territorial policy which, as amended, became known to history as the Ordinance of 1784, had antecedents that apparently have not been noted heretofore. Even its major features have been confused or misunderstood. The committee report as submitted 1 Mch. 1784 and as revised and resubmitted 22 Mch. 1784 should not, therefore, be presented alone and without commentary.

"The man chiefly responsible for the foundation of the first 'colonial policy' of the United States," a careful historian has stated, "was Thomas Jefferson. He had long been interested in the region west of the Alleghenies, not as a speculator, but as a statesman, a scientist, and a believer in agrarian democracy. Where others wanted to hand the West over to speculators, he wanted it to belong to actual settlers. Where others distrusted westerners as banditti and wanted them ruled by military force, he wanted them to govern themselves. Thus when he brought the Virginia cession to Congress, he had definite ideas about what should be done" (Merrill Jensen, *The New Nation*, p. 353, citing, as the most recent and best account of Jefferson's relation to the West, Anthony Marc Lewis' "Jefferson and Virginia's Pioneers, 1774-1781," MVHR, XXXIV [1948], 551-88). On the basic policy of establishing local autonomy and of employing the national domain for the encouragement of actual settlers, this was correct—though the resolution on a plan for the government of the western territory as Jefferson drew it contained no reference either to sale or gift of lands (cf. TJ's report on establishing a land office, 30 Apr. 1784). His unsuccessful effort to amend the Articles of Confederation in 1776, for example, would have provided that Congress control all purchases of lands from Indians in territories not claimed by any state and also that these lands "when purchased shall be given freely to those who may be permitted to seat them" (Vol. 1: 182).

The central concept in the Ordinance of 1784—that out of the western territories new states republican in nature should be formed and incorporated into the Union on a basis of equality with the original states—was also an idea that Jefferson had entertained from the beginning of the Revolution. His draft of a Constitution for Virginia in 1776 had provided for the establishment of new colonies west of the Alleghenies to be based on "the same fundamental laws contained in this instrument and . . . [to be] free and independant of this colony and of all the world" (Vol. 1: 363). This part of his draft, in modified form, was adopted by the Virginia Convention of 1776 (same, p. 383, 385 note 19). As Malone, *Jefferson*, I, 412, points out, the principle of admitting new states on an equal basis was by 1784 "generally accepted . . . and cannot be properly credited to any single man. Jefferson . . . if he did not originate it . . . was certainly one of those who held it first. It had been basic in his own thinking about the future of the Republic throughout the struggle for independence. He had no desire to break from the British Empire only to establish an American—in which the newer region should be subsidiary and tributary to the old. What he dreamed of was an expanding Union of self-governing commonwealths, joined as a group of peers."

Another dominant feature of the Ordinance of 1784 was that it applied to all parts of the national domain—those already acquired as well as those to be acquired in the future, not merely (as was the case with the more famous Ordinance of 1787) to the territory northwest of the Ohio. But it is now apparent that this feature of Jefferson's report of 1 Mch. 1784 was the result of progressive steps in his thinking. The earlier of these steps, so far as known documentary evidence of them is concerned, have no relation to principles or forms of territorial government or to the disposition of lands or to the relationship of new states with the United States: they are concerned only with the boundaries and location of "colonies" that Jefferson evidently planned or considered in the period 1783-1784 when he faced the problem of the West.

The first of these steps involves a "New Colony" covering roughly two degrees of latitude and "6. or 7. degrees of Longitude" (Document I). This fragment is undated, but it could scarcely have been written after the middle of Feb. 1784 when Jefferson had completed the report presented on 1 Mch. Its boundaries embraced most of the northern part of the present states of Indiana and Ohio, together with a slice of the southern part of what is now Michigan. The purpose that Jefferson had in mind in proposing this new "colony" may have been similar to (or even influenced by) that urged by Washington in the autumn of 1783 when, in response to inquiries from James Duane, chairman of a committee dealing with Indian affairs, he presented a long and thoughtful outline of policy concerning the western territory. In any case, the progressive evolution of Jefferson's plans can best be understood in light of discussions in Congress late in 1783 just before Jefferson took his seat. The principal object, thought Washington, was to establish order and regulation. "To suffer a wide extended Country to be over run with Land Jobbers, Speculators, and Monopolisers or even with scatter'd settlers," he declared, "is, in my opinion, inconsistent with that wisdom and policy which our true interest dictates, or that an enlightened People ought to adopt, and, besides, is pregnant of disputes both with the Savages, and among ourselves, the evils of which are easier to be conceived than described; and for what? but to aggrandize a few avaricious Men to the prejudice of many, and the embarrassment of Government." Therefore, he advised, let a line of demarcation between the two peoples be established, taking care "neither to yield nor to grasp at too much." Let it be proclaimed a felony to survey or settle beyond the line, and let the frontier garrison enforce the order. This would not only achieve peace with the Indians, but would enable Congress to "dispose of the Land to the best advantage; People the Country progressively, and check Land Jobbing and Monopolizing (. . . now going forward with great avidity) while the door would be open, and the terms known for every one to obtain what is reasonable and proper for himself upon legal and constitutional ground."

If this orderly mode of dealing with the Indians and the western territory were not adopted, Washington declared, one of two things would happen: "the settling, or rather overspreading the Western Country will take place, by a parcel of Banditti, who will bid defiance to all Authority," or there would be a renewal of Indian hostilities. Washington then proposed new states to be established in an extensive area: "from the Mouth of the Great Miami River which empties into the Ohio to its confluence with the Mad River, thence by a Line to the Miami Fort and Village on the other Miami River which empties into Lake Erie, and Thence by a Line to include the Settlement of Detroit would with Lake Erie to the No.ward Pensa. to the Eastwd. and the Ohio to the Soward form a Governmt. sufficiently extensive to fulfill all the public engagements, to receive moreover a large population by Emigrants, and to confine The Settlement of the New States within these bounds would . . . be infinitely better . . . than to suffer the same number of People to roam over a Country of at least 500,000 Square Miles contributing nothing to the support, but much perhaps to the Embarrassment of the Federal Government." If, however, Detroit were not to be included within such a governmental area, Washington thought that "a more compact and better shaped district for a State would be for the line to proceed from the Miami Fort and Village along the River of that name to Lake Erie, leaving In that case the Settlement of Detroit, and all the Territory No. of the Rivers Miami and St. Josephs between the Lakes Erie, St. Clair, Huron, and Michigan to form, hereafter, another State equally large compact and water bounded." Asked about Indian affairs, he had proposed the formation of new governments in the western territory. "At first view," he concluded in this remarkable and pivotal letter to Duane, "it may seem a little extraneous, when I am called upon to give an opinion upon the terms of a Peace proper to be made with the Indians, that I should go into the formation of New States; but the Settlemt. of the Western Country and making a Peace with the Indians are so analogous that there can be no definition of the one without involving considerations of the other" (Washington to Duane, 7 Sep. 1783, *Writings*, ed. Fitzpatrick, xxvii, 133-40).

This letter was written at Rocky Hill, New Jersey, and Congress was then sitting at nearby Princeton. The very next day the Virginia delegates in Congress reported that information had been received from the commander at Fort Pitt that a body of some 400 men "from the Western Frontier of Virginia, had passed the Ohio, in order to establish a settlement on the Muskingum" and that "The General" apprehended an immediate Indian war would be "among the first of the many evil consequences that must result from such lawless measures" (Mercer, Bland, and Lee to Benjamin Harrison, 8 Sep. 1783, Burnett, *Letters of Members*, vii, No. 350). Washington's letter and, no doubt more important, his conversations with Duane and other members of Congress influenced the report that Duane submitted on 15 Oct. 1783.

The members of Duane's committee were not sanguine that regulations of the Indian trade as proposed by them would be "a sufficient security against the increase of feeble, disorderly and dispersed settlements in those remote and wide extended territories; against the depravity of manners which they have a tendency to produce; the endless perplexities in which they must involve the administration of the affairs of the United States; or against the calamities of frequent and destructive wars with the Indians, which reciprocal animosities unrestrained by the interposition of legal authority must naturally excite." They were of opinion that "nothing can avert those complicated and impending mischiefs, or secure to the United States the just and important advantages which they ought to derive from those territories, but the speedy establishment of government and the regular administration of justice." This, in different words, was Washington's advice.

Congress thereupon resolved "That it will be wise and necessary, as soon as circumstances shall permit, to erect a district of the western territory into a distinct government, as well for doing justice to the army of the United States, who are entitled to lands as a bounty, or in reward for their services, as for the accommodation of such as may incline to become purchasers and inhabitants; and in the interim, that a committee be appointed to report a plan, consistent with the principles of the Confederation, for connecting with the Union by a temporary government, the purchasers and inhabitants of the said district, until their number and circumstances shall entitle them to form a permanent constitution for themselves, and as citizens of a free, sovereign and independent State, to be admitted to a representation in the Union; provided always, that such constitution shall not be incompatible with the republican principles, which are the basis of the constitutions of the respective states in the Union" (jcc, xxv, 693-4; also, 677-9, 690-1).

On the same day, 15 Oct., Congress appointed a committee of three to prepare an ordinance regulating the Indian trade and on 18 Dec. 1783, when that committee was renewed, it was also charged with the task of drawing up a plan for the temporary government of the western territory. Jefferson was chairman of the new committee and its other members were Cadwalader Morris and James McHenry; their responsibility was to draw up a form of government agreeable to the

basic principles laid down in the resolution of 15 Oct. (PCC: No. 186).
On 7 Jan. 1784 the committee on Indian affairs was again renewed.
Gaillard Hunt states (JCC, XXV, 693, note) that both matters—
Indian affairs and plan of government—were again referred to the
committee, which now consisted of Jefferson as chairman and Morris,
Jacob Read, Hugh Williamson, and Jeremiah Townley Chase as the
other members. But Thomson's journal of committee assignments under
7 Jan. shows only that the committee were directed to "prepare and
report an Ordinance for regulating the Indian Trade with a clause
prohibiting all civil and military Officers and all Commissioners and
Indian Agents from trading with the Indians or purchasing lands from
Indians except by express license and Authority of Congress" (PCC:
No. 186). There is no evidence that the committee reported such an
ordinance—though one regulating Indian affairs was adopted 7 Aug.
1786 (Clarence E. Carter, *Territorial Papers of the United States*, II,
19-22)—and Thomson's journal of committee assignments is blank in
the column under reports opposite this particular entry. Ford, III, 408,
note, makes the further mistake of saying that there "is no record of
the 'appointment' of the committee to draw up a plan of government
which reported on 1 Mch. 1784." But Thomson's journal of committee
assignments under date of 3 Feb. 1784 shows that Jefferson, Chase,
and Howell were appointed a committee to "prepare a plan for temporary government of western territory" and that they reported on 1 Mch.
(PCC: No. 186). However, Ford correctly conjectured, on the basis
of a letter from David Howell to Jonathan Arnold, that the committee
had been appointed prior to 21 Feb., for Howell on that date stated
that "A committee has been appointed to report a plan of government,
&c., for the western country. The report is agreed to by the committee,
but has not yet been made to Congress" (William R. Staples, *Rhode
Island in the Continental Congress*, Providence, 1870, p. 478-82).

Howell's letter is interesting for other reasons than the fact that it
proves Jefferson had completed the plan of government of the territories shortly after the committee was appointed and some days before
the Virginia Deed of Cession was accepted. In it he remarked: "Gov.
Jefferson, who is here a delegate from Virginia, and one of the best
members I have ever seen in Congress, has a good Library of French
books, and had been so good as to lend me." And Howell's appraisal
of the subject with which his committee was charged reveals agreement with Jeffersonian ideas if not a reflection of Jefferson's influence:
"There are at present many great objects before Congress; but none
of more importance, or which engage my attention more than that of the
Western Country. . . . The western world opens an amazing prospect
as a national fund, in my opinion; it is equal to our debt. As a source
of future population and strength, it is a guaranty to our independence.
As its inhabitants will be mostly cultivators of the soil, republicanism
looks to them as its guardians. When the states on the eastern shores,
or Atlantic, shall have become populous, rich and luxurious, and ready
to yield their liberties into the hands of a tyrant, the gods of the mountains will save us, for they will be stronger than the gods of the valleys.
Astraea will take her flight from the tops of the Alleghany when she

leaves the New World." This has very much the ring of Jefferson's faith in the "cultivators of the soil" and his "peculiar confidence in the men from the Western side of the mountains" (TJ to Muhlenberg, 31 Jan. 1781).

From the foregoing it is apparent that, some weeks before he had been instructed to draw up a plan for the government of the western territory, Jefferson had inherited the duty recommended by Duane's committee—"to erect a district of the western territory into a distinct government"—and it may be that soon after his appointment on 18 Dec. 1783 he outlined the boundaries of a "New Colony" conformable to these directions. He must have seen Washington's letter to Duane, for he no doubt inherited the previous committee's papers as well as its tasks. We know that during Jefferson's first days in Congress he was considering measures that would "cement us to our Western friends when they shall be formed into separate states" (TJ to Clark, 4 Dec. 1783), and that during December and January he had been in correspondence with Thomas Hutchins about western rivers and maps pertaining to that area (TJ to Hutchins, 29 Dec. 1783; Hutchins to TJ, 11 Feb. 1784). But the area of "distinct government" whose boundaries he described in the fragment presented here as Document I was different from and less extensive than either of the two new colonies proposed by Washington. (Cf. also TJ to Harrison, 11 Nov. 83.)

But Jefferson did not share the fears of Washington and others that a horde of "Banditti" would soon possess the western country (TJ to Hogendorp, 4 May 1784; cf. Appendix III, Document II). The orderly and progressive division of the whole of the existing and potential domain into new states to be incorporated into the Union on a basis of equality was too great an object to be hastened by the fear of squatters, the pressures of land companies, or even the claims of officers and soldiers. At any rate, Jefferson soon progressed beyond the idea of a single colony to an intermediate stage involving several divisions of the western territory.

This intermediate step, like that set forth in Document I, appears not to have been published hitherto. It provided for a cluster of six states lying to the westward of Pennsylvania, Virginia, and North Carolina. These were designated by the letters A, B, C, D, E, and F rather than by names. Their areas, in general, were defined by the natural boundaries of rivers and mountains rather than by lines of longitude and latitude. In these respects the intermediate plan (Document II) differed markedly from its successor. Neither the plan for the single "colony" nor for the cluster of six states is dated. On 1 Feb. 1784, two days before the appointment of the committee to draw up a plan of temporary government, David Howell remarked that "a district for *a new state* is to be marked out" (Howell to Greene, 1 Feb. 1784; Burnett, *Letters of Members*, VII, No. 501; italics supplied). This may mean that at that time he and perhaps Jefferson himself had not proceeded beyond the idea of a single governmental district suggested by Washington in the autumn of 1783. Both the first and second of these steps in the evolution of a plan of western government may therefore date from the appointment of the committee on 3 Feb. 1784.

It is certain that the third and final stage was reached before 20 Feb. 1784, for on that day Jefferson described in detail the principal features of his plan. It is almost equally certain that these stages occurred in the sequential order here given, for the "colony" defined in Document I was overlapped by the cluster of proposed states outlined in Document II, just as this cluster was subsequently overlapped by the territories provided for in the committee report (Document III). Each successive stage rendered irrelevant that which preceded it, not only in respect to number, size, and location of territories, but also in respect to its general conception.

All of these stages are remarkable because each transcended constitutional authority in at least one respect and the last was *ultra vires* in several important points. To most of these Jefferson was able to commit both his colleagues on the committee and in Congress. First, the report of 1 Mch. 1784 set boundaries to all states whose western limits touched the meridian of longitude that passed through the mouth of the Great Kanawha—this despite the fact that the Articles of Confederation specifically declared that "no State shall be deprived of territory for the benefit of the United States." The exact number of states that the resolution of 1 Mch. 1784 proposed—a much confused subject—will be discussed below. Second, it proposed to establish states within territory not ceded by any state, including Virginia; "Polypotamia" and "Pelisipia" each had a part of their territory within the area claimed but not ceded by Virginia. Third, though Jefferson's committee was specifically charged with the task of drawing up "a plan for *temporary* government of western territory" (PCC: No. 186; italics supplied)—and though the preamble to the report bears the same words, the resolutions proposed three stages of development whereby the settlers in a given area could proceed from (1) a temporary status of self-government to (2) a constitutionally organized statehood once a population of 20,000 had been reached, and, finally, to (3) full admission to the Union on a plane of equality with the original states once population had reached the total of the least populous member of the thirteen original states. This provision for a regular progression from temporary territorial status to permanent statehood was a concept of the Ordinance of 1784 that endured. It was reinforced by the solemn declaration that the terms constituted "a Charter of Compact"—Jefferson's rare use of capitals (departed from in the broadside text) underscored his sense of the fundamental importance of the declaration—that would stand as "fundamental constitutions between the thirteen original states, and those now newly described." Fourth, though, as noted above, the idea of establishing new states and admitting them into the Union was by 1784 generally accepted, there was nothing in the Articles of Confederation specifically authorizing such a procedure. As Madison declared in Number 38 of *The Federalist*: "Congress have undertaken . . . to form new States, to erect temporary governments, to appoint officers for them, and to prescribe the conditions on which such States shall be admitted into the Confederacy. All this has been done; and done without the least color of constitutional authority. . . . The public interest, the necessity of the case, imposed upon them the task of overleaping their constitutional limits." Here, but neither for the first nor the last time, Jefferson rested his action not on the narrow basis of a strict interpretation of delegated powers but on the higher law of national interest. Fifth—though this was a departure that Congress would not accept—Jefferson's plan as reported provided that, after the admission of the first new state, "the assent of two thirds of the United States in Congress assembled" would be necessary in all cases in which, by the Articles of Confederation, the assent of nine states was required. This, in effect, was an amendment of the Articles of Confederation, and Congress altered the passage by inserting the proviso that the substitution of two-thirds for nine states should be first "proposed to the legislatures of the" original states. Finally, there was nothing in the Articles of Confederation to warrant the abolition of slavery or the prohibition of hereditary titles, both of which were in Jefferson's original report and both of which were struck out by Congress.

The number and location of proposed states in the first two stages have never been presented cartographically and, in the final stage, have

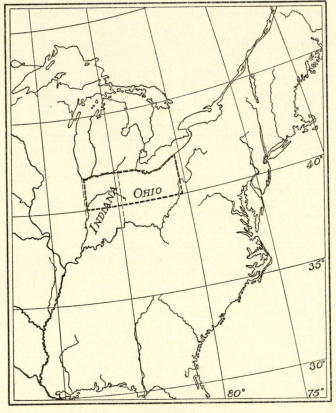

MAP I

(See Document 1)

been variously and confusedly stated. Hence there is a need for a series of outline maps to show each step. Each of these is given a designation corresponding to the Document in the present group to which it is related.

This proposal of a single colony requires no comment save that its eastern boundary would be either parallel to the meanders of the Delaware or would follow a meridian of longitude according to whatever settlement Pennsylvania and Virginia eventually made. An agreement had been made on 31 Aug. 1779 to make this western boundary a line of longitude, but actual settlement was not effected until 1785 (Vol. 3: 77; Paullin, *Atlas of the Historical Geography of the United States*, p. 77-8, Plate 97G). The names and boundaries of the present states of Ohio and Indiana are shown in this map, with heavy dotted lines indicating the proposed colony.

No satisfactory delineation of Jefferson's cluster of six states lying along the Ohio river can be made on a modern map. First, some of the boundaries would not close or would even be nonsensical, and, second, to place Jefferson's six states on an accurate modern map of the region would result in a distortion of their size and relationship, "B" for example becoming much larger than "A." Accordingly, the present outline is based on *A New and Correct Map of North America*, published in Thomas Jeffery's *American Atlas* (1779), which may have been employed by Jefferson. The first two of Jefferson's series, states "A" and "B," have such puzzling bounds that they are difficult to explain even on the basis of imperfect cartographical knowledge and may perhaps be accounted for only on the theory that Jefferson erred in setting them down (see note 1, Document II). Nevertheless, the approximate location and size of these six projected states lying along the Ohio river can be related generally to modern states: state "A" fell in what is now eastern Kentucky and Tennessee; "B" in Tennessee, Kentucky, and a strip of northern Alabama; "C" in northern Ohio and northwestern Indiana; "D" in southern Indiana and southwestern Ohio; "E" in southeastern Illinois and northern Indiana; and "F" in southern Illinois. Between this intermediate stage and that represented in the report of 1 Mch. 1784, Jefferson considered another step incorporating the main features of the report as ultimately drawn but applying these merely to the territory north of the Ohio river—that is, to the area embraced in the Virginia cession. The only evidence for this exists in Jefferson's letter to Madison of 20 Feb. 1784. If, as he pointed out there, the boundaries separating the three tiers of states followed the meridians of longitude "from the Ohio to L. Erie . . . allowing to each state an extent of 2°. from N. to South," there would still be one new state lying between "the meridian of Kanhaway . . . Pennsylva, the Ohio and L. Erie." This would have provided for a minimum of seven and a maximum of ten states depending upon the allocation of territory north of parallel 45° and south of parallel 39°. But Jefferson's letter to Madison made it clear that he was already contemplating the possibility of "crossing these [boundaries of meridians of longitude] by the parallels of latitude 37°. 39°. 41°. &c." But latitude 37°, as Jefferson knew, ran *below* the Ohio. Faced by the embarrassing meanders of that

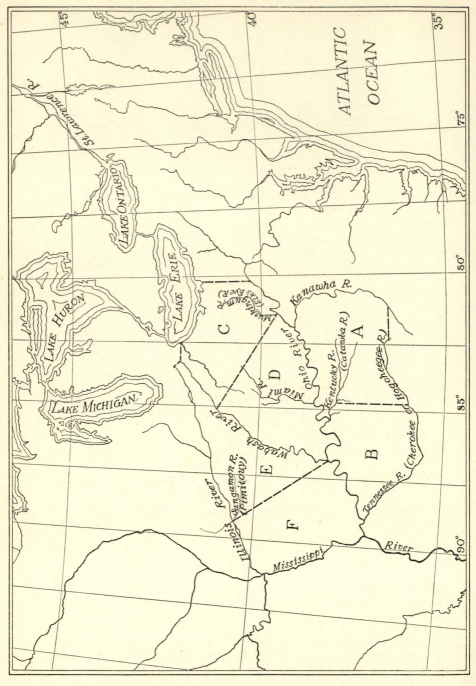

MAP II (See Document 11.)

river and by the hope of being able to provide for the government of all western territory, ceded and to be ceded, Jefferson looked beyond this stage of planning even in the letter to Madison which described it: "We hope N. Carola. will cede all beyond the same meridian of Kanhaway, and Virginia also. For god's sake push this at the next session of assembly." From this point it was an easy transition to the final stage as set forth in the report.

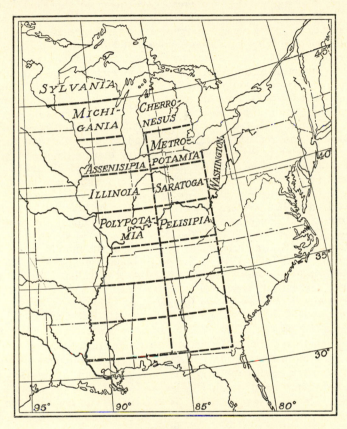

MAP III
(See Document III)

In respect to the number and location of proposed new states in the Ordinance of 1784, it is necessary to distinguish between what Jefferson proposed and what Congress finally approved. Jefferson has generally been credited with having proposed ten or fourteen new states. Actually, the number was not stated either in the report as submitted or in the Ordinance as adopted. If the bounds of colonies set forth in the report as submitted are plotted on a map—beginning at latitude 31° and going northward to latitude 47°, allowing two degrees for

[591]

each state, bounding the east and west lines of the first tier by lines of longitude running respectively through the mouth of the Great Kanawha and the Falls of Ohio, and bounding the east and west lines of the second tier by the western boundary of the first and the Mississippi—a maximum of sixteen states (one falling between the first tier and Pennsylvania) could be provided for, as shown in Map III. Ten of these were given names by Jefferson in the report as submitted. But the mere naming of these ten areas gave them no superior claim in law. They were no more "established" than any of the proposed states lying nameless in other parts of the western territory—all were limited by the same qualifying condition expressly stated in the report: that is, by cessions made or to be made by the states, and their bounds were to follow the terms of the report "as nearly as such cessions will admit."

It is true that Jefferson and the committee had in mind the laying off of fourteen new states, but this number appeared in private communications and not in the report as submitted. David Howell not only stated the number that the committee had in mind, but gave the best summary of the general concept developed by Jefferson and his colleagues: "It is proposed to divide the country into fourteen new states, in the following manner. There are to be three tiers of states:—One on the Atlantic, one on the Mississippi, and a middle tier. The middle tier is to be the smallest, and to form a balance betwixt the two more powerful ones. The western tier of states is to be bounded eastwardly by a meridianal line drawn through the lowest point of the rapids of the river Ohio, and the eastern tier is to be bounded westwardly by a meridianal line drawn through the west cape of the mouth of the great [Kanawha] from Lake Erie to the north boundary of South Carolina and Georgia to run west to the first mentioned meridianal line, as their Atlantic coast falls off west" (Howell to Arnold, 21 Feb. 1784; Staples, *Rhode Island in the Continental Congress*, p. 479).

This intent is made clear by the Jefferson-Hartley map, now in the David Hartley papers in The William L. Clements Library (see p. 593). Hartley must have obtained a copy of this map from Jefferson in Paris sometime after 6 Aug. 1784 and before 9 Jan. 1785 when he transmitted it to the British ministry, first making a copy for himself. Jefferson's original, from which Hartley evidently made his copy, is not known to be in existence. But it is not correct to say that "on this manuscript, in Hartley's hand, are the exact boundaries suggested by Jefferson in his report to Congress" (*Thomas Jefferson 1743-1943*, a pamphlet issued by the Clements Library describing an exhibit which included the Hartley map) or even that it shows "Jefferson's proposed division of the western territory into new states" (Malone, *Jefferson*, I, opposite p. 413). Rather, the Jefferson-Hartley map is a curious combination of what Jefferson and the committee privately intended, what they actually reported, and what Congress finally approved—plus a variation not attributable to any of these. As such, despite its great value and the interest compelled by its association with the remarkable man who copied it, it has been responsible for much of the confusion into which the subject has fallen.

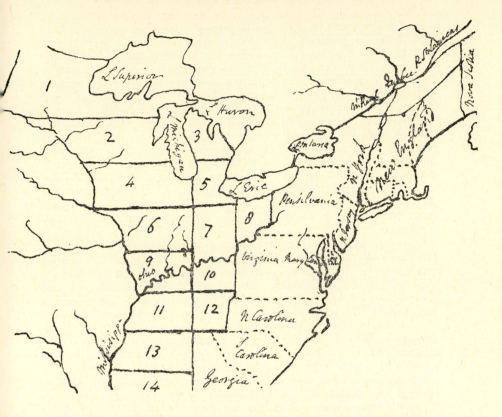

Congress in the Ordinance of 1784 retained Jefferson's two meridians of longitude. But whereas Jefferson proposed to begin with latitude 31° and proceed northward laying off states up to the end of latitude 47°, the amended report reversed the procedure by beginning at latitude 45° and going southward to an indeterminate limit. There was one other important difference. Congress made the Ohio river the southern boundary of the third state in the middle tier ("Saratoga" in Map III; number 7 in the Jefferson-Hartley map) instead of latitude 39°. The Jefferson-Hartley map incorporates and numbers the fourteen states that Jefferson and the committee intended and drops the two southernmost states of the middle tier west of South Carolina and Georgia; it also goes northward to latitude 47° (though parallels are not designated by number). In these respects it is a combination of what the committee privately intended and what they reported. But it also gives the Ohio river as the southern boundary of "Saratoga," thus agreeing with the amendment made by Congress. Furthermore, the Jefferson-Hartley map shows the eastern boundary of state number 12 as departing somewhat from its meridian of longitude. In this respect it may represent the eastern limit of what the North Carolina cession was expected to be, but neither this departure nor that of subsequent atlases and maps showing the bounds of cessions made by North Carolina, South Carolina, and Georgia can be properly described as representing what Jefferson proposed or what the Ordinance of 1784 provided. That Ordinance was repealed before any cessions south of the Ohio were made. It is therefore incorrect to show the eastern boundaries of states of the middle tier as departing from the meridian of longitude of the mouth of the Great Kanawha and to describe the result as states "proposed . . . according to the Ordinance of 1784." Paullin, *Atlas of the Historical Geography of the United States*, Plate 46B, makes this error, follows the Jefferson-Hartley map in other respects, and then goes even further by altering the eastern boundary of the two southern-most states in the third or western tier. Among the approximately correct modern representations of what the Ordinance of 1784 provided for are the maps in Andrew C. McLaughlin, *The Confederation and the Constitution*, p. 116, and E. M. Avery, *History of the United States*, VI, p. 403; the latter was made by David M. Matteson, but both contain errors.

Contemporary maps concerning the provisions of the Ordinance of 1784 are quite as confused. This was due in part, no doubt, to the fact that a copy of Jefferson's report as originally submitted fell into the hands of David C. Claypoole, editor of the *Pennsylvania Packet*, who printed it on 27 Apr. 1784 as if it had been adopted by Congress. The text used by Claypoole was that of the broadside printed soon after 1 Mch. 1784 for the use of members of Congress (see notes to Document III). Why he should have used this text when the report was recommitted on 17 Mch., reported as revised on 22 Mch., printed again in broadside form for use by Congress, and finally adopted, after being again amended, four days before the appearance of the 27 Apr. issue of the *Packet*, is an unexplained mystery. Whatever the cause, Claypoole's premature publication not only started a chain of errors but also disturbed Jefferson, who described it to Hopkinson as "this forgery" and to Gates as "a Report of a committee, erroneously said to be an act of Congress" (TJ to Hopkinson, 3 May 1784; TJ to Gates, 7 May 1784). Claypoole had introduced the report with these words: "The following are the Resolutions of Congress respecting the formation of ten new states. The Committee, consisting of Mr. Jefferson, Mr. Chace, and Mr. Howel, appointed to prepare a Plan for the temporary government of the Western Territory, have agreed to the following resolutions."

What appears to be the first published map to make use of the information revealed by the *Pennsylvania Packet* was *A Map of the United States of N. America* which appeared in Philadelphia in 1784 in Francis Bailey's *Pocket Almanac for 1785*. It contains the names of the ten states as proposed in Jefferson's original report, but it also shows the southern boundary of the state of "Saratoga" as lying along parallel 39° rather than the Ohio river. It shows the two meridians of longitude as running from the northern boundary of the United States to the southern, though the latter is undefined; but, below parallel 37°, it does not designate any of the bounds of districts that lay along parallels of latitude. It also represents the proposed district of "Washington" as projecting southward of the Ohio to a western boundary of Virginia running southwestwardly along the Blue Ridge Mountains—an error attributable to no known source. Thus it combines the facts of the report as submitted and of the Ordinance as adopted, plus something evidently drawn from the imagination of the cartographer (see accompanying illustration). This map, printed from the same plate, was used in John McCulloch's *Introduction to the History of America* (Phila., 1787); this in turn was reengraved for Johann David Schoepf's *Reise durch einige der mittlern und südlichen vereinigten nord Amerikanischen Staaten* (Erlangen, 1788); a reproduction of the last appears in Justin Winsor, *Narrative and Critical History of America*, VII, 529. William McMurray's map of 1784, *The United States According to the Definitive Treaty of Peace*, indicates that the "lines singly coloured N.W. of the Ohio, are the divisions of that Country into Ten new States, by a Resolve of Congress of April 23d. 1784." None of these is named in the map, but the Ordinance of 1784 did not designate ten or any other specific number of states and did not stipulate that those contemplated were to lie "N.W. of the Ohio." Moreover, McMurray was able to get ten states in that area only by bounding one state at parallel 47°, which was contrary to the Ordinance, and by counting as another the area lying northward of that parallel, which was contrary to Jefferson's report as submitted. He also bounded "Michigania" on the east by the meridian of longitude, not by Lake Michigan as called for by Jefferson's report. Further, the district that Jefferson proposed to call "Polypotamia" was bounded in McMurray's map on the north by parallel 39°, eastward by the meridian of the Falls of the Ohio, southward by the Ohio, and westward by the Mississippi—an area contemplated as a state neither in Jefferson's proposal nor in Congress' resolution. No boundaries were given in the map for the territory south of the Ohio. John Fitch's *Map of the North West Parts of the United States*, which was expressly derived from maps by Hutchins and McMurray, followed the latter's errors in designating the boundaries of the divisions north of the Ohio, but, by Fitch's calculations, the eastern boundary of "Michigania" included in that district a part of the Michigan peninsula that Jefferson's report had allocated exclusively to "Cherronesus." Fitch also stated that these boundaries represented "the form which that country is to be laid off into according to an ordinance of Congress May 20, 1785." But the ordinance of 20 May 1785 concerned the disposition of public lands and contained no divisions of proposed future states. Delamarche's *Etats-Unis de L'Amérique Septentrionale* (Paris, 1785) stated that "l'Etat de Vermont . . . a été reuni depuis le Congrès du 4 Juillet 1776" and added: "Il se forme encore 10 autres nouveaux Etats dans les Contrées comprises depuis le Lac des Bois, le Confluent de l'Ohio, et le Mississipi qu'on nomme Territoire Occidental." This, thought Delamarche, would give the Union twenty-four states in all and, with understandable confusion in spelling, he listed the Jeffersonian names of ten of the proposed new states.

Claypoole's premature publication of the committee report is no doubt responsible also for starting the long line of derisive and mirthful comments engendered by Jefferson's proposed names of ten of the new states. Except for the *Pennsylvania Packet*'s printing of the report and the consequent inclusion of the names in maps, Jefferson's nomenclature might have slumbered in the oblivion of the archives of the Continental Congress and thus escaped more or less partisan ridicule. But it is to be observed that most of these names were Indian derivatives, two were geographical features translated into classical form, and one was a tribute to Washington. This was a reflection of Jefferson's lifelong interest in Indian names—for example, he wisely revived the ancient aboriginal name of "Anacostia" and substituted it for "Eastern Branch" as applied to the Potomac at Washington (TJ to Ellicott, 15 Jan. 1793). The names of two modern states—Michigan and Illinois—are derived from the same source that Jefferson used, though he applied one to a different area and gave both a different form. "Pelisipi" seems quite as euphonious and has certainly as respectable an etymology as "Mississippi," and if Jefferson's addition of a classical ending to the former may seem unusual or offensive, it was no more so than the ending of the name of Georgia or of that of his own state or of the names proposed for new colonies such as "Charlotta," "Charlottina," and especially, "Vandalia."

But there is an even more important point about the proposed names as revealed by the texts presented in this group of documents. It has been assumed that because Jefferson's names were dropped by Congress and have been often ridiculed since, "his list was not liked" at the time he proposed it (Malone, *Jefferson*, I, 413; Burnett, *Letters of Members*, VII, xxxix). There does not seem to be any contemporary evidence to sustain this view. On the contrary, there is conclusive evidence in the text of Jefferson's report as printed for the members of Congress (Document III, notes 21-25) that Congress considered retaining all but one of Jefferson's names: the southern boundary of one of Jefferson's named districts ("Saratoga") was altered and all of the boundaries and the name of another ("Pelisipia") were deleted before the whole of this section was struck out of the report.

The fact that "Pelisipia" was the district singled out for elimination provides possibly the best explanation for the deletion of all of Jefferson's proposed nomenclature. This is not to suggest that "Pelisipia," considered solely as a name, was viewed with less favor than any of the other names on the list—or indeed that it or any of the proposed names, as one scholar has put it, "met with disapproval from unromantic members of Congress at the time" (Burnett, *Letters of Members*, xxxix). Such an inference, resting solely upon the fact that the names were ultimately eliminated from the report, becomes inadequate as an explanation in light of the knowledge that, at one stage of the debate, Congress considered the elimination of only one of the names. Since the name of that district, etymologically and euphonically, had as sound a basis as most of those Congress considered retaining, the explanation must be sought in some characteristic distinguishing it from the others. This distinction, it is suggested, lies in the boundaries and location of "Pelisipia." Its southern and northern boundaries were parallels 39° and 41° respectively. They embraced an area southward of the Ohio that had not been ceded, but this could not have been the cause of the elimination of Pelisipia for two reasons: (1) the report dealt with the entire national domain, ceded and to be ceded, not merely with that part of it lying northward of the Ohio; and (2) "Polypotamia" was also bounded by parallels 39° and 41° and ran southward of the Ohio —yet was carefully retained in the very paragraph from which, by amendment in Congress, "Pelisipia" and its bounds were deleted.

But there are two facts that distinguish the boundaries and area of "Pelisipia" from those of all of the remaining nine districts named by Jefferson. First, by an amendment in Congress that may well have been a part of that which eliminated "Pelisipia," the southern boundary of "Saratoga" was placed at the Ohio river, thus removing from "Pelisipia" and adding to its neighbor on the north that part of its territory lying between the Ohio and parallel 39°. All other northern and southern boundaries of the districts ran along odd-numbered parallels of latitude. Second, that part of "Pelisipia" southward of the Ohio embraced almost all of an area already known to the public in general and certainly to members of Congress as Kentucky; Filson's *Kentucke* appeared later in 1784 and referred to the region as "now called Kentucke, then [1767] but known to the Indians, by the name of the Dark and Bloody Ground" (Willard Rouse Jillson, ed., *Filson's Kentucke*, Filson Club Publications No. 35, Louisville, 1930, p. 8). Moreover, even while Jefferson's committee was drawing up its report, a petition had arrived at Annapolis from the inhabitants of that region asking Congress to "lay off Kentuckey Settlement westward of the Cumberland Mountains in a free, Independent State . . . and receive us into the fœderal Union" (Virginia delegates to Harrison, 20 Feb. 1784, and its enclosure; Howell to Arnold, 21 Feb. 1784, Burnett, *Letters of Members*, VII, 521).

Possibly these facts were pointed out in the debates in Congress on Jefferson's report as originally submitted. It may have been argued that the selection of a name for a region already settled, already known by an accepted designation, and already petitioning for admission to the Union might well be left to the inhabitants who referred to it by that name. It may have been suggested that Virginia, who had already erected three counties in that area (Lincoln, Jefferson, and Fayette), might herself establish the region of Kentucky as a separate state running northward and westward to the Ohio. It should not be overlooked that David Howell, Jefferson's colleague on the committee, reported that when the Kentucky petition was before Congress a motion was made to refer it to "the State of Virginia, *within whose jurisdiction the petitioners live*. The motion was opposed and finally rejected . . . the object was to establish their jurisdiction over that Country by a side wind, as the phrase is" (Howell to Arnold, 21 Feb. 1784; Staples, *Rhode Island in the Continental Congress*, 478-9). The cause of this maneuvering, Howell added, was that Col. George Morgan was expected, "and is now actually arrived here on the business of originating an action in behalf [of] the Indiana Company against the ancient dominion." Morgan's petition was read in Congress on 1 Mch. 1784, the very day that the Virginia Deed of Cession was made and the report on a plan for government of the western territory submitted. Jefferson and the other Virginia delegates voted unanimously against committing it, as they did against a motion to consider and prepare an answer to New Jersey for sponsoring Indiana's cause (JCC, XXVI, 110-12). It may well be that in the debates on Jefferson's report only a week later, the Virginia delegates themselves took the lead in amending the southern boundary of "Saratoga" and in eliminating "Pelisipia" because of the threat from the Indiana company. This explanation of the rejection of "Pelisipia" is, of course, conjectural, but so is the view that the "names met with disapproval from unromantic members of Congress"—and it squares better with the knowledge now available that Congress first deleted one name and then all.

But the question still remains why Jefferson threw out the name Kentucky (or even Ohio) in favor of "Pelisipia." Jefferson's report referred to "the Ohio, otherwise called the Pelisipi" (Document III), thereby proving that he deliberately rejected the better-known name of the river for one not so well known ("Pelesipi" or "Pelisipi" is the name usually given on 18th century maps to what is now the Clinch river, but Vaugondy's *Partie de l'Amerique Septentrionale*, 1755, gives the Ohio as "Ohio ou Splawacipiki" though it also designates the Clinch as "Pelesipi"; and *The Seat of the War in the Middle British Colonies*, Sayer and Bennett, 1776, refers to the "Ohio R. or Palawa-Thepiki"). He may have done this because of the difficulty presented by making Ohio's ending consistent with that chosen for the other districts—"Ohioia" would certainly have invited opposition.

A still more puzzling question remains: why, in fact, did Jefferson attempt to name any of the states? Contrary to the generally accepted view, the Ordinance of 1784 provided a greater measure of local autonomy than did the Ordinance of 1787 which repealed it. As Jensen has pointed out: "Jefferson's Ordinance provided for democratic self-government of western territories, and for that reason it was abolished in 1787 by the land speculators and their supporters who wanted congressional control of the West so that their interests could be protected from the actions of the inhabitants" (Merrill Jensen, *The New Nation*, p. 354). Evidences of this appear, in fact, in the amendments offered to Jefferson's report in the debates of 19-23 Apr. 1784 (see notes to Document IV). But if Jefferson provided a full measure of local autonomy while the Northwest Ordinance of 1787 established a centralized control and appointive power in Congress imitative in some respects of the kind of colonial administration prevailing before the Revolution, it is difficult to see why he was unwilling to grant to the inhabitants the right of naming a state that he was content to let them originate.

The debates in Congress on Jefferson's report were also undoubtedly influenced by consideration of a closely related problem—that of persuading the states to make further cessions of territory to the United States. On 8 Mch. 1784, the day on which Jefferson's report was brought up for discussion, Chase, Howell, and Sherman were appointed a committee "to consider and report what further measures are necessary on the part of Congress to obtain of the several states claiming western territory liberal cessions of such claims agreeably to the resolutions of 6 Sept. and 10 Octr. 1780" (PCC: No. 186). This action must have been prompted by the inclusion in Jefferson's report of all territories to be ceded as well as those already ceded. The fact that the committee personnel, except for the significant substitution of Sherman for Jefferson, was the same as that for the report on a plan for the government of the western territory seems to confirm this supposition. Though Chase was chairman, Sherman drew the report, which was presented on 15 Mch. (printed in JCC, XXVI, 142-3; the original in Sherman's hand is in PCC: No. 30, p. 47).

Sherman's report cited the cessions made by New York and Virginia and declared that they "have been accepted by the United States in Congress, but no act hath been done to quiet or recognize the right of said States to the residue." It then urged "an amicable settlement of all disputes respecting the territorial claims" as a measure calculated to "promote harmony among the States and strengthen their federal union." It also "earnestly recommended" to those states still claiming large tracts of western territory "to authorize their delegates in Congress to make liberal cessions . . . and instruct them previously to confer with a comittee of Congress in order to agree on what cessions it may be proper for such States to make, and the United States to accept . . . and the said States be entitled to the guaranty contained in the articles of Confederation for securing to them the residue of their claims." It is possible to interpret the purport of this resolution as being an effort to avoid by previous consultation such long negotiations as took place in the three years from 1781 to 1784 when Virginia and Congress finally arrived at a compromise on what was proper for the former "to make, and the United States to accept." But a more realistic appraisal, especially in the light of the concluding clause of the report, would refer Sherman's report to the context of his struggle with Jefferson over the Wyoming affair and to what some thought was "a State juggle contrived by old Roger Sherman to get a side wind confirmation to a thing [the Connecticut Western Reserve] they had no right to" (see documents pertaining to the Connecticut-Pennsylvania territorial dispute, printed under 21 Jan. 1784, and editorial note). This conjecture is further supported by the fact that, on 16 Mch., Gerry moved that Sherman's report be recommitted to the Grand Committee, of which Jefferson was chairman. It is significant that Jefferson seconded this motion, which was carried. The very next day Jefferson's report on the plan for the government of the western territory was also recommitted. Both reports were again brought up by Jefferson on 22 Mch. 1784 (JCC, XXVI, 143; PCC: Nos. 186, 191). In view of the relatedness of the subjects and of the parallel in timing, it is difficult to escape the conclusion that, in forcing Sherman's report to be recommitted to a committee of which he himself was chairman so that he could draft the report, Jefferson was merely carrying to a new plane the struggle with Sherman begun in the matter of the Wyoming business. This becomes even clearer when the report by Jefferson that displaced Sherman's is examined (see Document VI).

Whereas Sherman's report was one that opened the door to, if indeed it did not invite, "arrangements" between the delegates of a state and Congress as to what was proper for a state to offer and Congress to accept, Jefferson's report—as had the resolutions of 1780—merely appealed to the liberality of the states and urged the necessity of their complying with Congress' earlier solicitation, leaving the terms of cession in the hands of the state making it. In this phase of the struggle also, Sherman would appear to have lost to Jefferson, though the defeat was temporary and was reversed when the Connecticut cession was accepted in 1786.

Even more important than this was the object expressed in Jefferson's report that "this too is the time when our Confederacy with all the territory included within it's limits should assume it's ultimate and permanent form." Such a view merely brought the report on state cessions in line with the report on a plan for government of the whole of the national domain. Nevertheless, Congress refused to accept this concluding paragraph of the report and watered it down to the following: "That Congress still consider vacant territory as an important resource; and that therefore the said states be earnestly pressed, by immediate and liberal cessions, to forward these necessary ends, and to promote the harmony of the Union" (JCC, XXVI, 317; Document VI, note 8).

I. Bounds of a Proposed Northwest Colony

Bounded by a line of Longitude running from the most Southernly point of Lake Michigan to the Ouabache, then down the middle of the Ouabache to where it crosses a line of Latitude 40 degrees from the equator, thence along the said Line of Latitude to within five degrees of Longitude of the river Delaware, thence along a line five degrees of Longitude in every point of it from the said river Delaware, till it strikes Lake Erie, thence along the southern shore of Lake Erie to it's most Western point,[1] thence along a strait line[2] drawn to the nearest part of the river St. Joseph, thence down the said river to Lake Michigan, thence along the Southern shore of Lake Michigan to the beginning; (provided that if in the dispute between Virginia and Pennsylva. the western boundary of Pennsylva. should be settled[3] to be a line of Longitude, then the[4] same line of Longitude shall be the Eastern boundary of the New col[ony.]

This will be about 2°. degrees of Latitude and 6. or 7. degrees of Longitude.

[on verso:]

[. . .]'s map professed to be a copy from D'An[vil]le places the Southermost shore of Lake Erie 42° 30′

D'Anville's small map makes it 42° 50′

A map publishd by Jefferys makes it 41°. 40′

*A late map, published since the peace by Bowles makes it
    41°. 35′

The Northern boundary of Virga. is the end of 41° Lat.

Evans's last map makes S. shore of Lake Erie 41°.

*Mitchell's last map 41° 30′

Massachusets Western claim is to 42°. 2′ North Latitude.

Connecticut comes from that to 41° complete, i.e. to the
    beginning of the 42° degree.

Virginia then goes to 41°. complete and is coterminous with
    Connecticut.

MS (DLC: TJ Papers, 234: 41928); entirely in the hand of TJ; contains a number of deletions and interlineations, some of which are noted below; the lines on verso concerning boundaries may or may not have reference to the proposed "colony" and may be related only to TJ's investigations of the Virginia claim or to his drafting of the Virginia Deed of Cession; these lines are written at right angles to those on recto. MS is mutilated slightly, thus causing parts of two words to be lost. The date of this fragment is discussed in editorial note above, though it may be noted here that the text on verso is roughly placed at late 1783 or early 1784 by its reference to "A late map, published since the peace by Bowles"; this was presumably Carington Bowles' *New Map of North America* (London, 1783; Phillipps, 863). The editors are indebted to Dr. St. George L. Sioussat for examining the texts of Documents I and II in the present group and for bringing to bear upon them his extensive knowledge of the affairs of land companies, of cessions by the states, and of policies of Congress respecting the national domain. In a carefully prepared memorandum submitted to the editors on 1 Mch. 1949, Dr. Sioussat arrived at the conclusion that both of these documents "are recordings of ideas which were passing through Mr. Jefferson's mind in the uncertain period after his return to Congress in 1783, when the financial need of Congress, the demands of the Army, and the cessions of western lands were pressing problems." Mrs. Constance Thurlow, Mr. William Gaines, and Mr. Francis L. Berkeley, Jr. of the staff of the University of Virginia Library also concluded that the fragment represented by Document I was probably drawn up early in 1784 (Francis L. Berkeley, Jr. to the editors, 21 Jan. 1949).

[1] Preceding four words interlined in substitution for "fort Detroit," deleted.

[2] The following deleted at this point: "due West till it strikes the river St lo."

[3] This word interlined in substitution for "determined," deleted.

[4] The following deleted at this point: "the Eastern boundary of the said colony of ———— shall be."

II. Bounds of Six Proposed Northwest Colonies

Virginia to be bounded Westerly by the Ohio, Kanhaway, Kentucky and a meridian line from the most Southern spring of the Kentucky to the Carolina line.

N. Carolina by the Catawba and Kanhaway rivers and a line joining their nearest sources.

S. Carolina by the Cavetta river, the nearest water of the Hogohegee and a line joining them.

Georgia by the Cavetta and Flint rivers.

New Colonies

A. Kentucky[1] on the East, Ohio North, Meridian of the mouth of Myamis river[2] West, Hogohegee South.

B. By A. East, Ohio North, Hogohegee West and South.

C. Pennsylva. and Ohio East, Lake Erie North, Wabash West, and S. West[3] by a line running from mouth of Elk's eye somewhat North Westerly.

D. South Ohio, North East by C. West the Wabash.

E. The Wabash on the East, North the Ilinois river, South West a line from mouth of Pimitouy river to mouth of Wabash.

F. North East by E. South by Ohio, West by Missisipi, North by the Ilinois river.

MS (DLC: TJ Papers, 234: 41926); entirely in TJ's hand, with deletions and interlineations that are indicated in notes below. Accompanying this is another fragment in TJ's hand (DLC: TJ Papers, 234: 41927) giving the bounds of what may be another "colony" south of the Ohio that perhaps was drawn up around 1783-1784. These bounds coincide almost precisely with those of the colony of Transylvania of 1775 (see Vol. 1: 64-110), but since the fragment in TJ's hand contains deletions and interlineations as indicated, it is more likely that this may represent some idea he entertained early in 1784 concerning the possible bounds of Kentucky (see Virginia delegates to Harrison, 20 Feb. 1784): "Bounded on N.W. by Ohio. On N. E. by Louisa or Cantucky river to *Donaldson's line to* head spring of it. On E. by *Donaldson's line* a line from head of Cantucky to top of Powell's mountain. *On S.E. and S. by Cumberland river and all it's branches.* Then Westerly along top of Powell's mountain until a North West course will hit head spring of Cumberland river. Then by Cumberland river." The Kentucky river was also known as the Louisa; see reproduction of John Stuart's map of Vandalia in Abernethy, *Western Lands*, p. 54-5.

[1] This must be an error. TJ may have intended to write "Kanawha," for the Kentucky lies westward of all of the three rivers designated on maps available to TJ as "Great Miami," "Little Miami," or "Miami of the Lake" (also, "Myamis" or, as in Evans and Pownall, "Mineami"; e.g., Kitchin, *Map of the United States*, 1783). On the assumption that Kanawha was intended, the district "A" becomes approximately the general size of other districts contemplated; the accompanying map (Map II) is drawn on the basis of this assumption. See following note.

[2] These two words interlined in substitution for "Little Canhaway," deleted. The sentence as originally written apparently read: "Kentucky on the East, Ohio North, Meridian of the ⟨great⟩ mouth of Little Canhaway West, Hogohegee South." This also provides boundaries that do not enclose anything, and suggests that TJ made an error in writing "Kentucky on the East" instead of "Kentucky on the West." This is plausible, since it seems obvious that in deleting "great" TJ must have been thinking of the meridian he later established in the report —the meridian of the mouth of the Great Kanawha. If this is a correct assumption, TJ may then have decided to establish the meridian of the mouth of Miami river as the western boundary and made the appropriate change, but failed to change "Kentucky" to "Kanhawha."

[3] "S. West" interlined in substitution for "N. East," deleted.

III. Report of the Committee, 1 Mch. 1784

The Committee appointed to prepare a plan for the temporary government of the Western territory have agreed to the following resolutions.

Resolved, that[1] the territory ceded or to be ceded by Individual states to the United states[2] shall be formed into distinct states, bounded in the following manner as nearly as such cessions will admit, that is to say; Northwardly and Southwardly[3] by parallels of latitude so that each state shall comprehend from South to North two degrees of latitude beginning to count from the completion of thirty one degrees North of the Equator: but any territory Northwardly of the 47th. degree shall[4] make part of the state next below. And Eastwardly and Westwardly they shall be bounded, those on the Missisipi by that river on one side and the meridian of[5] the lowest point of the rapids of Ohio on[6] the other; and those adjoining on the East by the same meridian on their Western side, and on their Eastern by the meridian of[7] the Western cape of the mouth of the Great Kanhaway. And[8] the territory Eastward of this last meridian between the Ohio, Lake Erie, and Pennsylvania shall be one state.[9]

That the settlers within any of the said states[10] shall, either on their own petition, or on the order of Congress, receive authority from them, with appointments of time and place for their[11] free males of full age[12] to meet together for the purpose of establishing a temporary government, to adopt the constitution and laws of any one of these states,[13] so that such laws nevertheless shall be subject to alteration by their ordinary legislature, and to erect, subject to a like alteration, counties or townships for the election of members for their legislature.

That such temporary government shall only continue in force in any state until it shall have acquired 20.000. free inhabitants; when giving due proof thereof to Congress, they shall receive from them authority with appointments of time and place to call a Convention of representatives to establish a permanent constitution and government for themselves.

Provided that both the temporary and permanent governments be established on these principles as their basis. 1. That they shall for ever remain a part of[14] the United states of America.[15] 2. That in their persons, property and territory they shall be subject to the government of the United states in Congress assembled, and to the Articles of confederation in all those cases in which the original states shall be so subject. 3. That they shall be subject to pay a part of the federal debts contracted or to be contracted to be apportioned on them by Congress according to the same common rule and measure by which apportionments thereof shall be made on the other states. 4. That[16] their respective governments shall be in republican forms, and shall admit no person to be a citizen who holds any hereditary title. 5. That after the year 1800 of the Christian æra, there shall be neither slavery nor involuntary servitude in any of the said states, otherwise than in punishment of crimes, whereof the party shall have been duly convicted to have been personally guilty.

That whensoever any of the said states shall have, of free inhabitants, as many as shall then be in any one the least numerous of the thirteen original states, such state[17] shall be admitted by it's delegates into the Congress of the United states, on an equal footing with the said original states:[18] after which the assent of two thirds of the United states in Congress assembled shall be requisite in all those cases, wherein by the Confederation, the assent of nine states is now required. Provided the consent of nine states to such admission may be obtained according to the eleventh of the articles of Confederation. Until such admission by their delegates into Congress, any of the said states, after the establishment of their temporary government, shall have authority to keep a sitting member in Congress, with a right of debating, but not of voting.

That the territory Northward of the 45th. degree that is to say, of the completion of 45°. from the Equator, and extending to the Lake of the Woods[19] shall be called SYLVANIA:

That of the territory under the 45th and 44th degrees that which lies Westward of Lake Michigan shall be called MICHIGANIA, and that which is Eastward thereof within the peninsul formed[20] by the lakes and waters of Michigan, Huron, St. Clair and Erie, shall be called CHERRONESUS, and shall include any part of the peninsul which may extend above the 45th. degree.

Of the territory under the 43d and 42d degrees, that to the Westward thro' which the Assenisipi or Rock river runs shall be called ASSENISIPIA, and that to the Eastward in which are the fountains of the Muskingum, the two Miamis of Ohio, the Wabash, the Illinois, the Miami of the lake and Sandusky rivers shall be called METROPOTAMIA.

Of the territory which lies under the 41st. and 40th. degrees, the Western, thro' which the river Illinois runs, shall be called

By the UNITED STATES in CONGRESS Aſſembled,

A PROCLAMATION.

WHEREAS definitive articles of peace and friendſhip, between the United States of America and his Britannic majeſty, were concluded and ſigned at Paris, on the 3d day of September, 1783, by the plenipotentiaries of the ſaid United States, and of his ſaid Britannic Majeſty, duly and reſpectively authorized for that purpoſe; which definitive articles are in the words following.

In the Name of the Moſt Holy and Undivided TRINITY.

IT having pleaſed the Divine Providence to diſpoſe the hearts of the moſt ſerene and moſt potent Prince George the Third, by the Grace of God, King of Great-Britain, France and Ireland, Defender of the Faith, Duke of Brunſwick and Lunenburg, Arch-Treaſurer and Prince Elector of the Holy Roman Empire, &c. and of the United States of America, to forget all paſt miſunderſtandings and differences, that have unhappily interrupted the good correſpondence and friendſhip which they mutually wiſh to reſtore; and to eſtabliſh ſuch a beneficial and ſatisfactory intercourſe between the two countries, upon the ground of reciprocal advantages and mutual convenience, as may promote and ſecure to both perpetual peace and harmony: And having for this deſirable end, already laid the foundation of peace and reconciliation, by the proviſional articles, ſigned at Paris, on the 30th of November, 1782, by the commiſſioners empowered on each part, which articles were agreed to be inſerted in, and to conſtitute the treaty of peace propoſed to be concluded between the crown of Great-Britain and the ſaid United States, but which treaty was not to be concluded until terms of peace ſhould be agreed upon between Great-Britain and France, and his Britannic majeſty ſhould be ready to conclude ſuch treaty accordingly; and the treaty between Great-Britain and France, having ſince been concluded, his Britannic majeſty and the United States of America, in order to carry into full effect the proviſional articles abovementioned, according to the tenor thereof, have conſtituted and appointed, that is to ſay, His Britannic majeſty on his part, David Hartley, eſquire, member of the parliament of Great-Britain, and the ſaid United States on their part, John Adams, eſquire, late a commiſſioner of the United States of America at the court of Verſailles, late delegate in congreſs from the ſtate of Maſſachuſetts, and chief juſtice of the ſaid ſtate, and miniſter plenipotentiary of the ſaid United States, to their high mightineſſes the States General of the United Netherlands; Benjamin Franklin, eſquire, late delegate in congreſs from the ſtate of Pennſylvania, preſident of the convention of the ſaid ſtate, and miniſter plenipotentiary from the United States of America at the court of Verſailles; John Jay, eſquire, late preſident of congreſs, and chief juſtice of the ſtate of New-York, and miniſter plenipotentiary from the ſaid United States at the Court of Madrid, to be the plenipotentiaries for the concluding and ſigning the preſent definitive treaty; who after having reciprocally communicated their reſpective full powers, have agreed upon and confirmed the following articles.

ARTICLE 1ſt. His Britannic Majeſty acknowledges the ſaid United States, viz. New-Hampſhire, Maſſachuſetts-Bay, Rhode-Iſland and Providence Plantations, Connecticut, New-York, New-Jerſey, Pennſylvania, Delaware, Maryland, Virginia, North-Carolina, South-Carolina and Georgia, to be free, ſovereign and independent ſtates; that he treats with them as ſuch, and for himſelf, his heirs and ſucceſſors, relinquiſhes all claims to the government, propriety and territorial rights of the ſame, and every part thereof:

ARTICLE. 2d. And that all diſputes which might ariſe in future on the ſubject of the boundaries of the ſaid United States may be prevented, it is hereby agreed and declared, that the following are and ſhall be their boundaries, viz.

From the north weſt angle of Nova-Scotia, viz. that angle which is formed by a line drawn due north from the ſource of Saint-Croix river to the Highlands; along the ſaid Highlands which divide thoſe rivers that empty themſelves into the river Saint Lawrence from thoſe which fall into the Atlantic Ocean, to the north-weſternmoſt head of Connecticut river, thence down along the middle of that river to the forty-fifth degree of north latitude; from thence by a line due weſt on ſaid latitude, until it ſtrikes the river Iroquois or Cataraquy; thence along the middle of ſaid river into lake Ontario, through the middle of ſaid lake until it ſtrikes the communication by water between that lake and lake Erie; thence along the middle of ſaid communication into lake Erie, through the middle of ſaid lake until it arrives at the water communication between that lake and lake Huron; thence along the middle of ſaid water communication into the lake Huron; thence through the middle of ſaid lake to the water communication between that lake and lake Superior; thence through lake Superior northward of the iſles, Royal and Philipeaux to the long lake; thence through the middle of ſaid long lake and the water communication between it and the lake of the Woods, to the ſaid lake of the Woods; thence through the ſaid lake to the moſt north-weſtern point thereof, and from thence on a due weſt courſe to the river Miſſiſippi; thence by a line to be drawn along the middle of the ſaid river Miſſiſippi, until it ſhall interſect the northernmoſt part of the thirty-firſt degree of north latitude. South by a line to be drawn due eaſt from the determination of the line laſt mentioned, in the latitude of thirty-one degrees north of the equator, to the middle of the river Apalachicola or Catahouche; thence along the middle thereof to its junction with the Flint river; thence ſtraight to the head of Saint Mary's river; and thence down along the middle of Saint Mary's river to the Atlantic Ocean. Eaſt by a line to be drawn along the middle of the river Saint-Croix, from its mouth in the bay of Fundy to its ſource, and from its ſource directly north to the aforeſaid Highlands which divide the rivers that fall into the Atlantic Ocean from thoſe which fall into the river Saint Lawrence; comprehending all iſlands within twenty leagues of any part of the ſhores of the United States, and lying between lines to be drawn due eaſt from the points where the aforeſaid boundaries between Nova-Scotia on the one part, and Eaſt Florida on the other, ſhall reſpectively touch the bay of Fundy, and the Atlantic Ocean; excepting ſuch iſlands as now are or heretofore have been within the limits of the ſaid province of Nova Scotia.

ARTICLE. 3d. It is agreed that the people of the United Staets ſhall continue to enjoy unmoleſted the right to take fiſh of every kind on the Grand Bank, and on all the other banks of Newfoundland; alſo in the gulph of Saint Lawrence, and at all other places in the ſea, where the inhabitants of both countries uſed at any time heretofore to fiſh; and alſo that the inhabitants of the United States ſhall have liberty to take fiſh of every kind on ſuch part of the coaſt of Newfoundland as Britiſh fiſhermen ſhall uſe, (but not to dry or cure the ſame on that Iſland) and alſo on the coaſts, bays and creeks of all other of his Britannic Majeſty's dominions in America; and that the American fiſhermen ſhall have liberty to dry and cure fiſh in any of the unſettled bays, harbours and creeks of Nova-Scotia, Magdalen iſlands, and Labradore, ſo long as the ſame ſhall remain unſettled, but ſo ſoon as the ſame or either of them ſhall be ſettled, it ſhall not be lawful for the ſaid fiſhermen to dry or cure fiſh at ſuch ſettlement, without a previous agreement for that purpoſe with the inhabitants, proprietors or poſſeſſors of the ground.

ARTICLE 4th. It is agreed that creditors on either ſide, ſhall meet with no lawful impediment to the recovery of the full value in ſterling money, of all bona fide debts heretofore contracted.

ARTICLE 5th. It is agreed that the Congreſs ſhall earneſtly recommend it to the legiſlatures of the reſpective ſtates, to provide for the reſtitution of all eſtates, rights and properties, which have been confiſcated, belonging to real Britiſh ſubjects, and alſo of the eſtates, rights and properties of perſons reſident in diſtricts in the poſſeſſion of his majeſty's arms, and who have not borne arms againſt the ſaid United States. And that perſons of any other deſcription ſhall have free liberty to go to any part or parts of any of the Thirteen United States, and therein to remain twelve months unmoleſted in their endeavours to obtain the reſtitution of ſuch of their eſtates, rights and properties, as may have been confiſcated; and that Congreſs ſhall alſo earneſtly recommend to the ſeveral ſtates a reconſideration and reviſion of all acts or laws regarding the premiſes, ſo as to render the ſaid laws or acts perfectly conſiſtent, not only with juſtice and equity, but with that ſpirit of conciliation, which on the return of the bleſſings of peace ſhould univerſally prevail. And that Congreſs ſhall alſo earneſtly recommend to the ſeveral ſtates, that the eſtates, rights and properties of ſuch laſt mentioned perſons ſhall be reſtored to them; they refunding to any perſons who may be now in poſſeſſion the bona fide price (where any has been given) which ſuch perſons may have paid on purchaſing any of the ſaid lands, rights or properties ſince the confiſcation. And it is agreed that all perſons who have any intereſt in confiſcated lands, either by debts, marriage ſettlements, or otherwiſe, ſhall meet with no lawful impediment in the proſecution of their juſt rights.

ARTICLE 6th. That there ſhall be no future confiſcations made, nor any proſecutions commenced againſt any perſon or perſons for or by reaſon of the part which he or they may have taken in the preſent war; and that no perſon ſhall on that account, ſuffer any future loſs or damage, either in his perſon liberty or property, and that thoſe who may be in confinement on ſuch charges, at the time of the ratification of the treaty in America, ſhall be immediately ſet at liberty, and the proſecutions ſo commenced be diſcontinued.

ARTICLE 7th. There ſhall be a firm and perpetual peace between his Britannic Majeſty and the ſaid States, and between the ſubjects of the one, and the citizens of the other, wherefore all hoſtilities both by ſea and land ſhall from henceforth ceaſe: all priſoners on both ſides ſhall be ſet at liberty, and his Britannic Majeſty ſhall with all convenient ſpeed, and without cauſing any deſtruction, or carrying away any negroes or other property of the American inhabitants, withdraw all his armies, garriſons and fleets from the ſaid United States, and from every poſt place and harbour within the ſame; leaving in all fortifications the American artillery that may be therein, and ſhall alſo order and cauſe all archives, records deeds and papers, belonging to any of the ſaid ſtates, or their citizens, which in the courſe of the war may have fallen into the hands of his officers, to be forthwith reſtored and delivered to the proper ſtates and perſons to whom they belong.

ARTICLE 8th. The navigation of the river Miſſiſippi, from its ſource to the Ocean, ſhall forever remain free and open to the ſubjects of Great-Britain and the citizens of the United States.

ARTICLE 9th. In caſe it ſhould ſo happen that any place or territory belonging to Great-Britain or to the United States, ſhould have been conquered by the arms of either from the other, before the arrival of the ſaid proviſional articles in America, it is agreed, that the ſame ſhall be reſtored without difficulty, and without requiring any compenſation.

ARTICLE 10th. The ſolemn ratifications of the preſent treaty, expedited in good and due form, ſhall be exchanged between the contracting parties, in the ſpace of ſix months, or ſooner if poſſible, to be computed from the day of the ſignature of the preſent treaty. In witneſs whereof, we the underſigned, their miniſters plenipotentiary, have in their name and in virtue of our full powers, ſigned with our hands the preſent definitive treaty, and cauſed the ſeals of our arms to be affixed thereto.

DONE at Paris, this third day of September, in the year of our Lord one thouſand ſeven hundred and eighty-three.

(L. S.) D. HARTLEY, (L. S.) JOHN ADAMS,
(L. S.) B. FRANKLIN,
(L. S.) JOHN JAY.

AND we the United States in Congreſs aſſembled, having ſeen and duly conſidered the definitive articles aforeſaid, did by a certain act under the ſeal of the United States, bearing date this 14th day of January 1784, approve, ratify and confirm the ſame and every part and clauſe thereof, engaging and promiſing that we would ſincerely and faithfully perform and obſerve the ſame, and never ſuffer them to be violated by any one, or tranſgreſſed in any manner as far as ſhould be in our power: and being ſincerely diſpoſed to carry the ſaid articles into execution truly, honeſtly and with good faith, according to the intent and meaning thereof, we have thought proper by theſe preſents, to notify the premiſes to all the good citizens of theſe United States, hereby requiring and enjoining all bodies of magiſtracy, legiſlative, executive and judiciary, all perſons bearing office, civil or military, of whatever rank, degree or powers, and all others the good citizens of theſe States of every vocation and condition, that reverencing thoſe ſtipulations entered into on their behalf, under the authority of that fœderal bond by which their exiſtence as an independent people is bound up together, and is known and acknowledged by the nations of the world, and with that good faith which is every man's ſureſt guide within their ſeveral offices juriſdictions and vocations, they carry into effect the ſaid definitive articles, and every clauſe and ſentence thereof, ſincerely, ſtrictly and completely.

GIVEN under the Seal of the United States, Witneſs his Excellency THOMAS MIFFLIN, our Preſident, at Annapolis, this fourteenth day of January, in the year of our Lord one thouſand ſeven hundred and eighty-four, and of the ſovereignty and independence of the United States of America the eighth.

ANNAPOLIS: Printed by JOHN DUNLAP, Printer for the United States in Congreſs aſſembled.

Proclamation announcing ratification of Definitive Treaty

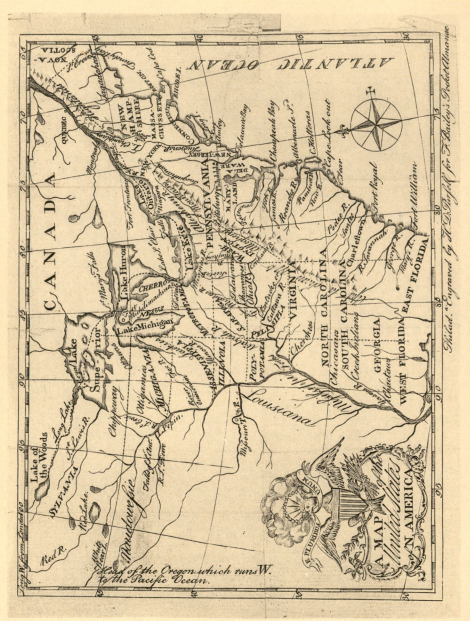

ILLINOIA; that next adjoining to the Eastward[21] SARATOGA, and that between this last and Pennsylvania and extending from the Ohio to Lake Erie, shall be called WASHINGTON.

Of[22] the territory which lies under the 39th. and 38th. degrees to which shall be added so much of the point of land within the fork of the Ohio and Missisipi as lies under the 37th. degree, that to the Westward[23] within and adjacent to which[24] are the confluences of the rivers Wabash, Shawanee, Tanissee, Ohio, Illinois, Missisipi and Missouri, shall be called POLYPOTAMIA, and that to the Eastward farther up the Ohio, otherwise called the Pelisipi shall be called PELISIPIA.[25]

That the preceding articles shall be formed into a Charter of Compact shall be duly executed by the President of the U.S. in Congress assembled under his hand and the seal of the United States, shall be promulgated, and shall stand as fundamental constitutions between the thirteen original states, and those now newly described, unalterable but by the joint consent of the U.S. in Congress assembled and of the particular state within which such alteration is proposed to be made.

MS (DLC); entirely in TJ's hand except for interlineations indicated in notes 2 and 10 below; endorsed by Thomson: "Report Mr Jefferson Mr Chase Mr Howell. Temporary governmt. of Western Country Delivered 1 March 1784. Entd. Read.—March 3. Monday next assigned for the consideration of this report. March 17. 1784 recommitted." Another text of the report as submitted 1 Mch. exists as a printed broadside (JCC, XXVI, 719, No. 426) and is in DLC: TJ Papers, 10: 1640; it bears numerous marginal corrections in TJ's hand which must have represented amendments offered in Congress in the discussion on 8 or 17 Mch. since all are incorporated in the report as resubmitted on 22 Mch. (see Document IV). The printed text, aside from differences of punctuation and capitalization, agrees precisely with the text of the MS before the interlineations indicated in notes 2 and 10 were made; hence those alternations occurred after the report was submitted. The broadside must have been printed sometime between 1 and 8 Mch. 1784, the latter being the date assigned for consideration of the report. A copy of it, together with the names of the committee, somehow fell into the hands of David C. Claypoole and was printed by him in the *Penna. Packet* for 27 Apr. 1784.

[1] The broadside text has interlined at this point the words "So much of"; this, of course, was part of the alteration described in note 2.

[2] The MS text has the following interlined at this point in the hand of Howell: "whensoever the same shall have been purchased of the Indian Inhabitants and offered for sale by the U.S." This was probably an alteration made by the committee rather than by Congress, for the broadside, which does not include these words, has, in TJ's hand in the margin, the phraseology of Howell's interlineation amended by TJ to read as it does in the revised report of 22 Mch.: "as shall ⟨at any time⟩ ⟨whensoever the same shall have⟩ be⟨en⟩ purchased of the Indian inhabitants and shall be opened for sale by ⟨the United States⟩ Congress." This alteration was made, obviously, in the light of TJ's report on instructions to the Indian commissioners (see under 4 Mch. 1784).

[3] The three preceding words deleted in broadside text.

[4] The following is deleted in MS at this point: "be added to and."

[5] In the printed text the words "but

any territory northwardly of the 47th degree . . . and the meridian of" are bracketed for deletion and the following words substituted in the margin by TJ: "and by meridians of longitude, one of which shall pass thro'."

6 This word altered to "and" in the broadside text to conform with the changes described in notes 5 and 7.

7 The words "and those adjoining on the east . . . by the meridian of" are bracketed for deletion in the printed text and the word "thro'" substituted in the margin by TJ.

8 This word deleted in printed text and "But" interlined by TJ in substitution.

9 At this point TJ added the following in the margin of the printed text: "whatsoever may be it's comprehension of latitude. That which may lie between the Ohio and completion of the 39th degree within the said meridians shall make part of the state adjoining on the north ⟨of that latitude⟩ ⟨degree⟩. That which may lie between the same meridians Nowd. of the completion of 45° shall make part of the state adjoining ⟨underneath 45th. and 44th. degrees⟩ on the south."

10 Preceding five words deleted in MS and the following interlined in the hand of Howell in substitution therefor: "the Territory so to be purchased and offered for Sale." In the right-hand margin of the printed text, imbedded in and therefore written prior to the alteration described in note 9, there is in TJ's hand an alteration corresponding with that made by Howell in MS; but in the left-hand margin of the printed text, also in TJ's hand, is the following: "on any territory which may have been so purchased and offered for sale." The latter, except for the deletion of the words "which may have been," is the reading employed by TJ in the revised report; this alteration thus bears a relationship to that described in note 2, and, for the reason there given, probably was made in committee rather than in Congress.

11 In printed text this word is deleted in part to read "the." This alteration, however, was not incorporated by TJ in the revised report.

12 In the printed text the following is interlined in TJ's hand: "within the limits of their state."

13 This phrase altered by interlineation in printed text to read: "the original states."

14 At this point TJ inserted a caret in MS and interlined the following:

"and confederated with." The interlined words, however, are faint and appear to have been erased; they are not in the printed text; see note 12, Document IV.

15 This clause number 1 in MS is enclosed in brackets. There are no corresponding brackets in the printed text or other marks to show that the passage was intended to be struck out.

16 The initial letter of the first word in this and the succeeding clause are capitalized in MS by Howell, who was also evidently responsible for inserting in the MS a large number of commas. These alterations may suggest that Howell had the duty of overseeing the printing of the report.

17 The text of the broadside reads "states," but the final letter is deleted by a mark, indicating that this was a typographical error; but it was not corrected when the type was corrected for the printing of the revised report.

18 At this point in the broadside a caret is inserted and the following is written opposite in the margin: "provided nine states agree to such admission ⟨as is req⟩ according to the reservation of the 11th of the Arts. of Confedn. And in order [to] ⟨accommodate⟩ adapt the said Articles of Confedn. to the state of Congress when it's numbers shall be thus increased, it shall [be] proposed to the legislatures of the states originally parties [there]to to require the assent of [two thirds of the] U.S. in C. ass. in all those [cases] wherein by the Articles the assent of 9. states is now required, which being agreed to by them shall be binding on the new states. Until such admission &c." This amendment, which was incorporated in the revised report, called for the deletion of the remainder of the sentence and all of the next sentence following the caret ("after which the assent of two thirds . . . of the articles of Confederation") but there is no indication on the broadside of such deletion.

19 Preceding seven words interlined in MS in substitution for "Westward of Lake Superior," deleted.

20 Preceding four words interlined in MS in substitution for "and nearly embraced," deleted. The first occurrence of "peninsul" in this paragraph seems to have the beginning of an "a" at its end, but the second is clearly "peninsul"; this form of spelling was employed by Samuel Purchas (see OED) and TJ may have been consciously or unconsciously following an author whose works he was familiar with and had no

doubt resorted to in the course of his investigations of Virginia's claim to western territory.

21 The broadside has a caret inserted at this point and the following written opposite in the margin: "and which shall be bounded on the south by the Ohio, whatsoever latitudes it may include, shall be called." This alteration shows that, even after the report had been printed and perhaps as an amendment offered in Congress, the southern boundary of "Saratoga" was changed to make it agree with what TJ represented in the Jefferson-Hartley map.

22 This word in the broadside is enclosed in rectangular lines; see note 25.

23 The preceding four words in the printed text are enclosed in rectangular lines; see note 25.

24 At this point in the printed text a caret is inserted and in the margin is written the single word "territory."

25 The final clause of this paragraph in the broadside is enclosed in rectangular lines; this and the preceding four paragraphs (beginning "That the territory Northward of the 45th degree," &c.) also have a vertical line drawn through them to indicate that they were to be deleted, as was, of course, done by amendment in Congress. But these rectangular enclosures in the final paragraph, as well as the changes indicated in notes 21 and 24, reveal a significant fact about the progress of the report through Congress that evidently has not been noted in previous accounts. If the words so enclosed as noted here and in notes 22 and 23 are eliminated from the paragraph, it reads as follows: "The territory which lies under the 39th. and 38th. degrees to which shall be added so much of the point of land within the fork of the Ohio and Missisipi as lies under the 37th degree, within and adjacent to which are the confluences of the rivers Wabash, Shawanee, Tanissee, Ohio, Illinois, Missisipi and Missouri, shall be called Polypotamia." In other words, during the debates in Congress the name of the proposed state of Pelisipia was eliminated from the group of ten proposed to be named in the Ordinance by TJ. The obvious inference is that, at least for a time, Congress considered retaining nine of the names but later deleted all of them.

IV. Revised Report of the Committee, 22 Mch. 1784

The Committee to whom was recommitted the report of a plan for a temporary government of the Western territory have agreed to the following resolutions.

Resolved that so much of the territory ceded or to be ceded by individual states to the United states, as is already purchased[1] or shall be purchased of the Indian inhabitants and offered for sale by Congress, shall be divided[2] into distinct states,[3] in the following manner, as nearly as such cessions will admit; that is to say, by parallels of latitude, so that each state shall comprehend from South to North[4] two degrees of latitude beginning to count from the completion of thirty one[5] degrees North of the equator; and by meridians of longitude, one of which shall pass thro' the lowest point of the rapids of Ohio, and the other thro' the Western cape of the mouth of the Great Kanhaway. But the territory Eastward of this last meridian, between the Ohio, lake Erie, and Pensylvania shall be one state whatsoever may be it's comprehension of latitude. That which may lie beyond the completion of the 45th.

degree between the said meridians shall make part of the state adjoining it on the South, and that part of the Ohio which is between the same meridians coinciding nearly with the parallel of 39°. shall be substituted so far in lieu of that parallel as a boundary line.[6]

That the settlers on any territory[7] so purchased and offered for sale shall, either on their own petition, or on the order of Congress, receive authority from them with appointments of time and place, for their free males of full age, within the limits of their state to meet together for the purpose of establishing a temporary government, to adopt the constitution and laws of any one of the original states,[8] so that such laws nevertheless shall be subject to alteration by their ordinary legislature; and to erect, subject to a like alteration, counties or townships[9] for the election of members for their legislature.[10]

That such temporary government shall only continue in force in any state until it shall have acquired 20,000 free inhabitants; when[11] giving due proof thereof to Congress, they shall receive from them authority, with appointments of time and place to call a convention of representatives to establish a permanent constitution and government for themselves.

Provided that both the temporary and permanent governments be established on these principles as their basis.[12] 1. That they shall for ever remain a part of this confederacy of the United states of America. 2. That in their persons, property and territory[13] they shall be subject to the government of the United states in Congress assembled, and[14] to the articles of Confederation in all those cases in which the original states shall be so subject.[15] 3.[16] That they shall be subject to pay a part of the federal debts contracted or to be contracted, to be apportioned on them by Congress, according to the same common rule and measure, by which apportionments thereof shall be made on the other states. 4.[17] That their respective governments shall be in[18] republican forms, and shall admit no person to be a citizen who holds any hereditary title.[19] 5. That after the year 1800. of the Christian æra, there shall be neither slavery nor involuntary servitude in any of the said states, otherwise than in punishment of crimes whereof the party shall have been[20] convicted to have been personally guilty.[21]

That whensoever any of the said states shall have, of free inhabitants, as many as shall then be in any one the least numerous of the thirteen original states, such state[22] shall be admitted by it's delegates into the Congress of the United states, on an equal footing with the said original states: provided nine states agree to such admission according to the reservation of the 11th of the articles of Confederation.[23] And in order to adapt[24] the said articles of confederation to the state of Congress when it's numbers shall be thus increased, it shall be proposed to the legislatures of the states originally parties thereto, to require the assent of two thirds of the United states in Congress assembled in all those cases wherein by the said articles the assent of nine states is now required; which being agreed to by them shall be binding on the new states. Until such admission by their delegates into Congress, any of the said states, after the establishment of their temporary government, shall have authority to keep a sitting[25] member in Congress, with a right of debating, but not of voting.[26]

That the preceding articles shall be formed into a charter of compact, shall be duly executed by the president of the United states in Congress assembled, under his hand, and the seal of the United states, shall be promulgated, and shall stand as fundamental constitutions between the thirteen original states and each of the several states now newly described, unalterable[27] but by the joint consent of the United states in Congress assembled, and of the particular state within which such alteration is proposed to be made.[28]

MS (DLC: PCC, No. 30, p. 55-7); entirely in TJ's hand, with a few alterations, all of which are described below; endorsed in Thomson's hand: "Report on Western territory Delivered 22 March 1784. read. Wednesday 24 Assigned for Consideration." A broadside printed text, corresponding exactly with the revised MS report as delivered (except in two typographical instances noted below), was made from the same type employed in producing the printed text of the original report (see notes to Document III), the amendments to that report made in Congress and the alterations in phraseology made by TJ in preparing the revision being incorporated in the standing type. Most of these changes were deletions, such as the elimination of the five paragraphs of named states, but some were additions. The official copy of this printed text is in PCC, No. 30, p. 53, to which a MS amendment in TJ's hand at p. 57½ belongs (see note 26, below). On the broadside, in the hand of Chase, are recorded the amendments proposed and adopted in Congress during the course of debate; it is endorsed in the

hand of Thomson: "Report of Mr Jefferson Mr Chase Mr Howell on Western territory. Delivered 1. March 1784. Passed April 23. 1784." In JCC, XXVI, 275-9, there is what is stated to be TJ's MS report as adopted with all amendments on 23 Apr. 1784; actually the text there employed is a combination of the MS and "alterations made during the debate" as recorded by Chase on the broadside; some of the differences between the two are indicated, but not all, with the result that deletions in the printed text as made by Congress are confusingly presented as deletions made in the MS report submitted by TJ. A more accurate description of this broadside is given in JCC, XXVII, 719, No. 427.

In addition to the official copy of this printed text, three others with marginal corrections have been found. (1) The first of these is reproduced in facsimile by Ford, III, facing p. 428, but has not been found. It includes deletions, interlineations, and marginal additions in TJ's hand representing the amended resolutions as adopted by Congress; at the bottom of the broadside is the following in TJ's hand: "Apr. 23. 1784. Passed in Congress by the votes of ten states out of eleven present." There are indications in the handwriting and in one or two deletions noted below that the amendments were entered by TJ during the course of debate, for the handwriting is TJ's "rough" hand, not the formal, regular hand employed in the MS of the revised report or in the third copy of this broadside. It is obvious, as the notation on the Jefferson broadside shows, that TJ must have sent that copy to someone to show what Congress had adopted. Since the *Va. Gaz.* (N & P) of 15 May 1784 printed the text of the Ordinance of 1784, under an Annapolis date line of 6 May, it may be that the Jefferson broadside was the one sent to Madison on 25 Apr. 1784 or possibly to Joseph Jones on the same date. (2) The second copy of the broadside bears the same deletions, interlineations, and marginal additions as the first (and are in TJ's hand), but the deletions are made by carefully drawn double rules and the handwriting is precise and regular. This copy was enclosed in TJ's letter to Hogendorp, 4 May 1784, as in the form "ultimately passed by Congress"; it is in the Hogendorp papers, Rijksarchief, The Hague, Holland. (3) The third is in PPHi and bears, in an unidentified hand, the same deletions, interlineations, and marginal additions as the first and second. Since it has no significant differences, this broadside is disregarded in the notes below.

The official broadside in PCC, No. 30, p. 53, the facsimile reproduced in Ford, III, facing p. 428, and the broadside sent to Hogendorp are referred to in the notes below as OB (official broadside), JB (Jefferson broadside), and HB (Hogendorp broadside), respectively. The phraseology of the amendments indicated in notes below is that recorded by Chase on OB; unless otherwise noted, the amendments as recorded on HB and JB agree with this phraseology.

1 Preceding four words interlined in MS and not included in the alteration described in note 2, Document III.

2 This word interlined in MS in substitution for "formed," deleted.

3 The word "bounded" is deleted in MS at this point.

4 This phrase altered in OB to read "from north to South."

5 Altered in OB to read: "forty five."

6 TJ first wrote this sentence so as to conform precisely to the phraseology quoted in note 9, Document III, except for substituting "beyond" for "Northward of." Then, on the MS, he altered this by deletion and interlineation to read: "That which may lie under the 41st. and 40th degrees ⟨of latitude⟩ between the meridians shall extend in every part [to the Ohio] as its Southern boundary whatever may be it's latitude ⟨and no further⟩, and that which may lie between the same meridians beyond the completion of the 45th. degree shall make part of the state adjoining on the South." Being still dissatisfied with this, TJ, on a separate slip of paper, wrote the passage as it appears above and wafered it to the first page of MS over the passage for which it was substituted. This slip has now been removed from the MS, but the wafers obscure the conjectural reading in square brackets.

7 The words "which may have been" are deleted in MS at this point (see note 10, Document III).

8 The passage "either on their own petition . . . of the original states" is bracketed and underscored in OB, but not in JB or HB. On 21 Apr. Gerry moved, seconded by TJ, that all of the first part of this clause down to and including the words "full age" be struck out and the following substituted: "That on the petition of the settlers on any territory so purchased of the Indians, or otherwise obtained and sold to individuals, or on the order of Congress, authority may be given by Congress with appointment of time and place, for all free males of full age, being residents of the United States, and owning lands or residing" (within the limits of their state, &c.). But only four states supported this motion and it failed (JCC, XXVI, 255-6).

9 This phrase altered in OB by deleting "or" and interlining "or other Divisions" after the word "townships."

10 The passage "and to erect . . . for their legislature" is underscored in OB, indicating that an amendment was offered in Congress, but no corresponding markings appear in JB or HB and there is no reference to such an attempted amendment in JCC.

11 The passage "such temporary government . . . inhabitants; when" is deleted in OB and the following interlined in substitution: "when any such State shall have acquired 20,000 free inhabitants on."

12 On 20 Apr. Williamson moved to

strike out the words "temporary and"; but Read of South Carolina was the only one of twenty-four delegates present to join him in supporting this motion (JCC, XXVI, 249-50). In the following sentence, the words "this confederacy" are not in the original report (Document III) and are not recorded there as among the amendments offered in Congress, which suggests that TJ inserted the words in MS in preparing the revised report.

13 Preceding six words deleted in OB; this was done before 20 Apr. 1784 (JCC, XXVI, 248).

14 Preceding eleven words deleted in OB. This amendment was offered by Sherman on 20 Apr.; TJ voted in favor of it (JCC, XXVI, 248-9).

15 At this point in OB there is the symbol # and in the margin a corresponding symbol followed by: "2d Article—and to all the Acts and Ordinances of the US in Congress assembled conformable thereto." The amendment as recorded in the margin of JB differs slightly: "and to all the acts and ordinances of Congress made conformable thereto." This difference supports the conjecture that TJ entered the notations on JB during Congress' debates and that in this as in another instance (note 16) copied an earlier form of an amendment and not the words as finally approved by Congress, despite his statement at the bottom of JB: "23 Apr. 1784 Passed in Congress. . . ." HB and the text from the Journals of Congress (Document V) both agree with the wording as given in the margin of OB.

16 This number changed to "4" by overwriting in all three broadsides. In the margin of OB is the following: "3d. That they in no Case interfere with the primary Disposal of the said Lands by the US in Congress assembled." This was then deleted and the following written below it: "3d Article [Th]at they in no Case shall with [inter]fere with the primary Disposal of the Soil by the US in Congress nor with the Ordinances and Regulations which Congress may find necessary for securing the Title in such Soil to the bona fide purchasers." In the margin of JB the word "soil" is interlined in substitution for the deleted words "said lands"; this corresponds to the change made in OB. But in JB the word "assembled" is struck out after the first use of "Congress" and in the revised amendment in OB the word does not appear. It does appear, however, in HB and also in

the text as finally adopted (Document V). This difference again supports the view that TJ entered amendments on JB during debates in Congress.

17 This number, not discernible in OB owing to mutilation, was changed by overwriting in JB and HB to "6" and then to "7."

18 This word deleted in OB, obviously as part of the amendment which involved also deletion of the word "forms." This amendment had already been made by 20 Apr. when the amendment described in note 19 was proposed (JCC, XXVI, 250).

19 Preceding fifteen words deleted in OB. This amendment was made on 20 Apr. (JCC, XXVI, 250-1). TJ reported that this was not because Congress entertained "an approbation of such honours, but because it was thought an improper place to encounter them" (TJ to Madison, 25 Apr. 1784).

At the bottom of OB is the following: "5th Article. That no Tax shall be imposed on Lands the property of the US." And immediately following the end of the paragraph is the amendment that became the seventh section: "That the Lands of Non Resident proprietors shall in no case be taxed higher than those of Residents within any new state before the admission thereof to a vote by its delegates in Congress." This amendment was inserted in margin of JB after the amendment described in note 23 had been adopted, as is proved both by its position on the page in OB and by the exceedingly crowded lines in JB, obviously squeezed in between passages already existing above and below. As originally proposed by Gerry and seconded by TJ, this amendment read: "That the lands and improvements thereon of non-resident proprietors," &c. Howell moved to delete the words "and improvements thereon"; TJ voted against this amendment to the amendment, but only six states could be mustered against it, so the question was lost and the words deleted. Howell then tried another amendment to the amendment—that the words "before the admission thereof to a vote by its delegates in Congress" be struck out, but this failed (JCC, XXVI, 257-9).

20 The word "duly" is deleted in MS at this point, though not indicated as an amendment in the alterations recorded in the printed text of Document III; hence probably deleted by TJ in preparing the revised report.

21 All of section 5 was deleted by

amendment in Congress and each of the broadsides shows the passage marked out. The motion to delete was made on 19 Apr. 1784 by Spaight of North Carolina and seconded by Read of South Carolina. Every delegate including and north of Pennsylvania voted for TJ's clause excluding slavery; Jefferson and Williamson were the only delegates southward of that state to vote with them. The lack of the vote of a single delegate determined the outcome; Beatty of New Jersey was ill (see TJ to Madison, 25 Apr. 1784). Sixteen delegates voted to retain the clause, whereas only seven voted to delete it; but the former represented only six states and the latter three. Thus a minority of states and of delegates' votes determined the issue, for on the question as to whether the words moved to be struck out should stand, the required seven states could not be mustered, the question was lost, and the words were deleted (JCC, XXVI, 247).

On the question of the exclusion of slavery, see Edward Coles, *History of the Ordinance of 1787* (Historical Society of Pennsylvania, 1856); the Society also has, in the Robins Collection, Edward Coles' correspondence with Henry Clay, Martin Van Buren, Henry S. Randall, Charles Sumner, and others concerning this and other matters (photocopies are in TJ Editorial Files). The reply of Sumner fairly sums up the long-drawn-out argument precipitated by Webster in the Webster-Hayne Debate as to whether Nathan Dane or TJ originated the proviso for the exclusion of slavery in the western territories: "To Jefferson belongs the honor of the first effort to prohibit slavery in the territories, to Dane belongs the honor of finally embodying this prohibition in the Ordinance drawn by his hand in 1787" (Sumner to Coles, 23 Aug. 1852, PHi).

22 Thus in MS, but the broadside text reads "states." This was obviously a typographical error, but TJ failed to correct it in HB or JB and it is also uncorrected in OB.

23 The passage "nine states agree . . . articles of Confederation" is deleted in OB and in the margin there is substituted the following: "the Consent of so many states in Congress is first obtained as may at the time be competent to such Admission." This amendment was made in Congress on 20 Apr. 1784. Gerry first moved that the proviso be altered to read: "Provided such admis-

sion be according to the articles of Confederation," but only five states could be mustered in support (TJ voting for the amendment) and the motion was lost. Williamson, seconded by Gerry, then moved the amendment recorded above and seven states supported the motion; TJ voted for it (JCC, XXVI, 251-2).

24 Another typographical error occurred in the broadside text with the printing of this word as "adopt." It was corrected in OB and JB, but TJ failed to make the correction in HB.

25 This word deleted in all three broadsides.

26 At this point in OB there is the symbol #, and in PCC: No. 30, p. 57½, there is a fragment with a corresponding symbol and the text in TJ's hand of an amendment described below. On 23 Apr. Gerry moved the following amendment: "That such measures as may from time to time be necessary not inconsistent with the principles of the confederation are reserved for and shall be taken by Congress to preserve peace and good order among the settlers in any of the said new States, previous to their assuming a temporary government as aforesaid" (JCC, XXVI, 274; MS in hand of Gerry in PCC: No. 36, IV, 563). Read, seconded by Spaight, then moved to postpone consideration of Gerry's motion in order to take up the following amendment that he had unsuccessfully moved two days earlier: "That until such time as the settlers aforesaid, shall have adopted the constitution and laws of some one of the original states as aforesaid, for a temporary government, the said settlers shall be ruled by magistrates to be appointed by the United States in Congress assembled, and under such laws and regulations as the United States in Congress assembled, shall direct" (JCC, XXVI, 259, 274-5; TJ had voted for the amendment on 21 Apr. possibly because he knew it would be defeated). But only Pennsylvania and Maryland voted for this postponement (TJ opposed it) and Read's motion was lost. At this point, though the Journals credit Gerry with the amendment as ultimately adopted, TJ came forward with a substitute motion on the fragment referred to above (PCC: No. 30, p. 57½); that this motion was written by TJ in Congress is proved by the fact that on its recto are various tally marks by Thomson which were clearly on the paper before TJ used it to compose his substitute motion; on its verso

is the tabulation of a balloting in Thomson's hand). As originally phrased this motion by TJ read: "That measures not inconsistent with the principles of the Confederation and necessary for the preservation of peace and good order among the settlers in any of the said new states until they shall assume a temporary government in the manner as aforesaid, may be taken by Congress from time to time." The latter part of this was altered (evidently in Congress, since the changes are in Thomson's hand) to read: ". . . a temporary government as aforesaid, may from time to time be taken by the US in C assembled." As thus altered, this substitute amendment was finally adopted (as noted by TJ on HB). However, the marginal insertion on JB begins: "That ⟨such⟩ measures ⟨as may from time to time be necessary⟩ not inconsistent with the principles of the Confederation and necessary for the preservation of peace and good order," &c.; the deleted words correspond exactly with those in Gerry's motion as originally introduced. This suggests that TJ may have drafted his substitute motion on JB and then copied it off on the slip of paper furnished by Thomson. But at any rate, though the Journals give Gerry credit

for the amendment, the final wording was TJ's.

The real issue, here, of course, was between the large measure of local control in the territories advocated by TJ and the augmentation of control by Congress advocated in Read's amendment, for which all of the Pennsylvania and Maryland delegates voted—states in which the leaders of the large western land companies were centered and whose policies prevailed in the Northwest Ordinance of 1787 that radically reversed the principles laid down by TJ in 1784.

[27] At this point a caret is inserted in OB and in the margin the following is written: "from and after the Sale of any part of the Territory of such state pursuant to this Resolve." Corresponding additions appear in JB and HB.

[28] At the bottom of OB are the words "Yeas and Nays Mr Beresford." This represented Beresford's request for a roll call vote on the entire revised report as amended down to 23 Apr. 1784. The result showed that ten states voted in favor of the amended report and only Read of South Carolina joined Beresford in casting their state's single vote in opposition.

V. The Ordinance of 1784

By the UNITED STATES in CONGRESS
assembled, April 23, 1784

CONGRESS resumed the consideration of the report of a committee on a plan for a temporary government of the western territory, which being amended, was agreed to as follows:

Resolved, That so much of the territory ceded or to be ceded by individual states to the United States, as is already purchased or shall be purchased of the Indian inhabitants, and offered for sale by Congress, shall be divided into distinct states in the following manner, as nearly as such cessions will admit; that is to say, by parallels of latitude, so that each state shall comprehend from north to south two degrees of latitude, beginning to count from the completion of forty five degrees north of the equator; and by meridians of longitude, one of which shall pass through the lowest point of the rapids of Ohio, and the other through the western cape of the mouth of the great Kanhaway; but the territory eastward of this last meridian, between the Ohio, Lake Erie, and Pennsylvania, shall be one state, whatsoever may be its comprehension of latitude. That which may lie beyond the completion of the 45th degree between the said meridians shall make part of the state adjoining it on the south; and that part of the Ohio, which is between the same meridians coinciding nearly with the parallel of 39° shall be substituted so far in lieu of that parallel as a boundary line.

That the settlers on any territory so purchased and offered for sale shall, either on their own petition or on the order of Congress, receive authority from them, with appointments of time and place, for their free males of full age within the limits of their state to meet together, for the purpose of establishing a temporary government, to adopt the constitution and laws of any one of the original states; so that such laws nevertheless shall be subject to alteration by their ordinary legislature; and to erect, subject to a like alteration, counties, townships, or other divisions, for the election of members for their legislature.

That when any such state shall have acquired twenty thousand free inhabitants, on giving due proof thereof to Congress, they shall receive from them authority with appointments of time and place, to call a Convention of representatives to establish a permanent constitution and government for themselves. Provided that both the temporary and permanent governments be established on these principles as their basis.

First. That they shall for ever remain a part of this confederacy of the United States of America.

Second. That they shall be subject to the articles of confederation in all those cases in which the original states shall be so subject, and to all the acts and ordinances of the United States in Congress assembled, conformable thereto.

Third. That they in no case shall interfere with the primary disposal of the soil by the United States in Congress assembled, nor with the ordinances and regulations which Congress may find necessary for securing the title in such soil to the bona fide purchasers.

Fourth. That they shall be subject to pay a part of the federal debts contracted or to be contracted, to be apportioned on them by Congress, according to the same common rule and measure by which apportionments thereof shall be made on the other states.

Fifth. That no tax shall be imposed on lands the property of the United States.

Sixth. That their respective governments shall be republican.

Seventh. That the lands of non resident proprietors shall in no case be taxed higher than those of residents within any new state, before the admission thereof to a vote by its delegates in Congress.

That whensoever any of the said states shall have of free inhabitants, as many as shall then be in any one the least numerous of the thirteen original states, such state[1] shall be admitted by its delegates into the Congress of the United States, on an equal footing with the said original states; provided the consent of so many states in Congress is first obtained as may at the time be competent to such admission. And in order to adapt[1] the said articles of confederation to the state of Congress when its numbers shall be thus increased, it shall be proposed to the legislatures of the states, originally parties thereto, to require the assent of two thirds of the United States in Congress assembled, in all those cases wherein by the said articles, the assent of nine states is now required, which being agreed to by them shall be binding on the new states. Until such admission by their Delegates into Congress, any of the said states after the establishment of their temporary government shall have authority to keep a member in Congress, with a right of debating, but not of voting.

That measures not inconsistent with the principles of the confederation, and necessary for the preservation of peace and good order among the settlers in any of the said new states, until they shall assume a temporary government as aforesaid, may from time to time be taken by the United States in Congress assembled.

That the preceding articles shall be formed into a charter of compact; shall be duly executed by the President of the United States in Congress assembled, under his hand, and the seal of the United States; shall be promulgated; and shall stand as fundamental constitutions between the thirteen original states, and each of the several states now newly described, unalterable from and after the sale of any part of the territory of such state, pursuant to this resolve, but by the joint consent of the United States in Congress assembled, and of the particular state within which such alteration is proposed to be made.

CHARLES THOMSON, Secretary

Text from *Va. Gaz.* (N & P), under the dateline "Annapolis May 6." This text was obviously printed from the two-leaf publication of the Ordinance of 1784 issued by authority of Congress, bearing the same title, and being circulated by Thomson (see Ford, III, 430, note). It varies from that in the manuscript Journals of Congress only in spelling and punctuation and, of course, in the fact that the latter lacks title, preamble, and attest.

[1] In copying this word in the Journals, Thomson committed the same error that the printer had made in the official broadside described in Document IV (see notes 22 and 24), but he

then corrected his mistake. From this it is clear that, in inserting the text in the Journal, Thomson must have been copying from the amended text described as OB in Document IV.

VI. Report on State Claims to Western Territory

[22 Mch. 1784]

The report of a Committee on the subject of Western territory having been referred to the Grand committee they have had the same under their consideration and agreed to the following report.

Congress by their resolution of Sep. 6. 1780. having thought it adviseable 'to press upon the states having claims to the Western country a liberal surrender of a portion of their territorial claims,' by that of the 10th. of Oct. in the same year having fixed[1] conditions to which the Union should be bound on receiving such cessions: and having again proposed the same subject to those states in their address of April   1783. wherein, stating the national debt[2] and expressing their reliance for it's discharge[3] on the prospect of vacant territory in aid of other resources[4] they, for that purpose, as well as to obviate disagreeable controversies and confusions included in the same recommendation a renewal of those of Sep. the 6th. and of Oct. the 10th. 1780: which several recommendations have not yet been finally complied with.

Resolved, that the same subject be again presented to the attention of the said states, that they be urged to consider that the war being now brought to a happy termination by the personal services of our souldiers, the supplies of property by our citizens, and loans of money from them as well as from foreigners, these several creditors have a right to expect that funds shall be provided[5] on which they may rely[6] for indemnification; that Congress still consider vacant territory as a[7] capital resource; that this too is the time when our Confederacy with all the territory included within it's limits should assume it's ultimate and permanent form; and that therefore the said states be earnestly pressed by immediate and liberal cessions to forward these necessary ends, and to remove those obstacles which disturb the harmony of the Union, which embarrass it's councils and obstruct it's operations.[8]

MS (DLC: PCC, No. 144, p. 81-2); entirely in TJ's hand; endorsed in Thomson's hand: "Report of grand Comee. delivered March 22. 1784. Monday 29 [i.e., 29 Mch.] assigned for Consideration"; contains some deletions and interlineations, all of which are indicated below.

This report was debated on 29 Apr. 1784. Spaight moved to delete that part of the first sentence of the report italicized in the following: ". . . having thought it adviseable to press upon the states *having claims to the* western country" (JCC, XXVI, 315; the words "western country" probably were included in the motion to delete, but they are not so indicated in the Journals). This was defeated by a vote of eight states to three; TJ was the only one of the Virginia delegation to oppose it. See note 8 for another amendment.

[1] TJ first wrote "having fixed the condition," and then altered the phrase to read as above.

[2] The following is deleted at this point: "and it's annual interest, they recommended for the discharge of the interest the plan of an impost on commerce now under consideration with the states, with such subsidiary 'funds as they might judge most convenient,' and for the discharge of the principal."

[3] As originally phrased, this passage read: "expressing some reliance on other resources, but chiefly," and then was altered to read as above.

[4] Preceding five words interlined.

[5] Preceding six words interlined in substitution for "call for a precise designation of the funds."

[6] This word interlined in substitution for "are to," deleted.

[7] This word interlined in substitution for "the," deleted.

[8] The concluding part of the report beginning "That Congress still consider vacant territory . . ." was amended by Congress to read as quoted above at the conclusion of the editorial note to the present group of documents; no mark on the MS, however, indicates that such an amendment was made (JCC, XXVI, 317).

Appendix I

The Legislative Request for an Inquiry
into the Conduct of General Steuben

EDITORIAL NOTE

The situation in Virginia at the close of Jefferson's administration as governor was such as to dispose the legislature to set on foot inquiries into the conduct of the executive and of those responsible for certain military events. Various documents in this and the preceding volume set forth the results of the inquiry into the conduct of the executive. Other documents printed in this volume under May and June, 1781, also take note of resolutions adopted by the General Assembly to influence military decisions directly, such as the action directing Jefferson to call on General Daniel Morgan to take the field. The notes and documents here presented belong to the same context. The editors feel justified in presenting them because of this fact and also because the affair at Point of Fork exhibits on Steuben's part an apparently fixed determination to leave Virginia and to rejoin Greene regardless of the exigencies in Virginia. This determination became dominant when the Governor and Council rejected Steuben's proposal of 29 March 1781 to lead the Virginia militia southward in an effort to trap Cornwallis. That proposal was a pivotal point in Steuben's relationship with Jefferson and with Virginia, and Steuben's behavior at Point of Fork seems related in greater or lesser degree to the animosities engendered when the proposal was rejected.

Steuben thought he had good reason to feel resentful that a proposal enthusiastically approved by Lafayette, Weedon, Gouvion, Greene, Washington, Richard Henry Lee, and others should have been rejected by civil officers. Almost all historians, including such a careful and dispassionate scholar as Gottschalk, have agreed that Jefferson and the Council made an unfortunate mistake. Certainly the point that Greene and Washington made—that broad strategy could not be planned if soldiers were restrained by state boundaries and held in check by what these two generals described as local and partial views—was a valid one. The other principal point insisted upon by Greene—that such decisions as those affecting Steuben's proposal should be left to the military and not determined by the civil authority—is less certain and involves a question that becomes perennial whenever the state has to call its military arm into active use. Jefferson never commented on Steuben's proposal or on his conduct at Point of Fork further than appears in the reasons given in the proceedings of the Council for 29 March 1781. But those who have accepted the hypothesis that Steuben's proposal was a good one and that the Executive's decision was dominated by local views have overlooked two facts: (1) Jefferson always subscribed to the broad strategy of General Greene that it was good policy to keep the war at a distance from Virginia and that Virginia's policy was to be purely defensive in order that she might give Greene every support possible; and (2) this concept of the war in the South carried with it the corollary concept of defense for Virginia as Greene's source of supplies, whereas Steuben's proposal was one that would have virtually stripped the state of all defense at a time when her waterways were commanded by an enemy whose forces would then have been free to invade the hinterland and destroy the sources needed by Greene.

Whether the decision influenced by these considerations was wise or not, it nevertheless strongly affected Steuben's attitude toward the government of Virginia and in turn influenced Greene's attitude also. It determined Steuben to leave Virginia at all costs and to rejoin Greene. By mid-April he himself was convinced that his usefulness in the state was at an end. He had become involved in many disputes and differences with officers both of the militia and of the Continental Line. Members of the legislative as well as the executive authority had been alienated by him. It is in this context, therefore, that his behavior at Point of Fork is to be understood and it is for this reason that documents relating to that episode are pertinent to the record of Jefferson's administration.

On 1 Nov. 1781 Baron Steuben, about to depart for the northward, wrote a letter of farewell to Governor Nelson in which he expressed regret that neither he nor Lafayette had been able to strike the brilliant stroke in the late campaign that they had wished, but he was nevertheless glad to have "participated in the glorious conclusion of it" at Yorktown. He added that he had received letters from Washington, Lafayette, and Greene expressing "their approbation of my Operations since I have been in Virginia." Almost as if it were an afterthought, he wrote: "I have to ask of your Excellency to inform me by an official Letter if Government have any complaint against me since I have had the honor of serving in Virginia that if there should be any I may Justify myself before my departure. A reputation acquired during 27 years service authorises me in this point of Delicacy."[1] Nelson made no reply to this request. Six weeks later Steuben repeated the inquiry in a letter to Governor Harrison, saying that before he left Virginia he had heard "by accident that a Resolve had some time before passed the House of Assembly requesting the Marquis to make an inquiry into the Conduct of the Officers under his command relative to the loss of

[1] Steuben to Nelson, 1 Nov. 1781 (Dft, NHi). No letter from Washington to Steuben such as is referred to in the letter to Nelson has been found, though the commander-in-chief, "by Affection Duty and Gratitude," in general orders on 20 Oct. 1781 did cite the baron along with Generals Lincoln and Lafayette for their disposition in the trenches before Yorktown (*Writings*, ed. Fitzpatrick, XXIII, 246). However, Washington appears to have been almost alone in still insisting in the autumn of 1781 that the inquiry called for should be held. Writing to Greene on 6 Oct. 1781, he declared: "The Baron, from the warmth of his temper, has got disagreeably involved with the State, and an enquiry into part of his conduct must one day take place, both for his own honor and their satisfaction. I have for the present given him a command in this Army which makes him happy" (same, XXIII, 190). For a general account of Steuben's behavior at Point of Fork, see Palmer, *Steuben*, p. 273-87; a more scholarly account is Gottschalk's *Lafayette and the Close of the American Revolution*, p. 237, 239, 240, 242, 246, 248-9. For the account written by Steuben's opposing commander at Point of Fork, see Simcoe's *Journal*, New York, 1844, p. 211-23.

the stores at the point of Fork."[2] To this Harrison replied briefly that the General Assembly had adopted such a resolution, that it had been forwarded to Lafayette, and that the marquis had replied that he had been too much engaged to enter upon an inquiry. "There the matter rests," Harrison concluded, "and I dare say will not be again taken up."[3] In this Harrison was correct. Steuben nevertheless, then or about that time, proceeded to draw up a defense of his conduct in Virginia (see Lafayette to Steuben, 26 Oct. 1781). But beyond this he apparently did not go in seeking vindication.

With Yorktown in the background, the Virginia legislature could afford to be more forgiving than it had been in the preceding June. At that time the House of Delegates had come to the following resolution: "It appearing that this State hath incurred great loss from the destruction of the public stores at the Point of Fork, on James River, by a small party of the enemy; and also from the shameful plundering the said stores by some of the adjacent inhabitants, and others: which loss, it is suggested, might have been prevented by the appointment of a small guard for their protection. *Resolved*, That the Honorable Major General Marquis La Fayette be requested to cause an inquiry to be made into the conduct of all persons under his command, who may be supposed, either by neglect or otherwise, to have been instrumental in the loss of the said stores."[4]

The official language of this resolution concealed much of the disgust and fury which the legislators felt. Benjamin Harrison, Speaker of the House of Delegates, wrote early in June to Joseph Jones, a Virginia delegate in Congress: "We have 600 fine men under Baron Steuben which he will not carry into action. What are his reasons, I know not, but I can assure you his Conduct gives universal disgust and injures the Service much, the People complaining and with reason that they are draged from their Families at a time when they are most wanted to make bread for them, whilst the Soldiers they have hired at very great expence lay Idle. In short, My Dr. Sir, his conduct does great mischief and will do more if he is not recalled, and I think it behoves you to bring it about. I assure you it is the wish and desire of every man that this Event should take place. I believe him a good officer on the Parade but the worst in every other respect in the American Army."[5] And the Speaker of the Senate, Archibald Cary, had

[2] Steuben to Harrison, 13 Dec. 1781 (Dft, NHi); in this letter Steuben explained that he had repeated his request in order that "I may have the Opportunity of Justifying myself not only to the State of Virginia but to the World" and he added that General Lawson and Colonels Davies and Meade would be witnesses to the propriety of his conduct at Point of Fork.

[3] Harrison to Steuben, 28 Dec. 1781 (RC, NHi). Harrison did not record this letter in the Executive Letter Book.

[4] JHD, May 1781, 1828 edn., p. 29.

[5] Harrison to Jones, Staunton, 8 June 1781, quoted in Jones' letter to Washington, 20 June 1781 (DLC: Washington Papers; also printed in part in Burnett, *Letters of Members*, VI, No. 165). Jones further inquired: "Could not Genl Greene be well spared from the South to take the Command in Virga. The scene of action is there, and as you cannot be present his Abilities and experience may be very useful." Washington replied on 10 July 1781 to Jones, in part: "from General Greenes Letters I had but little doubt but that he would have been in Virginia ere this, powerful causes may have detained him; but I am persuaded he will be there as soon as possible,

declared in a letter to Jefferson that three members of the Council—one of them was John Walker who had served on Steuben's staff in the spring of 1781—"observe that Baron Stuben deserves to be hanged for his Conduct."[6]

Colonel Davies attempted to soften the legislature's action by assuring the baron that "The Assembly were at first much mortified at the losses we had sustained by the rapid incursions of the enemy, and in their discontent they were really clamorous. They moderate in their vexation as they have since found that the mischief done by the enemy was inconsiderable compared with the plunder of the inhabitants, of whom we expect to recover a great deal, and the greater part of what was thrown in the water has been also recovered."[7] Davies was genuinely fond of the baron and his attempt to ameliorate the Assembly's blow does credit to his humane feelings. But he must have known that the legislature was aware of plundering by the public when its resolution was adopted. Moreover, in May, Davies had foreseen the danger to which the stores were being exposed and had made an eloquent plea to Steuben to give them more adequate protection, a plea that had its precedent a month earlier when both Jefferson and Greene had become concerned about the baron's inattention to such matters.[8] Others, though they were few, shared Davies' sympathy for the baron: Captain John Pryor wrote to Davies on 15 June: "I think the Public Clamour seems to be rather against the Baron. Pray mention that subject in your next to me, as I have charity for that venerable character."[9] But Davies' charity did not keep him from writing frankly to Greene that "The Baron has unfortunately become universally unpopular, and all ranks of people seem to have taken the greatest disgust at him, and carry it to such length as to talk of applying to Congress for his recall. A very little however, has raised all their clamour; but at all events his usefulness here is entirely over."[10]

As for Lafayette, it is quite clear that he had no relish for such an

---

as it is within his command, and now the principle theatre of action. In the mean while I am afraid to give any order in that quarter lest it should clash with his views, and produce confusion" (*Writings*, ed. Fitzpatrick, XXII, 353).

[6] Cary to TJ, 19 June 1781, printed above under that date. Steuben's letter of 3 June 1781 to the Speaker of the Senate had been presented in order to justify himself before that body and before the people of the state.

[7] William Davies to Steuben, 23 June 1781 (RC, NHi).

[8] Davies to Steuben, 12 May 1781, printed below. On 5 Sep. 1781 Davies wrote Steuben a farewell note in part as follows: "I shall always be solicitous to express my respect and my obligations to you, and shall often have occasion for your directions and advice. With the warmest emotions of

affectionate respect I bid you farewel, and beg you, my dear General, to accept of my most ardent wishes for your health and happiness, and a glorious reward for the very disinterested attachment you have shewn my country, in an unremitted series of faithful services" (RC, NHi).

[9] Pryor to Davies, 15 June 1781 (RC, Vi).

[10] Davies to Greene, 17 June 1781 (RC, NHi); Greene must have forwarded this letter to Steuben, since it is now among the baron's papers. In this letter Davies put an unexpected interpretation on the Greene strategy: "Lord Cornwallis certainly expected you would follow him. I am glad he has been disappointed. Distressed as the people are in this state, they applaud your conduct in the warmest terms of admiration."

inquiry as the legislature called upon him to make. "My respect to the Assembly," he explained to Governor Nelson later, "made me extremely desirous to comply with their wishes, but our situation before being joined by General Washington put it wholly out of my power."[11] The reason given is scarcely adequate and suggests that the true explanation lies elsewhere, perhaps in Lafayette's relationship with the baron.

From the afternoon of 14 Mch. 1781 when Lafayette came ashore at Yorktown until he finally departed from Virginia some months later, his relations with Steuben were so delicate as to require all of the marquis' well-known tact. Indeed, there is very good ground for supposing that Washington chose Lafayette for the Southern Department precisely because Steuben had angered Virginians so greatly and had built up such animosities.[12] Almost the first thing Lafayette did on touching Virginia soil was to write Washington: "In your first letter to the Baron, I wish, my dear General, you will write to him that I have been much satisfied with his preparations. I want to please him, and harmony shall be my first object."[13] If the common cause and the exacerbated state of feelings in Virginia had not required the "very conciliating temper" that Washington knew Lafayette possessed, the situation in which Lafayette found himself on confronting Steuben in March of 1781 would have made extraordinary tact essential. Here was a young French nobleman of twenty-three taking over the command from an officer who was more than twice his age, who was quite conscious of his own insubstantial claims either to nobility or to the distinguished service under Frederick the Great that had been the foundation for his preferment in the American army, and who, after months of disappointing service in Virginia, at last found himself facing the traitor Arnold with every reason to believe that he would soon achieve the glory of being his captor. And now the fame and glory would be Lafayette's, not Steuben's. The marquis met this situation in such a manner as fully to justify Washington's opinion of his sober and accommodating disposition.[14]

After the failure of the expedition against Portsmouth, Lafayette approved Steuben's proposal to lead the Virginia militia in a sudden enterprise against Cornwallis, just as he had thought Greene's comparable movement into South Carolina "a great piece of generalship."[15]

[11] Lafayette to Nelson, 31 Oct. 1781, printed in Chinard, *Lafayette in Virginia*, p. 60.

[12] Same, p. 6. Washington's opinion of Lafayette's tact, conciliatory temperament, and military ability is in his letter to Joseph Jones, 10 July 1781 (*Writings*, ed. Fitzpatrick, XXII, 353). In that same letter Washington remarked: "The complaints against the Baron de Steuben are not more distressing than unexpected, for I always viewed him in the light of a good officer. If he has formed a junction with the Marquis, he will be no longer Master of his own conduct, of course

the clamours against him will cease with his command."

[13] Lafayette to Washington, 15 Mch. 1781, printed in Gottschalk, *Letters of Lafayette to Washington*, New York, privately printed, 1944, p. 159-60. Lafayette added that the baron "wanted me to take the command immediately, but I thought it would be more polite not to do it untill the detachement arrives or operations are begun."

[14] Gottschalk, *Lafayette and the Close of the American Revolution*, p. 201.

[15] Historians generally have agreed with the verdict of approval given by

How much of this was genuine approval and how much was the product of a "very conciliating temper" is difficult to tell.[16] But by late May Lafayette was perfectly willing to have Steuben depart from the state to rejoin Greene, as the baron had long wanted to do. To La Luzerne on 22 May the marquis confided that he did not regret losing Steuben because "the hatred of the Virginians toward him was truly hurtful to the cause."[17] Lafayette fully realized the importance of protecting the stores at Point of Fork and, even after he had consented to have Steuben rejoin Greene, asked the baron to undertake that duty with new levies and Lawson's militia.[18]

After Steuben's failure to prevent the loss of those stores, Lafayette, whatever he might have told Steuben later, was privately aghast at the older general's behavior. On 18 June, the day before Steuben finally joined forces with him, Lafayette wrote a remarkable letter to Washington. Transmitting an account of military affairs in Virginia, he concluded this official part of his dispatch with the words: "So much I owe to my General, but with my friend I beg leave to be more confidential." Then, as friend to friend and not as one major general reporting another's delinquencies, he delivered himself of the following frank comment on Steuben: "The conduct of the Baron, my dear General, is to me unintelligible—every man woman and child in Virginia is roused against him. They dispute even on his courage but I cannot believe their assertions. I must however confess that he had 500 and odds new levies and some militia, that he was on the other side of a

military officers to Steuben's proposal. Even Gottschalk (same, p. 206) refers to "the unfortunate decision of the Virginia council" and Palmer (*Steuben*, p. 260), employing Steuben's words as his own, declared that "the civil authority had not an idea beyond local security" and concluded that the Executive's decision deprived Greene of an opportunity "to overwhelm Cornwallis before he could restore his shattered army. It also left Virginia at the mercy of Phillips." This may possibly be a sound interpretation. But it is just as plausible to think that Cornwallis, moving northward to join Phillips, would have caught Steuben between the two British forces and would have overwhelmed him as to conclude that Cornwallis would permit himself to be caught between the baron and Greene. In any case, Virginia was left at the mercy of Phillips with Steuben and the militia present and it is difficult to see how the situation would have been improved if he had taken both men and arms out of the state. See also Gottschalk, same, p. 215. Washington also approved of Steuben's proposal, adding that if Steuben had been able to carry it into effect "it would most prob-

ably have occasioned the ruin of Lord Cornwallis. But this is one of the thousand instances which daily shew the evils resulting from feeding and paying troops which can only be used for local purposes" (Washington to Steuben, 1 May 1781, *Writings*, ed. Fitzpatrick, XXII, 18-19).

16 See note 12.
17 Lafayette to La Luzerne, *Amer. Hist. Rev.*, XX (1915), p. 601. The next day Lafayette made the same statement in a letter to Alexander Hamilton (Palmer, *Steuben*, p. 269).
18 Lafayette to Steuben, 26 May 1781 (RC, NHi). On that day Steuben wrote Greene that he was preparing for his march southward; he also wrote friends in Germany, giving a fanciful account of his wealth in America in the form of land grants from various states (only one of which had a basis in actuality), stating that, by virtue of a special act of Congress vesting in him command of all the troops in Virginia, he had been confronted by superior numbers but had "always held the enemy in check and gained some minor advantages," and concluding: "I am now about to seek my revenge from Lord Cornwallis" (Palmer, *Steuben*, p. 270).

river which the freshet rendered very difficult to be crossed particularly by people that had no boats, that the greater part of the accounts make Simcoe 400 strong half of them dragoons, that our stores on the south side were destroied by about 30 or 40 men—that the Baron went to Staunton River about 70 [sic] miles from the Point of Fork—that the militia abandonned him and I am informed the new levies deserted from him, because they did not like his maneuvre. General Lawson and every officer and soldier both in the regulars and militia are so much exasperated again[st] the Baron and cover him with so many ridicules that after I have obtained a jonction with him I do not know where to employ him without giving offense."[19]

When Steuben joined him next day, Lafayette presumably learned at first hand the baron's own account of what had happened at Point of Fork. In a public letter to Greene, a copy of which he sent to Congress, Lafayette did not hint at the private conviction he held, though as Gottschalk remarks, "one could read between the lines of his matter-of-fact account of events since the beginning of June that he did not approve of Steuben's behavior."[20] But again his private views, as expressed in another communication to Greene, differed markedly from those destined for public consumption. "Had the Baron held 24 hours," Lafayette remarked, "every one of the articles might have been carried up as high as Albemarle Old Court House where they [the British] did not venture. Instead of it he went to Staunton River 15 miles from the Point of Fork and crossed it. General Lawson with the militia left him. The enemy laughed at him, and I cannot describe to you what my surprise has been."[21] Holding these views, Lafayette would seem to have been obligated to prefer charges against his subordinate even if the Assembly had not requested an investigation. But he wisely refrained from doing so, since the state of military affairs demanded harmony and united action. It was a delicate situation, relieved in part by Steuben's urgent desire to rejoin Greene and, later, by his illness. Late in October, only a week after Steuben had taken the honors that properly belonged to Lafayette, he transmitted to the marquis a flattering letter that he had received from General Greene and at the same time asked him to validate by signing his own narrative of events at Point of Fork. This Lafayette refused to do for cogent and obligatory reasons. Nevertheless, he wrote the baron a generous and—except on one point—somewhat equivocal letter of commendation. The unequivocal exception was Lafayette's flat assertion: "I was happy in your reunion with me." This was stretching magnanimity to the point where it collided with truth as revealed in Lafayette's confidential and private communications to Washington. (See Greene to Steuben, 17 Sep. 1781; Lafayette to Steuben, 26 Oct. 1781, both printed below.)

The loss of the stores at Point of Fork was not as severe as it seemed at first to be, but the uproar of the Virginians against Steuben was directed only partly at his failure in that matter. What angered the

[19] Gottschalk, *Letters of Lafayette to Washington*, p. 201-202.
[20] Gottschalk, *Lafayette and the* *Close of the American Revolution*, p. 251.
[21] Same, p. 252.

legislators and others quite as much was that Steuben had never for a moment given up his intent to leave Virginia at the first possible occasion, to rejoin Greene, and to take with him such arms and men as he could gather.[22] Gottschalk, in describing Lafayette's feeling in mid-June that Steuben's recent abandonment of the stores at Point of Fork and his tardiness in coming up despite frequent requests were perhaps in need of investigation, charitably remarks that Steuben was not altogether to blame and that the state of the mails, the frequent capture of dispatches, and the difficulty of communicating with Greene left him in some uncertainty as to whether the commander of the Southern Department wished him to stay in Virginia or not.[23]

It is true that communication between Greene and Steuben was slow and hazardous, but this would scarcely justify a soldier of the baron's experience in persisting stubbornly in his determination to follow a course of action that had obviously outlived its own purpose. Greene's decision in March to proceed into South Carolina and Steuben's proposal late the same month to move 4,000 (later reduced to 2,000) of the Virginia militia against Cornwallis in cooperation with Greene were both parts of the same strategy—to keep the war at a distance from Virginia, Greene's chief source of supplies. Cornwallis, however, left the American commander to march off against a series of minor posts and turned his own attention to Virginia. His primary aim in doing so was not to capture the forces under Lafayette and Steuben but to destroy such manufactories as Hunter's and such stores as Simcoe had destroyed at Petersburg and Manchester.[24] Thus it was the British general who, in the final analysis, paid one of the highest tributes to the effectiveness of Jefferson's administration as governor, for it was the accumulation of supplies already made and potential resources available that caused him to drive toward Virginia. Greene and Steuben had repeatedly called upon Virginia for arms, supplies, and men to support a strategy designed to keep the war at a distance from the state. This was a strategy to which Jefferson had given support, despite criticism from both Greene and Steuben to the effect that Virginia policy was dictated by local and partial views. But it was a strategy that became meaningless on 20 May when Cornwallis joined forces with the army of the late General Phillips at Petersburg: on that date the theater of war in the south shifted to the heart of Virginia and threatened Greene's source of supplies. This was an invasion far more serious than those of

[22] The House of Delegates on 29 May had already resolved that "a representation be made to the Hon. Major General Marquis La Fayette, by his excellency the Governor, stating the present state, quantity and condition of the public arms; the urgent reasons that appear for detaining the new levies now collected at Albemarle old courthouse, to oppose the invading enemy, until effectual exertions can be made for providing other means of defence, or the operations of the war shall, in the opinion of . . . La Fayette, render it more adviseable to detach them for southern service"; at the same time the House directed the Governor to urge upon Lafayette "that this State, under its present circumstances, can in no wise consent that the public arms in the hands of the said new levies, be sent out of the State" and that the Governor countermand any orders that may have been given for that purpose concerning state arms (JHD, May 1781, 1828 edn., p. 6).

[23] Gottschalk, *Lafayette and the Close of the American Revolution*, p. 249.

[24] Same, p. 238.

January and April that had been sufficient to keep Steuben from rejoining Greene. Confronted with this fact, which altered the whole basis of Greene's strategy, Steuben should have known without further communication with his commander that his presence was required more urgently with Lafayette than with Greene.

On 12 June Steuben wrote General Jethro Sumner a letter in which he seemed to give support to these considerations. He declared that he had had no word from Greene since 1 May and that Greene, in a letter bearing that date, had given him positive orders to move southward "with all possible dispatch with all the levies I could collect." However, Steuben added, "a change of circumstances" had determined him to halt at Cole's Ferry "till I could hear further from him or receive orders from the Marquis."[25] This appears to support the generally accepted explanation and justification for Steuben's behavior as being due to his failure to receive Greene's letter of 14 May authorizing him to remain with Lafayette. But Steuben's letter to Sumner must be read in the context of other letters and actions of a few days earlier.

On 3 June Steuben knew that Tarleton was at or near Charlottesville. Early the next morning, Major Call reported that Simcoe was approaching Point of Fork. Steuben thereupon crossed to the south side of the James, transporting and dispersing such stores as he had time to move. About noon on the 4th he observed the British move into Point of Fork. The next day at his "Camp near Forks,"[26] he dispatched an urgent letter to Governor Nash which was altogether different in tone from the one written a week later to General Sumner: "In the present situation of affairs here and by orders from General Greene to me, I find it expedient to march directly for North Carolina."[27] Steuben also asked Governor Nash to see that shirts, overalls, and shoes be provided for the Virginia levies under his command, for which, he said, "I will be answerable that the State of Virginia replaces every article North Carolina shall supply their troops with." The baron dispatched Captain Kirkpatrick to deliver this letter to Governor Nash, and then marched rapidly southward on his way to join Greene.

Captain Kirkpatrick arrived in Granville on Friday, 8 June. He found that Governor Nash had gone to New Bern about 150 miles away and therefore applied instead to General Sumner. Sumner was accommodating and ordered a commissary to lay in a supply of provisions for Steuben, along a route to be specified through North Carolina. Having thus discharged the real object of his mission, the intelligent captain braved Steuben's wrath by pointing out as delicately as he could that a movement southward under Greene's obsolete orders of 1 May was not a prudent military measure: "General Sumner," he began, "Shew'd me his last Orders from Genl Greene which directed him to march his new rais'd troops into Virga if Cornwallis should go into that State, which is the case. The Gentlemen here think it Verry extraordinary that Troops should march out of Virga. at a Time

<hr/>

25 Steuben to Sumner, 12 June 1781 (Dft, NHi).

26 Lafayette informed Greene that Steuben had moved fifteen miles the first night (see note 21 above); Burk-

Girardin, *Hist. of Va.* gives the distance as thirty miles.

27 Greene to Nash, 5 June 1781 (Dft, NHi).

when almost all the enemys force is there and Genl Greenes forces more than adequate to their Task in South Carolina, for at this time the Enemy dont hold any post in that State but Charlestown and I think he will not attempt anything against it. Besides, General Greene has more Troops than he can support and twill be only adding to the distress of both troops and inhabitants. The Gentlemen here think that in this state and the upper part of South Carolina there is not so much grain as twould average at one peck per man. . . . The country has been much laid waste and Virga. at the same time full of provisions Especially flour and daily falling into the Enemys hands." This argument, ascribed to the "Gentlemen here," had undeniable force. "But, my Dear Genl," Kirkpatrick concluded, "I don't mean to Dictate, but only to draw a true picture of the distresses of this Country. Carolina would I believe rather send Men out than any should come into it. I shall however proceed to see the Govr and execute the remaining part of your orders."[28]

Captain Kirkpatrick was no doubt inwardly relieved that he had orders obliging him to proceed 150 miles further on his journey after delivering himself of these opinions. Even so, he must have braced himself for the inevitable blast from his general. It came on 12 June. "It is the fate of a Genl in a republic," the baron began ominously, "to have his actions judged of by every person without their knowing either his reasons, or Orders. However, this we must submit to. I am happy that my conduct will bear a scrutiny. . . . My reasons for marching Southward, as I find a General must give reasons to every citizen for his conduct, were positive orders from Gen Greene, my own hopes that my moving this way would alarm Cornwallis and induce him to detach a part of his army after me, which would be of more essential advantage to the Marquis than if five times my number of recruits should join him. I shall risque disobeying my orders if the militia will enable me to cover this part of the state I shall stay in it. My reasons for altering my plan the people will not wish to know, it is sufficient for them that I act as they desire."[29] Despite this sarcasm, Steuben's actions showed that he had paid heed to the sensible counsel Captain Kirkpatrick had had the temerity to advance. For on the same day he wrote to Governor Nash explaining that Greene's orders to Sumner had given him an intimation of what Greene wished and therefore he had halted to gather militia and to form an opposition; to Sumner he wrote that he was very happy to hear "you are ordered to bring your levies this way—the sooner you can join me the better."[30]

The fact that Steuben did not depart precipitately from Point of Fork solely because of Greene's orders of 1 May is proved both by the logic of the situation on 5 June and by his own previous letters to Greene. In his defense here printed the baron gives no intimation that on that date his intention was to move straight through to Greene in

[28] Abraham Kirkpatrick to Steuben, 10 June 1781 (RC, NHi). Captain Kirkpatrick was transferred to the First Virginia Regiment, Continental Line, on 12 Feb. 1781 (Gwathmey, *Hist.* *Reg. of Virginians in the Revolution*).

[29] Steuben to Kirkpatrick, 12 June 1781 (Dft, NHi).

[30] Steuben to Sumner and to Nash, 12 June 1781 (Dfts, NHi).

South Carolina. He states only that he thought "it absurd to be making a Bravado with a small number of bad Troops against such a force" and he conveys the impression that it was his intent to retire from Point of Fork, gather the militia together, and reinforce the marquis. But his letter to Nash on 5 June proves otherwise, and his letters to the county lieutenants were not sent out until 11 June, perhaps after he had received Kirkpatrick's letter reporting the thoughts of the gentlemen in North Carolina. Moreover, a full month earlier he had assured Greene that he would remain in Virginia to assist the marquis as long as there was a probability of coming to action, "but when the Operations carry on too far from the Rendezvous, I shall think myself obliged to fulfill your instructions in accelerating by my presence the departure of the Levies for the southward." He added that he had already informed Lafayette of this course of action and had obtained his consent to it.[31] On 5 June when he set out toward Greene, however, the operations of the enemy were not carrying on "too far from the Rendezvous," but at it. Steuben had forgotten then the condition attached to this decision and, on the doubtful premise that Greene's orders of 1 May were fixed and immutable regardless of circumstances, departed precipitately.

For this Greene must bear a part of the responsibility. The orders that he sent Steuben on 1 May—issued partly at Steuben's urgent insistence, partly because of news that both Lafayette and Wayne were moving south—contained evidence of his inner feeling that the strategy of moving into South Carolina on the hope that Cornwallis would follow had not, after all, worked: "I know not in what light our movement will be viewed, but it was dictated by necessity and the only plan that promised any advantage. It is true it was hazardous, and I wish it may not prove unfortunate." To this was prefaced the lines that must have comforted Steuben in the midst of the torments he was experiencing in Virginia: "I find myself so beset with difficulties that I need the Council and assistance of an officer educated in the Prussian school, and persuade myself that I shall have in you both the friend and the General I want."[32] But in the orders of 14 May that Steuben did not receive, Greene still proceeded (though without conviction) on the assumption that Cornwallis might turn southward. He therefore expressed the hope that Steuben, Lafayette, and Wayne would prevent a junction of Cornwallis and Phillips, and if Cornwallis should then turn southward, the Pennsylvania line, the North Carolina regulars, and the Virginia levies should "follow him and form a junction with us," with Steuben taking command of these forces.[33] But Greene expressed it as his opinion that Cornwallis would stay "to the Northward." "If he should," Greene advised Steuben, "as soon as I have put things in a train here I propose to set out to join that Army, and leave this to compleat the reduction of the remaining posts."[34] This was certainly a proper position for the commander of the Southern Department

[31] Steuben to Greene, 5 May 1781 (Dft, NHi).

[32] Greene to Steuben, 1 May 1781 (RC, NHi).

[33] Greene to Steuben, 14 May 1781 (RC, NHi).

[34] This is what Washington expected Greene to do; see note 5, above.

to take, but Greene nevertheless continued what was in effect a mopping-up exercise in the partisan-ridden Carolinas while the great issue was being determined in the area where lay his chief hope of sustenance. More, he continued to demand that Virginia send militia to his support even in the face of the altered situation; the letter that he addressed to Jefferson on 27 June was a severe denunciation of the government for countermanding the order for militia to march southward.

On 19 July Greene sent Steuben a copy of the orders of 14 May and added: "I am happy to hear Lord Cornwallis has retired into the lower Country. I hope the new Governor and Council of Virga. will take more effectual measures for the defence of that state than has been. As soon as you can be spared from that quarter, I wish you to join me here, even if you should not be able to bring a man with you."[35] This letter came to Steuben early in August as he was emerging from illness, weakened by "an irruption of the blood which has covered my whole body." "If it had pleased God, my dear General, that this order had reached me four months sooner," Steuben concluded, "it would have saved me a great deal of pain and chagrin. What I have to say on that subject, I will reserve 'till I shall have the pleasure to see you."[36] But again Steuben was denied his wish to join Greene. Early in September he reported: "The whole country are flying to arms; at such a time as this I have reason to apprehend that my departure would be made to operate to my disadvantage by persons who seek to destroy the reputation of an honest man." De Grasse on 30 August had arrived at the Virginia capes, commanding a fleet of 28 line-of-battle ships and 6 frigates, with over three thousand marines. Lafayette had urged him to "hasten to his assistance." These facts altered the situation. Steuben declared that Greene's orders and his own wishes inclined him to proceed southward, but he begged his general's permission to join in the expedition then being mounted against Cornwallis.[37] Six weeks later Greene complied, but by then the surrender of Cornwallis had taken place.[38]

It was ironic that Steuben's detachment should have occupied the trenches while negotiations for surrender were in progress, but it was quite in character that Steuben should have refused to quit his post when it came his turn to be relieved, claiming that under the laws of war his men were entitled to remain until the close of negotiations and that they might thereby plant their divisional flags in the conquered town.[39] Thus the honors that should technically have gone to Lafayette's troops (he had been on duty when negotiations were begun and had been relieved by Steuben) went instead to the general who had spent

[35] Greene to Steuben, 19 July 1781 (RC, NHi).

[36] Steuben to Greene, 13 Aug. 1781 (Dft, NHi).

[37] This, it is to be noted, is the first request that Steuben made to be permitted to remain in Virginia. It is not clear how Steuben's leaving at that time, when the capture of Cornwallis seemed almost a certainty, could be used as a basis for injuring his reputation. Certainly his going to join Greene in September could not have occasioned the same kind of clamor that his precipitate flight from Point of Fork had raised. Steuben to Greene, 9 Sep. 1781 (Dft, NHi).

[38] Greene to Steuben, 25 Oct. 1781 (RC, NHi).

[39] Gottschalk, *Lafayette and the Close of the American Revolution*, p. 324.

several months trying desperately to keep away from Cornwallis. But these were empty honors.

With Cornwallis captured, Steuben suddenly lost interest in going to Greene's support. He announced that it was necessary for him to go northward instead in order to settle his accounts with Congress and to find out on what footing he stood. Thereafter his chief goals were lands and money. Lafayette generously withheld his own private feelings and gave "full approval of the baron's conduct during the entire campaign," a feat of magnanimity which indicates to what degree Washington was correct in describing the marquis as possessing "a very conciliatory temper." Greene also expressed complete confidence in the baron. His own difficulties, he reported in 1782, were much greater than could be imagined: "You had many in Virginia, but far less than we had. You made a short work of your business at last, ours continues. You got great glory, we only avoided disgrace. If ever we have the happiness to meet I have much to say to you. Your triumph over your enemies in Virginia afforded me great pleasure."[40]

[40] Same, p. 335.

William Davies to Steuben

DEAR GENERAL   Goochland May 12. 1781.

The enemy's horse have been employed in burning the mills round Petersburg. A man from below says they were at Manchester last night. They seize all the good horses they can get and mount infantry occasionally. There will not be one day's security for any stores below Carter's ferry; of course all of them will be centered there. The whole military stores of the state intended for the southern army, all the arms, powder, leather cloth and rum which for many months we have been laboring to collect will of necessity be brought to that place, besides the great quantity of continental stores which will be brought back from Prince Edward, sent up from Richmond and forwarded from Cumberland old courthouse. If these stores are lost, the whole wealth of the state in its present situation can never replace them, and the only dependences for General Greene's army will be almost totally cut off. The body of troops under Major Poulson would afford a security to so important an object which by no other means can be accomplished. All our powder and 1100 stand of arms must either be saved or lost according to the event of this application. There the whole of the new levies would be together, nor would there be any detachments; of course they would be every man with his proper officers. Their presence would not be required more than six days; in the mean time an officer with the carpenters and a few pioneers might be sent to Albemarle barracks; they want great repairs, the British intentionally injured them when they left them. I am very sorry to be importunate on any occasion; but I cannot refrain on this, when I am conscious the loss of these stores will prove the loss of this country. I have nothing personal to secure by this request; I am not asking to have my doors defended. If the stores were intended for the state alone, they would be worthy of attention; they must be more so to a continental officer, when he is told they are intended for the continent, altho' now in the possession of the state; but I fondly flatter myself that I shall prevail upon you without a doubt when you are informed that exclusive of the state stores, there are 500 stand of arms and other things belonging to the continent to a very considerable amount and of the most necessary kind. If I had an idea I was not soliciting for the preservation of the country, I would not take the liberty to be thus urgent with you; but if ever I thought myself clear in the propriety of a request, I think I am now. Pardon, my dear general, the warmth of my representation. You know my respect and attachment to you, and if I am wrong I am persuaded you will ascribe my zeal to an error in judgement.

In a letter from Captain Young just come to hand he says: "I think it may be depended on that Greene and Rawdon have had a severe action, in which Greene gained the field with great advantages." This is some encouragement.

I am with respectful regard, dear General, Your very obedient servt.,

WILLIAM DAVIES

P.S. The enemy sent from Petersburg yesterday morning 100 cavalry, 300 infantry double mounted on horses, and 400 infantry besides.

RC (NHi); endorsed.

Steuben's Narrative of His Movements on Leaving Point of Fork

[1781.]

A few days after my junction with the Marquis at Richmond we received the news of Lord Cornwallis's being on his march for Virginia. About the same time also I received a Letter from General Green desiring me to press the Levy of the recruits of this state, to assemble as many as possible, especially Cavalry, and to Join him with them as soon as possible. This letter was dated the 1st of May and I immediately communicated it to Governor Jefferson and the Marquis in the Council Chamber at Richmond.

The Draft had before this been put off till the Month of March. This was therefore the very time when the Counties should have been delivering in their Quotas. About 300 Men were however all that were yet collected. These were at Manchester badly armed and worse cloathed.

The place of Rendezvous had been at Chesterfield Court House. The Barracks at that place had been burnt by the Enemy and the Situation was no longer proper for the purpose. I mentioned therefore to Government the necessity of fixing on some place less exposed where we might Collect the recruits, Equip and form them and with the consent of the Marquis Albemarle Barracks was agreed on for the place. As the Governor had said that those Counties which had Militia in the Field could not proceed to Draft I asked him to what number would amount the Recruits from those Counties who were not so circumstanced. He informed me about 1500 men. At this conference the Marquis was present.

I determined therefore that the 300 men already collected should march immediately to Albemarle to be cloathed and Equipped for the Field, that the other Recruits should Join them as fast as they came in, and that they might afterwards Join General Green or the Marquis as circumstances might require. Orders were accordingly given for them to march by way of Carters ferry. The day after I received a letter from Colo. Davis Commissioner of War for the State in which he represented to me that Albemarle Barracks was a very improper place on many accounts, that great difficulty would occur in transporting Provision there, that there was no wood near it, and that the Barracks were nearly destroyed. He pointed out the Forks of James River as the most proper place, many of the Articles for Equipping the troops were he said already there and he promised to make every necessary arrangement for the reception of the troops at that place. On this I Joined the Marquis at Wilton and he having no objection that place was determined on and the Marquis desired me to repair there to hasten the Equipment of the 1500 Recruits we expected and who were to Join either Genl Green or the Marquis as I before said.

On my arrival at the Fork I was much surprized to find no more than 540 Men had yet come in and a great number of these not proper for the service. The whole were without cloathing and badly Equipped and were every day diminishing in number by desertion and sickness. They were also without arms and it was with some difficulty that I armed them with the Arms that just then arrived from Philadelphia.

Whilst I was thus occupied Lord Cornwallis crossed James River and the Marquis retreated up the Country.

The principal part of our Continental Stores were on the Southside the River at Prince Edward, Charlotte, and Halifax Court Houses. Those of the State were dispersed everywhere. A great part of them were at the Fork by order of Government. The Marquis's retreat induced me to represent to Colo. Davis and Mr. Ross Agent for the State the necessity of removing them higher up in the mountain. I told them that the troops were by no means destined to Guard the Stores but that I should move them as circumstances might direct. Great part of the stores were accordingly removed and the enclosed memorandum of their Store Keeper will show that those which by the negligence of their own Officers fell into the Enemies Hands were very inconsiderable.

Such was the situation of affairs when I received a Letter of 3 June from the Marquis dated near Raccoon ford on the Rappahanock 80 miles from the place where Lord Cornwallis then was and about the same distance from me.

The same night I received intelligence that the Enemy were at Goochland Court House moving up the River. This seemed to indicate an intention against me, but as the intelligence was not positive I only repeated my orders for moving the remainder of the stores and collecting all the Boats on both Rivers above and below me in order to cross should there be occasion.

At Five next morning Major Call of Washingtons [Continental Dragoons] arrived and informed me that the Enemy had divided their force into two parties, one of which had taken the route by Louisa Court Ho. and the other by Goochland Court House, that he had seen both columns on their march [and] with difficulty escaped being taken. This removed every doubt of their intention. I therefore gave immediate orders for crossing over the Baggage of the Troops, placed a picquet of 80 men on the point opposite which I expected Cornwallis would soon appear in order to draw our attention whilst the other party crossed the North branch above us in order to catch us between the two Rivers. I then marched the Batallion on the Road by which the party who I expected would cross above must come and waited there till the whole of the Baggage had crossed. I then left a Picket of 50 Men on the Road and crossed the Remainder of the Batallion. The same day Genl. Lawson arrived and informed me he had 250 militia, whereof 15 were Horsemen who were on the other side the River. I ordered them to Join the Recruits who were at that time reduced to 420 men as will appear by the return signed by Colo. Gaskins and sent to Govr. Nelson.

That Evening Colo. Davis arrived to secure the State Stores in which I gave every assistance in my power. I unloaded the Waggons of the Regiments and sent them to bring away the stores, but this business was very illy executed by the State Officers.

The morning of the 4th I sent Lt. Verdier of Armands Corps with four Dragoons up the Road on the Point of Fork to give intelligence of the Enemy's approach. Himself and party fell into their hands. About ten o'Clock I received intelligence that the Enemy were within four miles of the Point of Fork, on which I sent Mr. Fairlie one of my Aids to call in the Piquets which he did but was himself taken Prisoner.

About noon being on the bank of the River I perceived the Enemy arrive. As I afterwards Learnt Simcoe with about 4 or 500 Horse and foot. Tarleton was above him within supporting distance and Lord Cornwallis was on the other side James River about Six Miles below him.

As an instance of the dependance that could have been placed in the men I had under my Command, when the Enemy first arrived they fired only one shot from a three pounder they had with them and a piquet of 50 men I had at the Landing left their Post and it was with much persuasion and threats they were brought back again.

Contrary to my orders a number of Canoes were still left in the North Fork and consequently fell into the Enemy's hands and besides both Rivers are fordable at many places. I therefore determined to retire towards Willis creek which I did as soon as it was dark.

I sent back an officer to observe the movements of the Enemy, who reported that the morning of the 5th the Enemy had constructed two Rafts each capable of crossing from 80 to 100 men and that they had thrown a Bridge across the North fork by which they communicated with Lord Cornwallis then opposite Elk Island.

I have already observed that all our Continental Stores were at Prince Edward, Halifax, and Charlotte Court Houses. I did not see what could hinder the Enemy from detaching a sufficient party to disperse my force and render themselves masters of those stores. I thought it absurd to be making a Bravado with a small number of bad Troops against such a force whilst the Marquis being near a 100 Miles off could make no diversion on that side. I therefore gave orders for dispersing the stores in such a manner that only part could fall into the Enemies Hands in any Rout they could take and I sent off three Officers successively to Acquaint the Marquis of my Situation. I wrote Circular Letters to the County Lieutenants to call out their Militia and leaving Genl Lawson at Charlotte Court House I marched the recruits to Coles ferry on Staunton. Here I collected all the Boats on that River and sent an Officer to Genl. Sumner to collect what force he could and Join me.

Genl. Lawsons Militia were yet hardly 500 men, when I was advised of the Marquis Junction with Genl Wayne. On this I immediately and without waiting for orders advanced in four days to Carters ferry where I received the first Letter from the Marquis desiring me to Join him if possible by the 18th at Colo. Dandridges, which I did with 408 Recruits and about 500 Militia.

It must be remarked that these 408 Recruits were all that were in the field of 3000 which the Assembly had voted in february last.

Tr (NHi); in hand of Major William North, endorsed: "Copy of a relation of the Barons Movements on quitting the Point of Fork." Enclosure: There is in NHi a memorandum endorsed: "Memo of Stores lost at Point of Fork June 1781." This is probably a copy of "the enclosed memorandum of their Store Keeper." It reads as follows: "Memo of Cloathing supposed to have been lost at the Point of Fork June 4th 1781.

 68 boxes of coarse cloths
 60 pair leather breeches
 1 small bale linen belonging to Colonel Washington's Cavalry
2000 yards Canvas
 1 Hhd Soldiers Hatts
 1 Box containing some Linen, Checks and Coarse thread
 2 small bales of Blankets containing about 75
 2 Hogsheads of Coffee
 1 small case of Tea

 1 Box and 1 Barrell brown sugar
 40 Hhds Tierces and barrells of rum and Whiskey."
This memorandum does not quite agree with an inventory of clothing in the states stores at Point of Fork dated 24 May 1781 (also NHi). That memorandum reads:
"180 Yards russia Sheeting fit for Overhalls
 1 Peice Ozens
 80 pieces Irish linen
 60 ready made shirts
 20 pieces Bareskin 540 Yards
260 yards Plaid
 60 pair yarn Stockings
 70 yards white flannel
200 calf skins
 50 soldiers coats
 70 pair Leather breeches at Mr. Bollings Landing
 1 ps spotted Flannell
 5 ps Chec."

Burk-Girardin's Account of the Affair at Point of Fork

[1816]

In the mean time Lord Cornwallis, bent on the execution of the predatory plan which he had lately formed, made two considerable detachments from his army. One of these, amounting to 500 men, partly of the Queen's rangers, infantry and cavalry, and partly of the Yagers, he placed under the command of Lieutenant Colonel Simcoe, a partizan, whose indefatigable activity and singular fitness for stratagem, surprize and intrigue, we have already had occasion to mention.

At the confluence of the two branches of the James, in the county of Fluvanna, is a point of land, known under the appellation of the Point of Fork, where, during the late incursions of Phillips and Arnold, a State arsenal had been formed, and military stores collected, especially with a view to the prosecution of the war in the Carolinas. The protection of this important post had been entrusted to Baron Steuben, who, in this critical posture of affairs in Virginia, had, by the joint orders of La Fayette and Greene, repaired there from the borders of North Carolina, with about 600 new levies, originally destined for the Southern army! To the Point of Fork, the militia under General Lawson, amounting nearly to the same number, had also been directed to march. The plan of La Fayette was, at first, to unite the whole with the Pennsylvania line and the body under his immediate command, and make a combined effort against the enemy. The orders which he issued to bring this scheme into effect, unfortunately were intercepted. Cornwallis altered his movements; and this change, together with unexpected delays in the meditated junction with the Pennsylvania line, overthrew the project.

It was against Baron Steuben, and the magazines under his protection, that Lieutenant Colonel Simcoe now directed his efforts. His instructions were, suddenly to fall on the Baron, annihilate his force, or, at least, to drive the whole beyond the Southern branch of James river, and to destroy the arms and provisions known to have been collected at the Point of Fork.

The expedition of Tarleton, who was detached with 180 cavalry of the legion, and 70 mounted infantry of the 23d regiment, headed by Captain Champagne, embraced the following objects. He received orders to surprise, take or disperse the members of the General Assembly, then convened at Charlottesville as we have before mentioned, to seize on the person of the Governor, who resided in the neighborhood, to spread on his route devastation and terror, sparing no military stores or other resources likely to enable the Americans to prolong the existing struggle, and perhaps, to end it with success. He was ultimately to join Simcoe, and assist his intended operations.

With their accustomed eagerness and activity, the two indefatigable and dreaded partisans entered upon the execution of their respective tasks.

This double movement rendered Steuben's situation unusually perilous. The extreme difficulty of obtaining prompt and correct information respecting the British and their schemes, the severe precautions which Simcoe took for securing every person met or seen on his route, effectually concealed his march from the Baron. The latter, however, became apprized of Tarleton's rapid advance. Imagining himself the immediate object of it, he lost no time in transporting his stores to the South side of the Fluvanna, intending himself speedily to follow, with the whole division under his command. When Simcoe reached the Point of Fork, the American stores had been removed, and Steuben's detachment crossed the river, except about 30 men, then awaiting the return of the boats, to embark and join their friends. These men unavoidably fell into the hands of the British cavalry. The river was deep and unfordable; and all the boats had been secured on the South side of it. Simcoe's main object was, therefore, frustrated. Under the mortification arising from this disappointment, a singular stratagem occurred to his wily mind. It was to impress the Baron with the belief that the troops now at the Point of Fork were the advance of the British army, ready to overwhelm him; and thus to work upon his fears so far as to induce him to sacrifice most of the stores which had been transported over the Fluvanna. For this purpose he encamped on the heights opposite to Steuben's new station, advantageously display-ing his force, and by the number of his fires suggesting a probability of the main body, headed by Cornwallis, having actually reached the neighborhood. The Baron, who had been informed that the corps under Tarleton threatened his left, now fancied himself in imminent danger. Retreating precipitately during the night, he marched near 30 miles from the Point of Fork, abandoning to the enemy such stores as could not be removed. In the morning, Simcoe observing the success of his stratagem, and wishing to give it still further effect, procured some small canoes, and sent across the river Captain Stephenson, with a detachment of light infantry, and Cornet Wolsey with four hussars. The former was directed to destroy the stores and arms which the Baron had left behind in the hurry and confusion of his premature retreat; and the latter, to mount his hussars, who had carried their saddles over with them, on such straggling horses as he was likely to find, to patrole some miles on the route taken by Steuben; in short, to exhibit every appear-ance of eager and formidable pursuit. Both these orders were success-fully executed. Stephenson performed without delay or annoyance, the task of destruction assigned to him; and Wolsey so confirmed the belief of Steuben, that the whole British army was close in his rear, that he accelerated his march, retiring still further from the river. His object was to resume his original destination and join General Greene; but he received fresh orders not to leave the State, so long as Cornwallis should continue there. On the militia under Lawson, a similar injunc-tion was laid. British historians have greatly exaggerated the loss sustained by the Americans at the Point of Fork. Of their thrasonic accounts, undoubted evidence is in the hands of the author of this narrative.†

Text from *The History of Virginia*, Burk-Girardin, IV (1816), p. 496-8.

† Tarleton has magnified almost every circumstance. The official correspond-ence of Lord Cornwallis himself, is full of exaggerations of this sort. Stedman is not more correct—The evidence to which we allude has been furnished by persons on or near the spot, at the time. Much to that effect is also con-tained in the archives of the State.

Greene to Steuben

My Dear Baron   High Hills Santée 17th Septem 1781

Your letter of the 13th August gives me the most sensible pain. I am sorry that a mind so zealous of intent in promoting the public good, should be subject to chagrin and mortification for its well meant endeavors. But let me beg of you my Dear Baron not to feel too sensibly the illiberal attacks of a misguided populace. Merit is often veiled for a time and the best intentions subject to partial censure, and this more frequent in Republican governments than any others. But it rarely ever happens that a man of worth is long without his reward; for tho society may mistake for a time, men are generally willing to retract and approve when properly informed. And I am so confident of the propriety of your conduct, and of the justice of the people, that I have not the least doubt you will see this verified in your own case.

Our operations here and in Virginia have been not unlike cross purposes, the Marquis has been endeavoring to reinforce us but has been contravened by subsequent considerations. I beg leave to congratulate you on the arrival of the French fleet in Chesapeake, and of General Washington's arrival to take command in Virginia. Lord Cornwallis must tremble for his situation; and nothing can save him but a rapid retreat through North Carolina to Charles Town.

Since I wrote you before we have had a most bloody battle—and obtained a complete victory over the enemy, and have driven in near to the gates of Charles Town. We took five hundred prisoners and killed and wounded a greater number. We also took near a thousand stand of arms, but the stocks were all broken, and had it not been for one of those incidents to which military operations are subject, and against which there is no guarding, we should have taken the whole British army, notwithstanding our numbers were much inferior to theirs. The gallantry of the officers and the bravery of the troops would do honor even to the arms of his Prussian Majesty.

I will not trouble you with further particulars as doubtless you will see Captain Pearce one of my aids, who will be the bearer of this, and to whom I beg leave to refer you for further particulars.

With the most perfect esteem and regard, I am Dear Baron Your most obedient and humble servant   Nath. Greene

RC (NHi).

Lafayette to Steuben

Dear Sir   Camp near York Octbr 26th 1781

I have been honored with your letter of this date inclosing one from General Greene. The high terms in which he speaks particularly on the object you allude to are certainly sufficient for your satisfaction; so that I would think it needless for me to add anything to an opinion for which I have the highest veneration.

However to answer your wishes, I will mention some facts which were of my own knowlege. But as the journal comprehends things which happened at a distance, and of course was not within my observation; and as it is chiefly particular to your own movements, my signing it could not possibly add to its authority. I am enough convinced from your great exertions and precision when present with me, that these were the same at all times. I will therefore only speak of what can be supposed to have come under my immediate cognizance.

In the beginning of the campaign I considered you and the new levies as belonging to the Carolina army. The letters in which General Greene and myself were positive for your joining me have been intercepted by the enemy.

Lord Cornwallis's intention (as I have since still more particularly ascertained) was to manouvre me from a junction with Gen. Wayne. His endeavours were vain; but his movements towards our stores threw me for a little time at a pretty great distance from the enemy. The account you received was given by Major Call whom I had requested to watch in that quarter the motions of Lord Cornwallis. Your movements at that moment must have been directed by the intelligence you received, and what you conceived to be General Greene's intentions. I was happy in your reunion with me; and I think it determined Lord Cornwallis to a speedy evacuation of Richmond.

Let me add, that during all the time we served together, I have been so well satisfied with your assistance, that I was only sorry your health forced you to leave the army where your experience and exertions were so useful.

Should I have forgot anything that might add to your satisfaction, I will spare no pains to convince you of the sentiments I profess for you.

I have the honor to be, Dr Sr, your obd & hble sert   LAFAYETTE

RC (NHi).
The letter that Steuben enclosed FROM GENERAL GREENE was no doubt that printed above, 17 Sep. 1781. THE JOURNAL must have been Steuben's narrative of the circumstances surrounding his leaving Point of Fork, also printed above; it is significant that Steuben asked Lafayette to sign it and that the marquis refused to do so.

Appendix II

Commissions, Land Grants, Patents, Licenses, Loan Office Receipts, &c.

EDITORIAL NOTE

Under the Virginia Constitution of 1776 the Governor was given power in some cases to appoint and in all cases to issue commissions for various civil and military officials—judges of the various higher courts, justices of the peace, secretary, attorney general, sheriffs, coroners, county lieutenants and other militia officers, &c. In addition, various statutes calling for the appointment of officials also involved the issuance of commissions by the Governor, such as military agents, surveyors, clothier general, commissioners of the specific tax, escheators, inspectors, commercial agent, commissioner of the war office, commissioner of the navy, recruiting officers, and many other commissioners and officials of one sort or another. The Governor was also required on occasion to issue certain kinds of licenses, such as those permitting attorneys to practice. The Act of 1779 establishing a Land Office provided not only that surveyors in the various counties should be commissioned by the Governor, but also that the register of the Land Office should make out grants "by way of deed poll to the party having right" and this grant (or patent) the Governor was obligated to sign, since the Constitution of 1776 had stipulated that all "Commissions and Grants shall run, *In the Name of the Common Wealth of Virginia*, and bear teste by the Governour, with the Seal of the Common wealth annexed" (see Vol. 1: 382). Altogether the commissions, grants, patents, licenses, receipts, and other documents which the Governor was obliged to sign must have numbered not less than five or six thousand in the years 1779-1781. During these two years of Jefferson's governorship he signed approximately 2,500 land grants alone. In the first five months of 1780 it was necessary for him to sign no less than 337 Loan Office receipts, and he also signed during the governorship more than 300 Contingency Fund vouchers (see Vol. 4: 445).

It is obvious from these facts that the amount of paper work involved was burdensome. Its volume increased as the complexity of affairs increased; for example, the mounting tide of inflation in 1780 threw into the loan office a larger number of payments in five months than had been made in the two preceding years. With the shift of the war to the South during Jefferson's administration, emergency measures required that he and his clerks give more and more time to the multitudinous new details thrown upon his office. It was precisely at the time these emergencies developed that the flood of commissions, grants, receipts, and other documents needing attestation also rose to new levels. Within a year after Jefferson's term as governor had ended, "the Multiplicity of business" was such that the Council authorized the appointment of a prudent person to keep the seal of the Commonwealth "and affix it to all such instruments of writing as require it" (MS Va. Council Jour., 11 July 1782; the decision was made retroactive to 6

May 1782). But this "Multiplicity of business" must not have been greater than it had been in the years 1779-1781.

The commissions and grants signed by him may, of course, be considered from one point of view as Jefferson documents and therefore as comprehended within the scope of this edition. It would obviously be undesirable to attempt the inclusion of all such documents or even a listing of them, but some typical examples may be useful. Such a representative view of these commissions, grants, &c., may not only aid in understanding the kind of paper work that added greatly to Jefferson's burdens of office, but may also be instructive as to 18th-century usage respecting forms. The changing character of typography or the absence of available printed forms may also be noted. As to the last, it may be remarked that whereas the Constitution stipulated all such documents to run "In the name of the Commonwealth of Virginia," such a statute as the Act establishing a Land Office provided a phrasing of the form at variance with this requirement. Occasionally, practice also departed from statutory requirement, as for example when it was stipulated that the seal of the Commonwealth should be attached; necessity sometimes made a departure from this requirement inevitable.

The numbers and captions of documents described in the following notes correspond with numbers and captions of documents presented in facsimile form. The editors are obligated to Mr. William J. Van Schreeven, State Archivist of Virginia, for his kindness in assisting in the compilation of this representative group of documents and forms and for his care in having those in his custody flattened, pressed, and properly photographed in order to achieve more faithful reproductions. They are also indebted to the late Maude H. Woodfin for a survey of the Virginia Land Office papers. For the facsimiles, see p. 668ff.

Militia Officers

1. Commission for a Recruiting Officer

Williamsburg, 24 Jan. 1780. To Captain Edward Worthington of Col. George Rogers Clark's Illinois Regiment (DNA), authorizing him to recruit men to serve in the infantry and to offer bounties in accordance with the Act of May 1779 (Hening, x, 23-7; see also notes concerning TJ's part in the drafting of this Act, Vol. 2: 380-1). The following in the printed form was marked through in this commission: "So soon as you shall have enlisted and passed   men you shall be entitled to receive   commission." Worthington was directed by the commission to have his men rendezvoused at "Kaskaskais or at Such Other place as Col. Geo. Rs. shall derrect and are to be incorporated into his Battalion." The form was filled out in an unidentified hand and signed by TJ. Endorsed: "Recruiting Instructions" and in the same unidentified hand: "Mr. Hickes at Whitleys Station has a mare and Colt of mine."

It is to be noted that the Act of 1779 directed that "The field officers of every county shall, from time to time, during the continuance of the present war, appoint one or more persons . . . to the purpose of recruiting soldiers, sailors, and marines, under this act, who shall be remove-able at their will" (Hening, x, 25). Nothing was said in the Act about commissions being issued by the Governor to such recruiting officers. See TJ's reference in his letter of 29 Jan. 1780 to George Rogers Clark to "Captain Wotherington" and his (missing) letter to the Governor advising that he had raised a troop of horse for Clark (Vol. 3: 277). Since Worthington had already raised his men and since, as TJ pointed out, the Assembly had authorized only one troop of horse for the Illinois country, the present commission for recruitment of infantry may have been sent to Worthington by TJ to legalize the recruitment of horse already made but unauthorized by law.

2. *Commission for a Company Officer*

Richmond, 23 Oct. 1780. Issued to Richard Luttrell, Jr., as ensign of a company of Fauquier county militia (in possession of Mr. John A. Luttrell, Bowling Green, Virginia, by whose kind permission it is here reproduced). Blanks in form filled in by clerk; signed by TJ; wax seal.

Another copy, dated 2 Oct. 1780. Issued to William Latane as captain of a company of Essex county militia. Blanks in form filled in by clerk; signed by TJ; wax seal (ViU). Not reproduced.

Another copy, dated 21 Feb. 1781 (printed date at end of form altered by TJ by writing "one" after "Eighty."). Form also altered by deletion of printed words "in a Company" so as to make it applicable to a commission for a county lieutenant. Issued to Lewis Burwell as county lieutenant of Mecklenburg county. Blanks in form filled in by clerk; signed by TJ; wax seal (Vi). Not reproduced.

3. *Commission for a Company Officer*

Richmond, 11 May 1780. Issued to Thomas Walker as captain of militia in Princess Anne county. Blanks in form filled in in two different hands; signed by TJ; wax seal (Vi). This form was also applicable to regimental and brigade officers; it was issued on concurrence of the Council and not on recommendation of a county court; and it did not require the seal as in document No. 2.

4. *Commission for a Company Officer*

Charlottesville, 26 May 1781. Issued to Francis Walker as ensign in a company of militia of Albemarle county (ViU: Page Deposit). In the printed form the word "Richmond" is deleted and "Charlottesville" interlined in an unidentified hand. Blanks filled in by clerk; signed by TJ; seal impressed on paper affixed by wafer. This is among the last commissions signed by TJ as Governor; on 2 June 1781 he signed blank commissions for the officers of three battalions (TJ to Morgan, 2 June 1781).

5. *Commission for a County Lieutenant*

Richmond, 20 July 1780. Issued to Matthew Godfrey as county lieutenant of Norfolk county. Blanks in form filled in by clerk; signed by TJ (Vi). Substantially the same form as document No. 2 but with the clause "these our Letters are sealed, with the Seal of the Commonwealth, and made Patent" changed to read "these our Letters are made patent."

6. *Commission for a Regimental Officer*

Richmond, 5 June 1780. Issued to John Nicholas, Jr., as lieutenant colonel. Blanks in form filled in by clerk; signed by TJ (Vi). Seal impressed on paper affixed by wafer. Similar to document No. 3, above, but with the phrase "of Militia in the said County" changed to read "of the Militia embodying for the Relief of South Carolina, under an Act of the present session of General Assembly." Under the Act "to embody militia for the relief of South Carolina," passed at the session of May, 1780 (Hening, x, 221-6), the commanding brigadier general and field officers of the 2,500 infantry called out were to be "chosen by joint ballot of both houses, and commissioned by the governour" (same, p. 222). Thus the concurrence of the Council was not necessary and the words "with the Advice of the Council of State" were deleted by hand in the commission to field officers. The same Act required that captains and other inferior officers be appointed "in the manner prescribed by law for militia drawn into actual service" (same, p. 222). Hence this form was printed with the words "with the Advice of the Council of State" for use in commissioning the more numerous inferior officers.

7. *Commission for a Brigade Officer*

Richmond, [...] Nov. 1780. Issued to Robert Lawson as brigadier general (NcD). MS in clerk's hand; signed by TJ; wax seal. Similar to No. 6 except that Lawson is appointed "Brigadier General of the Volunteers raised under divers resolutions of Council passed in the months of September and October, one thousand seven hundred and eighty." The proceedings of Council for 6 Sep. 1780 contain, in part, the following: "The Governor laid before the board a proposition from Colo. Robert Lawson to raise a body of volunteers to march to the Southward whereon the board are of opinion that the service of such a corps be accepted on the following conditions. They shall serve during the present campaign. . . . They shall be subject to the Continental rules of war. . . . They shall be furnished with muskets, bayonets, cartouch boxes, medicine, rations, forage and such a proportion of waggons as is allowed in the Continental army. . . . Care shall be taken to preserve the rights acquired by the former rank born by any of the Officers; the volunteers when doing duty in Camp shall be under their own officers only. A troop of Cavalry will be accepted to each regiment of infantry to serve during the same time, and to be subject to Continental rules. They shall be furnished with a sword and pistol, each man, with rations and forage; and be officered by Colo. Lawson. If any of their horses be killed or unavoidably lost while in actual service, their value, to be previously settled in the mode pointed out by law in similar cases, shall be paid by the public, provided it do not exceed 50£ hard money at the current exchange and where it exceeds that sum, so much shall be paid and no more . . ." (attested copy in Weedon

Papers, PPAP). On 30 Nov. the House of Delegates came to the following resolutions: "*Resolved*, that the Assembly have an high sense of the patriotic exertions of the Volunteers under General Lawson and wish to render them every proof of their approbation but as the said Volunteers have been delayed in their march to Carolina by the Invasion of this State whereby their time of Service is considerably lessened, as a Scarcity of Provisions makes it necessary that every aid should be effected and as the great difficulty of procuring forage will make it imprudent to carry Cavalry into Carolina. *Resolved* that the Governor be desired to discharge the said Volunteers unless they shall agree to serve during the Southern Campaign to be ascertained by the Commanding Officer in that department or unless the Governor after consultation with the Baron Steuben shall be of opinion that the situation of our affairs will not admit of it" (attested copy in Steuben Papers, NHi). TJ received these resolutions on the afternoon of 1 Dec. 1780, immediately transmitted them to Steuben, Steuben approved, and, on 4 Dec., in a (missing) letter to Lawson, TJ directed him to dismiss the men (see Vol. 4: 176, 178).

Civil Officers

8. *Commission for Coroners*

This blank form, probably one of the earliest issued by TJ, is in DLC: TJ Papers, 4: 682. The printed words "Patrick Henry" and "under the Seal of the Commonwealth" are deleted and above the former, in a clerk's hand, is written "Thos. Jefferson." Below, also in a clerk's hand, the words "100 Copies" indicate that a copy of the form used during Henry's administration was here employed as printer's copy.

9. *Commission for Justices of the Peace*

Williamsburg, 12 Nov. 1779. Issued to Thomas Sanders, Lawrence Smith, John Nicholson, John Irby, Flood Nicholson, Green Hill, Nathaniel Dunn, Sterling Harwell, Cyrell Avery, and John Judkins as justices of the peace and of the court for Sussex county (Vi). Blanks filled in in an unidentified hand; signed by TJ.

Another copy (also Vi), dated at Williamsburg, 5 Nov. 1779. Issued to James Kemp of Princess Anne county. Blanks filled in in an unidentified hand; signed by TJ. Not reproduced.

10. *Commission for Commissioners of Oyer and Terminer for the Trial of Slaves*

Williamsburg, 5 Nov. 1779. Issued to James Kemp, justice of the peace for Princess Anne county, appointing him one of the commissioners of oyer and terminer for the trial of slaves in that county (Vi). Blanks filled in by clerk; signed by TJ.

Another copy (also Vi), issued to Thomas Sanders and nine other justices of the peace of Sussex county. Dated at Williamsburg, 12 Nov. 1779; blanks filled in by clerk; signed by TJ.

Under Bill No. 104 of the Revisal of Laws, adopted in 1786, it was stipulated that the justices of every county should also be justices of oyer and terminer for trying slaves charged with treason or felony; hence, a commission issued to a justice after the passage of the Act of 1786 made a separate and additional commission for this particular purpose unnecessary (see Vol. 2: 616-7).

11. *Commission for a Sheriff*

Richmond, 2 Nov. 1780. Issued to John Bowman as sheriff of Lincoln county (WHi). Blanks filled in by clerk; signed by TJ; wax seal.

Receipts, Land Grants, &c.

12. *Receipt for Loan Office Certificate*

Williamsburg, 17 Mch. 1780. Issued to Benjamin Waller to acknowledge receipt of a Loan Office certificate (ViWC). The form for Loan Office certificates was specified in an Act of May, 1777, "for establishing a Loan Office for the purpose of borrowing money for the use of the United States" (Hening, IX, 283). By an Act of Oct. 1777, it was made possible for any person owing money to a British subject to discharge all or part of the debt by payments into the Loan Office. The commissioner of the Loan Office was authorized to issue certificates covering such payments, and the Governor was required, on presentation of such a certificate, to issue a receipt which was the debtor's guarantee of the discharge of "so much of the debt" as mentioned in the face of the certificate and receipt (same, 379-80). In the present instance it appears that Benjamin Waller had paid into the loan office some "eleven thousand four hundred & thirty seven & seventeen seventy seconds dollars" toward the extinguishment of his indebtedness to "The Assignees of Thomas Knox & Company of the kingdom of *Great Britain*." From the time of the adoption of the Act of Sequestration to May 1780 when that Act was repealed because of mounting inflation, some 522 payments were made to the loan office on debts owed British subjects. TJ was obliged to sign receipts for certificates covering almost all of these payments, for few were made during Patrick Henry's administration. The increased amount of paper money and its consequent cheapness led to a larger number of payments. Thus in the first five months of 1780 (the last period in which the Act was operative) no less than 337 payments were made (Harrell, *Loyalism in Virginia*, p. 83; see also Vol. 2: 168-71). The present document, therefore, fell in the middle of TJ's busiest period in the signing of receipts for payments on British debts.

13. *Land Grant, manuscript on parchment*

Williamsburg, 23 Dec. 1779. Grant to Robert Rutherford, assignee of John Madison, and John West, Jr., "in consideration of Military Service performed by John Madison and John West, junr. in the late War between Great Britain and France, according to the terms of the

King of Great Britains Proclamation of One thousand seven hundred and sixty three," of 900 acres in Yohogania county, survey bearing date 10 Apr. 1775. Engrossed on parchment; signed by TJ; wax seal (PWW).

14. *Land Grant, manuscript on paper*

Richmond, 20 July 1780. Grant to Thomas Walker for 400 acres in Louisa and Albemarle counties "in Consideration of the Ancient Composition of Forty Shillings sterling." As recited in the grant, a patent for this land had issued to Nicholas Oliver under date of 5 July 1751 "on Condition of paying over Quitrents and Cultivateing and Improveing" the land, a condition which Oliver failed to meet by not paying quitrents, whereupon Walker Taliaferro sued for and obtained a grant which he assigned to Thomas Walker. In a clerk's hand; signed by TJ; wax seal (ViU: Page deposit). At bottom of text is the following in Thomas Walker's hand: "This Land was Nickason Olivers I bought of them and as the arrearage of quitrents was more then the expence of a Patton I got one. Thomas Walker 1784." Endorsed: "Thomas Walker is entitled to the within mentioned tract of Land. John Harvie Re: Ld. Off."

15. *Land Grant, printed form*

Richmond, 1 Sep. 1780. Issued to Martin Wetzel (variously spelled and given here as Wetsell), in consideration "of the ancient composition of Five Shillings Sterling," for 50 acres in Augusta county on a survey dated 26 Feb. 1773. Printed form; blanks filled in by clerk; signed by TJ; wax seal (ViU).

16. *Land Grant, printed form*

Williamsburg, 5 Jan. 1780. Issued to Nathaniel Gist in consideration of military service performed in accordance with the Proclamation of 1763, for 3,000 acres in Kentucky county on a survey dated June 1775. Printed form but with the place for the name of the Governor left blank; blanks filled in by clerk; signed by TJ (CtY).

Appendix III

Virginia's Claim to Western Territory

EDITORIAL NOTE

Of the two principal manuscripts presented here, both defended Virginia's charter claim as against the pretensions of privately organized companies of speculators in land. Neither is dated, but the first was written prior to the Revolution, probably in early 1774, and the second was written after Yorktown, probably in the spring of 1782. The latter was certainly written by Jefferson and was no doubt intended for publication in a newspaper or in pamphlet form. So far as is known, however, this defense of Virginia's rights to western territory never proceeded beyond the rough draft of a preamble and outline of argument; even so, it has not been previously identified or published. The former is among the Jefferson Papers in the Library of Congress but is in the handwriting of an unidentified clerk. Its author is unknown and at present no conclusive evidence points toward any given individual. But there are plausible reasons for supposing that Jefferson himself is not to be ruled out as a possible author of this highly interesting argument.

In examining this possibility, it is not necessary to explore the enormously complex and at times obscure history of the various land companies that attempted before the Revolution to purchase great tracts for speculation or for the purpose of erecting new colonies. Clarence W. Alvord's *Mississippi Valley in British Politics*, which examined trade and land speculation from the point of view of imperial politics, and Thomas Perkins Abernethy's *Western Lands and the American Revolution*, which brought together "in a single narrative an account of the American West from the time when its exploitation was begun by English colonists to the end of the Confederation period," are authoritative works covering the extended subject; both have excellent bibliographies.

Alvord and others inclined to the belief that Virginia was indignant over the attempt of a group led by Thomas Walpole, with the energetic prodding of Samuel Wharton and Benjamin Franklin, to obtain a royal grant to a vast tract of land south of the Ohio in territory acknowledged to be within Virginia's jurisdiction. Abernethy, however, has pointed out that, except for a condemnation of the project by George Washington, the nearest thing to a protest emanating from Virginia was the letter written to Lord Hillsborough by President William Nelson of the Virginia Council on 18 Oct. 1770. Abernethy points out that Nelson's letter could scarcely be considered a protest, since Nelson did not "presume to say to whom our gracious sovereign shall grant his vacant lands nor do I set myself as an opponent to Mr. Walpole and his associates. All that I can consistently with my duty hope for is, that all prior rights whether equitable or legal may be preserved and protected." Among these prior equitable and legal rights were the claims of Washington's regiment, of the Ohio Company of Virginia, of James Patton, and the Loyal Company. All save the last

two of these, at the time of Nelson's letter, had already been merged
with or protected by the Walpole group. Thomas Walker and the
Loyal Company, as Abernethy points out, "had more than once swayed
legislation" and "surely had enough influence to have secured some
kind of protest if they had wanted it. The fact that it was not forthcoming is very good evidence that they did not desire it" (Abernethy,
Western Lands, p. 73; maps showing the areas claimed by Vandalia
between 1769 and 1776 are in Alvord, II, frontispiece, and Abernethy,
p. 39). Thus the historian is faced with the anomalous fact of Virginia's indifference to the establishment of a new colony on her western
borders at the very time she was making strenuous effort at the treaty
of Lochaber to get a more extended territory from the Indians. Abernethy explains this on the ground that the Tidewater planters were
generally apathetic to the lure of the west or were actively hostile on the
ground that it involved the east in expensive Indian wars or were, with
a few exceptions, lacking in the necessary western connections to carry
on large-scale speculation in land.

Yet Document I in the present series was a vigorous protest aimed
at the Walpole Company and its object of establishing the colony of
Vandalia on the western waters. As such it deserves to be printed
quite aside from the question of authorship, for it throws new light on
the extent of Virginia's objection to the aim of the Walpole associates,
and it lends emphasis to Washington's vigorous denunciation of the
scheme.

In 1773 Washington wrote to Charles Mynn Thruston concerning
the officers' and soldiers' claims under the Dinwiddie proclamation of
1774 that "by, or before [March 1771] . . . our affairs, never in a very
promising way, began to grow very alarming, from the sollicitation of
a large Grant on the Ohio, by some of the most powerful men in England, and by Lord Botetourt" (12 Mch. 1773; *Writings*, ed. Fitzpatrick, III, 121). What is more, when he first heard of the Walpole
project, and before Hillsborough had brought it officially to the attention of Botetourt, Washington wrote on 15 Apr. 1770 to the governor
that he had been "encouraged in a . . . particular manner by a letter,
which I have just received from Mr. Blair (clerk of the Council), to
believe, that your Lordship is desirous of being fully informed how far
the grant of land solicited by Mr. Walpole and others will affect the
interests of this country in general." It is possible that this letter was
not sent, or, if sent, was not used by Botetourt. At any rate, Washington rewrote the same letter on 5 Oct. 1770, employing the phrases
quoted, and despatched it to Botetourt. By the latter date it must have
been known to Washington that Botetourt was seriously ill, probably
that he was not expected to recover (*Tyler's Quart.*, III [1922], p.
109). Botetourt died on 15 Oct. and Nelson immediately despatched
his own letter to Hillsborough, enclosing Washington's (Washington,
Writings, ed. Fitzpatrick, III, 9-12, 26-29). It is evident from this
that Blair had solicited the kind of protest that Nelson could not make
and Botetourt would not have been likely to make. In short, the circumstances surrounding Washington's protest magnify its significance
considerably: members of the Council, who were themselves interested

in various western land grants and speculations, must have been desirous of enlisting the support of someone in the colony to make an effective protest. For this purpose, no one could be found whose name, even at that date, would be more weighty than that of Washington.

In transmitting Washington's letter, William Nelson expressed the hope that "prior legal and equitable Rights" would be protected, such as those set forth by Washington and those claimed by the Loyal and other companies. The phrase is repeated in the present vindication of Virginia's claim, but given a very different context from that offered by Washington or even by Nelson. Even an exception of such prior legal and equitable rights, the anonymous author argued, would be nothing "more than a Nominal Security to Numbers of Poor People, in a Litigation with a Powerful Company" (see Document I). From this circumstance it seems certain that the author had access to Nelson's letter; it is to be noted in this connection that Jefferson in his post-war defense of Virginia's claim was familiar with that letter (Document III), as was Madison (Madison to TJ, 16 Apr. 1782). It is to be noted further that the Jefferson Papers in the Library of Congress contain important copies of documents pertaining to Vandalia, some furnished by Thomas Walker and some by James Madison. Most of these may have been acquired by him for the purpose of drawing up Document II, but it is possible that some were in his possession before the Revolution. The more important of these are listed below.

Perhaps the best reason for considering Jefferson as a possible author is the substance and nature of the argument advanced in Document I. The doctrine that title derives from right of discovery is challenged as an invasion of natural right, but such a title nevertheless had to be accepted *de facto* if not *de jure*. The argument also reveals its author to be quite familiar with the history of Virginia's charters, with English maps, and with various Acts of the Virginia legislature pertaining to the western claim. Jefferson, of course, had already by 1774 begun the formation of his extensive collection of copies of Virginia charters and statutes (see Vol. 1: 146-9; 164). Whereas Washington's protest was grounded primarily on the fact that the prior and equitable rights of soldiers, speculators, and private companies would be infringed, the author of the present document defended the charter claims on higher ground. Such a grant as that to the Walpole associates, he contended, would be "in direct Violation of the Virginia Charters" because it would "have taken away great Parts of the Territory of this Colony"; it would have removed from under the immediate protection of the crown and government of Virginia several thousand people who had settled on the Ohio "under the Faith of the said Charters"; it would have injured the College of William and Mary "by reducing one of the principal Branches of its Revenue"; and finally it would have introduced a "precedent of a very alarming and dangerous Nature to the Liberty, rights and Privileges of his Majestys Subjects of this Colony." On all of these grounds the manuscript has a Jeffersonian ring. The fact that it is not in his handwriting is not sufficient to dispel the assumption that he may possibly have been its author, for many statutes, bills, letters, and other documents—including the manuscript of *A*

Summary View of the Rights of British America of 1774—exist in the hand of others though written by Jefferson (a good example is the petition from Albemarle of 24 Dec. 1798, Vi; it is neither in Jefferson's hand nor includes his name among the signatories, though the original draft is entirely by him; DLC: TJ Papers, 232: 42018).

This, of course, is conjectural, but the presence of the document in Jefferson's papers and the obvious fact that it was written by a well-informed Virginian make it necessary that the hypothesis be considered. The remark made by George Mason in 1781 may also have reference to the authorship of the present manuscript. At that time, when "dangerous Schemes . . . for dismembering the Commonwealth of Virginia, and erecting a new State or States, to the westward of the Alleghany Mountains" were in contemplation by Congress rather than by the British ministry, Mason turned to Jefferson as if to an acknowledged authority on the Virginia claim. "I know," he wrote, "from some former Conversation, that you have heretofore turn'd your thoughts to this subject" (Mason to TJ, 27 Sep. 1781). This may have meant only that Jefferson had in mind the proviso concerning new colonies that he included in his draft of a constitution for Virginia in 1776. But it is possible also that it referred to such an investigation and defense of Virginia's charter claims as Document I sets forth. It should be pointed out, nevertheless, that in spelling, capitalization, and style—particularly the slavish copying of legal phrases from charters and statutes—the document is very unlike any drawn by Jefferson in 1774 (cf. Vol. 1: 121-35).

There can be no question, however, as to the authorship of Document II. Jefferson must have undertaken it as a result of prodding by Mason, Madison, and others. Early in 1782 Madison related to Jefferson the political maneuvers behind the report of the committee of Congress of 3 Nov. 1781 which rejected the cessions of Virginia and Connecticut, accepted that of New York, approved the Indiana Company's claim, recommended reimbursement to the American members of the Walpole associates, and disallowed the Illinois-Wabash claim (JCC, XXI, 1098; Abernethy, *Western Lands*, p. 246-7). The Virginia delegates remonstrated, but with no effect. Madison viewed this report as an "additional proof of the industry and perseverance with which the territorial rights of Virga. are persecuted and of the necessity of fortifying them with every precaution which their importance demands"; one of the obvious and necessary steps, he pointed out to Jefferson, was for the state authorities to gather "an accurate and full collection of the documents which relate to the subject" (Madison to TJ, 15 Jan. 1782).

When Madison also asked Jefferson to make available "such information as your researches have yielded, with the observations which you have made in the course of them," he reflected what must have been generally known among informed men in Virginia—that Jefferson had previously studied the problem and probably had made "observations" on it. In his reply on 24 Mch. 1782 Jefferson said that, on his return from the General Assembly in Dec. 1781, he had "thought . . . to have considered and stated our right and to have communicated to our

Delegates or perhaps to the public so much as I could trace, and expected to have derived some assistance from antient M.S.S. which I have been able to collect" (TJ to Madison, 24 Mch. 1782). Madison encouraged him to pursue this intention; at the same time he wrote to Edmund Randolph, who was in Richmond during the May session of the Assembly laden with his Indian treaties, newspapers, and other documents pertaining to the subject: "A letter which I received a few days ago from Mr. Jefferson gives me a hope that he will lend his succor in defending the title of Virginia. He professes ignorance of the ground on which the report of the committee places the controversy. I have exorted him not to drop his purpose, and referred him to you as a source of copious information on the subject. I wish much you and he could unite your ideas on it" (Madison to Randolph, 1 May 1781 [1782], *Writings*, ed. Hunt, I, 132-3; Madison's letter to Jefferson referring him to Randolph is that of 16 Apr. 1782). Randolph received this on his way to Richmond "and took Dr. [Arthur] Lee by the hand almost at the same moment." Randolph thought that Arthur and Richard Henry Lee would "probably give the tone to the politicks of this session, should Mr. Jefferson persist in his unpardonable rage for retirement, and Mr. Henry delay his attendance." He also informed Madison that "The Dr. [Arthur Lee] overflows with territorial zeal: and something will certainly fall from the pen of the legislature. Mr. Jefferson must undertake the guidance of the work; or, I fear, the deviation will be great from the path of argument, which ought to be trodden on this occasion. For the Dr. seems to think that general reasoning will be sufficient; but this, tho' powerful, does not comprehend those topics, which demonstrate the opinions of british sovereigns in favour of the existence of the charter of 1609, even after the abolition of the company's rights, and which exhibit their construction of the [terms?] of that charter. I am somewhat surpriz'd at Mr. Jefferson's 'want of information of the grounds on which the report of the committee places the controversy.' Dr. Lee enclosed a copy of it to him, and intrusted it to my care. The letter did, I am sure, reach him" (Randolph to Madison, 10 May 1782, DLC: Madison Papers; Lee's letter to TJ is that of 13 Mch. 1782, q.v.; Madison explained that he had expressed himself "ambiguously with respect to Mr. Jefferson. He does not allege ignorance of the report of the committee, but of the title of New York"; Madison to Randolph, 21 May 1782, DLC: Madison Papers).

Owing to the "territorial zeal" of Arthur Lee and others, the General Assembly was not slow to act upon Madison's suggestion concerning the necessary first step. "As soon as the Senate meets," Randolph informed Madison, "a resolution will be passed for the nomination of persons to collect documents concerning western territory" (Randolph to Madison, 21 May 1782, DLC: Madison Papers). This was done, and, in accordance with the resolution, Gov. Harrison issued a proclamation "requesting all persons in this state who have in their possession any original papers or authentic Copies of the same belonging to the records of the Council of Virginia previous to the present revolution to transmit the same to the clerk." The Council had already purchased from Randolph himself "a collection of Indian Treaties and the Virginia newspapers from the year 1766 to 1776 inclusive" that Randolph had acquired in Philadelphia; it had also directed the commercial agent to procure twelve copies of various publications including "a book published in London by Almon, containing the Charters and Title papers of the several Colonies in America" (MS, Va. Council Jour., 29 Apr., 11 May, 5 June 1782, Vi).

While the Assembly was in session Nicolson & Prentis' *Virginia Gazette* for 25 May added fuel to the flame by reprinting from the Philadelphia *Freeman's Journal* Thomas Paine's defense of his acceptance of a gift from the Indiana Company for writing the pamphlet *Public Good*. In defending himself, Paine declared that the documents shown him by George Morgan in support of the Indiana Company title proved that "the claim of Virginia to the western territory was ill founded either in right or reason" and stated that the object of his pamphlet had been "to wrest . . . the whole western territory from the unjust and enormous claims of Virginia." This was scarcely convincing to Virginians, and, in addition to making members of the General Assembly indignant, Paine flung out a challenge: *Public Good*, he declared, had been in print over a year and a half, but it had "never yet been answered by the advocates for the Virginia claims. I know it cannot be answered with success" (Paine was here replying to articles signed "Caractacus" which appeared in Bailey's *Freeman's Journal*, 24 Apr.; 8, 22 May; 19 June; and 31 July 1782).

The challenge was accepted, and Randolph promptly reported to Madison: "The day before yesterday Mr. Mason, Mr. Jefferson, Mr. A. Lee, myself and Dr. Walker were appointed to state the claims of Virginia to western territory. Our power extends to publication without consulting the Assembly, and I presume two or three months will produce something" (Randolph to Madison, 1 June 1782; Joseph Jones to Madison, 25 June 1783, both in DLC: Madison Papers; Abernethy, *Western Lands*, 271, note). But Randolph's estimate of the time required proved to be too optimistic. A month passed without an exchange of letters on the subject by members of the committee. Mason, so Randolph said, would "enter into the discussion . . . if he approves the acts of the present session. Mrs. Jefferson has been too near her flight to a happier station, to suffer her affectionate husband to do more than lament the prospect of a separation. . . . Of Dr. Lee I have not heard a syllable since his setting off for Phila. Dr. Walker has supplied a few rough materials only. I am pursuing the inquiry: but wait for the movements of my elders in the nomination" (Randolph to Madison, 5 July 1782, DLC: Madison Papers). A few days earlier he had promised to send Madison "a copy of a succinct state of the claim of Virginia to western territory, drawn by a certain violent Anti-Whartonian, together with its history" (Randolph to Madison, 20 June 1782, DLC: Madison Papers). This probably referred to Arthur Lee's "A Concise View of the Title of Virginia to the Western Lands in refutation of the pamphlet called Public Good," a partial MS of which, in Lee's hand, is in the Lee papers in the University of Virginia Library. By August Randolph feared the committee could not "accomplish our pamphlet as early as was expected" and later that month he informed Madison: "I have heard nothing from Mr. Jefferson lately. The imminent danger of his lady must be the cause of his silence on the subject of western territory" (Randolph to Madison, 6, 24 Aug. 1782, DLC: Madison Papers). Madison urged him nevertheless to "be furnished with all Mr. Jefferson's lights" on the subject and said he had lately seen a statement by him "which shows clearly the ideas entertained by Virginia with respect to her territorial limits subsequent to the resumption of the charter"; this was a reference to the articles of agreement entered into 12 Mch. 1651 by the Commissioners of the Council of State for the Commonwealth of England—a document included in full in Jefferson's *Notes on the State of Virginia*, which Madison saw and apparently copied from the manuscript then in Marbois' possession in Philadelphia (Madison to Randolph, 13 Aug., 26 Nov. 1782, DLC: Madison Papers; Ford, III, 218-19).

But George Mason declined membership on the committee, though, after several months' delay, he assured Randolph that he would be ready "to contribute his aid privately" (Randolph to Madison, 8 Nov. 1782, DLC: Madison Papers). Late in November Randolph explained to Madison why he could not attend Congress: "I shall probably be obliged to remain here [Richmond] some time in preparing the vindication of our title to the western country, and this, too, from the appointment of Mr. J[efferson as minister to France] on whose shoulders I wished to throw the penmanship of the work" (Randolph to Madison, 22 Nov. 1782, DLC: Madison Papers). At this time Jefferson was at Ampthill but Randolph reported that he was "irrevocable in his repugnance" to the idea of attending the session of the General Assembly "altho' the house have sent for him and he is now within six miles of the town." Randolph explained that the cause "of his being thus near is his attendance on his children whilst under inoculation" and conjectured that "from this circumstance . . . he is fitting them for an European climate." On 28 Nov. Randolph "saw Mr. Jefferson, to whom it was unnecessary to add incentives to his acceptance of his plenipotentiaryship. He purposes to enter upon it, and with as much expedition as his private affairs will suffer" (Randolph to Madison, 2, 8, and 29 Nov. 1782, DLC: Madison Papers). It is obvious that Jefferson gave no aid to the committee before departing for Philadelphia late in 1782.

Despite the fact that Randolph asserted his attendance on Congress was delayed by the necessity of writing the state of the case that he had expected Jefferson to draw up, he did not complete even a rough draft until late summer of 1783. Shortly afterward Gov. Harrison reported to the Virginia delegates in Congress that Randolph had informed him "his performance respecting our claim to the western country is ready for the inspection of the Committee and that as soon as it meets their approbation it will be transmitted to you" (Executive Letter Book, VI). There is evidence that the document was so transmitted. On 25 Nov. 1783 Randolph gave Harrison a detailed account of the work of the committee: "Of the five gentlemen appointed by the general assembly to vindicate the title of Virginia to western territory, three only professed to take an active part. Those were Mr. A. Lee, Dr. Walker and myself. At the solicitation of the two former gentlemen, I have prepared a draught, ready to be submitted to their revision. But it will be impossible to meet them together, so widely are we separated from each other. Mr. George Mason has already, however, perused and approved about a third of the composition. If the general Assembly will therefore permit the work to go into print under the correction of Mr. Mason and myself, we may probably be able soon to concert the measures necessary for its publication. . . . The draught in its present state was finished in August last. . . . The circumstances of our public records rendered it impossible to produce the work sooner" (Randolph to Harrison, 25 Nov. 1783, Vi). Harrison forwarded this letter to the Speaker of the House of Delegates. It was read and tabled (JHD, Oct. 1783, 1828 edn., p. 35).

From the foregoing it is clear that Jefferson did not participate in the drafting of the report, though he was named second on the committee and undoubtedly regarded the matter as of great importance. He may not even have seen Randolph's statement until after he left for Europe in 1784 (see Randolph to TJ, 15 May 1784; TJ to Randolph, 25 May 1784). His wife's illness and death must have been the primary cause, and by the time Randolph wrote to Harrison in Nov. 1783, Jefferson had just reentered Congress and was preparing to validate Virginia's claim as a legislator rather than as pamphleteer. Abernethy, *Western Lands*, p. 271, states that Randolph's vindication of the Virginia claim was laid before the General Assembly in May 1784, but the report itself has not been found among the Virginia State Archives nor do the journals of the House of Delegates of that session refer to it. By that date, of course, the compromise plan concerning the Virginia cession of territory north of the Ohio had been proposed by Congress and accepted by Virginia, and the formal Deed of Cession had been executed. By the time Jefferson entered Congress in Nov. 1783, the need for vindicating Virginia's title before the public was no longer as urgent as Madison had felt it to be in the spring of 1782.

In view of this sequence of events, it is very likely that the state of the case outlined in Document II was drawn up soon after Madison urged Jefferson early in 1782 to take up the defense of Virginia's claim. This manuscript was probably left incomplete by Jefferson because of his wife's illness and death and his withdrawal from public interests. Subsequent events made its completion unnecessary. (See Arthur Lee to TJ, 13 Mch. 1782.)

Among the Jefferson Papers in the Library of Congress are documents that Madison evidently transmitted to Jefferson for use in drafting his state of the case for Virginia. They are labelled "Papers relative to the Indiana Company obtained from Col. [John] Cox" and many are in Madison's hand. Among these are: a copy of the minutes of the Suffering Traders, 7 Dec. 1763, with the names of those who executed powers of attorney to William Trent; petition of David Franks and others to the Privy Council in 1768 opposing the maneuvers of Wharton and Trent, a copy described by Madison as having been "taken from an original put into the hands of the Virginia Delegates by Jno.

Cox Esqr. Philada. Feby. 23rd. 1782"; copies of various letters from David Franks, John Cox, William Trent, endorsed "Copies of Papers relating to the Indiana affair communicated by John Cox Esqr."; a copy in an unidentified hand of the petition of William Trent and Samuel Wharton "upon the subject of Vandalia," 28 Oct. 1781; a list in Madison's hand of the original shareholders of the Walpole Associates with comments about the subsequent disposition of some of the shares; a "List of the proprietors of Indiana as correct as can be made," also in the hand of Madison; and a list in an unidentified hand of "Members of the Illinois & Ouabache Companies at present" (DLC: TJ Papers, 1: 6-13; 7: 1164-7). There are also documents in the Jefferson Papers that were supplied by Dr. Thomas Walker, Jefferson's former guardian, neighbor, and colleague from 1769 to 1771 in the House of Burgesses (Archibald Henderson, "Dr. Thomas Walker and the Loyal Company," Am. Antiquarian Soc., *Procs.*, n.s., XL [1932], p. 77-178). Among these are the following: a 16-page copy in Walker's hand of minutes of the Treaty of Fort Stanwix of 1768 which, though incomplete, differs materially from the official version in *Docs. Rel. Col. Hist. N.Y.*, VIII, 111ff.; a clerk's copy of the deed from the Six Nations at Fort Stanwix, 5 Nov. 1768, with corrections in Walker's hand; clerk's copy of the petition of Thomas Walpole and others for a grant of 2,400,000 acres south of the Ohio; and a 12-page argument in an unidentified hand against the establishment of a new colony on the Ohio on the grounds that the "Amazing Extent of Country already included in the North American Provinces, will not be settled for Ages Yet to Come"; that acquiring large tracts of uncultivated lands "is a General Disease among the Farmers, and the lower sort of People are besides fond of settling far back on Lands to which they have no right by Patent . . . to be out of the reach of the Laws"; that it "would be Extremely hurtful to all the Middle Colonies in particular as a Great Number of the present Inhabitants would Certainly desert them"; that these people would of necessity become their own manufacturers; that the cost of defending and governing a people so separated from the other colonies would be great; that the lands of the middle colonies would depreciate because of migrations westward; that "the History . . . of the Persons who have set on foot the scheme" of petitioning for a grant of 2,400,000 acres and their motives would not bear inspection (DLC: TJ Papers, 1: 15-16, 17-22, 34-41, 43-46). The last was written "to be Useful to Administration," was obviously the performance of someone familiar with America but living in England, and reflects many of the arguments employed by Shelburne and his followers in opposing new colonies in the west (compare, for example, Franklin to William Franklin, 27 Sep. 1766, *Complete Works of Benjamin Franklin*, ed. John Bigelow, N.Y., 1887, IV, 138-9; Alvord, *Mississippi Valley in British Politics*, II, 97).

Vindication of Virginia's Claim Against the Proposed Colony of Vandalia

[ca. 1773-1774]

There are certain Maxims and customs in most Countrys, which tho' they will not stand the test of a strict examination into the Justice of their Origin, the Community is nevertheless obliged to support with the same strictness and regularity as if they had originated ever so fairly and unexceptionably.

Whoever shall attempt to trace the claims of the European Nations to the Countrys in America from the principles of Justice, or reconcile the invasions made on the native Indians to the natural rights of mankind, will find that he is pursueing a Chimera, which exists only in his own imagination, against the evidence of indisputable facts.

When America was first discovered by the Europeans, a general notion prevail'd, that the first discoverers of any particular part, had a right to take possession, in the name of that Kingdom or State of which they were Subjects; and that such discovery and formality of taking possession conferred a Title.

Exceptionable as such a maxim may seem in its first establishment, all our Titles in America are derived from it; and it is impossible to argue against it now, without renouncing the Claim of Europe to America and dissolving those principles, upon which the rights of Individuals as well as the Claims of the different European Nations have been adjusted and ascertained. And altho' upon any disputes between the inhabitants of the British Colonies in America and the Native Indians, it is certainly more consistant with Justice and Humanity and even with our own Interest to compromise matters amicably with them by purchases, rather than extort from them by force; Yet such purchases have never been considered as operating in the least against the original Title of the British Crown. The Inhabitants of these Colonies derive their Titles not from Indian, but British Monarchs.

It is upon these principles that the right of the Colony and Dominion of Virginia to the lands on the western waters, as far West as the British Dominions extend is deduced: for so far had the Crown a right to Grant. King James the first by Charter, or Letters Patent bearing date May 23d. 1609 granted to the Virginia Company all those lands; Countrys and Territories situate lying and being in that part of America called Virginia, from the point of Land called Cape or point Comfort all along the Sea Coast to the northward, two hundred Miles; and from the said Point of Cape Comfort, all along the Sea Coast, to the Southward, two hundred Miles, and all that space or circuit of Land lying from the Sea Coast of the precinct aforesaid, up into the Land, throughout from Sea to Sea, west and North west &c. with several priviledges and immunities to the people who had settled or should settle there, and their Posterity for ever.

The Virginia Company made considerable settlements in this Country, established a regular form of Government, and retained the possession for about fifteen years after the date of the said Charter.

But some partys and factions having arisen in the said Company, and several disputes having happened with the King and his Ministry; King James the first by Proclamation dated July 24th: 1624, forbid and suppressed the Courts of the said Company at their usual place of meeting in the City of London and soon after the Lords of his Majestys Privy-Council appointed a new Governor of the said Company; which being expressly contrary to their Charters, they refused to acquiesce in such appointment; and thus, rejecting the Officers nominated by the Ministry, and forbid to act under their own, their Courts and meetings were discontinued, and their business and proceedings stop'd, for tho' there had been a Quo Warranto brought in the Kings Bench and the process served on several of the members, the same were never brought to any decision or hearing: but the Company chagrined with the discouragements and opposition lately received from the King and Ministry, disgusted with the schisms and Factions in their own Body and wearied with so great and constant expense after some faint struggles submitted and quietly gave up, or rather forbore any further exercise of their rights; and the Government of the Colony was taken into the Kings hands. An Event (however illegally and arbitrarily brought about) very happy for the people of Virginia; who were thereby taken from under a Proprietary Government, and placed under the immediate Government and protection of the British Crown.

The Bounds of the Colony (as well as the form of Government) remained unaltered until King Charles the first, in the year 1632 by Charter to Cecilius Calvert Lord Baron of Baltimore, established the proprietary and province of Maryland; that Country being then uninhabited, the importance of it little known or attended to, and the scene of confusion introduced by the Civil war in England, prevented any opposition from the people of Virginia. In the succeeding Reign (with equal inattention in the Virginians) the Provinces Pensylvania and Carolina were erected, the Southern part of the first and the northern part of the latter being within the ancient Limits of Virginia. The Dutch and Sweeds having possessd themselves of the Country on the Sea Coast between New England and Maryland, King Charles the second in the year 1664 granted all the Country so usurped, to his brother the Duke of York, and an English Fleet having reduced the Dutch and Sweedish settlements; the Duke of York parcelled out that Country to under Proprietors; One of whom was William Penn the son of Admiral Penn. All these proprietors, except William Penn, afterwards sold or surrendered their Charters to the Crown. Mr. Penn retained his part; and had it increased and confirmed to him, in consideration of a Debt due from the King to his Father, and from thence arose the Province of Pensylvania.

There being few or no settlements on the Southern part of this Coast, a Grant was made in the year 1663 by King Charles the second to several of his Courtiers vizt. the Earl of Clarendon, the Duke of Albemarle, the Lord Craven, the Lord Berkely, the Lord Ashly Cooper, Sir George Carteret and Sir William Colleton, for the Country called Carolina, the greatest part of which (the Earl of Granville only retaining his Ancestors Sir George Carterets part) was sold by the heirs of these proprietors to the Crown: and out of it were formed the Provinces of North Carolina, South Carolina, and Georgia.

And by these means have the ancient and original Bounderies been contracted, and the Colony and Dominion of Virginia reduced to its present Limits.

In the year 1669 a grant was made by King Charles the second to Henry Earl of Saint Albans, John Lord Berkely, Sir William Moreton and John Tretheway Esqr. of all that tract of Land, or Teritory lying between Rappahanock and Potomack Rivers, commonly called the Northern neck (now in possession of the right honble the Lord Fairfax) and altho there was a Provisoe that the same should not infringe or prejudice any contract or grant whatsoever, before made or granted, by the Governor and Council of Virginia: and that the said Patentees, their heirs and assigns, and all the inhabitants of the said tract of Land or Teritory, shall be in all things subject and obedient to such Laws and constitutions, as were or should be made by the Governor, Council and Assembly of Virginia; yet some Royalties and considerable powers being thereby vested in the Patentees; it roused the attention of the General Assembly; who apprehensive that the people might be injured, or oppress'd by men of such powerful Interest, in the year 1674 passed an act of Address and supplication, asserting the rights and Priviledges granted to this Colony by his Majestys Ancestors, representing the dangers and ill consequences of such grants to Lords and others; and praying that his Majesty would be graciously pleased to revoke the said Grant; and for securing them from fears, in time to come, of being removed from his Majestys immediate protection, to confirm their Liberties, priviledges, Immunities, Rights and propertys, as aforesaid, by his Majestys Royal Charter. Certain Gentlemen were appointed to present this act; which procured the last Charter ever granted to this Colony, vizt. that from King Charles the second, and under the great Seal of England, bearing date the 10th day of October in the 28th year of his Reign Anno Dom. 1676.

By this Charter all the subjects of his Majesty, his heirs and Successours, from time to time inhabiting within the Colony and Plantation of Virginia, are to have their immediate dependance upon the Crown of England, under the rule and Government of such Governor or Governors as his Majesty his heirs and Successors shall from time to time appoint in that behalf; and of or upon no other person or persons whatsoever. The Governor for the time being is to be resident in that Country except his Majesty his heirs and Successors; shall at any time command his Attendance in England or elsewhere; with provision for the administration of the Government in his absence, or upon the Death of any Governor, until a new one shall be appointed by his Majesty, his heirs and Successors.

The titles to their lands are confirmed to the Inhabitants, Any Vacant Lands are from time to time to be granted for the importation of people, "according as the same hath been used from the first plantation, to be held of his Majesty, his heirs and Successors, as of their Manor of East Greenwich in the County Kent in free and common Soccage." All Lands which shall from time to time escheat are confirmed to the possessors and their heirs forever upon certain moderate terms.

The Governour and Council have full power to hear and determine all Treasons and other offences committed within the said Government; proceeding therein as near as may be to the Laws and Statutes of the Kingdom of England. And Lastly to continue to favour the Subjects who then did, or afterwards should inhabit the said Country of Virginia, and for the more liberal and ample encouragement of plantations there (that is to encourage the increase and extension of the settlement there) it is declared that all and every Clause, Article, and Sentance in his Majestys Letters-Patent contained, shall be from time to time, forever thereafter, as often as any Ambiguity, Doubt, or Question shall or may happen to arise thereupon, exponed, Construed, deemed and taken to be meant and intended and shall inure and take effect in the most beneficial and available sense, to all intents and purposes, for profit and advantage of the Subjects of his Majesty, his heirs and Successors of Virginia aforesaid as well against his Majesty, his Heirs and Successors as against all and every other person or persons whatsoever.

The Country of Virginia is only mentioned at large and in general terms in this Charter, and not described or ascertained by any particular Limits or Bounderies. It can't be confined to the Country then settled; for that would exclude more than nine tenths of the present Inhabitants of Virginia.

It can't mean the Country at that time purchased from, or ceded by the Indians, which, would be totally inconsistent with the design of giving encouragement to Plantations there, and would also exclude the greatest part of the present Inhabitants. Nor can posterior Purchases of Lands from the Indians be used as Arguments against the Extent of this Charter, without impeaching the Crowns right to these Lands, at the time of granting the said Charter. A Doctrin of a dangerous Nature, and diametrically opposite to the claims of Great Britain, in her Negotiations and Treaties with foreign Nations, as well as the reasons for which the King entered into the late war.

If such purchases cou'd operate against the extent of the Virginia Charter, they wou'd have operated against the Grant of the Northern Neck; for the greater part of which was possessed by the Indians, when the said Grant was made; and not purchased from them for many years after Queen Ann's Reign. The Blue Ridge of Mountains seperated the Possessions of the British Subjects here from those of the Indians; yet in the last reign, the King and Council gave Lord Fairfax a Judgement for the Lands to the Fountain Head of Potomack River, near fourscore Miles beyond the Blue Ridge.

As our Settlements were extended, and the wild Game destroyed, the Indians have been forced to remove further for the convenience of hunting: as they retired, purchase after purchase hath been made of them; and temporary Lines or Bounderies, from time to time accordingly settled between them and the English Inhabitants here. It is not above fifty Years, since the People of Virginia Settled beyond the Blue Ridge; It is near thirty Years since they first began to settle on the West side of the Alleghany or Apalatian[1] Mountains; and at this time there are several Thousand Familys settled to the West ward of the said Mountains, on the Branches and Waters of the Ohio River.

When the Colony of Virginia was settled, the Lands first purchased of the Indians were only upon and near the mouths and larger parts of the Rivers, then to the Falls of the said Rivers, then to the blue ridge of Mountains; afterwards to the Alleghany Mountains, and lately to the River Ohio. Many of these purchases have been made since the Charter of King Charles the Second. If the said Charter was not affected by the former purchases from the Indians, neither is it by the last, nor can it be by any purchase made hereafter.

For (not to mention the liberal and beneficial manner of construction which we have a right to) the plain natural and obvious meaning of the said Charter is, to grant and confirm certain rights privileges and Immunities to all his Majesty's Subjects, who then did, or ever shou'd inhabit that Tract of Country in America, called Virginia according to the description and Bounderies of the original Charters; not before otherwise appropriated, or disposed of by his Majesty or his Ancestors. In this situation hath it remained from the time of the last Charter; and in this manner hath Virginia been constantly laid down ever since, in all the English Maps; as well as those published by public authority, as others to wit, Bounded on the North by Maryland and Pensylvania; on the East by the Atlantic Ocean; on the South by Carolina; and on the West by the great South Sea, or by the Western Limits of the British Dominions; which were never clearly ascertained; until the late Treaty of Peace, in the Year 1763, fixed then by a Line drawn along the Middle of the River Missisippi. Several Acts of the British Crown and Goverment, as well as many Laws of this Colony (which receiving the Royall Assent, are also Acts of the British Crown and Government) have from time to time corresponded with, and confirmed these Bounds of Virginia. It will be sufficient to mention a few Instances; as there are none which contradict them.

In the 4th Year of the Reign of Queen Ann, Anno dom: 1705 an act of Assembly was made in Virginia, empowering the Governor, for the time being, with the Consent of the Council by Charter or Grant under the Seal of this Colony, to grant to any such Person or Persons, their Heirs Executors, Administrators or Assigns as shou'd at his or their own Charge, make Discovery of any Town or Nation of Indians, situate or inhabiting to the Westward of, or between the Apalatian Mountains, the sole liberty and right of Trading to, and with all and every such Town or Towns, Nation or Nations of Indians, so discovered aforesaid, for the space of fourteen Years, then next ensueing; with such Clauses or Articles of Restraint, or Prohibition of all other Persons from the said Trade, and under such Penaltys and Forfeitures, as shall be thought convenient.

In an additional Instruction from his late Majesty King George the Second, to Sir Wm Gooch Bart: Lieutenant Governor and Commander in Chief of the Colony and dominion of Virginia, or to the Commander in Chief of the said Colony for the time being, Given at the Court of Saint James's the 16th day of March 1748/9 in the 22d Year of his

Reign; reciting a Petition which had been presented to his Majesty by the Ohio Company, praying for a Grant of a large Quantity of Land beyond the Great Mountains, in his Majestys said Colony; situated betwixt Romanettos and Buffaloe Creeks on the South Side of the River Alleghany, otherwise the Ohio, and betwixt the two Creeks and the Yellow Creek on the North Side of the said River, or in such other Parts of the West of the said Mountains as shall be adjudged most proper by the said Petitioners for making settlements thereon &c. The said Governor is directed and required, forthwith to make a Grant or Grants to the said Petitioners and their Associates, of Two hundred Thousand Acres, betwixt Romanettos and Buffaloe Creeks, on the South Side the River Alleghany otherwise Ohio, and betwixt the two Creeks and the Yellow Creek on the North Side of the River or as aforesaid to the Westward of the Great Mountains within his Majestys Colony of Virginia &c.

In the Year 1753, an Act of Assembly was made in Virginia, for further encouraging Persons to settle on the Waters of the Missisippi, Declaring that it wou'd be a means of cultivating a better Correspondence with the Neighbouring Indians, if a further encouragement be given to Persons who have Settled or shall Settle on the Waters of the Missisippi, in the County of Augusta (which was then the Frontier County, to the Westward quite accross this Colony) and that a considerable number of Persons, as well his Majestys natural born Subjects, as foreign Protestants, were willing to come into this Colony, with their Familys and Effects, and settle upon the Lands near the said Waters, in case they can have encouragement for so doing; that Settling that part of the Country will add to the strength and security of the Colony in General, and be a means of Augmenting his Majestys revenue of Quitrents; and enacting: That all persons being Protestants who have already settled, or shall hereafter settle, and reside on any Lands situate to the Westward of the Ridge of Mountains that divides the Rivers Roanoke, James and Potomack, from the Missisippi, in the County of Augusta, shall be, and are exempted [and] discharged from the Payment of all public County and Parish Levys, for the term of fifteen Years next following. And in the Year 1754 another Act of Assembly was made, For the Encouragement and Protection of the Settlers upon the Waters of the Missisippi, Declaring that many of his Majestys faithfull subjects had been encouraged by the acts of the General Assembly heretofore made; to settle and inhabit on his Lands in this Colony, on and Near the Waters of the Missisippi, and that it hath been represented to the General Assembly, that the subjects of the French King and by their Instigation, the Indians in Alliance with them, had encroached on his Majestys said Lands, murder'd some of his subjects, and taken others Captive, and spoiled them of their Goods and Effects, empowering the Treasurer of this Colony to borrow a Sum of Money upon Interest, nominating certain directors (Members of both Houses of Assembly) and empowering them from time to time, with the Consent and approbation of the Governor, or Commander in chief for the time being, to direct and appoint how the said Money shall be applyed, towards protecting and defending his Majestys Subjects, who then were settled, or thereafter should settle on the Waters of the Missisippi; and laying Sundry duties and Taxes on the Inhabitants of this Colony, for raizing a Fund, to repay the Money to be so borrowed. And for the same purposes were several hundred Thousand Pounds Granted by the General Assembly and levy'd upon the People of Virginia, during the Course of the late War.

And soon after the conclusion of the War, to wit, in the Year 1769 it being thought expedient, in order to conciliate the Minds of the Indians, then but lately withdrawn from the French Interest to extend a Temporary Line or Boundery between the Inhabitants of this Colony and the Southern Indians, accross the Alleghany Mountains, to the Ohio River; the sum of £2500 Sterling was Granted by the General Assembly, and levy'd upon the People of Virginia, to defray the charge thereof; upon a Requisition made by the Crown for that Purpose. And lately two hundred Thousand Acres of Land in consequence of Governor Dinwiddies Proclamation of 1754 hath been regularly Granted, by Patents from his Majestys Land Office of Virginia to the Officers and Soldiers of the first Virginia Regiment, upon, and near the Ohio River besides the Patents and Warrants granted in Virginia to the Military Men, under his Majestys Proclamation of 1763. These Quotations and Examples are sufficient to shew in what sense the Charter of King Charles the Second respecting the boundary of this Colony, hath been always understood; and to demonstrate that the Country to the Westward of the Alleghany Mountains, on both sides of the Ohio River, is part of Virginia; and consequently that no new Goverment or proprietary can legally be established there. Nor hath any Attempt of that sort ever been made from the time of the said Charter, until the late extraordinary Application of Mr. Walpole, and his Associates, to the Crown, to Grant him a proprietary Charter and create a New Goverment, between the Alleghany Mountains and the River Ohio in direct Violation of the Virginia Charters, as it would not only have taken away great Parts of the Territory of this Colony; but wou'd have removed from under the imediate protection of the Crown, and the Goverment and Law of Virginia several thousand Inhabitants, settled there under the Faith of the said Charters, as well as many subsequent Acts of Goverment, and the encouragement of public Laws. It would also have greatly injured the only regular Seminary of Learning in Virginia, by reducing one of the principal Branches of its Revenue, the Profits accrueing from a Grant of the Office of Surveyor General of Virginia made by their Majestys King William and Queen Mary to the President and Professors of William and Mary College, and have introduced a precedent of a very alarming and dangerous Nature to the Liberty, rights and Privileges of his Majestys Subjects of this Colony. Nor would the Exception of all prior legal and equitable Rights be more than a Nominal Security to Numbers of Poor People, in a Litigation with a powerful Company.

NB The first Charter for Carolina, the Orders to the Commissioners for running the dividing Line between the [colonies of] North Carolina and Virginia, with their proceedings and report thereon; the Articles of the Peace of Utrecht, and Aix la Chapelle, with the proceedings of the Commissarys of the two Nations, respecting the Bounderies of the English and French Colonys; the royal Instructions from time to time to the Governors of Virginia; and other public documents, may perhaps, throw some Light on this important Subject.

MS (DLC); in an unidentified hand; eight numbered and closely written folio pages; undated, but written after 15 Dec. 1773, for on that date, under George Washington's prodding, an order in Council was adopted authorizing land grants to Virginia officers and soldiers under the Proclamation of 1763 (Alvord, *Mississippi Valley in British Politics*, II, 186; Washington, *Writings*, ed. Fitzpatrick, III, 149, 157-8, 158-63). This means that the reference in the present MS to "the Patents and Warrants granted in Virginia to the Military Men, under his Majestys Proclamation of 1763" could not have been made until some time after that date. Washington had forehandedly obtained surveys even before he knew that Dunmore and the Council would cause the terms of the Proclamation of 1763 to apply to Virginia soldiers, and the "Patents and Warrants granted in Virginia" were probably issued very soon after the order in Council of 15 Dec. 1773; Washington's own patents for lands to which he was entitled under the Proclamation of 1763 had not been issued by 28 Feb. 1774 (*Writings*, ed. Fitzpatrick, III, 191-2). It is very likely, therefore, that the present MS was written not earlier than the spring of 1774.

The LATE EXTRAORDINARY APPLICATION OF MR. WALPOLE for a proprietary charter and the establishment of a new government refers to the revised and enlarged plan approved by the Board of Trade on 6 May 1773 (Abernethy, *Western Lands*, p. 39, 54). The emphasis placed by the author upon the Acts of Assembly of 1753 and 1754 recalls the similar argument that Randolph evidently included in his state of the case. On 15 Feb. 1783 he wrote to Madison: "Among the records of 1710 I find an instruction from Queen Anne to her governor here to grant lands *according to the charter*. This expression plainly alludes, from the context, to that of 1609, not of 1676. The acts of Assembly in 1753 and 1754 concerning settlements on the Mississippi afford no mean argument in support of our title: they having been confirmed by the king. And a standing instruction to the governors farther shews that every act was sent over for royal inspection. Therefore every act referring to similar points with these may be considered as having equal force" (DLC: Madison Papers).

1 At this point there is an asterisk and, in the margin, the word "Appalachian."

Outline and Preamble of Argument on Virginia's Claim

[1782]

1. 2. 3. 4.

A brief history of the several charters.
Their extent.
Spiral.   Smith's map.
Resumption by the crown
    Whether there was such resumption
    It's effect only to change the form of government not lessen extent of country. See Record ⟨42⟩ pa. 3.
Encroachments of the crown by granting Maryld. Pennsylva. Carolina.
The opposition of Virginia
Stipulation with the Commissioners for limits
Subsequent assurances of the crown not to encroach again.

Treaty of Paris
Proclamation of 1763.
Ratification by Virga. at the forming new constitution
    Where shall be the bounds.
President Nelson's letter
Grants by King on Western Waters
Why he suspended those grants.
Acknolegement that our charter was in force by ministerial writers in
    beginning of late dispute
1631. The governor Virga. sends Besse to N.E. to invite to settle on
    Delaware.
(This belongs to 5.)
1685. At Albany[1] the Chiefs of the Pamonkies and Chickahominies
    tell the 5 nations expressly that the mountains of Virga. are their
    hunting grounds. The Senecas accordingly promise will not disturb
    them. Old M.S. What lands then did the government of Virga. get
    by this treaty if not those beyond the Alleganey. The 5 nations had
    no others to give.[2]

In the origin of the present revolution it was foretold that should
we succeed in our wishes it would be to our misfortune; for that the
controuling power which kept us in peace with one another being once
withdrawn, innumerable causes of internal contest would arise which
would bring on discords infinitely more distressing than any which
could be produced by foreign oppression or foreign war. In the zeal
of enmity to the one aggressing power in the first effusions of a new
passion for each other we fondly beleived these forebodings to be the
dreams of timid friends and wishes of our secret enemies. In the constitution of Congress too we thought we had provided a controuling
power[3] which standing as the universal and indifferent umpire between
state and state would forever prevent any two of them from
                Unfortunately we did not foresee and therefore did not
provide for a case which may certainly happen wherein Congress itself
shall be opposed as a party to the claims of one or more individual
states. [While the war remained in the Northern parts of our union the
questions which have lately occupied us were never agitated. The inhabitants of those states were emploied in the immediate work of self-
preservation while their Southern friends were busied in sending in
their aids of men and such other supplies as distance and the difficulties
of a land transportation would admit, and thought not of seizing
favourable opportunities to extend their own or invade the rights of
their neighbors. On the contrary it may be remembered that this was
the time in which they the most earnestly pressed the establishment of
our confederacy. In the course of the war however the scene shifted.
The Southern states became scenes of blood and devastation whilst our
Northern brethren were restored to the arms of peace and commerce,
and left at leisure to pursue their interests private and public. Then
first was generated an idea that it would be expedient to curtail the
limits   A happy enterprize of our great general
whose eye like that of his maker extended over all with equal care, the

generous aids of an ally to whom sufficient retributions can never be made, stopped in the hour of our distress and by one memorable blow][4]
                     still occupied with relieving the distresses which had been brought on us, and we were for some time inattentive to warnings duly received that schemes were in agitation for depriving us of rights which however unimportant as to the object first aimed at, were yet vitally so as to their consequences. For indeed it is a truth felt by the wiser part of our nation that the great extent of territory which remained to us even after our cession to Congress was far from adding either to our strength or wealth. Reason and reflection had already suggested to us that neither the disposition of the people in our Western extremity, turbulent and unruly as befits the inhabitants of a mountainous country, nor nature or distance of the country they occupy, nor yet the form of republican government rendered it productive[5] either of their or our happiness that we should remain under one government.[6] Nature had pronounced our separation and I think I may say it awaited only time when they should think themselves able to stand on their own legs, a period less distant in time than that of [. . .] in any other mode of[7] But when it came to be proposed that this avulsion, instead of awaiting it's natural maturity of our mutual consent, should be the act of a third power who could interfere on no principle which would leave us any thing of our own.[8] We are far from intimating or beleiving that Congress assume to themselves the exercise of any such power. That would indeed place us in a state of calamity which heaven I hope will for ever avert from these states. Nor would the opinion of individuals of that honourable body have commanded national notice had not their assemblage in the form of a committee of Congress given place to their opinion in the records of that honourable
for we are told that a committee of Congress to whom was referred the cession made by[9] Virginia at the request of Congress of all their territory North of the Ohio, have reported that
Whether expediency and power be not the real bottom of this enterprize on the rights of Virga. whilst the arguments under which it has been veiled are used because some must be used to pretend a belief of right which aggression itself must ever pretend, is now submitted to a candid world to whom the first appeal is to be made. Happy indeed shall we be if availing ourselves of this awful interval by fair examination and dispassionate   we lead men to the exercise of their reason and justice, we procure them time for information and reflection and for setting their judgments to rights before we are precipitated into those endless miseries which accompany civil dissension. With this view the writer of the following sheets asks the candid attention[10] while he examines the foundation of the territorial rights of Virginia and the claims which have *lately* been set up in opposition to them.

1. That the lands in question are comprehended within the chartered rights of Virga.
2. That such was the idea of the crown and grantees.
3. That this right tho' infringed by unjust kings have been afterwards recognised confirmed by themselves.

4. That such has been the uninterrupted opinion of this state.
5. That such has been (till very lately) the opinion and the assertions of our neighboring states.
6. That such was the opinion of the particular associations of men whose disappointment in certain interested views has produced the present question.[11]
7. And that such has been the uniform opinion of Congress itself.

[Perhaps better to arrange under this idea, having first shewn the natural import and construction of the words West and Northwest say] But it has been urged by some popular publications confessing that one of our lines is to be West while the other is N.W. that they have a right to say the Northern shall be West and the Southern N.W. But if the words honestly construed have not fixed this point from the beginning, let us see what acts have been done both by Grantor and grantees to fix it subsequently and to shew their concurring sense. Then state the uniform claim of Virginia and other acts on their part and[12]

IIdly. the declarations and acts of the grantor, i.e. the king shewing his sense.[13] And where both parties agree what third party has a right to controvert? But

IIIdly. shew the sense of those third parties, viz. Congress, Pennsva. &c.[14]

5.

Declarations and conduct of Maryland and Pennsylva. during last war. Frankl. Res. 188. 100.

Contest with Pennsylva. about F. Pitt.

Govr. Reid's letter to me acknowleging the generosity of Virga. in the ratification of their chartered boundary.

Final settlement of boundary with Pennsylva.

The reasons urged by Maryland for not acceding to Confederation.

Carolina lately running boundary.

New York

   Treaty of Lancaster 1744. See 2. Dougl. 317.

   Several Indian Treaties. 1684. 1701. 1726. 1744. 1754.

      Effect of the cessions by the Indians.

   Nature of chartered rights as to Indians, viz. pre-emption.

   The Iroquois at Albany Aug. 2. 1684. gave the Susquehanna river above the falls to D. of Y. Does this affect right of Pennsylva. See old M.S. They say expressly they will not join their lands to any other government by N.Y. that they are a free people and give the land to what sachem they please.

   The French deny that the Iroquois have any right South of Ohio, Wash's journ. p. 48

The English contra. ib. 314.

6.

Petitions of Indiana[15] Co.

      Henderson.

7.

Journals of Congr. passim.

Fort Pitt.

   Connoly.

Broadhead sued.
Letter when P. Reid attempted confusion.
Henderson's application for Kentucky.
Middleton's fable of the fox which lost his tail
Debates in Congr. on the declaration of independence.
8.

Rights of Congress.
    Consequence of urging this is in no state, viz.
    Gr. Br. will have it at peace.
Rights of N. York
    Their claim on head of expence.
Rights of Virga. under head of expence
    Conquest, Kaskaskias &c.
    Settlements

Dft (MHi); entirely in TJ's hand and filed with MS of TJ's *Notes on the State of Virginia*; it occupies eight unnumbered pages and is written with different pens and no doubt at different times; there are numerous deletions and interlineations, the more important of which are indicated in the notes below; square brackets are in Dft (except as indicated in note 4) and so are blank spaces following incomplete sentences; verso [2] is blank and numerals "1.2.3.4." at head of recto [1] must have been placed there after TJ had completed the preamble which, with the seven heads of arguments, occupies pages [3]-[6]; section 8 must have been added to the outline after TJ had completed these middle pages. The probable date of composition of this document is discussed in editorial note above; in addition to the facts presented there, it is to be noted that many of the facts concerning treaties with Indians, &c., outlined by Madison in his letter to TJ of 16 Apr. 1782, are also to be found in the MS, hence it is likely that TJ did not begin the present outline until after he had received that letter.

PRESIDENT NELSON'S LETTER was the letter from William Nelson to Hillsborough, 18 Oct. 1770 (Abernethy, *Western Lands*, p. 49, 72; Alvord, *Mississippi Valley in British Politics*, II, 115-16). The POPULAR PUBLICATIONS must have included Samuel Wharton's *Plain Facts* and Thomas Paine's *Public Good* (see Madison to TJ, 16 Apr. 1782).

1 This word interlined in substitution for "Lancaster," deleted.
2 At this point TJ added in square brackets: "I have confounded treaty of Albany with Lancaster."
3 TJ interlined the following and then deleted it: "equal both in justice and force."
4 TJ first wrote "stroke," then "capital stroke," and finally "memorable blow." A vertical line in Dft is drawn through the passage in square brackets (supplied), indicating that on reflection TJ decided to omit an argument that was sectional and divisive rather than national.
5 This word interlined in substitution for "expedient," deleted.
6 Preceding three words interlined in substitution for "united," deleted.
7 This sentence is apparently unfinished, though the Dft is so heavily scored and interlined at this point that it is difficult to determine whether or not TJ intended to delete all following the words "their own legs."
8 This sentence has a caret inserted at the end, indicating that TJ may have intended to make an addition.
9 TJ interlined "Connecticut N.York &" at this point and then deleted the words.
10 The following deleted at this point: "of his fellow citizens of the United States." This indicates that TJ must have intended the MS to be published as a pamphlet.
11 Section 6 was interlined after section 7 (first designated "6") had been written.
12 This sentence is followed by the numerals "1.2.4." in different ink.
13 This sentence is followed by the numerals "2.3." in different ink.
14 This sentence is followed by the numerals "5.8." in different ink.
15 TJ first wrote "Van" (intending "Vandalia") and then deleted it.

Preamble to a State of the Case

[1782-1783]

'A judicious state of our right to the lands we claim, comprehending the progression of grants and settlements under the government of Virginia from at least the period or some time before the Lancaster treaty shewing the expence we have been at from time to time in treaties with the Indians and protecting the Frontier and the extent of our exercising jurisdiction in that country down to the time of the revolution when Independance was declared, will serve' &c.

MS (DLC); entirely in TJ's hand. This document was quoted above in the footnote to TJ's letter to Samuel Huntington, 17 Jan. 1781 (Vol. 4: 390), as possibly having been drawn up to be inserted in some document pertaining to Virginia's claim to western territory and as perhaps relevant to Virginia's conditional cession of 2 Jan. 1781, though, as suggested there, the fact that TJ enclosed the passage in quotation marks may indicate that he was not the author but the transcriber from another document. It is more likely that this MS belongs to the period of 1782; it may even have been copied from or for Randolph's state of the case.

Commissions, Land Grants, &c.

To Capt _Lw Hathington of the Illinois Battalion_

WILLIAMSBURG, _January 24th 1780._

Gentleman:

YOU are appointed, and forthwith are to proceed, to recruit men to serve in the _infantry_ —— of this commonwealth.

Each man is to receive at the time of enlistment a bounty of seven hundred and fifty dollars to serve during the war, and the following articles of clothing, that is to say: A coat, waistcoat, a pair of overalls, two shirts, a pair of shoes, and a hat; to be delivered at the place of rendezvous, and with the like articles every year after during his service, to be delivered at his station; and will be entitled to the same pay and rations as are allowed by Congress to the like soldiers in continental service, and during his continuance in the service will be supplied with goods by this state, at the following rates, viz. Osnabrugs at 1s. 6d. per yard, coarse hats at 7s. 6d. each, coarse shoes at 8s. per pair, coarse yarn stockings at 5s. per pair, rum or brandy at the rate of 10s. per gallon, whiskey at the rate of 5s. per gallon, and such other imported articles as may be necessary at the rate of 120 per centum upon the first cost. At the end of the war he will be entitled to one hundred acres of unimproved land, within the commonwealth. All soldiers who may be disabled in the service will be entitled to receive pensions during life. You are to be allowed one hundred and fifty dollars for each able-bodied soldier you shall enlist and pass with the officer of review to be appointed for that purpose. You are to make return of your enlistments within _two months_ from the date hereof, in person, or by letter, and continue to make _Monthly_ returns thereof afterwards. ~~So soon as you shall have enlisted and passed~~ men you shall be entitled to.

~~to~~ The men you are to enlist are to be rendezvoused at _Northumberland_ ~~such other place as Colo G. R. Clark Barrack or at to comprehend in to~~ _his Battalion_

1. Commission for a Recruiting Officer

The Commonwealth of VIRGINIA

To *Richard Littlepage* Gentleman, greeting:

KNOW YOU that our GOVERNOUR, on Recommendation from the Court of the County of *Pamunkey* hath constituted and appointed you *Ensign* in a Company of Militia in the said County. In Testimony whereof, these our Letters are sealed, with the Seal of the Commonwealth, and made Patent.

Witness THOMAS JEFFERSON, Esquire, our said Governour, at Richmond, the *23* Day of *October* in the Year of our Lord One Thousand Seven Hundred and Eighty.

Th: Jefferson

2. Commission for a Company Officer

The COMMONWEALTH OF VIRGINIA to *Thomas Walker* Gentleman, greeting:

KNOW YOU that our GOVERNOUR, on the special Truft and Confidence which is repofed in your Fidelity, Courage, Activity, and good Conduct, hath, with the Advice of the COUNCIL OF STATE, conftituted and appointed you *Captain* of Militia in the County of *Princefs Anne* IN TESTIMONY whereof thefe our Letters are made patent. Witnefs THOMAS JEFERSON, Efquire, our faid Governour at *Richmond* the *Eleventh* Day of *May* in the Year of our Lord One Thoufand Seven Hundred and *Eighty*

Th: Jefferson

3. Commission for a Company Officer

The Commonwealth of Virginia

To Francis Walker — GENTLEMAN, greeting:

KNOW you that our Governour, on recommendation from the court of the county of Albemarle hath constituted and appointed you an ensign — in a company of militia in the said county. In testimony whereof, these our letters are sealed with the seal of the commonwealth, and made patent. Witness, THOMAS JEFFERSON, Esquire, our said Governour, at Charlottesville, the twenty ninth day of May in the year of our Lord, one thousand seven hundred and eighty one

Th: Jefferson

4. Commission for a Company Officer

THE COMMONWEALTH OF VIRGINIA to Matthew Godfrey — Gentleman, greeting: KNOW YOU that our GOVERNOUR, on Recommendation from the Court of the County of a Norfolk , hath constituted and appointed you County Lieutenant of Militia in the said County. IN TESTIMONY whereof these our Letters are made patent. Witness THOMAS JEFFERSON, Esquire, our said Governour at Richmond the Twentieth Day of July in the Year of our Lord One Thousand Seven Hundred and Eighty

5. Commission for a County Lieutenant

The Commonwealth of Virginia

To John Nicholas jun.

Gentleman, greeting:

K NOW you that from the special Trust and Confidence which is reposed in your Fidelity, Courage, Activity, and good Conduct, our Governour, with the Advice of the Council of State, doth hereby constitute and appoint you the said John Nicholas _____ a Lieutenant Colonel of a Regiment of the Militia embodying for the Relief of South Carolina, under an Act of the present session of General Assembly. In Testimony whereof these our Letters are made patent.

Witness THOMAS JEFFERSON, Esquire, our said Governour at Richmond on the Fifth Day of June _____ in the Year of our Lord One Thousand Seven Hundred and eighty.

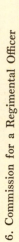

The Commonwealth of Virginia.

To Robert Lawson Esquire _____ greeting _____

Know you that from the special trust and confidence which is reposed in your fidelity, courage, activity, and good conduct, our Governour with the advice of the Council of State, doth hereby constitute & appoint

you Brigadier General of the Volunteers raised under divers resolutions of Council passed in the months of September

ber and October one thousand seven hundred and eighty, _____ "" _____ "" _____ "" _____ "" _____ "" _____ ?"!

In testimony whereof these our

Jefferson Esquire our said Governour at ___ of November

the year of our Lord one thousand seven h___

7. Commission for a Brigade Officer

The Commonwealth of Virginia

To

YOU the faid
County of
Coroner of the faid County of   are by thefe Prefentsco nftituted and appointed to be Coroners of the
in this State: **TO HAVE, HOLD**, exercife, and enjoy the faid Office of
                    with all Fees, Profits, and Advantages whatfoever, to
the fame belonging, or in any Wife appertaining. **WITNESS PATRICK HENRY**, Efquire, Governour or Chief Magiftrate of the faid
State, at *Williamsburg*, under the Seal of the Commonwealth, the   Day of
        Year of the **Commonwealth**, *Annoque Domini* 177

682

8. Commission for Coroners

The COMMONWEALTH of VIRGINIA

TO all Perſons to whom theſe Preſents ſhall come, greeting: KNOW YE that our GOVERNOUR, on Recommendation from the Court of the County of _Tyler_ hath, with Advice of our COUNCIL OF STATE, conſtituted and appointed _Thomas_ _____ _____ _____ _____ _____ _____ _____ _____ _____ _____ _____ Gentlemen, Juſtices of the Peace in and for the ſaid County, in Addition to thoſe now holding that Office, with Authority as well to execute within the Limits of the ſaid County the other Duties of the ſaid Office preſcribed by Law as to be of any Court to be held for the ſaid County; of which Court one of the ſaid Juſtices heretofore commiſſioned and now holding the ſaid Office ſhall be one. IN TESTIMONY whereof theſe our Letters are made patent. Witneſs THOMAS JEFFERSON, Eſq; our ſaid Governour at _Williamſburg_ in the Year of our Lord One Thouſand Seven Hundred and _Seventy-nine_ on the _twelfth_ Day of _November_ —————

The COMMONWEALTH of VIRGINIA

TO all to whom these present Letters shall come, greeting: KNOW YE that our GOVERNOUR, on Recommendation from the Court of the County of *Princess Anne* having, with Advice of our COUNCIL OF STATE, this Day issued a Commission constituting and appointing *James Kemps* Gentlemen, Justices of the Peace in and for the said County, in Addition to those then holding the said Office, doth now also constitute and appoint the said *James Kemps* Gentlemen, Commissioners of Oyer and Terminer for the Trial of Slaves in the said County, in Addition to those now holding the said Office, with Authority to be of any Court of Oyer and Terminer to be held for the said County, from Time to Time, for the Purpose of trying, condemning, and executing, or otherwise punishing or acquitting any Slave committing a capital Crime within the said County; of which Court one of the said Commissioners heretofore appointed and now holding the said Office shall be one. IN TESTIMONY whereof these our Letters are made patent. Witness THOMAS JEFFERSON, Esq; our said Governour at *Williamsburg* on the *fifth* —— Day of *November* in the Year of our Lord One Thousand Seven Hundred and *Seventy-ninth*

Th: Jefferson

10. Commission for Commissioners of Oyer and Terminer for the Trial of Slaves

THE COMMONWEALTH OF VIRGINIA to all Persons to whom these present Letters shall come, greeting: KNOW YE that on the special Trust and Confidence reposed in the Activity, Punctuality, Prudence, and Integrity of *John Bowman* ————— Gentleman, one of our Justices of the Peace for the County of *Lincoln* ————— , our GOVERNOUR, with Advice of the COUNCIL OF STATE, doth hereby constitute and appoint the said *John Bowman* ————— , Gentleman, SHERIFF for the said County. IN TESTIMONY whereof these our Letters are made patent. Witness THOMAS JEFFERSON, Esq; our Governour at *Richmond* ————— on the *second* ————— Day of *November* ————— in the Year of our Lord One Thousand Seven Hundred and *eighty.*

11. Commission for a Sheriff

WILLIAMSBURG, Mar. 17. 1780

RECEIVED from the hands of *Benjamin Waller*

a LOAN OFFICE CERTIFICATE for *eleven thousand four hundred thirty seven hundred* dollars, being so much money due from the said *Benjamin Waller* to *The Assignees of Thomas Shore & Company* of the kingdom of *Great Britain*, and sequestered according to the act of Assembly for that purpose made. Given under my hand date above.

£. 3401..3..5

12. Receipt for Loan Office Certificate

13. Land Grant, manuscript on parchment

Thomas Jefferson Esquire Governor of the Commonwealth of Virginia to all whom these presents shall come greeting Whereas by one patent under the seal of this our Colony and Dominion of Virginia bearing date the fifth day of July One Thousand seven hundred and fifty one there was granted to Nicholas Oliver one certain tract or parcel of Land Containing Four hundred Acres lying and being in the County of Louisa (now in the Counties of Louisa and Albemarle) on Great Creek and the Branches thereof and bounded as followeth to wit Beginning at Pointers in the Line of Benjamin Johnson running thence on his line North forty two degrees East forty five poles to his corner Red Oak ~~~~~~ thence on his other line North thirty eight degrees East forty eight poles to his and Timothy Dalton's their corner two white Oaks and red Oak standing on both sides Great Creek thence up the Creek and along a line of Marked Trees North forty seven degrees East sixty four poles to Dalton's corner Red Oak thence on his line North twenty three degrees East Eighty four poles to his corner thence on his line North thirty nine degrees East seventy six poles to his corner Pine thence on his line North six degrees East fifty six poles to his corner pine thence North thirty six degrees East six poles to a corner pine in his the said Dalton's line thence a new line South fifty four degrees East at One hundred and twenty four poles a Branch of Great Creek at One hundred and Eighty nine poles to Pointers thence South thirty two degrees West at One hundred and four poles a branch of Great Creek at One hundred and fifty nine another of the same at two hundred and twenty two another at three hundred and twenty four poles a corner large Pine in a draw of the said Creek thence North fifty four degrees West One hundred and Ninety four poles to the Beginning which said Tract or parcel of Land was granted on Condition of Paying our Quitrents and cultivating and improving as in the said Patent is expressed and whereas the said Nicholas Oliver hath failed to pay such Quitrents and Walter Taliaferro have made humble suit to our late Governor and Commander in Chief of our said Colony and Dominion and hath Obtained a grant for the same the right and title whereof he hath assigned to Thomas Walker Now Therefore Know ye that in Consideration of the Ancient Composition of Forty Shillings sterling paid into the Treasury of this Commonwealth by the said Thomas Walker there is granted by the said Commonwealth unto the said Thomas Walker and to his heirs and assigns forever all the said Tract or parcel of land with its Appurtenances to have and to hold the said tract or parcel of Land with its Appurtenances to the said Thomas Walker and his heirs forever In Witness whereof the said Thomas Jefferson Esquire Governor of the Commonwealth of Virginia hath hereunto set his hand and Caused the seal of the said Commonwealth to be affixed at Richmond on the twentieth day of July in the Year of our Lord One Thousand seven hundred and Eighty and of the Commonwealth the fifth

This Land was Nicholas
Olivers bought of him &
as the arrearage of quitrents
was more then the value of a Dalton
I got one Thomas Walker 1784

14. Land Grant, manuscript on paper

THOMAS JEFFERSON, Esq. Governour of the commonwealth of *Virginia*, to all to whom these presents shall come greeting: KNOW YE that in consideration of the ancient composition of *Five Shillings Sterling* ⸺ paid by *Martin Wetsell* ⸺ into the treasury of this commonwealth there is granted by the said commonwealth unto *the said Martin Wetsell*

a certain tract or parcel of land containing *Eighty Acres by Survey bearing date the twenty sixth day of February one Thousand seven hundred and Seventy three lying and being in the County Augusta on the ⸺ upper South fork in West Gap Beginning at three White Oakes in a flat place on the South side of a Survey of Thomas West and Thence South Sixty seven degrees East one hundred and twenty poles to two hickories near fair line South Seventy seven degrees West one hundred and eight poles to a line on a Ridge Thence South thirtyseven degrees West Ninety poles to a White Oak in a flat North Seventy degrees West thirtytwo poles to a White Oak by a branch North Sixteen degrees East Eighty poles to a White Oak and Pine North Eightysix Degrees East one hundred and three Poles to the Beginning*

with its appurtenances; to have and to hold the said tract or parcel of land, with its appurtenances, to the said *Martin Wetsell* ⸺

and his heirs for ever. IN WITNESS whereof, the said THOMAS JEFFERSON, Esq; Governour of the commonwealth of *Virginia*, hath hereunto set his hand, and caused the seal of the said commonwealth to be affixed at *Richmond* on the *first* ⸺ day of *September* ⸺ in the year of our Lord One Thousand Seven Hundred and Eighty ⸺ and of the ⸺ year of the commonwealth, the *fifth* ⸺

15. Land Grant, printed form

Thomas Jefferson, Esq; Governour of the commonwealth of Virginia, to all whom these presents shall come greeting: **KNOW YE** that in consideration *of Military Service performed by Nathaniel Gist in the late War between Great Britain and France, according to the Terms of the King of Great Britain Proclamation of 1763.* there is granted by the said commonwealth unto the said *Nathaniel Gist*

a certain tract or parcel of land containing *three thousand acres by Survey bearing date June 1775 lying and being in the County of Kentucky on the North side of the Kentucky River on Gists Creek, the waters of the Ohio River, joining on the North side of a Tract Surveyed for him and is bounded as followeth, towit, Beginning at two white Oaks & a Sugar Tree, and runneth South seventy West one thousand two hundred poles to two Sugar Trees and Elm, thence South twenty East four hundred poles to three white Oaks, thence North seventy East one thousand two hundred poles to a Spanish Oak and hickory, thence North twenty West four hundred poles to the Beginning*

with its appurtenances; to have and to hold the said tract or parcel of land, with its appurtenances, to the said *Nathaniel Gist*

and his heirs forever. **IN WITNESS** whereof the said *Thomas Jefferson* ~~Governour of the commonwealth Virginia, hath~~

hereunto set his hand, and caused the seal of the said commonwealth to be affixed at *Williamsburg* on the *fifth* day of *January* in the year of our **Lord** *one thousand seven hundred & eighty* and of the commonwealth. *the fifth*

Th Jefferson

16. Land Grant, printed form

Preliminary indexes will be issued periodically for groups of volumes. A comprehensive index of persons, places, subjects, etc., arranged in a single consolidated sequence, will be issued at the conclusion of the series.

THE PAPERS OF THOMAS JEFFERSON is composed in Monticello, a type specially designed by the Mergenthaler Linotype Company for this series. Monticello is based on a type design originally developed by Binny & Ronaldson, the first successful typefounding company in America. It is considered historically appropriate here because it was used extensively in American printing during the last thirty years of Jefferson's life, 1796 to 1826; and because Jefferson himself expressed cordial approval of Binny & Ronaldson types.

❖

Composed and printed by Princeton University Press. Illustrations are reproduced in collotype by Meriden Gravure Company, Meriden, Connecticut. Paper for the series is made by W. C. Hamilton & Sons, at Miquon, Pennsylvania; cloth for the series is made by Holliston Mills, Inc., Norwood, Massachusetts. Bound by the J. C. Valentine Company, New York.

DESIGNED BY P. J. CONKWRIGHT